Life Studies

An Analytic Reader

Life Studies

AN ANALYTIC READER

FIFTH EDITION

EDITED BY

David Cavitch

Tufts University

Bedford Books *of* St. Martin's Press

BOSTON

For Bedford Books
President and Publisher: Charles H. Christensen
General Manager and Associate Publisher: Joan E. Feinberg
Managing Editor: Elizabeth M. Schaaf
Developmental Editor: Beth Castrodale
Production Editor: Jonathan R. Burns
Editorial Assistant: Verity Winship
Copyeditor: Kathleen Smith
Text Design: Anna Post-George
Cover Design: Hannus Design Associates
Cover Painting: Robert Anderson, *Tile Walls–Strange Angels*, 1991.

Library of Congress Catalog Card Number: 94–65162
Copyright © 1995 by Bedford Books *of* St. Martin's Press

Manufactured in the United States of America.

9 8 7 6 5
f   e   d   c   b

For information, write: St. Martin's Press, Inc.
175 Fifth Avenue, New York, NY 10010

Editorial Offices: Bedford Books *of* St. Martin's Press
75 Arlington Street, Boston, MA 02116

ISBN: 0–312–10202–X

Part Opening Photographs
Self-Images (page 12): © Dion Ogust/The Image Works, P.O. Box 443, Woodstock, NY 12498. All rights reserved.
Family Ties (page 62): Jeff Dunn/The Picture Cube
Significant Others (page 126): Steven Stone/The Picture Cube
Lessons (page 182): Ellis Herwig/Stock, Boston
Group Pictures (page 240): Paul Fortin/Stock, Boston
Possessions (page 292): © Mikki Ferrill, P.O. Box 4060, Berkeley, CA 94704
Media Images (page 338): © Topham-PA/The Image Works, P.O. Box 443, Woodstock, NY 12498. All rights reserved.
Dilemmas (page 390): Fredrik D. Bodin/Stock, Boston

Acknowledgments
Diane Ackerman, "The Face of Beauty." Excerpted from *A Natural History of the Senses* by Diane Ackerman. Copyright © 1990 by Diane Ackerman. Reprinted by permission of Random House, Inc.
Marcia Aldrich, "Hair." The essay first apeared in *Northwest Review* (1992, Vol 30, No. 2), and is reprinted here with the permission of the editor.
Maya Angelou, "Graduation." From *I Know Why the Caged Bird Sings* by Maya Angelou. Copyright © 1969 by Maya Angelou. Reprinted by permission of Random House, Inc.

TO INSTRUCTORS

◇

Life Studies has been a popular reader chiefly because students like the selections. Students using the book avidly "read around" on their own initiative. They enjoy the readings, are moved by them, and are stimulated into thinking. They then strive to attain in their writing the interesting effects of the essays. The fifth edition continues the book's distinctive emphasis on examining individual experience in its larger-than-personal dimensions. But it also recognizes that instructors want students to move beyond personal reactions, to formulate more complex, analytic responses to readings. New questions and writing assignments encourage students to make the transition from expressive immediate responses to equally empathic but more analytic considerations. This new emphasis of the fifth edition is reflected in the new subtitle: "An Analytic Reader."

Although the revisions are pervasive, this new edition of *Life Studies* reconfirms the original premise that students learn to write well when they try to understand matters that are truly significant to them. They will work hard at articulating their ideas and feelings only if they have something that they really want to say clearly and convincingly. The works included here offer students varied and challenging perspectives on topics they care about, encouraging them to read with heightened attention, to respond knowledgeably in class discussions, and to write with a strong purpose to learn about themselves and their world.

Two new part topics, "Lessons" and "Media Images," examine mixed messages received from education — both inside and outside the class-room — and from popular culture. In addition, "Group Pictures" has been substantially revised to explore the personal, political, and socioeconomic significance of being part of a religious, racial, or ethnic group. Other parts have been recast in major ways, with the addition of new selections and many new topics for writing. Of the fifty-eight selections, twenty-five are new to this edition, and nineteen of the new pieces have never before appeared in a composition reader.

The organization of the book into eight thematic parts treats a progression of experience from personal to general awareness. The topics address our self-images; our family relationships; our love for people outside the family; education that we get inside and outside the classroom; our identification with religious, ethnic, and racial groups; our connection to valued possessions; our cultural images reflected by films, magazines, and pop music; and our dilemmas over moral issues that cannot be sidestepped. Each part opens with a number of Insights — succinct, often controversial statements by well-known writers whose colloquy of opinions offer a lively approach to the theme. Each group of Insights includes a poem expressing a highly personal viewpoint related to the theme. The longer works that follow include contemporary essays, memoirs, social criticism, and reportage. The authors provide diverse perspectives — including those of the journalist, sociologist, screenwriter, philosopher, and satirist, among others — and represent a broad range of ethnic and cultural backgrounds. In addition to the essays, each part contains one short story that develops the theme imaginatively.

Throughout *Life Studies*, the generous editorial apparatus places new emphasis on critical thinking and analysis, encouraging students to move beyond their personal experience and to examine, analyze, and take a stand on issues. To motivate and encourage students, the book opens with a new introduction that stresses the importance of attentive and critical reading in order to improve writing. "Finding a Trail: An Introduction to Reading and Writing Analytically" offers guidelines and specific practical advice for reading with better comprehension. The introduction is built around a new essay, Linda Hogan's "Walking," which is annotated to show how a student might respond to it during close reading. Following this essay, a clarification of the style and content shows students how to use margin annotations to increase their understanding of a reading and to develop viewpoints for writing. The introduction also includes composition advice that identifies and illustrates common writing problems.

Each part of *Life Studies* opens with Focusing by Writing, warm-up questions that can be used for in-class writing exercises or to generate class discussion. The Focusing topics are framed to show students that they — like the authors of the Insights — possess knowledge and opinions about the topics in the chapter. The questions raise students' awareness of the issues and suggest the significance of their own experience. Instructors may wish to use some Focusing topics for longer writing assignments as well.

Preceding each selection is a biographical and introductory headnote. Each selection is then followed by three categories of questions that promote analytic reading and writing. First come *Analyzing This Selection* questions, which encourage students to consider the reading's content and meaning as well as the writer's methods and approaches. These are followed by *Analyzing Connections* questions, which ask students to connect, integrate, and analyze the reading with earlier material. (Because many instructors flexibly assign their own order of readings, other links are suggested in the instructor's manual, *Resources for Teaching Life Studies*. But as a model for students, a pattern of progressive, expansive reflectiveness is built into the book itself.) Finally, *Analyzing by Writing* offers one or two writing topics that invite students to write papers that explain, analyze, or take a stand on issues raised by the selection.

A rhetorical index to the selections appears in the back of the book, and *Resources for Teaching Life Studies*, co-authored by Debra Spark, offers suggestions for dealing with each piece in class. The significantly expanded instructor's manual also offers further writing suggestions and comments on the photographs, suggesting ways to use them for class discussion and writing assignments.

Many instructors helped improve this book by responding to a questionnaire on the fourth edition. Several of the respondents and their colleagues also responded to ideas for the fifth edition by phone. I am grateful for the careful consideration given by Helen Aron, Union County College; Kathleen Aguero, Pine Manor College; Debra Boyd, Winthrop University; Jerry Bradley, New Mexico Institute of Mining and Technology; Mark Braley, U.S. Air Force Academy; Gayle Burkowski, Glenville State College; Sara King Brown, George Mason University; Margaret Cruikshank, City College of San Francisco; J. Arthur Faber, Wittenberg University; Regina R. Flynn, Salem State College; Michele Fry, Arizona State University; Paul deGategno, North Carolina Wesleyan College; Luc Gilleman, Indiana University; Susan Gorman, Tufts University; David Goslee, University of Tennessee at Knoxville; Andrea Green, Union County College; Margaret Grissom, Saint Mary's College; Elizabeth Grove, Ithaca College; Raouf J. Halaby, Ouachita Baptist University; Sarah Holben, State University of New York, Cortland; Dorothy W. Howell, University of North Carolina at Charlotte; Barbara Jensen, Modesto Junior College; Joanne Johnson, Jefferson Community College; Carole Keller, University of Akron; Rosemarie Lewandowski, Union County College; Gerald McCarthy of St. Thomas Aquinas College; Marie McCarthy, Union County College; Jerry Nelson, University of Nebraska at Lincoln; Elizabeth Otten, Northeast Missouri State University; Kathleen Patterson, California State University of Fullerton; Katherine Payant, Northern Michigan University; Richard Potter, Roger Williams University; Jon Quitslund, George Washington University; David Rivard, Tufts University; Beth Romano, Adrian College; Wayne de Rosset, Glenville State College; Connie Rothwell, University of North Carolina at Charlotte; and Edward Wiltse, Tufts University. In addition, special thanks go to David Goslee of the University of Tennessee at Knoxville and Kathleen Aguero of Pine Manor College for their thoughtful reviews of the introduction.

Friends and colleagues made helpful suggestions. I am grateful for thoughtful advice from Sylvan Barnet, Judith Brown, Abby Faux, Morse Hamilton, and Marcia Stubbs. The exceptionally capable people at Bedford Books provided much assistance. Beth Castrodale guided the development of this edition. Her astute judgment, abundant contributions, and careful management of the revising process made the current edition a true collaboration. Verity Winship did helpful research and tirelessly tracked down photographs for the fifth edition. Kimberly Chabot and Audrey Murfin also provided valuable editorial assistance, and Lori Chong cleared permissions with efficiency and cheer. Kathleen Smith copyedited the manuscript with a light and skillful touch. Jonathan Burns ably piloted the book through production, and Elizabeth Schaaf carefully managed the production process. Once again, Charles Christensen and Joan Feinberg gave their imaginative vision and high standards to the entire endeavor.

CONTENTS

◇

4. *Lessons*   183

5. GROUP PICTURES   241

6. POSSESSIONS   293

7. MEDIA IMAGES   339

8. DILEMMAS   391

Becoming an American citizen raises problems of conscience for this scholar and advocate of nonviolence.

When an incident that at first seems amusing gets out of control, a young Englishman learns a lesson about the fear, hatred, and suspicion that a colonial power and a native people feel toward each other.

A bully shatters a fragile peace, and everyone appears to do the wrong thing about it.

A nurse in an abortion clinic searches for a moral outlook that transcends simple judgments.

This scholar of constitutional law argues that, in our efforts to keep religion out of politics and education, we are denying an important part of our culture.

Life Studies

AN ANALYTIC READER

FINDING A TRAIL

An Introduction to Reading and Writing Analytically

It takes good reading to learn good writing. And every attentive response to good reading stimulates new possibilities of improvement in our writing.

Reading is the most important, and the most pleasurable, training for writers. From essays, fiction, and poetry we acquire a vastly increased vocabulary of knowledge and an array of models for more expressive, analytical ways of thinking about our world and ourselves. From reading we take in special verbal tools and methods that we use in writing. But we can't just swallow words and digest the meanings and uses of them. We have to become active intellectually and imaginatively in order to read with clear perception and firm emotional response. This introduction offers some practical advice on how to read and write more *analytically*, an approach explained in the next paragraph. The particular suggestions will prove effective as you practice them again and again. Like playing the piano, reading and writing are acquired abilities that no one is born with. But as we become good at what we're doing, the pleasure of doing it grows deeper and richer.

The literary meaning of *analysis* is to examine the parts and details of a piece of writing in order to explain their function and effects when all the parts work together. The basic premise of analysis is that style and form work together with ideas and emotions. The analytic reader clarifies what an author says by taking note of matters such as particular words, figures of speech, sentence structures, and links between sentences, paragraph development, the order of paragraphs, the structure of the piece as a whole, and the author's explicit and implicit attitudes — called *tone* — toward the subject and toward the reader.

That's a lot of parts and details to analyze. To keep track of them, a reader has to be systematic, and the full analysis must accumulate step by step. For instance, an observation about a writer's use of the colloquial word *spiffy* may lead to another observation about her chummy tone toward the reader, and discovering that attitude may further illuminate how she controls the flow of ideas from one paragraph to the next. Good writers are always in control of their writing, even when they sound casual and spontaneous. They want readers to grasp their intended meaning. They lay out as clear a path as they can to define their exact meaning, which is often not simple or easy to arrive at. This introduction demonstrates ways to pick up and follow the trail of the author's intentions.

When you read, give an essay your undivided attention. It is probably a good idea to turn off the radio or stereo or television. You need to be able to hear how an essay sounds in your head. Read one or two paragraphs aloud to help you discover and express spoken inflections to the writing. Then return to reading silently, and listen for the tones of the written voice. "Heard melodies are sweet," wrote John Keats, "but those unheard are sweeter." The poet was not urging students to turn off the stereo, but nevertheless follow his suggestion to open your mind to the vibes of silent things.

Approach a selection with an intention to read it word by word. Don't skim and don't skip over details. At least once through the whole essay, take it *all* in, so that its full meaning will be accessible in your mind for you to consider. There is nothing in this anthology that takes very long to read. You are reading not for the broad outline or vague gist of what is said, but to grasp the full substance, both explicit and implicit, and to see how an essay is developed.

Begin with the title, because the title is part of an essay. Paying attention to the title is a good first step in analytic reading. Be aware of what the title tells you or leads you to expect. For example, from the title of Nora Ephron's essay, "Shaping Up Absurd," you can foresee the author's critical attitude toward her subject, an attitude that comes across throughout the essay. The title of Raymond Carver's essay, "My Father's Life," defines the subject matter but does not hint at the author's attitude. Carver's title fittingly withholds that suggestion, because the essay explores his ambivalent, hard-to-define attitudes about his father. Some titles intrigue us with their ambiguity. Joan Didion's title, "In Bed," may cleverly mislead a reader into expecting a racier subject than the author presents. Andrew Holleran's title, "The Fear," is deliberately general. Such titles acquire their specific meaning only after you plunge into the essay. Some titles reveal their appropriateness, or lack of it, only after you have reached the conclusion. All titles are worth reconsidering after you know where the whole essay leads.

Continue your analytic methods when you get going in the essay. Give close attention to details by making observations as you read. Read with a pencil in hand and use the pages of your anthology (only in your own copy, please!) to jot down your responses. Underline or circle whatever sounds important as you read. Words, phrases, and suggestions of meaning that stick out prominently as you read are reliable indicators of what is important in the essay. Circle words you don't understand, and try to figure out what they mean from the context. The circles will remind you to look them up later. When you compare the dictionary definition with your initial sense of the word, you will discover the precise shade of meaning that the author attains in that particular word choice. Write comments in the margins. You will come back to them too. Some of your comments will refer directly to the essay's contents, and some will record your own associations or reactions.

If you begin with good intentions to read analytically but find that your attention is waning and your mind wandering, perhaps the selection itself is at fault. When you are too bored to read well, ask yourself, Why is this writing so uninteresting? What is the author doing here that makes it harder to pay attention? Whether the fault is in the essay or in your reading of it, don't succumb to passivity, reading pages without noting or remembering what they are about. Like half-conscious driving, half-conscious reading can lead to no good end.

As you read, reformulate in your mind what the author is saying. Try to put the author's point into your words, even if you doubt or don't like what is said. Get the ideas up off the page and into your head. The more conscious you are of the author's thoughts, the more energized you will be to respond with thoughts of your own, in either agreement or disagreement. Be sure to record in the margin wherever you balk over an assertion or concept. Are you disagreeing? Are you puzzled? Take your mental pulse and note it. The good thing about questions is that they provoke response. Perhaps your question can be dealt with in class discussion. Sometimes you will want to answer your own question later — perhaps by writing on the topic.

Don't hesitate to include personal associations in your margin comments. Does a passage remind you of something that once happened to you? something you read or heard? something you learned in another class? Make a note of it. If the connection can be expressed briefly, your margin note will suffice. But sometimes the connections that occur as you read are worth pursuing later with a more lengthy response in a notebook or journal. The mark or note in your margin will lead you back to the thought for further development. Connections you make while reading help you to assimilate and thoroughly comprehend new material. They also frequently lead to terrific writing topics.

A good way to proceed analytically is to note how each paragraph serves the writer's purpose. Writers shape their thoughts into paragraphs in order to focus concentrated attention (theirs and yours). Identify what seems to be the main substance of important paragraphs, even when you are unsure that you grasp the point. You will later return to the paragraph to understand its purpose better. Of course you know the usefulness of locating a topic sentence in a paragraph, when you can find one. A topic sentence states the main substance, and other sentences help make it convincing by arguing or illustrating the point. The topic often appears in the first or second sentence, or in the final sentence. Note where the paragraph's strongest emphasis occurs. Does the paragraph lead off with an emphatic assertion followed by sentences supporting it, or does the paragraph progressively build up to a conclusive statement at the end? Either pattern can give effective *development* to the main point.

Identifying the substance and development of each paragraph helps you to notice also how the paragraphs fit together — that is, how the essay is organized. Look for the connecting link, or "transition," which is usually but not always in the first sentence, that echoes or refers to the preceding paragraph. What is added to the subject as the author proceeds? Now you need to note the new paragraph's purpose.

The sequence, or order, of paragraphs establishes the author's path or direction of thought. Paragraphs cannot be jumbled into another sequence and still work effectively in an essay. They are not in random order like items on a list; they are more like chapters in a novel. They make full sense only in their intended sequence.

As you observe an author's paragraph development and organization, you will acquire a sense of the author's goal in writing the essay. You will begin to say, "I see what this is getting at." Or, if the essay is a narration of events, "I see what's shaping up here." This impression of the essay's overall coherence may build up clearly during your first careful reading. But often it comes after repeated study. In this book the questions on "Analyzing This Selection" can help you reconsider the content and approach of essays.

One constant guide to the author's intended meaning is his or her tone. In the margin, try to describe the writer's voice that is heard silently inside your head. Any voice includes tones that convey more than the words themselves mean — that impart the speaker's attitudes and implications. The tones of voice in written language are more subtle than in spoken language, but they are nevertheless essential to the meaning. You can begin to identify the writer's tone of voice if you first approach it as a more general quality, one of "manner." Is the writer formal? humorous? solemn? earnest? casual? authoritative? ironic? straightforward? playful? argumentative? Come up with two or three adjectives that best describe the writer's general manner and jot them down in the margin. Then closely examine the passage that prompted your observation and find the specific words and phrases that fit your description of the writer. Underline those words. Try to hear them as spoken words in order to check the accuracy of your description. Do they illustrate the manner you noted? Perhaps you will need to adjust your initial description of the writer's manner as you recognize the nuances of the language that express the tone of voice.

A writer's word choice expresses a particular slant, or viewpoint, toward the subject. A specialized or technical vocabulary establishes the tone of an expert authority, such as a sportswriter who addresses an audience of fans who understand the lingo of baseball or horse racing. Sportswriters also use many figures of speech to suggest the excitement of the game. The statement "Rice exploded the horsehide into the stands" doesn't make much sense to an ordinary reader, or even to any too literal-minded fan. The selections in this anthology seldom use such jargon. But even common diction and more comprehensible figures of speech indicate the writer's attitude toward the subject. Look at the first paragraph of Maya Angelou's "Graduation" (on p. 193). Words and phrases like "glorious release," "nobility," "exotic destinations," and "rites" indicate Angelou's — and the black community's — feelings about the school graduation.

Keep noticing the tone to see where and how it changes within a selection.

Sometimes it is possible to underline the sentence, or circle a pivotal word or phrase, where the tone shifts to express a different attitude. For example, in "Graduation" the intense, poetic language continues until the entrance of the white man who gives the speech at the ceremony. Now the language changes to officialese — boring generalities and flat clichés — revealing the white speaker's attitude toward the event. Angelou is making a point about race relations by this change in the essay's tone.

It is especially important to identify the tone at the conclusion of a selection, because you want to recognize the writer's final attitude. On what note does the essay end? How does the ending affect you? Has the writer been building up to this effect all along? Or is it a slight surprise? Even a relatively short essay such as Brent Staples's "Black Men and Public Space" can achieve a shift in tone from beginning to end. Carver's essay "My Father's Life" includes several changes of tone and ends on a note that is still unexpected. The concluding paragraph of Terry Galloway's "I'm Listening as Hard as I Can" introduces a new tone to the essay that suggests another dimension of the subject.

Paying close attention to the conclusion's tone gives you a way to pull together your observations about the entire essay. Your reconsideration of the whole is the most fruitful step in making sense of your reading. It is often an exciting synthesis of the material that leads to discoveries and fresh insights. From your overview of *all* the material, you can determine what the whole essay conveys through its ideas and techniques. Reaching that kind of comprehensive viewpoint about an essay is what you want to achieve from your analytic examination.

To demonstrate these reading suggestions, we have annotated an essay as you might do when reading it on your own. Important points and connotative words are underlined, and varied comments or questions are noted in the margins. Puzzling words are circled, as are clues to vague or puzzling matters. As you read the following essay, you may find that your reactions differ from what you see in the margins. Freely add your own.

Linda Hogan

WALKING

For exercise? Fun? Where?

◇

Will I know what's going on?

LINDA HOGAN (b. 1947) grew up in Oklahoma and graduated from the University of Colorado, where she also earned a master's degree. As a poet, fiction writer, and essayist, Hogan frequently draws on her American Indian culture, including tribal traditions. Her books of poetry include *Calling Myself Home* (1979), *Eclipse* (1983), and *Seeing Through the Sun* (1985). Her stories are collected in *That Horse* (1985), which was a collaboration with her Chickasaw father, and *The Big Woman* (1987). After teaching at Colorado College and the University of Minnesota, Hogan returned to her alma mater, where she is a professor of Native American and American Studies. She lives in the mountains near Boulder, Colorado. The following essay appeared first in *Parabola* magazine in 1990.

Sounds sinister. What?

A rebel?

1 It began in dark and underground weather, a slow hunger moving toward light. It grew in a dry gully beside the road where I live, a place where entire hillsides are sometimes yellow, windblown tides of sunflower plants. But this one was different. It was alone, and larger than the countless others who had established their lives further up the hill. This one was a traveler, a settler, and like a dream beginning in conflict, it grew where the land had been disturbed.

Buggy!

Will it live?

2 I saw it first in early summer. It was a green and sleeping bud, raising itself toward the sun. Ants worked around the unopened bloom, gathering aphids and sap. A few days later, it was a tender young flower, soft and new, with a pale green center and a troop of silver gray insects climbing up and down the stalk.

More positive tone, She likes it.

3 Over the summer this sunflower grew into a plant of incredible beauty, turning its face daily toward the sun in the most subtle of ways, the black center of it dark and alive with a deep blue light, as if flint had sparked an elemental fire there, in community with rain, mineral, mountain air, and sand.

She knows but does not see micro-thing.

4 As summer changed from green to yellow there were new visitors daily: the lace-winged insects, the bees whose legs were fat with pollen, and grasshoppers with their clattering wings and desperate hunger. There were other lives I missed, lives too small or hidden to see. It was as if this plant with its host of lives was a society, one in which moment by moment, depending on light and moisture, there was great and diverse change.

Like Thoreau at Walden.
Sinister again.

There were changes in the next larger world around the plant as well. One day I rounded a bend in the road to find the disturbing sight of a dead horse, black and still against a hillside, eyes rolled back. Another day I was nearly lifted by a wind and sandstorm so fierce and hot that I had to wait for it to pass before I could return home. On this day the faded dry petals of the sunflower were swept across the land. That was when the birds arrived to carry the new seeds to another future.

A summary.
Very impersonal.

In this one plant, in one summer season, a drama of need and survival took place. Hungers were filled. Insects coupled. There was escape, exhaustion, and death. Lives touched down a moment and were gone.

She jumps to the human angle.

I was an outsider. I only watched. I never learned the sunflower's golden language or the tongues of its citizens. I had a small understanding, nothing more than a shallow observation of the flower, insects, and birds. But they knew what to do, how to live. An old voice from somewhere, gene or cell, told the plant how to evade the pull of gravity and find its way upward, how to open. It was instinct, intuition, necessity. A certain knowing directed the seedbearing birds on paths to ancestral homelands they had never seen. They believed it. They followed.

Is she afraid that she doesn't know.

instinct ≠ belief

Strange doings.

There are other summons and calls, some even more mysterious than those commandments to birds or those survival journeys of insects. In bamboo plants, for instance, with their thin green canopy of light and golden stalks that creak in the wind. Once a century, all of a certain kind of bamboo flower on the same day. Whether they are in Malaysia or in a greenhouse in Minnesota makes no difference, nor does the age or size of the plant. They flower. Some current of an inner language passes between them, through space and separation, in ways we cannot explain in our language. They are all, somehow, one plant, each with a share of communal knowledge.

Can this be true?

This is also what she says.

John Hay, in *The Immortal Wilderness*, has written: "There are occasions when you can hear the mysterious language of the Earth, in water, or coming through the trees, emanating from the mosses, seeping through the undercurrents of the soil, but you have to be willing to wait and receive."

Heard it. Is she high?

Is she always alone?

Sometimes I hear it talking. The light of the sunflower was one language, but there are others, more audible. Once, in the redwood forest, I heard a beat, something like a drum or heart coming from the ground and trees and wind. That underground current stirred a kind of knowing inside me, a kinship and longing, a dream barely remembered that disappeared back to the body.

Another time, there was the booming voice of an ocean storm thundering from far out at sea, telling about what lived in the distance, about the rough water that would arrive, wave after wave revealing the disturbance at center.

Like on the lake, the beach, the storm coming up the shore

Tonight I walk. I am watching the sky. I think of the people who came before me and how they knew the placement of stars in the sky, watched the moving sun long and hard enough to witness how a certain angle of light touched a stone only once a year. Without written records, they knew the

Indians

The first other people in this essay.

5

6

7

8

9

10

11

12

gods of every night, the small, fine details of the world around them and of immensity above them.

Walking, I can almost hear the redwoods beating. And the oceans are above me here, rolling clouds, heavy and dark, considering snow. On the dry, red road, I pass the place of the sunflower, that dark and secret location where creation took place. I wonder if it will return this summer, if it will multiply and move up to the other stand of flowers in a territorial struggle.

It's winter and there is smoke from the fires. The square, lighted windows of houses are fogging over. It is a world of elemental attention, of all things working together, listening to what speaks in the blood. Whichever road I follow, I walk in the land of many gods, and they love and eat one another.

Walking, I am listening to a deeper way. Suddenly all my ancestors are behind me. Be still, they say. Watch and listen. You are the result of the love of thousands.

Handwritten margin notes:
She wants it to come back. Wistful.
Always a struggle?
Love + eat?!
More personal.
But she is still alone at the end.

Line numbers: 13, 14, 15

This essay is likely to produce some confusion or even bafflement. Few students will be confident about the overall point, goal, purpose, or tone of the essay from a first, unassisted reading. It is surprising to be left partly in the dark by such a familiar subject as just walking in nature and looking at things. We all have done that, and we expect to understand other people doing the same thing. But this writer's ordinary experience does not occur in commonplace, familiar ways. Her perceptions and responses are unusual. And she doesn't offer much helpful explanation of her particular or peculiar experiences.

Recognizing where you *are* at the conclusion of an essay, even if it is in a state of some confusion, is a good plateau on which to pull your thoughts together. The comments in the margin leave a record of reactions while reading. Go back to the beginning and pick up the trail.

The comments indicate that even the title is indefinite and uninformative. It is so general that it could cover many different kinds of walking. Adding to the indefiniteness at the beginning of the essay, the first sentence is deliberately mystifying. We could not possibly know what is referred to by the pronoun "It." The second sentence refers again to "it" without clearing up the mystery, but we begin to surmise that "it" is some kind of plant. We are led to this supposition by the word "grew" and the image of the hillside covered with flowers. The third sentence still doesn't name the plant, but suggests that "this one was different." Apparently, "it" must be a sunflower like the others but different because it grows alone instead of within the usual cluster. The author has deliberately puzzled us in order to prevent our routine, overly familiar response to this experience. Hogan wants us to perceive ordinary things in her special way.

In the first paragraph the indefiniteness combines with powerful figures of speech. Hogan gives the sunflower very human connotations by her poetic word choice. The diction personifies the sunflower by suggesting that it has human attributes. It has "hunger," and it seems motivated by human inclinations to launch out on its own. It has *dreams* and feels *conflicts*, according to Hogan. The motions of the flower as it turns with the sun suggest a spirit within the plant.

Comments on the next paragraphs help us recognize that the author continues her method of humanizing, or personifying, the sunflower. We are given a close-up view, as focused as a film close-up shot. Hogan lingers over the flower's pretty face, thrilled with its "incredible beauty." The face seems almost to have deeply luminous eyes in it. It looks vibrant with human qualities.

Yet, in other paragraphs, the author sees the plant as a complex organism that hosts a colony of insects. She sees it teeming with natural life on a minute scale. From both perspectives, Hogan emphasizes the intense vitality, the aliveness, of the flower. The vitality of nature includes danger and death, as the threatening storm and the nearby dead horse indicate. By paragraph 6 she is filled with wonder over the magnitude of what she witnessed. Her sentences are short and reverential in tone. They are general and impersonal, as if she is overcome with awe over things that are greater than herself.

As the essay develops, Hogan's sense of nature's vitality expands. The settings broaden to include wider territory, and the power of nature increases. Nature's vitality becomes more than human. It becomes divine. The author develops a religious attitude toward the trees, the ocean, and the stars. Nature reveals a spirit that feels holy to her. It makes perfect sense to her that her American Indian ancestors believed in gods, divine spirits that lived in nature. When she goes for her solitary walks, she feels the presence of divine spirits that her ancestors also knew. Her link with ancient generations is renewed and strengthened by this deep response to the natural world. In the concluding paragraph, she feels loved and supported by other human beings, not just the natural world.

After recognizing the central importance of Hogan's American Indian background, it is easier to grasp the purpose or the effect of other details. Throughout the essay, the author appears solitary and quiet in her rambles. Her walks are not for entertainment, relaxation, exercise, or even for ordinary nature appreciation. They are different from Thoreau's, for instance, though he comes to mind. Her walks are more like religious observances. They are her rituals. They are similar to taking communion in a Christian church, or saying a blessing over bread and wine. These associations with other religious rituals explain why Hogan says in paragraph 14 that the gods "love and eat one another." That surprising combination sounded bizarre on first reading. Now we can link it to the ritual or blessing of giving and receiving sustenance. Every religion makes a solemn ritual out of *eating* what is god-given in life.

Hogan's religious attitude might be an interesting topic to write about. An analytic reading usually turns up several such topics to pursue in writing where the ideas can be fully developed. The process of making sense is not complete until you write out your views in an analytic essay. You never really know what you think until you see what you say. The topic of Hogan's religious attitude might stimulate surprising, fresh opinions about similarities and differences with your own outlook. Not many of us are familiar with a traditional religion, such as hers, that promotes direct worship of nature. Yet, we all respond deeply to special and beautiful places, which we revere or hallow. Our suppositions about the natural world are probably different from Hogan's spiritual outlook. To compare and contrast Hogan's religious sense and your own view of nature, you can draw on your personal experiences and your religious and/or scientific background. You have an abundance of material you can examine.

Don't trap yourself into feeling blocked over writing. You can always begin to write by jotting down fleeting phrases. Don't worry about connecting up the jumble of thoughts that may cover your sheet of paper. Keep writing even if you are formulating only fragments. As you continue to energize your mind into forming phrases and sentences, you will soon begin to write longer passages and more cohesive thoughts. The important activity is to make your mind use words that you write down. The object of writing at any stage of preparation or revision is to get thoughts out of your head and onto paper. To achieve this goal you must work on the page. If you have trouble focusing your attention and getting started, push yourself to articulate one thought and then another. (It also helps to have privacy and silence where you write.)

What you get down onto paper during your first hour or two of effort will be patchy and often vague. Don't be disheartened. You can't construct the complicated network of ideas in an essay as easily and methodically as you knit a scarf or add a column of figures. You have to work further on the material you produce, adding what you need in order to be clear and convincing, and trimming away what you don't need.

To turn your rough material into a well-formed draft, think of yourself laying out a trail that your reader must be able to follow. You are in charge of the meaning now, and you want to make yourself fully understood.

Try to establish a purpose or central idea for each paragraph. Explain your idea so that your thoughts expand into a developed paragraph with a main point and supporting discussion. Often you will have to pull together a couple of brief, fragmentary paragraphs in your rough material and synthesize them into a longer paragraph that contributes a substantive point. Do not hesitate to write paragraphs that are longer than what you find in newspapers and most magazines. You want to learn to sustain and control extended thought processes. Add concrete details and illustrations that make your writing more convincing. Paragraph by paragraph, spell out what you mean.

And emphasize what *you* mean. Don't just repeat the author. Present your ideas. Students tend to summarize what is written without adding much personal comment on it, instead of forming an idea or attitude about the selection. For example, the following sentence merely reports what happened:

> When she walks, Hogan hears voices in the redwood trees.

Turn this kind of sentence into one that includes more of your own interpretation:

> When she walks among redwood trees, Hogan hears voices that are not hallucinations but sensations of vitality in these huge, ancient plants.

The revised sentence still summarizes the event, but includes an explanation of its significance. The sentence is more analytic in its purpose. The following sentence does not summarize at all. It refers to the event but does not recount it.

> By her silent communication with redwood trees, Hogan draws us into her reverence for their ancient vitality.

That sentence is fully analytic because it explains how Hogan achieves her purpose and effect.

Your sentences are the very flesh and muscle of your writing. Making them strong and energetic is probably the semester goal of classroom instruction. Commonly, sentences are too inactive and do not convey specific information. Using active instead of passive verbs can galvanize lazy sentences. As you shape up your sentences, listen critically for the dull sound of flab that arises from using vague words and too many words. A sentence does not need fatty tissue taking the place of substantive content.

Remember that your intended meaning is expressed by both what you say and how you say it. Your own tone of voice should be faintly audible in your head as you write. Is it a voice that sounds worth listening to on this particular topic? Is it a voice with a purpose?

When you think that you are finished, muster up the energy and courage to take one more critical look at your introduction and conclusion. These paragraphs have special functions that cannot be achieved until you have fully understood the point of your essay and your purpose in writing. You should make last-minute adjustments to your introduction and conclusion so that they serve your intentions. Remember from your readings that there is a rich variety of ways to begin and end an essay. Don't be humdrum in your introduction and conclusion. You owe it to yourself to win some attention to your fully developed views.

This brief bit of advice about writing should remind you that readers and writers confront much the same problems. But writing is more difficult. Writing is difficult for everyone, so you should never lose your nerve. The frustrations you face are the same frustrations that experienced writers face in their work. The standards you strive to attain are the same goals set by authors in this anthology. The work of writing is very democratic work: students, teachers, authors — we are all on this path together. If it is your turn to blaze a trail, take us to see something interesting.

PART 1

SELF-IMAGES

INSIGHTS

I conceive a man's body as a kind of flame, like a candle flame, forever upright and yet flowing: and the intellect is just the light that is shed on to the things around. And I am not so much concerned with the things around — which is really mind — but with the mystery of the flame forever flowing, coming God knows how from out of practically nowhere, and being *itself*, whatever there is around it, that it lights up. We have got so ridiculously mindful that we never know that we ourselves are anything — we think there are only the objects we shine upon. And there the poor flame goes on burning ignored, to produce this light. And instead of chasing the mystery in the fugitive, half-lighted things outside us, we ought to look at ourselves, and say "My God, I am myself!"

— D. H. LAWRENCE

◇

We are creatures of *outside influences* — we originate *nothing* within. Whenever we take a new line of thought and drift into a new line of belief and action, the impulse is *always* suggested from the *outside*.

— MARK TWAIN

◇

The Eagle-Feather Fan

The eagle is my power,
And my fan is an eagle.
It is strong and beautiful
In my hand. And it is real.
My fingers hold upon it
As if the beaded handle
Were the twist of bristlecone.
The bones of my hands are fine
And hollow; the fan bears them.
My hand veers in the thin air
Of the summits. All morning
It scuds on the cold currents;
All afternoon it circles
To the singing, to the drums.

— N. SCOTT MOMADAY

◇

The nicknames children bestow on one another can confer power. Like ancient Rome, the playground republic marks off the inner core of citizens from barbarians. Those who have no nicknames have no social existence; they are the nonpeople. . . . To be nicknamed is to be seen as having an attribute that entitles one to social attention, even if that attention is unpleasant. Thus, it may be better to be called "Sewage" than merely John.

— ROM HARRÉ

◇

My advice to everyone is to change their name at once if they're the least unhappy with their lives. In [my] Utopia everyone will choose a new name at seven, at eleven, at sixteen, and at twenty-four. And naturally women at forty-five, or when the last child has grown up and left home, whichever is the earliest. . . . Then life will be seen to start over, not finish. It is a perfectly legal thing to do. . . . So long as there is no intent to defraud. . . . But so many of us, either feeling our identities to be fragile, or out of misplaced loyalty to our parents, feel we must stick with the names we start out with. The given name is a dead giveaway of our parents' ambition for us — whether to diminish or enhance, ignore us as much as possible or control us forever. . . . No, it will not do. It will have to change.

— FAY WELDON

◇

This consciousness of self, this capacity to see one's self as though from the outside, is the distinctive characteristic of man. A friend of mine has a dog who waits at his studio door all morning and, when anybody comes to the door, he jumps up and barks, wanting to play. My friend holds that the dog is saying in his barking: "Here is a dog who has been waiting all morning for someone to come to play with him. Are you the one?" This is a nice sentiment, and all of us who like dogs enjoy projecting such cozy thoughts into their heads. But actually this is exactly what the dog cannot say. He can show that he wants to play and entice you into throwing his ball for him, but he cannot stand outside himself and see himself as a dog doing these things. He is not blessed with the consciousness of self.

— ROLLO MAY

◇

Show me a sensible person who likes himself or herself! I know myself too well to like what I see. I know but too well that I'm not what I'd like to be.

— GOLDA MEIR

FOCUSING BY WRITING

1. People are apt to think of their personal identities as resembling either *artichoke* or *onion*. The outer leaves of an artichoke are inedible; they shield and nurture the vegetable but are easily peeled away. The essence of the vegetable appears closer to the innermost core, the heart of the artichoke. An onion, by contrast, has concentric layers of homogenous identity. It extends uniformly from its inner rings to its outermost. Which are you? Explain why one metaphor reflects your sense of self better than the other.

2. If you were going to write an autobiography, where would you start? at some point in your own experience, or in someone else's experience? or with some place, such as a town, a house, or a country? Explain your reason for deciding on a particular beginning. Do not write it — merely explain why you would start your life story at that point.

3. As a child, did you ever create an imaginary name for yourself? Could you create one for yourself as you are at present? Recalling or inventing an imaginary name, explain its attractions and advantages over your given name.

4. Write about the pleasures and other possible effects of looking at old photographs, as in leafing through an album including pictures of yourself among those of other people. Do the photographic images evoke special reactions?

Nora Ephron

SHAPING UP ABSURD[1]

◇

NORA EPHRON (b. 1941) grew up in Hollywood amid an adult world of screen-writers, entertainers, and celebrities. This background may have had more to do with shaping her self-image than the physical trait of flat-chestedness that she writes about in this essay. She wanted to be a writer, and her letters from Wellesley College to her parents became the basis of a comedy they wrote. Ephron began a career as a journalist in New York by writing for *Newsweek* and contributing articles to entertainment magazines, before joining the edi-torial staff of magazines such as *New York* and *Esquire*. Her essays have been collected in *Wallflower at the Orgy* (1970) and *Crazy Salad* (1975). Her comic novel about a failed marriage, *Heartburn* (1983), was made into a popular film, and she also wrote screenplays for *Silkwood* (1983) and *When Harry Met Sally* (1989). Recently Ephron directed the film *Sleepless in Seattle* (1992).

I have to begin with a few words about androgyny. In grammar school, in 1
the fifth and sixth grades, we were all tyrannized by a rigid set of rules that supposedly determined whether we were boys or girls. The episode in *Huck-leberry Finn* where Huck is disguised as a girl and gives himself away by the way he threads a needle and catches a ball — that kind of thing. We learned that the way you sat, crossed your legs, held a cigarette and looked at your nails, your wristwatch, the way you did these things instinctively was absolute proof of your sex. Now obviously most children did not take this literally, but I did. I thought that just one slip, just one incorrect cross of my legs or flick of an imaginary cigarette ash would turn me from whatever I was into the other thing; that would be all it took, really. Even though I was outwardly a girl and had many of the trappings generally associated with the field of girldom — a girl's name, for example, and dresses, my own telephone, an autograph book — I spent the early years of my adolescence absolutely certain that I might at any point gum it up. I did not feel at all like a girl. I was boyish. I was athletic, ambitious, outspoken, competitive, noisy, ram-bunctious. I had scabs on my knees and my socks slid into my loafers and I could throw a football. I wanted desperately not to be that way, not to be a mixture of both things but instead just one, a girl, a definite indisputable girl.

[1]Editor's title.

17

As soft and as pink as a nursery. And nothing would do that for me, I felt, but breasts.

I was about six months younger than everyone in my class, and so for 2 about six months after it began, for six months after my friends had begun to develop — that was the word we used, develop — I was not particularly worried. I would sit in the bathtub and look down at my breasts and know that any day now, any second now, they would start growing like everyone else's. They didn't. "I want to buy a bra," I said to my mother one night. "What for?" she said. My mother was really hateful about bras, and by the time my third sister had gotten to that point where she was ready to want one, my mother had worked the whole business into a comedy routine. "Why not use a Band-Aid instead?" she would say. It was a source of great pride to my mother that she had never even had to wear a brassiere until she had her fourth child, and then only because her gynecologist made her. It was incomprehensible to me that anyone would ever be proud of something like that. It was the 1950s, for God's sake. Jane Russell. Cashmere sweaters. Couldn't my mother see that? *"I am too old to wear an undershirt."* Scream-ing. Weeping. Shouting. "Then don't wear an undershirt," said my mother. "But I want to buy a bra." "What for?"

I suppose that for most girls, breasts, brassieres, that entire thing, has more 3 trauma, more to do with the coming of adolescence, of becoming a woman, than anything else. Certainly more than getting your period, although that too was traumatic, symbolic. But you could *see* breasts; they were there; they were visible. Whereas a girl could claim to have her period for months before she actually got it and nobody would ever know the difference. Which is exactly what I did. All you had to do was make a great fuss over having enough nickels for the Kotex machine and walk around clutching your stomach and moaning for three to five days a month about The Curse and you could convince anybody. There is a school of thought somewhere in the women's lib/women's mag/gynecology establishment that claims that men-strual cramps are purely psychological, and I lean toward it. Not that I didn't have them finally. Agonizing cramps, heating-pad cramps, go-down-to-the-school-nurse-and-lie-on-the-cot cramps. But unlike any pain I had ever suffered, I adored the pain of cramps, welcomed it, wallowed in it, bragged about it. "I can't go. I have cramps." "I can't do that. I have cramps." And most of all, gigglingly, blushingly: "I can't swim. I have cramps." Nobody ever used the hard-core word. Menstruation. God, what an awful word. Never that. "I have cramps."

The morning I first got my period, I went into my mother's bedroom to 4 tell her. And my mother, my utterly-hateful-about-bras mother, burst into tears. It was really a lovely moment, and I remember it so clearly not just because it was one of the two times I ever saw my mother cry on my account (the other was when I was caught being a six-year-old kleptomaniac), but also because the incident did not mean to me what it meant to her. Her little girl, her firstborn, had finally become a woman. That was what she was crying about. My reaction to the event, however, was that I might well be a woman in some scientific, textbook sense (and could at least stop faking every month and stop wasting all those nickels). But in another sense — in a visible sense — I was as androgynous and as liable to tip over into boyhood as ever.

I started with a 28AA bra. I don't think they made them any smaller in those days, although I gather that now you can buy bras for five year olds that don't have any cups whatsoever in them; trainer bras they are called. My first brassiere came from Robinson's Department Store in Beverly Hills. I went there alone, shaking, positive they would look me over and smile and tell me to come back next year. An actual fitter took me into the dressing room and stood over me while I took off my blouse and tried the first one on. The little puffs stood out on my chest. "Lean over," said the fitter (to this day I am not sure what fitters in bra departments do except to tell you to lean over). I leaned over, with the fleeting hope that my breasts would miraculously fall out of my body and into the puffs. Nothing.

"Don't worry about it," said my friend Libby some months later, when things had not improved. "You'll get them after you're married."

"What are you talking about?" I said.

"When you get married," Libby explained, "your husband will touch your breasts and rub them and kiss them and they'll grow."

That was the killer. Necking I could deal with. Intercourse I could deal with. But it had never crossed my mind that a man was going to touch my breasts, that breasts had something to do with all that, petting, my God they never mentioned petting in my little sex manual about the fertilization of the ovum. I became dizzy. For I knew instantly — as naive as I had been only a moment before — that only part of what she was saying was true: the touching, rubbing, kissing part, not the growing part. And I knew that no one would ever want to marry me. I had no breasts. I would never have breasts.

My best friend in school was Diana Raskob. She lived a block from me in a house full of wonders. English muffins, for instance. The Raskobs were the first people in Beverly Hills to have English muffins for breakfast. They also had an apricot tree in the back, and a badminton court, and a subscription to *Seventeen* magazine, and hundreds of games like Sorry and Parcheesi and Treasure Hunt and Anagrams. Diana and I spent three or four afternoons a week in their den reading and playing and eating. Diana's mother's kitchen was full of the most colossal assortment of junk food I have ever been exposed to. My house was full of apples and peaches and milk and homemade chocolate-chip cookies — which were nice, and good for you, but-not-right-before-dinner-or-you'll-spoil-your-appetite. Diana's house had nothing in it that was good for you, and what's more, you could stuff it in right up until dinner and nobody cared. Bar-B-Q potato chips (they were the first in them, too), giant bottles of ginger ale, fresh popcorn with melted butter, hot fudge sauce on Baskin-Robbins jamoca ice cream, powdered-sugar doughnuts from Van de Kamps. Diana and I had been best friends since we were seven; we were about equally popular in school (which is to say, not particularly), we had about the same success with boys (extremely intermittent), and we looked much the same. Dark. Tall. Gangly.

It is September, just before school begins. I am eleven years old, about to   11
enter the seventh grade, and Diana and I have not seen each other all summer. I have been to camp and she has been somewhere like Banff with her parents. We are meeting, as we often do, on the street midway between our two houses and we will walk back to Diana's and eat junk and talk about what has happened to each of us that summer. I am walking down Walden Drive in my jeans and my father's shirt hanging out and my old red loafers with the socks falling into them and coming toward me is . . . I take a deep breath . . . a young woman. Diana. Her hair is curled and she has a waist and hips and a bust and she is wearing a straight skirt, an article of clothing I have been repeatedly told I will be unable to wear until I have the hips to hold it up. My jaw drops, and suddenly I am crying, crying hysterically, can't catch my breath sobbing. My best friend has betrayed me. She has gone ahead without me and done it. She has shaped up.

Here are some things I did to help: 12
Bought a Mark Eden Bust Developer.   13
Slept on my back for four years.   14
Splashed cold water on them every night because some French actress said   15
in *Life* magazine that that was what *she* did for her perfect bustline.

Ultimately, I resigned myself to a bad toss and began to wear padded bras.   16
I think about them now, think about all those years in high school I went around in them, my three padded bras, every single one of them with different sized breasts. Each time I changed bras I changed sizes: one week nice perky but not too obtrusive breasts, the next medium-sized slightly pointed ones, the next week knockers, true knockers; all the time, whatever size I was, carrying around this rubberized appendage on my chest that occasionally crashed into a wall and was poked inward and had to be poked outward — I think about all that and wonder how anyone kept a straight face through it. My parents, who normally had no restraints about needling me — why did they say nothing as they watched my chest go up and down? My friends, who would periodically inspect my breasts for signs of growth and reassure me — why didn't they at least counsel consistency?

And the bathing suits. I die when I think about the bathing suits. That was   17
the era when you could lay an uninhabited bathing suit on the beach and someone would make a pass at it. I would put one on, an absurd swimsuit with its enormous bust built into it, the bones from the suit stabbing me in the rib cage and leaving little red welts on my body, and there I would be, my chest plunging straight downward absolutely vertically from my collar-bone to the top of my suit and then suddenly, wham, out came all that padding and material and wiring absolutely horizontally.

Buster Klepper was the first boy who ever touched them. He was my 18
boyfriend my senior year of high school. There is a picture of him in my
high-school yearbook that makes him look quite attractive in a Jewish,
horn-rimmed glasses sort of way, but the picture does not show the pimples,
which were air-brushed out, or the dumbness. Well, that isn't really fair. He
wasn't dumb. He just wasn't terribly bright. His mother refused to accept it,
refused to accept the relentlessly average report cards, refused to deal with her
son's inevitable destiny in some junior college or other. "He was tested," she
would say to me, apropos of nothing, "and it came out 145. That's near-
genius." Had the word underachiever been coined, she probably would have
lobbed that one at me, too. Anyway, Buster was really very sweet — which
is, I know, damning with faint praise, but there it is. I was the editor of the
front page of the high-school newspaper and he was editor of the back page;
we had to work together, side by side, in the print shop, and that was how it
started. On our first date, we went to see *April Love* starring Pat Boone. Then
we started going together. Buster had a green coupe, a 1950 Ford with an
engine he had handchromed until it shone, dazzled, reflected the image of
anyone who looked into it, anyone usually being Buster polishing it or the
gas-station attendants he constantly asked to check the oil in order for them
to be overwhelmed by the sparkle on the valves. The car also had a boot
stretched over the back seat for reasons I never understood; hanging from the
rearview mirror, as was the custom, was a pair of angora dice. A previous
girlfriend named Solange who was famous throughout Beverly Hills High
School for having no pigment in her right eyebrow had knitted them for him.
Buster and I would ride around town, the two of us seated to the left of the
steering wheel. I would shift gears. It was nice.

There was necking. Terrific necking. First in the car, overlooking Los 19
Angeles from what is now the Trousdale Estates. Then on the bed of his
parents' cabana at Ocean House. Incredibly wonderful, frustrating necking,
I loved it, really, but no further than necking, please don't, please, because
there I was absolutely terrified of the general implications of going-a-step-
further with a near-dummy and also terrified of his finding out there was next
to nothing there (which he knew, of course; he wasn't that dumb).

I broke up with him at one point. I think we were apart for about two 20
weeks. At the end of that time I drove down to see a friend at a boarding
school in Palos Verdes Estates and a disc jockey played *April Love* on the
radio four times during the trip. I took it as a sign. I drove straight back to
Griffith Park to a golf tournament Buster was playing in (he was the sixth-
seeded teenage golf player in Southern California) and presented myself back
to him on the green of the 18th hole. It was all very dramatic. That night we
went to a drive-in and I let him get his hand under my protuberances and
onto my breasts. He really didn't seem to mind at all.

"Do you want to marry my son?" the woman asked me. 21
"Yes," I said. 22

I was nineteen years old, a virgin, going with this woman's son, this big 23
strange woman who was married to a Lutheran minister in New Hampshire
and pretended she was Gentile and had this son, by her first husband, this
total fool of a son who ran the hero-sandwich concession at Harvard Business
School and whom for one moment one December in New Hampshire I
said — as much out of politeness as anything else — that I wanted to marry.

"Fine," she said. "Now, here's what you do. Always make sure you're on 24
top of him so you won't seem so small. My bust is very large, you see, so I
always lie on my back to make it look smaller, but you'll have to be on top
most of the time."

I nodded. "Thank you," I said. 25

"I have a book for you to read," she went on. "Take it with you when you 26
leave. Keep it." She went to the bookshelf, found it, and gave it to me. It was
a book on frigidity.

"Thank you," I said. 27

That is a true story. Everything in this article is a true story, but I feel 28
I have to point out that that story in particular is true. It happened on
December 30, 1960. I think about it often. When it first happened, I
naturally assumed that the woman's son, my boyfriend, was responsible. I
invented a scenario where he had had a little heart-to-heart with his
mother and confessed that his only objection to me was that my breasts
were small; his mother then took it upon herself to help out. Now I think
I was wrong about the incident. The mother was acting on her own, I
think: That was her way of being cruel and competitive under the guise
of being helpful and maternal. You have small breasts, she was saying;
therefore you will never make him as happy as I have. Or you have small
breasts; therefore you will doubtless have sexual problems. Or you have
small breasts; therefore you are less woman than I am. She was, as it
happens, only the first of what seems to me to be a never-ending string of
women who have made competitive remarks to me about breast size. "I
would love to wear a dress like that," my friend Emily says to me, "but
my bust is too big." Like that. Why do women say these things to me? Do
I attract these remarks the way other women attract married men or alcoholics or homosexuals? This summer, for example, I am at a party in East
Hampton and I am introduced to a woman from Washington. She
is a minor celebrity, very pretty and Southern and blonde and outspoken
and I am flattered because she has read something I have written. We are
talking animatedly, we have been talking no more than five minutes,
when a man comes up to join us. "Look at the two of us," the woman
says to the man, indicating me and her. "The two of us together couldn't
fill an A cup." Why does she say that? It isn't even true, dammit, so
why? Is she even more addled than I am on this subject? Does she honestly believe there is something wrong with her size breasts, which, it
seems to me, now that I look hard at them, are just right? Do I uncon-

sciously bring out competitiveness in women? In that form? What did I do
to deserve it?

As for men.   29

There were men who minded and let me know they minded. There were   30
men who did not mind. In any case, I always minded.

And even now, now that I have been countlessly reassured that my figure   31
is a good one, now that I am grown up enough to understand that most of my
feelings have very little to do with the reality of my shape, I am nonetheless
obsessed by breasts. I cannot help it. I grew up in the terrible Fifties — with
rigid stereotypical sex roles, the insistence that men be men and dress like men
and women be women and dress like women, the intolerance of androgyn-
y — and I cannot shake it, cannot shake my feelings of inadequacy. Well, that
time is gone, right? All those exaggerated examples of breast worship are gone,
right? Those women were freaks, right? I know all that. And yet, here I am,
stuck with the psychological remains of it all, stuck with my own peculiar
version of breast worship. You probably think I am crazy to go on like this: Here
I have set out to write a confession that is meant to hit you with the shock of
recognition and instead you are sitting there thinking I am thoroughly warped.
Well, what can I tell you? If I had had them, I would have been a completely
different person. I honestly believe that.

After I went into therapy, a process that made it possible for me to tell total   32
strangers at cocktail parties that breasts were the hang-up of my life, I was
often told that I was insane to have been bothered by my condition. I was also
frequently told, by close friends, that I was extremely boring on the subject.
And my girlfriends, the ones with nice big breasts, would go on endlessly
about how their lives had been far more miserable than mine. Their bra
straps were snapped in class. They couldn't sleep on their stomachs. They
were stared at whenever the word "mountain" cropped up in geography. And
Evangeline, good God what they went through every time someone had to
stand up and recite the Prologue to Longfellow's *Evangeline:* ". . . *stand like
druids of eld . . . /With beards that rest on their bosoms."* It was much worse
for them, they tell me. They had a terrible time of it, they assure me. I don't
know how lucky I was, they say.

I have thought about their remarks, tried to put myself in their place,   33
considered their point of view. I think they are full of shit.

Analyzing This Selection

1. Ephron establishes a very informal, colloquial tone right from the start. Underline the key words and phrases in the opening paragraph that help set this tone.
   What is the correlation between this tone and the subject of her essay?

2. As a child, Ephron felt sure that her every distress would lead to a large, fateful
   disaster. In addition to her flat-chestedness, what does she worry about? How does
   she express these worries?

3. What is the point of the section about her friend Diana? Does her name fit the effect that she has on Ephron? Similarly, what is the point of the section about Buster Klepper? And what are the connotations of his name? Do they fit his effect on her?

Analyzing Connections

4. Two contrasting metaphors for personal identity are mentioned in the first topic of Focusing by Writing (see p. 16). Which metaphor suggests Ephron's image of herself?

Analyzing by Writing

5. Being unusually tall or short, thin or fat, red-haired, freckled, pretty, or thoroughly average can seem to be the most important fact in your existence. Write an essay explaining how one trait came to have exaggerated importance for some period of your life. Recount the circumstances, and examine the reasons for their importance at that time.

Terry Galloway

I'M LISTENING
AS HARD AS I CAN

◇

TERRY GALLOWAY (b. 1950) was born in Stuttgart, Germany and grew up in Berlin and Austin, Texas. She graduated from the University of Texas. She is a writer, director, and performer of one-woman performance pieces. Her first play, *Heart of a Dog*, was produced in New York and won the Villager Award; it was published in 1983. Galloway has toured the United States, Canada, and the United Kingdom with two performance pieces, *Out All Night and Lost My Shoes* and *Lardo Weeping*. She has taught performance at various schools, including the University of Texas, Florida State University, Vassar College, and the California Institute of the Arts. In addition to her work in theater, Galloway has published a book of poems, *Buncha Crocs in Surch of Snac* (1980). She has written for a public television series about handicapped children. For the following essay about her own handicap, Galloway always liked the title "Huh?" — but no editor has yet agreed with her.

At the age of twelve I won the swimming award at the Lions Camp for 1 Crippled Children. When my name echoed over the PA system the girl in the wheelchair next to me grabbed the box speaker of my hearing aid and shouted, "You won!" My ear quaking, I took the cue. I stood up straight — the only physically unencumbered child in a sea of braces and canes — affixed a pained but brave grin to my face, then limped all the way to the stage.

Later, after the spotlight had dimmed, I was overcome with remorse, but 2 not because I'd played the crippled heroine. The truth was that I was ashamed of my handicap. I wanted to have something more visibly wrong with me. I wanted to be in the same league as the girl who'd lost her right leg in a car accident; her artificial leg attracted a bevy of awestruck campers. I, on the other hand, wore an unwieldy box hearing aid buckled to my body like a dog halter. It attracted no one. Deafness wasn't, in my eyes, a blue-ribbon handicap. Mixed in with my envy, though, was an overwhelming sense of guilt; at camp I was free to splash in the swimming pool, while most of the other children were stranded at the shallow end, where lifeguards floated them in lazy circles. But seventeen years of living in the "normal" world has diminished my guilt considerably, and I've learned that every handicap has its own particular hell.

I'm something of an anomaly in the deaf world. Unlike most deaf 3 people, who were either born deaf or went deaf in infancy, I lost my hearing in chunks over a period of twelve years. Fortunately I learned to speak before my loss grew too profound, and that ability freed me from the most severe problem facing the deaf — the terrible difficulty of making themselves understood. My opinion of deafness was just as biased as that of a person who can hear. I had never met a deaf child in my life, and I didn't know how to sign. I imagined deaf people to be like creatures from beyond: animal-like because their language was so physical, threatening because they were unable to express themselves with sophistication — that is, through speech. I *could* make myself understood, and because I had a talent for lipreading it was easy for me to pass in the wider world. And for most of my life that is exactly what I did — like a black woman playing white, I passed for something other than what I was. But in doing so I was avoiding some very painful facts. And for many years I was inhibited not only by my deafness but my own idea of what it meant to be deaf.

My problems all started when my mother, seven months pregnant with 4 me, developed a serious kidney infection. Her doctors pumped her full of antibiotics. Two months later I was born, with nothing to suggest that I was anything more or less than a normal child. For years nobody knew that the antibiotics had played havoc with my fetal nervous system. I grew up bright, happy, and energetic.

But by the time I was ten I knew, if nobody else did, that something 5 somewhere had gone wrong. The people around me had gradually developed fuzzy profiles, and their speech had taken on a blurred and foreign character. But I was such a secure and happy child that it didn't enter my mind to question my new perspective or mention the changes to anyone else. Finally, my behavior became noticeably erratic — I would make nonsensical replies to ordinary questions or simply fail to reply at all. My teachers, deciding that I was neither a particularly creative child nor an especially troublesome one, looked for a physical cause. They found two: I wasn't quite as blind as a bat, but I was almost as deaf as a doornail.

My parents took me to Wilford Hall Air Force Hospital in San Antonio, 6 where I was examined from ear to ear. My tonsils were removed and studied, ice water was injected into my inner ear, and I underwent a series of inexplicable and at times painful exploratory tests. I would forever after associate deafness with kind attention and unusual punishment. Finally a verdict was delivered: "Congenital interference has resulted in a neural disorder for which there is no known medical or surgical treatment." My hearing loss was severe and would grow progressively worse.

I was fitted with my first hearing aid and sent back home to resume my 7 childhood. I never did. I had just turned twelve, and my body was undergoing enormous changes. I had baby fat, baby breasts, hairy legs, and thick pink cat-eye glasses. My hearing aid was about the size of a small transistor radio and rode in a white linen pouch that hit exactly at breast level. It was not a welcome addition to my pubescent woe.

As a vain child trapped in a monster's body, I was frantic for a way to 8 survive the next few years. Glimpsing my reflection in mirrors became such agony that I acquired a habit of brushing my teeth and hair with my eyes closed. Everything I did was geared to making my body more inhabitable, but I only succeeded in making it less so. I kept my glasses in my pocket and developed an unbecoming squint; I devised a smile that hid two broken front teeth, but it looked disturbingly like the grin of a piranha; I kept my arms folded over my would-be breasts. But the hearing aid was a different story. There was no way to disguise it. I could tuck it under my blouse, but then all I could hear was the static of cotton. Besides, whenever I took a step the box bounced around like a third breast. So I resigned myself: A monster I was, a monster I would be.

I became more withdrawn, more suspicious of other people's intentions. 9 I imagined that I was being deliberately excluded from school-yard talk because the other children didn't make much of an effort to involve me — they simply didn't have the time or patience to repeat snatches of gossip ten times and slowly. Conversation always reached the point of ridiculousness before I could understand something as simple as "The movie starts at five." (The groovy shark's alive? The moving stars that thrive?) I didn't make it to many movies. I cultivated a lofty sense of superiority, and I was often brutal with people who offered the "wrong" kind of help at the "wrong" time. Right after my thirteenth birthday some well-meaning neighbors took me to a revivalist faith healing. I already had doubts about exuberant religions, and the knee-deep hysteria of the preacher simply confirmed them. He bounded to my side and put his hands on my head. "O Lord," he cried, "heal this poor little lamb!"

I leaped up as if transported and shouted, "I can walk!"   10

For the first few years my parents were as bewildered as I was. Nothing 11 had prepared them for a handicapped child on the brink of adolescence. They sensed a whole other world of problems, but in those early stages I still seemed so normal that they just couldn't see me in a school for the deaf. They felt that although such schools were there to help, they also served to isolate. I have always been grateful for their decision. Because of it, I had to contend with public schools, and in doing so I developed two methods of survival: I learned to read not just lips but the whole person, and I learned the habit of clear speech by taking every speech and drama course I could.

That is not to say my adolescent years were easygoing — they were misery. 12 The lack of sound cast a pall on everything. Life seemed less fun than it had been before. I didn't associate that lack of fun with the lack of sound. I didn't begin to make the connection between the failings of my body and the failings of the world until I was well out of college. I simply did not admit to myself that deafness caused certain problems — or even that I was deaf.

From the time I was twelve until I was twenty-four, the loss of my 13
hearing was erratic. I would lose a decibel or two of sound and then my
hearing would stabilize. A week or a year later there would be another slip
and then I'd have to adjust all over again. I never knew when I would hit
bottom. I remember going to bed one night still being able to make out
the reassuring purr of the refrigerator and the late-night conversation of my
parents, then waking the next morning to nothing — even my own voice
was gone. These fits and starts continued until my hearing finally dropped
to the last rung of amplifiable sound. I was a college student at the time,
and whenever anyone asked about my hearing aid, I admitted to being
only slightly hard of hearing.

My professors were frequently alarmed by my almost maniacal intensity in 14
class. I was petrified that I'd have to ask for special privileges just to achieve
marginal understanding. My pride was in flames. I became increasingly
bitter and isolated. I was terrified of being marked a deaf woman, a label that
made me sound dumb and cowlike, enveloped in a protective silence that
denied me my complexity. I did everything I could to hide my handicap. I
wore my hair long and never wore earrings, thus keeping attention away from
my ears and their riders. I monopolized conversations so that I wouldn't slip
up and reveal what I was or wasn't hearing; I took on a disdainful air at large
parties, hoping that no one would ask me something I couldn't instantly reply
to. I lied about the extent of my deafness so I could avoid the stigma of being
thought "different" in a pathetic way.

It was not surprising that in my senior year I suffered a nervous collapse 15
and spent three days in the hospital crying like a baby. When I stopped crying
I knew it was time to face a few things — I had to start asking for help when
I needed it because I couldn't handle my deafness alone, and I had to quit
being ashamed of my handicap so I could begin to live with its consequences
and discover what (if any) were its rewards.

When I began telling people that I was *really* deaf, I did so with grim 16
determination. Some were afraid to talk to me at any length, fearing perhaps
that they were talking into a void; others assumed that I was somehow an
unsullied innocent and always inquired in carefully enunciated sentences:
"Dooooooooo youuuuuuuu driiiinnk liquor?" But most people were surpris-
ingly sympathetic — they wanted to know the best way to be understood,
they took great pains to talk directly to my face, and they didn't insult me by
using only words of one syllable.

It was, in part, that gentle acceptance that made me more curious about 17
my own deafness. Always before it had been an affliction to wrestle with as
one would with angels, but when I finally accepted it as an inevitable part of
my life, I relaxed enough to do some exploring. I would take off my hearing
aid and go through a day, a night, an hour or two — as long as I could take
it — in absolute silence. I felt as if I were indulging in a secret vice because
I was perceiving the world in a new way — stripped of sound.

Of course I had always known that sound is vibration, but I didn't know, 18
until I stopped straining to hear, how truly sound is a refinement of feeling.
Conversations at parties might elude me, but I seldom fail to pick up on
moods. I enjoy watching people talk. When I am too far away to read lips I
try reading postures and imagining conversations. Sometimes, to everyone's
horror, I respond to things better left unsaid when I'm trying to find out
what's going on around me. I want to see, touch, taste, and smell everything
within reach; I especially have to curb a tendency to judge things by their
smell — not just potato salad but people as well — a habit that seems to some
people entirely too barbaric for comfort. I am not claiming that my other
senses stepped up their work to compensate for the loss, but the absence of
one does allow me to concentrate on the others. Deafness has left me acutely
aware of both the duplicity that language is capable of and the many expressions the body cannot hide.

Nine years ago I spent the summer at the University of Texas's experi- 19
mental Shakespeare workshop at Winedale, and I went back each year for
eight years, first as a student and then as a staff associate. Off and on for the
last four years I have written and performed for Esther's Follies, a cabaret
theater group in Austin. Some people think it's odd that, as deaf as I am, I've
spent so much of my life working in the theater, but I find it to be a natural
consequence of my particular circumstance. The loss of sound has enhanced
my fascination with language and the way meaning is conveyed. I love to
perform. Exactly the same processes occur onstage as off — except that
onstage, once I've memorized the script, I know what everybody is saying as
they say it. I am delighted to be so immediately in the know. It has provided
a direct way to keep in touch with the rest of the world despite the imposed
isolation.

Silence is not empty; it is simply more sobering than sound. At times I 20
prefer the sobriety. I can still "hear" with a hearing aid — that is, I can
discern noise, but I can't tell you where it's coming from or if it is laughter
or a faulty drain. When there are many people talking together I hear a
strange music, a distant rumbling in my consciousness. But when I take off
my hearing aid at night and lie in bed surrounded by my fate, I wonder,
"What is this — a foul subtraction or a blessing in disguise?" For despite my
fears there is a kind of peace in the silence — albeit an uneasy one. There is,
after all, less to distract me from my thoughts.

But I know what I've lost. The process of becoming deaf has at times been 21
frightening, akin perhaps to dying, and early in life it took away my happy
confidence in the image of a world where things always work right. When I
first came back from the Lions Camp that summer I cursed heaven and earth
for doing such terrible wrong to me and to my friends. My grandmother tried
to comfort me by promising, "Honey, God's got something special planned
for you."

But I thought, "Yes. He plans to make me deaf." 22

Analyzing This Selection

1. How does the author's deafness differ from that of most other deaf people? In what ways has this difference made her problems both easier and more burdensome?

2. At the end of paragraph 5, the author uses two clichés about herself. What emotions in the twelve-year-old child do the clichés suggest?

3. In high school and college, why did Galloway refuse to acknowledge the serious consequences of her deafness? What other important considerations were at stake for her? Do you think that her denials were wise or immature for her age?

4. How has deafness influenced the author's adult awareness of the world? How has it influenced her self-awareness?

5. In paragraphs 21 and 22, is the interchange between the author and her grandmother an appropriate or disappointing conclusion to the essay? What attitudes and feelings does it suggest the author has found beneficial?

Analyzing Connections

6. Both Galloway and Ephron (see the preceding essay) suffer mortifications. Compare the kinds of humiliation they endure. What similarities and differences do you find in their self-images?

Analyzing by Writing

7. Helen Keller, who became deaf and blind when she was nineteen months old, said that deafness was the more difficult of her two misfortunes. Which deprivation would be more threatening to you? Are you primarily visually or aurally oriented? Explain how the complete loss of sight or hearing would disconnect you from what you now value most in the world and in yourself.

Diane Ackerman

THE FACE OF BEAUTY

◇

DIANE ACKERMAN (b. 1948), a poet and natural history writer, earned a doctorate in English from Cornell University. Her collections of verse include *Jaguar of Sweet Laughter* (1991). She has won various awards including two fellowships from the National Endowment for the Arts (1976, 1986). Ackerman is a contributing writer for *The New Yorker*. The following essay is excerpted from *A Natural History of the Senses* (1990), a book about experiencing each of the five senses. Her most recent book is A *Natural History of Love* (1994).

In a study in which men were asked to look at photographs of pretty 1 women, it was found they greatly preferred pictures of women whose pupils were dilated. Such pictures caused the pupils of the men's eyes to dilate as much as 30 percent. Of course, this is old news to women of the Italian Renaissance and Victorian England alike, who used to drop belladonna (a poisonous plant in the nightshade family, whose name means "beautiful woman") into their eyes to enlarge their pupils before they went out with gentlemen. Our pupils expand involuntarily when we're aroused or excited; thus, just seeing a pretty woman with dilated pupils signaled the men that she found them attractive, and that made their pupils begin a body-language tango in reply. When I was on shipboard recently, traveling through the ferocious winds and waves of Drake Passage and the sometimes bouncy waters around the Antarctic peninsula, the South Orkneys, South Georgia, and the Falklands, I noticed that many passengers wore a scopolamine patch behind one ear to combat seasickness. Greatly dilated pupils, a side effect of the patch, began to appear a few days into the trip; everybody one met had large, welcoming eyes, which no doubt encouraged the feeling of immediate friendship and camaraderie. Some people grew to look quite zombielike, as they drank in wide gulps of light, but most seemed especially open and warm.[1] Had they checked, the women would have discovered that their cervixes were dilated, too. In professions where emotion or sincere interests

---

[1] An alkaloid extracted from henbane and various other plants of the nightshade family, scopolamine has also been used as truth serum. What a perfect cocktail for a cruise: large pupils continuously signaling interest in everyone they see, and a strong urge to be uninhibited and open to persuasion. [Au.]

need to be hidden, such as gambling or jade-dealing, people often wear dark glasses to hide intentions visible in their telltale pupils.

We may pretend that beauty is only skin deep, but Aristotle was right   2
when he observed that "beauty is a far greater recommendation than any letter of introduction." The sad truth is that attractive people do better in school, where they receive more help, better grades, and less punishment; at work, where they are rewarded with higher pay, more prestigious jobs, and faster promotions; in finding mates, where they tend to be in control of the relationships and make most of the decisions; and among total strangers, who assume them to be interesting, honest, virtuous, and successful. After all, in fairy tales, the first stories most of us hear, the heroes are handsome, the heroines are beautiful, and the wicked sots are ugly. Children learn implicitly that good people are beautiful and bad people are ugly, and society restates that message in many subtle ways as they grow older. So perhaps it's not surprising that handsome cadets at West Point achieve a higher rank by the time they graduate, or that a judge is more likely to give an attractive criminal a shorter sentence. In a 1968 study conducted in the New York City prison system, men with scars, deformities, and other physical defects were divided into three groups. The first group received cosmetic surgery, the second intensive counseling and therapy, and the third no treatment at all. A year later, when the researchers checked to see how the men were doing, they discovered that those who had received cosmetic surgery had adjusted the best and were less likely to return to prison. In experiments conducted by corporations, when different photos were attached to the same résumé, the more attractive person was hired. Prettier babies are treated better than homelier ones, not just by strangers but by the baby's parents as well. Mothers snuggle, kiss, talk to, play more with their baby if it's cute; and fathers of cute babies are also more involved with them. Attractive children get higher grades on their achievement tests, probably because their good looks win praise, attention, and encouragement from adults. In a 1975 study, teachers were asked to evaluate the records of an eight-year-old who had a low IQ and poor grades. Every teacher saw the same records, but to some the photo of a pretty child was attached, and to others that of a homely one. The teachers were more likely to recommend that the homely child be sent to a class for retarded children. The beauty of another can be a valuable accessory. One particularly interesting study asked people to look at a photo of a man and a woman, and to evaluate only the man. As it turned out, if the woman on the man's arm was pretty, the man was thought to be more intelligent and successful than if the woman was unattractive.

Shocking as the results of these and similar experiments might be, they   3
confirm what we've known for ages: Like it or not, a woman's face has always been to some extent a commodity. A beautiful woman is often able to marry her way out of a lower class and poverty. We remember legendary beauties like Cleopatra and Helen of Troy as symbols of how beauty can be powerful enough to cause the downfall of great leaders and change the career of

empires. American women spend millions on makeup each year; in addition, there are the hairdressers, the exercise classes, the diets, the clothes. Handsome men do better as well, but for a man the real commodity is height. One study followed the professional lives of 17,000 men. Those who were at least six feet tall did much better — received more money, were promoted faster, rose to more prestigious positions. Perhaps tall men trigger childhood memories of looking up to authority — only our parents and other adults were tall, and they had all the power to punish or protect, to give absolute love, set our wishes in motion, or block our hopes.

The human ideal of a pretty face varies from culture to culture, of course, 4 and over time, as Abraham Cowley noted in the seventeenth century:

> Beauty, thou wild fantastic ape
> Who dost in every country change thy shape!

But in general what we are probably looking for is a combination of mature and immature looks — the big eyes of a child, which make us feel protective, the high cheekbones and other features of a fully developed woman or man, which make us feel sexy. In an effort to look sexy, we pierce our noses, elongate our earlobes or necks, tattoo our skin, bind our feet, corset our ribs, dye our hair, have the fat liposuctioned from our thighs, and alter our bodies in countless other ways. Throughout most of western history, women were expected to be curvy, soft, and voluptuous, real earth mothers radiant with sensuous fertility. It was a preference with a strong evolutionary basis: A plump woman had a greater store of body fat and the nutrients needed for pregnancy, was more likely to survive during times of hunger, and would be able to protect her growing fetus and breastfeed it once it was born. In many areas of Africa and India, fat is considered not only beautiful but prestigious for both men and women. In the United States, in the Roaring Twenties and also in the Soaring Seventies and Eighties, when ultrathin was in, men wanted women to have the figures of teenage boys, and much psychological hay could be made from how this reflected the changing role of women in society and the work place. These days, most men I know prefer women to have a curvier, reasonably fit body, although most women I know would still prefer to be "too" thin.

But the face has always attracted an admirer's first glances, especially the 5 eyes, which can be so smoldery and eloquent, and throughout the ages people have emphasized their facial features with makeup. Archaeologists have found evidence of Egyptian perfumeries and beauty parlors dating to 4,000 B.C., and makeup paraphernalia going back to 6,000 B.C. The ancient Egyptians preferred green eye shadow topped with a glitter made from crushing the iridescent carapaces of certain beetles; kohl eye liner and mascara; blue-black lipstick; red rouge; and fingers and feet stained with henna. They shaved their eyebrows and drew in false ones. A fashionable Egyptian woman of those days outlined the veins on her breasts in blue and coated her nipples with gold. Her nail polish signaled social status, red indicating the highest. Men also indulged in elaborate potions and beautifiers; and not only for a night out: Tutankhamen's tomb included jars of makeup and beauty creams for his use in the afterlife. Roman men adored cosmetics, and commanders had their hair coiffed and perfumed and their nails lacquered before they went into battle. Cosmetics appealed even more to Roman women, to one of whom Martial wrote in the first century A.D., "While you remain at home, Galla, your hair is at the hairdresser's; you take out your teeth at night and sleep tucked away in a hundred cosmetic boxes — even your face does not sleep with you. Then you wink at men under an eyebrow you took out of a drawer that same morning." A second-century Roman physician invented cold cream, the formula for which has changed little since then. We may remember from the Old Testament that Queen Jezebel painted her face before embarking on her wicked ways, a fashion she learned from the high-toned Phoenicians in about 850 B.C. In the eighteenth century, European women were willing to eat Arsenic Complexion Wafers to make their skin whiter; it poisoned the hemoglobin in the blood so that they developed a fragile, lunar whiteness. Rouges often contained such dangerous metals as lead and mercury, and when used as lipstain they went straight into the bloodstream. Seventeenth-century European women and men sometimes wore beauty patches in the shape of hearts, suns, moons, and stars, applying them to their breasts and face, to draw an admirer's eye away from any imperfections, which, in that era, too often included smallpox scars.

Studies conducted recently at the University of Louisville asked college 6 men what they considered to be the ideal components in a woman's face, and fed the results into a computer. They discovered that their ideal woman had wide cheekbones; eyes set high and wide apart; a smallish nose; high eyebrows; a small neat chin; and a smile that could fill half of the face. On faces deemed "pretty," each eye was one-fourteenth as high as the face, and three-tenths its width; the nose didn't occupy more than five percent of the face; the distance from the bottom lip to the chin was one fifth the height of the face, and the distance from the middle of the eye to the eyebrow was one-tenth the height of the face. Superimpose the faces of many beautiful women onto these computer ratios, and none will match up. What this geometry of beauty boils down to is a portrait of an ideal mother — a young, healthy woman. A mother had to be fertile, healthy, and energetic to protect her young and continue to bear lots of children, many of whom might die in infancy. Men drawn to such women had a stronger chance of their genes surviving. Capitalizing on the continuing subleties of that appeal, plastic surgeons sometimes advertise with extraordinary bluntness. A California surgeon, Dr. Vincent Forshan, once ran an eight-page color ad in *Los Angeles* magazine showing a gorgeous young woman with a large, high bosom, flat stomach, high, tight buttocks, and long sleek legs posing beside a red Ferrari. The headline over the photo ran: "Automobile by Ferrari . . . *body by Forshan.*" Question: What do those of us who aren't tall, flawlessly sculpted adolescents do? Answer: Console ourselves with how relative beauty can be. Although it wins our first praise and the helpless gift of our attention, it can curdle before our eyes in a matter of moments. I remember seeing Omar Sharif in *Doctor Zhivago* and *Lawrence of Arabia*, and thinking him astoundingly handsome. When I saw him being interviewed on television some months later, and heard him declare that his only interest in life was playing bridge, which is how he spent most of his spare time, to my great amazement he was transformed before my eyes into an unappealing man. Suddenly his eyes seemed rheumy and his chin stuck out too much and none of the pieces of his anatomy fell together in the right proportions. I've watched this alchemy work in reverse, too, when a not-particularly-attractive stranger opened his mouth to speak and became ravishing. Thank heavens for the arousing qualities of zest, intelligence, wit, curiosity, sweetness, passion, talent, and grace. Thank heavens that, though good looks may rally one's attention, a lasting sense of a person's beauty reveals itself in stages. Thank heavens, as Shakespeare puts it in *A Midsummer Night's Dream*: "Love looks not with the eyes, but with the mind."

Analyzing This Selection

1. If dilated pupils signal excitement, why is concealing eyes behind sunglasses also considered sexy or glamorous? How might Ackerman explain this apparent contradiction in our responses to a nice face?

2. Ackerman says research shows that good-looking persons always receive preferential treatment. Should educators, employers, and other influential people try to correct this bias? Why or why not?

3. According to Ackerman, what are the basic components of male and female beauty? Do you agree with her analysis?

Analyzing Connections

4. In the photograph at the beginning of this section (see p. 12), what contrasting or conflicting ideals of beauty are evident in the young woman's preoccupations and appearance?

Analyzing by Writing

5. What is the currently popular ideal of attractiveness in women and men? Does this style glamorize health and sportiness? Or does it glamorize subtlety and mystery? What other terms may more accurately describe the current fashionable image? What are the potential depersonalizing and stereotyping effects of this ideal?

Marcia Aldrich

HAIR

◇

Marcia Aldrich, a professor at Michigan State University, received her doctorate in English from the University of Washington. She has published poems in various journals and written articles about modern poets. The following essay is part of a book-in-progress that might be titled *Girl Rearing*, according to the author. "Hair" was selected for inclusion in *The Best American Essays of 1993*.

I've been around and seen the Taj Mahal and the Grand Canyon and Marilyn Monroe's footprints outside Grauman's Chinese Theater, but I've never seen my mother wash her own hair. After my mother married, she never washed her own hair again. As a girl and an unmarried woman — yes — but, in my lifetime, she never washed her hair with her own two hands. Upon matrimony, she began weekly treks to the beauty salon where Julie washed and styled her hair. Her appointment on Fridays at two o'clock was never canceled or rescheduled; it was the bedrock of her week, around which she pivoted and planned. These two hours were indispensable to my mother's routine, to her sense of herself and what, as a woman, she should concern herself with — not to mention their being her primary source of information about all sorts of things she wouldn't otherwise come to know. With Julie my mother discussed momentous decisions concerning hair color and the advancement of age and what could be done about it, hair length and its effect upon maturity, when to perm and when not to perm, the need to proceed with caution when a woman desperately wanted a major change in her life like dumping her husband or sending back her newborn baby and the only change she could effect was a change in her hair. That was what Julie called a "dangerous time" in a woman's life. When my mother spoke to Julie, she spoke in conspiratorial, almost confessional, tones I had never heard before. Her voice was usually tense, on guard, the laughter forced, but with Julie it dropped much lower, the timbre darker than the upper-register shrills sounded at home. And most remarkably, she listened to everything Julie said.

As a child I was puzzled by the way my mother's sense of self-worth and mood seemed dependent upon how she thought her hair looked, how the search for the perfect hair style never ended. Just as Mother seemed to like her latest color and cut, she began to agitate for a new look. The cut seemed to have become a melancholy testimony, in my mother's eyes, to time's inexorable passage. Her hair never stood in and of itself; it was always moored to a complex set of needs and desires her hair couldn't in itself satisfy. She wanted her hair to illuminate the relationship between herself and the idea of motion while appearing still, for example. My mother wanted her hair to be fashioned into an event with a complicated narrative past. However, the more my mother attempted to impose a hair style pulled from an idealized image of herself, the more the hair style seemed to be at odds with my mother. The more the hair style became substantial, the more the woman underneath was obscured. She'd riffle through women's magazines and stare for long dreamy hours at a particular woman's coiffure. Then she'd ask my father in an artificially casual voice: "How do you think I'd look with really short hair?" or "Would blonde become me?" My father never committed himself to an opinion. He had learned from long experience that no response he made could turn out well; anything he said would be used against him, if not in the immediate circumstances, down the line, for my mother never forgot anything anyone ever said about her hair. My father's refusal to engage the "hair question" irritated her.

So too, I was puzzled to see that unmarried women washed their own 3 hair, and married women, in my mother's circle at least, by some unwritten dictum never touched their own hair. I began studying before and after photographs of my mother's friends. These photographs were all the same. In the pre-married mode, their hair was soft and unformed. After the wedding, the women's hair styles bore the stamp of property, looked constructed from grooming talents not their own, hair styles I'd call produced, requiring constant upkeep and technique to sustain the considerable loft and rigidity — in short, the antithesis of anything I might naively call natural. This was hair no one touched, crushed, or ran fingers through. One poked and prodded various hair masses back into formation. This hair presented obstacles to embrace, the scent of the hair spray alone warded off man, child, and pests. I never saw my father stroke my mother's head. Children whimpered when my mother came home fresh from the salon with a potent do. Just when a woman's life was supposed to be opening out into daily affection, *the* sanctioned affection of husband and children, the women of my mother's circle encased themselves in a helmet of hair not unlike Medusa's.

In so-called middle age, my mother's hair never moved, never blew, never 4 fell in her face: her hair became a museum piece. When she went to bed, she wore a blue net, and when she took short showers, short because, after all, she wasn't washing her hair and she was seldom dirty, she wore a blue plastic cap for the sake of preservation. From one appointment to the next, the only change her hair could be said to undergo was to become crestfallen. Taking extended vacations presented problems sufficiently troublesome to rule out countries where she feared no beauty parlors existed. In the beginning, my parents took overnighters, then week jaunts, and thereby avoided the whole hair dilemma. Extending their vacations to two weeks was eventually managed by my mother applying more hair spray and sleeping sitting up. But after the two-week mark had been reached, she was forced to either return home or venture into an unfamiliar salon and subject herself to scrutiny, the kind of scrutiny that leaves no woman unscathed. Then she faced Julie's disapproval, for no matter how expensive and expert the salon, my mother's hair was to be lamented. Speaking just for myself, I had difficulty distinguishing Julie's cunning from the stranger's. In these years my mother's hair looked curled, teased, and sprayed into a waved tossed monument with holes poked through for glasses. She believed the damage done to her hair was tangible proof she had been somewhere, like stickers on her suitcases.

My older sisters have worked out their hair positions differently. My oldest 5 sister's solution has been to fix upon one hair style and never change it. She wants to be thought of in a singular fashion. She may vary the length from long to longer, but that is the extent of her alteration. Once, after having her first baby, the "dangerous time" for women, she recklessly cut her hair to just below the ear. She immediately regretted the decision and began growing it back as she walked home from the salon, vowing not to repeat the mistake. Her signature is dark, straight hair pulled heavily off her face in a large silver clip, found at any Woolworth's. When one clip breaks, she buys another just like it. My mother hates the timelessness of my sister's hair. She equates it with a refusal to face growing old. My mother says, "It's immature to wear your hair the same way all your life."

My sister replies, "It's immature to never stop thinking about your hair. If 6 this hair style was good enough when I was twenty, it's good enough when I'm forty, if not better."

"But what about change?" my mother asks.   7

"Change is overrated," my sister says, flipping her long hair over her 8 shoulder definitively. "I feel my hair."

My other sister was born with thin, lifeless, nondescript hair: a cross she 9 has had to bear. Even in the baby pictures, the limp strands plastered on her forehead in question marks wear her down. Shame and self-effacement are especially plain in the pictures where she posed with our eldest sister, whose dark hair dominates the frame. She's spent her life attempting to disguise the real state of her hair. Some years she'd focus on style, pulling it back in ponytails so that from the front no one could see there wasn't much hair in the back. She tried artless, even messy styles — as if she had just tied it up any old way before taking a bath or bunched it to look deliberately snarled. There were the weird years punctuated by styles that looked as if she had taken sugar water and lemon juice and squeezed them onto her wet hair and then let them crystallize. The worst style was when she took her hair and piled it on the top of her head in a cone shape and then crimped the ponytail into a zigzag. Personally, I thought she had gone too far. No single approach solved the hair problem, and so now, in maturity, she combines the various phases of attack in hope something will work. She frosts both the gray strands and the pale brown, and then perms for added body and thickness. She's forced to keep her hair short because chemicals do tend to destroy. My mother admires my sister's determination to transform herself, and never more than in my sister's latest assault upon middle age. No one has known for many years nor does anyone remember what the untreated color or texture of either my mother's or my sister's hair might be.

As the youngest by twelve years, there was little to distract Mother's 10 considerable attention from the problem of my hair. I had cowlicks, a remarkable number of them, which like little arrows shot across my scalp. They refused to be trained, to lie down quietly in the same direction as the rest of my hair. One at the front insisted on sticking straight up while two on either side of my ears jutted out seeking sun. The lack of uniformity, the fact that my hair had a mind of its own, infuriated my mother and she saw to it that Julie cut my hair as short as possible in order to curtail its wanton expression. Sitting in the swivel chair before the mirror while Julie snipped, I felt invisible, as if I was unattached to my hair.

Just when I started to menstruate, my mother decided the battle plan 11 needed a change, and presto, the page boy replaced the pixie. Having not outgrown the thicket of cowlicks, Mother bought a spectrum of brightly colored stretch bands to hold my hair back off my face. Then she attached thin pink plastic curlers with snap-on lids to the ends of my hair to make them flip up or under, depending on her mood. The stretch bands pressed my hair flat until the very bottom, at which point the ends formed a tunnel with ridges from the roller caps — a point of emphasis, she called it. Coupled with the aquamarine eyeglasses, newly acquired, I looked like an overgrown insect that had none of its kind to bond with.

However, I was not alone. Unless you were the last in a long line of sisters, 12 chances were good that your hair would not go unnoticed by your mother. Each of my best friends was subjected to her mother's hair dictatorship, although with entirely different results. Perry Jensen's mother insisted that all five of her daughters peroxide their hair blonde and pull it back into high ponytails. All the girls' hair turned green in the summer from chlorine. Melissa Matson underwent a look-alike "home perm" with her mother, an experience she never did recover from. She developed a phobic reaction to anything synthetic, which made life very expensive. Not only did mother and daughter have identical tight curls and wear mother-daughter outfits, later they had look-alike nose jobs.

In my generation, many women who survived hair bondage to their 13 mothers now experiment with hair styles as one would test a new design: to see how it works, what it will withstand, and how it can be improved. Testing requires boldness, for often the style fails dramatically, as when I had my hair cut about a half inch long at the top, and it stood straight up like a tacky shag carpet. I had to live with the results, bear daily witness to the kinks in its design for nine months until strategies of damage control could be deployed.

But sometimes women I know create a look that startles in its originality and suggests a future not yet realized.

The women in my family divide into two general groups: those who fasten 14 upon one style, become identified with a look, and are impervious to change, weathering the years steadfastly, and those who, for a variety of reasons, are in the business of transforming themselves. In my sister's case, the quest for perfect hair originates in a need to mask her own appearance; in my mother's case, she wants to achieve a beauty of person unavailable in her own life story. Some women seek transformation, not out of dissatisfaction with themselves, but because hair change is a means of moving along in their lives. These women create portraits of themselves that won't last forever, a new hair style will write over the last.

Since my mother dictated my hair, I never took a stand on the hair issue. 15 In maturity, I'm incapable of assuming a coherent or consistent philosophy. I have wayward hair: it's always becoming something else. The moment it arrives at a recognizable style, it begins to undo itself, it grows, the sun colors it, it waves. When one hair pin goes in, another seems to come out. Sometimes I think I should follow my oldest sister — she claims to never give more than a passing thought to her hair and can't see what all the angst is about. She asks, "Don't women have better things to think about than their hair?"

I bite back: "But don't you think hair should reflect who you are?" 16

"To be honest, I've never thought about it. I don't think so. Cut your hair 17 the same way, and lose yourself in something else. You're distracted from the real action."

I want to do what my sister says, but when I walk out into shop-lined 18 streets, I automatically study women's hair and always with the same question: How did they arrive at their hair? Lately, I've been feeling more and more like my mother. I hadn't known how to resolve the dilemma until I found Rhonda. I don't know if I found Rhonda or made her up. She is not a normally trained hairdresser: she has a different set of eyes, unaffected. One day while out driving around to no place in particular, at the bottom of a hill, I found: "Rhonda's Hair Salon — Don't Look Back" written on a life-size cardboard image of Rhonda. Her shop was on the top of this steep orchard-planted hill, on a plateau with a great view that opened out and went on forever. I parked my car at the bottom and walked up. Zigzagging all the way up the hill, leaning against or sticking out from behind the apple trees, were more life-size cardboard likenesses of Rhonda. Except for the explosive sunbursts in her hair, no two signs were the same. At the bottom, she wore long red hair falling below her knees and covering her entire body like a shawl. As I climbed the hill, Rhonda's hair gradually became shorter and shorter, and each length was cut differently, until when I reached the top, her head was shaved and glistening in the sun. I found Rhonda herself out under one of the apple trees wearing running shoes. Her hair was long and red and looked as if it had never been cut. She told me she had no aspirations to be a hairdresser, "she just fell into it." "I see hair," she continued, "as an extension of the head and therefore I try to do hair with a lot of thought." Inside there were no mirrors, no swivel chairs, no machines of torture with their accompanying stink. She said, "Nothing is permanent, nothing is forever. Don't feel hampered or hemmed in by the shape of your face or the shape of your past. Hair is vital, sustains mistakes, can be born again. You don't have to marry it. Now tip back and put your head into my hands."

Analyzing This Selection

1. What varied roles does Julie the hairdresser serve in Aldrich's mother's life? Does the author view Julie's role as a necessity or a luxury to her mother?

2. As a child, what was Aldrich's view of women's married life? In paragraphs 2 and 3, what does the author imply about herself in childhood?

3. At what points in the essay did you begin to notice that the author deliberately exaggerates her mother's obsession with hair? What details and word choices seem exaggerated? Identify some overstatements. What seems valid despite the exaggeration?

4. Is Rhonda "made up" (p. 40)? Does her philosophy of hair express the author's views or not? Why doesn't Aldrich ever articulate her own views in her own voice?

Analyzing Connections

5. How would Diane Ackerman (in the preceding selection) explain the purpose of hairdressing? How does Ackerman's viewpoint confirm, modify, or contradict Aldrich's analysis?

Analyzing by Writing

6. Men and women send messages about themselves through hairstyles. There are messages visible in the crewcut, the bouffant, the lacquered spike, the metallic dyes, buns, mohawks, men's ponytails, women's butch cuts, and other styles, whether modest or outlandish. Hair can convey political, racial, ethnic, or religious meanings. Analyze the meaning of the hairstyle of your *alter ego* — that is, either your ideal self, a suppressed self, or some identity you would like to try out. Explain your similarities to and differences from this alter ego's appearance.

Joan Didion

IN BED

◇

Joan Didion (b. 1934) was raised in California and graduated from the University of California at Berkeley. Her career in journalism has included work as an editor and columnist for magazines such as *Vogue* and *Saturday Evening Post*. Her essays are collected in *Slouching Towards Bethlehem* (1969), *The White Album* (1979), and *After Henry* (1992). She has written several novels and screenplays, and she has published reportage on international issues in *Salvador* (1983) and *Miami* (1987). Currently Didion contributes essays to the *New York Review of Books* and *The New Yorker*. Didion says about her work, "I write entirely to find out what I'm thinking, what I'm looking at, what I see, and what it means." This analytic viewpoint is evident in the following essay about her suffering from migraine headaches.

Three, four, sometimes five times a month, I spend the day in bed with 1 a migraine headache, insensible to the world around me. Almost every day of every month, between these attacks, I feel the sudden irrational irritation and flush of blood into the cerebral arteries which tell me that migraine is on its way, and I take certain drugs to avert its arrival. If I did not take the drugs, I would be able to function perhaps one day in four. The physiological error called migraine is, in brief, central to the given of my life. When I was fifteen, sixteen, even twenty-five, I used to think that I could rid myself of this error by simply denying it, character over chemistry. "Do you have headaches *sometimes? frequently? never?*" the application forms would demand. "Check one." Wary of the trap, wanting whatever it was that the successful circumnavigation of that particular form could bring (a job, a scholarship, the respect of mankind, and the grace of God), I would check one. "*Sometimes,*" I would lie. That in fact I spent one or two days a week almost unconscious with pain seemed a shameful secret, evidence not merely of some chemical inferiority but of all my bad attitudes, unpleasant tempers, wrongthink.

For I had no brain tumor, no eyestrain, no high blood pressure, nothing 2 wrong with me at all: I simply had migraine headaches, and migraine headaches were, as everyone who did not have them knew, imaginary. I fought migraine then, ignored the warnings it sent, went to school and later to work in spite of it, sat through lectures in Middle English and presentations to advertisers with involuntary tears running down the right side of my face, threw up in washrooms, stumbled home by instinct, emptied ice trays onto my bed and tried to freeze the pain in my right temple, wished only for a neurosurgeon who would do a lobotomy on house call, and cursed my imagination.

It was a long time before I began thinking mechanistically enough to 3 accept migraine for what it was: something with which I would be living, the way people live with diabetes. Migraine is something more than the fancy of a neurotic imagination. It is an essentially hereditary complex of symptoms, the most frequently noted but by no means the most unpleasant of which is a vascular headache of blinding severity, suffered by a surprising number of women, a fair number of men (Thomas Jefferson had migraine, and so did Ulysses S. Grant, the day he accepted Lee's surrender), and by some unfortunate children as young as two years old. (I had my first when I was eight. It came on during a fire drill at the Columbia School in Colorado Springs, Colorado. I was taken first home and then to the infirmary at Peterson Field, where my father was stationed. The Air Corps doctor prescribed an enema.) Almost anything can trigger a specific attack of migraine: stress, allergy, fatigue, an abrupt change in barometric pressure, a contretemps over a parking ticket. A flashing light. A fire drill. One inherits, of course, only the predisposition. In other words I spent yesterday in bed with a headache not merely because of my bad attitudes, unpleasant tempers, and wrongthink, but because both my grandmothers had migraine, my father has migraine, and my mother has migraine.

No one knows precisely what it is that is inherited. The chemistry of 4 migraine, however, seems to have some connection with the nerve hormone named serotonin, which is naturally present in the brain. The amount of serotonin in the blood falls sharply at the onset of migraine, and one migraine drug, methysergide, or Sansert, seems to have some effect on serotonin. Methysergide is a derivative of lysergic acid (in fact Sandoz Pharmaceuticals first synthesized LSD-25 while looking for a migraine cure), and its use is hemmed about with so many contraindications and side effects that most doctors prescribe it only in the most incapacitating cases. Methysergide, when it is prescribed, is taken daily, as a preventive; another preventive which works for some people is old-fashioned ergotamine tartrate, which helps to constrict the swelling blood vessels during the "aura," the period which in most cases precedes the actual headache.

Once an attack is under way, however, no drug touches it. Migraine gives 5 some people mild hallucinations, temporarily blinds others, shows up not only as a headache but as a gastrointestinal disturbance, a painful sensitivity to all sensory stimuli, an abrupt overpowering fatigue, a strokelike aphasia, and a crippling inability to make even the most routine connections. When I am in a migraine aura (for some people the aura lasts fifteen minutes, for others several hours), I will drive through red lights, lose the house keys, spill whatever I am holding, lose the ability to focus my eyes or frame coherent sentences, and generally give the appearance of being on drugs, or drunk. The actual headache, when it comes, brings with it chills, sweating, nausea, a debility that seems to stretch the very limits of endurance. That no one dies of migraine seems, to someone deep into an attack, an ambiguous blessing.

My husband also has migraine, which is unfortunate for him but fortu-   6 nate for me: Perhaps nothing so tends to prolong an attack as the accusing eye of someone who has never had a headache. "Why not take a couple of aspirin," the unafflicted will say from the doorway, or "I'd have a headache, too, spending a beautiful day like this inside with all the shades drawn." All of us who have migraine suffer not only from the attacks themselves but from this common conviction that we are perversely refusing to cure ourselves by taking a couple of aspirin, that we are making ourselves sick, that we "bring it on ourselves." And in the most immediate sense, the sense of why we have a headache this Tuesday and not last Thursday, of course we often do. There certainly is what doctors call a "migraine personality," and that personality tends to be ambitious, inward, intolerant of error, rather rigidly organized, perfectionist. "You don't look like a migraine personality," a doctor once said to me. "Your hair's messy. But I suppose you're a compulsive housekeeper." Actually my house is kept even more negligently than my hair, but the doctor was right nonetheless: Perfectionism can also take the form of spending most of a week writing and rewriting and not writing a single paragraph.

But not all perfectionists have migraine, and not all migrainous people   7 have migraine personalities. We do not escape heredity. I have tried in most of the available ways to escape my own migrainous heredity (at one point I learned to give myself two daily injections of histamine with a hypodermic needle, even though the needle so frightened me that I had to close my eyes when I did it), but I still have migraine. And I have learned now to live with it, learned when to expect it, how to outwit it, even how to regard it, when it does come, as more friend than lodger. We have reached a certain understanding, my migraine and I. It never comes when I am in real trouble. Tell me that my house is burned down, my husband has left me, that there is gunfighting in the streets and panic in the banks, and I will not respond by getting a headache. It comes instead when I am fighting not an open but a guerrilla war with my own life, during weeks of small household confusions, lost laundry, unhappy help, canceled appointments, on days when the telephone rings too much and I get no work done and the wind is coming up. On days like that my friend comes uninvited.

And once it comes, now that I am wise in its ways, I no longer fight it. I   8 lie down and let it happen. At first every small apprehension is magnified, every anxiety a pounding terror. Then the pain comes, and I concentrate only on that. Right there is the usefulness of migraine, there in that imposed yoga, the concentration on the pain. For when the pain recedes, ten or twelve hours later, everything goes with it, all the hidden resentments, all the vain anxieties. The migraine has acted as a circuit breaker, and the fuses have emerged intact. There is a pleasant convalescent euphoria. I open the windows and feel the air, eat gratefully, sleep well. I notice the particular nature of a flower in a glass on the stair landing. I count my blessings.

Analyzing This Selection

1. Why did Didion for many years try to ignore her migraines and to deny having them? What realizations finally changed her mind?

2. In paragraphs 4 and 5, Didion gives an objective account of migraines, and at the same time she suggests her subjective responses as a migraine sufferer. What words and phrases give us her personal response, despite the air of objective detachment?

3. What is a "migraine personality"? Does Didion believe that she has one?

4. In the final two paragraphs, Didion personifies her migraines as she learns to live with her affliction. How does the personification help make her problem more tolerable?

Analyzing Connections

5. Didion and Galloway (see p. 25) write about severe physical afflictions that changed their self-images. What personal qualities do the writers appear to have developed in response to their impairments? Compare their redefined personalities.

Analyzing by Writing

6. Seasonal Affective Disorder. Chronic Fatigue Syndrome. Attention Deficit Disorder. These terms are used to describe familiar kinds of distress or incapacity. How is a person's self-image affected by the application of such terms? Consider both positive and negative effects.

Brent Staples

BLACK MEN AND PUBLIC SPACE

◇

BRENT STAPLES (b. 1951) was born in Chester, Pennsylvania. He earned his undergraduate degree at Widener University and a Ph.D. in psychology from the University of Chicago. After working at the *Chicago Sun-Times* and several Chicago periodicals, he became an assistant metropolitan editor at the *New York Times* in 1985. He is now on the editorial board of that newspaper. Staples has published a memoir, *Parallel Time: Growing Up in Black and White* (1994). The following essay, which appeared first in *Ms.* magazine, describes his experience of "being ever the suspect" in urban America.

My first victim was a woman — white, well dressed, probably in her early 1 twenties. I came upon her late one evening on a deserted street in Hyde Park, a relatively affluent neighborhood in an otherwise mean, impoverished section of Chicago. As I swung onto the avenue behind her, there seemed to be a discreet, uninflammatory distance between us. Not so. She cast back a worried glance. To her, the youngish black man — a broad six feet two inches with a beard and billowing hair, both hands shoved into the pockets of a bulky military jacket — seemed menacingly close. After a few more quick glimpses, she picked up her pace and was soon running in earnest. Within seconds she disappeared into a cross street.

That was more than a decade ago. I was twenty-two years old, a graduate 2 student newly arrived at the University of Chicago. It was in the echo of that terrified woman's footfalls that I first began to know the unwieldy inheritance I'd come into — the ability to alter public space in ugly ways. It was clear that she thought herself the quarry of a mugger, a rapist, or worse. Suffering a bout of insomnia, however, I was stalking sleep, not defenseless wayfarers. As a softy who is scarcely able to take a knife to a raw chicken — let alone hold one to a person's throat — I was surprised, embarrassed, and dismayed all at once. Her flight made me feel like an accomplice in tyranny. It also made it clear that I was indistinguishable from the muggers who occasionally seeped into the area from the surrounding ghetto. That first encounter, and those that followed, signified that a vast, unnerving gulf lay between night-time pedestrians — particularly women — and me. And I soon gathered that being perceived as dangerous is a hazard in itself. I only needed to turn a corner into a dicey situation, or crowd some frightened, armed person in a foyer somewhere, or make an errant move after being pulled over by a policeman. Where fear and weapons meet — and they often do in urban America — there is always the possibility of death.

In that first year, my first away from my hometown, I was to become 3 thoroughly familiar with the language of fear. At dark, shadowy intersections, I could cross in front of a car stopped at a traffic light and elicit the *thunk, thunk, thunk, thunk* of the driver — black, white, male, or female — hammering down the door locks. On less traveled streets after dark, I grew accustomed to but never comfortable with people crossing to the other side of the street rather than pass me. Then there were the standard unpleasantries with policemen, doormen, bouncers, cabdrivers, and others whose business it is to screen out troublesome individuals *before* there is any nastiness.

I moved to New York nearly two years ago and I have remained an avid 4 night walker. In central Manhattan, the near-constant crowd cover minimizes tense one-on-one street encounters. Elsewhere — in SoHo, for example, where sidewalks are narrow and tightly spaced buildings shut out the sky — things can get very taut indeed.

After dark, on the warrenlike streets of Brooklyn where I live, I often see 5 women who fear the worst from me. They seem to have set their faces on neutral, and with their purse straps strung across their chests bandolier-style, they forge ahead as though bracing themselves against being tackled. I understand, of course, that the danger they perceive is not a hallucination. Women are particularly vulnerable to street violence, and young black males are drastically overrepresented among the perpetrators of that violence. Yet these truths are no solace against the kind of alienation that comes of being ever the suspect, a fearsome entity with whom pedestrians avoid making eye contact.

It is not altogether clear to me how I reached the ripe old age of twenty- 6 two without being conscious of the lethality nighttime pedestrians attributed to me. Perhaps it was because in Chester, Pennsylvania, the small, angry industrial town where I came of age in the 1960s, I was scarcely noticeable against a backdrop of gang warfare, street knifings, and murders. I grew up one of the good boys, had perhaps a half-dozen fistfights. In retrospect, my shyness of combat has clear sources.

As a boy, I saw countless tough guys locked away; I have since buried several, 7 too. They were babies, really — a teenage cousin, a brother of twenty-two, a childhood friend in his mid-twenties — all gone down in episodes of bravado played out in the streets. I came to doubt the virtues of intimidation early on. I chose, perhaps unconsciously, to remain a shadow — timid, but a survivor.

The fearsomeness mistakenly attributed to me in public places often has 8 a perilous flavor. The most frightening of these confusions occurred in the late 1970s and early 1980s, when I worked as a journalist in Chicago. One day, rushing into the office of a magazine I was writing for with a deadline story in hand, I was mistaken for a burglar. The office manager called security and, with an ad hoc posse, pursued me through the labyrinthine halls, nearly to my editor's door. I had no way of proving who I was. I could only move briskly toward the company of someone who knew me.

Another time I was on assignment for a local paper and killing time before 9 an interview. I entered a jewelry store on the city's affluent Near North Side. The proprietor excused herself and returned with an enormous red Doberman pinscher straining at the end of a leash. She stood, the dog extended toward me, silent to my questions, her eyes bulging nearly out of her head. I took a cursory look around, nodded, and bade her good night.

Relatively speaking, however, I never fared as badly as another black male 10 journalist. He went to nearby Waukegan, Illinois, a couple of summers ago to work on a story about a murderer who was born there. Mistaking the reporter for the killer, police officers hauled him from his car at gunpoint and but for his press credentials would probably have tried to book him. Such episodes are not uncommon. Black men trade tales like this all the time.

Over the years, I learned to smother the rage I felt at so often being taken 11 for a criminal. Not to do so would surely have led to madness. I now take precautions to make myself less threatening. I move about with care, particularly late in the evening. I give a wide berth to nervous people on subway platforms during the wee hours, particularly when I have exchanged business clothes for jeans. If I happen to be entering a building behind some people who appear skittish, I may walk by, letting them clear the lobby before I return, so as not to seem to be following them. I have been calm and extremely congenial on those rare occasions when I've been pulled over by the police.

And on late-evening constitutionals I employ what has proved to be an 12 excellent tension-reducing measure: I whistle melodies from Beethoven and Vivaldi and the more popular classical composers. Even steely New Yorkers hunching toward nighttime destinations seem to relax, and occasionally they even join in the tune. Virtually everybody seems to sense that a mugger wouldn't be warbling bright, sunny selections from Vivaldi's *Four Seasons*. It is my equivalent of the cowbell that hikers wear when they know they are in bear country.

Analyzing This Selection

1. What is the effect of the opening paragraph?
2. How does the author's presence "alter public space in ugly ways"? Describe the difference between Staples's image of himself and how he is perceived by others.
3. Why doesn't Staples see the suspicion he elicits from being a young black man on the street as solely the result of racial attitudes?

4. How does the author defuse the explosive tensions his presence produces in other people? Do his methods compromise his own self-image and integrity?

5. What is the essay's overall purpose? Does Staples propose any remedies for the unjust assumptions he describes?

Analyzing Connections

6. Staples and Galloway (see p. 25) each relate a brief incident in their opening paragraphs. Compare the themes and tones they introduce within these anecdotal openings. Both essays conclude by echoing the opening anecdotes. What is the effect of such endings?

Analyzing by Writing

7. In what way have you been stereotyped? Perhaps as "a brain" or "a jock"; or as a black, a Jew, an Italian; or as someone who is always "good-natured" or always "responsible." In an essay, examine the stereotype that falsifies and denigrates something that is true in your nature.

Stephen Dixon

INTERSTATE 7

◇

STEPHEN DIXON (b. 1936) was raised in New York City and graduated from City College. As a fiction writer he has won various awards, including a fellowship from the National Endowment for the Arts (1975) and a Guggenheim Fellowship (1985). In 1980 Dixon joined the faculty of Johns Hopkins University, where he is a professor of fiction. His ten books of short stories have been collected in *The Stories of Stephen Dixon* (1994). The following new story was printed in the *Boston Review* (1994).

Guy in the car to the left of ours looking at me. I didn't see the car till just 1 before this second, nod to him, eyes back on the road, car he's in stays beside ours maybe four-five feet away; maybe six. "Yes," I think, "what?" looking at him. No answer. "You're awfully close, any reason to be?" No answer. Wouldn't think so. Just the look, the straight stare, oh you're a toughie, bet your kids are scared shit of ya, and look front and steer the car closer to the right lane line. Few seconds later I feel — sense — he's doing something with his hand, motioning, or waving something and maybe even from outside and I look over and car he's in has moved over to almost cross the lane into mine and his window's down and he's pointing out it at me and has this smirk or sneer or I don't know what, not the noncommittal plain know-nothing to even dopey look from before trying to be hard but some smart-ass scorning sarcastic smile if I want to say it in a mouthful, and I think "Why, what's with him, did I do something with my driving he didn't like and for all I know might have, or he thought so, endangered their car for a moment or maybe the driver thought this and told him to let me know for he's closer?" and say through my window "Yes?" and Margo in back says "What's the man pointing at you for, Daddy?" and I say "Beats me. — Yes sir, what, something wrong?" I mouth to him now, raising my eyebrows to show, or by doing that making lots of folds in my forehead, but that I'm asking a serious question and am no wiseguy and maybe something's wrong with my car that he's spotted and he wants to tell me but doesn't know how to look at people or really deal with them in any way, or just strangers, but how he's doing, or possibly just normal rather conventional looking guys with kids in tow who he thinks might be some threat to him for some reason, that they do seem so normal and content and polite and nice while he's such a roughneck who can't keep anything, job, woman, family, but I'm no doubt going too far into it, and he starts laughing riotously while pointing at me, to even shutting his eyes and opening his mouth wide and probably making haw-haw noises it's all so funny and then says something to the driver who starts laughing normally — I'm looking back and forth at the road and them — but almost as if he doesn't really want to laugh, his face I mean, but feels he has to for the other guy's sake — honor, whatever — or so the other guy doesn't think he hasn't a sense of humor or something. In other words, his heart's not in it, and out of friendship or fellowship, I mean. They beat up people the same way, I bet: even if you think the guy who's arguing with your friend is absolutely right and your friend's dead wrong you still stomp the guy with your friend. And I look front and I don't know why, out of nowhere perhaps but maybe more so from some nervousness with these guys keeping up this thing with me like they are and their car being closer than I like and still almost in my lane, maybe straddling the in-between line now and staying even with us so long, but I say "So what do you think they find so funny, girls?" — asking them this to distract myself from those guys, is what I'm saying — "and don't look, no staring, don't give them any more cause for continuing whatever it is they're continuing," and Julie says "What is it that they're doing, Daddy, and the driver's doing it too?" and I say "That's just it, I don't know what it is, playing goofy loony games with me is all I can see. There are all sorts of stupid people in this world I'm afraid to tell you, but when they get on the road they're even worse. The car seems to bring something out in people that nothing else does, and it isn't just the speed and enclosure of the thing either — you know, being contained in it, inside, windows shut, cut off from other people. For even the bumper cars at the amusement park do it to people — excite them, make them reckless. But that's a bad example since they're made for craziness and you pay to get in them and drive wildly, but I guess I was saying that those things are wide open and aren't fast at all while most real cars are the opposite. Meaning, fast or slow, open or enclosed, just being in a car, even a kiddy car when you're a kid — I remember how reckless and adult I felt in them — does it. And in a way, though you can't get in them but they can make kids wild and strange a little, those miniature toy cars kids have — Matchboxes, because they come in them or that's the size they are — that they roll against the wall or smash into other tiny cars like it, or off a table and that sort of stuff. So it's cars of all kinds we can say — kiddy and bumper ones, toy cars and real convertibles and Jeeps. Two-seaters, six-seaters, racing and stock cars of course, probably not blood- and bookmobiles and golf carts, panel trucks, minivans, though not as much, I'd think, possibly because families are usually in them. They're made for parents with their kids, you can say, and families can be kind of inhibiting on the road. Restraining. You know, they keep control of the driver's most reckless and wild emotions when he's outside, while inside, meaning in the house and not the car, it could be another story where all sorts of violent terrible stuff can go on. But anyway, you don't want to drive too fast and carelessly and take chances — that's it — take chances with your wife and kids in the car, so almost any car or minitruck when they're in it and also your cats and dogs and so on. Oh, do I know what I'm talking about? Nobody answer but I'm afraid not. Though what was I talking about way before I started all that about cars and pets?" and Julie says "I don't know, you lost me long ago," and I say "Thank ye, thank ye — oh yeah, about what do you girls think those men found so funny before from their car, anyone have an idea now?" "Not me," Julie says and I say "My face, right? Maybe my face. Got to be that, for we all know it's funny, and can't be your faces for yours are gorgeous and who laughs at that? So, fine, my funny-looking spongy face and maybe my balding scalp — they both had big hairy clumps on theirs — and we'll leave it at that," and Julie says "I don't think your face is so funny, and you have hair," and I say "Not in the right head places, but thanks. And Margo, you've been noticeably quiet, anything wrong?" and she says "I've lost interest in the subject," and I say "Oh, well, that's — uh," for I see without looking right at it that a car's alongside us again when one hasn't been there for a couple of minutes or so, not that I saw the guys' car go, I was too caught up in my talking, and I say "Listen, and I'm serious, I've a funny feeling those same two palookas are beside us again on my side, anyone want to sneak a peak for me and report back? — maybe it's a different car," and Julie says "The same, they're there for lots more seconds than just now, something the matter, Daddy?" and I say "Are they — do this from memory, neither of you look — were they staring or laughing again?" and Margo says "Staring, at you, the man not the driver was. And now kind of trying to talk to you through your window. And now making these hand movements as if rolling down a car window while also pointing to you as if you should do it with yours too," and I say "I told you not to look, goddamnit," and she says "I'm sorry, Daddy, I didn't mean to; I'm now looking straight ahead at only nothing, but are you worried by him?" and I say "The truth is, without trying to scare your kids, and the good thing is they're not so dangerously close as they were the first time — And continue not to look at them, just as I'm not and won't, for sooner we completely ignore them I'm sure quicker they'll go away. But I just didn't like the looks of those guys. Not the looks so much as what they did and are still doing, distracting my attention, or trying to, really, and just being dumb, but real dumb dumb dumb, as if they want to spook me off the road, for who the fuck they think they are? — excuse me, but I'm mad at them and with good reason — I got my kids with me," and I speed up and Margo says "I hope I didn't make you feel bad before by what I said about losing interest," and I yell "Please, not now," for their car stays beside ours, "I've got too much to do driving, and sit back tight, make sure you're buckled in good in case they try to do something crazy with their car — they could," and Margo yells "Oh no," and I say "What's wrong?" and Julie says "My gosh, Daddy, what?" and I shout "It's okay, nothing will happen, but do what I say, and let me drive," and slow down and their car continues as fast and the guy sticks his head out and turns it around to me and gives this sinister big grin and then sticks his hand out the window and points it at me into sort of a pistol shape and takes aim, one eye cocked, and I think says "Bang bang," his mouth moves like that, or maybe "Pop pop," and then puts the pistol hand up to his mouth and blows gunsmoke off his fingertip and brings his head back into the car and faces front and they're now about a hundred feet in front of us, his pistol hand open and dangling down the door, and now a hundred-fifty, two hundred, and their car cuts into my lane without signaling and slows down a little and I think "What're they up to now?" and slow down some more and then shoots across the next center lane into the slow one and really speeds up till it must be doing 85, 90, no car's in front of it, even a hundred, it seems to be going so fast. I look around for a patrol car same time I'm keeping my eyes on the men, or an unmarked car with a trooper in it in trooper's clothes and maybe the hat. I'd love to see those bastards caught. If one went after them with the roof light or siren going I'd follow at a reasonable clip just to stay near and pull up behind on the shoulder once the trooper stopped them and explain to him why I was speeding like that myself: what those guys tried doing to me and my kids, the scare tactics and driving close and so on. By now their car's way off, half a mile or so, quarter-mile, third of one, anyway, pretty far in front and still speeding it seems and now no threat to us, for I just can't think of them slowing down so much where they'd come back and resume what they were doing, and soon they're out of sight or just mixed in with lots of tiny dots that are cars and buses and trucks. "It's okay, girls, you can relax, those idiots are gone," slowing down even more and moving into the slow lane to be out of the way of any cars that might want to get around me, for my body has that feeling of having just gone through something very scary, heart pumping where I can feel it, the stuff in the larynx or neck, and of course the sweat, and Margo says "It wasn't really ever that bad, was it, Daddy?" and I say, "Nah, though just for a moment I thought so, but I'll tell you, if I ever saw those guys stopped off the road by some cop for speeding, which they should be, but you know, as they say, try and find a cop when you truly need one, well I'd pull over and tell the policeman what they did. But okay, good riddance and may we never see them or anything like them again," and Julie says "What's 'good riddance'?" and Margo tells her though her definition's all wrong — something like riders no longer riding — I don't correct her. What would I say to the policeman though? That they drove alongside us a while, sort of were following us, tried to screw up my driving by trying to frighten me with those sinister grins and getting too close and also that thing with the hand shaped like a gun when they tore off? It would be nothing; they could give all sorts of innocent and plausible reasons why they did it: they like kids, at least the passenger does, but in a good way and he was trying to make my sourpusses laugh by making faces. Or he thought my door wasn't closed all the way and was pointing it out to me, that's why their car got so close, because I didn't seem to hear him and they thought it was too important to just let pass, and that's also what his so-called shooting finger meant: it was pointing to my door, and they never crossed the lane line into mine either, and so forth. The trooper might just laugh at me or tell me to be a good guy and forget it, even if he half believed me, and move on, for he has more important business to take care of, like writing out a speeding ticket — that he has clocked on his radar — and calling in on them to see if their car's stolen or they owe for past traffic violations in this state.

Analyzing This Selection

1. What is the father's reaction to the first provocations of the men in the other car?

2. How does the father try to reassure his daughters? How do his attempts at reassurance affect him? How can we discern these changes in his composure?

3. How does the father convince himself that it would be futile to complain to the police?

Analyzing Connections

4. Brent Staples (in the preceding selection) deals with many hostile encounters in daily life. What advice might he pass along to the father in this story? Considering the differences in their personalities, would his advice work?

Analyzing by Writing

5. Define a common term for some aspect of self-awareness such as *self-possessed, self-evolved, self-esteem, self-respect,* or *self-love.* Write concretely about the abstraction, giving examples when useful. Consider the shades of meaning covered by the term.

Andrew Holleran

THE FEAR

◇

ANDREW HOLLERAN (b. 1943) has written two novels about gay life, *Dancer from the Dance* (1978) and *Nights in Aruba* (1983). His essays dealing with public and personal issues surrounding AIDS have been collected in *Ground Zero* (1988). The following essay appeared in a collection of writers' responses to the AIDS crisis titled *Personal Dispatches* (1989). Holleran examines the anxiety and distrust that grip people facing the threat of communicable disease and death.

The Fear is of course unseemly — as most fear is. People behave at worst 1
with demonic cruelty — at best oddly. Even among those who are good-hearted, the madness breaks out in small ways that bring friendships of long standing to an abrupt end. When the plague began and the television crews of certain TV stations refused to work on interviews with people with AIDS, I wanted to get their names, write them down, publish them on a list of cowards. When the parents in Queens picketed and refused to send their kids to school; when they kicked Ryan White[1] out of class in Indiana; when people called in to ask if it was safe to ride the subway; when Pat Buchanan[2] called for a quarantine of homosexuals; when they burned down the house in Arcadia, Florida, I felt a thrilling disgust, a contempt, an anger at the shrill, stupid, mean panic, the alacrity with which people are converted to lepers and the lepers cast out of the tribe, the fact that if Fear is contemptible, it is most contemptible in people who have no reason to fear.

Even within the homosexual community, however, there was despicable 2
behavior: men who would not go to restaurants, hospital rooms, wakes, for fear that any contact with other homosexuals might be lethal. At dinner one night in San Francisco in 1982, a friend said, "There's a crack in the glass," after I'd taken a sip of his lover's wine, and took the glass back to the kitchen to replace it — a reaction so swift it took me a moment to realize there was no crack in the glass; the problem was my lips' touching it — homosexual

---

[1]Ryan White, a child who contracted AIDS through a blood transfusion, was not allowed to continue elementary school. Legal action eventually reversed his school's action. He died from the disease in 1990. [Ed.]

[2]Patrick Buchanan, a political journalist, was a presidential aide to Ronald Reagan. [Ed.]

lips, from New York: the kiss of death. I was furious then, but the behavior no longer surprises me. AIDS, after all, belongs to the Age of Anxiety. My friend was a germophobe to begin with, who, though homosexual himself, after five years in San Francisco, had come to loathe homosexuals. The idea that they could now kill him, or his lover, fit in. AIDS fed on his free-floating anxiety about the rest of modern life: the fertilizers, pesticides, toxic wastes, additives in food, processing of food, steroids given cattle, salmonella in chickens, killer bees moving up from Brazil, Mediterranean fruit fly, poisoned water, lead in our pipes, radon in our homes, asbestos in our high schools, danger of cigarette smoke, mercury in tuna, auto emissions in the air, Filipinos on the bus, Mexicans sneaking across the border. The society that could make sugar sinister was ready, it would seem, to panic over AIDS, so that when Russia put out the disinformation in its official press that AIDS was the work of a germ-warfare laboratory run by the Pentagon, it was only repeating a charge made by homosexuals convinced that AIDS is a right-wing program to eradicate queers.

God only knows what AIDS will turn out to be, years and years from now — perhaps, in 2005, "Sixty Minutes" will reveal it *was* a CIA foul-up. But this general panic, this unease, this sense that the world is out of control and too intimately connected, is not *all* the Fear is among homosexuals. The Fear among homosexuals is personal, physical, and real. It is easy enough to dismiss the idea that the CIA set out to exterminate homosexuals; it is not easy to dismiss the fact that — having lived in New York during the seventies as a gay man — one can reasonably expect to have been infected. "We've all been exposed," a friend said to me in 1981 on the sidewalk one evening before going off to Switzerland to have his blood recycled — when "exposed" was still the word to spare the feelings of those who were, someone finally pointed out, "infected." The idea — that everyone had been swimming in the same sea — made little impression on us at the time; nor did I grasp the implications — because then the plague was still so new, and its victims so (relatively) few, that most homosexuals could still come up with a list of forty to fifty things to distinguish their past, their habits, from those of the men they knew who had it. Now, five years later, that list is in shreds; one by one, those distinguishing features or habits have been taken away, and the plague reveals itself as something infinitely larger, more various, more random, than was suspected at the start — as common as the flu — indeed, the thing the doctors are predicting a repeat of: the Spanish influenza following World War I.

Predictions like these, above all, intensify the Fear, to the point that one tenses when a news story comes on the evening news about AIDS — and wonders: What new sadistic detail? What new insoluble problem? One looks away when the word is in the newspaper headline and turns to the comics instead. One hopes the phone will not ring with news of yet another friend diagnosed, because one can always trace a flare-up of the Fear — an AIDS anxiety attack: that period when you are certain you have *It*, and begin making plans for your demise — to some piece of news, or several, that came through the television or the telephone. Sometimes they are so numerous, and all at once, that you are undone — like the man walking down the boardwalk on Fire Island with a friend one evening on their way to dance, who, after a quiet conversation at dinner, suddenly threw himself down on the ground and began screaming: "We're all going to die, we're all going to die!" He did. Sometimes it hits like that. It appears in the midst of the most ordinary circumstances — like the man on that same beach, who in the middle of a cloudless summer afternoon turned to my friend and said: "What is the point of going on?" ("To bear witness," my friend responded.) The Fear is there all the time, but it comes in surges, like electricity — activated, triggered, almost always by specific bad news.

The media are full of bad news, of course — the stories of breakthroughs, 5 of discoveries, of new drugs seem to have subsided now into a sea of disappointment. They do not sound the note of relief and hope and exultation they once did — that dream that one evening you would be brushing your teeth, and your roommate, watching the news in the living room, would shout: "It's over!" and you would run down the hall and hear the Armistice declared. Instead, the media carry the *pronunciamientos* of the Harvard School of Public Health, the World Health Organization, dire beyond our wildest nightmares: What began as a strange disease ten or twelve homosexuals in New York had contracted becomes the Black Death. Of course, journalists, as Schopenhauer said, are professional alarmists, and have only fulfilled their usual role: scaring their readers. They are scaring them so that the readers will protect themselves, of course; they are at the same time inducing despair in those already infected. There's the dilemma: They're all watching the same TV, reading the same newspapers.

After a while, the Fear is so ugly you feel like someone at a dinner party 6 whose fellow guests are being taken outside and shot as you concentrate politely on your salad. There is the school of thought that says the Fear is a form of stress, and stress enhances the virus. Like the man so afraid of muggers he somehow draws them to him, the Fear is said to make itself come true, by those who believe in mind control. As a friend of mine (so fearful of the disease he refused to have sex for four years) said, "I got everything I resisted." So one becomes fearful even of the Fear. The Fear can be so wearing, so depressing, so constant that a friend who learned he had AIDS said, on hearing the diagnosis, "Well, it's a lot better than worrying about it."

He also said, "I wasn't doing anything anyone else wasn't." Which ex- 7 plains the Fear more succinctly than anything else: Tens of thousands were doing the same thing in the seventies. Why, then, should some get sick and not others? Isn't it logical to expect everyone will, eventually? The Fear is so strong it causes people to change cities, to rewrite their pasts in order to imagine they were doing less than everyone else; because the most unnerving thing about the plague is its location in the Past, the Time allotted to it.

Were AIDS a disease which, once contracted, brought death within 8 forty-eight hours of exposure, it would be a far more easily avoided illness — but because it is not — because it is invisible, unknown, for such a long period of time, because it is something people got before they even knew it existed (with each passing year, the Time Lag gets longer), the Fear of AIDS is limitless. Who has not had sex within the last seven years — once? (The nun in San Francisco who got AIDS from a blood transfusion given her during an operation to set her broken leg, and died, her superiors said, without anger or bitterness.) (The babies who get it in the womb.) There's a memory — of an evening, an incident — to justify every Fear. And nothing exists that will guarantee the fearful that even if they are functioning now, they will not get caught in the future. The phrase that keeps running through the fearful mind is: Everyone was healthy before he got sick. One has to have two programs, two sets of responses, ready at all times: (a) Life, (b) Death. The switch from one category to the other can come at any moment, in the most casual way. At the dentist's, or putting on your sock. Did that shin bruise a little too easily? Is that a new mole? Is the sinus condition that won't go away just a sinus condition? Do you feel a bit woozy standing at the kitchen sink? Do you want to lie down? Is the Fear making you woozy, or the virus? Have you had too many colds this past spring to be just colds? Thus the hyperconsciousness of the body begins. Your body — which you have tended, been proud of — is something you begin to view with suspicion, mistrust. Your body is someone you came to a party with and you'd like to ditch, only you promised to drive him home. Your body is a house — there's a thief inside it who wants to rob you of everything. Your body could be harboring It, even as you go about your business. This keeps you on edge. You stop, for instance, looking in mirrors. Or at your body in the shower — because the skin, all of a sudden, seems as vast as Russia: a huge terrain, a monumental wall, on which tiny handwriting may suddenly appear. The gums, the tongue, the face, the foot, the forearm, the leg: *billions* of cells waiting to go wrong. Because you read that sunburn depresses the immune system, you no longer go out in the sun. You stay in the house — as if already an invalid — you cancel all thoughts of traveling in airplanes because you heard flights can trigger the pneumonia and because you want to be home when it happens, not in some hotel room in Japan or San Diego.

And so the Fear constricts Life. It suffocates, till one evening its prey 9 snaps — gets in the car and drives to the rest stop, or bar, or baths to meet another human being; and has sex. Sometimes has sex; sometimes just talks about the Fear, because a conversation about the danger of sex sometimes replaces sex itself. The Fear is a god to which offerings must be made before sex can commence. Sometimes it refuses the offering. If it does not, it takes its share of the harvest afterward. Sex serves the Fear more slavishly than anything. Even safe sex leads to the question: Why was I even doing something that *required* condoms? The aftermath of sex is fear *and* loathing. AIDS is a national program of aversion therapy. Sex and terror are twins. Death is a hunk, a gorgeous penis. And fear is self-centered, is above all personal, and you vent your terror before you realize how insensitive this is. One day you spill out your fears about the sex you had to a friend who — you realize too late — has had AIDS for a couple of years now. He has lived with his own fear for two years. Your friend merely listens calmly, says what you did does not seem unsafe, and then remarks: "What I'm getting from what you've been saying is that you're still afraid." Of course, you want to reply, *of course* I'm still afraid! "But you have no reason to be," he says, from the height, the eminence of his own fear, digested, lived with, incorporated into his own life by now. "If you don't have it now, you won't." (Your other friend has told you, "The doctors think we're about to see a second wave of cases, the ones who contracted it in 1981.") Going home on the subway, your fear takes the form of superstition: He should never have said that! He himself had said (a remark you've never forgotten) that he was diagnosed just at the point when — after three years of abstinence — he thought he had escaped. It's the Time Lag, of course, the petri dish in which the Fear thrives. Of course, you are afraid; every male homosexual who lived in New York during the seventies is scared shitless. And a bit unstable, withdrawn, and crazy. The tactlessness of venting your fear to a friend who already has been diagnosed is symptomatic of this behavior. People who are afraid are seldom as considerate as those who are unafraid. The ironic thing about my last visit to New York was that the two men I knew who have AIDS were cheerful, calm, gracious, well behaved. Those who did not were nervous wrecks: depressed, irritable, isolated, withdrawn, unwilling to go out at night, in bed by ten under a blanket, with terror and a VCR. The Fear is not fun to live with, though when shared, it can produce occasional, hysterical laughter. The laughter vanishes, however, the moment you leave the apartment building and find yourself alone on the street. Falls right off your face as you slip instantly back into the mood you were in before you went to visit your friend. The Fear breeds depression. The depression breeds anger. (Not to mention the anger of people who have it toward those who don't. Why me? Why should *he* escape?) Friendships come to an end over incidents which would have been jokes before. People withdraw from each other so they don't have to go through the suffering of each other's illness. People behave illogically: One night a friend refuses to eat from a buffet commemorating a dead dancer because so many of the other guests have AIDS ("They shouldn't have served finger food"), but he leaves the wake with a young handsome Brazilian who presumably doesn't, goes home, and has sex. We all have an explanation for our private decisions, our choices of what we will do and what we won't; we all have a rationale for our superstitions. Most of it *is* superstition, because that is what the Fear produces and always has. Some of it is just muddled thinking, like the nightclub patrons in Miami who said they did not worry about AIDS there because it cost ten dollars to get in. And some of it is perfectly rational, like that which convinces people they should not take the Test because they would rather not live with the knowledge they have antibodies to the virus. (Today, the news announces a home test that will tell you in three minutes if you do, or don't; not much time for counseling!) The Test is the most concentrated form of the Fear that there is — which 10 is why people are advised not to take it if they think they will have trouble handling the results. Why should we know? The fact is things are happening in our bodies, our blood, all the time we know nothing of; the hole in the dike of our immune systems may appear at any moment, and is always invisible, silent, unadvertised.

When does a person begin to develop cancer? When does a tumor start to   11 grow? When does the wall of the heart begin to weaken? Do you want to know? With AIDS, there is presumably something in hiding, in the brain, the tissues, waiting for some moment to begin its incredibly fast and protean reproduction. It may be waiting — or reproducing — as I type this. This is the Fear that is finally selfish. That is perhaps worse in the imagining than in the reality. This is what makes you think: I must know, I can't bear this, I'll take the Test. So you drive over one hot afternoon to do it, thinking of the letter from a woman whose nephew just died at home of AIDS: "Tony even tested Negative two months before he died." What fun. You feel as if you are driving not toward the county health department but the Day of Judgment. In my right hand, I give you Life, in my left, Death. What will you do, the voice asks, when you find out? How will you live? How do people with AIDS drive the car, fall asleep at night, face the neighbors, deal with solitude? The stupendous cruelty of this disease crashes in upon you. And so you bargain with God. You apologize, and make vows. Ask, How could this have happened? How could I have reached this point? Where did I make the turn that got me on *this* road? Every test you have ever taken, written or oral — the book reports; the thesis exam- inations; the spelling bees; those afternoons walking home from school as far as you could before turning the page of your test to see the grade, on a corner where no one could see your reaction; the day you got drafted; the day you found out whether you were going to Vietnam — all pale, or come back, in one single concentrated tsunami of terror at this moment.

In eighteenth-century Connecticut, Jonathan Edwards preached a sermon   12 called "Sinners in the Hands of an Angry God," which was so terrifying that women in the congregation fainted. Some things never change. The Fear, like the sermon, feeds on the Imagination. And the moment you know someone who faces this disease daily with composure, calm, humor, and his or her own personality intact, you realize how deforming, how demeaning, how subject to the worst instincts Fear is.

Analyzing This Selection

1. How does Holleran focus on the experience of fear rather than on the AIDS disease? Point out details from the first three paragraphs that maintain this focus.

2. Identify and define several of Holleran's diverse attitudes toward the behavior of various fearful people. Is Holleran inconsistent in his responses to fearfulness?

3. How does Holleran try to deal with "the Fear" in himself? Give examples of his successful and unsuccessful efforts to cope.

4. In your opinion, what passages in the essay best clarify or illustrate the way fear, of any sort, affects people in general?

Analyzing Connections

5. Holleran, Brent Staples (see p. 46), and the father in "Interstate 7" (see the preceding selection) each encounter a different fear that pervades society. Compare their examinations of the disintegrative effects of fear itself. Evaluate their actual or implied remedies.

Analyzing by Writing

6. In your secondary school, what measures were taken to educate students about AIDS? Did the education program include acknowledgment of "the Fear"? In an essay, evaluate the health information you received about AIDS, including its likelihood of reducing or increasing the Fear.

PART 2

FAMILY TIES

Thomas Simmons, *Motorcycle Talk*
Nancy Friday, *Competition*
Joy Harjo, *Three Generations of Native American Women's Birth Experience*
Raymond Carver, *My Father's Life*
Jamaica Kincaid, *A Walk to the Jetty*
Steven Harvey, *The Nuclear Family*
Calvin Trillin, *It's Just Too Late*
Kazuo Ishiguro, *A Family Supper*

INSIGHTS

The family, not the individual, is the real molecule of society, the key link in the social chain of being.

— ROBERT NISBET

◇

The family is a subversive organization. In fact, it is the ultimate and only consistently subversive organization. Only the family has continued throughout history and still continues to undermine the State. The family is the enduring permanent enemy of all hierarchies, churches, and ideologies. Not only dictators, bishops, and commissars, but also humble parish priests and café intellectuals find themselves repeatedly coming up against the stony hostility of the family and its determination to resist interference to the last.

— FERDINAND MOUNT

◇

No people are ever as divided as those of the same blood.

— MAVIS GALLANT

◇

But what we think of as a social crisis of this generation — the rapid growth of divorce, the emancipation of women and adolescents, the sexual and educational revolutions, even the revolution in eating which is undermining the family as the basis of nourishment, for over a hundred years ago the majority of Europeans never ate in public in their lives — all of these things, which are steadily making the family weaker and weaker, are the inexorable result of the changes in society itself. The family as a unit of social organization was remarkably appropriate for a less complex world of agriculture and craftsmanship, a world which stretches back some seven thousand years, but ever since industry and highly urbanized societies began to take its place, the social functions of the family have steadily weakened — and this is a process that is unlikely to be halted. And there is no historical reason to believe that human beings could be less or more happy, less or more stable.

— J. H. PLUMB

The family is the basic cell of government: it is where we are trained to believe that we are human beings or that we are chattel, it is where we are trained to see the sex and race divisions and become callous to injustice even if it is done to ourselves, to accept as biological a full system of authoritarian government.

— GLORIA STEINEM

◇

Those Winter Sundays

Sundays too my father got up early
and put his clothes on in the blueblack cold,
then with cracked hands that ached
from labor in the weekday weather made
banked fires blaze. No one ever thanked him.

I'd wake and hear the cold splintering, breaking.
When the rooms were warm, he'd call,
and slowly I would rise and dress,
fearing the chronic angers of that house,

Speaking indifferently to him,
who had driven out the cold
and polished my good shoes as well.
What did I know, what did I know
of love's austere and lonely offices?

— ROBERT HAYDEN

◇

Children become attached to parents whatever the parents' characteristics, so long as the parents are adequately accessible and attentive. It does not matter to the intensity of the children's attachment, though it may matter greatly in the development of their personalities, whether their parents are reliable, consistently loving, or considerate of the children's health and welfare. Nor does it matter whether the children admire their parents or even whether they feel friendly toward them. Children who are battered and bruised by parents will continue to feel attached to them. Attachment, like walking or talking, is an intrinsic capacity that is developed under appropriate circumstances; it is not willed into being after a calculation of its advantages.

— ROBERT WEISS

FOCUSING BY WRITING

1. Do you have too many brothers and sisters, or too few? Almost everyone sometimes wishes for a few changes in that area of fate. Explain one way your life might have been improved by changing the number, sex, or ages of your siblings.

2. It usually requires more than one person's adverse behavior to produce a black sheep in any family. A child or adult who is consistently a maverick or a delinquent may be relegated to that role by other family members who maintain stereotypical attitudes and expectations. Examine an example of family stereotyping that contributed to the formation of a black sheep you know.

3. Does family life encourage independence or dependence? Does it promote liberty or authority? Present at least two good reasons why in your view the effects of family life support mainly a free individual or mainly a cohesive society.

4. Adolescents and their parents customarily go through a period of sustained bickering, which may last a few years, over simple issues such as household cleanliness, going out, studying, or spending money. In your family, what were the recurrent themes or persistent issues during this period of mutual irritation? Were the differences ever resolved? In a brief essay, clarify both sides of the key issue in your own passage through the valley of family harassment.

Thomas Simmons

MOTORCYCLE TALK

◇

THOMAS SIMMONS (b. 1956) lived his first thirteen years in West Chester, Pennsylvania, where he developed an enduring passion for motorcycles. At thirteen he moved with his family to Los Altos, California. Simmons graduated from Stanford University and went on to graduate study in English at the University of California at Berkeley. He has taught writing at the Massachusetts Institute of Technology and at the University of Iowa. The following essay about his father is part of his memoir about struggling with religious upbringing, *The Unseen Shore, Memories of a Christian Science Childhood* (1991). His autobiography continues in his most recent book, *A Season in the Air* (1993), which recounts his learning how to fly. Simmons has two children, as well as a motorcycle and a small airplane.

My father, who suffered from so many private griefs, was not an easy man 1 to get along with, but in one respect he was magnificent: he was unfailing in his devotion to machines of almost any variety. When he chose to, he could talk to me at length on the virtues of, say, the 1966 Chevrolet four-barrel carburetor or the drawbacks of the Wankel rotary engine. Talking, however, was not his strongest suit: he was a man of action. As he liked to point out, talking would never make an engine run more smoothly.

On weekends sometimes, or on his rare summer days of vacation, he 2 would encourage me in my first and last steps toward automotive literacy. He would allow me to stand beside him as he worked on the car, and when he needed a simple tool — a crescent wrench or needlenose pliers — I would be allowed to hand them to him. And when I was 12, he and my daring mother bought me a motorcycle.

It was a 50cc Benelli motocross bike — neither new, nor large, nor 3 powerful, nor expensive. But it gave form and life to my imaginings. No longer did I have to confine myself wistfully to magazine photos of high-speed turns and hair-raising rides through rough country. I had the thing itself — the device that would make these experiences possible, at least to some degree.

And, although I did not know it at the time, I also had a new kind of 4 lexicon. The motorcycle was a compendium of gears and springs and sprockets and cylinder heads and piston rings, which between my father and me acquired the force of more affectionate words that we could never seem to use in each other's presence.

Almost immediately the Benelli became a meeting ground, a magnet for 5 the two of us. We would come down to look at it — even if it was too late in the day for a good ride — and my father would check the tension of the chain, or examine the spark plug for carbon, or simply bounce the shock absorbers a few times as he talked. He'd tell me about compression ratios and ways of down-shifting smoothly through a turn; I'd tell him about my latest ride, when I leaped two small hummocks or took a spill on a tight curve.

More rarely, he'd tell the stories of his youth. His favorite, which he 6 recounted in slightly different versions about four times a year, had to do with the go-kart he built from scrap parts in his father's basement during the Depression. It was by any account a masterful performance: he managed to pick up a small, broken gasoline engine for free, and tinkered with it until it came back to life. The wheels, steering gear, axles, chassis — all were scrounged for a few cents, or for free, from junkyards and vacant lots in and around Philadelphia.

Winter was in full swing when my father had his go-kart ready for a 7 test-drive; snow lay thick on the ground. But he'd built the go-kart in his father's large basement, and given the weather he felt it made sense to make the trial run indoors. His engineering skills were topnotch. Assembled from orphaned parts, the go-kart performed like a well-tuned race car. My father did what any good 13-year-old would have done: he got carried away. He laid on the power coming around the corner of the basement, lost control, and smashed head-on into the furnace. It was a great loss for him. The jagged wood and metal cut and bruised him; he had destroyed his brand-new car. Far worse was the damage to the furnace. In 1933 such damage was almost more than the family finances could sustain. Furious, my father's father called him names, upbraided him for his stupidity and irresponsibility, and made him feel worthless. Years later, as he would tell this story to me, my father would linger over those words — "stupid," "irresponsible" — as if the pain had never gone away.

In these moments he and I had a common stake in something. Though 8 he might not know whether I was reading at the eighth-grade level or the twelfth-grade level — or whether my math scores lagged behind those of the rest of the class — he was delighted to see that I knew how to adjust a clutch cable or stop after a low-speed, controlled skid. These skills were a source of genuine adventure for me, and I came to life when he observed my progress.

But this was only part of our rapport with the motorcycle. My father found 9 few occasions to be overtly tender with the family, but he could be tender with a machine. I began to notice this in the countless small adjustments he regularly made. His touch on the cranky carburetor settings for gas and air was gentle, even soothing; at least it seemed to soothe the motorcycle, which ran smoothly under his touch but not under mine.

I found that, from time to time, this tenderness buoyed me up in its wake. 10

If my father was, in his dreams, a flat-track mechanic, then I was his driver: he owed me the best he could give me; that was his job. This dream of his bound us in a metaphor which, at its heart, was not so different from the kind of straightforward love another child might have received from a more accessible father. I did not know this then, not exactly. But I knew, when we both hovered over the Benelli's cylinder head or gearbox, adjusting a cam or replacing a gasket, that he would not have worked on this machine for himself alone.

Yet there was a secret to our new language, a secret that only slowly 11 revealed itself. What we shared through the motorcycle contradicted most of our other encounters in the family. It was almost as if we lived in another world when we came together over this machine, and for a time I hoped that that world might be the new one, the ideal on the horizon. I was wrong. The bands of our words were strong, but too narrow to encompass the worlds rising before me.

Almost without knowing it I began to acquire other vocabularies — the 12 tough, subtle speech of girls, the staccato syllables of independence, the wrenching words of love and emptiness. In this I began to leave him behind. He could not talk of these things with me. He remained with his engines; and long after I had ceased to ride it, he would occasionally open the gas jets, prime the carburetor, and take my motorcycle for a spin around the block.

But as it seems that nothing is ever wholly lost, this vocabulary of the 13 garage and the flat-track speed-way has a kind of potency, a place in the scheme of things. When, recently, I had dinner with my father, after not having seen him for nearly a year, we greeted each other with the awkward-ness of child cousins: we hardly knew what to say. I had almost given up on the possibility of a prolonged conversation until I happened to mention that my car needed a new clutch. Suddenly we were safe again, as we moved from the clutch to the valves on his souped-up VW and the four-barrel carburetor on the '66 Chevrolet Malibu, still pouring on the power after all these years. We had moved back to the language of our old country. And though one of us had journeyed far and had almost forgotten the idioms, the rusty speech still held, for a time, the words of love.

Analyzing This Selection

1. The first sentence carries many implications about the author and his family. Which suggestions are fully considered in the rest of the essay? Which remain implied?

2. How does the motorcycle change the son's and father's perceptions of each other?

3. How does the father appear different from the adult writer? What resemblances are visible?

Analyzing Connections

4. In the Insights (p. 65), psychologist Robert Weiss theorizes about the development of a child's attachment to his or her parents. Test out the strengths and weaknesses of the theory by applying it to Simmons's relationship with his father.

Analyzing by Writing

5. In many families, a sport or hobby provides the vocabulary for talk between the generations. Baseball, basketball, tennis, hockey, skiing, photography, camping, each can become the medium for relationships that do not flow as smoothly without this shared interest. Examine a shared interest that bridges the generation gap in your family (or in another family you know well). As if you were examining the dialect of another tribe, clarify the vocabulary that the family uses to discuss the interest. For instance, does custom allow for praise and criticism from young to old? — not just from old to young. Explain the forms and limits of expressiveness in this family idiom.

Nancy Friday

COMPETITION

◇

Nᴀɴᴄʏ Fʀɪᴅᴀʏ (b. 1937) worked as a journalist after attending Wellesley College. As a feminist writer, she has helped re-examine woman's identity by writing about the way sexual roles are enforced and expressed in everyday life. These concerns are reflected in several of her books: *Men in Love, Male Sexual Fantasies: The Triumph of Love over Rage* (1981), *Forbidden Flowers* (1982), and *Jealousy* (1985). *My Secret Garden* (1983) considers the prominence of fantasies in the sexual development of young people. Her most recent study of connections between sexual fantasy and people's real circumstances is *Women on Top: How Real Life Has Changed Women's Sexual Fantasies* (1993). This excerpt from her autobiography, *My Mother/My Self* (1977), recounts the way that as an early adolescent she reacted to the presence of older, more sexually defined and attractive women in her family.

Although I didn't realize it at the time, my mother was getting prettier. 1
My sister was a beauty. My adolescence was the time of our greatest estrangement.

I have a photo of the three of us when I was twelve: my mother, my sister 2
Susie, and I, on a big chintz sofa, each on a separate cushion, leaning away from one another with big spaces in between. I grew up fired with a sense of family spirit, which I loved and needed, with aunts and uncles and cousins under the omnipotent umbrella of my grandfather. "All for one and one for all," he would say at summer reunions, and no one took it more seriously than I. I would have gone to war for any one of them, and believed they would do the same for me. But within our own little nucleus, the three of us didn't touch much.

Now, when I ask her why, my mother sighs and says she supposes it was 3
because that was how she was raised. I remember shrinking from her Elizabeth Arden night-cream kiss, mumbling from under the blanket that yes, I had brushed my teeth. I had not. I had wet the toothbrush in case she felt it, feeling that would get even with her. For what? The further we all get from childhood, the more physically affectionate we try to be with one another. But we are still shy after all these years.

I was a late bloomer, like my mother. But my mother bloomed so late, or 4
had such a penetrating early frost, that she believed it even less than I would

71

in my turn. When she was a freckled sixteen and sitting shyly on her unfortunate hands, her younger sister was already a famous beauty. That is still the relationship between them. Grandmothers both, in their eyes my aunt is still the sleek-haired belle of the ball, immaculately handsome on a horse. My mother's successes do not count. They will argue at 2:00 A.M. over whether one of my aunt's many beaux ever asked my mother out. My mother could never make up a flattering story about herself. I doubt that she so much as heard the nice things men told her once she had grown into the fine-looking woman who smiles at me in family photos. But she always gives in to my aunt, much I'm sure as she gave in to the old self-image after my father died. He — that one splendidly handsome man — may have picked her out from all the rest, but his death just a few years later must have felt like some punishment for having dared to believe for a moment that her father was wrong: Who could possibly want her? She still blushes at a compliment.

I think she was at her prettiest in her early thirties. I was twelve and at my   5
nadir. Her hair had gone a delicate auburn red and she wore it brushed back from her face in soft curls. Seated beside her and Susie, who inherited a raven version of her beautiful hair, I look like an adopted person. But I had already defended myself against my looks. They were unimportant. There was a distance between me and the mirror commensurate with the growing distance between me and my mother and sister. My success with my made-up persona was proof: I didn't need them. My titles at school, my awards and achievements, so bolstered my image of myself that until writing this book I genuinely believed that I grew up feeling sorry for my sister. What chance had she alongside The Great Achiever and Most Popular Girl in the World? I even worked up some guilt about outshining her. Pure survival instinct? My dazzling smile would divert the most critical observer from comparing me to the cute, petite girls with whom I grew up. I switched the contest: Don't look at my lank hair, my 5' 10", don't notice that my right eye wanders bizarrely (though the eye doctor said it was useless to keep me in glasses); watch me tap dance, watch me win the game, let me make you happy! When I describe myself in those days my mother laughs. "Oh, Nancy, you were such a darling little girl." But I wasn't little anymore.

I think my sister, Susie, was born beautiful, a fact that affected my mother   6
and me deeply, though in different ways. I don't think it mattered so much until Susie's adolescence. She turned so lush one ached to look at her. Pictures of Susie then remind me of the young Elizabeth Taylor in *A Place in the Sun*. One has to almost look away from so much beauty. It scared my mother to death. Whatever had gone on between them before came to a head and has never stopped. Their constant friction determined me to get away from this house of women, to be free of women's petty competitions, to live on a bigger scale. I left home eventually but I've never gotten away from feeling how wonderful to be so beautiful your mother can't take her eyes off you, even if only to nag.

I remember an amazing lack of any feeling about my only sibling, with   7 whom I shared a room for years, whose clothes were identical to mine until I was ten. Except for feelings of irritation when she tried to cuddle me when I was four, bursts of anger that erupted into fist fights which I started and won at ten, and after that, indifference, a calculated unawareness that has resulted in a terrible and sad absence of my sister in my life.

My husband says his sister was the only child his father ever paid any 8 attention to: "You have done to Susie what I did to my sister," he says. "You made her invisible." Me, jealous of Susie, who never won a single trophy or had as many friends as I? I must have been insanely jealous.

I only allowed myself to face it twice. Both times happened in that twelfth 9 year, when my usual defenses couldn't take the emotional cross currents of adolescence. When I did slash out it wasn't very glorious, no well-chosen words or contest on the tennis courts. I did it like a thief in the night. Nobody ever guessed it was I who poured the red nail polish down the front of Susie's new white eyelet evening dress the day of her first yacht club dance. When I stole her summer savings and threw her wallet down the sewer, mother blamed Susie for being so careless. I watched my sister accept the criticism with her mother's own resignation, and I felt some relief from the angry emotions that had hold of me.

When Susie went away to boarding school, I made jokes about how glad 10 I was to be rid of her. It was our first separation. Conflicting urges, angers, and envies were coming at me from every direction; I had nothing left over to handle my terrible feelings of loss at her going. It was the summer I was plagued by what I called "my thoughts."

I read every book in the house as a talisman against thinking. I was afraid 11 that if my brain were left idle for even one minute, these "thoughts" would take over. Perhaps I feared they already had. Was my sister's going away the fulfillment of my own murderous wishes against her? I wrote in my first and only diary: "Susie, come home, please come home!!!!!!! I'm sorry, I'm sorry!!!!!!!"

When I outgrew the Nancy Drew books for perfect attendance at Sunday 12 school, and the Girl Scout badges for such merits as selling the most rat poison door to door, I graduated to prizes at the community theater. I won a plastic wake-up radio for the I Speak for Democracy contest. I was captain of the athletic association, president of the student government, and had the lead in the class play, all in the same year. In fact, I wrote the class play. It might have been embarrassing, but no one else wanted these prizes. Scoring home runs and getting straight A's weren't high on the list of priorities among my friends. (The South takes all prizes for raising noncompetitive women.) In the few cases where anyone did give me a run for the money, I had an unbeatable incentive: my grandfather's applause. It was he for whom I ran.

I can't remember ever hearing my grandfather say to my mother, "Well 13 done, Jane." I can't remember my mother ever saying to my sister, "Well done, Susie." And I never gave my mother the chance to say it to me. She was the last to hear of my achievements, and when she did, it was not from me but from her friends. Did she really notice so little that I was leaving her out? Was she so hurt that she pretended not to care? My classmates who won second prize or even no prize at all asked their families to attend the award ceremonies. I, who won first prize, always, did so to the applause of no kin at all. Was I spiting her? I know I was spiting myself. Nothing would have made me happier than to have her there; nothing would induce me to invite her. It is a game I later played with men: "Leave!" I would cry, and when they did, "How could you hurt me so?" I'd implore.

If I deprived her of the chance to praise me, she never criticized me.   14 Criticism was the vehicle by which she could articulate her relationship to my sister. No matter what it was, Susie could never get it right — in my mother's eyes. It continues that way to this day. Difficult as it is to think of my mother as competitive with anyone, how else could she have felt about her beautiful, ripe fourteen-year-old daughter? My mother was coming into her own mature, full bloom but perhaps that only made her more sensitive to the fact that Susie was simultaneously experiencing the same sexual flush. A year later, my mother remarried. Today, only the geography has changed: The argument begins as soon as they enter the same room. But they are often in the same room. They have never been closer.

How often the dinner table becomes the family battleground. When I met   15 Bill he had no table you could sit around in his vast bachelor apartment. The dinner table was where his father waged war; it was the one time the family was together. In Charleston, dinner was served at 2:00. I have this picture of our midday meals: Susie on my right, mother on my left, and me feeling that our cook, Ruth, had set this beautiful table for me alone.

No one else seemed to care about the golden squash, the crisp chicken, the   16 big silver pitcher of iced tea. While I proceeded to eat my way from one end of the table to the other, Susie and mother would begin: "Susie, that lipstick is too dark. . . . Must you pluck your eyebrows? . . . Why did you buy high-heeled, open-toe shoes when I told you to get loafers? . . . Those pointy bras make you look a, like a — " But my mother couldn't say the word. At this point one of them would leave the table in tears, while the other shuddered in despair at the sound of the slammed bedroom door. Meanwhile, I pondered my problem of whose house to play at that afternoon. I would finish both their desserts and be gone before Ruth had cleared the table. Am I exaggerating? Did it only happen once a week? Does it matter?

I was lucky to have escaped those devastating battles. "I never had to worry   17 about Nancy," my mother has always said. "She could always take care of herself." It became true. Only my husband has been allowed to see the extent of my needs. But the competitive drive that made me so self-sufficient was fired by more than jealousy of my sister. If my mother wasn't going to acknowledge me, her father would. If she couldn't succeed in his eyes, I would. It's my best explanation for all those years of trophies and presidencies, for my ability to "reach" my grandfather as my mother never could. I not only won what she had wanted all her life — his praise — I learned with the canniness of the young that this great towering man loved to be loved, to be touched. He couldn't allow himself to reach out first to those he loved most, but he couldn't resist an overture of affection.

I greeted his visits with embraces, took the kisses I had won, and sat at his 18 feet like one of his Dalmatians, while my sister stood shyly in the background and my mother waited for his criticism. But I was no more aware of competing with my mother than of being jealous of my sister. Two generations of women in my family have struggled for my grandfather's praise. Perhaps I became his favorite because he sensed I needed it most. The price I paid was that I had to beat my mother and my sister. I am still guilty for that.

In the stereotyping of the sexes, men are granted all the competitive 19 drives, women none. The idea of competitive women evokes disturbing images — the darker, dykey side of femininity, or cartoons of "ladies" in high heels, flailing at each other ineffectively with their handbags. An important step has been left out of our socialization: Mother raises us to win people's love. She gives us no training in the emotions of rivalry that would lose it for us. With no practical experience in the rules that make competition safe, we fear its ferocity. Never having been taught to win, we do not know how to lose. Women are not raised to compete like gentlemen.

Analyzing This Selection

1. What sort of person was the author as a twelve-year-old? Describe her appearance and personality. Of her likeable and unlikeable traits, which qualities would have mattered most to you as a twelve-year-old acquaintance?

2. What does Friday's mother fear? Identify several things in her life that contribute to those fears. Do Friday's insights into her mother's character seem fair?

3. Explain the difference between "hating to lose" and "loving to win."

4. This selection is about competitiveness, and it is also about the author's family past. Which focus seems to be guiding the author's purpose in writing?

Analyzing Connections

5. As an early adolescent, how was Nancy Friday different from Nora Ephron (see "Shaping Up Absurd," p. 17) or from Terry Galloway (see "I'm Listening as Hard as I Can," p. 25)?

Analyzing by Writing

6. Among adolescents, how does competitiveness differ for males and females? How openly are achievements pursued and displayed? What hypocrisies about abilities are generally accepted? Are the differences for young males and females defined more sharply at home or at school? Write an essay about how your sense of competition differs from the competitiveness you observe in the opposite sex.

Joy Harjo

THREE GENERATIONS OF
NATIVE AMERICAN WOMEN'S
BIRTH EXPERIENCE

◇

Joy Harjo (b. 1951), a member of the Creek tribe, grew up in Tulsa, Oklahoma. She intended to become a painter, and attended high school at the Institute of American Indian Arts in Santa Fe, New Mexico. During her college years at the University of New Mexico, her interest switched from art to poetry. "Poetry-speaking 'called me' in a sense. And I couldn't say no." Harjo completed a master's degree at the University of Iowa Writers' Workshop. Her books of poetry include *The Last Song* (1973), *What Moon Drove Me to This* (1980), *She Had Some Horses* (1983), and *The Woman Who Fell From the Sky* (1994). She is currently a professor of English at the University of New Mexico.

It was still dark when I awakened in the stuffed back room of my mother- 1
in-law's small rented house with what felt like hard cramps. At 17 years of age
I had read everything I could from the Tahlequah Public Library about
pregnancy and giving birth. But nothing prepared me for what was coming.
I awakened my child's father and then ironed him a shirt before we walked
the four blocks to the Indian hospital because we had no car and no money
for a taxi. He had been working with another Cherokee artist silk-screening
signs for specials at the supermarket and making $5 a day, and had to leave
me alone at the hospital because he had to go to work. We didn't awaken his
mother. She had to get up soon enough to fix breakfast for her daughter and
granddaughter before leaving for her job at the nursing home. I knew my life
was balanced at the edge of great, precarious change and I felt alone and
cheated. Where was the circle of women to acknowledge and honor this
birth?

It was still dark as we walked through the cold morning, under oaks that 2
symbolized the stubbornness and endurance of the Cherokee people who had
made Tahlequah their capital in the new lands. I looked for handholds in the
misty gray sky, for a voice announcing this impending miracle. I wanted to
change everything; I wanted to go back to a place before childhood, before
our tribe's removal to Oklahoma. What kind of life was I bringing this child

into? I was a poor, mixed-blood woman heavy with a child who would suffer the struggle of poverty, the legacy of loss. For the second time in my life I felt the sharp tug of my own birth cord, still connected to my mother. I believe it never pulls away, until death, and even then it becomes a streak in the sky symbolizing that most important warrior road. In my teens I had fought my mother's weaknesses with all my might, and here I was at 17, becoming as my mother, who was in Tulsa, cooking breakfasts and preparing for the lunch shift at a factory cafeteria as I walked to the hospital to give birth. I should be with her; instead, I was far from her house, in the house of a mother-in-law who later would try to use witchcraft to destroy me.

After my son's father left me I was prepped for birth. This meant my pubic   3
area was shaved completely and then I endured the humiliation of an enema, all at the hands of strangers. I was left alone in a room painted government green. An overwhelming antiseptic smell emphasized the sterility of the hospital, a hospital built because of the U.S. government's treaty and responsibility to provide health care to Indian people.

I intellectually understood the stages of labor, the place of transition, of   4
birth — but it was difficult to bear the actuality of it, and to bear it alone. Yet in some ways I wasn't alone, for history surrounded me. It is with the birth of children that history is given form and voice. Birth is one of the most sacred acts we take part in and witness in our lives. But sacredness seemed to be far from my lonely labor room in the Indian hospital. I heard a woman screaming in the next room with her pain, and I wanted to comfort her. The nurse used her as a bad example to the rest of us who were struggling to keep our suffering silent.

The doctor was a military man who had signed on this watch not for the   5
love of healing or out of awe at the miracle of birth, but to fulfill a contract for medical school payments. I was another statistic to him; he touched me as if he were moving equipment from one place to another. During my last visit I was given the option of being sterilized. He explained to me that the moment of birth was the best time to do it. I was handed the form but chose not to sign it, and am amazed now that I didn't think too much of it at the time. Later I would learn that many Indian women who weren't fluent in English signed, thinking it was a form giving consent for the doctor to deliver their babies. Others were sterilized without even the formality of signing. My light skin had probably saved me from such a fate. It wouldn't be the first time in my life.

When my son was finally born I had been deadened with a needle in my   6
spine. He was shown to me — the incredible miracle nothing prepared me for — then taken from me in the name of medical progress. I fell asleep with the weight of chemicals and awoke yearning for the child I had suffered for, had anticipated in the months proceeding from his unexpected genesis when I was still 16 and a student at Indian school. I was not allowed to sit up or walk because of the possibility of paralysis (one of the drug's side effects), and when I finally got to hold him, the nurse stood guard as if I would hurt him.

I felt enmeshed in a system in which the wisdom that had carried my people from generation to generation was ignored. In that place I felt ashamed I was an Indian woman. But I was also proud of what my body had accomplished despite the rape by the bureaucracy's machinery, and I got us out of there as soon as possible. My son would flourish on beans and fry bread, and on the dreams and stories we fed him.

My daughter was born four years later, while I was an art student at the 7 University of New Mexico. Since my son's birth I had waitressed, cleaned hospital rooms, filled cars with gas (while wearing a miniskirt), worked as a nursing assistant, and led dance classes at a health spa. I knew I didn't want to cook and waitress all my life, as my mother had done. I had watched the varicose veins grow branches on her legs, and as they grew, her zest for dancing and sports dissolved into utter tiredness. She had been born with a caul over her face, the sign of a gifted visionary.

My earliest memories are of my mother writing songs on an ancient 8 Underwood typewriter after she had washed and waxed the kitchen floor on her hands and knees. She too had wanted something different for her life. She had left an impoverished existence at age 17, bound for the big city of Tulsa. She was shamed in a time in which to be even part Indian was to be an outcast in the great U.S. system. Half her relatives were Cherokee full-bloods from near Jay, Oklahoma, who for the most part had nothing to do with white people. The other half were musically inclined "white trash" addicted to country-western music and Holy Roller fervor. She thought she could disappear in the city; no one would know her family, where she came from. She had dreams of singing and had once been offered a job singing on the radio but turned it down because she was shy. Later one of her songs would be stolen before she could copyright it and would make someone else rich. She would quit writing songs. She and my father would divorce and she would be forced to work for money to feed and clothe four children, all born within two years of each other.

As a child growing up in Oklahoma, I liked to be told the story of my 9 birth. I would beg for it while my mother cleaned and ironed. "You almost killed me," she would say. "We almost died." That I could kill my mother filled me with remorse and shame. And I imagined the push-pull of my life, which is a legacy I deal with even now when I am twice as old as my mother was at my birth. I loved to hear the story of my warrior fight for my breath. The way it was told, it had been my decision to live. When I got older, I realized we were both nearly casualties of the system, the same system flourishing in the Indian hospital where later my son Phil would be born.

My parents felt lucky to have insurance, to be able to have their children 10 in the hospital. My father came from a fairly prominent Muscogee Creek family. *His* mother was a full-blood who in the early 1920s got her degree in art. She was a painter. She gave birth to him in a private hospital in

Oklahoma City; at least that's what I think he told me before he died at age 53. It was something of which they were proud.

This experience was much different from my mother's own birth. She and five of her six brothers were born at home, with no medical assistance. The only time a doctor was called was when someone was dying. When she was born her mother named her Wynema, a Cherokee name my mother says means beautiful woman, and Jewell, for a can of shortening stored in the room where she was born.

I wanted something different for my life, for my son, and for my daughter, who later was born in a university hospital in Albuquerque. It was a bright summer morning when she was ready to begin her journey. I still had no car, but I had enough money saved for a taxi for a ride to the hospital. She was born "naturally," without drugs. I could look out of the hospital window while I was in labor at the bluest sky in the world. I had support. Her father was present in the delivery room — though after her birth he disappeared on a drinking binge. I understood his despair, but did not agree with the painful means to describe it. A few days later Rainy Dawn was presented to the sun at her father's pueblo and given a name so that she will always be recognized as a part of the people, as a child of the sun.

That's not to say that my experience in the hospital reached perfection. The clang of metal against metal in the delivery room had the effect of a tuning fork reverberating fear in my pelvis. After giving birth I held my daughter, but they took her from me for "processing." I refused to lie down to be wheeled to my room after giving birth; I wanted to walk out of there to find my daughter. We reached a compromise and I rode in a wheelchair. When we reached the room I stood up and walked to the nursery and demanded my daughter. I knew she needed me. That began my war with the nursery staff, who deemed me unknowledgeable because I was Indian and poor. Once again I felt the brushfire of shame, but I'd learned to put it out much more quickly, and I demanded early release so I could take care of my baby without the judgment of strangers.

I wanted something different for Rainy, and as she grew up I worked hard to prove that I could make "something" of my life. I obtained two degrees as a single mother. I wrote poetry, screenplays, became a professor, and tried to live a life that would be a positive influence for both of my children. My work in this life has to do with reclaiming the memory stolen from our peoples when we were dispossessed from our lands east of the Mississippi; it has to do with restoring us. I am proud of our history, a history so powerful that it both destroyed my father and guarded him. It's a history that claims my mother as she lives not far from the place her mother was born, names her as she cooks in the cafeteria of a small college in Oklahoma.

When my daughter told me she was pregnant, I wasn't surprised. I had known it before she did, or at least before she would admit it to me. I felt despair, as if nothing had changed or ever would. She had run away from

Indian school with her boyfriend and they had been living in the streets of Gallup, a border town notorious for the suicides and deaths of Indian peoples. I brought her and her boyfriend with me because it was the only way I could bring her home. At age 16, she was fighting me just as I had so fiercely fought my mother. She was making the same mistakes. I felt as if everything I had accomplished had been in vain. Yet I felt strangely empowered, too, at this repetition of history, this continuance, by a new possibility of life and love, and I steadfastly stood by my daughter.

I had a university job, so I had insurance that covered my daughter. She 16 saw an obstetrician in town who was reputed to be one of the best. She had the choice of a birthing room. She had the finest care. Despite this, I once again battled with a system in which physicians are taught the art of healing by dissecting cadavers. My daughter went into labor a month early. We both knew intuitively the baby was ready, but how to explain that to a system in which numbers and statistics provide the base of understanding? My daughter would have her labor interrupted; her blood pressure would rise because of the drug given to her to stop the labor. She would be given an unneeded amniocentesis and would have her labor induced — after having it artificially stopped! I was warned that if I took her out of the hospital so her labor could occur naturally my insurance would cover nothing.

My daughter's induced labor was unnatural and difficult, monitored by 17 machines, not by touch. I was shocked. I felt as if I'd come full circle, as if I were watching my mother's labor and the struggle of my own birth. But I was there in the hospital room with her, as neither my mother had been for me, nor her mother for her. My daughter and I went through the labor and birth together.

And when Krista Rae was born she was born to her family. Her father was 18 there for her, as were both her grandmothers and my friend who had flown in to be with us. Her paternal great-grandparents and aunts and uncles had also arrived from the Navajo Reservation to honor her. Something *had* changed.

Four days later, I took my granddaughter to the Saguaro forest before 19 dawn and gave her the name I had dreamed for her just before her birth. Her name looks like clouds of mist settling around a sacred mountain as it begins to speak. A female ancestor approaches on a horse. We are all together.

Analyzing This Selection

1. What details in the first paragraph establish the economic and social conditions of the author?

2. What is Harjo's main dissatisfaction with the three birth experiences?

3. Describe the author's style, and find details that illustrate your description. What does the style contribute, or fail to contribute, to the essay's purpose?

Analyzing Connections

4. In the Insights (p. 64), Ferdinand Mount asserts that a family is a subversive organization. In what ways is Harjo's family orientation subversive?

Analyzing by Writing

5. Explain a clash you have had with "family values," or a challenge to your "family values" by another standard. In what ways did a sense-of-family resist outside influences? What was at stake for you? Examine the issues and explain the goals upheld on opposing sides.

Raymond Carver

MY FATHER'S LIFE

◇

RAYMOND CARVER (1938–1988), acclaimed for his poetry and for his short stories about hardscrabble contemporary lives, was born in a logging town in Oregon. He graduated from California State University at Humboldt and spent a year at the Writers' Workshop at the University of Iowa. He taught writing at the University of California at Santa Cruz and at Syracuse University. His poetry and short stories appeared in magazines such as *Esquire, Harper's, The Atlantic,* and *The New Yorker.* His fiction has been collected in *What We Talk About When We Talk About Love* (1981) — see the story on page 152 — *Cathedral* (1984), and *Where I'm Calling From* (1988). His verse is collected in three books, *Where Water Comes Together with Other Water* (1985), *Ultramarine* (1986), and the posthumously published *A New Path to the Waterfall* (1989). In this memoir of his father, which first appeared in *Esquire* in 1984, Carver emphasizes the hardships that his father faced as a laborer during the Great Depression of the 1930s and later during the years of his psychological depression.

My dad's name was Clevie Raymond Carver. His family called him 1 Raymond and friends called him C.R. I was named Raymond Clevie Carver, Jr. I hated the "Junior" part. When I was little my dad called me Frog, which was okay. But later, like everybody else in the family, he began calling me Junior. He went on calling me this until I was thirteen or fourteen and announced that I wouldn't answer to that name any longer. So he began calling me Doc. From then until his death, on June 17, 1967, he called me Doc, or else Son.

When he died, my mother telephoned my wife with the news. I was away 2 from my family at the time, between lives, trying to enroll in the School of Library Science at the University of Iowa. When my wife answered the phone, my mother blurted out, "Raymond's dead!" For a moment, my wife thought my mother was telling her that I was dead. Then my mother made it clear *which* Raymond she was talking about and my wife said, "Thank God. I thought you meant *my* Raymond."

My dad walked, hitched rides, and rode in empty boxcars when he went 3 from Arkansas to Washington State in 1934, looking for work. I don't know whether he was pursuing a dream when he went out to Washington. I doubt it. I don't think he dreamed much. I believe he was simply looking for steady work at decent pay. Steady work was meaningful work. He picked apples for a time and then landed a construction laborer's job on the Grand Coulee Dam. After he'd put aside a little money, he bought a car and drove back to Arkansas to help his folks, my grandparents, pack up for the move west. He said later that they were about to starve down there, and this wasn't meant as a figure of speech. It was during that short while in Arkansas, in a town called Leola, that my mother met my dad on the sidewalk as he came out of a tavern.

"He was drunk," she said. "I don't know why I let him talk to me. His eyes   4 were glittery. I wish I'd had a crystal ball." They'd met once, a year or so before, at a dance. He'd had girlfriends before her, my mother told me. "Your dad always had a girlfriend, even after we married. He was my first and last. I never had another man. But I didn't miss anything."

They were married by a justice of the peace on the day they left for   5 Washington, this big, tall country girl and a farmhand-turned-construction worker. My mother spent her wedding night with my dad and his folks, all of them camped beside the road in Arkansas.

In Omak, Washington, my dad and mother lived in a little place not   6 much bigger than a cabin. My grandparents lived next door. My dad was still working on the dam, and later, with the huge turbines producing electricity and the water backed up for a hundred miles into Canada, he stood in the crowd and heard Franklin D. Roosevelt when he spoke at the construction site. "He never mentioned those guys who died building that dam," my dad said. Some of his friends had died there, men from Arkansas, Oklahoma, and Missouri.

He then took a job in a sawmill in Clatskanie, Oregon, a little town   7 alongside the Columbia River. I was born there, and my mother has a picture of my dad standing in front of the gate to the mill, proudly holding me up to face the camera. My bonnet is on crooked and about to come untied. His hat is pushed back on his forehead, and he's wearing a big grin. Was he going in to work or just finishing his shift? It doesn't matter. In either case, he had a job and a family. These were his salad days.

In 1941 we moved to Yakima, Washington, where my dad went to work   8 as a saw filer, a skilled trade he'd learned in Clatskanie. When war broke out, he was given a deferment because his work was considered necessary to the war effort. Finished lumber was in demand by the armed services, and he kept his saws so sharp they could shave the hair off your arm.

After my dad had moved us to Yakima, he moved his folks into the same   9 neighborhood. By the mid-1940s the rest of my dad's family — his brother, his sister, and her husband, as well as uncles, cousins, nephews, and most of their extended family and friends — had come out from Arkansas. All because my dad came out first. The men went to work at Boise Cascade, where my dad worked, and the women packed apples in the canneries. And in just a little while, it seemed — according to my mother — everybody was better off than my dad. "Your dad couldn't keep money," my mother said. "Money burned a hole in his pocket. He was always doing for others."

The first house I clearly remember living in, at 1515 South Fifteenth   10
Street, in Yakima, had an outdoor toilet. On Halloween night, or just any night, for the hell of it, neighbor kids, kids in their early teens, would carry our toilet away and leave it next to the road. My dad would have to get somebody to help him bring it home. Or these kids would take the toilet and stand it in somebody else's backyard. Once they actually set it on fire. But ours wasn't the only house that had an outdoor toilet. When I was old enough to know what I was doing, I threw rocks at the other toilets when I'd see someone go inside. This was called bombing the toilets. After a while, though, everyone went to indoor plumbing until, suddenly, our toilet was the last outdoor one in the neighborhood. I remember the shame I felt when my third-grade teacher, Mr. Wise, drove me home from school one day. I asked him to stop at the house just before ours, claiming I lived there.

I can recall what happened one night when my dad came home late to   11
find that my mother had locked all the doors on him from the inside. He was drunk, and we could feel the house shudder as he rattled the door. When he'd managed to force open a window, she hit him between the eyes with a colander and knocked him out. We could see him down there on the grass. For years afterward, I used to pick up this colander — it was as heavy as a rolling pin — and imagine what it would feel like to be hit in the head with something like that.

It was during this period that I remember my dad taking me into the   12
bedroom, sitting me down on the bed, and telling me that I might have to go live with my Aunt LaVon for a while. I couldn't understand what I'd done that meant I'd have to go away from home to live. But this, too — whatever prompted it — must have blown over, more or less, anyway, because we stayed together, and I didn't have to go live with her or anyone else.

I remember my mother pouring his whiskey down the sink. Sometimes   13
she'd pour it all out and sometimes, if she was afraid of getting caught, she'd only pour half of it out and then add water to the rest. I tasted some of his whiskey once myself. It was terrible stuff, and I don't see how anybody could drink it.

After a long time without one, we finally got a car, in 1949 or 1950, a   14
1938 Ford. But it threw a rod the first week we had it, and my dad had to have the motor rebuilt.

"We drove the oldest car in town," my mother said. "We could have had   15
a Cadillac for all he spent on car repairs." One time she found someone else's tube of lipstick on the floorboard, along with a lacy handkerchief. "See this?" she said to me. "Some floozy left this in the car."

Once I saw her take a pan of warm water into the bedroom where my dad   16
was sleeping. She took his hand from under the covers and held it in the water. I stood in the doorway and watched. I wanted to know what was going

on. This would make him talk in his sleep, she told me. There were things she needed to know, things she was sure he was keeping from her.

Every year or so, when I was little, we would take the North Coast Limited 17 across the Cascade Range from Yakima to Seattle and stay in the Vance Hotel and eat, I remember, at a place called the Dinner Bell Cafe. Once we went to Ivar's Acres of Clams and drank glasses of warm clam broth.

In 1956, the year I was to graduate from high school, my dad quit his job 18 at the mill in Yakima and took a job in Chester, a little sawmill town in northern California. The reasons given at the time for his taking the job had to do with a higher hourly wage and the vague promise that he might, in a few years' time, succeed to the job of head filer in this new mill. But I think, in the main, that my dad had grown restless and simply wanted to try his luck elsewhere. Things had gotten a little too predictable for him in Yakima. Also, the year before, there had been the deaths, within six months of each other, of both his parents.

But just a few days after graduation, when my mother and I were packed 19 to move to Chester, my dad penciled a letter to say he'd been sick for a while. He didn't want us to worry, he said, but he'd cut himself on a saw. Maybe he'd got a tiny sliver of steel in his blood. Anyway, something had happened and he'd had to miss work, he said. In the same mail was an unsigned postcard from somebody down there telling my mother that my dad was about to die and that he was drinking "raw whiskey."

When we arrived in Chester, my dad was living in a trailer that belonged 20 to the company. I didn't recognize him immediately. I guess for a moment I didn't want to recognize him. He was skinny and pale and looked bewildered. His pants wouldn't stay up. He didn't look like my dad. My mother began to cry. My dad put his arm around her and patted her shoulder vaguely, like he didn't know what this was all about, either. The three of us took up life together in the trailer, and we looked after him as best we could. But my dad was sick, and he couldn't get any better. I worked with him in the mill that summer and part of the fall. We'd get up in the mornings and eat eggs and toast while we listened to the radio, and then go out the door with our lunch pails. We'd pass through the gate together at eight in the morning, and I wouldn't see him again until quitting time. In November I went back to Yakima to be closer to my girlfriend, the girl I'd made up my mind I was going to marry.

He worked at the mill in Chester until the following February, when he 21 collapsed on the job and was taken to the hospital. My mother asked if I would come down there and help. I caught a bus from Yakima to Chester, intending to drive them back to Yakima. But now, in addition to being physically sick, my dad was in the midst of a nervous breakdown, though none of us knew to call it that at the time. During the entire trip back to Yakima, he didn't speak, not even when asked a direct question. ("How do you feel, Raymond?" "You okay, Dad?") He'd communicate, if he communicated at all, by moving his head or by turning his palms up as if to say he didn't know or care. The only time he said anything on the trip, and for nearly a month afterward, was when I was speeding down a gravel road in Oregon and the car muffler came loose. "You were going too fast," he said.

Back in Yakima a doctor saw to it that my dad went to a psychiatrist. My 22 mother and dad had to go on relief, as it was called, and the county paid for the psychiatrist. The psychiatrist asked my dad, "Who is the President?" He'd had a question put to him that he could answer. "Ike," my dad said. Nevertheless, they put him on the fifth floor of Valley Memorial Hospital and began giving him electroshock treatments. I was married by then and about to start my own family. My dad was still locked up when my wife went into this same hospital, just one floor down, to have our first baby. After she had delivered, I went upstairs to give my dad the news. They let me in through a steel door and showed me where I could find him. He was sitting on a couch with a blanket over his lap. *Hey,* I thought. *What in hell is happening to my dad?* I sat down next to him and told him he was a grandfather. He waited a minute and then he said, "I feel like a grandfather." That's all he said. He didn't smile or move. He was in a big room with a lot of other people. Then I hugged him, and he began to cry.

Somehow he got out of there. But now came the years when he couldn't 23 work and just sat around the house trying to figure what next and what he'd done wrong in his life that he'd wound up like this. My mother went from job to crummy job. Much later she referred to that time he was in the hospital, and those years just afterward, as "when Raymond was sick." The word *sick* was never the same for me again.

In 1964, through the help of a friend, he was lucky enough to be hired on 24 at a mill in Klamath, California. He moved down there by himself to see if he could hack it. He lived not far from the mill, in a one-room cabin not much different from the place he and my mother had started out living in when they went west. He scrawled letters to my mother, and if I called she'd read them aloud to me over the phone. In the letters, he said it was touch and go. Every day that he went to work, he felt like it was the most important day of his life. But every day, he told her, made the next day that much easier. He said for her to tell me he said hello. If he couldn't sleep at night, he said, he thought about me and the good times we used to have. Finally, after a couple of months, he regained some of his confidence. He could do the work and didn't think he had to worry that he'd let anybody down ever again. When he was sure, he sent for my mother.

He'd been off from work for six years and had lost everything in that 25 time — home, car, furniture, and appliances, including the big freezer that had been my mother's pride and joy. He'd lost his good name too — Raymond Carver was someone who couldn't pay his bills — and his self-respect was gone. He'd even lost his virility. My mother told my wife, "All during that time Raymond was sick we slept together in the same bed, but we didn't have relations. He wanted to a few times, but nothing happened. I didn't miss it, but I think he wanted to, you know."

During those years I was trying to raise my own family and earn a living. 26

But, one thing and another, we found ourselves having to move a lot. I couldn't keep track of what was going down in my dad's life. But I did have a chance one Christmas to tell him I wanted to be a writer. I might as well have told him I wanted to become a plastic surgeon. "What are you going to write about?" he wanted to know. Then, as if to help me out, he said, "Write about stuff you know about. Write about some of those fishing trips we took." I said I would, but I knew I wouldn't. "Send me what you write," he said. I said I'd do that, but then I didn't. I wasn't writing anything about fishing, and I didn't think he'd particularly care about, or even necessarily understand, what I was writing in those days. Besides, he wasn't a reader. Not the sort, anyway, I imagined I was writing for.

Then he died. I was a long way off, in Iowa City, with things still to say 27 to him. I didn't have the chance to tell him goodbye, or that I thought he was doing great at his new job. That I was proud of him for making a comeback.

My mother said he came in from work that night and ate a big supper. 28 Then he sat at the table by himself and finished what was left of a bottle of whiskey, a bottle she found hidden in the bottom of the garbage under some coffee grounds a day or so later. Then he got up and went to bed, where my mother joined him a little later. But in the night she had to get up and make a bed for herself on the couch. "He was snoring so loud I couldn't sleep," she said. The next morning when she looked in on him, he was on his back with his mouth open, his cheeks caved in. *Graylooking*, she said. She knew he was dead — she didn't need a doctor to tell her that. But she called one anyway, and then she called my wife.

Among the pictures my mother kept of my dad and herself during those 29 early days in Washington was a photograph of him standing in front of a car, holding a beer and a stringer of fish. In the photograph he is wearing his hat back on his forehead and has this awkward grin on his face. I asked her for it and she gave it to me, along with some others. I put it up on my wall, and each time we moved, I took the picture along and put it up on another wall. I looked at it carefully from time to time, trying to figure out some things about my dad, and maybe myself in the process. But I couldn't. My dad just kept moving further and further away from me and back into time. Finally, in the course of another move, I lost the photograph. It was then that I tried to recall it, and at the same time make an attempt to say something about my dad, and how I thought that in some important ways we might be alike. I wrote the poem when I was living in an apartment house in an urban area south of San Francisco, at a time when I found myself, like my dad, having trouble with alcohol. The poem was a way of trying to connect up with him.

Photograph of My Father in His Twenty-Second Year

> *October.* Here in this dank, unfamiliar kitchen
> I study my father's embarrassed young man's face.
> Sheepish grin, he holds in one hand a string
> of spiny yellow perch, in the other
> a bottle of Carlsberg beer.

In jeans and flannel shirt, he leans
against the front fender of a 1934 Ford.
He would like to pose brave and hearty for his posterity,
wear his old hat cocked over his ear.
All his life my father wanted to be bold.

But the eyes give him away, and the hands
that limply offer the string of dead perch
and the bottle of beer. Father, I love you,
yet how can I say thank you, I who can't hold my liquor either
and don't even know the places to fish.

The poem is true in its particulars, except that my dad died in June and ³⁰ not October, as the first word of the poem says. I wanted a word with more than one syllable to it to make it linger a little. But more than that, I wanted a month appropriate to what I felt at the time I wrote the poem — a month of short days and failing light, smoke in the air, things perishing. June was summer nights and days, graduations, my wedding anniversary, the birthday of one of my children. June wasn't a month your father died in.

After the service at the funeral home, after we had moved outside, a ³¹ woman I didn't know came over to me and said, "He's happier where he is now." I stared at this woman until she moved away. I still remember the little knob of a hat she was wearing. Then one of my dad's cousins — I didn't know the man's name — reached out and took my hand, "We all miss him," he said, and I knew he wasn't saying it just to be polite.

I began to weep for the first time since receiving the news. I hadn't been ³² able to before. I hadn't had the time, for one thing. Now, suddenly, I couldn't stop. I held my wife and wept while she said and did what she could do to comfort me there in the middle of that summer afternoon.

I listened to people say consoling things to my mother, and I was glad that ³³ my dad's family had turned up, had come to where he was. I thought I'd remember everything that was said and done that day and maybe find a way to tell it sometime. But I didn't. I forgot it all, or nearly. What I do remember is that I heard our name used a lot that afternoon, my dad's name and mine. But I knew they were talking about my dad. *Raymond*, these people kept saying in their beautiful voices out of my childhood. *Raymond*.

Analyzing This Selection

1. In paragraphs 1 and 2, the author implicitly suggests some of the effects of having a name similar to his father's. What were these effects? Define his reaction explicitly.

2. In paragraphs 3 through 6, how does Carver's attitude about both his parents differ

from his mother's attitude about her husband and herself? In your opinion, who seems to have a better understanding of the past, the mother or the son?

3. What episodes and details in Carver's early life indicate that he and his father felt closely connected?

4. In Carver's poem about his father he writes, "All his life my father wanted to be bold." Do you think that line sums up the father fairly accurately? Does the essay indicate other things that the father also wanted to be? Was he more successful or less successful in those other aspirations?

5. In the final paragraph, Carver again notes the similarity of their names. How has his attitude toward this similarity changed from his attitude at the beginning of the essay?

Analyzing Connections

6. Both Carver and Simmons (see "Motorcycle Talk," p. 67) express mixed attitudes toward their difficult fathers. Compare their mixture of admiration and blame. Compare Carver and Robert Hayden (see "Those Winter Sundays," p. 65). Which writer identifies more closely with his father?

Analyzing by Writing

7. Write an extended description of the person in your family whom you most closely resemble in physical appearance. Be precise and detailed about his or her features that are like your own. If it is useful, include matters such as the person's tone of voice, way of walking, gestures and mannerisms, or other physical characteristics. Be sure to differentiate yourself at some point or at various points in your essay. In what ways do the similarities please or disturb you?

Jamaica Kincaid

A WALK TO THE JETTY

◊

JAMAICA KINCAID (b. 1949) was born in Antigua in the West Indies. As a child she felt that her Caribbean surroundings were "almost overwhelming," and much of her fiction reflects her early life on the island. She came to the United States at seventeen. Her stories have appeared in the *Paris Review, Rolling Stone,* and *The New Yorker.* They were collected in *At the Bottom of the River* (1984). Her novels include *Lucy* (1990) and *Autobiography of My Mother* (1994). Her interrelated stories about Annie John, a fictional character much like herself, were collected in *Annie John* (1985). The following selection is about the day of Annie's departure from Antigua.

"My name is Annie John." These were the first words that came into my mind as I woke up on the morning of the last day I spent in Antigua, and they stayed there, lined up one behind the other, marching up and down, for I don't know how long. At noon on that day, a ship on which I was to be a passenger would sail to Barbados, and there I would board another ship, which would sail to England, where I would study to become a nurse. My name was the last thing I saw the night before, just as I was falling asleep; it was written in big, black letters all over my trunk, sometimes followed by my address in Antigua, sometimes followed by my address as it would be in England. I did not want to go to England, I did not want to be a nurse, but I would have chosen going off to live in a cavern and keeping house for seven unruly men rather than go on with my life as it stood. I never wanted to lie in this bed again, my legs hanging out way past the foot of it, tossing and turning on my mattress, with its cotton stuffing all lumped just where it wasn't a good place to be lumped. I never wanted to lie in my bed again and hear Mr. Ephraim driving his sheep to pasture — a signal to my mother that she should get up to prepare my father's and my bath and breakfast. I never wanted to lie in my bed and hear her get dressed, washing her face, brushing her teeth, and gargling. I especially never wanted to lie in my bed and hear my mother gargling again.

Lying there in the half-dark of my room, I could see my shelf, with my books — some of them prizes I had won in school, some of them gifts from my mother — and with photographs of people I was supposed to love forever no matter what, and with my old thermos, which was given to me for my eighth birthday, and some shells I had gathered at different times I spent at the sea. In one corner stood my washstand and its beautiful basin of white enamel with blooming red hibiscus painted at the bottom and an urn that matched. In another corner were my old school shoes and my Sunday shoes. In still another corner, a bureau held my old clothes. I knew everything in this room, inside out and outside in. I had lived in this room for thirteen of my seventeen years. I could see in my mind's eye even the day my father was adding it onto the rest of the house. Everywhere I looked stood something that had meant a lot to me, that had given me pleasure at some point, or could remind me of a time that was a happy time. But as I was lying there my heart could have burst open with joy at the thought of never having to see any of it again.

If someone had asked me for a little summing up of my life at that 3 moment as I lay in bed, I would have said, "My name is Annie John. I was born on the fifteenth of September, seventeen years ago, at Holberton Hospital, at five o'clock in the morning. At the time I was born, the moon was going down at one end of the sky and the sun was coming up at the other. My mother's name is Annie also; I am named after her, and that is why my parents call me Little Miss. My father's name is Alexander, and he is thirty-five years older than my mother. Two of his children are four and six years older than she is. Looking at how sickly he has become and looking at the way my mother now has to run up and down for him, gathering the herbs and barks that he boils in water, which he drinks instead of the medicine the doctor has ordered for him, I plan not only never to marry an old man but certainly never to marry at all. The house we live in my father built with his own hands. The bed I am lying in my father built with his own hands. If I get up and sit on a chair, it is a chair my father built with his own hands. When my mother uses a large wooden spoon to stir the porridge we sometimes eat as part of our breakfast, it will be a spoon that my father has carved with his own hands. The sheets on my bed my mother made with her own hands. The curtains hanging at my window my mother made with her own hands. The nightie I am wearing, with scalloped neck and hem and sleeves, my mother made with her own hands. When I look at things in a certain way, I suppose I should say that the two of them made me with their own hands. For most of my life, when the three of us went anywhere together I stood between the two of them. But then I got too big, and there I was, shoulder to shoulder with them more or less, and it became not very comfortable to walk down the street together. And so now there they are together and here I am apart. I don't see them now the way I used to, and I don't love them now the way I used to. The bitter thing about it is that they are just the same and it is I who have changed, so all the things I used to be and all the things I used to feel are as false as the teeth in my father's head. Why, I wonder, didn't I see the hypocrite in my mother when, over the years, she said that she loved me and could hardly live without me, while at the same time proposing and arranging separation after separation, including this one, which, unbeknownst to her, *I* have arranged to be permanent? So now, I, too, have hypocrisy, and breasts (small ones), and hair growing in the appropriate places, and sharp eyes, and I have made a vow never to be fooled again."

Lying in my bed for the last time, I thought, This is what I add up to. At that, I felt as if someone had placed me in a hole and was forcing me first down and then up against the pressure of gravity. I shook myself and prepared to get up. I said to myself, "I am getting up out of this bed for the last time." Everything I would do that morning until I got on the ship that would take me to England I would be doing for the last time, for I had made up my mind that, come what might, the road for me now went only in one direction: away from my home, away from my mother, away from my father, away from the everlasting blue sky, away from the everlasting hot sun, away from people who said to me, "This happened during the time your mother was carrying you." If I had been asked to put into words why I felt this way, if I had been given years to reflect and come up with the words of why I felt this way, I would not have been able to come up with so much as the letter "A." I only knew that I felt the way I did, and that this feeling was the strongest thing in my life.

The Anglican church bell struck seven. My father had already bathed and dressed and was in his workshop puttering around. As if the day of my leaving were something to celebrate, they were treating it as a holiday, and as if nothing usual would take place. My father would not go to work at all. When I got up, my mother greeted me with a big, bright "Good morning" — so big and bright that I shrank before it. I bathed quickly in some warm bark water that my mother had prepared for me. I put on my underclothes — all of them white and all of them smelling funny. Along with my earrings, my neck chain, and my bracelets, all made of gold from British Guiana, my underclothes had been sent to my mother's obeah woman, and whatever she had done to my jewelry and underclothes would help protect me from evil spirits and every kind of misfortune. The things I never wanted to see or hear or do again now made up at least three weeks' worth of grocery lists. I placed a mark against obeah women, jewelry, and white underclothes. Over my underclothes, I put on an around-the-yard dress of my mother's. The clothes I would wear for my voyage were a dark-blue pleated skirt and a blue-and-white checked blouse (the blue in the blouse matched exactly the blue of my skirt) with a large sailor collar and with a tie made from the same material as the skirt — a blouse that came down a long way past my waist, over my skirt. They were lying on a chair, freshly ironed by my mother. Putting on my clothes was the last thing I would do just before leaving the house. Miss Cornelia came and pressed my hair and then shaped it into what felt like a hundred corkscrews, all lying flat against my head so that my hat would fit properly.

At breakfast, I was seated in my usual spot, with my mother at one end of the table, my father at the other, and me in the middle, so that as they talked to me or to each other I would shift my head to the left or to the right and get a good look at them. We were having a Sunday breakfast, a breakfast as if we had just come back from Sunday-morning services: salt fish and antroba and souse and hard-boiled eggs, and even special Sunday bread from Mr. Daniel, our baker. On Sundays, we ate this breakfast at eleven o'clock, and then we didn't eat again until four o'clock, when we had our big Sunday dinner. It was the best breakfast we ate, and the only breakfast better than that was the one we ate on Christmas morning. My parents were in a festive mood, saying what a wonderful time I would have in my new life, what a wonderful opportunity this was for me, and what a lucky person I was. They were eating away as they talked, my father's false teeth making a *clop-clop* sound like a horse on a walk as he talked, my mother's mouth going up and down like a horse eating hay as she chewed each mouthful thirty-two times. (I had long ago counted, because it was something she made me do also, and I was trying to see if this was just one of her rules that applied only to me.) I was looking at them with a smile on my face but disgust in my heart when my mother said, "Of course, you are a young lady now, and we won't be surprised if in due time you write to say that one day soon you are to be married."

Without thinking, I said, with bad feeling that I didn't hide very well, 7 "How absurd!"

My parents immediately stopped eating and looked at me as if they had 8 not seen me before. My father was the first to go back to his food. My mother continued to look. I don't know what went through her mind, but I could see her using her tongue to dislodge food stuck in the far corners of her mouth.

Many of my mother's friends now came by to say good-bye to me, and to 9 wish me God's blessings. I thanked them and showed the proper amount of joy at the glorious things they pointed out to me that my future held and showed the proper amount of sorrow at how much my parents and everyone else who loved me would miss me. My body ached a little at all this false going back and forth, at all this taking in of people gazing at me with heads tilted, love and pity on their smiling faces. I could have left without saying any good-byes to them and I wouldn't have missed it. There was only one person I felt I should say good-bye to, and that was my former friend Gwen. We had long ago drifted apart, and when I saw her now my heart nearly split in two with embarrassment at the feelings I used to have for her and things I had shared with her. She had now degenerated into complete silliness, hardly able to complete a sentence without putting in a few giggles. Along with the giggles, she had developed some other schoolgirl traits that she did not have when she was actually a schoolgirl, so beneath her were such things then. When we were saying our good-byes, it was all I could do not to say cruelly, "Why are you behaving like such a monkey?" Instead, I put everything into a friendly, plain wishing her well and the best in the future. It was then that she told me that she was more or less engaged to a boy she had known while growing up early on in Nevis, and that soon, in a year or so, they would be married. My reply to her was "Good luck," and she thought I meant her well, so she grabbed me and said, "Thank you. I knew you would be happy about it." But to me it was as if she had shown me a high point from which she was going to jump and hoped to land in one piece on her feet. We parted, and when I turned away I didn't look back.

My mother had arranged with a stevedore to take my trunk to the jetty 10 ahead of me. At ten o'clock on the dot, I was dressed, and we set off for the jetty. An hour after that, I would board a launch that would take me out to sea, where I then would board the ship. Starting out, as if for old time's sake and without giving it a thought, we lined up in the old way: I walking between my mother and my father. I loomed way above my father and could see the top of his head. I wasn't so much taller than my mother that it could bring me any satisfaction. We must have made a strange sight: a grown girl all dressed up in the middle of a morning, in the middle of the week, walking in step in the middle between her two parents, for people we didn't know stared at us. It was all of half an hour's walk from our house to the jetty, but I was passing through most of the years of my life. We passed by the house where Miss Lois, the seamstress that I had been apprenticed to for a few years, lived, and just as I was passing by a wave of bad feeling for her came over me, because I suddenly remembered that the first year I spent with her all she had me do was sweep the floor, which was always full of threads and pins and needles, and I never seemed to sweep it clean enough to please her. Then she would send me to the store to buy buttons or thread, though I was only allowed to do this if I was given a sample of the button or thread, and then she would find fault even though they were an exact match of the samples she had given me. And all the while she said to me, "You'll never sew, you know." At the time, I don't suppose I minded it, because it was customary to treat the first-year apprentice with such scorn, but now I placed on the dustheap of my life Miss Lois and everything that I had had to do with her.

We were soon on the road that I had taken to school, to church, to 11 Sunday school, to choir practice, to Brownie meetings, to Girl Guide meetings, to meet a friend. I was five years old when I first walked on this road unaccompanied by someone to hold my hand. My mother had placed three pennies in my little basket, which was a duplicate of her bigger basket, and sent me to the chemist's shop to buy a pennyworth of senna, a pennyworth of eucalyptus leaves, and a pennyworth of camphor. She then instructed me on what side of the road to walk, where to make a turn, where to cross, and to look carefully before I crossed, and if I met anyone that I knew to politely pass greetings and keep on my way. I was wearing a freshly ironed yellow dress that had printed on it scenes of acrobats flying through the air and swinging on a trapeze. I had just had a bath, and after it, instead of powdering me with my baby-smelling talcum powder, my mother had, as a special favor, let me use her own talcum powder, which smelled quite perfumy and came in a can that had painted on it people going out to dinner in nineteenth-century London and was called Mazie. How it pleased me to walk out the door and bend my head down to sniff at myself and see that I smelled just like my mother. I went to the chemist's shop, and he had to come from behind the counter and bend down to hear what it was that I wanted to buy, my voice was so little and timid then. I went back just the way I had come, and when I walked into the yard and presented my basket with its three packages to my mother her eyes filled with tears and she swooped me up and held me high in the air and said that I was wonderful and good and that there would never be anybody better. If I had just conquered Persia, she couldn't have been more proud of me.

We passed by our church — the church in which I had been christened 12 and received and had sung in the junior choir. We passed by a house in which a girl I used to like and was sure I couldn't live without had lived. Once, when she had mumps, I went to visit her against my mother's wishes, and we sat on her bed and ate the cure of roasted, buttered sweet potatoes that had been placed on her swollen jaws, held there by a piece of white cloth. I don't know how, but my mother found out about it, and I don't know how, but she put an end to our friendship. Shortly after, the girl moved with her family across the sea to somewhere else. We passed the doll store where I would go with my mother when I was little and point out the doll I wanted that year for Christmas. We passed the store where I bought the much-fought-over shoes I wore to church to be received in. We passed the bank. On my sixth birthday, I was given, among other things, the present of a sixpence. My mother and I then went to this bank, and with the sixpence I opened my own savings account. I was given a little gray book with my name in big letters on it, and in the balance column it said "6d." Every Saturday morning after that, I was given a sixpence — later, a shilling, and later a two-and-sixpence piece — and I would take it to the bank for deposit. I had never been allowed to withdraw even a farthing from my bank account until just a few weeks before I was to leave; then the whole account was closed out, and I received from the bank the sum of six pounds, ten shillings, and two and a half pence.

We passed the office of the doctor who told my mother three times that I 13 did not need glasses, that if my eyes were feeling weak a glass of carrot juice a day would make them strong again. This happened when I was eight. And so every day at recess I would run to my school gate and meet my mother, who was waiting for me with a glass of juice from carrots she had just grated and then squeezed, and I would drink it and then run back to meet my chums. I knew there was nothing at all wrong with my eyes, but I had recently read a story in "A Girl's Own Annual" in which the heroine, a girl a few years older than I was then, cut such a figure to my mind with the way she was always adjusting her small, round horn-rimmed glasses that I felt I must have a pair exactly like them. When it became clear that I didn't need glasses, I began to complain about the glare of the sun being too much for my eyes, and I walked around with my hands shielding them — especially in my mother's presence. My mother then bought for me a pair of sunglasses with the exact horn-rimmed frames I wanted, and how I enjoyed the gestures of blowing on the lenses, wiping them with the hem of my uniform, adjusting the glasses when they slipped down my nose, and just removing them from their case and putting them on. In three weeks, I grew tired of them and they found a nice resting place in a drawer, along with some other things that at one time or another I couldn't live without. We passed the store that sold only grooming aids, all imported from England. This store had in it a large porcelain dog — white, with black spots all over and a red ribbon of satin tied around its neck. The dog sat in front of a white porcelain bowl that was always filled with fresh water, and it sat in such a way that it looked as if it had just taken a long drink. When I was a small child, I would ask my mother, if ever we were near this store, to please take me to see the dog, and I would stand in front of it, bent over slightly, my hands resting on my knees, and stare at it and stare at it. I thought this dog more beautiful and more real than any dog I had ever seen or any dog I would ever see. I must have outgrown my interest in the dog, for when it disappeared I never asked what became of it. We passed the library, and if there was anything on this walk that I might have wept over leaving this most surely would have been the thing. My mother had been a member of the library long before I was born. And since she took me everywhere with her when I was quite little, when she went to the library she took me along here, too. I would sit in her lap very quietly as she read books that she did not want to take home with her. I could not read the words yet, but just the way they looked on the page was interesting to me. Once, a book she was reading had a large picture of a man in it, and when I asked her who he was she told me that he was Louis Pasteur and that the book was about his life. It stuck in my mind, because she said it was because of him that she boiled my milk to purify it before I was allowed to drink it, that it was his idea, and that that was why the process was called pasteurization. One of the things I had put away in my mother's old trunk in which she kept all my childhood things was my library card. At that moment, I owed sevenpence in overdue fees.

As I passed by all these places, it was as if I were in a dream, for I didn't   14
notice the people coming and going in and out of them, I didn't feel my feet touch ground. I didn't even feel my own body — I just saw these places as if they were hanging in the air, not having top or bottom, and as if I had gone in and out of them all in the same moment. The sun was bright; the sky was blue and just above my head. We then arrived at the jetty.

My heart now beat fast, and no matter how hard I tried I couldn't keep my   15
mouth from falling open and my nostrils from spreading to the ends of my face. My old fear of slipping between the boards of the jetty and falling into the dark-green water where the dark-green eels lived came over me. When

my father's stomach started to go bad, the doctor had recommended a walk every evening right after he ate his dinner. Sometimes he would take me with him. When he took me with him, we usually went to the jetty, and there he would sit and talk to the night watchman about cricket or some other thing that didn't interest me, because it was not personal; they didn't talk about their wives, or their children, or their parents, or about any of their likes and dislikes. They talked about things in such a strange way, and I didn't see what they found funny, but sometimes they made each other laugh so much that their guffaws would bound out to sea and send back an echo. I was always sorry when we got to the jetty and saw that the night watchman on duty was the one he enjoyed speaking to; it was like being locked up in a book filled with numbers and diagrams and what-ifs. For the thing about not being able to understand and enjoy what they were saying was I had nothing to take my mind off my fear of slipping in between the boards of the jetty.

Now, too, I had nothing to take my mind off what was happening to me. 16 My mother and my father — I was leaving them forever. My home on an island — I was leaving it forever. What to make of everything? I felt a familiar hollow space inside. I felt I was being held down against my will. I felt I was burning up from head to toe. I felt that someone was tearing me up into little pieces and soon I would be able to see all the little pieces as they floated out into nothing in the deep blue sea. I didn't know whether to laugh or cry. I could see that it would be better not to think too clearly about any one thing. The launch was being made ready to take me, along with some other passengers, out to the ship that was anchored in the sea. My father paid our fares, and we joined a line of people waiting to board. My mother checked my bag to make sure that I had my passport, the money she had given me, and a sheet of paper placed between some pages in my Bible on which were written the names of the relatives — people I had not known existed — with whom I would live in England. Across from the jetty was a wharf, and some stevedores were loading and unloading barges. I don't know why seeing that struck me so, but suddenly a wave of strong feeling came over me, and my heart swelled with a great gladness as the words "I shall never see this again" spilled out inside me. But then, just as quickly, my heart shrivelled up and the words "I shall never see this again" stabbed at me. I don't know what stopped me from falling in a heap at my parents' feet.

When we were all on board, the launch headed out to sea. Away from the 17 jetty, the water became the customary blue, and the launch left a wide path in it that looked like a road. I passed by sounds and smells that were so familiar that I had long ago stopped paying any attention to them. But now here they were, and the ever-present "I shall never see this again" bobbed up and down inside me. There was the sound of the seagull diving down into the water and coming up with something silverish in its mouth. There was the smell of the sea and the sight of small pieces of rubbish floating around in it. There were boats filled with fishermen coming in early. There was the sound of their voices as they shouted greetings to each other. There was the hot sun, there was the blue sea, there was the blue sky. Not very far away, there was the white sand of the shore, with the run-down houses all crowded in next to each other, for in some places only poor people lived near the shore. I was seated in the launch between my parents, and when I realized that I was gripping their hands tightly I glanced quickly to see if they were looking at me with scorn, for I felt sure that they must have known of my never-see-this-again feelings. But instead my father kissed me on the forehead and my mother kissed me on the mouth, and they both gave over their hands to me, so that I could grip them as much as I wanted. I was on the verge of feeling that it had all been a mistake, but I remembered that I wasn't a child anymore, and that now when I made up my mind about something I had to see it through. At that moment, we came to the ship, and that was that.

The good-byes had to be quick, the captain said. My mother introduced   18
herself to him and then introduced me. She told him to keep an eye on me, for I had never gone this far away from home on my own. She gave him a letter to pass on to the captain of the next ship that I would board in Barbados. They walked me to my cabin, a small space that I would share with someone else — a woman I did not know. I had never before slept in a room with someone I did not know. My father kissed me good-bye and told me to be good and to write home often. After he said this, he looked at me, then looked at the floor and swung his left foot, then looked at me again. I could see that he wanted to say something else, something that he had never said to me before, but then he just turned and walked away. My mother said, "Well," and then she threw her arms around me. Big tears streamed down her face, and it must have been that — for I could not bear to see my mother cry — which started me crying, too. She then tightened her arms around me and held me to her close, so that I felt that I couldn't breathe. With that, my tears dried up, and I was suddenly on my guard. "What does she want now?" I said to myself. Still holding me close to her, she said, in a voice that raked across my skin, "It doesn't matter what you do or where you go. I'll always be your mother and this will always be your home."

I dragged myself away from her and backed off a little, and then I shook   19
myself, as if to wake myself out of a stupor. We looked at each other for a long time with smiles on our faces, but I know the opposite of that was in my heart. As if responding to some invisible cue, we both said, at the same moment, "Well." Then my mother turned around and walked out the cabin door. I stood there for I don't know how long, and then I remembered that it was customary to stand on deck and wave to your relatives who were returning to shore. From the deck, I could not see my father, but I could see my mother facing the ship, her eyes searching to pick me out. I removed from my bag a red cotton handkerchief that she had earlier given me for just this purpose, and I waved it wildly in the air. Recognizing me immediately, she waved back just as wildly, and we continued to do this until she became just a dot in the matchbox-size launch swallowed up in the big blue sea.

I went back to my cabin and lay down on my berth. Everything trembled   20
as if it had a spring at its very center. I could hear the small waves lap-lapping
around the ship. They made an unexpected sound, as if a vessel filled with
liquid had been placed on its side and now was slowly emptying out.

Analyzing This Selection

1. In the first paragraph, what phrase is repeated with only slight variations until it
   expresses Annie John's basic attitude? How does the repetition affect our response
   to her situation?

2. Why does she object to the fact that all their belongings are handmade?

3. What is the point of her sarcasm about saying good-bye to her mother's friends
   and to her own friend Gwen? What qualities in these people does she scorn?

4. While Annie John is walking to the jetty, what memory begins to change her
   attitude toward this leave-taking? Why would that particular memory have special
   meaning for her now?

5. Remembering that as a child she used to be frightened on the jetty, she says in
   paragraph 16, "Now, too, I had nothing to take my mind off what was happening
   to me." What is the connection between her childhood fear and her present state
   of mind?

6. Do you think that Annie John has just been disguising her real feelings? Does she
   really want to go or doesn't she?

7. Do you think this selection is a story or a personal essay? That is, does it strike you
   as mostly fictional or as mostly a direct recollection? What details give you this
   impression?

Analyzing Connections

8. Compare the hypocrisies and constraints that Annie John faced in her life and the
   hypocrisies and constraints that Nancy Friday faced (see "Competition," p. 71).
   Which limitations arise within a particular family, and which arise from society?

Analyzing by Writing

9. Some people have more trouble than others when it comes to saying good-bye,
   but everyone finds it difficult at some time. Analyze a particularly tense experience of saying good-bye to someone in your family circle (not to your former or
   present heartthrobs), when your own or someone else's uptight feelings were
   expressed by unusual or inappropriate behavior. A first day at camp or at school
   might serve as your example of leave-taking.

Steven Harvey

THE NUCLEAR FAMILY

◇

STEVEN HARVEY (b. 1949) grew up in many different places, as he acknowledges in this essay. He graduated from Wake Forest University in North Carolina and earned a doctorate in English from the University of Virginia. His essays and poems have appeared in magazines such as *Harper's*, the *Beloit Poetry Journal*, and the *Georgia Review*. "The Nuclear Family" is a chapter from his first book, *A Geometry of Lilies: Life and Death in an American Family* (1993). Harvey teaches at Young Harris College in northern Georgia.

A witch cackles from my family tree. That is the word I got in the mail the other day when a family genealogy arrived. In addition to the good news that a progenitor fought beside William the Conqueror in 1066 and some other distant relative is a distant relative of Captain John Smith, comes this juicy bit from one of my American ancestors: "Rebecca Shelly, hanged herself on August 26, 1692, in prison, Cambridge, Massachusetts, where she was held on a charge of witchcraft." 1

The rest of the genealogy pales by comparison, with the possible exception of a Tory sympathizer whose remains were "burned on the common" in Worcester, Massachusetts, in 1790 and the headstone of his grave "put under the sod." Most of the genealogy is given over to a list of farmers, burghers, and professionals who braved life's common tragedies and wrote letters about prairie migration thick with — ho hum — everyday heartaches. But there *is* a witch and a hanging! It made our day. 2

In fact, the genealogy came just in time. Nessa needed it for a school assignment on her family history. Before she finished everyone in the house was caught up in the project — everyone except me. Matt drew the chart, the single slot which held Nessa's name swelling geometrically into a thicket of lines, branches on the family tree. Barbara searched boxes of old photos and spent time sitting at the kitchen table bouncing a pencil tip on her forehead and racking her brains for names. Nessa printed each entry carefully, marveling over the way maiden names cropped up later as middle names in our family and proud that her old-fashioned first name, Agnes, belonged to her grandmother and great-great-grandmother. 3

There were many smiles when the work was done, each name perched 4 properly on a branch. Only I hung back, nonplussed. So many of the names were just that, names — no stories, no words, no memories, no faces. Holding the chart up, after the rest had gone to sleep, I saw that this family tree was all grid, a genealogy reduced to geometry. Who *are* these people? I wondered. Who *were* we?

Family photos have the same effect on me. Flattened out on the dining 5 room table their glossy surfaces turn liquid and tempting under my fingertips but remain stubbornly opaque, oddly distant artifacts of familiar faces in strange places and strange faces among familiar ones. What do these silent, smiling people, drowned in the past and sealed within a photograph, have to do with me? A chin, a nose, a grin — I isolate these between my fingernails and patch together a semblance of faces I know, but, like scraps of today's torn picture blown and scattered into the past, these parts cannot be assembled into a coherent whole.

I think of those staged pictures made in tourist traps throughout the West: 6 a painted backdrop of some frontier scene with holes in it for the faces. Poke your face through the hole and you are a cowboy or a cowgirl or — for an extra laugh — a cow. Are my family photos any less odd? The bits of me and the ones I love superimposed on unfamiliar backdrops?

And what about the faces I know well? They belong to people I love, true, 7 but I took the photographs precisely because their images are not mine to keep. They are faces I visit — not the ones I live with — and there is always about their glossy expressions the look of someone surprised by a guest. I may call where they live home, but I am never at home when I'm there.

So where *is* home? My own biography, the severed ends of many genea- 8 logical lines, sputters and thrashes about the eastern half of the country trying to find its own place. Born in Dodge City, Kansas, I moved, age one, with my family to New York, was raised in Chicago, Kentucky, and New Jersey by two mothers, went to school in North Carolina and — after living briefly in three more states — settled in Georgia. I have attended colleges in North Carolina, New York, Maryland, Vermont, and Virginia, accumulating so many transcripts that the dread of paper work alone keeps me from applying for a new job. Since then, my wife and I have had four children born in three states. With a record like that it is pretty hard for the past, rumbling along at the leisurely pace of a Conestoga, to catch up.

Most of us have little choice in all this. A friend of mine, living out his 9 version of the tale common to us all (an Indiana boy who married a Californian before settling down in Georgia) tells a story about his father. One morning before dawn, the father roused him out of bed and took him to the middle of a corn field. It was cold, the sky iridescent like mother of pearl. The boy was soon to go to college — never to live on this farm again. His father bent down in the stubble, grabbed a handful of black dirt, and put it in his son's hands.

"This is your mother," he said. "This is your father." 10

When he tells the story, my friend — who is now a biologist — bends over 11 and makes a scooping motion, his hand inches from the carpet. He holds the fist out and cannot keep from smiling at the glory of the memory, and then shakes his head, opens his hand, the dust of his imaginings drifting through his fingers, blown away by the winds of reality. My friend is in red-clay country now, far from the good soil of his midwestern "mother" and "father." In our world, his father's injunction is little more than a wish, a longing.

There are stories in my family too — stories intended to connect me to a   12 heritage — but they also sift through my fingers leaving me empty-handed. In June of 1870 my great-great-grandmother made the five-hundred-mile journey from Pella, Iowa, to Glen Elder, Kansas. Her memoir of the move, recorded by my grandmother in 1928, is rich with stories, humorous and moving by turns. *Item* — the heartbreak of packing: "I insisted on a dresser, a commode, and carpet for my bedroom and sitting room, but we finally cut it down to the commode and carpet with a full set of nice dishes. Then we filled every available place with loose oats for the horses." *Item* — the terror of locusts: "On August 1, 1874, there was an eclipse of the sun. Later, one of our men got up from the dinner table, went to the door and said, 'there must be another eclipse.' I looked up at the sun and said, 'it is the largest swarm of bees I ever saw.' In less than 10 minutes everything was covered with grasshoppers. At 2 o'clock we went to the cornfield, you could hear them chomping like pigs. They ate the covers, husks, cobs and leaves, leaving the bare stalk. They even ate the onions into the ground." *Item* — the joy of new birth: "My first child was born during the winter of 1870 with the assistance of a neighbor woman. That morning the snow sifted through the roof into my bed."

These are wonderful stories, my heritage, but they do not belong to me.   13 I have moved so far from them — in place and spirit — that they are some-one *else's* tale, no more real to me than the history of William the Conqueror.

I live, like most Americans, in a "nuclear family," a term best defined as   14 "the contents of a mini-van or less." Grandparents keep out. For sociologists who coined the phrase a nuclear family is "an independent, autonomous unit" in which "each marriage marks the start of a new conjugal family, separate in residence, self-supporting, and in control of its affairs." In short, a nuclear family is one without a place or history.

The term seems apt, suggestive of the kinds of annihilation common to   15 family life in America, especially these days. It is nuclear, in the literal sense, because it is a core family, shrinking away from the sustaining larger family of grandparents, uncles, aunts, and cousins. It is nuclear, too, because, under the pressure of modern life it is prone to split, with devastating effects to all involved. The phrase is a comment on the chances of survival, a reckoning of the odds. And, as the words suggest, the odds are terrible. Few families can take each other for the span of a generation these days without one partner packing up the mini-van and heading west.

The result: families become names in a book, genealogies compiled by   16
experts that have no place in the heart, passion without an object for some,
mere curiosity for most.

Something is missing in the nuclear family. I sense the absence most   17
concretely, I think, when I am in the midst of a family fight and realize, in
my fury, that there is no one outside this throbbing nucleus to turn to.
Shouts, slammed doors, and angry thumpings reverberate in the house's
shell and return uncushioned by the long faces of a larger family. No one
hears what I say or cares; no one is there to rescue me from myself. When
the fight is over, I look out my picture window and see my image fill with the
darkness of the alien landscape that, by default, I call home.

What is remarkable here — as always — is the resilience of the human   18
spirit, the resourcefulness of Americans cut off from a nurturing family
culture. "There was no lumber this side of Junction City and very little
there," my great-great-grandmother said. "So we built our house of rock with
dirt roof, holes for windows and doors. To close these we used my carpet."
She knew the meaning of nuclear family. Cut off from supplies in Pella, she
"made do" — to use a phrase familiar to Kansans — and built her house into
the ground.

We make do, too. Far from any home or history, the nuclear family   19
invents traditions on the spot and by its own lights — nonce rituals, the
free-verse of family life. Like suckers rising from the roots of felled family
trees, these ersatz ceremonies have the beauty of a blossom mixed with
pathos of a stump. They may not brighten the night, but they gladden the
day, serving by their newness as a reminder of lost grandeur. Traditional
rituals — the Moravian Feast of Lights, for instance — honor the past by
codifying it. The cookies must be baked this way. The candles must be lit at
this hour. Re-enactment, repetition is the point. Nonce rituals, on the other
hand, make up for lost historical richness with spontaneity. Silliness is never
codified out of nonce rituals nor are these on-the-spot rites battened down by
martinets of tradition. Silliness is, in fact, the defining ingredient.

One of the best nonce rituals I know of was invented by a family who live   20
near us, a nuclear family of the fundamentalist stripe, one that adds to its
isolation by keeping the children out of public schools and enforcing strict
codes of learning and behavior. In this family there is no TV or rock and
roll. And yet the family, especially the children, never seems stiff or doctri-
naire — quite the opposite, in fact, as though the isolation from conventional society allows for true idiosyncrasy. Each summer this family
celebrates itself by an odd ritual: the father wakes the children in the middle
of the night, takes the whole bunch to a park, and lets the children, armed
with flashlights, play on the swingsets, slides, and climbing toys in the pitch
dark. I imagine them playing into the early morning, the shadows of the
swingset elongating into a tripod for the moon, the see-saw jutting a dark
plank into a glitter of stars, and the bobbing heads of children casting flashlit

shadows against the Milky Way. How different their giggles must sound at night — more like whinnies in the wind than laughter! The activity, so simple and yet so subversive of the quotidian, is a nonce ritual.

In our family, I announce the first snow by whistling "Dixie." No one 21 knows how this started, exactly, although it, too, was invented to handle the problem of having children home from school. We live in the Georgia mountains, only a few miles from the border of North Carolina, and get a couple of bus-stopping snows each year. When that happens, I trudge off to work wrapped in a scarf and bundled to the chin, carrying my suitcase and looking respectably bound. The kids, snowed-in, are left behind for the day. I'm whistling, oh, say, some bit from Beethoven's Seventh. No sooner am I out of sight than the kids begin plotting, making piles of snowballs and settling down for the day in some hiding place behind a tree or a snow-drifted wheelbarrow, waiting for my return.

They know I'm coming when they hear me whistling "Dixie" — the 22 signal that I've shed my briefcase and am ready for battle. Why "Dixie"? Why whistling? Who knows? But I certainly am not *just* whistling "Dixie": I'm a moving target. Suddenly there is a blur of white in the sky as my bundled body absorbs the first blows. I trudge forward — throwing a few hastily packed snowballs of my own — awaiting the next volley. Along the way I may upright a little kid who, turned over in a snowsuit, rocks in the drifts like a flipped turtle, my good deed rewarded by a direct hit to my rear! The rest of the time I trudge ahead, occasionally catching a snowball and tossing it back. The important thing is that I never miss a beat. Red cheeks puffed and lips stoically puckered, I keep on whistling.

Maybe I whistle "Dixie" because I'm a lost cause against children armed 23 with snow and ice. At any rate, by the time I totter up the steps I look like Frosty, white from top to bottom, with a hint of rebel red in my cheeks. My wife greets me at the door with a stiff Jack Daniels.

The nonce ritual that fits our family best is Birthday Bird. Most of the year 24 this puppet droops in tangles in a downstairs closet. But on our birthdays we hang it for a week from the lamp over the dining room table where it serves as a daffy reminder that someone is a year older. Matt brought it home as a shop project when he was in sixth grade. "The other class made guns," he complained. "We made these dumb ducks!" He held his duck up for all to see. It twisted under his fist, legs crossed, head drooped, and tail high in the air.

"I think it's *perfect*," his mother said, taking the toy from Matt and shaking 25 a few kinks out. "I know *just* what to do with it." She hung it from the dining room lamp where it stayed until somebody had a birthday. From then on it was Birthday Bird.

Although Matt called it a duck, Birthday Bird is more properly classified 26 as a generic bird. Each of its parts — tinker-toy feet, yarn legs, ovoid body and pointed head — is unrecognizable as anything birdlike by itself, but bobbing above the cake candles in graceless consort, the bits of string and wood do come to resemble *some* kind of bird. Proto-bird, perhaps. *Birth*day bird. Touch one piece and all parts dance and jiggle like a tickled baby. Let it stand for hours and breezes still play on it causing the body to twist with rotisserie slowness, the feet rising and falling, the head nodding. Often it seems to be watching you, the black eye swimming your way momentarily, but soon this apparent attention is shown for the sham it is as the eye — like a lawn sprinkler set on slow — keeps moving along its path, ruled not by sympathy but by the inner compulsion of its strings and parts, oblivious to all outside.

I think of the solar system, suspended mid-space, each part hanging free 27 and moving in harmony. I think of snow swirling down on a baby's brow and a witch turning in the noose of her own sheets. I think of the atom, electrons whirling in a sub-visible blur around a miniscule nuclear core. Looking at Birthday Bird I think of all things tangled, goofy, doomed and suspended in space. For our family it is, as Barbara said, "perfect."

All rituals are about loss, the insubstantiality of life, but nonce rituals tug 28 at us in other ways, too. They take on a fresh poignancy since they are as flimsy as the flesh they represent. The Feast of Lights will last as long as there are Moravians to celebrate it, long after Birthday Bird slumps in rotting strings and tumbles from the perch. Birthday Bird is a symbol of all that flops out of our grasp. Rather than commemorate life, as traditional rituals do, the ritual of Birthday Bird ratifies loss.

In this it is like words, pictures, and all other reminders of life's passing 29 masked as mementos. I line up the kids for a picture in a kind of frenzy, sacrificing the tranquility of the present to an uncertain future, saving forever a moment lost to posing. Even then I suspect I'm in trouble. When the pictures come back from the drugstore I flip through them registering all that is missing, the absences and gaps in these visual memorials. Built out of the fear that all is insubstantial and tentative, they are no balm, but symptoms of the problem. They offer no solace.

Words are no better. "After you've written, you can no longer remember 30 anything but the writing," Annie Dillard complains. "After I've written about any experience, my memories — those elusive, fragmentary patches of color and feeling — are gone; they've been replaced by the work. The work is a sort of changeling on the doorstep." Photos, words — they, like nonce rituals, shadow reality. A word to the wise is never enough, and a picture worth a thousand of them merely multiples the insufficiency. With Birthday Bird at hand, the bird in the bush gets away.

On the night of a recent birthday of mine, I stayed up alone and watched 31 the old bird twist in its strings. There was no wind, but eyes and head floated slowly, propelled by some inner restlessness or some otherwise invisible agitation. Suspended in glittering nylon the painted eye caught mine. I glanced away; it kept spinning, oblivious to me as always. No comfort. Suddenly I saw how little of our lives we keep and was afraid. Like the mourner walking away from the grave, I was alone with loss. "This is *it?*" I asked, setting down my drink and casting a cold eye on the dumb bird. Against the inevitable losses of family life — of all life — I bring a marionette and whistle "Dixie" in the dark?

There is, after all, a sorcery in all this hocus-pocus of the everyday. Like 32 a witch, I surround myself with owl, cat, and bat — beasts of nocturnal solidarity. Whistling "Dixie" is my incantation for another season and Birthday Bird is my eye-of-frog-and-tail-of-newt concoction for another year. With this witchcraft I hope to untangle my life's strings and fly by night. I steal children, taking them far from any home, until one day — *presto!* — I too vanish into thin air. Looking at Birthday Bird I think of a black figure twisting undiscovered in a dark-lit cell. Maybe there really *is* a witch in my past.

A picture comes to mind: a mini-van hurtling down a black highway, 33 illuminating a patch of road ahead and followed by the reddish dark it drags close behind. *This* is the nuclear family, and our pictures and rituals and words are never enough to redeem the losses. No witchcraft will keep the noose from drawing tight.

Nonce, noose, nuclear — our losses, it is true, are never redeemed. All 34 that you love, you lose.

And yet I come back the next night as I do on any night the bird hangs from 35 the ceiling light, to watch its silent spin yet again. Gazing into its mingle of threads and bobbers, midnight snack in hand, I feel happier, better, awash perhaps but still afloat and less alone. Our tawdry ceremonies — patch and paste for families with no past — draw us in quiet moments as if they had one more thing to whisper from the gloom. Draped from a pole here, hung on the wall there, or riding a breath into a cold night sky, these decorations of the present serve as reminders that the beauty of the modern family is not its success in the face of death but the quixotic nature of its resistance, the goofy defenses it has made against oblivion. They drape uncertain beginnings — weekends, seasons, birthdays — in the familiar and bear this message: the world may or may not outlive us and our children, but it will, in all probability, survive tomorrow, and most of us will have the humor necessary to cope.

For the nonce, that had better be enough.   36

Analyzing This Selection

1. What reactions and phrases indicate the author's detachment from his family past? Describe his attitude and tone.

2. According to Harvey, what are the origins and causes of his detachment?

3. What connotative overtones does Harvey add to the sociological definition of a "nuclear family"?

4. What is the purpose of nonce rituals? How do they differ from and resemble traditional rituals?

5. What "witchcraft" would Harvey like to perform? Why does he think of it as witchcraft? Can you give it another name or description?

Analyzing Connections

6. Harvey writes from a father's viewpoint. How does he differ from the fathers who are portrayed by their sons in "Motorcycle Talk" (p. 67) and "My Father's Life" (p. 82)? From an imaginary son's viewpoint, what praise and criticism would you have for this father?

Analyzing by Writing

7. Harvey worries about the instabilities of the family. As J. H. Plumb points out in the Insights (see p. 64), families could become completely obsolete in highly technological and affluent societies. If you were designing an utopian society, how would you change the family's role in bearing, nurturing, socializing, educating, and financing children? What would you eliminate, preserve, or strengthen in the family? Explain the reasons for your position about one or two current features of family life; don't get caught up in working out the details of an alternative plan.

8. Analyze a ritual that your family observes. Is it a nonce ritual, a traditional ritual, or a mixture of both? What meanings and purposes does it have in your family? Would you like to alter the ritual in any way?

Calvin Trillin

IT'S JUST TOO LATE

◊

CALVIN TRILLIN (b. 1935) grew up in Kansas City, Missouri, and attended Yale University. He worked as a reporter for *Time* magazine, and from 1963 to 1982 he was a staff writer for *The New Yorker*. His regular reports of his travels around the United States focused on daily life, including where and how Americans eat. These observations were collected in three books on food in America: *American Fried* (1974), *Alice, Let's Eat* (1978), and *Third Helpings* (1983). His widely syndicated humorous columns are collected in *If You Can't Say Something Nice* (1987) and *Enough's Enough* (1990). On the darker side, Trillin wrote a memoir of a Yale classmate who committed suicide, *Remembering Denny* (1993). Believing that the way people die can illuminate the way they lived, Trillin reported about deadly crimes and accidents in *Killings* (1984), which included the following account of the death of a teenage girl.

Knoxville, Tennessee
March 1979

Until she was sixteen, FaNee Cooper was what her parents sometimes 1 called an ideal child. "You'd never have to correct her," FaNee's mother has said. In sixth grade, FaNee won a spelling contest. She played the piano and the flute. She seemed to believe what she heard every Sunday at the Beaver Dam Baptist Church about good and evil and the hereafter. FaNee was not an outgoing child. Even as a baby, she was uncomfortable when she was held and cuddled. She found it easy to tell her parents she loved them but difficult to confide in them. Particularly compared to her sister, Kristy, a cheerful, open little girl two and a half years younger, she was reserved and introspective. The thoughts she kept to herself, though, were apparently happy thoughts. Her eighth-grade essay on Christmas — written in a remarkably neat hand — talked of the joys of helping put together toys for her little brother, Leo, Jr., and the importance of her parents' reminder that Christmas is the birthday of Jesus. Her parents were the sort of people who might have been expected to have an ideal child. As a boy, Leo Cooper had been called "one of the greatest high-school basketball players ever developed in Knox County." He went on to play basketball at East Tennessee State, and he married the homecoming queen, JoAnn Henson. After college, Cooper became a high-school basketball coach and teacher and, eventually, an administrator. By the time FaNee turned thirteen, in 1973, he was in his

108

third year as the principal of Gresham Junior High School, in Fountain City — a small Knox County town that had been swallowed up by Knoxville when the suburbs began to move north. A tall man, with curly black hair going on gray, Leo Cooper has an elaborate way of talking ("Unless I'm very badly mistaken, he has never related to me totally the content of his conversation") and a manner that may come from years of trying to leave errant junior-high-school students with the impression that a responsible adult is magnanimous, even humble, about invariably being in the right. His wife, a high-school art teacher, paints and does batik, and created the name FaNee because she liked the way it looked and sounded — it sounds like "Fawnee" when the Coopers say it — but the impression she gives is not of artiness but of soft-spoken small-town gentility. When she found, in the course of cleaning up FaNee's room, that her ideal thirteen-year-old had been smoking cigarettes, she was, in her words, crushed. "FaNee was such a perfect child before that," JoAnn Cooper said some time later. "She was angry that we found out. She knew we knew that she had done something we didn't approve of, and then the rebellion started. I was hurt. I was very hurt. I guess it came through as disappointment."

Several months later, FaNee's grandmother died. FaNee had been de- 2 voted to her grandmother. She wrote a poem in her memory — an almost joyous poem, filled with Christian faith in the afterlife ("Please don't grieve over my happiness / Rejoice with me in the presence of the Angels of Heaven"). She also took some keepsakes from her grandmother's house, and was apparently mortified when her parents found them and explained that they would have to be returned. By then, the Coopers were aware that FaNee was going to have a difficult time as a teenager. They thought she might be self-conscious about the double affliction of glasses and braces. They thought she might be uncomfortable in the role of the principal's daughter at Gresham. In ninth grade, she entered Halls High School, where JoAnn Cooper was teaching art. FaNee was a loner at first. Then she fell in with what could only be considered a bad crowd.

Halls, a few miles to the north of Fountain City, used to be known as 3 Halls Crossroads. It is what Knoxville people call "over the ridge" — on the side of Black Oak Ridge that has always been thought of as rural. When FaNee entered Halls High, the Coopers were already in the process of building a house on several acres of land they had bought in Halls, in a sparsely settled area along Brown Gap Road. Like two or three other houses along the road, it was to be constructed basically of huge logs taken from old buildings — a house that Leo Cooper describes as being, like the name FaNee, "just a little bit different." Ten years ago, Halls Crossroads was literally a crossroads. Then some of the Knoxville expansion that had swollen Fountain City spilled over the ridge, planting subdivisions here and there on roads that still went for long stretches with nothing but an occasional house with a cow or two next to it. The increase in population did not create a town. Halls has no center. Its commercial area is a series of two or three shopping centers strung together on the Maynardville Highway, the four-lane that leads north into Union County — a place almost synonymous in east Tennessee with mountain poverty. Its restaurant is the Halls Freezo Drive-In. The gathering place for the group FaNee Cooper eventually found herself in was the Maynardville Highway Exxon station.

At Halls High School, the social poles were represented by the Jocks and   4
the Freaks. FaNee found her friends among the Freaks. "I am truly enlighted upon irregular trains of thought aimed at strange depots of mental wards," she wrote when she was fifteen. "Yes! Crazed farms for the mental off — Oh! I walked through the halls screams & loud laughter fill my ears — Orderlys try to reason with me — but I am unreasonable! The joys of being a FREAK in a circus of imagination." The little crowd of eight or ten young people that FaNee joined has been referred to by her mother as "the Union County group." A couple of the girls were from backgrounds similar to FaNee's, but all the boys had the characteristics, if not the precise address, that Knoxville people associate with the poor whites of Union County. They were the sort of boys who didn't bother to finish high school, or finished it in a special program for slow learners, or got ejected from it for taking a swing at the principal.

"I guess you can say they more or less dragged us down to their level   5
with the drugs," a girl who was in the group — a girl who can be called Marcia — said recently. "And somehow we settled for it. It seems like we had to get ourselves in the pit before we could look out." People in the group used marijuana and Valium and LSD. They sneered at the Jocks and the "prim and proper little ladies" who went with Jocks. "We set ourselves aside," Marcia now says. "We put ourselves above everyone. How we did that I don't know." In a Knox County high school, teenagers who want to get themselves in the pit need not mainline heroin. The Jocks they mean to be compared to do not merely show up regularly for classes and practice football and wear clean clothes; they watch their language and preach temperance and go to prayer meetings on Wednesday nights and talk about having a real good Christian witness. Around Knoxville, people who speak of well-behaved high-school kids often seem to use words like "perfect," or even "angels." For FaNee's group, the opposite was not difficult to figure out. "We were into wicked things, strange things," Marcia says. "It was like we were on some kind of devil trip." FaNee wrote about demons and vultures and rats. "Slithering serpents eat my sanity and bite my ass," she wrote in an essay called "The Lovely Road of Life," just after she turned sixteen, "while tornadoes derail and ever so swiftly destroy every car in my train of thought." She wrote a lot about death.

FaNee's girlfriends spoke of her as "super-intelligent." Her English teacher   6
found some of her writing profound — and disturbing. She was thought to be not just super-intelligent but super-mysterious, and even, at times, super-weird — an introverted girl who stared straight ahead with deep-brown, nearly black eyes and seemed to have thoughts she couldn't share. Nobody

really knew why she had chosen to run with the Freaks — whether it was loneliness or rebellion or simple boredom. Marcia thought it might have had something to do with a feeling that her parents had settled on Kristy as their perfect child. "I guess she figured she couldn't be the best," Marcia said recently. "So she decided she might as well be the worst."

Toward the spring of FaNee's junior year at Halls, her problems seemed 7 to deepen. Despite her intelligence, her grades were sliding. She was what her mother called "a mental dropout." Leo Cooper had to visit Halls twice because of minor suspensions. Once, FaNee had been caught smoking. Once, having ducked out of a required assembly, she was spotted by a favorite teacher, who turned her in. At home, she exchanged little more than short, strained formalities with Kristy, who shared their parents' opinion of FaNee's choice of friends. The Coopers had finished their house — a large house, its size accentuated by the huge old logs and a great stone fireplace and outsize "Paul Bunyan"–style furniture — but FaNee spent most of her time there in her own room, sleeping or listening to rock music through earphones. One night, there was a terrible scene when FaNee returned from a concert in a condition that Leo Cooper knew had to be the result of marijuana. JoAnn Cooper, who ordinarily strikes people as too gentle to raise her voice, found herself losing her temper regularly. Finally, Leo Cooper asked a counselor he knew, Jim Griffin, to stop in at Halls High School and have a talk with FaNee — unofficially.

Griffin — a young man with a warm, informal manner — worked for the 8 Juvenile Court of Knox County. He had a reputation for being able to reach teenagers who wouldn't talk to their parents or to school administrators. One Friday in March of 1977, he spent an hour and a half talking to FaNee Cooper. As Griffin recalls the interview, FaNee didn't seem alarmed by his presence. She seemed to him calm and controlled — Griffin thought it was something like talking to another adult — and, unlike most of the teenagers he dealt with, she looked him in the eye the entire time. Griffin, like some of FaNee's friends, found her eyes unsettling — "the coldest, most distant, but, at the same time, the most knowing eyes I'd ever seen." She expressed affection for her parents, but she didn't seem interested in exploring ways of getting along better with them. The impression she gave Griffin was that they were who they were, and she was who she was, and there didn't happen to be any connection. Several times, she made the same response to Griffin's suggestions: "It's too late."

That weekend, neither FaNee nor her parents brought up the subject of 9 Griffin's visit. Leo Cooper has spoken of the weekend as being particularly happy; a friend of FaNee's who stayed over remembers it as particularly strained. FaNee stayed home from school on Monday because of a bad headache — she often had bad headaches — but felt well enough on Monday evening to drive to the library. She was to be home at nine. When she wasn't, Mrs. Cooper began to phone her friends. Finally, around ten, Leo

Cooper got into his other car and took a swing around Halls — past the teenage hangouts like the Exxon station and the Pizza Hut and the Smoky Mountain Market. Then he took a second swing. At eleven, FaNee was still not home.

She hadn't gone to the library. She had picked up two girlfriends and   10
driven to the home of a third, where everyone took five Valium tablets. Then the four girls drove over to the Exxon station, where they met four boys from their crowd. After a while, the group bought some beer and some marijuana and reassembled at Charlie Stevens's trailer. Charlie Stevens was five or six years older than everyone else in the group — a skinny, slow-thinking young man with long black hair and a sparse beard. He was married and had a child, but he and his wife had separated; she was back in Union County with the baby. Stevens had remained in their trailer — parked in the yard near his mother's house, in a back-road area of Knox County dominated by decrepit, unpainted sheds and run-down trailers and rusted-out automobiles. Stevens had picked up FaNee at home once or twice — apparently, more as a driver for the group than as a date — and the Coopers, having learned that his unsuitability extended to being married, had asked her not to see him.

In Charlie's trailer, which had no heat or electricity, the group drank beer   11
and passed around joints, keeping warm with blankets. By eleven or so, FaNee was what one of her friends has called "super-messed-up." Her speech was slurred. She was having trouble keeping her balance. She had decided not to go home. She had apparently persuaded herself that her parents intended to send her away to some sort of home for incorrigibles. "It's too late," she said to one of her friends. "It's just too late." It was decided that one of the boys, David Munsey, who was more or less the leader of the group, would drive the Coopers' car to FaNee's house, where FaNee and Charlie Stevens would pick him up in Steven's car — a worn Pinto with four bald tires, one light, and a dragging muffler. FaNee wrote a note to her parents, and then, perhaps because her handwriting was suffering the effects of beer and marijuana and Valium, asked Stevens to rewrite it on a large piece of paper, which would be left on the seat of the Coopers' car. The Stevens version was just about the same as FaNee's, except that Stevens left out a couple of sentences about trying to work things out ("I'm willing to try") and, not having won any spelling championship himself, he misspelled a few words, like "tomorrow." The note said, "Dear Mom and Dad. Sorry I'm late. Very late. I left your car because I thought you might need it tomorrow. I love you all, but this is something I just had to do. The man talked to me privately for one and a half hours and I was really scared, so this is something I just had to do, but don't worry. I'm with a very good friend. Love you all. FaNee. P.S. Please try to understand I love you all very much, really I do. Love me if you have a chance."

At eleven-thirty or so, Leo Cooper was sitting in his living room, looking   12
out the window at his driveway — a long gravel road that runs almost four hundred feet from the house to Brown Gap Road. He saw the car that FaNee

had been driving pull into the driveway. "She's home," he called to his wife, who had just left the room. Cooper walked out on the deck over the garage. The car had stopped at the end of the driveway, and the lights had gone out. He got into his other car and drove to the end of the driveway. David Munsey had already joined Charlie Stevens and FaNee, and the Pinto was just leaving, traveling at a normal rate of speed. Leo Cooper pulled out on the road behind them.

Stevens turned left on Crippen Road, a road that has a field on one side   13 and two or three small houses on the other, and there Cooper pulled his car in front of the Pinto and stopped, blocking the way. He got out and walked toward the Pinto. Suddenly, Stevens put the car in reverse, backed into a driveway a hundred yards behind him, and sped off. Cooper jumped in his car and gave chase. Stevens raced back to Brown Gap Road, ran a stop sign there, ran another stop sign at Maynardville Highway, turned north, veered off onto the old Andersonville Pike, a nearly abandoned road that runs parallel to the highway, and then crossed back over the highway to the narrow, dark country roads on the other side. Stevens sometimes drove with his lights out. He took some of the corners by suddenly applying his hand brake to make the car swerve around in a ninety-degree turn. He was in familiar territory — he actually passed his trailer — and Cooper had difficulty keeping up. Past the trailer, Stevens swept down a hill into a sharp left turn that took him onto Foust Hollow Road, a winding, hilly road not much wider than one car.

At a fork, Cooper thought he had lost the Pinto. He started to go right and   14 then saw what seemed to be a spark from Stevens's dragging muffler off to the left, in the darkness. Cooper took the left fork, down Salem Church Road. He went down a hill and then up a long, curving hill to a crest, where he saw the Stevens car ahead. "I saw the car airborne. Up in the air," he later testified. "It was up in the air. And then it completely rolled over one more time. It started to make another flip forward, and just as it started to flip to the other side it flipped back this way, and my daughter's body came out."

Cooper slammed on his brakes and skidded to a stop up against the Pinto.   15 "Book!" Stevens shouted — the group's equivalent of "Scram!" Stevens and Munsey disappeared into the darkness. "It was dark, no one around, and so I started yelling for FaNee," Cooper had testified. "I thought it was an eternity before I could find her body, wedged under the back end of that car. . . . I tried everything I could, and saw that I couldn't get her loose. So I ran to a trailer back up to the top of the hill back up there to try to get that lady to call to get me some help, and then apparently she didn't think that I was serious. . . . I took the jack out of my car and got under, and it was dark, still couldn't see too much what was going on . . . and started prying and got her loose, and I don't know how. And then I dragged her over to the side, and, of course, at the time I felt reasonably assured that she was gone, because her head was completely — on one side just as if you had taken a sledgehammer and just hit it and bashed it in. And I did have the pleasure of one thing. I had the pleasure of listening to her breathe about the last three times she ever breathed in her life."

David Munsey did not return to the wreck that night, but Charlie Stevens 16 did. Leo Cooper was kneeling next to his daughter's body. Cooper insisted that Stevens come close enough to see FaNee. "He was kneeling down next to her," Stevens later testified. "And he said, 'Do you know what you've done? Do you really know what you've done?' Like that. And I just looked at her, and I said, 'Yes,' and just stood there. Because I couldn't say nothing." There was, of course, a legal decision to be made about who was responsible for FaNee Cooper's death. In a deposition, Stevens said he had been fleeing for his life. He testified that when Leo Cooper blocked Crippen Road, FaNee had said that her father had a gun and intended to hurt them. Stevens was bound over and eventually indicted for involuntary manslaughter. Leo Cooper testified that when he approached the Pinto on Crippen Road, FaNee had a strange expression that he had never seen before. "It wasn't like FaNee, and I knew something was wrong," he said. "My concern was to get FaNee out of the car." The district attorney's office asked that Cooper be bound over for reckless driving, but the judge declined to do so. "Any father would have done what he did," the judge said. "I can see no criminal act on the part of Mr. Cooper."

Almost two years passed before Charlie Stevens was brought to trial. Part 17 of the problem was assuring the presence of David Munsey, who had joined the Navy but seemed inclined to assign his own leaves. In the meantime, the Coopers went to court with a civil suit — they had "uninsured-motorist coverage," which requires their insurance company to cover any defendant who has no insurance of his own — and they won a judgment. There were ways of assigning responsibility, of course, which had nothing to do with the law, civil or criminal. A lot of people in Knoxville thought that Leo Cooper had, in the words of his lawyer, "done what any daddy worth his salt would have done." There were others who believed that FaNee Cooper had lost her life because Leo Cooper had lost his temper. Leo Cooper was not among those who expressed any doubts about his actions. Unlike his wife, whose eyes filled with tears at almost any mention of FaNee, Cooper seemed able, even eager to go over the details of the accident again and again. With the help of a school-board security man, he conducted his own investigation. He drove over the route dozens of times. "I've thought about it every day, and I guess I will the rest of my life," he said as he and his lawyer and the prosecuting attorney went over the route again the day before Charlie Stevens's trial finally began. "But I can't tell any alternative for a father. I simply wanted her out of that car. I'd have done the same thing again, even at the risk of losing her."

Tennessee law permits the family of a victim to hire a special prosecutor 18 to assist the district attorney. The lawyer who acted for the Coopers in the civil case helped prosecute Charlie Stevens. Both he and the district attorney assured the jurors that the presence of a special prosecutor was not to be construed to mean that the Coopers were vindictive. Outside the courtroom, Leo Cooper said that the verdict was of no importance to him — that he felt sorry, in a way, for Charlie Stevens. But there were people in Knoxville who thought Cooper had a lot riding on the prosecution of Charlie Stevens. If Stevens was not guilty of FaNee Cooper's death — found so by twelve of his peers — who was?

At the trial, Cooper testified emotionally and remarkably graphically about 19 pulling FaNee out from under the car and watching her die in his arms. Charlie Stevens had shaved his beard and cut his hair, but the effort did not transform him into an impressive witness. His lawyer — trying to argue that it would have been impossible for Stevens to concoct the story about FaNee's having mentioned a gun, as the prosecution strongly implied — said, "His mind is such that if you ask him a question you can hear his mind go around, like an old mill creaking." Stevens did not deny the recklessness of his driving or the sorry condition of his car. It happened to be the only car he had available to flee in, he said, and he had fled in fear for his life.

The prosecution said that Stevens could have let FaNee out of the car when 20 her father stopped them, or could have gone to the commercial strip on the Maynardville Highway for protection. The prosecution said that Leo Cooper had done what he might have been expected to do under the circumstances — alone, late at night, his daughter in danger. The defense said precisely the same about Stevens: He had done what he might have been expected to do when being pursued by a man he had reason to be afraid of. "I don't fault Mr. Cooper for what he did, but I'm sorry he did it," the defense attorney said. "I'm sorry the girl said what she said." The jury deliberated for eighteen minutes. Charlie Stevens was found guilty. The jury recommended a sentence of from two to five years in the state penitentiary. At the announcement, Leo Cooper broke down and cried, JoAnn Cooper's eyes filled with tears; she blinked them back and continued to stare straight ahead.

In a way, the Coopers might still strike a casual visitor as an ideal 21 family — handsome parents, a bright and bubbly teenage daughter, a little boy learning the hook shot from his father, a warm house with some land around it. FaNee's presence is there, of course. A picture of her, with a small bouquet of flowers over it, hangs in the living room. One of her poems is displayed in a frame on a table. Even if Leo Cooper continues to think about that night for the rest of his life, there are questions he can never answer. Was there a way that Leo and JoAnn Cooper could have prevented FaNee from choosing the path she chose? Would she still be alive if Leo Cooper had not jumped into his car and driven to the end of the driveway to investigate? Did she in fact tell Charlie Stevens that her father would hurt them — or even that her father had a gun? Did she want to get away from her family even at the risk of tearing around dark country roads in Charlie Stevens's dismal Pinto? Or did she welcome the risk? The poem of FaNee's that the Coopers have displayed is one she wrote a week before her death:

> I think I'm going to die
> And I really don't know why.
> But look in my eye
> When I tell you good-bye.
> I think I'm going to die.

Analyzing This Selection

1. In the first paragraph, what bearing do the parents' backgrounds and earlier life probably have on their attitude toward their children?

2. In the second paragraph, how do the parents react to the problems that FaNee faces?

3. What is the author's purpose in giving detailed descriptions, as in paragraph 3 and other places, of the setting and the local conditions of life?

4. What is the effect of the two full paragraphs that recount the car chase? What would be lost by condensing paragraphs 13 and 14 into a short statement that reports what happened?

5. FaNee's own writings, including her farewell note, show sharp contrasts between her different outlooks on life. Does this contrast make her any more sympathetic as a person? Or does it turn her into more of a freak?

6. If Mr. Cooper had been able to stop Charlie Stevens's car (immediately after paragraph 12), what might have happened? Use your insight into the characters and your sense of the situation to explain the most likely reactions of each of the main characters.

Analyzing Connections

7. In Focusing by Writing (see p. 66), the second topic suggests that families sometimes play an unwitting role in the formation of "a black sheep." Considering FaNee as a "black sheep," do you think this role was partly created by her family? Why or why not?

Analyzing by Writing

8. The essay presents the difficulties of assigning legal and moral blame for the death of FaNee. Do you think the author is too harsh or too soft in his judgment of who is guilty? who is responsible? who is victimized? In a short essay, explain the author's implied judgment in this accidental death. Include at least one point on which your judgment differs from the author's viewpoint.

9. The only viewpoint missing from Trillin's account is, of course, FaNee's. Offer some possible explanations for FaNee's withdrawal from her family. You might want to draw on insights from the other daughters and sons described in this chapter.

Kazuo Ishiguro

A FAMILY SUPPER

◇

KAZUO ISHIGURO (b. 1954) was born in Nagasaki. At the age of six, he was brought by his parents to live in England. Raised in a Japanese-speaking household, he was required to read a monthly quota of books from Japan, a country he knows almost solely from reading about it. Ishiguro studied at the University of Kent. After hitchhiking throughout Canada and the United States, he studied fiction writing at the University of East Anglia. His first novel, *A Pale View of Hills* (1982), won the Whitbread Book of the Year award in England. His most recent novel, *The Remains of the Day* (1989), was made into a popular film. Like his novels, the story "A Family Supper" (1990) deals with a perplexing situation filled with unuttered sentiments. "I try to put in as little plot as possible," he has said about his fiction.

Fugu is a fish caught off the Pacific shores of Japan. The fish has held a special significance for me ever since my mother died after eating one. The poison resides in the sex glands of the fish, inside two fragile bags. These bags must be removed with caution when preparing the fish, for any clumsiness will result in the poison leaking into the veins. Regrettably, it is not easy to tell whether or not this operation has been carried out successfully. The proof is, as it were, in the eating. 1

Fugu poisoning is hideously painful and almost always fatal. If the fish has been eaten during the evening, the victim is usually overtaken by pain during his sleep. He rolls about in agony for a few hours and is dead by morning. The fish became extremely popular in Japan after the war. Until stricter regulations were imposed, it was all the rage to perform the hazardous gutting operation in one's own kitchen, then to invite neighbors and friends round for the feast. 2

At the time of my mother's death, I was living in California. My relationship with my parents had become somewhat strained around that period and consequently I did not learn of the circumstances of her death until I returned to Tokyo two years later. Apparently, my mother had always refused to eat fugu, but on this particular occasion she had made an exception, having been invited by an old school friend whom she was anxious not to offend. It was my father who supplied me with the details as we drove from the airport to his house in the Kamakura 3 district. When we finally arrived, it was nearing the end of a sunny autumn day.

"Did you eat on the plane?" my father asked. We were sitting on the   4
tatami floor of his tearoom.

"They gave me a light snack."   5

"You must be hungry. We'll eat as soon as Kikuko arrives."   6

My father was a formidable-looking man with a large stony jaw and   7
furious black eyebrows. I think now, in retrospect, that he much resembled Chou En-lai, although he would not have cherished such a comparison, being particularly proud of the pure samurai blood that ran in the family. His general presence was not one that encouraged relaxed conversation; neither were things helped much by his odd way of stating each remark as if it were the concluding one. In fact, as I sat opposite him that afternoon, a boyhood memory came back to me of the time he had struck me several times around the head for "chattering like an old woman." Inevitably, our conversation since my arrival at the airport had been punctuated by long pauses.

"I'm sorry to hear about the firm," I said when neither of us had spoken   8
for some time. He nodded gravely.

"In fact, the story didn't end there," he said. "After the firm's collapse,   9
Watanabe killed himself. He didn't wish to live with the disgrace."

"I see."   10

"We were partners for seventeen years. A man of principle and honor. I   11
respected him very much."

"Will you go into business again?" I asked.   12

"I am . . . in retirement. I'm too old to involve myself in new ventures   13
now. Business these days has become so different. Dealing with foreigners. Doing things their way. I don't understand how we've come to this. Neither did Watanabe." He sighed. "A fine man. A man of principle."

The tearoom looked out over the garden. From where I sat I could make   14
out the ancient well that as a child I had believed to be haunted. It was just visible now through the thick foliage. The sun had sunk low and much of the garden had fallen into shadow.

"I'm glad in any case that you've decided to come back," my father said.   15
"More than a short visit, I hope."

"I'm not sure what my plans will be."   16

"I, for one, am prepared to forget the past. Your mother, too, was always   17
ready to welcome you back — upset as she was by your behavior."

"I appreciate your sympathy. As I say, I'm not sure what my plans are."   18

"I've come to believe now that there were no evil intentions in your   19
mind," my father continued. "You were swayed by certain . . . influences. Like so many others."

"Perhaps we should forget it, as you suggest."   20

"As you will. More tea?"   21

Just then a girl's voice came echoing through the house.   22

"At last." My father rose to his feet. "Kikuko has arrived."   23

Despite our difference in years, my sister and I had always been close. 24
Seeing me again seemed to make her excessively excited, and for a while she
did nothing but giggle nervously. But she calmed down somewhat when my
father started to question her about Osaka and her university. She answered
him with short, formal replies. She in turn asked me a few questions, but she
seemed inhibited by the fear that her question might lead to awkward topics.
After a while, the conversation had become even sparser than prior to
Kikuko's arrival. Then my father stood up, saying: "I must attend to the
supper. Please excuse me for being burdened by such matters. Kikuko will
look after you."

My sister relaxed quite visibly once he had left the room. Within a few 25
minutes, she was chatting freely about her friends in Osaka and about her
classes at university. Then quite suddenly she decided we should walk in the
garden and went striding out onto the veranda. We put on some straw sandals
that had been left along the veranda rail and stepped out into the garden. The
light in the garden had grown very dim.

"I've been dying for a smoke for the last half hour," she said, lighting a 26
cigarette.

"Then why didn't you smoke?" 27

She made a furtive gesture back toward the house, then grinned mischie- 28
vously.

"Oh, I see," I said. 29

"Guess what? I've got a boyfriend now." 30

"Oh, yes?" 31

"Except I'm wondering what to do. I haven't made up my mind yet." 32

"Quite understandable." 33

"You see, he's making plans to go to America. He wants me to go with 34
him as soon as I finish studying."

"I see. And you want to go to America?" 35

"If we go, we're going to hitchhike." Kikuko waved a thumb in front of my 36
face. "People say it's dangerous, but I've done it in Osaka and it's fine."

"I see. So what is it you're unsure about?" 37

We were following a narrow path that wound through the shrubs and 38
finished by the old well. As we walked, Kikuko persisted in taking unneces-
sarily theatrical puffs on her cigarette.

"Well, I've got lots of friends now in Osaka. I like it there. I'm not sure 39
I want to leave them all behind just yet. And Suichi . . . I like him, but I'm
not sure I want to spend so much time with him. Do you understand?"

"Oh, perfectly." 40

She grinned again, then skipped on ahead of me until she had reached the 41
well. "Do you remember," she said as I came walking up to her, "how you
used to say this well was haunted?"

"Yes, I remember." 42

We both peered over the side. 43

"Mother always told me it was the old woman from the vegetable store 44 you'd seen that night," she said. "But I never believed her and never came out here alone."

"Mother used to tell me that too. She even told me once the old woman 45 had confessed to being the ghost. Apparently, she'd been taking a shortcut through our garden. I imagine she had some trouble clambering over these walls."

Kikuko gave a giggle. She then turned her back to the well, casting her 46 gaze about the garden.

"Mother never really blamed you, you know," she said, in a new voice. 47 I remained silent. "She always used to say to me how it was their fault, hers and Father's, for not bringing you up correctly. She used to tell me how much more careful they'd been with me, and that's why I was so good." She looked up and the mischievous grin had returned to her face. "Poor Mother," she said.

"Yes. Poor Mother." 48

"Are you going back to California?" 49

"I don't know. I'll have to see." 50

"What happened to . . . to her? To Vicki?" 51

"That's all finished with," I said. "There's nothing much left for me now 52 in California."

"Do you think I ought to go there?" 53

"Why not? I don't know. You'll probably like it." I glanced toward the 54 house. "Perhaps we'd better go in soon. Father might need a hand with the supper."

But my sister was once more peering down into the well. "I can't see any 55 ghosts," she said. Her voice echoed a little.

"Is Father very upset about his firm collapsing?" 56

"Don't know. You never can tell with Father." Then suddenly she 57 straightened up and turned to me. "Did he tell you about old Watanabe? What he did?"

"I heard he committed suicide." 58

"Well, that wasn't all. He took his whole family with him. His wife and 59 his two little girls."

"Oh, yes?" 60

"Those two beautiful little girls. He turned on the gas while they were all 61 asleep. Then he cut his stomach with a meat knife."

"Yes, Father was just telling me how Watanabe was a man of principle." 62

"Sick." My sister turned back to the well. 63

"Careful. You'll fall right in." 64

"I can't see any ghost," she said. "You were lying to me all that time." 65

"But I never said it lived down the well." 66

"Where is it then?" 67

We both looked around at the trees and shrubs. The daylight had almost 68 gone. Eventually I pointed to a small clearing some ten yards away.

"Just there I saw it. Just there." 69

We stared at the spot.   70
"What did it look like?"   71
"I couldn't see very well. It was dark."   72
"But you must have seen something."   73
"It was an old woman. She was just standing there, watching me."   74
We kept staring at the spot as if mesmerized.   75
"She was wearing a white kimono," I said. "Some of her hair came   76
undone. It was blowing around a little."

Kikuko pushed her elbow against my arm. "Oh, be quiet. You're trying to   77
frighten me all over again." She trod on the remains of her cigarette, then for
a brief moment stood regarding it with a perplexed expression. She kicked
some pine needles over it, then once more displayed her grin. "Let's see if
supper's ready," she said.

We found my father in the kitchen. He gave us a quick glance, then   78
carried on with what he was doing.

"Father's become quite a chef since he's had to manage on his own,"   79
Kikuko said with a laugh.

He turned and looked at my sister coldly. "Hardly a skill I'm proud of,"   80
he said. "Kikuko, come here and help."

For some moments my sister did not move. Then she stepped forward and   81
took an apron hanging from a drawer.

"Just these vegetables need cooking now," he said to her. "The rest just   82
needs watching." Then he looked up and regarded me strangely for some
seconds. "I expect you want to look around the house," he said eventually.
He put down the chopsticks he had been holding. "It's a long time since
you've seen it."

As we left the kitchen I glanced toward Kikuko, but her back was turned.   83
"She's a good girl," my father said.   84

I followed my father from room to room. I had forgotten how large the   85
house was. A panel would slide open and another room would appear. But
the rooms were all startlingly empty. In one of the rooms the lights did not
come on, and we stared at the stark walls and tatami in the pale light that
came from the windows.

"This house is too large for a man to live in alone," my father said. "I   86
don't have much use for most of these rooms now."

But eventually my father opened the door to a room packed full of books   87
and papers. There were flowers in vases and pictures on the walls. Then I
noticed something on a low table in the corner of the room. I came nearer
and saw it was a plastic model of a battleship, the kind constructed by
children. It had been placed on some newspaper; scattered around it were
assorted pieces of gray plastic.

My father gave a laugh. He came up to the table and picked up the model.   88
"Since the firm folded," he said, "I have a little more time on my hands."   89
He laughed again, rather strangely. For a moment his face looked almost
gentle. "A little more time."

"That seems odd," I said. "You were always so busy." 90

"Too busy, perhaps." He looked at me with a small smile. "Perhaps I 91 should have been a more attentive father."

I laughed. He went on contemplating his battleship. Then he looked up. 92 "I hadn't meant to tell you this, but perhaps it's best that I do. It's my belief that your mother's death was no accident. She had many worries. And some disappointments."

We both gazed at the plastic battleship. 93

"Surely," I said eventually, "my mother didn't expect me to live here 94 forever."

"Obviously you don't see. You don't see how it is for some parents. Not 95 only must they lose their children, they must lose them to things they don't understand." He spun the battleship in his fingers. "These little gunboats here could have been better glued, don't you think?"

"Perhaps. I think it looks fine." 96

"During the war I spent some time on a ship rather like this. But my 97 ambition was always the air force. I figured it like this: If your ship was struck by the enemy, all you could do was struggle in the water hoping for a lifeline. But in an airplane — well, there was always the final weapon." He put the model back onto the table. "I don't suppose you believe in war."

"Not particularly." 98

He cast an eye around the room. "Supper should be ready by now," he 99 said. "You must be hungry."

Supper was waiting in a dimly lit room next to the kitchen. The only 100 source of light was a big lantern that hung over the table, casting the rest of the room in shadow. We bowed to each other before starting the meal.

There was little conversation. When I made some polite comment about 101 the food, Kikuko giggled a little. Her earlier nervousness seemed to have returned to her. My father did not speak for several minutes. Finally he said:

"It must feel strange for you, being back in Japan." 102

"Yes, it is a little strange." 103

"Already, perhaps, you regret leaving America." 104

"A little. Not so much. I didn't leave behind much. Just some empty 105 rooms."

"I see." 106

I glanced across the table. My father's face looked stony and forbidding in 107 the half-light. We ate on in silence.

Then my eye caught something at the back of the room. At first I 108 continued eating, then my hands became still. The others noticed and looked at me. I went on gazing into the darkness past my father's shoulder.

"Who is that? In that photograph there?" 109

"Which photograph?" My father turned slightly, trying to follow my gaze. 110

"The lowest one. The old woman in the white kimono." 111

My father put down his chopsticks. He looked first at the photograph, then 112 at me.

"Your mother." His voice had become very hard. "Can't you recognize 113
your own mother?"

"My mother. You see, it's dark. I can't see it very well." 114

No one spoke for a few seconds, then Kikuko rose to her feet. She took the 115
photograph down from the wall, came back to the table, and gave it to me.

"She looks a lot older," I said. 116

"It was taken shortly before her death," said my father. 117

"It was the dark. I couldn't see very well." 118

I looked up and noticed my father holding out a hand. I gave him the 119
photograph. He looked at it intently, then held it toward Kikuko. Obedi-
ently, my sister rose to her feet once more and returned the picture to the
wall.

There was a large pot left unopened at the center of the table. When 120
Kikuko had seated herself again, my father reached forward and lifted the lid.
A cloud of steam rose up and curled toward the lantern. He pushed the pot
a little toward me.

"You must be hungry," he said. One side of his face had fallen into 121
shadow.

"Thank you." I reached forward with my chopsticks. The steam was 122
almost scalding. "What is it?"

"Fish." 123

"It smells very good." 124

In the soup were strips of fish that had curled almost into balls. I picked 125
one out and brought it to my bowl.

"Help yourself. There's plenty." 126

"Thank you." I took a little more, then pushed the pot toward my father. 127
I watched him take several pieces to his bowl. Then we both watched as
Kikuko served herself.

My father bowed slightly. "You must be hungry," he said again. He took 128
some fish to his mouth and started to eat. Then I, too, chose a piece and put
it in my mouth. It felt soft, quite fleshy against my tongue.

The three of us ate in silence. Several minutes went by. My father lifted 129
the lid and once more steam rose up. We all reached forward and helped
ourselves.

"Here," I said to my father, "you have this last piece." 130

"Thank you." 131

When we had finished the meal, my father stretched out his arms and 132
yawned with an air of satisfaction. "Kikuko," he said, "prepare a pot of tea,
please."

My sister looked at him, then left the room without comment. My father 133
stood up.

"Let's retire to the other room. It's rather warm in here." 134

I got to my feet and followed him into the tearoom. The large sliding 135
windows had been left open, bringing in a breeze from the garden. For a
while we sat in silence.

"Father," I said, finally.   136

"Yes?"   137

"Kikuko tells me Watanabe-san took his whole family with him."   138

My father lowered his eyes and nodded. For some moments he seemed   139
deep in thought. "Watanabe was very devoted to his work," he said at last.
"The collapse of the firm was a great blow to him. I fear it must have
weakened his judgment."

"You think what he did . . . it was a mistake?"   140

"Why, of course. Do you see it otherwise?"   141

"No, no. Of course not."   142

"There are other things besides work," my father said.   143

"Yes."   144

We fell silent again. The sound of locusts came in from the garden. I   145
looked out into the darkness. The well was no longer visible.

"What do you think you will do now?" my father asked. "Will you stay in   146
Japan for a while?"

"To be honest, I hadn't thought that far ahead."   147

"If you wish to stay here, I mean here in this house, you would be very   148
welcome. That is, if you don't mind living with an old man."

"Thank you. I'll have to think about it."   149

I gazed out once more into the darkness.   150

"But of course," said my father, "this house is so dreary now. You'll no   151
doubt return to America before long."

"Perhaps. I don't know yet."   152

"No doubt you will."   153

For some time my father seemed to be studying the back of his hands.   154
Then he looked up and sighed.

"Kikuko is due to complete her studies next spring," he said. "Perhaps she   155
will want to come home then. She's a good girl."

"Perhaps she will."   156

"Things will improve then."   157

"Yes, I'm sure they will."   158

We fell silent once more, waiting for Kikuko to bring the tea.   159

Analyzing This Selection

1. Describe the narrator's tone in the first three paragraphs. What phrases and attitudes contribute to this tone?

2. Over what specific issues do the father and son appear to be in opposition? Identify two or three instances of their opposition. How do the father and son deal with their differences?

3. Characterize Kikuko, the sister. How does the reader come to infer so much about her character? What details seem to reveal more than is explained?

4. If the story did not include mention of fugu, the poison fish, what would be lost from its overtones and suggestions?

5. By the end of the dinner, has the son's attitude toward his father changed? How can you tell? Does your final attitude toward the father differ from the narrator's?

Analyzing Connections

6. Compare Ishiguro and Joy Harjo (see p. 76) on the roles and values of highly traditional families. How would Steven Harvey (see "The Nuclear Family," p. 100) react to these traditional situations?

Analyzing by Writing

7. Analyze the conflict of generations in this family. How does each generation appear in the eyes of the other? Be sure to include the mother, a continuing presence, though dead.

8. Write a character study (that is, a *life study*) of the most solitary or the most private person in your extended family (which can include aunts, uncles, cousins, grandparents). Give details that will make the person vivid to the reader, and try to explain or suggest this person's inner values and separate outlook.

PART 3

Significant Others

INSIGHTS

All love is self-love.

— FRANÇOIS DE LA ROCHEFOUCAULD

◇

The word love has by no means the same sense for both sexes, and this is one of the serious misunderstandings that divide them.

— SIMONE DE BEAUVOIR

◇

Christ, here's my discovery. You have got hold of the wrong absolutes and infinities. God as absolute? God as infinity? I don't even understand the words. I'll tell you what's absolute and infinite. Loving a woman. But how would you know? You see, your church knows what it's doing: Rule out one absolute so you have to look for another.

Do you know what it's like to be a self-centered not unhappy man who leads a tolerable finite life, works, eats, drinks, hunts, sleeps, then one fine day discovers that the great starry heavens have opened to him and that his heart is bursting with it. It? She. Her. Woman. Not a category, not a sex, not one of two sexes, a human female creature, but an infinity. $♀ = ∞$. What else is infinity but a woman become meat and drink to you, life and your heart's own music, the air you breathe? Just to be near her is to live and have your soul's own self. Just to open your mouth on the skin of her back. What joy just to wake up with her beside you in the morning. I didn't know there was such happiness.

But there is the dark converse: Not having her is not breathing. I'm not kidding: I couldn't get my breath without her.

What else is man made for but this? I can see you agree about love but you look somewhat ironic. Are we talking about two different things? In any case, there's a catch. Love is infinite happiness. Losing it is infinite unhappiness.

— WALKER PERCY

◇

During the first six months, the baby has the rudiments of a love language available to him. There is the language of the embrace, the language of the eyes, the language of the smile, vocal communications of pleasure and distress. It is the essential vocabulary of love before we can speak of love. Eighteen years later, when this baby is full grown and "falls in love" for the first time, he will woo his partner through the language of the eyes, the language of the smile, through the utterance of endearments, and the joy of the embrace. In his declarations of love he will use such phrases as "When I first looked into your eyes," "When you smiled at me," "When I held you in my arms." And naturally, in his exalted state, he will believe that he invented this love song.

— SELMA FRAIBERG

◇

No one can fall in love if he is even partially satisfied with what he has or who he is. The experience of falling in love originates in an extreme depression, an inability to find something that has value in everyday life. The "symptom" of the predisposition to fall in love is not the conscious desire to do so, the intense desire to enrich our lives; it is the profound sense of being worthless and of having nothing that is valuable and the shame of not having it. This is the first sign that we are prepared for the experience — the feeling of nothingness and shame over our own nothingness. For this reason, falling in love occurs more frequently among young people, since they are profoundly uncertain, unsure of their worth, and often ashamed of themselves. The same thing applies to people of other ages when they lose something in their lives — when their youth ends or when they start to grow old. There is an irreparable loss of something in the self, a feeling that we will inevitably become devoid of value or degraded, compared with what we have been. It isn't the longing for an affair that makes us fall in love, but the conviction that we have nothing to lose by becoming whatever we will become; it is the prospect of nothingness stretching before us. Only then do we develop the inclination for the different and the risky, that propensity to hurl ourselves into all or nothing which those who are in any way satisfied with their lives cannot feel.

— FRANCESCO ALBERONI

◇

Sex Without Love

How do they do it, the ones who make love
without love? Beautiful as dancers,
gliding over each other like ice skaters
over the ice, fingers hooked
inside each other's bodies, faces
red as steak, wine, wet as the
children at birth whose mothers are going to
give them away. How do they come to the

come to the   come to the   God   come to the
still waters, and not love
the one who came there with them, light
rising slowly as steam off their joined
skin? These are the true religious,
the purists, the pros, the ones who will not
accept a false Messiah, love the
priest instead of the God. They do not
mistake the lover for their own pleasure,
they are like great runners: they know they are alone
with the road surface, the cold, the wind,
the fit of their shoes, their over-all cardio-
vascular health — just factors, like the partner
in the bed, and not the truth, which is the
single body alone in the universe
against its own best time.

— SHARON OLDS

◇

We are too ego-centered. The ego-shell in which we live is the hardest thing to outgrow. We seem to carry it all the time from childhood up to the time we finally pass away. We are, however, given many chances to break through this shell, and the first and greatest of them is when we reach adolescence. This is the first time the ego really comes to recognize the "other." I mean the awakening of sexual love. An ego, entire and undivided, now begins to feel a sort of split in itself. Love hitherto dormant deep in his heart lifts its head and causes a great commotion in it. For the love now stirred demands at once the assertion of the ego and its annihilation. Love makes the ego lose itself in the object it loves, and yet at the same time it wants to have the object as its own. This is a contradiction, and a great tragedy of life.

— D. T. SUZUKI

FOCUSING BY WRITING

1. Is your campus preparing you for equality or for war between the sexes? How were sex roles and sexual expectations discussed by college officials during your freshman orientation program? What possible positive or negative results do you foresee from the presentation of the issues?

2. Children of early elementary school age often develop a heavy "crush" on somebody — frequently a teacher, sometimes another child two or three years older. Characterize the person you had a crush on. How did the object of your crush resemble or differ from your family members? Examine the wishes and ideas that your crush expressed to you.

3. A "fan" is usually involved in an imaginary romantic relationship. A fan cherishes the star's face and image; a fan delights in knowing details of the star's life; a fan identifies with the star's successes and tribulations; and a fan often fantasizes reciprocated attention and affection. Define one specific imaginary relationship that you have had as a fan. Do not just reminisce; keep your attention on examining the behavior and responses of a fan.

4. What is your favorite song that deals with love? Write down the lyrics you can remember and examine the attitude about love that the song expresses both explicitly and implicitly.

Susan Allen Toth

BOYFRIENDS

◊

SUSAN ALLEN TOTH (b. 1940) grew up in Ames, Iowa, and was graduated from Smith College before she returned to the Midwest for a Ph.D. in English and a college teaching career. She describes her college years in *Ivy Days: Making My Way Out East* (1984). Toth writes for magazines such as *Redbook* and *Harper's*, and her scholarly articles have appeared in professional journals. She recounts her precollege years in *Blooming: A Small Town Girlhood* (1981), from which this excerpt is taken. In regard to boyfriends generally, she writes, "I can't remember when I didn't want one."

Just when I was approaching sixteen, I found Peter Stone. Or did he find 1
me? Perhaps I magicked him into existence out of sheer need. I was spooked by the boys who teased us nice girls about being sweet-sixteen-and-never-been-kissed. I felt that next to being an old maid forever, it probably was most demeaning to reach sixteen and not to have experienced the kind of ardent embrace Gordon MacRae periodically bestowed on Kathryn Grayson between choruses of "Desert Song." I was afraid I would never have a real boyfriend, never go parking, never know true love. So when Peter Stone asked his friend Ted to ask Ted's girlfriend Emily who asked me if I would ever neck with anyone, I held my breath until Emily told me she had said to Ted to tell Peter that maybe I would.

Not that Peter Stone had ever necked with anyone either. But I didn't 2
realize that for a long time. High-school courtship usually was meticulously slow, progressing through inquiry, phone calls, planned encounters in public places, double or triple dates, single dates, handholding, and finally a good-night kiss. I assumed it probably stopped there, but I didn't know. I had never gotten that far. I had lots of time to learn about Peter Stone. What I knew at the beginning already attracted me. He was a year ahead of me, vice-president of Hi-Y, a shot-putter who had just managed to earn a letter sweater. An older man, *and* an athlete. Tall, heavy, and broad-shouldered, Peter had a sweet slow smile. Even at a distance there was something endearing about the way he would blink nearsightedly through his glasses and light up with pleased recognition when he saw me coming toward him down the hall.

For a long while I didn't come too close. Whenever I saw Peter he was in 3
the midst of his gang, a group of five boys as close and as self-protective as
any clique we girls had. They were an odd mixture: Jim, an introspective son
of a lawyer; Brad, a sullen hot-rodder; Ted, an unambitious and gentle boy
from a poor family; Andy, a chubby comedian; and Peter. I was a little afraid
of all of them, and they scrutinized me carefully before opening their circle
to admit me, tentatively, as I held tight to Peter's hand. The lawyer's son had
a steady girl, a fast number who was only in eighth grade but looked eighteen;
the hot-rodder was reputed to have "gone all the way" with his adoring girl,
a coarse brunette with plucked eyebrows; gentle Ted pursued my friend
Emily with hangdog tenacity; but Peter had never shown real interest in a
girlfriend before.

Although I had decided to go after Peter, I was hesitant about how to plot 4
my way into the interior of his world. It was a thicket of strange shrubs and
tangled branches. Perhaps I see it that way because I remember the day Peter
took me to a wild ravine to shoot his gun. Girls who went with one of "the
guys" commiserated with each other that their boyfriends all preferred two
other things to them: their cars and their guns. Although Peter didn't hunt
and seldom went to practice at the target range, still he valued his gun.
Without permits, "the guys" drove outside of town to fire their guns illegally.
I had read enough in my *Seventeen* about how to attract boys to know I
needed to show enthusiasm about Peter's hobbies, so I asked him if someday
he would take me someplace and teach me how to shoot.

One sunny fall afternoon he did. I remember rattling over gravel roads 5
into a rambling countryside that had surprising valleys and woods around
cultivated farmland. Eventually we stopped before a barred gate that led to an
abandoned bridge, once a railroad trestle, now a splintering wreck. We had
to push our way through knee-high weeds to get past the gate. I was afraid of
snakes. Peter took my hand; it was the first time he had ever held it, and my
knees weakened a little. I was also scared of walking onto the bridge, which
had broken boards and sudden gaps that let you look some fifty feet down into
the golden and rust-colored brush below. But I didn't mind being a little
scared as long as Peter was there to take care of me.

I don't think I had ever held a gun until Peter handed me his pistol, a 6
heavy metal weapon that looked something like the ones movie sheriffs
carried in their holsters. I was impressed by its weight and power. Peter fired
it twice to show me how and then stood close to me, watching carefully,
while I aimed at an empty beer can he tossed into the air. I didn't hit it. The
noise of the gun going off was terrifying. I hoped nobody was walking in the
woods where I had aimed. Peter said nobody was, nobody ever came here.
When I put the gun down, he put his arm around me, very carefully. He had
never done that before, either. We both just stood there, looking off into the
distance, staring at the glowing maples and elms, dark red patches of sumac,
brown heaps of leaves. The late afternoon sun beat down on us. It was hot,
and after a few minutes Peter shifted uncomfortably. I moved away, laughing

nervously, and we walked back to the car, watching the gaping boards at our feet.

What Peter and I did with our time together is a mystery. I try to picture   7
us at movies or parties or somebody's house, but all I can see is the two of us in Peter's car. "Going for a drive!" I'd fling at my mother as I rushed out of the house; "rinking" was our high-school term for it, drawn from someone's contempt for the greasy "hoods" who hung out around the roller-skating rink and skidded around corners on two wheels of their souped-up cars. Peter's car barely made it around a corner on all four wheels. Though he had learned something about how to keep his huge square Ford running, he wasn't much of a mechanic. He could make jokes about the Ford, but he didn't like anyone else, including me, to say it looked like an old black hearse or remind him it could scarcely do forty miles an hour on an open stretch of highway. Highways were not where we drove, anyway, nor was speed a necessity unless you were trying to catch up with someone who hadn't seen you. "Rinking" meant cruising aimlessly around town, looking for friends in *their* cars, stopping for conversations shouted out of windows, maybe parking somewhere for a while, ending up at the A&W Root Beer Stand or the pizza parlor or the Rainbow Cafe.

Our parents were often puzzled about why we didn't spend time in each   8
other's homes. "Why don't you invite Peter in?" my mother would ask a little wistfully, as I grabbed my billfold and cardigan and headed toward the door. Sometimes Peter would just pause in front of the house and honk; if I didn't come out quickly, he assumed I wasn't home and drove away. Mother finally made me tell him at least to come to the door and knock. I couldn't explain to her why we didn't want to sit in the living room, or go down to the pine-paneled basement at the Harbingers', or swing on the Harrises' front porch. We might not have been bothered at any of those places, but we really wouldn't have been alone. Cars were our private space, a rolling parlor, the only place we could relax and be ourselves. We could talk, fiddle with the radio if we didn't have much to say, look out the window, watch for friends passing by. Driving gave us a feeling of freedom.

Most of my memories of important moments with Peter center in that old   9
black Ford. One balmy summer evening I remember particularly because my friend Emily said I would. Emily and Ted were out cruising in his rusty two-tone Chevy, the lawyer's son Jim and his girl had his father's shiny Buick, and Peter and I were out driving in the Ford. As we rumbled slowly down the Main Street, quiet and dark at night, Peter saw Ted's car approaching. We stopped in the middle of the street so the boys could exchange a few laconic grunts while Emily and I smiled confidentially at each other. We were all in a holiday mood, lazy and happy in the warm breezes that swept through the open windows. One of us suggested that we all meet later at Camp Canwita, a wooded park a few miles north of town. Whoever saw Jim would tell him to join us too. We weren't sure what we would do there, but it sounded like an adventure. An hour or so later, Peter and I bumped over

the potholes in the road that twisted through the woods to the parking lot. We were the first ones there. When Peter turned off the motor, we could hear grasshoppers thrumming on all sides of us and leaves rustling in the dark. It was so quiet, so remote, I was a little frightened, remembering one of my mother's unnerving warnings about the dangerous men who sometimes preyed upon couples who parked in secluded places. We didn't have long to wait, though, before Ted's car coughed and sputtered down the drive. Soon Jim arrived too, and then we all pulled our cars close together in a kind of circle so we could talk easily out the windows. Someone's radio was turned on, and Frank Sinatra's mournful voice began to sing softly of passing days and lost love. Someone suggested that we get out of the cars and dance. It wouldn't have been Peter, who was seldom romantic. Ted opened his door so the overhead light cast a dim glow over the tiny area between the cars. Solemnly, a little self-consciously, we began the shuffling steps that were all we knew of what we called "slow dancing." Peter was not a good dancer, nor was I, though I liked putting my head on his bulky shoulder. But he moved me around the small lighted area as best he could, trying not to bump into Ted and Emily or Jim and his girl. I tried not to step on his toes. While Sinatra, Patti Page, and the Four Freshmen sang to us about moments to remember and Cape Cod, we all danced, one-two back, one-two back. Finally Emily, who was passing by my elbow, looked significantly at me and said, "This is something we'll be able to tell our grandchildren." Yes, I nodded, but I wasn't so sure. The mosquitoes were biting my legs and arms, my toes hurt, and I was getting a little bored. I think the others were too, because before long we all got into our cars and drove away.

Not all the time we spent in Peter's car was in motion. After several 10 months, we did begin parking on deserted country roads, side streets, even sometimes my driveway, if my mother had heeded my fierce instructions to leave the light turned off. For a while we simply sat and talked with Peter's arm draped casually on the back of the seat. Gradually I moved a little closer. Soon he had his arm around me, but even then it was a long time before he managed to kiss me good-night. Boys must have been as scared as we girls were, though we always thought of them as having much more experience. We all compared notes, shyly, about how far our boyfriends had gone; was he holding your hand yet, or taking you parking, or . . . ? When a girl finally got kissed, telephone lines burned with the news next day. I was getting a little embarrassed about how long it was taking Peter to get around to it. My sixteenth birthday was only a few weeks away, and so far I had nothing substantial to report. I was increasingly nervous too because I still didn't know quite how I was going to behave. We girls joked about wondering where your teeth went and did glasses get in the way, but no one could give a convincing description. For many years I never told anyone about what *did* happen to me that first time. I was too ashamed. Peter and I were parked down the street from my house, talking, snuggling, listening to the radio. During a silence I turned my face toward him, and then he kissed me, tentatively and quickly. I was exhilarated but frightened. I wanted to respond in an adequate way but my instincts did not entirely cooperate. I leaned towards Peter, but at the last moment I panicked. Instead of kissing him, I gave him a sudden lick on the cheek. He didn't know what to say. Neither did I.

Next morning I was relieved that it was all over. I dutifully reported my 11 news to a few key girlfriends who could pass it on to others. I left out the part about the lick. That was my last bulletin. After a first kiss, we girls also respected each other's privacy. What more was there to know? We assumed that couples sat in their cars and necked, but nice girls, we also assumed, went no farther. We knew the girls who did. Their names got around. We marveled at them, uncomprehending as much as disapproving. Usually they talked about getting married to their boyfriends, and eventually some of them did. A lot of "nice" girls suffered under this distinction. One of them told me years later how she and her steady boyfriend had yearned and held back, stopped just short, petted and clutched and gritted their teeth. "When we went together to see the movie *Splendor in the Grass*, we had to leave the theater," she said ruefully. "The part about how Natalie Wood and Warren Beatty wanted to make love so desperately and couldn't. . . . Well, that was just how we felt."

My mother worried about what was going on in the car during those long 12 evenings when Peter and I went "out driving." She needn't have. Amazing as it seems now, when courting has speeded up to a freeway pace, when I wonder if a man who doesn't try to get me to bed immediately might possibly be gay, Peter and I gave each other hours of affection without ever crossing the invisible line. We sat in his car and necked, a word that was anatomically correct. We hugged and kissed, nuzzling ears and noses and hairlines. But Peter never put a hand on my breast, and I wouldn't have known whether Peter had an erection if it had risen up and thwapped me in the face. I never got that close. Although we probably should have perished from frustration, in fact I reveled in all that holding and touching. Peter seemed pleased too, and he never demanded more. Later, I suppose, he learned quickly with someone else about what he had been missing. But I remember with gratitude Peter's awkward tenderness and the absolute faith I had in his inability to hurt me.

After Peter graduated and entered the university, our relationship 13 changed. Few high-school girls I knew went out with college men; it was considered risky, like dating someone not quite in your social set or from another town. You were cut off. At the few fraternity functions Peter took me to, I didn't know anyone there. I had no idea what to talk about or how to act. So I refused to go, and I stopped asking Peter to come with me to parties or dances at the high school. I thought he didn't fit in there either. When I was honest with myself, I admitted that romance had gone. Already planning to go away to college, I could sense new vistas opening before me, glowing horizons whose light completely eclipsed a boyfriend like Peter. When I got on the Chicago & Northwestern train to go east to Smith, I felt with relief that the train trip was erasing one problem for me. I simply rode away from Peter.

On my sixteenth birthday, Peter gave me a small cross on a chain. All the guys had decided that year to give their girlfriends crosses on chains, even though none of them was especially religious. It was a perfect gift, they thought, intimate without being soppy. Everyone's cross cost ten dollars, a lot of money, because it was real sterling silver. Long after Peter and I stopped seeing each other, I kept my cross around my neck, not taking it off even when I was in the bathtub. Like my two wooden dolls from years before, I clung to that cross as a superstitious token. It meant that someone I had once cared for had cared for me in return. Once I had had a boyfriend.

Analyzing This Selection

1. What moved Toth into her first romance? What was apparently *not* part of the impetus?

2. Where did Toth learn the appropriate way for her to interest Peter? What indicates her present attitude toward the episode with the gun?

3. Why didn't they ever come into each other's houses? What were the reasons for being in cars all the time?

4. Is there any part of this account that strikes you as probably oversimplified or idealized? What additions might make it more true to life without changing the main points of her memoir?

5. What was the lasting effect of this romance after it ended? Was it different from what she sought or expected?

Analyzing Connections

6. Toth, born in 1940, and Nora Ephron, born in 1941, grew up during the same period, the 1950s (see "Shaping Up Absurd," p. 17). What are some similarities in their adolescent experiences? What differences arise in the authors' tones and attitudes toward their adolescence?

Analyzing by Writing

7. Many high schools distribute condoms in order to reduce the likelihood of teenage pregnancies. How would, or did, this sort of prevention program affect student attitudes in the school you attended? Explain the impact on high-school attitudes toward romance and sexuality.

Alice Walker

BROTHERS AND SISTERS

◇

ALICE WALKER (b. 1944) was the youngest of eight children, a situation that made her acutely aware of the formative influence of siblings, which is the topic of the following essay. Raised in a Georgia sharecropper's family, she attended Spelman College in Atlanta, then transferred to and graduated from Sarah Lawrence College in New York. She became active in the civil rights movement and in feminism. Her literary work as a poet, essayist, and fiction writer includes the novel *The Color Purple* (1982), which won the Pulitzer Prize and the American Book Award, and two collections of essays, *In Search of Our Mothers' Gardens: Womanist Prose* (1983) and *Living by the Word* (1988). Walker has taught at Wellesley College, Yale University, Brandeis University, and the University of California at Berkeley. She now lives in San Francisco. "Brothers and Sisters" was first published in *Ms.* magazine (1975) under a pseudonym.

We lived on a farm in the South in the fifties, and my brothers, the four 1 of them I knew (the fifth had left home when I was three years old), were allowed to watch animals being mated. This was not unusual; nor was it considered unusual that my older sister and I were frowned upon if we even asked, innocently, what was going on. One of my brothers explained the mating one day, using words my father had given him: "The bull is getting a little something on his stick," he said. And he laughed. "What stick?" I wanted to know. "Where did he get it? How did he pick it up? Where did he put it?" All my brothers laughed.

I believe my mother's theory about raising a large family of five boys and 2 three girls was that the father should teach the boys and the mother teach the girls the facts, as one says, of life. So my father went around talking about bulls getting something on their sticks and she went around saying girls did not need to know about such things. They were "womanish" (a very bad way to be in those days) if they asked.

The thing was, watching the matings filled my brothers with an aimless 3 sort of lust, as dangerous as it was unintentional. They knew enough to know that cows, months after mating, produced calves, but they were not bright enough to make the same connection between women and their offspring.

Sometimes, when I think of my childhood, it seems to me a particularly 4
hard one. But in reality, everything awful that happened to me didn't seem
to happen to *me* at all, but to my older sister. Through some incredible power
to negate my presence around people I did not like, which produced invisi-
bility (as well as an ability to appear mentally vacant when I was nothing of
the kind), I was spared the humiliation she was subjected to, though at the
same time, I felt every bit of it. It was as if she suffered for my benefit, and
I vowed early in my life that none of the things that made existence so
miserable for her would happen to me.

The fact that she was not allowed at official matings did not mean she 5
never saw any. While my brothers followed my father to the mating pens on
the other side of the road near the barn, she stationed herself near the pigpen,
or followed our many dogs until they were in a mating mood, or, failing to
witness something there, she watched the chickens. On a farm it is impossible *not* to be conscious of sex, to wonder about it, to dream . . . but to
whom was she to speak of her feelings? Not to my father, who thought all
young women perverse. Not to my mother, who pretended all her children
grew out of stumps she magically found in the forest. Not to me, who never
found anything wrong with this lie.

When my sister menstruated she wore a thick packet of clean rags between 6
her legs. It stuck out in front like a penis. The boys laughed at her as she
served them at the table. Not knowing any better, and because our parents
did not dream of actually *discussing* what was going on, she would giggle
nervously at herself. I hated her for giggling, and it was at those times I would
think of her as dim-witted. She never complained, but she began to have
strange fainting fits whenever she had her period. Her head felt as if it were
splitting, she said, and everything she ate came up again. And her cramps
were so severe she could not stand. She was forced to spend several days of
each month in bed.

My father expected all of his sons to have sex with women. "Like bulls," 7
he said, "a man *needs* to get a little something on his stick." And so, on
Saturday nights, into town they went, chasing the girls. My sister was rarely
allowed into town alone, and if the dress she wore fit too snugly at the waist,
or if her cleavage dipped too far below her collarbone, she was made to stay
home.

"But why can't I go too," she would cry, her face screwed up with the 8
effort not to wail.

"They're boys, your brothers, *that's* why they can go." 9

Naturally, when she got the chance, she responded eagerly to boys. But 10
when this was discovered she was whipped and locked up in her room.

I would go in to visit her. 11

"Straight Pine," she would say, "you don't know what it *feels* like to want 12
to be loved by a man."

"And if this is what you get for feeling like it I never will," I said, with — I 13
hoped — the right combination of sympathy and disgust.

"Men smell so good," she would whisper ecstatically. "And when they 14
look into your eyes, you just melt."

Since they were so hard to catch, naturally she thought almost any of 15
them terrific.

"Oh, that Alfred!" she would moon over some mediocre, square-headed 16
boy, "he's so *sweet!*" And she would take his ugly picture out of her bosom
and kiss it.

My father was always warning her not to come home if she ever found 17
herself pregnant. My mother constantly reminded her that abortion was a
sin. Later, although she never became pregnant, her period would not come
for months at a time. The painful symptoms, however, never varied or
ceased. She fell for the first man who loved her enough to beat her for
looking at someone else, and when I was still in high school, she married
him.

My fifth brother, the one I never knew, was said to be different from the 18
rest. He had not liked matings. He would not watch them. He thought the
cows should be given a choice. My father had disliked him because he was
soft. My mother took up for him. "Jason is just tender-hearted," she would
say in a way that made me know he was her favorite; "he takes after me." It
was true that my mother cried about almost anything.

Who was this oldest brother? I wondered. 19

"Well," said my mother, "he was someone who always loved you. Of 20
course he was a great big boy when you were born and out working on his
own. He worked on a road gang building roads. Every morning before he left
he would come in the room where you were and pick you up and give you
the biggest kisses. He used to look at you and just smile. It's a pity you don't
remember him."

I agreed. 21

At my father's funeral I finally "met" my oldest brother. He is tall and 22
black with thick gray hair above a young-looking face. I watched my sister cry
over my father until she blacked out from grief. I saw my brothers sobbing,
reminding each other of what a great father he had been. My oldest brother
and I did not shed a tear between us. When I left my father's grave he came
up and introduced himself. "You don't ever have to walk alone," he said,
and put his arms around me.

One out of five ain't *too* bad, I thought, snuggling up. 23

But I didn't discover until recently his true uniqueness: He is the only 24
one of my brothers who assumes responsibility for all his children. The
other four all fathered children during those Saturday-night chases of
twenty years ago. Children — my nieces and nephews whom I will probably never know — they neither acknowledge as their own, provide for, or
even see.

It was not until I became a student of women's liberation ideology that I 25 could understand and forgive my father. I needed an ideology that would define his behavior in context. The black movement had given me an ideology that helped explain his colorism (he *did* fall in love with my mother partly because she was so light; he never denied it). Feminism helped explain his sexism. I was relieved to know his sexist behavior was not something uniquely his own, but, rather, an imitation of the behavior of the society around us.

All partisan movements add to the fullness of our understanding of society as a whole. They never detract; or, in any case, one must not allow them to do so. Experience adds to experience. "The more things the better," as O'Connor and Welty both have said, speaking, one of marriage, the other of Catholicism.   26

I desperately needed my father and brothers to give me male models I could respect, because white men (for example; being particularly handy in this sort of comparison) — whether in films or in person — offered man as dominator, as killer, and always as hypocrite.   27

My father failed because he copied the hypocrisy. And my brothers — except for one — never understood they must represent half the world to me, as I must represent the other half to them.   28

Analyzing This Selection

1. Explain the author's analogy between animal mating and human sexual behavior. What main points does Walker emphasize with this comparison?

2. In Walker's childhood, how much did she know about her absent brother? How did thoughts of him affect her development?

3. Consider specific social and historical differences between Walker's family and your family. In your opinion, how importantly do the differences affect family attitudes toward sexuality? Do general circumstances have profound or only superficial effects on family sexual attitudes?

4. How did Walker's adult participation in the black movement and feminism change her attitudes toward her family? In her view, what are the benefits and risks of an ideology?

Analyzing Connections

5. The first question in Focusing by Writing for *Family Ties* (see p. 66) asks about your preferred number of siblings. In this essay, did Walker in her childhood feel that she had too many or too few brothers and sisters? What place did she have among them?

6. Compare and contrast Walker's portrayal of youthful sexuality with Susan Allen Toth's views in "Boyfriends" (the preceding selection). Along with differences, what values and outlooks do these authors share?

Analyzing by Writing

7. Sex roles may not be as coarsely defined or as cruelly enforced as they were for Walker, but young male and female sex roles are still dictated by family and society. How are gender patterns for sexual activity currently articulated and enforced? Are the roles separate-but-equal? Or are they wholly unequal?

8. In your opinion, how important are children's attitudes toward brothers and sisters in the development of their adult attitudes toward the opposite sex? Expand Walker's thesis about sibling role models by supporting or disagreeing with her point.

Bernard Cooper

PICKING PLUMS

◊

Bᴇʀɴᴀʀᴅ Cᴏᴏᴘᴇʀ (b. 1951) was born in Hollywood, California. He studied visual arts at the California Institute of the Arts, where he took both his undergraduate and master's degrees in fine arts. His essays have been published in magazines such as *Grand Street, Georgia Review,* and *Harper's,* where the following selection first appeared. Cooper has published a collection of essays, *Maps to Anywhere* (1992), and a novel, *A Year of Rhymes* (1993). He teaches writing at the University of California at Los Angeles.

It has been nearly a year since my father fell while picking plums. The 1
bruises on his leg have healed, and except for a vague absence of pigmentation where the calf had blistered, his recovery is complete. Back in the habit of evening constitutionals, he navigates the neighborhood with his usual stride — "Brisk," he says, "for a man of eighty-five" — dressed in a powder blue jogging suit that bears the telltale stains of jelly doughnuts and Lipton tea, foods which my father, despite doctor's orders, hasn't the will to forsake.

He broke his glasses and his hearing aid in the fall, and when I first 2
stepped into the hospital room for a visit, I was struck by the way my father — head cocked to hear, squinting to see — looked so much older and more remote, a prisoner of his failing senses. "Boychik?" he asked, straining his face in my general direction. He fell back into a stack of pillows, sighed a deep sigh, and without my asking described what had happened:

"There they are, all over the lawn. Purple plums, dozens of them. They 3
look delicious. So what am I supposed to do? Let the birds eat them? Not on your life. It's my tree, right? First I fill a bucket with the ones from the ground. Then I get the ladder out of the garage. I've climbed the thing a hundred times before. I make it to the top, reach out my hand, and . . . who knows what happens. Suddenly I'm an astronaut. Up is down and vice versa. It happened so fast I didn't have time to piss in my pants. I'm flat on my back, not a breath in me. Couldn't have called for help if I tried. And the pain in my leg — you don't want to know."

"Who found you?" 4

"What?" 5

I move closer, speak louder.   6

"Nobody found me," he says, exasperated. "Had to wait till I could get up   7
on my own. It seemed like hours. I'm telling you, I thought it was all over.
But eventually I could breathe normal again and — don't ask me how; God
only knows — I got in the car and drove here myself." My father shifted his
weight and grimaced. The sheet slid off his injured leg, the calf swollen,
purple as a plum, what the doctor called "an insult to the tissue."

Throughout my boyhood my father possessed a surplus of energy, or it   8
possessed him. On weekdays he worked hard at the office, and on weekends
he gardened in our yard. He was also a man given to unpredictable episodes
of anger. These rages were never precipitated by a crisis — in the face of
illness or accident my father remained steady, methodical, even optimistic;
when the chips were down he was an incorrigible joker, an inveterate
backslapper, a sentry at the bedside — but something as simple as a drinking
glass left out on the table could send him into a frenzy of invective. Spittle
shot from his lips. Blood ruddied his face. He'd hurl the glass against the
wall.

His temper rarely intimidated my mother. She'd light a Tareyton, stand   9
aside, and watch my father flail and shout until he was purged of the last
sharp word. Winded and limp, he'd flee into the living room, where he
would draw the shades, sit in his wing chair, and brood for hours.

Even as a boy, I understood how my father's profession had sullied his   10
view of the world, had made him a wary man, prone to explosions. He spent
hours taking depositions from jilted wives and cuckolded husbands. He
conferred with a miserable clientele: spouses who wept, who spat accusa-
tions, who pounded his desk in want of revenge. At the time, California law
required that grounds for divorce be proven in court, and toward this end my
father carried in his briefcase not only the usual legal tablets and manila files
but bills for motel rooms, matchbooks from bars, boxer shorts blooming with
lipstick stains.

After one particularly long and vindictive divorce trial, he agreed to a   11
weekend out of town. Mother suggested Palm Springs, rhapsodized about the
balmy air, the cacti lit by colored lights, the street named after Bob Hope.
When it finally came time to leave, however, my mother kept thinking of
things she forgot to pack. No sooner would my father begin to back the car
out of the driveway than my mother would shout for him to stop, dash into
the house, and retrieve what she needed. A carton of Tareytons. An aerosol
can of Solarcaine. A paperback novel to read by the pool. I sat in the
backseat, motionless and mute; with each of her excursions back inside, I felt
my father's frustration mount. When my mother insisted she get a package
of Saltine crackers in case we got hungry along the way, my father glared at
her, bolted from the car, wrenched every piece of luggage from the trunk,
and slammed it shut with such a vengeance the car rocked on its springs.

Through the rear window, my mother and I could see him fling two   12 suitcases, a carryall, and a makeup case yards above his balding head. The sky was a huge and cloudless blue; gray chunks of luggage sailed through it, twisting and spinning and falling to earth like the burned-out stages of a booster rocket. When a piece of luggage crashed back to the asphalt, he'd pick it up and hurl it again. With every effort, an involuntary, animal grunt issued from the depths of his chest.

Finally, the largest suitcase came unlatched in mid-flight. Even my father 13 was astonished when articles of his wife's wardrobe began their descent from the summer sky. A yellow scarf dazzled the air like a tangible strand of sunlight. Fuzzy slippers tumbled down. One diaphanous white slip drifted over the driveway and, as if guided by an invisible hand, draped itself across a hedge. With that, my father barreled by us, veins protruding on his temple and neck, and stomped into the house. "I'm getting tired of this," my mother grumbled. Before she stooped to pick up the mess — a vast and random geography of clothes — she flicked her cigarette onto the asphalt and ground the ember out.

One evening, long after I'd moved away from home, I received a phone 14 call from my father telling me that my mother had died the night before. "But I didn't know it happened," he said.

He'd awakened as usual that morning, ruminating over a case while he 15 showered and shaved. My mother appeared to be sound asleep, one arm draped across her face, eyes sheltered beneath the crook of her elbow. When he sat on the bed to pull up his socks, he'd tried not to jar the mattress and wake her. At least he *thought* he'd tried not to wake her, but he couldn't remember, he couldn't be sure. Things looked normal, he kept protesting — the pillow, the blanket, the way she lay there. He decided to grab a doughnut downtown and left in a hurry. But that night my father returned to a house suspiciously unlived-in. The silence caused him to clench his fists, and he called for his wife — "Lillian, Lillian" — as he drifted through quiet, unlit rooms, walking slowly up the stairs.

I once saw a photograph of a woman who had jumped off the Empire 16 State Building and landed on the roof of a parked car. What is amazing is that she appears merely to have leapt into satin sheets, to be deep in a languid and absolute sleep. Her eyes are closed, lips slightly parted, hair fanned out on a metal pillow. Nowhere is there a trace of blood, her body caught softly in its own impression.

As my father spoke into the telephone, his voice about to break — "I 17 should have realized. I should have known" — that's the state in which I pictured my mother: a long fall of sixty years, an uncanny landing, a miraculous repose.

My father and I had one thing in common after my mother's heart attack: 18 we each maintained a secret life. Secret, at least, from each other.

I'd fallen for a man named Travis Mask. Travis had recently arrived in Los 19

Angeles from Kentucky, and everything I was accustomed to — the bill-boards lining the Sunset strip, the 7-Elevens open all night — stirred in him a strong allegiance; "I love this town," he'd say every day. Travis's job was to collect change from food vending machines throughout the city. During dinner he would tell me about the office lobbies and college cafeterias he had visited, the trick to opening different machines, the noisy cascade of nickels and dimes. Travis Mask was enthusiastic. Travis Mask was easy to please. In bed I called him by his full name because I found the sound of it exciting.

My father, on the other hand, had fallen for a woman whose identity he meant to keep secret. I knew of her existence only because of a dramatic change in his behavior: he would grow mysterious as quickly and inexplicably as he had once grown angry. Though I resented being barred from this central fact of my father's life, I had no intention of telling him I was gay. It had taken me thirty years to achieve even a modicum of intimacy with the man, and I didn't want to risk a setback. It wasn't as if I was keeping my sexual orientation a secret; I'd told relatives, co-workers, friends. But my father was a man who whistled at waitresses, flirted with bank tellers, his head swiveling like a radar dish toward the nearest pair of breasts and hips. Ever since I was a child my father reminded me of the wolf in cartoons whose ears shoot steam, whose eyes pop out on springs, whose tongue unfurls like a party favor whenever he sees a curvaceous dame. As far as my father was concerned, desire for women fueled the world, compelled every man without exception — his occupation testified to that — was a force as essential as gravity. I didn't want to disappoint him.

Eventually, Travis Mask was transferred to Long Beach. In his absence my nights grew long and ponderous, and I tried to spend more time with my father in the belief that sooner or later an opportunity for disclosure would present itself. We met for dinner once a month in a restaurant whose interior was dim and crimson, our interaction friendly but formal, both of us cautiously skirting the topic of our private lives; we'd become expert at the ambiguous answer, the changed subject, the half-truth. Should my father ask if I was dating, I'd tell him yes, I had been seeing someone. I'd liked them very much, I said, but they were transferred to another city. Them. They. My attempt to neuter the pronouns made it sound as if I were courting people en masse. Just when I thought this subterfuge was becoming obvious, my father began to respond in kind: "Too bad I didn't get a chance to meet them. Where did you say they went?"

Avoidance also worked in reverse: "And how about you, Dad? Are you seeing anybody?"

"Seeing? I don't know if you'd call it *seeing*. What did you order, chicken or fish?"

During one dinner we discovered that we shared a fondness for nature programs on television, and from that night on, when we'd exhausted our comments about the meal or the weather, we'd ask if the other had seen the show about the blind albino fish who live in underwater caves, or the one about the North American moose whose antlers, coated with green moss, provide camouflage in the underbrush. My father and I had adapted like those creatures to the strictures of our shared world.

And then I met her.   25

I looked up from a rack of stationery at the local Thrifty one afternoon and   26 there stood my father with a willowy black woman in her early forties. As she waited for a prescription to be filled, he drew a finger through her hair, nuzzled the nape of her neck, the refracted light of his lenses causing his cheeks to glow. I felt like a child who was witness to something forbidden: his father's helpless, unguarded ardor for an unfamiliar woman. I didn't know whether to run or stay. Had he always been attracted to young black women? Had I ever known him well? Somehow I managed to move myself toward them and mumble hello. They turned around in unison. My father's eyes widened. He reached out and cupped my shoulder, struggled to say my name. Before he could think to introduce us, I shook the woman's hand, startled by its softness. "So you're the son. Where've you been hiding?" She was kind and cordial, though too preoccupied to engage in much conversation, her handsome features furrowed by a hint of melancholy, a sadness which I sensed had little to do with my surprise appearance. Anna excused herself when the pharmacist called her name.

Hours after our encounter, I could still feel the softness of Anna's hand,   27 the softness that stirred my father's yearning. He was seventy-five years old, myopic and hard of hearing, his skin loose and liver-spotted, but one glimpse of his impulsive public affection led me to the conclusion that my father possessed, despite his age, a restless sexual energy. The meeting left me elated, expectant. My father and I had something new in common: the pursuit of our unorthodox passions. We were, perhaps, more alike than I'd realized. After years of relative estrangement, I'd been given grounds for a fresh start, a chance to establish a stronger connection.

But none of my expectations mattered. Later that week, they left the   28 country.

The prescription, it turned out, was for a psychotropic drug. Anna had   29 battled bouts of depression since childhood. Her propensity for unhappiness gave my father a vital mission: to make her laugh, to wrest her from despair. Anna worked as an elementary-school substitute teacher and managed a few rental properties in South-Central Los Angeles, but after weeks of functioning normally, she would take to my father's bed for days on end, blank and immobile beneath the quilt she had bought to brighten up the room, unaffected by his jokes, his kisses and cajoling. These spells of depression came without warning and ended just as unexpectedly. Though they both did their best to enjoy each other during the periods of relative calm, they lived, my father later lamented, like people in a thunderstorm, never knowing when lightning would strike. Thinking that a drastic change might help Anna shed a recent depression, they pooled their money and flew to Europe.

They returned with snapshots showing the two of them against innumer- 30
able backdrops: the Tower of London, the Vatican, Versailles; monuments,
obelisks, statuary. In every pose their faces were unchanged, the faces of
people who want to be happy, who try to be happy, and somehow can't.

As if in defiance of all the photographic evidence against them, they 31
were married the following month at the Church of the Holy Trinity. I
was one of only two guests at the wedding. The other was an uncle of
Anna's. Before the ceremony began, he shot me a glance which attested,
I was certain, to an incredulity as great as mine. The vaulted chapel rang
with prerecorded organ music, an eerie and pious overture. Light filtered
through stained-glass windows, chunks of sweet color that reminded me of
Jell-O. My old Jewish father and his Episcopalian lover appeared at opposite ends of the dais, walking step by measured step toward a union in the
center. The priest, swimming in white vestments, was somber and almost
inaudible. Cryptic gestures, odd props; I watched with a powerful, wordless amazement. Afterward, as if the actual wedding hadn't been surreal
enough, my father and Anna formed a kind of receiving line (if two
people can constitute a line) in the church parking lot, where the four of
us, bathed by hazy sunlight, exchanged pleasantries before the newlyweds
returned home for a nap; their honeymoon in Europe, my father joked,
had put the cart before the horse.

During the months after the wedding, when I called my father, he 32
answered as though the ringing of the phone had been an affront. When
I asked him what the matter was he'd bark, "What makes you think there's
something the matter?" I began to suspect that my father's frustration had
given rise to those ancient rages. But my father had grown too old and
frail to sustain his anger for long. When we saw each other — Anna was
always visiting relatives or too busy or tired to join us — he looked worn,
embattled, and the pride I had in him for attempting an interracial marriage, for risking condemnation in the eyes of the world, was overwhelmed
now by concern. He lost weight. His hands began to shake. I would sit
across from him in the dim, red restaurant and marvel that this bewildered
man had once hurled glasses against a wall and launched Samsonite into
the sky.

Between courses I'd try to distract my father from his problems by pressing 33
him to unearth tidbits of his past, as many as memory would allow. He'd
often talk about Atlantic City, where his parents had owned a small grocery.
Sometimes my mother turned up in the midst of his sketchy regressions. He
would smooth wrinkles from the tablecloth and tell me no one could take her
place. He eulogized her loyalty and patience, and I wondered whether he
could see her clearly — her auburn hair and freckled hands — wondered
whether he wished she were here to sweep up after his current mess. "Remember," he once asked me, without a hint of irony or regret, "what fun we
had in Palm Springs?" Then he snapped back into the present and asked what
was taking so long with our steaks.

The final rift between my father and Anna must have happened suddenly; 34 she left behind several of her possessions, including the picture of Jesus that sat on the sideboard in the dining room next to my father's brass menorah. And along with Anna's possessions were stacks of leather-bound books, *Law of Torts, California Jurisprudence,* and *Forms of Pleading and Practice,* embossed along their spines. Too weak and distracted to practice law, my father had retired, and the house became a repository for the contents of his former office. I worried about him being alone, wandering through rooms freighted with history, crowded with the evidence of two marriages, fatherhood, and a long and harrowing career; he had nothing to do but pace and sigh and stir up dust. I encouraged him to find a therapist, but as far as my father was concerned, psychiatrists were all conniving witch doctors who fed off the misery of people like Anna.

Brian, the psychotherapist I'd been living with for three years (and live 35 with still), was not at all fazed by my father's aversion to his profession. They'd met only rarely — once we ran into my father at a local supermarket, and twice Brian accompanied us to the restaurant — but when they were together, Brian would draw my father out, compliment him on his plaid pants, ask questions regarding the fine points of law. And when my father spoke, Brian listened intently, embraced him with his cool, blue gaze. My father relished my lover's attention; Brian's cheerfulness and steady disposition must have been refreshing in those troubled, lonely days. "How's that interesting friend of yours?" he sometimes asked. If he was suspicious that Brian and I shared the same house, he never pursued it — until he took his fall from the plum tree.

I drove my father home from the hospital, trying to keep his big unwieldy 36 car, bobbing like a boat, within the lane. I bought him a pair of seersucker shorts because long pants were too painful and constricting. I brought over groceries and my wok, and while I cooked dinner my father sat at the dinette table, leg propped on a vinyl chair, and listened to the hissing oil, happy, abstracted. I helped him up the stairs to his bedroom, where we watched *Wheel of Fortune* and *Jeopardy* on the television and where, for the first time since I was a boy, I sat at his feet and he rubbed my head. It felt so good I'd graze his good leg, contented as a cat. He welcomed my visits with an eagerness bordering on glee and didn't seem to mind being dependent on me for physical assistance; he leaned his bulk on my shoulder wholly, and I felt protective, necessary, inhaling the scents of salve and Old Spice and the base, familiar odor that was all my father's own.

"You know those hostages?" asked my father one evening. He was sitting 37 at the dinette, dressed in the seersucker shorts, his leg propped on the chair. The bruises had faded to lavender, his calf back to its normal size.

I could barely hear him over the broccoli sizzling in the wok. "What 38 about them?" I shouted.

"I heard on the news that some of them are seeing a psychiatrist now that 39 they're back."

"So?"   40

"Why a psychiatrist?"   41

I stopped tossing the broccoli. "Dad," I said, "if you'd been held hostage 42 in the Middle East, you might want to see a therapist, too."

The sky dimmed in the kitchen windows. My father's face was a silhou- 43 ette, his lenses catching the last of the light. "They got their food taken care of, right? And a place to sleep. What's the big deal?"

"You're at gunpoint, for God's sake. A prisoner. I don't think it's like 44 spending a weekend at the Hilton."

"Living alone," he said matter-of-factly, "is like being a prisoner."   45

I let it stand. I added the pea pods.   46

"Let me ask you something," said my father. "I get this feeling — I'm not 47 sure how to say it — that something isn't right. That you're keeping some-thing from me. We don't talk much, I grant you that. But maybe now's the time."

My heart was pounding. I'd been thoroughly disarmed by his interpreta- 48 tion of world events, his minefield of non sequiturs, and I wasn't prepared for a serious discussion. I switched off the gas. The red jet sputtered. When I turned around, my father was staring at his outstretched leg. "So?" he said.

"You mean Brian?"   49

"Whatever you want to tell me, tell me."   50

"You like him, don't you?"   51

"What's not to like."   52

"He's been my lover for a long time. He makes me happy. We have a 53 home." Each declaration was a stone in my throat. "I hope you understand. I hope this doesn't come between us."

"Look," said my father without skipping a beat, "you're lucky to have 54 someone. And he's lucky to have you, too. It's no one's business anyway. What the hell else am I going to say?"

But my father thought of something else before I could speak and express 55 my relief. "You know," he said, "when I was a boy of maybe sixteen, my father asked me to hold a ladder while he trimmed the tree in our backyard. So I did, see, when I suddenly remember I have a date with this bee-yoo-tiful girl, and I'm late, and I run out of the yard. I don't know what got into me. I'm halfway down the street when I remember my father, and I think, 'Oh, boy. I'm in trouble now.' But when I get back I can hear him laughing way up in the tree. I'd never heard him laugh like that. 'You must like her a lot,' he says when I help him down. Funny thing was, I hadn't told him where I was going."

I pictured my father's father teetering above the earth, a man hugging the 56 trunk of a tree and watching his son run down the street in pursuit of sweet, ineffable pleasure. While my father reminisced, night obscured the branches of the plum tree, the driveway where my mother's clothes once floated down like enormous leaves. When my father finished telling the story, he looked at me, then looked away. A moment of silence lodged between us, an old and obstinate silence. I wondered whether nothing or everything would change. I spooned our food onto separate plates. My father carefully pressed his leg to test the healing flesh.

Analyzing This Selection

1. What is the relevance of the father's profession? What perspective does it introduce?

2. What is the author's view of his parents' marriage?

3. Why doesn't Cooper tell his father about Travis Mask?

4. How does his father's involvement with Anna change Cooper's view of him? Look for some mixed responses, but try to sum up their effect.

5. The father says "Living alone is like being a prisoner." Why is the son surprised by this observation?

6. The essay starts by recounting the father's fall from a plum tree. In paragraph 8, Cooper begins to recount events that occurred before the accident, including some in the distant past. At the end of paragraph 35, the author returns to the present time with the phrase "until he took his fall from the plum tree." Why does the author use that detail to focus from present to past and back to the present?

Analyzing Connections

7. In their early lives, both Cooper and Raymond Carver (see "My Father's Life, p. 82) suffered from their fathers' shortcomings, yet both come to love their fathers. What different recognitions arise in their father-son relationships? To which son is the father a more "significant other"?

Analyzing by Writing

8. Are parents ever impartial and detached about their children's romantic interests? How do they express or signal approval and disapproval? Consider the code of allowable direct or indirect parental "interference" that operates in your family, and explain the subtleties, the anxieties, and the limits of this form of participation.

9. Keeping secrets from those who are closest to you gets out of bounds sometimes, and can become a disturbing part of a relationship. Under certain circumstances, parents are secretive in front of their children; children keep secrets from parents and other family members; and friends at school keep secrets from one another. Analyze the patterns and purposes of habitual secrecy in a group of your friends or in your family.

Raymond Carver

WHAT WE TALK ABOUT
WHEN WE TALK ABOUT LOVE

◇

See the earlier headnote about Raymond Carver on page 82. This selection is the title story of his volume What We Talk About When We Talk About Love *(1981). The story is a contemporary symposium (Plato's* Symposium, *an after-dinner conversation about love, seems to loom in the background) in which four people half-drunkenly discuss the peculiarities of loves they have known and witnessed.*

My friend Mel McGinnis was talking. Mel McGinnis is a cardiologist, 1 and sometimes that gives him the right.

The four of us were sitting around his kitchen table drinking gin. 2 Sunlight filled the kitchen from the big windows behind the sink. There were Mel and me and his second wife, Teresa — Terri, we called her — and my wife, Laura. We lived in Albuquerque then. But we were all from somewhere else.

There was an ice bucket on the table. The gin and the tonic water kept 3 going around, and we somehow got on the subject of love. Mel thought real love was nothing less than spiritual love. He said he'd spent five years in a seminary before quitting to go to medical school. He said he still looked back on those years in the seminary as the most important years in his life.

Terri said the man she lived with before she lived with Mel loved her so 4 much he tried to kill her. Then Terri said, "He beat me up one night. He dragged me around the living room by my ankles. He kept saying, 'I love you, I love you, you bitch.' He went on dragging me around the living room. My head kept knocking on things." Terri looked around the table. "What do you do with love like that?"

She was a bone-thin woman with a pretty face, dark eyes, and brown hair 5 that hung down her back. She liked necklaces made of turquoise, and long pendant earrings.

"My God, don't be silly. That's not love, and you know it," Mel said. "I 6 don't know what you'd call it, but I sure know you wouldn't call it love."

"Say what you want to, but I know it was," Terri said. "It may sound crazy 7 to you, but it's true just the same. People are different, Mel. Sure, sometimes he may have acted crazy. Okay. But he loved me. In his own way maybe, but he loved me. There was love there, Mel. Don't say there wasn't."

Mel let out his breath. He held his glass and turned to Laura and me. 8 "The man threatened to kill me," Mel said. He finished his drink and reached for the gin bottle. "Terri's a romantic. Terri's of the kick-me-so-I'll-know-you-love-me school. Terri, hon, don't look that way." Mel reached across the table and touched Terri's cheek with his fingers. He grinned at her.

"Now he wants to make up," Terri said. 9

"Make up what?" Mel said. "What is there to make up? I know what I 10 know. That's all."

"How'd we get started on this subject, anyway?" Terri said. She raised her 11 glass and drank from it. "Mel always has love on his mind," she said. "Don't you, honey?" She smiled, and I thought that was the last of it.

"I just wouldn't call Ed's behavior love. That's all I'm saying, honey," 12 Mel said. "What about you guys?" Mel said to Laura and me. "Does that sound like love to you?"

"I'm the wrong person to ask," I said. "I didn't even know the man. I've only 13 heard his name mentioned in passing. I wouldn't know. You'd have to know the particulars. But I think what you're saying is that love is an absolute."

Mel said, "The kind of love I'm talking about is. The kind of love I'm 14 talking about, you don't try to kill people."

Laura said, "I don't know anything about Ed, or anything about the 15 situation. But who can judge anyone else's situation?"

I touched the back of Laura's hand. She gave me a quick smile. I picked 16 up Laura's hand. It was warm, the nails polished, perfectly manicured. I encircled the broad wrist with my fingers, and I held her.

"When I left, he drank rat poison," Terri said. She clasped her arms with 17 her hands. "They took him to the hospital in Santa Fe. That's where we lived then, about ten miles out. They saved his life. But his gums went crazy from it. I mean they pulled away from his teeth. After that, his teeth stood out like fangs. My God," Terri said. She waited a minute, then let go of her arms and picked up her glass.

"What people won't do!" Laura said. 18

"He's out of the action now," Mel said. "He's dead." 19

Mel handed me the saucer of limes. I took a section, squeezed it over my 20 drink, and stirred the ice cubes with my finger.

"It gets worse," Terri said. "He shot himself in the mouth. But he bungled 21 that too. Poor Ed," she said. Terri shook her head.

"Poor Ed nothing," Mel said. "He was dangerous." 22

Mel was forty-five years old. He was tall and rangy with curly soft hair. His 23 face and arms were brown from the tennis he played. When he was sober, his gestures, all his movements, were precise, very careful.

"He did love me though, Mel. Grant me that," Terri said. "That's all I'm 24 asking. He didn't love me the way you love me. I'm not saying that. But he loved me. You can grant me that, can't you?"

"What do you mean, he bungled it?" I said.   25

Laura leaned forward with her glass. She put her elbows on the table and   26
held her glass in both hands. She glanced from Mel to Terri and waited with
a look of bewilderment on her open face, as if amazed that such things
happened to people you were friendly with.

"How'd he bungle it when he killed himself?" I said.   27

"I'll tell you what happened," Mel said. "He took his twenty-two pistol   28
he'd bought to threaten Terri and me with. Oh, I'm serious, the man was
always threatening. You should have seen the way we lived in those days.
Like fugitives. I even bought a gun myself. Can you believe it? A guy like
me? But I did. I bought one for self-defense and carried it in the glove
compartment. Sometimes I'd have to leave the apartment in the middle of
the night. To go to the hospital, you know? Terri and I weren't married then,
and my first wife had the house and kids, the dog, everything, and Terri and
I were living in this apartment here. Sometimes, as I say, I'd get a call in the
middle of the night and have to go into the hospital at two or three in the
morning. It'd be dark out there in the parking lot, and I'd break into a sweat
before I could even get to my car. I never knew if he was going to come up
out of the shrubbery or from behind a car and start shooting. I mean, the
man was crazy. He was capable of wiring a bomb, anything. He used to call
my service at all hours and say he needed to talk to the doctor, and when I'd
return the call, he'd say, 'Son of a bitch, your days are numbered.' Little
things like that. It was scary, I'm telling you."

"I still feel sorry for him," Terri said.   29

"It sounds like a nightmare," Laura said. "But what exactly happened after   30
he shot himself?"

Laura is a legal secretary. We'd met in a professional capacity. Before we   31
knew it, it was a courtship. She's thirty-five, three years younger than I am.
In addition to being in love, we like each other and enjoy one another's
company. She's easy to be with.

"What happened?" Laura said.   32

Mel said, "He shot himself in the mouth in his room. Someone heard the   33
shot and told the manager. They came in with a passkey, saw what had
happened, and called an ambulance. I happened to be there when they
brought him in, alive but past recall. The man lived for three days. His head
swelled up to twice the size of a normal head. I'd never seen anything like it,
and I hope I never do again. Terri wanted to go in and sit with him when she
found out about it. We had a fight over it. I didn't think she should see him
like that. I didn't think she should see him, and I still don't."

"Who won the fight?" Laura said.   34

"I was in the room with him when he died," Terri said. "He never came   35
up out of it. But I sat with him. He didn't have anyone else."

"He was dangerous," Mel said. "If you call that love, you can have it."   36

"It was love," Terri said. "Sure, it's abnormal in most people's eyes. But 37 he was willing to die for it. He did die for it."

"I sure as hell wouldn't call it love," Mel said. "I mean, no one knows 38 what he did it for. I've seen a lot of suicides, and I couldn't say anyone ever knew what they did it for."

Mel put his hands behind his neck and tilted his chair back. "I'm not 39 interested in that kind of love," he said. "If that's love, you can have it."

Terri said, "We were afraid. Mel even made a will out and wrote to his 40 brother in California who used to be a Green Beret. Mel told him who to look for if something happened to him."

Terri drank from her glass. She said, "But Mel's right — we lived like 41 fugitives. We were afraid. Mel was, weren't you, honey? I even called the police at one point, but they were no help. They said they couldn't do anything until Ed actually did something. Isn't that a laugh?" Terri said.

She poured the last of the gin into her glass and waggled the bottle. Mel 42 got up from the table and went to the cupboard. He took down another bottle.

"Well, Nick and I know what love is," Laura said. "For us, I mean," 43 Laura said. She bumped my knee with her knee. "You're supposed to say something now," Laura said, and turned her smile on me.

For an answer, I took Laura's hand and raised it to my lips. I made a big 44 production out of kissing her hand. Everyone was amused.

"We're lucky," I said. 45

"You guys," Terri said. "Stop that now. You're making me sick. You're 46 still on the honeymoon, for God's sake. You're still gaga, for crying out loud. Just wait. How long have you been together now? How long has it been? A year? Longer than a year?"

"Going on a year and a half," Laura said, flushed and smiling. 47

"Oh, now," Terri said. "Wait awhile." 48

She held her drink and gazed at Laura. 49

"I'm only kidding," Terri said. 50

Mel opened the gin and went around the table with the bottle. 51

"Here, you guys," he said. "Let's have a toast. I want to propose a toast. 52 A toast to love. To true love," Mel said.

We touched glasses. 53

"To love," we said. 54

Outside in the backyard, one of the dogs began to bark. The leaves of the 55 aspen that leaned past the window ticked against the glass. The afternoon sun was like a presence in this room, the spacious light of ease and generosity. We could have been anywhere, somewhere enchanted. We raised our glasses again and grinned at each other like children who had agreed on something forbidden.

"I'll tell you what real love is," Mel said. "I mean, I'll give you a good   56
example. And then you can draw your own conclusions." He poured more
gin into his glass. He added an ice cube and a sliver of lime. We waited and
sipped our drinks. Laura and I touched knees again. I put a hand on her
warm thigh and left it there.

"What do any of us really know about love?" Mel said. "It seems to me   57
we're just beginners at love. We say we love each other and we do, I don't
doubt it. I love Terri and Terri loves me, and you guys love each other
too. You know the kind of love I'm talking about now. Physical love, that
impulse that drives you to someone special, as well as love of the other
person's being, his or her essence, as it were. Carnal love and, well, call
it sentimental love, the day-to-day caring about the other person. But
sometimes I have a hard time accounting for the fact that I must have
loved my first wife too. But I did, I know I did. So I suppose I am like
Terri in that regard. Terri and Ed." He thought about it and then he went
on. "There was a time when I thought I loved my first wife more than life
itself. But now I hate her guts. I do. How do you explain that? What
happened to that love? What happened to it, is what I'd like to know. I
wish someone could tell me. Then there's Ed. Okay, we're back to Ed.
He loves Terri so much he tries to kill her and he winds up killing
himself." Mel stopped talking and swallowed from his glass. "You guys
have been together eighteen months and you love each other. It shows all
over you. You glow with it. But you both loved other people before you
met each other. You've both been married before, just like us. And you
probably loved other people before that too, even. Terri and I have been
together five years, been married for four. And the terrible thing, the
terrible thing is, but the good thing too, the saving grace, you might say,
is that if something happened to one of us — excuse me for saying this
— but if something happened to one of us tomorrow, I think the other
one, the other person, would grieve for a while, you know, but then the
surviving party would go out and love again, have someone else soon
enough. All this, all of this love we're talking about, it would just be a
memory. Maybe not even a memory. Am I wrong? Am I way off base?
Because I want you to set me straight if you think I'm wrong. I want to
know. I mean, I don't know anything, and I'm the first one to admit it."

"Mel, for God's sake," Terri said. She reached out and took hold of his   58
wrist. "Are you getting drunk? Honey? Are you drunk?"

"Honey, I'm just talking," Mel said. "All right? I don't have to be drunk   59
to say what I think. I mean, we're all just talking, right?" Mel said. He fixed
his eyes on her.

"Sweetie, I'm not criticizing," Terri said.   60

She picked up her glass.   61

"I'm not on call today," Mel said. "Let me remind you of that. I am not   62
on call," he said.

"Mel, we love you," Laura said.   63

Mel looked at Laura. He looked at her as if he could not place her, as if   64
she was not the woman she was.

"Love you too, Laura," Mel said. "And you, Nick, love you too. You   65
know something?" Mel said. "You guys are our pals," Mel said.

He picked up his glass.   66

Mel said, "I was going to tell you about something. I mean, I was going   67
to prove a point. You see, this happened a few months ago, but it's still going
on right now, and it ought to make us feel ashamed when we talk like we
know what we're talking about when we talk about love."

"Come on now," Terri said. "Don't talk like you're drunk if you're not   68
drunk."

"Just shut up for once in your life," Mel said very quietly. "Will you do   69
me a favor and do that for a minute? So as I was saying, there's this old
couple who had this car wreck out on the interstate. A kid hit them and they
were all torn to shit and nobody was giving them much chance to pull
through."

Terri looked at us and then back at Mel. She seemed anxious, or maybe   70
that's too strong a word.

Mel was handing the bottle around the table.   71

"I was on call that night," Mel said. "It was May or maybe it was June.   72
Terri and I had just sat down to dinner when the hospital called. There'd
been this thing out on the interstate. Drunk kid, teenager, plowed his dad's
pickup into this camper with this old couple in it. They were up in their
mid-seventies, that couple. The kid — eighteen, nineteen, something — he
was DOA. Taken the steering wheel through his sternum. The old couple,
they were alive, you understand. I mean, just barely. But they had everything. Multiple fractures, internal injuries, hemorrhaging, contusions, lacerations, the works, and they each of them had themselves concussions.
They were in a bad way, believe me. And, of course, their age was two strikes
against them. I'd say she was worse off than he was. Ruptured spleen along
with everything else. Both kneecaps broken. But they'd been wearing their
seatbelts and, God knows, that's what saved them for the time being."

"Folks, this is an advertisement for the National Safety Council," Terri   73
said. "This is your spokesman, Dr. Melvin R. McGinnis, talking." Terri
laughed. "Mel," she said, "sometimes you're just too much. But I love you,
hon," she said.

"Honey, I love you," Mel said.   74

He leaned across the table. Terri met him halfway. They kissed.   75

"Terri's right," Mel said as he settled himself again. "Get those seatbelts   76
on. But seriously, they were in some shape, those oldsters. By the time I got
down there, the kid was dead, as I said. He was off in a corner, laid out on
a gurney. I took one look at the old couple and told the ER nurse to get me
a neurologist and an orthopedic man and a couple of surgeons down there
right away."

He drank from his glass. "I'll try to keep this short," he said. "So we took   77
the two of them up to the OR and worked like fuck on them most of the
night. They had these incredible reserves, those two. You see that once in a
while. So we did everything that could be done, and toward morning we're
giving them a fifty-fifty chance, maybe less than that for her. So here they
are, still alive the next morning. So, okay, we move them into the ICU,
which is where they both kept plugging away at it for two weeks, hitting it
better and better on all the scopes. So we transfer them out to their own
room."

Mel stopped talking. "Here," he said, "let's drink this cheapo gin the hell   78
up. Then we're going to dinner, right? Terri and I know a new place. That's
where we'll go, to this new place we know about. But we're not going until
we finish up this cut-rate, lousy gin."

Terri said, "We haven't actually eaten there yet. But it looks good. From   79
the outside, you know."

"I like food," Mel said. "If I had it to do all over again, I'd be a chef, you   80
know? Right? Terri?" Mel said.

He laughed. He fingered the ice in his glass.   81

"Terri knows," he said. "Terri can tell you. But let me say this. If I could   82
come back again in a different life, a different time and all, you know what?
I'd like to come back as a knight. You were pretty safe wearing all that armor.
It was all right being a knight until gunpowder and muskets and pistols came
along."

"Mel would like to ride a horse and carry a lance," Terri said.   83

"Carry a woman's scarf with you everywhere," Laura said.   84

"Or just a woman," Mel said.   85

"Shame on you," Laura said.   86

Terri said, "Suppose you came back as a serf. The serfs didn't have it so   87
good in those days," Terri said.

"The serfs never had it good," Mel said. "But I guess even the knights   88
were vessels to someone. Isn't that the way it worked? But then everyone is
always a vessel to someone. Isn't that right? Terri? But what I liked about
knights, besides their ladies, was that they had that suit of armor, you know,
and they couldn't get hurt very easy. No cars in those days, you know? No
drunk teenagers to tear into your ass."

"Vassals," Terri said.   89

"What?" Mel said.   90

"Vassals," Terri said. "They were called vassals, not vessels."   91

"Vassals, vessels," Mel said, "what the fuck's the difference? You knew   92
what I meant anyway. All right," Mel said. "So I'm not educated. I learned
my stuff. I'm a heart surgeon, sure, but I'm just a mechanic. I go in and fuck
around and fix things. Shit," Mel said.

"Modesty doesn't become you," Terri said.   93

"He's just a humble sawbones," I said. "But sometimes they suffocated in   94 all that armor, Mel. They'd even have heart attacks if it got too hot and they were too tired and worn out. I read somewhere that they'd fall off their horses and not be able to get up because they were too tired to stand with all that armor on them. They got trampled by their own horses sometimes."

"That's terrible," Mel said. "That's a terrible thing, Nicky. I guess they'd   95
just lay there and wait until somebody came along and made a shish kebab out of them."

"Some other vessel," Terri said.   96

"That's right," Mel said. "Some vassal would come along and spear the   97
bastard in the name of love. Or whatever the fuck it was they fought over in those days."

"Same things we fight over these days," Terri said.   98

Laura said, "Nothing's changed."   99

The color was still high in Laura's cheeks. Her eyes were bright. She   100
brought her glass to her lips.

Mel poured himself another drink. He looked at the label closely as if   101
studying a long row of numbers. Then he slowly put the bottle down on the table and slowly reached for the tonic water.

"What about the old couple?" Laura said. "You didn't finish that story   102
you started."

Laura was having a hard time lighting her cigarette. Her matches kept   103
going out.

The sunshine inside the room was different now, changing, getting thin-   104
ner. But the leaves outside the window were still shimmering, and I stared at the pattern they made on the panes and on the Formica counter. They weren't the same patterns, of course.

"What about the old couple?" I said.   105

"Older but wiser," Terri said.   106

Mel stared at her.   107

Terri said, "Go on with your story, hon. I was only kidding. Then what   108
happened?"

"Terri, sometimes," Mel said.   109

"Please, Mel," Terri said. "Don't always be so serious, sweetie. Can't you   110
take a joke?"

"Where's the joke?" Mel said.   111

He held his glass and gazed steadily at his wife.   112

"What happened?" Laura said.   113

Mel fastened his eyes on Laura. He said, "Laura, if I didn't have Terri and   114
if I didn't love her so much, and if Nick wasn't my best friend, I'd fall in love with you. I'd carry you off, honey," he said.

"Tell your story," Terri said. "Then we'll go to that new place, okay?"   115

"Okay?" Mel said. "Where was I?" he said. He stared at the table and then   116
he began again.

"I dropped in to see each of them every day, sometimes twice a day if I was   117 up doing other calls anyway. Casts and bandages, head to foot, the both of them. You know, you've seen it in the movies. That's just the way they looked, just like in the movies. Little eye-holes and nose-holes and mouth-holes. And she had to have her legs slung up on top of it. Well, the husband was very depressed for the longest while. Even after he found out that his wife was going to pull through, he was still very depressed. Not about the accident, though. I mean, the accident was one thing, but it wasn't everything. I'd get up to his mouth-hole, you know, and he'd say no, it wasn't the accident exactly but it was because he couldn't see her through his eye-holes. He said that was what was making him feel so bad. Can you imagine? I'm telling you, the man's heart was breaking because he couldn't turn his goddamn head and *see* his goddamn wife."

Mel looked around the table and shook his head at what he was going to   118
say.

"I mean, it was killing the old fart just because he couldn't *look* at the   119
fucking woman."

We all looked at Mel.   120

"Do you see what I'm saying?" he said.   121

Maybe we were a little drunk by then. I know it was hard keeping things   122
in focus. The light was draining out of the room, going back through the window where it had come from. Yet nobody made a move to get up from the table to turn on the overhead light.

"Listen," Mel said. "Let's finish this fucking gin. There's about enough   123
left here for one shooter all around. Then let's go eat. Let's go to the new place."

"He's depressed," Terri said. "Mel, why don't you take a pill?"   124

Mel shook his head. "I've taken everything there is."   125

"We all need a pill now and then," I said.   126

"Some people are born needing them," Terri said.   127

She was using her finger to rub at something on the table. Then she   128
stopped rubbing.

"I think I want to call my kids," Mel said. "Is that all right with everybody?   129
I'll call my kids," he said.

Terri said, "What if Marjorie answers the phone? You guys, you've heard   130
us on the subject of Marjorie? Honey, you know you don't want to talk to Marjorie. It'll make you feel even worse."

"I don't want to talk to Marjorie," Mel said. "But I want to talk to my   131
kids."

"There isn't a day goes by that Mel doesn't say he wishes she'd get married   132
again. Or else die," Terri said. "For one thing," Terri said, "She's bank-rupting us. Mel says it's just to spite him that she won't get married again. She has a boyfriend who lives with her and the kids, so Mel is supporting the boyfriend too."

"She's allergic to bees," Mel said. "If I'm not praying she'll get married   133 again, I'm praying she'll get herself stung to death by a swarm of fucking bees."

"Shame on you," Laura said.   134

"Bzzzzzzz," Mel said, turning his fingers into bees and buzzing them at   135 Terri's throat. Then he let his hands drop all the way to his sides.

"She's vicious," Mel said. "Sometimes I think I'll go up there dressed like   136 a beekeeper. You know, that hat that's like a helmet with the plate that comes down over your face, the big gloves, and the padded coat? I'll knock on the door and let a loose hive of bees in the house. But first I'd make sure the kids were out, of course."

He crossed one leg over the other. It seemed to take him a lot of time to   137 do it. Then he put both feet on the floor and leaned forward, elbows on the table, his chin cupped in his hands.

"Maybe I won't call the kids, after all. Maybe it isn't such a hot idea.   138 Maybe we'll just go eat. How does that sound?"

"Sounds fine to me," I said. "Eat or not eat. Or keep drinking. I could   139 head right on out into the sunset."

"What does that mean, honey?" Laura said.   140

"It just means what I said," I said. "It means I could just keep going.   141 That's all it means."

"I could eat something myself," Laura said. "I don't think I've ever been   142 so hungry in my life. Is there something to nibble on?"

"I'll put out some cheese and crackers," Terri said.   143

But Terri just sat there. She did not get up to get anything.   144

Mel turned his glass over. He spilled it out on the table.   145

"Gin's gone," Mel said.   146

Terri said, "Now what?"   147

I could hear my heart beating. I could hear everyone's heart. I could hear   148 the human noise we sat there making, not one of us moving, not even when the room went dark.

Analyzing This Selection

1. Think of three adjectives that together summarize Mel's character in the first half of the story. Would you change the adjectives to fit his character at the end of the story?

2. At what times and how do the characters express their love for their partners and for their friends during the conversation? What motives or satisfactions enter into their expressions of love? Examine the details closely.

3. What aspect of love is especially troubling to Mel? What bearing does it have on his earlier intention to become a priest and his present vocation as a cardiologist?

4. Why does Mel's language become more vulgar as he tells his story about the old people? What is agitating him?

5. What do Nick and Laura find disturbing about Mel's story? How do we know?

6. Mel divides love into "carnal" and "sentimental." Does his example of true love fit either category? How would you define it?

Analyzing Connections

7. Add another participant to this conversation around the kitchen table: If Simone de Beauvoir contributed her viewpoint in the Insights (see p. 128), how would the other characters respond?

Analyzing by Writing

8. Our commonly used expressions about love indicate that love is not just an emotion: It is also a whole set of ideas and beliefs about that emotion. Is love something to "work on"? Is it something to "share"? Is it "communication"? or a "commitment"? Is it a "feeling"? or a "trip"? Consider the assumptions and implications surrounding the concept of love that is current among a group of people you know. Examine the specific words, gestures, and reactions that indicate their assumed view of love.

Barbara Ehrenreich

IN PRAISE OF "BEST FRIENDS"

◇

BARBARA EHRENREICH (b. 1941) was born in Butte, Montana. After graduating from Reed College and earning her Ph.D. at Rockefeller University, she taught at the State University of New York at Old Westbury. She has edited *Seven Days* magazine in Washington, D.C., where she is a fellow at the Institute for Policy Studies. Since 1981 Ehrenreich has also been a contributing editor to *Ms.* magazine, where this article first appeared (1987). Her commentaries on social history, popular culture, and contemporary issues have been published in a variety of magazines, including *Mother Jones*, the *Nation*, the *New York Times Magazine*, and *The New Republic*. Her book-length critiques of American society include *Fear of Falling: The Inner Life of the Middle Class* (1989) and *The Worst Years of Our Lives: Irreverent Notes from a Decade of Greed* (1990).

All the politicians, these days, are "profamily," but I've never heard of one 1 who was "profriendship." This is too bad and possibly shortsighted. After all, most of us would never survive our families if we didn't have our friends.

I'm especially concerned about the fine old institution of "best friends." I 2 realized that it was on shaky ground a few months ago, when the occasion arose to introduce my own best friend (we'll call her Joan) at a somewhat intimidating gathering. I got as far as saying, "I am very proud to introduce my best friend, Joan . . ." when suddenly I wasn't proud at all. I was blushing. "Best friend," I realized as soon as I heard the words out loud, sounds like something left over from sixth-grade cliques: the kind of thing where if Sandy saw you talking to Stephanie at recess, she might tell you after school that she wasn't going to be your best friend anymore, and so forth. Why couldn't I have just said "my good friend Joan" or something *grown-up* like that?

But Joan is not just any friend, or even a "good friend"; she is my best 3 friend. We have celebrated each other's triumphs together, nursed each other through savage breakups with the various men in our lives, discussed the Great Issues of Our Time, and cackled insanely over things that were, objectively speaking, not even funny. We have quarreled and made up; we've lived in the same house and we've lived thousands of miles apart. We've learned to say hard things, like "You really upset me when . . ." and even

"I love you." Yet, for all this, our relationship has no earthly weight or status. I can't even say the name for it without sounding profoundly silly.

Why is best friendship, particularly between women, so undervalued and 4 unrecognized? Partly, no doubt, because women themselves have always been so undervalued and unrecognized. In the Western tradition, male best friendships are the stuff of history and high drama. Reread Homer, for example, and you'll realize that Troy did not fall because Paris, that spoiled Trojan prince, loved Helen, but because Achilles so loved Patroclus. It was Patroclus's death, at the hands of the Trojans, that made Achilles snap out of his sulk long enough to slay the Trojans' greatest warrior and guarantee victory to the Greeks. Did Helen have a best friend, or any friend at all? We'll never know, because the only best friendships that have survived in history and legend are man-on-man: Alexander and Hephaestion, Orestes and Pylades, Heracles and Iolas.

Christianity did not improve the status of female friendship. "Every 5 woman ought to be filled with shame at the thought that she is a woman," declaimed one of the early church fathers, Clement of Alexandria, and when two women got together, the shame presumably doubled. Male friendship was still supposed to be a breeding ground for all kinds of upstanding traits — honor, altruism, courage, faith, loyalty. Consider Arthur's friendship with Lancelot, which easily survived the latter's dalliance with Queen Guinevere. But when two women got together, the best you could hope for, apparently, was bitchiness, and the worst was witchcraft.

Yet, without the slightest encouragement from history, women have per- 6 sisted in finding best friends. According to recent feminist scholarship, the nineteenth century seems to have been a heyday of female best friendship. In fact, feminism might never have gotten off the ground at all if it hadn't been for the enduring bond between Elizabeth Cady Stanton, the theoretician of the movement, and Susan B. Anthony, the movement's first great pragmatist.

And they are only the most famous best friends. According to Lillian 7 Faderman's book *Surpassing the Love of Men*, there were thousands of anonymous female couples who wrote passionate letters to each other, exchanged promises and tokens of love, and suffered through the separations occasioned by marriage and migration. Feminist scholars have debated whether these great best friendships were actually lesbian, sexual relationships — a question that I find both deeply fascinating (if these were lesbian relationships, were the women involved conscious of what a bold and subversive step they had taken?) and somewhat beside the point. What matters is that these women honored their friendships, and sought ways to give them the kind of coherence and meaning that the larger society reserved only for marriage.

In the twentieth century, female best friendship was largely eclipsed by the 8 new ideal of the "companionate marriage." At least in the middle-class culture that celebrated "togetherness," your *husband* was now supposed to be your best friend, as well, of course, as being your lover, provider, coparent, housemate, and principal heir. My own theory (profamily politicians please take note) is that these expectations have done more damage to the institution of marriage than no-fault divorce and the sexual revolution combined. No man can be all things to even one woman. And the foolish idea that one could has left untold thousands of women not only divorced, but what is in the long run far worse — friendless.

Yet even feminism, when it came back to life in the early seventies, did 9 not rehabilitate the institution of female best friendship. Lesbian relationships took priority, for the good and obvious reason that they had been not only neglected, but driven underground. But in our zeal to bring lesbian relationships safely out of the closet, we sometimes ended up shoving best friendships further out of sight. "Best friends?" a politically ever-so-correct friend once snapped at me, in reference to Joan, "why aren't you lovers?" In the same vein, the radical feminist theoretician Shulamith Firestone wrote that after the gender revolution, there would be no asexual friendships. The coming feminist Utopia, I realized sadly, was going to be a pretty lonely place for some of us.

Then, almost before we could get out of our jeans and into our corporate 10 clone clothes, female friendship came back into fashion — but in the vastly attenuated form of "networking." Suddenly we were supposed to have dozens of women friends, hundreds if time and the phone bill allow, but each with a defined function: mentors, contacts, connections, allies, even pretty ones who might be able to introduce us, now and then, to their leftover boyfriends. The voluminous literature on corporate success for women is full of advice on friends: whom to avoid ("turkeys" and whiners), whom to cultivate (winners and potential clients), and how to tell when a friend is moving from the latter category into the former. This is an advance, because it means we are finally realizing that women are important enough to be valued friends and that friendship among women is valuable enough to write and talk about. But in the pushy new dress-for-success world, there's less room than ever for best friendships that last through thick and thin, through skidding as well as climbing.

Hence my campaign to save the institution of female best friendship. I am 11 not asking you to vote for anyone, to pray to anyone, or even to send me money. I'm just suggesting that we all begin to give a little more space, and a little more respect, to the best friendships in our lives. To this end, I propose three rules:

1. Best friendships should be given social visibility. If you are inviting Pat 12 over for dinner, you would naturally think of inviting her husband, Ed. Why not Pat's best friend, Jill? Well, you may be thinking, how childish! They don't have to go everywhere together. Of course they don't, but neither do Pat and Ed. In many settings, including your next dinner party or potluck, Pat and Jill may be the combination that makes the most sense and has the most fun.

2. Best friends take time and nurturance, even when that means taking 13

time and nurturance away from other major relationships. Everyone knows that marriages require "work." (A ghastly concept, that. "Working on a marriage" has always sounded to me like something on the order of lawn maintenance.) Friendships require effort, too, and best friendships require our very best efforts. It should be possible to say to husband Ed or whomever, "I'm sorry I can't spend the evening with you because I need to put in some quality time with Jill." He will only be offended if he is a slave to heterosexual couple-ism — in which case you shouldn't have married him in the first place.

3. Best friendship is more important than any work-related benefit that 14 may accrue from it, and should be treated accordingly. Maybe your best friend will help you get that promotion, transfer, or new contract. That's all well and good, but the real question is: Will that promotion, transfer, or whatever help your best friendship? If it's a transfer to San Diego, and your best friend's in Cincinnati, it may not be worth it. For example, as a writer who has collaborated with many friends, including "Joan," I am often accosted by strangers exclaiming, "It's just amazing that you got through that book [article, or other project] together and you're still friends!" The truth is, in nine cases out of ten, that the friendship was always far more important than the book. If a project isn't going to strengthen my friendship — and might even threaten it — I'd rather not start.

When I was thinking through this column — out loud of course, with a 15 very good friend on the phone — she sniffed, "So what exactly do you want — formal, legalized friendships, with best-friend licenses and showers and property settlements in case you get in a fight over the sweaters you've been borrowing from each other for the past ten years?" No, of course not, because the beauty of best friendship, as opposed to, say, marriage, is that it's a totally grass-roots, creative effort that requires no help at all from the powers-that-be. Besides, it would be too complicated. In contrast to marriage — and even to sixth-grade cliques — there's no rule that says you can have only one "best" friend.

Analyzing This Selection

1. According to Ehrenreich, why would a name for "best friendship" improve its status in society? What other significant relationships lack names that confer positive status?

2. According to the author, society respects friendships between men but denigrates women's friendships. Do you agree? Without using examples from literature, provide contemporary publicly known illustrations that support or dispute her point.

3. What gains and losses to friendship does Ehrenreich attribute to women's greater participation in careers?

4. Of the three rules Ehrenreich proposes to upgrade friendships, the third might cause the most difficulties, especially for young people facing choices about education and careers. Are you prepared to follow such a rule?

Analyzing Connections

5. Ehrenreich treats female friendships as simple harmonies. Reconsider Nancy Friday's view of competitiveness among women who love one another (see "Competition," p. 71). Is rivalry a serious threat to women's friendships? Do best friends have to play noncompeting roles?

Analyzing by Writing

6. Write an account of how your overall view of someone (not necessarily a friend) was changed by your recognition of particular new qualities about him or her. The person may have been a stranger who gave you an impression that was modified upon further observation; or the person may be someone long familiar to you in a different way. Was the person aware of your earlier view and your later view? Be detailed and precise about your different perceptions.

Marc Feigen Fasteau

FRIENDSHIPS AMONG MEN

◇

Marc Feigen Fasteau (b. 1942) is a lawyer who specializes in sex discrimination cases. He attended Harvard Law School, where he was editor of the *Harvard Law Review*. Upon graduation, he returned to Washington, D.C., where he had been born, to work in government service. Moving to New York City, he then combined a law career with a political interest in legislation to reduce sex discrimination. He lectures widely on the topic of sexual stereotypes, and his articles have appeared in feminist magazines, such as *Ms.*, as well as journals for scientists. His book *The Male Machine* (1974) is a study of the masculine stereotype in our society. As the title suggests, the author believes that men are partly dehumanized by our idea of masculinity: "the male machine . . . is functional, designed mainly for work." In the following selection from that book, Fasteau argues that men remain unemotional and impersonal even in their friendships.

There is a long-standing myth in our society that the great friendships are 1 between men. Forged through shared experience, male friendship is portrayed as the most unselfish, if not the highest, form of human relationship. The more traditionally masculine the shared experience from which it springs, the stronger and more profound the friendship is supposed to be. Going to war, weathering crises together at school or work, playing on the same athletic team, are some of the classic experiences out of which friendships between men are believed to grow.

By and large, men do prefer the company of other men, not only in their 2 structured time but in the time they fill with optional, nonobligatory activity. They prefer to play games, drink, and talk, as well as work and fight together. Yet something is missing. Despite the time men spend together, their contact rarely goes beyond the external, a limitation which tends to make their friendships shallow and unsatisfying.

My own childhood memories are of doing things with my friends — play- 3 ing games or sports, building walkie-talkies, going camping. Other people and my relationships to them were never legitimate subjects for attention. If someone liked me, it was an opaque, mysterious occurrence that bore no analysis. When I was slighted, I felt hurt. But relationships with people just happened. I certainly had feelings about my friends, but I can't remember a single instance of trying consciously to sort them out until I was well into college.

For most men this kind of shying away from the personal continues into adult life. In conversations with each other, we hardly ever use ourselves as reference points. We talk about almost everything except how we ourselves are affected by people and events. Everything is discussed as though it were taking place out there somewhere, as though we had no more felt response to it than to the weather. Topics that can be treated in this detached, objective way become conversational mainstays. The few subjects which are fundamentally personal are shaped into discussions of abstract general questions. Even in an exchange about their reactions to liberated women — a topic of intensely personal interest — the tendency will be to talk in general, theoretical terms. Work, at least its objective aspects, is always a safe subject. Men also spend an incredible amount of time rehashing the great public issues of the day. Until early 1973, Vietnam was the work-horse topic. Then came Watergate. It doesn't seem to matter that we've all had a hundred similar conversations. We plunge in for another round, trying to come up with a new angle as much to impress the others with what we know as to keep from being bored stiff.

Games play a central role in situations organized by men. I remember a weekend some years ago at the country house of a law-school classmate as a blur of softball, football, croquet, poker, and a dice-and-board game called Combat, with swimming thrown in on the side. As soon as one game ended, another began. Taken one at a time, these "activities" were fun, but the impression was inescapable that the host, and most of his guests, would do anything to stave off a lull in which they would be together without some impersonal focus for their attention. A snapshot of almost any men's club would show the same thing, 90 percent of the men engaged in some activity — ranging from backgammon to watching the tube — other than, or at least as an aid to, conversation.[1]

My composite memory of evenings spent with a friend at college and later when we shared an apartment in Washington is of conversations punctuated by silences during which we would internally pass over any personal or emotional thoughts which had arisen and come back to the permitted track. When I couldn't get my mind off personal matters, I said very little. Talks with my father have always had the same tone. Respect for privacy was the rationale for our diffidence. His questions to me about how things were going at school or at work were asked as discreetly as he would have asked a friend about someone's commitment to a hospital for the criminally insane. Our conversations, when they touched these matters at all, to say nothing of more sensitive matters, would veer quickly back to safe topics of general interest.

---

[1] Women may use games as a reason for getting together — bridge clubs, for example. But the show is more for the rest of the world — to indicate that they are doing *something* — and the games themselves are not the only means of communication. [Au.]

In our popular literature, the archetypal male hero embodying this personal muteness is the cowboy. The classic mold for the character was set in 1902 by Owen Wister's novel *The Virginian* where the author spelled out, with an explicitness that was never again necessary, the characteristics of his protagonist. Here's how it goes when two close friends the Virginian hasn't seen in some time take him out for a drink: 7

All of them had seen rough days together, and they felt guilty with emotion.

"It's hot weather," said Wiggin.

"Hotter in Box Elder," said McLean. "My kid has started teething."

Words ran dry again. They shifted their positions, looked in their glasses, read the labels on the bottles. They dropped a word now and then to the proprietor about his trade, and his ornaments.

One of the Virginian's duties is to assist at the hanging of an old friend as a horse thief. Afterward, for the first time in the book, he is visibly upset. The narrator puts his arm around the hero's shoulders and describes the Virginian's reaction:

I had the sense to keep silent, and presently he shook my hand, not looking at me as he did so. He was always very shy of demonstration.

And, for explanation of such reticence, "As all men know, he also knew that many things should be done in this world in silence, and that talking about them is a mistake."

There are exceptions, but they only prove the rule. 8

One is the drunken confidence. "Bob, ole boy, I gotta tell ya — being divorced isn't so hot. . . . [and see, I'm too drunk to be held responsible for blurting it out]." Here, drink becomes an excuse for exchanging confidences and a device for periodically loosening the restraint against expressing a need for sympathy and support from other men — which may explain its importance as a male ritual. Marijuana fills a similar need. 9

Another exception is talking to a stranger — who may be either someone the speaker doesn't know or someone who isn't in the same social or business world. (Several black friends told me that they have been on the receiving end of personal confidences from white acquaintances that they were sure had not been shared with white friends.) In either case, men are willing to talk about themselves only to other men with whom they do not have to compete or whom they will not have to confront socially later. 10

Finally, there is the way men depend on women to facilitate certain conversations. The women in a mixed group are usually the ones who make the first personal reference, about themselves or others present. The men can then join in without having the onus for initiating a discussion of "personalities." Collectively, the men can "blame" the conversation on the women. 11

They can also feel in these conversations that since they are talking "to" the women instead of "to" the men, they can be excused for deviating from the masculine norm. When the women leave, the tone and subject invariably shift away from the personal.

The effect of these constraints is to make it extraordinarily difficult for 12
men to really get to know each other. A psychotherapist who has conducted a lengthy series of encounter groups for men summed it up:

> With saddening regularity [the members of these groups] described how much they wanted to have closer, more satisfying relationships with other men: "I'd settle for having one really close man friend. I supposedly have some close men friends now. We play golf or go for a drink. We complain about our jobs and our wives. I care about them and they care about me. We even have some physical contact — I mean we may even give a hug on a big occasion. But it's not enough."

The sources of this stifling ban on self-disclosure, the reasons why men hide from each other, lie in the taboos and imperatives of the masculine stereotype.

To begin with, men are supposed to be functional, to spend their time 13
working or otherwise solving or thinking about how to solve problems. Personal reaction, how one feels about something, is considered dysfunctional, at best an irrelevant distraction from the expected objectivity. Only weak men, and women, talk about — i.e., "give in," to their feelings. "I group my friends in two ways," said a business executive:

> those who have made it and don't complain and those who haven't made it. And only the latter spend time talking to their wives about their problems and how bad their boss is and all that. The ones who concentrate more on communicating . . . are those who have realized that they aren't going to make it and therefore they have changed the focus of attention.

In a world which tells men they have to choose between expressiveness and manly strength, this characterization may be accurate. Most of the men who talk personally to other men *are* those whose problems have gotten the best of them, who simply can't help it. Men not driven to despair don't talk about themselves, so the idea that self-disclosure and expressiveness are associated with problems and weakness becomes a self-fulfilling prophecy.

Obsessive competitiveness also limits the range of communication in male 14
friendships. Competition is the principal mode by which men relate to each other — at one level because they don't know how else to make contact, but more basically because it is the way to demonstrate, to themselves and others, the key masculine qualities of unwavering toughness and the ability to dominate and control. The result is that they inject competition into situations which don't call for it.

In conversations, you must show that you know more about the subject 15
than the other man, or at least as much as he does. For example, I have often engaged in a contest that could be called My Theory Tops Yours, disguised

as a serious exchange of ideas. The proof that it wasn't serious was that I was willing to participate even when I was sure that the participants, including myself, had nothing fresh to say. Convincing the other person — victory — is the main objective, with control of the floor an important tactic. Men tend to lecture at each other, insist that the discussion follow their train of thought, and are often unwilling to listen. As one member of a men's rap group said,

> When I was talking I used to feel that I had to be driving to a point, that it had to be rational and organized, that I had to persuade at all times, rather than exchange thoughts and ideas.

Even in casual conversation some men hold back unless they are absolutely sure of what they are saying. They don't want to have to change a position once they have taken it. It's "just like a woman" to change your mind, and, more important, it is inconsistent with the approved masculine posture of total independence.

Competition was at the heart of one of my closest friendships, now 16 defunct. There was a good deal of mutual liking and respect. We went out of our way to spend time with each other and wanted to work together. We both had "prospects" as "bright young men" and the same "liberal but tough" point of view. We recognized this about each other, and this recognition was the basis of our respect and of our sense of equality. That we saw each other as equals was important — our friendship was confirmed by the reflection of one in the other. But our constant and all-encompassing competition made this equality precarious and fragile. One way or another, everything counted in the measuring process. We fought out our tennis matches as though our lives depended on it. At poker, the two of us would often play on for hours after the others had left. These *mano a mano* poker marathons seem in retrospect especially revealing of the competitiveness of the relationship: Playing for small stakes, the essence of the game is in outwitting, psychologically beating down the other player — the other skills involved are negligible. Winning is the only pleasure, one that evaporates quickly, a truth that struck me in inchoate form every time our game broke up at four A.M. and I walked out the door with my five-dollar winnings, a headache, and a sense of time wasted. Still, I did the same thing the next time. It was what we did together, and somehow it counted. Losing at tennis could be balanced by winning at poker; at another level, his moving up in the federal government by my getting on the *Harvard Law Review*.

This competitiveness feeds the most basic obstacle to openness between 17 men, the inability to admit to being vulnerable. Real men, we learn early, are not supposed to have doubts, hopes and ambitions which may not be realized, things they don't (or even especially do) like about themselves, fears, and disappointments. Such feelings and concerns, of course, are part of everyone's inner life, but a man must keep quiet about them. If others know how you really feel, you can be hurt, and that in itself is incompatible with manhood. The inhibiting effect of this imperative is not limited to disclosures of major personal problems. Often men do not share even ordinary uncertainties and half-formulated plans of daily life with their friends. And when they do, they are careful to suggest that they already know how to proceed — that they are not really asking for help or understanding but simply for particular bits of information. Either way, any doubts they have are presented as external, carefully characterized as having to do with the issue as distinct from the speaker. They are especially guarded about expressing concern or asking a question that would invite personal comment. It is almost impossible for men to simply exchange thoughts about matters involving them personally in a comfortable, noncrisis atmosphere. If a friend tells you of his concern that he and a colleague are always disagreeing, for example, he is likely to quickly supply his own explanation — something like "different professional backgrounds." The effect is to rule out observations or suggestions that do not fit within this already reconnoitered protective structure. You don't suggest, even if you believe it is true, that in fact the disagreements arise because he presents his ideas in a way which tends to provoke a hostile reaction. It would catch him off guard; it would be something he hadn't already thought of and accepted about himself and, for that reason, no matter how constructive and well-intentioned you might be, it would put you in control for the moment. He doesn't want that; he is afraid of losing your respect. So, sensing he feels that way, because you would yourself, you say something else. There is no real give-and-take.

It is hard for men to get angry at each other honestly. Anger between 18 friends often means that one has hurt the other. Since the straightforward expression of anger in these situations involves an admission of vulnerability, it is safer to stew silently or find an "objective" excuse for retaliation. Either way, trust is not fully restored.

Men even try not to let it show when they feel good. We may report the 19 reasons for our happiness, if they have to do with concrete accomplishments, but we try to do it with straight face, as if to say, "Here's what happened, but it hasn't affected my grown-up unemotional equilibrium, and I am not asking for any kind of response." Happiness is a precarious, "childish" feeling, easy to shoot down. Others may find the event that triggers it trivial or incomprehensible, or even threatening to their own self-esteem — in the sense that if one man is up, another man is down. So we tend not to take the risk of expressing it.

What is particularly difficult for men is seeking or accepting help from 20 friends. I, for one, learned early that dependence was unacceptable. When I was eight, I went to a summer camp I disliked. My parents visited me in the middle of the summer and, when it was time for them to leave, I wanted to go with them. They refused, and I yelled and screamed and was miserably unhappy for the rest of the day. That evening an older camper comforted me, sitting by my bed as I cried, patting me on the back soothingly and saying whatever it is that one says at times like that. He was in some way clumsy or funny-looking, and a few days later I joined a group of kids in cruelly making fun of him, an act which upset me, when I thought about it, for years. I can only explain it in terms of my feeling, as early as the age of eight, that by needing and accepting his help and comfort I had compromised myself, and took it out on him.

"You can't express dependence when you feel it," a corporate executive 21 said, "because it's a kind of absolute. If you are loyal 90 percent of the time and disloyal 10 percent, would you be considered loyal? Well, the same happens with independence: You are either dependent or independent; you can't be both." "Feelings of dependence," another explained, "are identified with weakness or 'untoughness' and our culture doesn't accept those things in men." The result is that we either go it alone or "act out certain games or rituals to provoke the desired reaction in the other and have our needs satisfied without having to ask for anything."

Somewhat less obviously, the expression of affection also runs into emo- 22 tional barriers growing out of the masculine stereotype. When I was in college, I was suddenly quite moved while attending a friend's wedding. The surge of feeling made me uncomfortable and self-conscious. There was nothing inherently difficult or, apart from the fact of being moved by a moment of tenderness, "unmasculine" about my reaction. I just did not know how to deal with or communicate what I felt. "I consider myself a sentimentalist," one man said, "and I think I am quite able to express my feelings. But the other day my wife described a friend of mine to some people as my best friend and I felt embarrassed when I heard her say it."

A major source of these inhibitions is the fear of being, of being thought, 23 homosexual. Nothing is more frightening to a heterosexual man in our society. It threatens, at one stroke, to take away every vestige of his claim to a masculine identity — something like knocking out the foundation of a building — and to expose him to the ostracism, ranging from polite tolerance to violent revulsion, of his friends and colleagues. A man can be labeled as homosexual not just because of an overt sexual act but because of almost any sign of behavior which does not fit the masculine stereotype. The touching of another man, other than shaking hands, or, under emotional stress, an arm around the shoulder, is taboo. Women may kiss each other when they meet; men are uncomfortable when hugged even by close friends. Onlookers might misinterpret what they saw, and more important, what would we think of ourselves if we feel a twinge of sexual pleasure from the embrace.

Direct verbal expressions of affection or tenderness are also something that 24 only homosexuals and women engage in. Between "real" men affection has to be disguised in gruff, "you old son-of-a-bitch" style. Paradoxically, in some instances, terms of endearment between men can be used as a ritual badge of manhood, dangerous medicine safe only for the strong. The flirting with homosexuality that characterizes the initiation rites of many fraternities and men's clubs serves this purpose. Claude Brown wrote about black life in New York City in the 1950s:

The term ["baby"] had a hip ring to it. . . . It was like saying, "Man, look at me. I've got masculinity to spare. . . . I can say 'baby' to another cat and he can say 'baby' to me, and we can say it with strength in our voices." If you could say it, this meant that you really had to be sure of yourself, sure of your masculinity.

Fear of homosexuality does more than inhibit the physical display of affection. One of the major recurring themes in the men's groups led by psychotherapist Don Clark was:

A large segment of my feelings about other men are unknown or distorted because I am afraid they might have something to do with homosexuality. Now I'm lonely for other men and don't know how to find what I want with them.

As Clark observes, "The specter of homosexuality seems to be the dragon at the gateway to self-awareness, understanding, and acceptance of male-male needs. If a man tries to pretend the dragon is not there by turning a blind eye to erotic feelings for all other males, he also blinds himself to the rich variety of feelings that are related."

The few situations in which men do acknowledge strong feelings of 25 affection and dependence toward other men are exceptions which prove the rule. With "cop couples," for example, or combat soldier "buddies," intimacy and dependence are forced on the men by their work — they have to ride in the patrol car or be in the same foxhole with somebody — and the jobs themselves have such highly masculine images that the man can get away with behavior that would be suspect under any other conditions.

Furthermore, even these combat-buddy relationships, when looked at 26 closely, turn out not to be particularly intimate or personal. Margaret Mead has written:

During the last war English observers were confused by the apparent contradiction between American soldiers' emphasis on the buddy, so grievously exemplified in the breakdowns that followed a buddy's death, and the results of detailed inquiry which showed how transitory these buddy relationships were. It was found that men actually accepted their buddies as derivatives from their outfit, and from accidents of association, rather than because of any special personality characteristics capable of ripening into friendship.

One effect of the fear of appearing to be homosexual is to reinforce the practice that two men rarely get together alone without a reason. I once called a friend to suggest that we have dinner together. "O.K.," he said. "What's up?" I felt uncomfortable telling him that I just wanted to talk, that there was no other reason for the invitation.

Men get together to conduct business, to drink, to play games and sports, 27 to re-establish contact after long absences, to participate in heterosexual social occasions — circumstances in which neither person is responsible for actually wanting to see the other. Men are particularly comfortable seeing each other in groups. The group situation defuses any possible assumptions about the intensity of feeling between particular men and provides the safety of numbers — "All the guys are here." It makes personal communication, which requires a level of trust and mutual understanding not generally shared by all members of a group, more difficult and offers an excuse for avoiding this dangerous territory. And it provides what is most sought after in men's friendships: mutual reassurance of masculinity.

Analyzing This Selection

1. Are the first two paragraphs contradictory? If male friendships are superficial, why are they widely regarded as models of great friendship? Explain the author's point in paragraphs 1 and 2, adding whatever you think needs to be clarified in his argument.

2. According to the author, what are the satisfactions that games provide that make them more important to men than to women? Do you agree?

3. What example does the author give of society's archetypal male hero? Can you substitute a more up-to-date popular image of admired masculinity? (Pick a type, not an individual.) Is your example similar to or different from Fasteau's type of hero?

4. What does Fasteau say are the barriers to better friendships among men? Do you regard them as mainly social or mainly personal barriers? Does Fasteau suggest how the barriers can be overcome?

5. In restating his thesis about men, in the final paragraph Fasteau implies that women have different reasons for seeking friendship with other women. Which, if any, of these differences do you accept as self-evident? or as valid?

Analyzing Connections

6. Apply La Rouchefoucauld's maxim (Insights, p. 128) to Fasteau's analysis of friendship among men. Does the remark fit Fasteau's view of male friendship? Does it fit your view?

Analyzing by Writing

7. Fasteau and Barbara Ehrenreich (see the preceding selection) assume that friendship has very different meaning and value for men and women. To what extent would you support, reject, update, or modify this assumption held by both authors?

8. Fasteau's views about male friendship may be relevant also to father-son relationships. Apply Fasteau's views to two or more preceding selections portraying strained or limited connections between sons and fathers. (See Carver, p. 82; Cooper, p. 143; Ishiguro, p. 117; and Simmons, p. 67.) What traits that Fasteau ascribes to male friendships are visible in these family ties? What traits are not visible? Do you think Fasteau's views deal with principal or minor issues between fathers and sons?

Lindsy Van Gelder

MARRIAGE AS A
RESTRICTED CLUB

◇

LINDSY VAN GELDER (b. 1944) was born in New Jersey. She attended Northwestern University for two years and earned her B.A. at Sarah Lawrence
College. After graduating, she worked as a reporter for United Press International and then for the *New York Post*. She has been a staff writer for *Ms.* and
contributes articles to periodicals including *Esquire, New York, Redbook,
Rolling Stone,* and the *Village Voice*. The following article originally appeared
in *Ms.* Van Gelder has described one of her major concerns as a writer this
way: "I constantly worry about how to convey seemingly radical ideas to an
unconvinced audience."

Several years ago, I stopped going to weddings. In fact, I no longer 1
celebrate the wedding anniversaries or engagements of friends, relatives, or
anyone else, although I might wish them lifelong joy in their relationships.
My explanation is that the next wedding I attend will be my own — to the
woman I've loved and lived with for nearly six years.

Although I've been legally married to a man myself (and come close to 2
marrying two others), I've come, in these last six years with Pamela, to see
heterosexual marriage as very much a restricted club. (Nor is this likely to
change in the near future, if one can judge by the recent clobbering of what
was actually a rather tame proposal to recognize "domestic partnerships" in
San Francisco.) Regardless of the *reason* people marry — whether to save on
real estate taxes or qualify for married student housing or simply to express
love — lesbians and gay men can't obtain the same results should they desire
to do so. It seems apparent to me that few friends of Pamela's and mine
would even join a club that excluded blacks, Jews, or women, much less
assume that they could expect their black, Jewish, or female friends to toast
their new status with champagne. But probably no other stand of principle
we've ever made in our lives has been so misunderstood, or caused so much
bad feeling on both sides.

Several people have reacted with surprise to our views, it never having 3
occurred to them that gay people *can't* legally marry. (Why on earth did they
think that none of us had bothered?) The most common reaction, however,

is acute embarrassment, followed by a denial of our main point — that the about-to-be-wed person is embarking on a privileged status. (One friend of Pamela's insisted that lesbians are "lucky" not to have to agonize over whether or not to get married.) So wrapped in gauze is the institution of marriage, so ingrained the expectation that brides and grooms can enjoy the world's delighted approval, that it's hard for me not to feel put on the defensive for being so mean-spirited, eccentric, and/or politically rigid as to boycott such a happy event.

Another question we've fielded more than once (usually from our most   4 radical friends, both gay and straight) is why we'd want to get married in the first place. In fact, I have mixed feelings about registering my personal life with the state, but — and this seems to me to be the essence of radical politics — I'd prefer to be the one making the choice. And while feminists in recent years have rightly focused on puncturing the Schlaflyite[1] myth of the legally protected homemaker, it's also true that marriage does confer some very real dollars-and-cents benefits. One example of inequity is our inability to file joint tax returns, although many couples, both gay and straight, go through periods when one partner in the relationship is unemployed or makes considerably less money than the other. At one time in our relationship, Pamela — who is a musician — was between bands and earning next to nothing. I was making a little over $37,000 a year as a newspaper reporter, a salary that put me in the 42 percent tax bracket — about $300 a week taken out of my paycheck. If we had been married, we could have filed a joint tax return and each paid taxes on half my salary, in the 25 or 30 percent bracket. The difference would have been nearly $100-a-week in our pockets.

Around the same time, Pamela suffered a months'-long illness which would   5 have been covered by my health insurance if she were my spouse. We were luckier than many; we could afford it. But on top of the worry and expense involved (and despite the fact that intellectually we believe in the ideal of free medical care for everyone), we found it almost impossible to avoid internalizing a sense of personal failure — the knowledge that *because of who we are, we can't take care of each other.* I've heard of other gay people whose lovers were deported because they couldn't marry them and enable them to become citizens; still others who were barred from intensive-care units where their lovers lay stricken because they weren't "immediate family."

I would never begrudge a straight friend who got married to save a lover   6 from deportation or staggering medical bills, but the truth is that I no longer sympathize with most of the less tangible justifications. This includes the oft-heard "for the sake of the children" argument, since (like many gay people, especially women) I *have* children, and I resent the implication that some families are more "legitimate" than others. (It's important to safeguard

---

[1]Phyllis Schlafly, a political activist, opposed the Equal Rights Amendment. [Ed.]

one's children's rights to their father's property, but a legal contract will do the same thing as marriage.)

But the single most painful and infuriating rationale for marriage, as far as I'm concerned, is the one that goes: "We wanted to stand up and show the world that we've made a *genuine* commitment." When one is gay, such sentiments are labeled "flaunting." My lover and I almost never find ourselves in public settings outside the gay ghetto where we are (a) perceived to be a couple at all (people constantly ask us if we're sisters, although we look nothing like each other), and (b) valued as such. Usually we're forced to choose between being invisible and being despised. "Making a genuine commitment" in this milieu is like walking a highwire without a net — with most of the audience not even watching and a fair segment rooting for you to fall. A disproportionate number of gay couples do.

I think it's difficult for even my closest, most feminist straight women friends to empathize with the intensity of my desire to be recognized as Pamela's partner. (In fact, it may be harder for feminists to understand than for others; I know that when I was straight, I often resented being viewed as one half of a couple. My struggle was for an independent identity, not the cojoined one I now crave.) But we are simply not considered *authentic*, and the reminders are constant. Recently at a party, a man I'd known for years spied me across the room and came over to me, arms outstretched, big happy-to-see-you grin on his face. Pamela had a gig that night and wasn't at the party; my friend's wife was there but in another room, and I hadn't seen her yet. "How's M———?" I asked the man. "Oh, she's fine," he replied, continuing to smile pleasantly. "Are you and Pam still together?"

Our sex life itself is against the law in many states, of course, and like all lesbians and gay men, we are without many other rights, both large and small. (In Virginia, for instance, it's technically against the law for us to buy liquor.) But as a gay couple, we are also most likely to be labeled and discriminated against in those very settings that, for most heterosexual Americans, constitute the most relaxed and personal parts of life. Virtually every tiny public act of togetherness — from holding hands on the street to renting a hotel room to dancing — requires us constantly to risk humiliation (I think, for example, of the two California women who were recently thrown out of a restaurant that had special romantic tables for couples), sexual harassment (it's astonishing how many men can't resist coming on to a lesbian couple), and even physical assault. A great deal of energy goes into just expecting possible trouble. It's a process which, after six years, has become second nature for me — but occasionally, when I'm in Provincetown or someplace else with a large lesbian population, I experience the *absence* of it as a feeling of virtual weightlessness.

What does all this have to do with my friends' weddings? Obviously, I can't expect my friends to live my life. But I do think that lines are being drawn in this "profamily" Reagan era, and I have no choice about what side

I'm placed on. My straight friends do, and at the very least, I expect them to acknowledge that. I certainly expect them to understand why I don't want to be among the rice-throwers and well-wishers at their weddings; beyond that, I would hope that they would commit themselves to fighting for my rights — preferably in personally visible ways, like marching in gay pride parades. But I also wish they wouldn't get married, period. And if that sounds hard-nosed, I hope I'm only proving my point — that not being able to marry isn't a minor issue.

Not that my life would likely be changed as the result of any individual 11 straight person's symbolic refusal to marry. (Nor, for that matter, do all gay couples want to be wed.) But it's a political reality that heterosexual live-together couples are among our best tactical allies. The movement to repeal state sodomy laws has profited from the desire of straight people to keep the government out of *their* bedrooms. Similarly, it was a heterosexual New York woman who went to court several years ago to fight her landlord's demand that she either marry her live-in boyfriend or face eviction for violating a lease clause prohibiting "unrelated" tenants — and whose struggle led to the recent passage of a state rent law that had ramifications for thousands of gay couples, including Pamela and me.

The right wing has seized on "homosexual marriage" as its bottom-line 12 scare phrase in much the same way that "Would you want your sister to marry one?" was brandished twenty-five years ago. *They* see marriage as their turf. And so when I see feminists crossing into that territory of respectability and "sinlessness," I feel my buffer zone slipping away. I feel as though my friends are taking off their armbands, leaving me exposed.

Analyzing This Selection

1. Explain whether or not you think Van Gelder is "mean-spirited, eccentric, and/or politically rigid" for boycotting engagements, weddings, and anniversaries and for not wanting her friends to marry.

2. What reasons does the author give for wanting to marry her gay lover? Which is the most important reason to her?

3. Van Gelder sees herself as an outsider, one who does not share equal privileges with the rest of society. How does she cope with the problems of her "minority" status?

Analyzing Connections

4. Van Gelder and Barbara Ehrenreich ("In Praise of 'Best Friends' " p. 163) advocate higher public visibility and status for friends and lovers. Compare and evaluate their reasons for recommending new customs and laws to acknowledge personal ties.

Analyzing by Writing

5. Do anniversaries sometimes create myths? Consider the meaning and validity of wedding anniversaries as they are celebrated in your family. Do children or grandparents have a role? Do the observances emphasize romance? Do the celebrations include and preserve family history, or do they emphasize the present and future? Explain the customs, symbolism, and other kinds of significance that you have witnessed in these events.

PART 4

LESSONS

Edward C. Martin, *Being Junior High*
Maya Angelou, *Graduation*
Maxine Hong Kingston, *The Misery of Silence*
Richard Rodriguez, *Reading for Success*
Michael Moffatt, *Coming of Age in a College Dorm*
Virginia Woolf, *Professions for Women*
Amy Tan, *Mother Tongue*
Tillie Olsen, *I Stand Here Ironing*

INSIGHTS

Education! Which of the various me's do you propose to educate, and which do you propose to suppress?

Anyhow I defy you. I defy you, oh society, to educate me or to suppress me, according to your dummy standards. . . .

There are other men in me, besides this patient ass who sits here in a tweed jacket. What am I doing, playing the patient ass in a tweed jacket? Who am I talking to? Who are you, at the other end of this patience?

Who are you? How many selves have you? And which of these selves do you want to be?

Is Yale College going to educate the self that is in the dark of you, or Harvard College?

— D. H. LAWRENCE

◇

You go to a great school not for knowledge so much as for arts and habits; for the habit of attention, for the art of expression, for the art of assuming at a moment's notice a new intellectual posture, for the art of entering quickly into another person's thought, for the habit of submitting to censure and refutation, for the art of indicating assent or dissent in graduated terms, for the habit of regarding minute points of accuracy, for the habit of working out what is possible in a given time, for taste, for discrimination, for mental courage and mental soberness. Above all, you go to a great school for self-knowledge.

— WILLIAM CORY

◇

Books are the best of things, well used; abused, among the worst. What is the right use? What is the one end which all means go to effect? They are for nothing but to inspire. I had better never see a book than to be warped by its attraction clean out of my own orbit, and made a satellite instead of a system. The one thing in the world, of value, is the active soul. This every man is entitled to; this every man contains within him, although in almost all men obstructed and as yet unborn. The soul active sees absolute truth and utters truth, or creates. In this action it is genius; not the privilege of here and there a favorite, but the sound estate of every man. In its essence it is progressive.

The book, the college, the school of art, the institution of any kind, stop with some past utterance of genius. This is good, say they, — let us hold by this. They pin me down. They look backward and not forward. But genius looks forward: the eyes of man are set in his forehead, not in his hindhead: man hopes: genius creates. Whatever talents may be, if the man create not, the pure efflux of the Deity is not his; — cinders and smoke there may be, but not yet flame. There are creative manners, there are creative actions, and creative words; manners, actions, words, that is, indicative of no custom or authority, but springing spontaneous from the mind's own sense of good and fair.

— RALPH WALDO EMERSON

◊

But it is not hard work which is dreary; it is superficial work. That is always boring in the long run, and it has always seemed strange to me that in our endless discussions about education so little stress is ever laid on the pleasure of becoming an educated person, the enormous interest it adds to life. To be able to be caught up into the world of thought — that is to be educated.

— EDITH HAMILTON

◊

If you hear a voice within you saying, "You are not a painter," *then by all means paint*, boy, and that voice will be silenced, but only by working. He who goes to friends and tells his troubles when he feels like that loses part of his manliness, part of the best that's in him; your friends can only be those who themselves struggle against it, who raise your activity by their own example of action. One must undertake it with confidence, with a certain assurance that one is doing a reasonable thing, like the farmer drives his plow, or like our friend in the scratch below, who is harrowing, and even drags the harrow himself. If one hasn't a horse, one is one's own horse — many people do so here.

— VINCENT VAN GOGH

◊

A change of heart is the essence of all other change and it is brought about by a re-education of the mind.

— EMMELINE PETHICK-LAWRENCE

◊

Beginning My Studies

Beginning my studies the first step pleas'd me so much,
The mere fact consciousness, these forms, the power of motion,
The least insect or animal, the senses, eyesight, love,

The first step I say awed me and pleas'd me so much,
I have hardly gone and hardly wish'd to go any farther,
But stop and loiter all the time to sing it in ecstatic songs.

— WALT WHITMAN

◇

The plots and stories in the novels did not interest me so much as the point of view revealed. I gave myself over to each novel without reserve, without trying to criticize it; it was enough for me to see and feel something different. And for me, everything was something different. Reading was like a drug, a dope. The novels created moods in which I lived for days. But I could not conquer my sense of guilt, my feeling that the white men around me knew that I was changing, that I had begun to regard them differently.

— RICHARD WRIGHT

FOCUSING BY WRITING

1. Consider the obstacles between you and an appealing but unlikely choice of profession. Freely imagine yourself in that profession fifteen years from now, and explain why it is genuinely attractive to you. Differentiate between limitations or barriers that would be particularly your own and hurdles in the profession itself. How would you or the world need to be different for you to pursue that course?

2. Reconsider a book that for a while was your favorite reading. What about it appealed strongly to you at that time? What was its main contrast with or similarity to your actual life?

3. Write your own newspaper obituary, taking note of some present accomplishments and of future details that you would like your life to have included.

4. The Insights quotes a letter from Vincent Van Gogh to his brother Theo. Write a letter back to Vincent explaining why you sometimes feel that you are deluding yourself about your abilities or ambitions.

Edward C. Martin

BEING JUNIOR HIGH

◊

EDWARD C. MARTIN (b. 1937) is an educational administrator and an author of
social science textbooks such as *The People Make a Nation* (1971). He has
taught in both high schools and junior high schools. In this essay on the early
adolescent student, he discusses some of the special difficulties that a twelve-
to fourteen-year-old has in being an individual and also a member of a group.
This essay is a condensation of an article that originally appeared in *Daedalus*
under the title "Reflections on the Early Adolescent in School."

What is it like to be in school if you are twelve to fourteen years of age? 1
What does and doesn't it mean to you?

. . . Fundamentally, for most American twelve-year-olds, school is *where* 2
it's at. School occupies the time and concerns of all the people you
know — your friends, your parents, people you meet. People are always
asking what you do in school and how you like school. School is often a
source of contention between you and adults. Why did you get low grades?
Why did you play hooky? Why don't you play school sports or join clubs or
work harder or work less, and so forth? You are always telling people you
don't like school, but often you don't mean it because school is comfortable
and they at least want you around. Also you think school is important and
even fun. But these things can't be said too openly.

Friends and enemies are a large part of school, perhaps the largest. One 3
comes to school to see friends, one fears school because enemies are there
also. Some of the most important parts of the school day are the walk or ride
there, changing between classes, the few minutes before the class gets started,
the study hall, and the end of school. These times are the intense periods of
"seeing other kids," or realizing you have no one to see. One of those
unwritten rules of teaching is "begin the class on time." It makes the teacher
appear efficient and purposeful and gives the task to be done a sense of
importance. When I started teaching in junior high I still believed this rule,
until I began to realize how much there is to learn about students by
observing or participating in the three minutes before class started. . . . My
interest in the friendship group has been not to join in but to figure out ways

188

to tap it when it made sense to do so. The usual separation of the interests of these groups and the classroom is not necessarily a bad separation. Doing the peer group's thing all the time would be as deadly as doing the teacher's thing all the time.

The case of a student staying home, being ill, or skipping a class because   4 he fears some group of students is more common than most adults imagine. Threats are used frequently by students although fortunately not often carried through. For two weeks a group of girls were harassing another girl in and out of classes. The girl under attack was literally terrified, although she sought to hold her ground by appearing casual and unafraid. When this failed she would seek the help of adults or just burst into tears. For the group of antagonists, this aggressiveness was a source of unity and camaraderie. They relished the times of confrontation and the times of subtle teasing. Individuals took pride and received group praise devising more exciting methods of taunting their foe. There was always the daring aspect of avoiding that line where the full force of adult intervention would be imposed. The several adults involved did not know what to do. One teacher tried to give some perspective on the situation by showing the long-run absurdity of such behavior, another by attempting disciplinary tactics — essentially tongue-lashing and keeping the aggressive group after school. The guidance counselor tried to talk it through with all the students involved. The situation improved on the surface, but we all knew the individual girl's fear remained and the group's resentment toward her and power over her continued. We also realized that there was very little we could do about it but make sure it did not become violent. I am always surprised at how brutal students this age can be toward each other. It reminds me again of how important a book Golding's novel *Lord of the Flies* is for teachers.

The intense friendship groupings in junior high obviously have another   5 side — the youngster who has no friends, no group to which he has allegiance or which sees him as a part. Several kinds of students in my experience fall into this category and it means different things to each. John was an outgoing intellectual student who spoke in an affected way and assumed he had the right answers. Other students saw him as a "freak" and made it clear to him that was how they regarded him. Sharon was a quiet withdrawn girl who talked with no one and to whom no one talked. She seemed not to be bothered by this isolation. Bob was a class leader. He demanded everyone's attention and when he did not get it was bound to provoke it. Although the students saw him as an important person to be reckoned with, he was really not part of any group. Adults at one time or another are isolated from others by choice or happenstance, but the isolation of a twelve-, thirteen-, or fourteen-year-old is particularly difficult. There is a pain brought on by not being like everyone else when it is important that you be like others. This comes at a time in physical, emotional, and intellectual development when change is so rapid that many individual youngsters are either behind or ahead of the mass of their peers. Aggravating these gaps is the intolerance of this age group toward diversity and their delight in making an issue over those who are different. The boy who does not start to spurt in physical stature is called a "shrimp" and sees himself as a shrimp. The girl who gets seriously interested in a boy does not quite fit with her giggly friends. The peer group of the twelve- to fourteen-year-old has most of the mechanisms of keeping members in line but often lacks the moral, ethical, and intellectual substance of the so-called "youth culture" of older students. . . .

In schools, the classroom is seen as the center of the educational experi-   6 ence. Whether or not it is in effect is beside the point. Students see it as such. . . .

In the center of the classroom experience is the teacher. Students most   7 often describe and define their courses in terms of the teacher. He or she is the one who makes a class great or terrible. Curriculum reform projects of the past ten years in the academic disciplines have tried to improve schools by producing better materials, some of which could be taught by *any* teacher. Most of them now realize that with a bad teacher students will feel the new course is as bad as the old. Parents, principals, and guidance counselors keep telling youngsters it should not matter who the teacher is. They say you should be able to learn from someone you do not like. This is true only when personal dislike is mild and is overpowered by respect for the teacher's fairness and competence. Most teachers accept the necessity of being liked by their students; some turn this into an end in itself. Students want a positive personal relationship with their teachers, but they want more.

The teacher, whether or not he considers himself a benevolent despot or   8 a partner in learning, is a model. He is usually the only adult in a room of thirty people. He is the one most different and the one who is expected to do something to make that class good. If he does not, he is not a good teacher. He is the one turned to when the going gets rough. One day I brought six candy bars into class for a lesson on the distribution of goods. I put the candy bars on the desk and told the class they were welcome to have them and should agree on how to divide them. For the rest of the period and part of the next, alternatives were presented and discussed. Several boys from the track team suggested, only half in jest, that the candy be placed at one end of the room and the class race for it. Generally, this solution was opposed. Other proposals were made including equal division, grades, fighting, working, bidding, and drawing lots. None, by the way, suggested that I as teacher decide. Finally, drawing lots was agreed upon as the best method. As I moved the candy bars to another spot in the room, the elected class chairman grabbed at one. I asked him why, since all had agreed to do the division by lots. He said he wanted one. I held out the bars and he took one, opened it, and proceeded to eat it. The universal reaction of the class was silent confusion. I thought they would be outraged and I suppose they were, but in this case they expected me to take action, to stop the violation of their hard-reached decision. I finally did ask the boy why he disregarded the class's decision, rather mildly chewed him out, and ruled him out of the drawing of lots.

The incident illustrates many things and raises many questions. Clearly I 9 had violated the expectations of the students, either by letting their classmate take the candy or by not acting when he did. They expected me to handle this situation even though all but the assignment of the task was in their control and they had made the decisions. Perhaps I had asked them to step too far out of their notions of authority and the security that a teacher is expected to provide in the classroom. Another reason I was surprised at the class's lack of reaction was their usual strong reactions to injustice. Students measure teachers, generally with a high degree of accuracy, on a continuum from just to unjust in treatment of people. Twelve-year-olds often use a double standard — canons of fairness are strictly applied to others, much less strictly applied to themselves. Connected to both the security and justice issues is the whole question of authority. Although much less sensitive about authority than sixteen-year-olds, the twelve-year-old in school is keenly aware of who makes decisions and what role he has in the process. In the case of the candy bars, I was expected to act as the authority. No doubt I was naive about how students viewed the authority relationships in class to think they would exercise some control on their classmate. This age student is more committed to the distinction between himself and adults. He is more willing to go along with the authorities, but is beginning to question. By the time he leaves junior high school, the question of legitimate authority is a central part of things about which he is "bugged."

A final point about the candy bar incident. The actions of the boy 10 represent, in the extreme, a serious problem for most youngsters in junior high school: *How do I establish and develop individuality in an institution that treats me as one of a group with similar characteristics?* Most of the students I teach want to be seen as individuals, just as we all do. A school is a difficult if not impossible place to get a great deal of individual treatment. The students want to be members of the group, but they also want to be someone unique. Since all the children have this problem and since there is considerable pressure toward group conformity, they are not much able to give each other this sense of individuality. The teacher is often the only one able to legitimize pluralism, but he is hampered because he deals with so many children and almost always as a group.

Analyzing This Selection

1. Martin recognizes that "seeing other kids" is important in the school day, but he does not look into what makes it important. Based on your own observations, what interests and activities do seventh and eighth graders share with friends in school? How do they spend time together? Are they always with the same friends?

2. What qualities do junior high students generally expect from a teacher? How did Martin meet or fail their expectations?

3. Throughout the essay, Martin mentions several differences between junior high students and older, high-school students. What are the differences he notes, and do you find his observations accurate?

4. In the final sentence, what does Martin mean by "legitimize pluralism"? Paraphrase him, and add an illustration of how the teacher might be able to do this. Why don't the students do the same for one another?

Analyzing Connections

5. Martin believes that for his students "school is *where it's at.*" When Nancy Friday was the age of Martin's students (see "Competition," p. 71), what was the center of life? Which writer has a more valid view of that age group?

Analyzing by Writing

6. What is the strongest peer pressure on most students in grades 8 through 10? Does it focus on drinking? drugs? sex? or friendship grouping? Explain how the pressure operates in school. Try to generalize about student experience, without emphasizing your own.

Maya Angelou

GRADUATION

◇

MAYA ANGELOU (b. 1928) was raised by her grandmother, who ran a small store for blacks in the town of Stamps, Arkansas. She survived a childhood that seemed certain to defeat her, and as she once told an interviewer: "One would say of my life — born loser — had to be; from a broken family, raped at eight, unwed mother at sixteen." During her adult life, she became a dancer, an actress, a poet, a television writer and producer, and a coordinator in Martin Luther King's Southern Christian Leadership Conference. She is most widely known for her autobiographical books, beginning with *I Know Why the Caged Bird Sings* (1970), from which this selection is taken. Her most recent memoir is *All God's Children Need Traveling Shoes* (1986).

The children in Stamps trembled visibly with anticipation. Some adults 1
were excited too, but to be certain the whole young population had come down with graduation epidemic. Large classes were graduating from both the grammar school and the high school. Even those who were years removed from their own day of glorious release were anxious to help with preparations as a kind of dry run. The junior students who were moving into the vacating classes' chairs were tradition-bound to show their talents for leadership and management. They strutted through the school and around the campus exerting pressure on the lower grades. Their authority was so new that occasionally if they pressed a little too hard it had to be overlooked. After all, next term was coming, and it never hurt a sixth grader to have a play sister in the eighth grade, or a tenth-year student to be able to call a twelfth grader Bubba. So all was endured in a spirit of shared understanding. But the graduating classes themselves were the nobility. Like travelers with exotic destinations on their minds, the graduates were remarkably forgetful. They came to school without their books, or tablets, or even pencils. Volunteers fell over themselves to secure replacements for the missing equipment. When accepted, the willing workers might or might not be thanked, and it was of no importance to the pregraduation rites. Even teachers were respectful of the now quiet and aging seniors, and tended to speak to them, if not as equals, as beings only slightly lower than themselves. After tests were returned and grades given, the student body, which acted like an extended family, knew who did well, who excelled, and what piteous ones had failed.

Unlike the white school, Lafayette County Training School distinguished   2
itself by having neither lawn, nor hedges, nor tennis court, nor climbing ivy.
Its two buildings (main classrooms, the grade school, and home economics)
were set on a dirt hill with no fence to limit either its boundaries or those of
bordering farms. There was a large expanse to the left of the school which
was used alternately as a baseball diamond or a basketball court. Rusty hoops
on the swaying poles represented the permanent recreational equipment,
although bats and balls could be borrowed from the P.E. teacher if the
borrower was qualified and if the diamond wasn't occupied.

Over this rocky area relieved by a few shady tall persimmon trees the   3
graduating class walked. The girls often held hands and no longer bothered to
speak to the lower students. There was a sadness about them, as if this old world
was not their home and they were bound for higher ground. The boys, on the
other hand, had become more friendly, more outgoing. A decided change
from the closed attitude they projected while studying for finals. Now they
seemed not ready to give up the old school, the familiar paths and classrooms.
Only a small percentage would be continuing on to college — one of the
South's A & M (agricultural and mechanical) schools, which trained Negro
youths to be carpenters, farmers, handymen, masons, maids, cooks, and baby
nurses. Their future rode heavily on their shoulders, and blinded them to the
collective joy that had pervaded the lives of the boys and girls in the grammar
school graduating class.

Parents who could afford it had ordered new shoes and ready-made clothes   4
for themselves from Sears and Roebuck or Montgomery Ward. They also
engaged the best seamstresses to make the floating graduating dresses and to
cut down secondhand pants which would be pressed to a military slickness for
the important event.

Oh, it was important, all right. Whitefolks would attend the ceremony,   5
and two or three would speak of God and home, and the Southern way of
life, and Mrs. Parsons, the principal's wife, would play the graduation march
while the lower-grade graduates paraded down the aisles and took their seats
below the platform. The high school seniors would wait in empty classrooms
to make their dramatic entrance.

In the Store I was the person of the moment. The birthday girl. The   6
center. Bailey[1] had graduated the year before, although to do so he had had
to forfeit all pleasures to make up for his time lost in Baton Rouge.

My class was wearing butter-yellow piqué dresses, and Momma launched   7
out on mine. She smocked the yoke into tiny crisscrossing puckers, then
shirred the rest of the bodice. Her dark fingers ducked in and out of the
lemony cloth as she embroidered raised daisies around the hem. Before she
considered herself finished she had added a crocheted cuff on the puff
sleeves, and a pointy crocheted collar.

[1]The author's brother. The children help out in their grandmother's store. [Ed.]

I was going to be lovely. A walking model of all the various styles of fine 8 hand sewing and it didn't worry me that I was only twelve years old and merely graduating from the eighth grade. Besides, many teachers in Arkansas Negro schools had only that diploma and were licensed to impart wisdom.

The days had become longer and more noticeable. The faded beige of 9 former times had been replaced with strong and sure colors. I began to see my classmates' clothes, their skin tones, and the dust that waved off pussy willows. Clouds that lazed across the sky were objects of great concern to me. Their shiftier shapes might have held a message that in my new happiness and with a little bit of time I'd soon decipher. During that period I looked at the arch of heaven so religiously my neck kept a steady ache. I had taken to smiling more often, and my jaws hurt from the unaccustomed activity. Between the two physical sore spots, I suppose I could have been uncomfortable, but that was not the case. As a member of the winning team (the graduating class of 1940) I had outdistanced unpleasant sensations by miles. I was headed for the freedom of open fields.

Youth and social approval allied themselves with me and we trammeled 10 memories of slights and insults. The wind of our swift passage remodeled my features. Lost tears were pounded to mud and then to dust. Years of withdrawal were brushed aside and left behind, as hanging ropes of parasitic moss.

My work alone had awarded me a top place and I was going to be one of 11 the first called in the graduating ceremonies. On the classroom blackboard, as well as on the bulletin board in the auditorium, there were blue stars and white stars and red stars. No absences, no tardinesses, and my academic work was among the best of the year. I could say the preamble to the Constitution even faster than Bailey. We timed ourselves often: "WethepeopleoftheUnitedStatesinordertoformamoreperfectunion . . ." I had memorized the Presidents of the United States from Washington to Roosevelt in chronological as well as alphabetical order.

My hair pleased me too. Gradually the black mass had lengthened and 12 thickened, so that it kept at last to its braided pattern, and I didn't have to yank my scalp off when I tried to comb it.

Louise and I had rehearsed the exercises until we tired out ourselves. 13 Henry Reed was class valedictorian. He was a small, very black boy with hooded eyes, a long, broad nose, and an oddly shaped head. I had admired him for years because each term he and I vied for the best grades in our class. Most often he bested me, but instead of being disappointed I was pleased that we shared top places between us. Like many Southern Black children, he lived with his grandmother, who was as strict as Momma and as kind as she knew how to be. He was courteous, respectful, and soft-spoken to elders, but on the playground he chose to play the roughest games. I admired him. Anyone, I reckoned, sufficiently afraid or sufficiently dull could be polite. But to be able to operate at a top level with both adults and children was admirable.

His valedictory speech was entitled "To Be or Not to Be." The rigid 14
tenth-grade teacher had helped him to write it. He'd been working on the
dramatic stresses for months.

The weeks until graduation were filled with heady activities. A group of 15
small children were to be presented in a play about buttercups and daisies
and bunny rabbits. They could be heard throughout the building practicing
their hops and their little songs that sounded like silver bells. The older girls
(nongraduates, of course) were assigned the task of making refreshments for
the night's festivities. A tangy scent of ginger, cinnamon, nutmeg, and
chocolate wafted around the home economics building as the budding cooks
made samples for themselves and their teachers.

In every corner of the workshop, axes and saws split fresh timber as the 16
woodshop boys made sets and stage scenery. Only the graduates were left out
of the general bustle. We were free to sit in the library at the back of the
building or look in quite detachedly, naturally, on the measures being taken
for our event.

Even the minister preached on graduation the Sunday before. His subject 17
was, "Let your light so shine that men will see your good works and praise
your Father, Who is in Heaven." Although the sermon was purported to be
addressed to us, he used the occasion to speak to backsliders, gamblers, and
general ne'er-do-wells. But since he had called our names at the beginning
of the service we were mollified.

Among Negroes the tradition was to give presents to children going only 18
from one grade to another. How much more important this was when the
person was graduating at the top of the class. Uncle Willie and Momma had
sent away for a Mickey Mouse watch like Bailey's. Louise gave me four
embroidered handkerchiefs. (I gave her three crocheted doilies.) Mrs. Sneed,
the minister's wife, made me an underskirt to wear for graduation, and nearly
every customer gave me a nickel or maybe even a dime with the instruction
"Keep on moving to higher ground," or some such encouragement.

Amazingly the great day finally dawned and I was out of bed before I knew 19
it. I threw open the back door to see it more clearly, but Momma said,
"Sister, come away from that door and put your robe on."

I hoped the memory of that morning would never leave me. Sunlight was 20
itself still young, and the day had none of the insistence maturity would bring
it in a few hours. In my robe and barefoot in the backyard, under cover of
going to see about my new beans, I gave myself up to the gentle warmth and
thanked God that no matter what evil I had done in my life He had allowed
me to live to see this day. Somewhere in my fatalism I had expected to die,
accidentally, and never have the chance to walk up the stairs in the auditorium and gracefully receive my hard-earned diploma. Out of God's merciful
bosom I had won reprieve.

Bailey came out in his robe and gave me a box wrapped in Christmas 21
paper. He said he had saved his money for months to pay for it. It felt like

a box of chocolates, but I knew Bailey wouldn't save money to buy candy when we had all we could want under our noses.

He was as proud of the gift as I. It was a soft-leather-bound copy of a 22 collection of poems by Edgar Allan Poe, or, as Bailey and I called him, "Eap." I turned to "Annabel Lee" and we walked up and down the garden rows, the cool dirt between our toes, reciting the beautifully sad lines.

Momma made a Sunday breakfast although it was only Friday. After we 23 finished the blessing, I opened my eyes to find the watch on my plate. It was a dream of a day. Everything went smoothly and to my credit. I didn't have to be reminded or scolded for anything. Near evening I was too jittery to attend to chores, so Bailey volunteered to do all before his bath.

Days before, we had made a sign for the Store and as we turned out the 24 lights Momma hung the cardboard over the doorknob. It read clearly: CLOSED. GRADUATION.

My dress fitted perfectly and everyone said that I looked like a sunbeam in 25 it. On the hill, going toward the school, Bailey walked behind with Uncle Willie, who muttered, "Go on, Ju." He wanted him to walk ahead with us because it embarrassed him to have to walk so slowly. Bailey said he'd let the ladies walk together, and the men would bring up the rear. We all laughed, nicely.

Little children dashed by out of the dark like fireflies. Their crepepaper 26 dresses and butterfly wings were not made for running and we heard more than one rip, dryly, and the regretful "uh uh" that followed.

The school blazed without gaiety. The windows seemed cold and un- 27 friendly from the lower hill. A sense of ill-fated timing crept over me, and if Momma hadn't reached for my hand I would have drifted back to Bailey and Uncle Willie, and possibly beyond. She made a few slow jokes about my feet getting cold, and tugged me along to the now-strange building.

Around the front steps, assurance came back. There were my fellow 28 "greats," the graduating class. Hair brushed back, legs oiled, new dresses and pressed pleats, fresh pocket handkerchiefs and little handbags, all homesewn. Oh, we were up to snuff, all right. I joined my comrades and didn't even see my family go in to find seats in the crowded auditorium.

The school band struck up a march and all classes filed in as had been 29 rehearsed. We stood in front of our seats, as assigned, and on a signal from the choir director, we sat. No sooner had this been accomplished than the band started to play the national anthem. We rose again and sang the song, after which we recited the pledge of allegiance. We remained standing for a brief minute before the choir director and the principal signaled to us, rather desperately I thought, to take our seats. The command was so unusual that our carefully rehearsed and smooth-running machine was thrown off. For a full minute we fumbled for our chairs and bumped into each other awkwardly. Habits change or solidify under pressure, so in our state of nervous tension we had been ready to follow our usual assembly pattern: the American National Anthem, then the pledge of allegiance, then the song every Black person I knew called the Negro National Anthem. All done in the same key, with the same passion and most often standing on the same foot.

Finding my seat at last, I was overcome with a presentiment of worse   30 things to come. Something unrehearsed, unplanned, was going to happen, and we were going to be made to look bad. I distinctly remember being explicit in the choice of pronoun. It was "we," the graduating class, the unit, that concerned me then.

The principal welcomed "parents and friends" and asked the Baptist   31 minister to lead us in prayer. His invocation was brief and punchy, and for a second I thought we were getting back on the high road to right action. When the principal came back to the dais, however, his voice had changed. Sounds always affected me profoundly and the principal's voice was one of my favorites. During assembly it melted and lowed weakly into the audience. It had not been in my plan to listen to him, but my curiosity was piqued and I straightened up to give him my attention.

He was talking about Booker T. Washington, our "late great leader," who   32 said we can be as close as the fingers on the hand, etc. . . . Then he said a few vague things about friendship and the friendship of kindly people to those less fortunate than themselves. With that his voice nearly faded, thin, away. Like a river diminishing to a stream and then to a trickle. But he cleared his throat and said, "Our speaker tonight, who is also our friend, came from Texarkana to deliver the commencement address, but due to the irregularity of the train schedule, he's going to, as they say, 'speak and run.'" He said that we understood and wanted the man to know that we were most grateful for the time he was able to give us and then something about how we were willing always to adjust to another's program, and without more ado — "I give you Mr. Edward Donleavy."

Not one but two white men came through the door offstage. The shorter   33 one walked to the speaker's platform, and the tall one moved over to the center seat and sat down. But that was our principal's seat, and already occupied. The dislodged gentleman bounced around for a long breath or two before the Baptist minister gave him his chair, then with more dignity than the situation deserved, the minister walked off the stage.

Donleavy looked at the audience once (on reflection, I'm sure that he   34 wanted only to reassure himself that we were really there), adjusted his glasses, and began to read from a sheaf of papers.

He was glad "to be here and to see the work going on just as it was in the   35 other schools."

At the first "Amen" from the audience I willed the offender to immediate   36 death by choking on the word. But Amens and Yes, sir's began to fall around the room like rain through a ragged umbrella.

He told us of the wonderful changes we children in Stamps had in store.   37 The Central School (naturally, the white school was Central) had already been granted improvements that would be in use in the fall. A well-known artist was coming from Little Rock to teach art to them. They were going to have the newest microscopes and chemistry equipment for their laboratory. Mr. Donleavy didn't leave us long in the dark over who made these improvements available to Central High. Nor were we to be ignored in the general betterment scheme he had in mind.

He said that he had pointed out to people at a very high level that one of 38 the first-line football tacklers at Arkansas Agricultural and Mechanical College had graduated from good old Lafayette County Training School. Here fewer Amen's were heard. Those few that did break through lay dully in the air with the heaviness of habit.

He went on to praise us. He went on to say how he had bragged that "one 39 of the best basketball players at Fisk sank his first ball right here at Lafayette County Training School."

The white kids were going to have a chance to become Galileos and 40 Madame Curies and Edisons and Gauguins, and our boys (the girls weren't even in on it) would try to be Jessie Owenses and Joe Louises.

Owens and the Brown Bomber were great heroes in our world, but what 41 school official in the white-goddom of Little Rock had the right to decide that those two men must be our only heroes? Who decided that for Henry Reed to become a scientist he had to work like George Washington Carver, as a bootblack, to buy a lousy microscope? Bailey was obviously always going to be too small to be an athlete, so which concrete angel glued to what country seat had decided that if my brother wanted to become a lawyer he had to first pay penance for his skin by picking cotton and hoeing corn and studying correspondence books at night for twenty years?

The man's dead words fell like bricks around the auditorium and too 42 many settled in my belly. Constrained by hard-learned manners I couldn't look behind me, but to my left and right the proud graduating class of 1940 had dropped their heads. Every girl in my row had found something new to do with her handkerchief. Some folded the tiny squares into love knots, some into triangles, but most were wadding them, then pressing them flat on their yellow laps.

On the dais, the ancient tragedy was being replayed. Professor Parsons sat, 43 a sculptor's reject, rigid. His large, heavy body seemed devoid of will or willingness, and his eyes said he was no longer with us. The other teachers examined the flag (which was draped stage right) or their notes, or the windows which opened on our now-famous playing diamond.

Graduation, the hush-hush magic time of frills and gifts and congratula- 44 tions and diplomas, was finished for me before my name was called. The accomplishment was nothing. The meticulous maps, drawn in three colors of ink, learning and spelling decasyllabic words, memorizing the whole of *The Rape of Lucrece* — it was nothing. Donleavy had exposed us.

We were maids and farmers, handymen and washerwomen, and anything 45 higher that we aspired to was farcical and presumptuous. Then I wished that Gabriel Prosser and Nat Turner had killed all whitefolks in their beds and that Abraham Lincoln had been assassinated before the signing of the Emancipation Proclamation, and that Harriet Tubman had been killed by that blow on her head and Christopher Columbus had drowned in the *Santa Maria.*

It was awful to be Negro and have no control over my life. It was brutal 46 to be young and already trained to sit quietly and listen to charges brought against my color with no chance of defense. We should all be dead. I thought I should like to see us all dead, one on top of the other. A pyramid of flesh with the whitefolks on the bottom, as the broad base, then the Indians with their silly tomahawks and teepees and wigwams and treaties, the Negroes with their mops and recipes and cotton sacks and spirituals sticking out of their mouths. The Dutch children should all stumble in their wooden shoes and break their necks. The French should choke to death on the Louisiana Purchase (1803) while silkworms ate all the Chinese with their stupid pigtails. As a species, we were an abomination. All of us.

Donleavy was running for election, and assured our parents that if he won 47 we could count on having the only colored paved playing field in that part of Arkansas. Also — he never looked up to acknowledge the grunts of acceptance — also, we were bound to get some new equipment for the home economics building and the workshop.

He finished, and since there was no need to give any more than the most 48 perfunctory thank-you's, he nodded to the men on the stage, and the tall white man who was never introduced joined him at the door. They left with the attitude that now they were off to something really important. (The graduation ceremonies at Lafayette County Training School had been a mere preliminary.)

The ugliness they left was palpable. An uninvited guest who wouldn't 49 leave. The choir was summoned and sang a modern arrangement of "Onward, Christian Soldiers," with new words pertaining to graduates seeking their place in the world. But it didn't work. Elouise, the daughter of the Baptist minister, recited "Invictus," and I could have cried at the impertinence of "I am the master of my fate, I am the captain of my soul."

My name had lost its ring of familiarity and I had to be nudged to go and 50 receive my diploma. All my preparations had fled. I neither marched up to the stage like a conquering Amazon, nor did I look in the audience for Bailey's nod of approval. Marguerite Johnson, I heard the name again, my honors were read, there were noises in the audience of appreciation, and I took my place on the stage as rehearsed.

I thought about colors I hated: ecru, puce, lavender, beige, and black. 51

There was shuffling and rustling around me, then Henry Reed was giving 52 his valedictory address, "To Be or Not to Be." Hadn't he heard the whitefolks? We couldn't *be,* so the question was a waste of time. Henry's voice came out clear and strong. I feared to look at him. Hadn't he got the message? There was no "nobler in the mind" for Negroes because the world didn't think we had minds, and they let us know it. "Outrageous fortune"?

Now, that was a joke. When the ceremony was over I had to tell Henry Reed some things. That is, if I still cared. Not "rub," Henry, "erase." "Ah, there's the erase." Us.

Henry had been a good student in elocution. His voice rose on tides of 53 promise and fell on waves of warnings. The English teacher had helped him to create a sermon winging through Hamlet's soliloquy. To be a man, a doer, a builder, a leader, or to be a tool, an unfunny joke, a crusher of funky toadstools. I marveled that Henry could go through the speech as if we had a choice.

I had been listening and silently rebutting each sentence with my eyes 54 closed; then there was a hush, which in an audience warns that something unplanned is happening. I looked up and saw Henry Reed, the conservative, the proper, the A student, turn his back to the audience and turn to us (the proud graduating class of 1940) and sing, nearly speaking,

> Lift ev'ry voice and sing
> Till earth and heaven ring
> Ring with the harmonies of Liberty . . .

It was the poem written by James Weldon Johnson. It was the music composed by J. Rosamond Johnson. It was the Negro National Anthem. Out of habit we were singing it.

Our mothers and fathers stood in the dark hall and joined the hymn of 55 encouragement. A kindergarten teacher led the small children onto the stage and the buttercups and daisies and bunny rabbits marked time and tried to follow:

> Stony the road we trod
> Bitter the chastening rod
> Felt in the days when hope, unborn, had died.
> Yet with a steady beat
> Have not our weary feet
> Come to the place for which our fathers sighed?

Every child I knew had learned that song with his ABCs and along with 56 "Jesus Loves Me This I Know." But I personally had never heard it before. Never heard the words, despite the thousands of times I had sung them. Never thought they had anything to do with me.

On the other hand, the words of Patrick Henry had made such an 57 impression on me that I had been able to stretch myself tall and trembling and say, "I know not what course others may take, but as for me, give me liberty or give me death."

And now I heard, really for the first time: 58

> We have come over a way that with tears has been watered,
> We have come, treading our path through the blood
>   of the slaughtered.

While echoes of the song shivered in the air, Henry Reed bowed his head, 59
said "Thank you," and returned to his place in the line. The tears that
slipped down many faces were not wiped away in shame.

We were on top again. As always, again. We survived. The depths had 60
been icy and dark, but now a bright sun spoke to our souls. I was no longer
simply a member of the proud graduating class of 1940; I was a proud
member of the wonderful, beautiful Negro race.

Oh, Black known and unknown poets, how often have your auctioned 61
pains sustained us? Who will compute the lonely nights made less lonely by
your songs, or by the empty pots made less tragic by your tales?

If we were a people much given to revealing secrets, we might raise 62
monuments and sacrifice to the memories of our poets, but slavery cured us
of that weakness. It may be enough, however, to have it said that we survive
in exact relationship to the dedication of our poets (include preachers,
musicians, and blues singers).

Analyzing This Selection

1. What changes come over the student body as the time for graduation approaches?
   What phrases convey a special atmosphere? What changes come over Angelou in
   particular?

2. What details indicate the involvement of the entire black community in the
   student graduations? Does the selection seem to exaggerate the public importance
   of the event, or is the account entirely believable? Does Angelou as an eighth
   grader appear too impressionable to be storing up accurate memories?

3. What details in the narrative contribute to the suspense and the worry that
   something might go wrong? What kind of a calamity are we led to anticipate?

4. How do you explain Angelou's immediate response to Donleavy's speech? Does
   it seem excessive?

5. In what sense is this graduation truly a "commencement" for Angelou? Make
   your answer detailed and explicit.

Analyzing Connections

6. Angelou and Nora Ephron (see "Shaping Up Absurd," p. 17) recapture the style
   of adolescent impulsiveness and exaggeration. Compare their uses of humor in
   dealing with serious subjects.

Analyzing by Writing

7. Songs often become popular unofficial "anthems" for school-age clubs, gangs,
   and cliques. Singing them expresses friendship, as well as other feelings such as
   unity, hope, rebellion, or nostalgia. Explain how a song attained the status of an
   anthem in your experience. Analyze the lyrics and the circumstances that were
   meaningful.

Maxine Hong Kingston

THE MISERY OF SILENCE[1]

◇

MAXINE HONG KINGSTON (b. 1940) grew up in a Chinese immigrant community in Stockton, California, where her parents ran a laundry. Kingston graduated from the University of California at Berkeley. As a first-generation American, Kingston had to learn how to live in two distinctly contrasting societies. This was confusing and difficult for a five- to seven-year-old child, as she recalls in this selection from her autobiography, *The Woman Warrior: Memoirs of a Girlhood Among Ghosts* (1976). The immigrants regarded all non-Chinese as "ghosts" — pale, insubstantial, and threatening. *China Men* (1980) extends her story of Chinese-American girlhood by describing the lives of the fathers and sons in China and America. Kingston published her first novel, *Tripmaster Monkey: His Fake Book*, in 1989.

When I went to kindergarten and had to speak English for the first time, 1 I became silent. A dumbness — a shame — still cracks my voice in two, even when I want to say "hello" casually, or ask an easy question in front of the check-out counter, or ask directions of a bus driver. I stand frozen, or I hold up the line with the complete, grammatical sentence that comes squeaking out at impossible length. "What did you say?" says the cab driver, or "Speak up," so I have to perform again, only weaker the second time. A telephone call makes my throat bleed and takes up that day's courage. It spoils my day with self-disgust when I hear my broken voice come skittering out into the open. It makes people wince to hear it. I'm getting better, though. Recently I asked the postman for special-issue stamps; I've waited since childhood for postmen to give me some of their own accord. I am making progress, a little every day.

My silence was thickest — total — during the three years that I covered 2 my school paintings with black paint. I painted layers of black over houses and flowers and suns, and when I drew on the blackboard, I put a layer of chalk on top. I was making a stage curtain, and it was the moment before the curtain parted or rose. The teachers called my parents to school, and I saw they had been saving my pictures, curling and cracking, all alike and black.

[1]Editor's title.

The teachers pointed to the pictures and looked serious, talked seriously too, but my parents did not understand English. ("The parents and teachers of criminals were executed," said my father.) My parents took the pictures home. I spread them out (so black and full of possibilities) and pretended the curtains were swinging open, flying up, one after another, sunlight underneath, mighty operas.

During the first silent year I spoke to no one at school, did not ask before going to the lavatory, and flunked kindergarten. My sister also said nothing for three years, silent in the playground and silent at lunch. There were other quiet Chinese girls not of our family, but most of them got over it sooner than we did. I enjoyed the silence. At first it did not occur to me I was supposed to talk or to pass kindergarten. I talked at home and to one or two of the Chinese kids in class. I made motions and even made some jokes. I drank out of a toy saucer when the water spilled out of the cup, and everybody laughed, pointing at me, so I did it some more. I didn't know that Americans don't drink out of saucers.

I liked the Negro students (Black Ghosts) best because they laughed the loudest and talked to me as if I were a daring talker too. One of the Negro girls had her mother coil braids over her ears Shanghai-style like mine; we were Shanghai twins except that she was covered with black like my paintings. Two Negro kids enrolled in Chinese school, and the teachers gave them Chinese names. Some Negro kids walked me to school and home, protecting me from the Japanese kids, who hit me and chased me and stuck gum in my ears. The Japanese kids were noisy and tough. They appeared one day in kindergarten, released from concentration camp, which was a tic-tac-toe mark, like barbed wire, on the map.

It was when I found out I had to talk that school become a misery, that the silence became a misery. I did not speak and felt bad each time that I did not speak. I read aloud in first grade, though, and heard the barest whisper with little squeaks come out of my throat. "Louder," said the teacher, who scared the voice away again. The other Chinese girls did not talk either, so I knew the silence had to do with being a Chinese girl.

Reading out loud was easier than speaking because we did not have to make up what to say, but I stopped often, and the teacher would think I'd gone quiet again. I could not understand "I." The Chinese "I" has seven strokes, intricacies. How could the American "I," assuredly wearing a hat like the Chinese, have only three strokes, the middle so straight? Was it out of politeness that this writer left off the strokes the way a Chinese has to write her own name small and crooked? No, it was not politeness; "I" is a capital and "you" is lower-case. I stared at that middle line and waited so long for its black center to resolve into tight strokes and dots that I forgot to pronounce it. The other troublesome word was "here," no strong consonant to hang on to, and so flat, when "here" is two mountainous ideographs. The teacher, who had already told me every day how to read "I" and "here," put me in the low corner under the stairs again, where the noisy boys usually sat.

When my second grade class did a play, the whole class went to the 7
auditorium except the Chinese girls. The teacher, lovely and Hawaiian,
should have understood about us, but instead left us behind in the classroom.
Our voices were too soft or nonexistent, and our parents never signed the
permission slips anyway. They never signed anything unnecessary. We
opened the door a crack and peeked out, but closed it again quickly. One of
us (not me) won every spelling bee, though.

I remember telling the Hawaiian teacher, "We Chinese can't sing 'land 8
where our fathers died.' " She argued with me about politics, while I meant
because of curses. But how can I have that memory when I couldn't talk? My
mother says that we, like the ghosts, have no memories.

After American school, we picked up our cigar boxes, in which we had 9
arranged books, brushes, and an inkbox neatly, and went to Chinese school,
from 5:00 to 7:30 P.M. There we chanted together, voices rising and falling,
loud and soft, some boys shouting, everybody reading together, reciting
together and not alone with one voice. When we had a memorization test,
the teacher let each of us come to his desk and say the lesson to him privately,
while the rest of the class practiced copying or tracing. Most of the teachers
were men. The boys who were so well behaved in the American school
played tricks on them and talked back to them. The girls were not mute.
They screamed and yelled during recess, when there were no rules; they had
fistfights. Nobody was afraid of children hurting themselves or of children
hurting school property. The glass doors to the red and green balconies with
the gold joy symbols were left wide open so that we could run out and climb
the fire escapes. We played capture-the-flag in the auditorium, where Sun
Yat-sen and Chiang Kai-shek's pictures hung at the back of the stage, the
Chinese flag on their left and the American flag on their right. We climbed
the teak ceremonial chairs and made flying leaps off the stage. One flag
headquarters was behind the glass door and the other on stage right. Our feet
drummed on the hollow stage. During recess the teachers locked themselves
up in their office with the shelves of books, copybooks, inks from China.
They drank tea and warmed their hands at a stove. There was no play
supervision. At recess we had the school to ourselves, and also we could roam
as far as we could go — downtown, Chinatown stores, home — as long as we
returned before the bell rang.

At exactly 7:30 the teacher again picked up the brass bell that sat on his 10
desk and swung it over our heads, while we charged down the stairs, our
cheering magnified in the stairwell. Nobody had to line up.

Not all of the children who were silent at American school found voice 11
at Chinese school. One new teacher said each of us had to get up and
recite in front of the class, who was to listen. My sister and I had memorized the lesson perfectly. We said it to each other at home, one chant-
ing, one listening. The teacher called on my sister to recite first. It was the
first time a teacher had called on the second-born to go first. My sister was
scared. She glanced at me and looked away; I looked down at my desk. I

hoped that she could do it because if she could, then I would have to. She opened her mouth and a voice came out that wasn't a whisper, but it wasn't a proper voice either. I hoped that she would not cry, fear breaking up her voice like twigs underfoot. She sounded as if she were trying to sing through weeping and strangling. She did not pause or stop to end the embarrassment. She kept going until she said the last word, and then she sat down. When it was my turn, the same voice came out, a crippled animal running on broken legs. You could hear splinters in my voice, bones rubbing jagged against one another. I was loud, though. I was glad I didn't whisper.

How strange that the emigrant villagers are shouters, hollering face to   12 face. My father asks, "Why is it I can hear Chinese from blocks away? Is it that I understand the language? Or is it they talk loud?" They turn the radio up full blast to hear the operas, which do not seem to hurt their ears. And they yell over the singers that wail over the drums, everybody talking at once, big arm gestures, spit flying. You can see the disgust on American faces looking at women like that. It isn't just the loudness. It is the way Chinese sounds, ching-chong ugly, to American ears, not beautiful like Japanese sayonara words with the consonants and vowels as regular as Italian. We make guttural peasant noise and have Ton Duc Thang names you can't remember. And the Chinese can't hear Americans at all; the language is too soft and western music unhearable. I've watched a Chinese audience laugh, visit, talk-story, and holler during a piano recital, as if the musician could not hear them. A Chinese-American, somebody's son, was playing Chopin, which has no punctuation, no cymbals, no gongs. Chinese piano music is five black keys. Normal Chinese women's voices are strong and bossy. We American-Chinese girls had to whisper to make ourselves American-feminine. Apparently we whispered even more softly than the Americans. Once a year the teachers referred my sister and me to speech therapy, but our voices would straighten out, unpredictably normal, for the therapists. Some of us gave up, shook our heads, and said nothing, not one word. Some of us could not even shake our heads. At times shaking my head no is more self-assertion than I can manage. Most of us eventually found some voice, however faltering. We invented an American-feminine speaking personality.

Analyzing This Selection

1. What was the connection between Kingston's silence and her paintings? What did the paintings signify to *her*?

2. Why did the English pronouns "I" and "you" strike Kingston as unnatural? How do they differ from their Chinese equivalents? What looks wrong about the word "here"?

3. Does this account reinforce a stereotype of the Asian woman? What does Kingston suggest that Chinese women are like when they are among Chinese?

4. In the concluding sentence Kingston refers to "an American-feminine speaking personality." What would that be? Can you describe or imitate the tone and manner she suggests?

Analyzing Connections

5. Kingston was obviously a "problem student" in class. If you had been her teacher, what might you have done? How might the problem have been handled by a teacher like Edward C. Martin? (See "Being Junior High," p. 188.)

Analyzing by Writing

6. At the beginning of this selection, Kingston says that even today she has trouble speaking up in public situations. Does her style of writing indicate any hesitation or absence of assertiveness in using English for writing to the public? Is her language easy or hard to read? What is the tone of her voice? Write about Kingston's style in relation to her childhood experience.

Richard Rodriguez

READING FOR SUCCESS

◇

RICHARD RODRIGUEZ (b. 1944) grew up in San Francisco, where as the child of Spanish-speaking Mexican Americans he received his education in a language that was not spoken at home. His attraction to English and to English-speaking culture became his avenue to a promising future, but he felt torn away from the people he loved. He received a Ph.D. in English from the University of California at Berkeley and remained there as a teacher, until he decided to write about the conflicting aspirations that divided him between two worlds. This selection from his autobiography, *Hunger of Memory* (1982), recalls the origin of his passion for reading. Rodriguez has continued his memoir in *Days of Obligation: An Argument with My Mexican Father* (1992).

From an early age I knew that my mother and father could read and write 1 both Spanish and English. I had observed my father making his way through what, I now suppose, must have been income tax forms. On other occasions I waited apprehensively while my mother read onion-paper letters air-mailed from Mexico with news of a relative's illness or death. For both my parents, however, reading was something done out of necessity and as quickly as possible. Never did I see either of them read an entire book. Nor did I see them read for pleasure. Their reading consisted of work manuals, prayer books, newspapers, recipes. . . .

In our house each school year would begin with my mother's careful 2 instruction: "Don't write in your books so we can sell them at the end of the year." The remark was echoed in public by my teachers, but only in part: "Boys and girls, don't write in your books. You must learn to treat them with great care and respect."

OPEN THE DOORS OF YOUR MIND WITH BOOKS, read the red and white poster 3 over the nun's desk in early September. It soon was apparent to me that reading was the classroom's central activity. Each course had its own book. And the information gathered from a book was unquestioned. READ TO LEARN, the sign on the wall advised in December. I privately wondered: What was the connection between reading and learning? Did one learn something only by reading it? Was an idea only an idea if it could be written down? In June, CONSIDER BOOKS YOUR BEST FRIENDS. Friends? Reading was, at best, only a chore. I needed to look up whole paragraphs of words in a dictionary. Lines of type were dizzying, the eye having to move slowly across the page, then down, and across. . . . The sentences of the first books I read were coolly impersonal. Toned hard. What most bothered me, however, was the isolation reading required. To console myself for the loneliness I'd feel when I read, I tried reading in a very soft voice. Until: "Who is doing all that talking to his neighbor?" Shortly after, remedial reading classes were arranged for me with a very old nun.

At the end of each school day, for nearly six months, I would meet 4 with her in the tiny room that served as the school's library but was actually only a storeroom for used textbooks and a vast collection of *National Geographics*. Everything about our sessions pleased me: the smallness of the room; the noise of the janitor's broom hitting the edge of the long hallway outside the door; the green of the sun, lighting the wall; and the old woman's face blurred white with a beard. Most of the time we took turns. I began with my elementary text. Sentences of astonishing simplicity seemed to me lifeless and drab: "The boys ran from the rain. . . . She wanted to sing. . . . The kite rose in the blue." Then the old nun would read from her favorite books, usually biographies of early American presidents. Playfully she ran through complex sentences, calling the words alive with her voice, making it seem that the author somehow was speaking directly to me. I smiled just to listen to her. I sat there and sensed for the very first time some possibility of fellowship between a reader and a writer, a communication, never *intimate* like that I heard spoken words at home convey, but one nonetheless *personal*.

One day the nun concluded a session by asking me why I was so reluctant 5 to read by myself. I tried to explain; said something about the way written words made me feel all alone — almost, I wanted to add but didn't, as when I spoke to myself in a room just emptied of furniture. She studied my face as I spoke; she seemed to be watching more than listening. In an uneventful voice she replied that I had nothing to fear. Didn't I realize that reading would open up whole new worlds? A book could open doors for me. It could introduce me to people and show me places I never imagined existed. She gestured toward the bookshelves. (Bare-breasted African women danced, and the shiny hubcaps of automobiles on the back covers of the *Geographic* gleamed in my mind.) I listened with respect. But her words were not very influential. I was thinking then of another consequence of literacy, one I was too shy to admit but nonetheless trusted. Books were going to make me "educated." *That* confidence enabled me, several months later, to overcome my fear of the silence.

In fourth grade I embarked upon a grandiose reading program. "Give 6 me the names of important books," I would say to startled teachers. They soon found out that I had in mind "adult books." I ignored their suggestion of anything I suspected was written for children. (Not until I was in college, as a result, did I read *Huckleberry Finn* or *Alice's Adventures in Wonderland*.) Instead, I read *The Scarlet Letter* and Franklin's *Autobiog-*

raphy. And whatever I read I read for extra credit. Each time I finished a book, I reported the achievement to a teacher and basked in the praise my effort earned. Despite my best efforts, however, there seemed to be more and more books I needed to read. At the library I would literally tremble as I came upon whole shelves of books I hadn't read. So I read and I read and I read: *Great Expectations*; all the short stories of Kipling; *The Babe Ruth Story*; the entire first volume of the *Encyclopedia Britannica* (A-ANSTEY); the *Iliad*; *Moby-Dick*; *Gone with the Wind*; *The Good Earth*; *Ramona*; *Forever Amber*; *The Lives of the Saints*; *Crime and Punishment*; *The Pearl*. . . . Librarians who initially frowned when I checked out the maximum ten books at a time started saving books they thought I might like. Teachers would say to the rest of the class, "I only wish the rest of you took reading as seriously as Richard obviously does."

But at home I would hear my mother wondering, "What do you see in   7 your books?" (Was reading a hobby like her knitting? Was so much reading even healthy for a boy? Was it the sign of "brains"? Or was it just a convenient excuse for not helping around the house on Saturday mornings?) Always, "What do you see . . . ?"

What *did* I see in my books? I had the idea that they were crucial for my   8 academic success, though I couldn't have said exactly how or why. In the sixth grade I simply concluded that what gave a book its value was some major idea or theme it contained. If that core essence could be mined and memorized, I would become learned like my teachers. I decided to record in a notebook the themes of the books that I read. After reading *Robinson Crusoe*, I wrote that its theme was "the value of learning to live by oneself." When I completed *Wuthering Heights*, I noted the danger of "letting emotions get out of control." Rereading these brief moralistic appraisals usually left me disheartened. I couldn't believe that they were really the source of reading's value. But for many years, they constituted the only means I had of describing to myself the educational value of books.

In spite of my earnestness, I found reading a pleasurable activity. I came   9 to enjoy the lonely good company of books. Early on weekday mornings, I'd read in my bed. I'd feel a mysterious comfort then, reading in the dawn quiet — the blue-gray silence interrupted by the occasional churning of the refrigerator motor a few rooms away or the more distant sounds of a city bus beginning its run. On weekends I'd go to the public library to read, surrounded by old men and women. Or, if the weather was fine, I would take my books to the park and read in the shade of a tree. Neighbors would leave for vacation and I would water their lawns. I would sit through the twilight on the front porches or in backyards, reading to the cool, whirling sounds of the sprinklers.

I also had favorite writers. But often those writers I enjoyed most I was   10 least able to value. When I read William Saroyan's *The Human Comedy*, I was immediately pleased by the narrator's warmth and the charm of his story. But as quickly I became suspicious. A book so enjoyable to read couldn't be very "important." Another summer I determined to read all the novels of Dickens. Reading his fat novels, I loved the feeling I got — after the first hundred pages — of being at home in a fictional world where I knew the names of the characters and cared about what was going to happen to them. And it bothered me that I was forced away at the conclusion, when the fiction closed tight, like a fortune-teller's fist — the futures of all the major characters neatly resolved. I never knew how to take such feelings seriously, however. Nor did I suspect that these experiences could be part of a novel's meaning. Still, there were pleasures to sustain me after I'd finish my books. Carrying a volume back to the library, I would be pleased by its weight. I'd run my fingers along the edge of the pages and marvel at the breadth of my achievement. Around my room, growing stacks of paperback books reinforced my assurance.

I entered high school having read hundreds of books. My habit of 11 reading made me a confident speaker and writer of English. Reading also enabled me to sense something of the shape, the major concerns, of Western thought. (I was able to say something about Dante and Descartes and Engels and James Baldwin in my high school term papers.) In these various ways, books brought me academic success as I hoped that they would. But I was not a good reader. Merely bookish, I lacked a point of view when I read. Rather, I read in order to acquire a point of view. I vacuumed books for epigrams, scraps of information, ideas, themes — anything to fill the hollow within me and make me feel educated. When one of my teachers suggested to his drowsy tenth-grade English class that a person could not have a "complicated idea" until he had read at least two thousand books, I heard the remark without detecting either its irony or its very complicated truth. I merely determined to compile a list of all the books I had ever read. Harsh with myself, I included only once a title I might have read several times. (How, after all, could one read a book more than once?) And I included only those books over a hundred pages in length. (Could anything shorter be a book?)

There was yet another high school list I compiled. One day I came 12 across a newspaper article about the retirement of an English professor at a nearby state college. The article was accompanied by a list of the "hundred most important books of Western Civilization." "More than anything else in my life," the professor told the reporter with finality, "these books have made me all that I am." That was the kind of remark I couldn't ignore. I clipped out the list and kept it for the several months it took me to read all of the titles. Most books, of course, I barely understood. While reading Plato's *Republic*, for instance, I needed to keep looking at the book jacket comments to remind myself what the text was about. Nevertheless, with the special patience and superstition of a scholarship boy, I looked at every word of the text. And by the time I reached the last word, relieved, I convinced myself that I had read *The Republic*. In a ceremony of great pride, I solemnly crossed Plato off my list.

Analyzing This Selection

1. What were the reasons Rodriguez did not enjoy his early reading? What do you think was the greatest single barrier to his enjoyment? What leads you to this conclusion?

2. Do you agree with his remark that "I was not a good reader"? What does he think was wrong? Is his self-criticism justified?

3. Rodriguez implies that early reading experiences would be different for a child in a middle-class, English-speaking family. What specific matters do you think might be just the same?

Analyzing Connections

4. Rodriguez and Terry Galloway (see "I'm Listening as Hard as I Can," p. 25) temporarily became overachievers. What goals do you think they were striving for?

5. Rodriguez and the young Richard Wright (p. 186) responded differently to books. Which adolescent's responses to reading were like yours at that age? Explain the similarities you find.

Analyzing by Writing

6. In the household you grew up in, what attitudes toward personal achievement were taken for granted or explicitly defined? Were there any disagreements among family members' views about the importance of being outstanding? How were variations from the dominant view expressed and treated? Explain the background of your motivation to excel.

Michael Moffatt

COMING OF AGE
IN A COLLEGE DORM[1]

◇

MICHAEL MOFFATT (b. 1944) attended Dartmouth College, then transferred to
and graduated from Reed College. His double exposure to undergraduate life
may have been the origin of his long-lasting interest in the customs of students
and other subcastes. He is a professor of cultural anthropology. After studying
at Oxford University, Moffatt earned his Ph.D. from the University of Chicago. His first published research was on the low-status "untouchables" in
India, *An Untouchable Community in South India* (1979). Turning his attention closer to Rutgers University, where he has taught since 1973, Moffatt
began studying student life in the college dormitories, from the perspective of
a resident anthropologist. He lived for two years in a number of dorms and later
continued his research by interviews and other methods. His observations are
published in *Coming of Age in New Jersey: College and American Culture*
(1989). In the following excerpt, Moffatt is in his second year of living among
the "natives" and his first semester at this site, the fourth floor of a dormitory
that he fictitiously calls (to protect the guilty) Hasbrouck Hall.

Most of the freshmen on Hasbrouck Fourth, interviewed privately in the 1
first weeks of the semester, said they were impressed and relieved by the
general friendliness of the other students on the floor, especially of
the knowledgeable upperclassmen. They were grateful for the chance to
establish personal relationships so quickly in college, particularly given the
size, impersonality, and confusion of most of Rutgers outside the dorms. A
few of them also said, however, that the ambience of the dorms was more
juvenile than they had expected in college, and a few others were surprised
at how little studying some of their upperclass exemplars appeared to do. Half
a dozen freshmen said they were particularly surprised at the amount of
drinking that went on.

The sophomores and some of the other upperclassmen also set examples 2
for the sensible use of daily and weekly time for the freshmen. Avoid classes
before eleven or so in the morning. Look for floor friends for lunches and
dinners; nap in the afternoon if a morning schedule was absolutely necessary;

[1]Editor's title.

spend some friendly time in the lounge every day, especially before an early dinner (around four in the afternoon) and after an evening of studying. To bed at one or two in the morning after quieter talks with closer friends, or perhaps after a little "David Letterman" or some other late-night TV comic. Avoid Friday classes. Thursday nights were the big party nights; then home or somewhere else for the long weekend, and back to campus Sunday afternoon, perhaps warming up for the next week with the first real studying of the weekend. . . .

You were not a bad person if you did not hang out on the floor; you were just a nonperson. A much worse thing to be was a person who was around a lot but not friend*ly*. Then you were in trouble. Then you were a snob. If you didn't watch it, you might open your door one day to find some local vigilantes "mooning" you in disapproval, or someone might fill a large garbage can with water, balance it against your door, knock, and disappear.

Accordingly, most of the remaining forty-six residents of Hasbrouck Fourth spent varying amounts of time together in the fall of 1984 in the lounges, in private rooms, at Commons, going out visiting or partying with one another at night, going to classes together when they happened to have them in common, and so on. This was friendly time. You necessarily spent some of it with floor acquaintances you were not especially crazy about as individuals, but you tried to spend more of it with your "real" friends on the floor.

In the lounges, the sophomores also soon taught the freshmen to talk the dominant mode of discourse in the undergraduate peer group. It might be labeled "Undergraduate Cynical." In different forms, it is probably a very old speech genre in American college culture. It can be seen as the polar opposite of Deanly Officialese, or of Faculty Lofty. Its attitudinal stance is "wise to the ways of the world." In it, moral, ethical, and intellectual positions are rapidly reduced to the earthiest possible motives of those who articulate them; in it, everyone who participates or is referred to is treated in the same way — leveled — made equal by the joke-and-insult-impregnated discourse of contemporary American friendly busting.

As the students spoke Undergraduate Cynical in the dorms, friends and acquaintances and one's own self were mocked at firsthand, and other people and other kinds of pretension were made fun of at a distance. The students might complain to one another about the rigors of higher education:

> I really hate the teaching in my poly sci classes. They give you a lot of reading and lectures and then tell you to figure things out for yourself. There's a thousand questions the professor can ask. "Relate this to that." . . . I wish they'd have textbooks that just told you everything you need to know. Enough of this enlightened bullshit! — Freshman male, Erewhon Third, 1978.

Or they might discuss among themselves various ways of beating the system, as did two upperclassmen on Hasbrouck Fourth in the spring of 1985.

Al: Hey, John, how was the exam? Was it a cake exam?
John: Yeah. The prof said up to five answers were correct for every question.
Al: Good, good. That means you can definitely argue points with him.

At first I mistook Undergraduate Cynical for a privileged form of truth, for   7
what the undergraduates really thought among themselves when all their
defenses were down. Eventually I realized that, as a code of spoken discourse, Undergraduate Cynical could be just as mandatory and just as
coercive as other forms of discourse. You could say some very important
things in it, things that you really were not allowed to say elsewhere. It was
definitely fun to talk it once you learned its rules, and I certainly enjoyed my
regular bouts of it throughout my research. But you could not necessarily say
everything that you really thought in it, any more than a dean speaking in
public could easily stop emphasizing consensus and community among all
those who "worked together" at Rutgers and suddenly start ventilating her or
his personal animosities toward a particular administrative rival.

Imagine, for instance, that you were an undergraduate who had been   8
reading a sonnet by the poet Shelley for a classroom assignment, and that it
had really swept you away. Unless you enjoyed being a figure of fun, you
would not have dared to articulate your feelings for the poem with any
honesty in the average peer-group talk in the average dorm lounge. You
might, on the other hand, have discussed such sentiments more privately
with trusted friends. Ordinarily, the dorm lounge and its near-mandatory
code did not allow you to say what the "real you" believed, either intellectually or in other ways. The dorm lounge was more often an arena for
peer-group posing in which, acting friend*ly*, you presented the "as if" you.

There were many nuances, subtleties, and variations in the modes of   9
lounge talk, however. In unpredictable ways, peer-group talk could shift
from purely cynical into more sincere, earnest expressions of meanings and
feelings, even when it was not between close friends. In mid-September,
while I was still getting to know the residents of Hasbrouck Fourth and while
they were still sorting each other out, I touched off one of these talk sessions.
In it, the student voices moved back and forth through a number of stances.
Sometimes they were bullshitting. Sometimes they were simply being playful. Sometimes they were talking from the heart, evidently trying to present
the "real me." Often they were trying to seize conversational control. And
almost always, they were performing.

Louie had been hustling as usual, in an ironic mode he often used,   10
simultaneously making fun of himself for hustling as he hustled: "Here I am,
Mike, an unknown college sophomore, lost in the dorms at Rutgers. You're
my big chance. You can make me famous. When are you gonna interview
me? You *gotta* interview me!" So I decided to give him an interview I had
been developing privately to elicit some simple cultural meanings. Except, as
an experiment, I decided to give it to Louie around his peers rather than in
private. We sat down with a tape recorder in a corner of the high-side lounge

at about seven o'clock one evening early in the semester. Fifteen feet away, Carrie was quietly reading a book and apparently minding her own business; two freshmen girls sat near her.

I led off with my standard opening question in this interview. I was a man 11 from Mars, I told Louis. I understood about colleges educationally. Earthlings did not have preprogrammed knowledge like we did on Mars. But I did not understand about college "dorms" on Earth. Why did young Earthlings leave big comfortable homes a few miles away, where all their needs were provided for by their parents, and come to live in these crowded, noisy confines, packed together like sardines?

> *Louie:* Well, part of college is to grow, and not only to grow intellectually but to grow independently wise. . . . When you come to college, it's not exactly the real world but it's one step toward it, it's kinda like a plateau. You become more independent. You have to do your own laundry. . . . And you feel a togetherness because there's sixty of you on the floor and all stuck in the same boat. . . .

Louie went on in this vein for five minutes, answering a few of my 12 Martian's follow-up questions. Then, possibly aware that Carrie and the freshmen women were listening in, he paused and soliloquized: "How I bullshit! You want some real answers now? I don't know why anyone's here. They're all just getting ripped off!"

This gave Carrie her opening. "Do you really believe all that stuff you just 13 said, Louie?" she asked. Louie moved over closer to Carrie, and I followed him, carrying my tape recorder in a visible position. Louie said that he really did not know what he believed, so Carrie offered her answer to the Martian's question:

> College is a place where suburban brats come, to hang out for four years. . . . I think it's a step *away* from the real world. . . . I don't think a lot of people here *want* an education, whether from college itself or from interacting with other people. . . . And when they get out of here, they're just going into Mom and Dad's business, or Mom and Dad is going to pay for their apartment for three years until they get a real job. . . . Which is really fucked up.

Louie recognized the critique, but he did not consider himself a spoiled 14 college kid. He answered Carrie by telling her that his father was divorced from his mother and was not putting him through Rutgers; he had to work hard at several jobs to stay in school. He talked about how hard he worked and how much money he made. A lot of other Rutgers undergraduates were serious, hardworking youths like him, he concluded. Carrie agreed that she was, but she was not sure about many others; and whatever the state of Louie's finances, she still thought his opinions were screwy: "I don't know, I see a lot of bullshit and a lot of bullshit people here. . . . And a lot of that stuff you were saying, I thought that was pretty *zorbo*. I said to myself, Louie man, if that's the way you think, I don't know. . . ."

Louie challenged her to tell him what in the world was *not* bullshit? She 15 made a case for the caring self, for "how you feel about yourself and how you feel about those closest to you. That's all that really matters." "*I'm* proud of myself," Louie replied, "so that's not bullshit, right? According to your definition?" Carrie agreed that it was good that Louie was proud of himself, but she thought Louie's pride was misplaced, since it was really just rooted in his ability to make money. And that, she said, still struck her as "zorbo bullshit."

At this point, one of the freshman listeners cut in. "What exactly is 16 'zorbo'?" she asked deferentially. "I've never heard the phrase." "Bullshit," Louie explained in a dismissive tone. "Nothing," Carrie added. Later I discovered that Louie had never heard the word either and was bluffing. Carrie had coined it the year before in an old clique on a different dorm floor. It was her synonym for "nerd." A real loser, she had decided for some private reason, a hopeless case, should have the name "Zorbo McBladeoff." Anything that such a character did was a "zorbo" thing to do. She was not able to sell the word to Hasbrouck Fourth in 1984, however; despite Louie's implication that it was a perfectly ordinary term in the talk of knowledgeable upperclassmen at Rutgers, I never heard it again.

Carrie and Louie went back to their argument. Carrie thought that the 17 most important things in life had nothing to do with money. Finding something you really wanted to do was more important. So was helping and influencing others. "If you can do that for a friend, and one friend starts to think the way you do, that's two of you now, and if two of you can go out. . . . I want to be able to change the way America is. I'm serious! This place is so fucked up."

Louie replied that helping others often did you no good at all: "Like, if you 18 believe in something, and every time you try to do it, nine times out of ten it gets pushed back in your face. . . . Where does that get you? That and fifty cents and you can buy a cup of coffee." Right now, Louie decided, what *he* believed in was "*nothin'*." And he got bored easily, he said, so he liked to try lots of different jobs and he liked to date lots of different girls. In deference to Carrie, Louie did not refer to his erotic prey with his normal label for them, "chicks."

While Carrie and Louie were in the middle of this colloquy, Jay walked in 19 and sat down. He had been working on a paper for an English course; "Does anyone here understand Isaac Babel?" he asked the group at large. "No," Carrie answered abruptly, and went back to her argument. Jay did not like being ignored; he listened for a minute and then tried to change the mood of the session: "Oh, I get it, we're being *cosmic*!" Carrie told him to shut up, so he began busting on her directly. She had been talking about personal satisfaction through an artistic vocation. "Carrie wants to be a really incredible actress," Jay declared to the group, now augmented by three more passing residents, "perhaps on the order of Bo Derek or Ursula Andress." Carrie did not look much like either of these two ridiculous Nordic icons. That ploy did not succeed either, however, and a few minutes later Jay walked away.

Carrie and Louie went on arguing, and after another ten minutes, an 20 upperclassman strode confidently into the lounge from the elevators. He was a skinny, self-assured young man wearing a worn black sports jacket; I had never seen him before on the floor, and I never saw him again. Carrie stopped talking and gave him a big hello, without introducing him to anyone else, and they alluded briefly to unexplained old intimacies:

Carrie: Heeey! It's you! It's the crazy man! What's up?
Stranger: So good to see you alive, kid.
Carrie: I know. I got through it.

Then Carrie went back to the meaning of life with Louie. The stranger listened for a few minutes, apparently felt he had caught the drift, and then stood up and actually danced around the lounge intoning the following paean to the self. He had a certain hypnotic charm, reinforced by the reiterative phrases he used, and a man-of-the-world authority reinforced by the density of his easy vulgarisms:

If you want to go out and be a success, you're gonna have to go to school and do well, you're gonna go to college, and you're gonna find out you can live on your own [Louie: "You're 150 percent right!"] And you're gonna find out it's you! You know that song [croons]: "It is yoooou, Oh yeah, Oh yeah"? [Back to normal voice] I can tell a person what's gone right for me, how I've gotten where I've gotten, how I've fucked up.

And that's all I can do. It's them, you know, it's got to come from them. . . . If they want to benefit, that's great. If they want to say, "You're an asshole," that's fine too. It hurts me to see them fuck up, but that's the way it's gonna be. And I don't get upset and say [tone of fake emotion], "You're fuckin' up, you're fuckin' up." I walk up calmly and say [calm tone], "You're fuckin' up." You know, "You could do it this way or you could do it that way." And it's gonna come from you. Nobody's gonna hand you anything.

That's the way I feel. You know, it's different for everyone, but that's the way I feel.

I was not sure what this tone poem had to do with the substance of Carrie and Louie's debate. But the stranger had captured everybody's attention, including my own. Everyone sat in rapt silence as he ended his spiel. Then, apparently deliberately, he punctured the mildly reverent mood he himself had created: "Yeah, and there's another thing. I don't like to *dog* anyone. I present myself, not *degrade* somebody else. And you know, it's rush week, everybody. And this is a lot of what my fraternity's all about. . . ." The audience guffawed. The stranger laughed happily and made a quick exit. He had achieved what Jay had failed to do. He had popped the "cosmic" bubble. This little talk session was over, and the participants wandered off to other interests of the evening.

Analyzing This Selection

1. In the first four paragraphs, how do the freshman impressions of dorm life compare with or differ from your own impressions? For what reasons would you prefer to live in Hasbrouck or in your own dorm?

2. According to the author, what are the basic elements of "Undergraduate Cynical"? Do you agree with Moffatt that it can be a "coercive" language?

3. On what points do Louie and Carrie disagree? What views do they hold in common?

4. What is the substance of the stranger's monologue? What words suggest Moffatt's implied attitude toward the stranger's talk and performance?

Analyzing Connections

5. Moffatt and Edward C. Martin, in "Being Junior High" (p. 188), describe different age-groups of students. How do the younger students in Martin's essay differ from the Hasbrouck residents? Compare the main traits that each author observes. Which students would you rather teach?

Analyzing by Writing

6. For the evening of interviews in the lounge, Moffatt adopts the viewpoint of a detached observer, a Martian, who appears sometimes not to grasp the situation intuitively. Write a letter to Moffatt in which you explain, as an insider, the interactions among the people in the lounge, including the connections among their views, their performances, and their personalities. Try to clarify for Moffatt whether the evening produced real coherence or just bullshit.

7. Collect and examine examples of the type of speech called Undergraduate Cynical, as it is spoken among your acquaintances. Give details of the vocabulary, explaining the uses and tones of three or four key words or phrases. Illustrate your points with bits of dialogue, if helpful. Try to analyze what the language disguises as well as what it declares.

Virginia Woolf

PROFESSIONS FOR WOMEN

◊

VIRGINIA WOOLF (1882–1941) was an important British novelist noted for her emphasis on the subjective meaning of events rather than the outward circumstances of plot and appearance. Her novels include *Mrs. Dalloway* (1925) and *To the Lighthouse* (1927). Born into a distinguished literary family, she was educated at home and began her writing career as a book reviewer for the London *Times Literary Supplement*. With her husband she lived among a group of artists and intellectuals known as the Bloomsbury group — a group that included E. M. Forster, John Maynard Keynes, Bertrand Russell, and Lytton Strachey. She spoke out consistently for freedom and equality for women in works such as *A Room of One's Own* (1929) and the following address to the Women's Service League. Her essays are collected in four volumes of *Collected Essays* (1967).

When your secretary invited me to come here, she told me that your Society 1 is concerned with the employment of women and she suggested that I might tell you something about my own professional experiences. It is true I am a woman; it is true I am employed; but what professional experiences have I had? It is difficult to say. My profession is literature; and in that profession there are fewer experiences for women than in any other, with the exception of the stage — fewer, I mean, that are peculiar to women. For the road was cut many years ago — by Fanny Burney, by Aphra Behn, by Harriet Martineau, by Jane Austen, by George Eliot[1] — many famous women, and many more unknown and forgotten, have been before me, making the path smooth, and regulating my steps. Thus, when I came to write, there were very few material obstacles in my way. Writing was a reputable and harmless occupation. The family peace was not broken by the scratching of a pen. No demand was made upon the family purse. For ten and sixpence one can buy paper enough to write all the plays of Shakespeare — if one has a mind that way. Pianos and models, Paris, Vienna and Berlin, masters and mistresses, are not needed by a writer. The cheapness of writing paper is, of course, the reason why women have succeeded as writers before they succeeded in the other professions.

But to tell you my story — it is a simple one. You have only got to figure 2

[1]British women novelists of the eighteenth and nineteenth centuries. [Ed.]

to yourselves a girl in a bedroom with a pen in her hand. She had only to move that pen from left to right — from ten o'clock to one. Then it occurred to her to do what is simple and cheap enough after all — to slip a few of those pages into an envelope, fix a penny stamp in the corner, and drop the envelope into the red box at the corner. It was thus that I became a journalist; and my effort was rewarded on the first day of the following month — a very glorious day it was for me — by a letter from an editor containing a check for one pound ten shillings and sixpence. But to show you how little I deserve to be called a professional woman, how little I know of the struggles and difficulties of such lives, I have to admit that instead of spending that sum upon bread and butter, rent, shoes and stockings, or butcher's bills, I went out and bought a cat — a beautiful cat, a Persian cat, which very soon involved me in bitter disputes with my neighbors.

What could be easier than to write articles and to buy Persian cats with the profits? But wait a moment. Articles have to be about something. Mine, I seem to remember, was about a novel by a famous man. And while I was writing this review I discovered that if I were going to review books I should need to do battle with a certain phantom. And the phantom was a woman, and when I came to know her better I called her after the heroine of a famous poem, The Angel in the House. It was she who used to come between me and my paper when I was writing reviews. It was she who bothered me and wasted my time and so tormented me that at last I killed her. You who come of a younger and happier generation may not have heard of her — you may not know what I mean by the Angel in the House. I will describe her as shortly as I can. She was intensely sympathetic. She was immensely charming. She was utterly un-selfish. She excelled in the difficult arts of family life. She sacrificed herself daily. If there was chicken, she took the leg; if there was a draught, she sat in it — in short she was so constituted that she never had a mind or a wish of her own, but preferred to sympathize always with the minds and wishes of others. Above all — I need not say it — she was pure. Her purity was supposed to be her chief beauty — her blushes, her great grace. In those days — the last of Queen Victoria — every house had its Angel. And when I came to write I encountered her with the very first words. The shadow of her wings fell on my page; I heard the rustling of her skirts in the room. Directly, that is to say, I took my pen in hand to review that novel by a famous man, she slipped behind me and whispered: "My dear, you are a young woman. You are writing about a book that has been written by a man. Be sympathetic; be tender; flatter; deceive; use all the arts and wiles of our sex. Never let anybody guess that you have a mind of your own. Above all, be pure." And she made as if to guide my pen. I now record the one act for which I take some credit to myself, though the credit rightly belongs to some excellent ancestors of mine who left me a certain sum of money — shall we say five hundred pounds a year? — so that it was not necessary for me to depend solely on charm for my living.

I turned upon her and caught her by the throat. I did my best to kill her. My excuse, if I were to be had up in a court of law, would be that I acted in self-defense. Had I not killed her she would have killed me. She would have plucked the heart out of my writing. For, as I found, directly I put pen to paper, you cannot review even a novel without having a mind of your own, without expressing what you think to be the truth about human relations, morality, sex. And all these questions, according to the Angel in the House, cannot be dealt with freely and openly by women; they must charm, they must conciliate, they must — to put it bluntly — tell lies if they are to succeed. Thus, whenever I felt the shadow of her wing or the radiance of her halo upon my page, I took up the inkpot and flung it at her. She died hard. Her fictitious nature was of great assistance to her. It is far harder to kill a phantom than a reality. She was always creeping back when I thought I had despatched her. Though I flatter myself that I killed her in the end, the struggle was severe; it took much time that had better have been spent upon learning Greek grammar; or in roaming the world in search of adventures. But it was a real experience; it was an experience that was bound to befall all women writers at that time. Killing the Angel in the House was part of the occupation of a woman writer.

But to continue my story. The Angel was dead; what then remained? You 4 may say that what remained was a simple and common object — a young woman in a bedroom with an inkpot. In other words, now that she had rid herself of falsehood, that young woman had only to be herself. Ah, but what is "herself"? I mean, what is a woman? I assure you, I do not know. I do not believe that you know. I do not believe that anybody can know until she has expressed herself in all the arts and professions open to human skill. That indeed is one of the reasons why I have come here — out of respect for you, who are in process of showing us by your experiment what a woman is, who are in process of providing us, by your failures and successes, with that extremely important piece of information.

But to continue the story of my professional experiences. I made one 5 pound ten and six by my first review; and I bought a Persian cat with the proceeds. Then I grew ambitious. A Persian cat is all very well, I said; but a Persian cat is not enough. I must have a motor car. And it was thus that I became a novelist — for it is a very strange thing that people will give you a motor car if you will tell them a story. It is a still stranger thing that there is nothing so delightful in the world as telling stories. It is far pleasanter than writing reviews of famous novels. And yet, if I am to obey your secretary and tell you my professional experiences as a novelist, I must tell you about a very strange experience that befell me as a novelist. And to understand it you must try first to imagine a novelist's state of mind. I hope I am not giving away professional secrets if I say that a novelist's chief desire is to be as unconscious as possible. He has to induce in himself a state of perpetual lethargy. He wants life to proceed with the utmost quiet and regularity. He wants to see the same faces, to read the same books, to do the same things day after day, month after month, while he is writing, so that nothing may break the illusion in which he is living — so that nothing may disturb or disquiet the mysterious nosings about, feelings round, darts, dashes, and sudden discoveries of that very shy and illusive spirit, the imagination. I suspect that this state is the same both for men and women. Be that as it may, I want you to imagine me writing a novel in a state of trance. I want you to figure to yourselves a girl sitting with a pen in her hand, which for minutes, and indeed for hours, she never dips into the inkpot. The image that comes to my mind when I think of this girl is the image of a fisherman lying sunk in dreams on the verge of a deep lake with a rod held out over the water. She was letting her imagination sweep unchecked round every rock and cranny of the world that lies submerged in the depths of our unconscious being. Now came the experience, the experience that I believe to be far commoner with women writers than with men. The line raced through the girl's fingers. Her imagination had rushed away. It had sought the pools, the depths, the dark places where the largest fish slumber. And then there was a smash. There was an explosion. There was foam and confusion. The imagination had dashed itself against something hard. The girl was roused from her dream. She was indeed in a state of the most acute and difficult distress. To speak without figure she had thought of something, something about the body, about the passions which it was unfitting for her as a woman to say. Men, her reason told her, would be shocked. The consciousness of what men will say of a woman who speaks the truth about her passions had roused her from her artist's state of unconsciousness. She could write no more. The trance was over. Her imagination could work no longer. This I believe to be a very common experience with women writers — they are impeded by the extreme conventionality of the other sex. For though men sensibly allow themselves great freedom in these respects, I doubt that they realize or can control the extreme severity with which they condemn such freedom in women.

These then were two very genuine experiences of my own. These were 6 two of the adventures of my professional life. The first — killing the Angel in the House — I think I solved. She died. But the second, telling the truth about my own experiences as a body, I do not think I solved. I doubt that any woman has solved it yet. The obstacles against her are still immensely powerful — and yet they are very difficult to define. Outwardly, what is simpler than to write books? Outwardly, what obstacles are there for a woman rather than for a man? Inwardly, I think, the case is very different; she has still many ghosts to fight, many prejudices to overcome. Indeed it will be a long time still, I think, before a woman can sit down to write a book without finding a phantom to be slain, a rock to be dashed against. And if this is so in literature, the freest of all professions for women, how is it in the new professions which you are now for the first time entering?

Those are the questions that I should like, had I time, to ask you. And   7
indeed, if I have laid stress upon these professional experiences of mine, it is
because I believe that they are, though in different forms, yours also. Even
when the path is nominally open — when there is nothing to prevent a
woman from being a doctor, a lawyer, a civil servant — there are many
phantoms and obstacles, as I believe, looming in her way. To discuss and
define them is I think of great value and importance; for thus only can the
labor be shared, the difficulties be solved. But besides this, it is necessary also
to discuss the ends and the aims for which we are fighting, for which we are
doing battle with these formidable obstacles. Those aims cannot be taken for
granted; they must be perpetually questioned and examined. The whole
position, as I see it — here in this hall surrounded by women practicing for
the first time in history I know not how many different professions — is one
of extraordinary interest and importance. You have won rooms of your own
in the house hitherto exclusively owned by men. You are able, though not
without great labor and effort, to pay the rent. You are earning your five
hundred pounds a year. But this freedom is only a beginning; the room is
your own, but it is still bare. It has to be furnished; it has to be decorated; it
has to be shared. How are you going to furnish it, how are you going to
decorate it? With whom are you going to share it, and upon what terms?
These, I think, are questions of the utmost importance and interest. For the
first time in history you are able to ask them; for the first time you are able
to decide for yourselves what the answers should be. Willingly would I stay
and discuss those questions and answers — but not tonight. My time is up;
and I must cease.

Analyzing This Selection

1. In the first two paragraphs, what relation does Woolf establish with her audience?
   What details make her appear ingratiating? condescending? earnest?

2. Does the Angel in the House still exist? What has changed, and what remains the
   same, in present-day expectations of women?

3. Does Woolf assume that men writers encounter no difficulties or conflicts in
   thinking independently and expressing themselves? Is Woolf a female sexist in
   some of her observations?

4. What relationships between men and women are implied in Woolf's many
   references to women in a house and a room? What changes in the future are
   suggested by the metaphorical use of "house" in the final paragraph?

Analyzing Connections

5. Describe the qualities of the Angel that Nancy Friday encountered in her house
   (see "Competition," p. 71). Did Friday kill it?

Analyzing by Writing

6. Should young men and women ever be educated separately for part of their lives? At what age can it do the most good or the most harm to change or reinforce gender roles through separate schools or separate classes? Draw on any of your relevant experiences in single-sex associations such as scouting, sports, clubs, and being with just "the boys" or "the girls." Consider what it has meant to you to have these associations, and how they might have been more beneficial, or less limiting, than they were.

Amy Tan

MOTHER TONGUE

◊

AMY TAN (b. 1952), the daughter of Chinese immigrants, grew up in California and graduated from San Jose State University. She began a business career writing speeches and reports for corporate executives. She turned to fiction writing as part of her remedy for workaholism. Tan's first novel, *The Joy Luck Club* (1989), recounts interconnected stories of conflict and loyalty between Chinese mothers and their American-born daughters. The novel was made into a popular movie. Tan's second novel, *The Kitchen God's Wife* (1991), focuses on a Chinese woman resembling Tan's mother in the following essay, which appeared first in *Threepenny Review* (1990).

I am not a scholar of English or literature. I cannot give you much more 1
than personal opinions on the English language and its variations in this
country or others.

I am a writer. And by that definition, I am someone who has always loved 2
language. I am fascinated by language in daily life. I spend a great deal of my
time thinking about the power of language — the way it can evoke an
emotion, a visual image, a complex idea, or a simple truth. Language is the
tool of my trade. And I use them all — all the Englishes I grew up with.

Recently, I was made keenly aware of the different Englishes I do use. I 3
was giving a talk to a large group of people, the same talk I had already given
to half a dozen other groups. The nature of the talk was about my writing,
my life, and my book, *The Joy Luck Club*. The talk was going along well
enough, until I remembered one major difference that made the whole talk
sound wrong. My mother was in the room. And it was perhaps the first time
she had heard me give a lengthy speech, using the kind of English I have
never used with her. I was saying things like, "The intersection of memory
upon imagination" and "There is an aspect of my fiction that relates to
thus-and-thus" — a speech filled with carefully wrought grammatical
phrases, burdened, it suddenly seemed to me, with nominalized forms, past
perfect tenses, conditional phrases, all the forms of standard English that I
had learned in school and through books, the forms of English I did not use
at home with my mother.

Just last week, I was walking down the street with my mother, and I again 4
found myself conscious of the English I was using, the English I do use with

her. We were talking about the price of new and used furniture and I heard myself saying this: "Not waste money that way." My husband was with us as well, and he didn't notice any switch in my English. And then I realized why. It's because over the twenty years we've been together I've often used that same kind of English with him, and sometimes he even uses it with me. It has become our language of intimacy, a different sort of English that relates to family talk, the language I grew up with.

So you'll have some idea of what this family talk I heard sounds like, 5 I'll quote what my mother said during a recent conversation which I videotaped and then transcribed. During this conversation, my mother was talking about a political gangster in Shanghai who had the same last name as her family's, Du, and how the gangster in his early years wanted to be adopted by her family, which was rich by comparison. Later, the gangster became more powerful, far richer than my mother's family, and one day showed up at my mother's wedding to pay his respects. Here's what she said in part:

"Du Yusong having business like fruit stand. Like off the street kind. He 6 is Du like Du Zong — but not Tsung-ming Island people. The local people call putong, the river east side, he belong to that side local people. That man want to ask Du Zong father take him in like become own family. Du Zong father wasn't look down on him, but didn't take seriously, until that man big like become a mafia. Now important person, very hard to inviting him. Chinese way, came only to show respect, don't stay for dinner. Respect for making big celebration, he shows up. Mean gives lots of respect. Chinese custom. Chinese social life that way. If too important won't have to stay too long. He come to my wedding. I didn't see, I heard it. I gone to boy's side, they have YMCA dinner. Chinese age I was nineteen."

You should know that my mother's expressive command of English belies 7 how much she actually understands. She reads the *Forbes* report, listens to *Wall Street Week*, converses daily with her stockbroker, reads all of Shirley MacLaine's books with ease — all kinds of things I can't begin to understand. Yet some of my friends tell me they understand 50 percent of what my mother says. Some say they understand 80 to 90 percent. Some say they understand none of it, as if she were speaking pure Chinese. But to me, my mother's English is perfectly clear, perfectly natural. It's my mother tongue. Her language, as I hear it, is vivid, direct, full of observation and imagery. That was the language that helped shape the way I saw things, expressed things, made sense of the world.

Lately, I've been giving more thought to the kind of English my mother 8 speaks. Like others, I have described it to people as "broken" or "fractured" English. But I wince when I say that. It has always bothered me that I can think of no way to describe it other than "broken," as if it were damaged and needed to be fixed, as if it lacked a certain wholeness and soundness. I've heard other terms used, "limited English," for example. But they seem just as bad, as if everything is limited, including people's perceptions of the limited English speaker.

I know this for a fact, because when I was growing up, my mother's 9 "limited" English limited *my* perception of her. I was ashamed of her English. I believed that her English reflected the quality of what she had to say. That is, because she expressed them imperfectly her thoughts were imperfect. And I had plenty of empirical evidence to support me: the fact that people in department stores, at banks, and at restaurants did not take her seriously, did not give her good service, pretended not to understand her, or even acted as if they did not hear her.

My mother has long realized the limitations of her English as well. When 10 I was fifteen, she used to have me call people on the phone to pretend I was she. In this guise, I was forced to ask for information or even to complain and yell at people who had been rude to her. One time it was a call to her stockbroker in New York. She had cashed out her small portfolio and it just so happened we were going to go to New York the next week, our very first trip outside California. I had to get on the phone and say in an adolescent voice that was not very convincing, "This is Mrs. Tan."

And my mother was standing in the back whispering loudly, "Why he 11 don't send me check, already two weeks late. So mad he lie to me, losing me money."

And then I said in perfect English, "Yes, I'm getting rather concerned. 12 You had agreed to send the check two weeks ago, but it hasn't arrived."

Then she began to talk more loudly. "What he want, I come to New York 13 tell him front of his boss, you cheating me?" And I was trying to calm her down, make her be quiet, while telling the stockbroker, "I can't tolerate any more excuses. If I don't receive the check immediately, I am going to have to speak to your manager when I'm in New York next week." And sure enough, the following week there we were in front of this astonished stockbroker, and I was sitting there red-faced and quiet, and my mother, the real Mrs. Tan, was shouting at his boss in her impeccable broken English.

We used a similar routine just five days ago, for a situation that was far less 14 humorous. My mother had gone to the hospital for an appointment, to find out about a benign brain tumor a CAT scan had revealed a month ago. She said she had spoken very good English, her best English, no mistakes. Still, she said, the hospital did not apologize when they said they had lost the CAT scan and she had come for nothing. She said they did not seem to have any sympathy when she told them she was anxious to know the exact diagnosis, since her husband and son had both died of brain tumors. She said they would not give her any more information until the next time and she would have to make another appointment for that. So she said she would not leave until the doctor called her daughter. She wouldn't budge. And when the doctor finally called her daughter, me, who spoke in perfect English — lo and behold — we had assurances the CAT scan would be found, promises that a conference call on Monday would be held, and apologies for any suffering my mother had gone through for a most regrettable mistake.

I think my mother's English almost had an effect on limiting my possi- 15
bilities in life as well. Sociologists and linguists probably will tell you that a person's developing language skills are more influenced by peers. But I do think that the language spoken in the family, especially in immigrant families which are more insular, plays a large role in shaping the language of the child. And I believe that it affected my results on achievement tests, IQ tests, and the SAT. While my English skills were never judged as poor, compared to math, English could not be considered my strong suit. In grade school I did moderately well, getting perhaps B's, sometimes B-pluses, in English and scoring perhaps in the sixtieth or seventieth percentile on achievement tests. But those scores were not good enough to override the opinion that my true abilities lay in math and science, because in those areas I achieved A's and scored in the ninetieth percentile or higher.

This was understandable. Math is precise; there is only one correct answer. 16
Whereas, for me at least, the answers on English tests were always a judgment call, a matter of opinion and personal experience. Those tests were constructed around items like fill-in-the-blank sentence completion, such as, "Even though Tom was_____, Mary thought he was_____." And the correct answer always seemed to be the most bland combinations of thoughts, for example, "Even though Tom was shy, Mary thought he was charming," with the grammatical structure "even though" limiting the correct answer to some sort of semantic opposites, so you wouldn't get answers like, "Even though Tom was foolish, Mary thought he was ridiculous." Well, according to my mother, there were very few limitations as to what Tom could have been and what Mary might have thought of him. So I never did well on tests like that.

The same was true with word analogies, pairs of words in which you were 17
supposed to find some sort of logical, semantic relationship — for example, "*Sunset* is to *nightfall* as _____ is to _____." And here you would be presented with a list of four possible pairs, one of which showed the same kind of relationship: *red* is to *stoplight*, *bus* is to *arrival*, *chills* is to *fever*, *yawn* is to *boring*. Well, I could never think that way. I knew what the tests were asking, but I could not block out of my mind the images already created by the first pair, "*sunset* is to *nightfall*" — and I would see a burst of colors against a darkening sky, the moon rising, the lowering of a curtain of stars. And all the other pairs of words — red, bus, stoplight, boring — just threw up a mass of confusing images, making it impossible for me to sort out something as logical as saying: "A sunset precedes nightfall" is the same as "a chill precedes a fever." The only way I would have gotten that answer right would have been to imagine an associative situation, for example, my being disobedient and staying out past sunset, catching a chill at night, which turns into feverish pneumonia as punishment, which indeed did happen to me.

I have been thinking about all this lately, about my mother's English, 18
about achievement tests. Because lately I've been asked, as a writer, why
there are not more Asian Americans represented in American literature.
Why are there few Asian Americans enrolled in creative writing programs?
Why do so many Chinese students go into engineering? Well, these are
broad sociological questions I can't begin to answer. But I have noticed in
surveys — in fact, just last week — that Asian students, as a whole, always do
significantly better on math achievement tests than in English. And this
makes me think that there are other Asian-American students whose English
spoken in the home might also be described as "broken" or "limited." And
perhaps they also have teachers who are steering them away from writing and
into math and science, which is what happened to me.

Fortunately, I happen to be rebellious in nature and enjoy the challenge 19
of disproving assumptions made about me. I became an English major my
first year in college, after being enrolled as pre-med. I started writing
nonfiction as a freelancer the week after I was told by my former boss that
writing was my worst skill and I should hone my talents toward account
management.

But it wasn't until 1985 that I finally began to write fiction. And at first I 20
wrote using what I thought to be wittily crafted sentences, sentences that
would finally prove I had mastery over the English language. Here's an
example from the first draft of a story that later made its way into *The Joy
Luck Club*, but without this line: "That was my mental quandary in its
nascent state." A terrible line, which I can barely pronounce.

Fortunately, for reasons I won't get into today, I later decided I should 21
envision a reader for the stories I would write. And the reader I decided upon
was my mother, because these were stories about mothers. So with this
reader in mind — and in fact she did read my early drafts — I began to write
stories using all the Englishes I grew up with: the English I spoke to my
mother, which for lack of a better term might be described as "simple"; the
English she used with me, which for lack of a better term might be described
as "broken"; my translation of her Chinese, which could certainly be described as "watered down"; and what I imagined to be her translation of her
Chinese if she could speak in perfect English, her internal language, and for
that I sought to preserve the essence, but neither an English nor a Chinese
structure. I wanted to capture what language ability tests can never reveal: her
intent, her passion, her imagery, the rhythms of her speech and the nature
of her thoughts.

Apart from what any critic had to say about my writing, I knew I had 22
succeeded where it counted when my mother finished reading my book and
gave me her verdict: "So easy to read."

Analyzing This Selection

1. The author starts by emphasizing her professional viewpoint. What focus and freedoms does she claim through her profession?

2. In paragraph 7, Tan says: "It's my mother tongue." To be more precise, it is her *mother's* tongue. What is the difference? And why does Tan make this pun?

3. What is Tan's tone toward her mother? Find details that indicate her feelings and attitudes in their relationship. How have they changed through the years?

4. Explain why the author had so much trouble with SAT tests. What is her criticism of language ability tests?

5. How would you translate the mother's verdict on Tan's novel?

Analyzing Connections

6. Tan and Virginia Woolf (in the preceding selection) faced different barriers to becoming writers. What similar lessons did they have to learn?

Analyzing by Writing

7. Should schools offer bilingual education to children of minority groups? Or perhaps to everyone? Consider positive and negative effects of having a single public language in a multicultural society. Tan points out some of the routine or extreme mistreatment endured by people (both old and young) who do not speak standard English. Richard Rodriguez (see "Reading for Success," p. 208) points out effects of schools excluding the language used at home. What do you think should be a school's policy about using English?

Tillie Olsen

I STAND HERE IRONING

◇

TILLIE OLSEN (b. 1913) dropped out of high school in Nebraska at fifteen in order to help support her family during the Depression. She held jobs as a factory worker or secretary while she organized labor unions, got married, raised four children, and continued to read prodigiously. "Public libraries were my college," she has said. When she was forty, she resumed her early efforts to write fiction. She enrolled in a class in fiction writing at San Francisco State College, and later she won a writing fellowship at Stanford University. Her volume of stories, *Tell Me a Riddle* (1961), established her as a sensitively compassionate and politically radical champion of the poor and overburdened. In *Silences* (1978), a collection of essays, Olsen examines the injustices of social class, racism, and sexism that hinder creativity, particularly in women. The cruelty of harmful social conditions is a theme in all her work, including the following story, which reflects harsh realities she faced in her own life.

I stand here ironing, and what you asked me moves tormented back and forth with the iron.

"I wish you would manage the time to come in and talk with me about your daughter. I'm sure you can help me understand her. She's a youngster who needs help and whom I'm deeply interested in helping."

"Who needs help." . . . Even if I came, what good would it do? You think because I am her mother I have a key, or that in some way you could use me as a key? She has lived for nineteen years. There is all that life that has happened outside of me, beyond me.

And when is there time to remember, to sift, to weigh, to estimate, to total? I will start and there will be an interruption and I will have to gather it all together again. Or I will become engulfed with all I did or did not do, with what should have been and what cannot be helped.

She was a beautiful baby. The first and only one of our five that was beautiful at birth. You do not guess how new and uneasy her tenancy in her now-loveliness. You did not know her all those years she was thought homely, or see her poring over her baby pictures, making me tell her over and over how beautiful she had been — and would be, I would tell her — and was now, to the seeing eye. But the seeing eyes were few or nonexistent. Including mine.

I nursed her. They feel that's important nowadays. I nursed all the 6
children, but with her, with all the fierce rigidity of first motherhood, I did
like the books then said. Though her cries battered me to trembling and my
breasts ached with swollenness, I waited till the clock decreed.

Why do I put that first? I do not even know if it matters, or if it explains 7
anything.

She was a beautiful baby. She blew shining bubbles of sound. She loved 8
motion, loved light, loved color and music and textures. She would lie on
the floor in her blue overalls patting the surface so hard in ecstasy her hands
and feet would blur. She was a miracle to me, but when she was eight
months old I had to leave her daytimes with the woman downstairs to whom
she was no miracle at all, for I worked or looked for work and for Emily's
father, who "could no longer endure" (he wrote in his good-bye note)
"sharing want with us."

I was nineteen, it was the pre-relief, pre-WPA world of the Depression. I 9
would start running as soon as I got off the streetcar, running up the stairs,
the place smelling sour, and awake or asleep to startle awake, when she saw
me she would break into a clogged weeping that could not be comforted, a
weeping I can hear yet.

After a while I found a job hashing at night so I could be with her days, 10
and it was better. But it came to where I had to bring her to his family and
leave her.

It took a long time to raise the money for her fare back. Then she got 11
chicken pox and I had to wait longer. When she finally came, I hardly knew
her, walking quick and nervous like her father, looking like her father, thin,
and dressed in a shoddy red that yellowed her skin and glared at the pock-
marks. All the baby loveliness gone.

She was two. Old enough for nursery school they said, and I did not know 12
then what I know now — the fatigue of the long day, and the lacerations of
group life in the kinds of nurseries that are only parking places for children.

Except that it would have made no difference if I had known. It was the 13
only place there was. It was the only way we could be together, the only way
I could hold a job.

And even without knowing, I knew. I knew the teacher that was evil 14
because all these years it has curdled into my memory, the little boy hunched
in the corner, her rasp, "why aren't you outside, because Alvin hits you?
that's no reason, go out, scaredy." I knew Emily hated it even if she did not
clutch and implore "don't go Mommy" like the other children, mornings.

She always had a reason why we should stay home. Momma, you look 15
sick. Momma, I feel sick. Momma, the teachers aren't there today, they're
sick. Momma, we can't go, there was a fire there last night. Momma, it's a
holiday today, no school, they told me.

But never a direct protest, never rebellion. I think of our others in their 16
three-, four-year-oldness — the explosions, the tempers, the denunciations,
the demands — and I feel suddenly ill. I put the iron down. What in me

demanded that goodness in her? And what was the cost, the cost to her of such goodness?

The old man living in the back once said in his gentle way: "You should 17 smile at Emily more when you look at her." What *was* in my face when I looked at her? I loved her. There were all the acts of love.

It was only with the others I remembered what he said, and it was the face 18 of joy, and not of care or tightness or worry I turned to them — too late for Emily. She does not smile easily, let alone almost always as her brothers and sisters do. Her face is closed and somber, but when she wants, how fluid. You must have seen it in her pantomimes, you spoke of her rare gift for comedy on the stage that rouses a laughter out of the audience so dear they applaud and applaud and do not want to let her go.

Where does it come from, that comedy? There was none of it in her when 19 she came back to me that second time, after I had had to send her away again. She had a new daddy now to learn to love, and I think perhaps it was a better time.

Except when we left her alone nights, telling ourselves she was old 20 enough.

"Can't you go some other time, Mommy, like tomorrow?" she would ask. 21 "Will it be just a little while you'll be gone? Do you promise?"

The time we came back, the front door open, the clock on the floor in the 22 hall. She rigid awake. "It wasn't just a little while. I didn't cry. Three times I called you, just three times, and then I ran downstairs to open the door so you could come faster. The clock talked loud. I threw it away, it scared me what it talked."

She said the clock talked loud again that night I went to the hospital to 23 have Susan. She was delirious with the fever that comes before red measles, but she was fully conscious all the week I was gone and the week after we were home when she could not come near the new baby or me.

She did not get well. She stayed skeleton thin, not wanting to eat, and night 24 after night she had nightmares. She would call for me, and I would rouse from exhaustion to sleepily call back: "You're all right, darling, go to sleep, it's just a dream," and if she still called, in a sterner voice, "now go to sleep, Emily, there's nothing to hurt you." Twice, only twice, when I had to get up for Susan anyhow, I went in to sit with her.

Now when it is too late (as if she would let me hold and comfort her like 25 I do the others) I get up and go to her at once at her moan or restless stirring. "Are you awake, Emily? Can I get you something?" And the answer is always the same. "No, I'm all right, go back to sleep, Mother."

They persuaded me at the clinic to send her away to a convalescent home 26 in the country where "she can have the kind of food and care you can't manage for her, and you'll be free to concentrate on the new baby." They still send children to that place. I see pictures on the society page of sleek young women planning affairs to raise money for it, or dancing at the affairs, or decorating Easter eggs or filling Christmas stockings for the children.

They never have a picture of the children so I do not know if the girls still 27 wear those gigantic red bows and the ravaged looks on the every other Sunday when parents can come to visit "unless otherwise notified" — as we were notified the first six weeks.

Oh it is a handsome place, green lawns and tall trees and fluted flower 28 beds. High up on the balconies of each cottage the children stand, the girls in their red bows and white dresses, the boys in white suits and gigantic red ties. The parents stand below shrieking up to be heard and the children shriek down to be heard, and between them the invisible wall "Not To Be Contaminated by Parental Germs or Physical Affection."

There was a tiny girl who always stood hand in hand with Emily. Her 29 parents never came. One visit she was gone. "They moved her to Rose Cottage," Emily shouted in explanation. "They don't like you to love anybody here."

She wrote once a week, the labored writings of a seven-year-old. "I am 30 fine. How is the baby. If I write my leter nicly I will have a star. Love." There never was a star. We wrote every other day, letters she could never hold or keep but only hear read — once. "We simply do not have room for children to keep any personal possessions," they patiently explained when we pieced one Sunday's shrieking together to plead how much it would mean to Emily, who loved so to keep things, to be allowed to keep her letters and cards.

Each visit she looked frailer. "She isn't eating," they told us. 31

(They had runny eggs for breakfast or mush with lumps, Emily said later, 32 I'd hold it in my mouth and not swallow. Nothing ever tasted good, just when they had chicken.)

It took us eight months to get her released home, and only the fact that 33 she gained back so little of her seven lost pounds convinced the social worker.

I used to try to hold and love her after she came back, but her body would 34 stay stiff, and after a while she'd push away. She ate little. Food sickened her, and I think much of life too. Oh she had physical lightness and brightness, twinkling by on skates, bouncing like a ball up and down up and down over the jump rope, skimming over the hill; but these were momentary.

She fretted about her appearance, thin and dark and foreign-looking at a 35 time when every little girl was supposed to look or thought she should look like a chubby blonde replica of Shirley Temple. The doorbell sometimes rang for her, but no one seemed to come and play in the house or be a best friend. Maybe because we moved so much.

There was a boy she loved painfully through two school semesters. Months 36 later she told me how she had taken pennies from my purse to buy him candy. "Licorice was his favorite and I brought him some every day, but he still liked Jennifer better'n me. Why, Mommy?" The kind of question for which there is no answer.

School was a worry to her. She was not glib or quick in a world where 37 glibness and quickness were easily confused with ability to learn. To her overworked and exasperated teachers she was an over-conscientious "slow learner" who kept trying to catch up and was absent entirely too often.

I let her be absent, though sometimes the illness was imaginary. How 38 different from my now-strictness about attendance with the others. I wasn't working. We had a new baby, I was home anyhow. Sometimes, after Susan grew old enough, I would keep her home from school, too, to have them all together.

Mostly Emily had asthma, and her breathing, harsh and labored, would fill 39 the house with a curiously tranquil sound. I would bring the two old dresser mirrors and her boxes of collections to her bed. She would select beads and single earrings, bottle tops and shells, dried flowers and pebbles, old postcards and scraps, all sorts of oddments; then she and Susan would play Kingdom, setting up landscapes and furniture, peopling them with action.

Those were the only times of peaceful companionship between her and 40 Susan. I have edged away from it, that poisonous feeling between them, that terrible balancing of hurts and needs I had to do between the two, and did so badly, those earlier years.

Oh there are conflicts between the others too, each one human, needing, 41 demanding, hurting, taking — but only between Emily and Susan, no, Emily toward Susan that corroding resentment. It seems so obvious on the surface, yet it is not obvious. Susan, the second child, Susan, golden- and curly-haired and chubby, quick and articulate and assured, everything in appearance and manner Emily was not; Susan, not able to resist Emily's precious things, losing or sometimes clumsily breaking them; Susan telling jokes and riddles to company for applause while Emily sat silent (to say to me later: That was *my* riddle, Mother, I told it to Susan); Susan, who for all the five years' difference in age was just a year behind Emily in developing physically.

I am glad for that slow physical development that widened the difference 42 between her and her contemporaries, though she suffered over it. She was too vulnerable for that terrible world of youthful competition, of preening and parading, of constant measuring of yourself against every other, of envy, "If I had that copper hair," "If I had that skin. . . ." She tormented herself enough about not looking like the others, there was enough of the unsureness, the having to be conscious of words before you speak, the constant caring — what are they thinking of me? without having it all magnified by the merciless physical drives.

Ronnie is calling. He is wet and I change him. It is rare there is such a cry 43 now. That time of motherhood is almost behind me when the ear is not one's own but must always be racked and listening for the child cry, the child call. We sit for a while and I hold him, looking out over the city spread in charcoal with its soft aisles of light. "*Shoogily,*" he breathes and curls closer. I carry him back to bed, asleep. *Shoogily.* A funny word, a family word, inherited from Emily, invented by her to say: *comfort.*

In this and other ways she leaves her seal, I say aloud. And startle at me 44
saying it. What do I mean? What did I start to gather together, to try and
make coherent? I was at the terrible, growing years. War years. I do not
remember them well. I was working, there were four smaller ones now, there
was not time for her. She had to help be a mother, and housekeeper, and
shopper. She had to set her seal. Mornings of crisis and near hysteria trying
to get lunches packed, hair combed, coats and shoes found, everyone to
school or Child Care on time, the baby ready for transportation. And always
the paper scribbled on by a smaller one, the book looked at by Susan then
mislaid, the homework not done. Running out to that huge school where she
was one, she was lost, she was a drop; suffering over her unpreparedness,
stammering and unsure in her classes.

There was so little time left at night after the kids were bedded down. She 45
would struggle over books, always eating (it was in those years she developed
her enormous appetite that is legendary in our family) and I would be
ironing, or preparing food for the next day, or writing V-mail to Bill, or
tending the baby. Sometimes, to make me laugh, or out of her despair, she
would imitate happenings or types at school.

I think I said once: "Why don't you do something like this in the school 46
amateur show?" One morning she phoned me at work, hardly understandable through the weeping: "Mother, I did it. I won, I won; they gave me first
prize; they clapped and clapped and wouldn't let me go."

Now suddenly she was Somebody, and as imprisoned in her difference as 47
she had been in anonymity.

She began to be asked to perform at other high schools, even in colleges, 48
then at city and statewide affairs. The first one we went to, I only recognized
her that first moment when thin, shy, she almost drowned herself into the
curtains. Then: Was this Emily? The control, the command, the convulsing
and deadly drowning, the spell, then the roaring, stamping audience, unwilling to let this rare and precious laughter out of their lives.

Afterwards: You ought to do something about her with a gift like that — but 49
without money or knowing how, what does one do? We have left it all to her,
and the gift has as often eddied inside, clogged and clotted, as been used and
growing.

She is coming. She runs up the stairs two at a time with her light graceful 50
step, and I know she is happy tonight. Whatever it was that occasioned your
call did not happen today.

"Aren't you ever going to finish the ironing, Mother? Whistler painted his 51
mother in a rocker. I'd have to paint mine standing over an ironing board."
This is one of her communicative nights and she tells me everything and
nothing as she fixes herself a plate of food out of the icebox.

She is so lovely. Why did you want me to come in at all? Why were you 52
concerned? She will find her way.

She starts up the stairs to bed. "Don't get me up with the rest in the 53 morning." "But I thought you were having midterms." "Oh, those," she comes back in, kisses me, and says quite lightly, "in a couple of years when we'll be all atom-dead they won't matter a bit."

She has said it before. She *believes* it. But because I have been dredging the past, and all that compounds a human being is so heavy and meaningful in me, I cannot endure it tonight. 54

I will never total it all. I will never come in to say: She was a child seldom smiled at. Her father left me before she was a year old. I had to work her first six years when there was work, or I sent her home and to his relatives. There were years she had care she hated. She was dark and thin and foreign-looking in a world where the prestige went to blondeness and curly hair and dimples, she was slow where glibness was prized. She was a child of anxious, not proud, love. We were poor and could not afford for her the soil of easy growth. I was a younger mother, I was a distracted mother. There were the other children pushing up, demanding. Her younger sister seemed all that she was not. There were years she did not want me to touch her. She kept too much in herself, her life was such she had to keep too much in herself. My wisdom came too late. She has much to her and probably little will come of it. She is a child of her age, of depression, of war, of fear. 55

Let her be. So all that is in her will not bloom — but in how many does it? There is still enough left to live by. Only help her to know — help make it so there is cause for her to know — that she is more than this dress on the ironing board, helpless before the iron. 56

Analyzing This Selection

1. Who has phoned Emily's mother? How has the caller's request affected the mother?

2. Does the mother blame herself too much or too little for causing Emily's hardships? At which points do you disagree with the mother's judgment of her own actions?

3. How did Emily differ from her brothers and sisters? What explanations does the mother have for Emily's difference? Which of her explanations do you think are most valid and important?

4. In the final two paragraphs, why does the mother refuse to consult about Emily?

5. Does the story reflect specific political views toward particular social conditions and historical events? What social attitudes, if any, does the story stimulate in the reader?

6. To what extent do the mother's aspirations for Emily reflect her own?

Analyzing Connections

7. Emily and FaNee (see "It's Just Too Late," p. 108) cause problems for their parents. What lessons have the parents learned?

Analyzing by Writing

8. How would a child like Emily perceive her mother's conflict of responsibilities? What problems do you think the child faced? Adopt Emily's viewpoint in a monologue (like this story) that explores Emily's thoughts during any one incident or situation suggested in the fiction.

PART 5

GROUP PICTURES

INSIGHTS

No man is an island, entire of itself; every man is a piece of the continent, a part of the main; if a clod be washed away by the sea, Europe is less, as well as if a promontory were, as well as if a manor of thy friends or of thine own were; any man's death diminishes me, because I am involved in mankind; and therefore never send to know for whom the bell tolls: it tolls for thee.

— JOHN DONNE

◇

Hell is other people.

— JEAN-PAUL SARTRE

◇

Society everywhere is in conspiracy against the manhood of every one of its members. Society is a joint-stock company, in which the members agree, for the better securing of his bread to each shareholder, to surrender the liberty and culture of the eater. The virtue in most request is conformity. Self-reliance is its aversion. It loves not realities and creators, but names and customs. Who would be a man, must be a nonconformist.

— RALPH WALDO EMERSON

◇

Being ashamed of one's parents is, psychologically, not identical with being ashamed of one's people. I believe every one of us will, if he but digs deeply enough into the realm of unconscious memories, remember having been ashamed of his parents. Being ashamed of our people must have another psychological meaning. It must be the expression of a tendency to disavow the most essential part of ourself. To be ashamed of being Jewish means not only to be a coward and insincere in disavowing the proud inheritance of an old people who have made an eternal contribution to the civilization of mankind. It also means to disavow the best and the most precious part we get from our parents, their parents, and their ancestors, who continue to live in us. It means, furthermore, to renounce oneself. When the Jewish proverb proclaims that he who is ashamed of his family will have no luck in life, it must mean just that: he cannot have that self-confidence which makes life worth living. Strange that the folklore of an oriental people

242

coincides here with the viewpoint of Goethe; any life can be lived if one does not miss oneself, if one but remains oneself.

The thought that my children are sometimes ashamed of the human faults and failings of their father does not sadden me; but, for their own sake, I wish that they will never be ashamed that their father was Jewish. The one feeling concerns only the personal shortcomings of an individual who was striving, sometimes succeeding and often failing. The other shame concerns something superpersonal, something beyond the narrow realm of the individual. It concerns the community of fate, it touches the bond that ties one generation to those preceding it and those following it.

— THEODOR REIK

◇

It is difficult to let others see the full psychological meaning of caste segregation. It is as though one, looking out from a dark cave in a side of an impending mountain, sees the world passing and speaks to it; speaks courteously and persuasively, showing them how these entombed souls are hindered in their natural movement, expression, and development; and how their loosening from prison would be a matter not simply of courtesy, sympathy, and help to them, but aid to all the world. One talks on evenly and logically in this way, but notices that the passing throng does not even turn its head, or if it does, glances curiously and walks on. It gradually penetrates the minds of the prisoners that the people passing do not hear; that some thick sheet of invisible but horribly tangible plate glass is between them and the world. They get excited; they talk louder; they gesticulate. Some of the passing world stop in curiosity; these gesticulations seem so pointless; they laugh and pass on. They still either do not hear at all, or hear but dimly, and even what they hear, they do not understand. Then the people within may become hysterical. They may scream and hurl themselves against the barriers, hardly realizing in their bewilderment that they are screaming in a vacuum unheard and that their antics may actually seem funny to those outside looking in. They may even, here and there, break through in blood and disfigurement, and find themselves faced by a horrified, implacable, and quite overwhelming mob of people frightened for their own very existence.

— W. E. B. DUBOIS

◇

The New Colossus

Not like the brazen giant of Greek fame,
With conquering limbs astride from land to land;
Here at our sea-washed, sunset gates shall stand
A mighty woman with a torch, whose flame
Is the imprisoned lightning, and her name

Mother of Exiles. From her beacon-hand
Glows world-wide welcome; her mild eyes command
The air-bridged harbor that twin cities frame.
"Keep, ancient lands, your storied pomp!" cries she
With silent lips. "Give me your tired, your poor,
Your huddled masses yearning to breathe free,
The wretched refuse of your teeming shore.
Send these, the homeless, tempest-tost to me,
I lift my lamp beside the golden door!"

— EMMA LAZARUS

◇

The brotherhood of man is not a mere poet's dream; it is a most depressing
and humiliating reality.

— OSCAR WILDE

◇

Among aristocratic nations families maintain the same station for centuries and often live in the same place. So there is a sense in which all the
generations are contemporaneous. A man almost always knows about his
ancestors and respects them; his imagination extends to his great-
grandchildren, and he loves them. He freely does his duty by both ancestors
and descendants and often sacrifices personal pleasures for the sake of beings
who are no longer alive or are not yet born.

Moreover, aristocratic institutions have the effect of linking each man
closely with several of his fellows.

Each class is an aristocratic society, being clearly and permanently limited, forms, in a sense, a little fatherland for all its members, to which they
are attached by more obvious and more precious ties than those linking them
to the fatherland itself.

Each citizen of an aristocratic society has his fixed station, one above
another, so that there is always someone above him whose protection he
needs and someone below him whose help he may require.

So people living in an aristocratic age are almost always closely involved
with something outside themselves, and they are often inclined to forget
about themselves. It is true that in these ages the general conception of
human fellowship is dim and that men hardly ever think of devoting themselves to the cause of humanity, but men do often make sacrifices for the sake
of certain other men.

In democratic ages, on the contrary, the duties of each to all are much
clearer but devoted service to any individual much rarer. The bonds of
human affection are wider but more relaxed.

Among democratic peoples new families continually rise from nothing
while others fall, and nobody's position is quite stable. The woof of time is

ever being broken and the track of past generations lost. Those who have gone before are easily forgotten, and no one gives a thought to those who will follow. All a man's interests are limited to those near himself.

As each class catches up with the next and gets mixed with it, its members do not care about one another and treat one another as strangers. Aristocracy links everybody, from peasant to king, in one long chain. Democracy breaks the chain and frees each link.

As social equality spreads there are more and more people who, though neither rich nor powerful enough to have much hold over others, have gained or kept enough wealth and enough understanding to look after their own needs. Such folk owe no man anything and hardly expect anything from anybody. They form the habit of thinking of themselves in isolation and imagine that their whole destiny is in their own hands.

Thus, not only does democracy make men forget their ancestors, but also clouds their view of their descendants and isolates them from their contemporaries. Each man is forever thrown back on himself alone, and there is danger that he may be shut up in the solitude of his own heart.

— ALEXIS DE TOCQUEVILLE

◇

The "natural" approach to human relations presumes to know any person well enough is to love him, that the only human problem is a communication problem. This denies that people might be separated by basic, genuinely irreconcilable differences — philosophical, political, or religious — and assumes that all such differences are no more than misunderstandings.

Many forms of etiquette are employed precisely to disguise those antipathies that arise from irreconcilable differences, in order to prevent mayhem. The reason that diplomacy, for example, is so stilted is that its purpose is to head off the most natural social relation between countries in conflict, namely war.

The idea that people can behave "naturally" without resorting to an artificial code tacitly agreed upon by their society is as silly as the idea that they can communicate by using a language without commonly accepted semantic and grammatical rules. Like language, a code of manners can be used with more or less skill, for laudable or evil purposes, to express a great variety of ideas and emotions. Like language, manners continually undergo slow changes and adaptations, but these changes have to be global, not atomic. For if everyone improvises his own manners, no one will understand the meaning of anyone else's behavior, and the result will be social chaos and the end of civilization, or about what we have now.

— JUDITH MARTIN ("Miss Manners")

FOCUSING BY WRITING

1. If you had to choose among the natural dwelling places of animals, what fantasy home would be suitable for you? You might prefer to live in a robin's nest, a beaver lodge, a rabbit warren, a bear's cave, an ant colony, a beehive, an eagle's aerie, a wasp's nest, a fox's lair, a lion's den. (Do not pick manmade places such as a doghouse or fishbowl.) Describe some concrete details of your primal dwelling place. Why would it feel good to live there?

2. You must know someone you could call a "total jerk" — that is, someone who never knows the right way to act. Explain the code of behavior that this person does not follow. Do not just relate an anecdote that ridicules someone. Focus on explaining the accepted standard of behavior that this person consistently violates.

3. What particular place has made you aware of your entire country? It might be a historical site, a busy city street, or a wilderness area, a schoolyard, a game, a mall, or any place that at a specific moment epitomized America — for better or worse. Describe the place, giving the concrete details that affected you with their national symbolism.

4. As a tourist in a foreign country, as a visitor to a large city, or as a prefreshman interviewee on a college campus, were you self-conscious about being an outsider? Were you embarrassed to be seen as distinguishable from the local people? What kind of exposure did you wish to cover up? Conversely, what did you try to emphasize or exaggerate about yourself?

Barbara Grizzuti Harrison

GROWING UP APOCALYPTIC

◇

BARBARA GRIZZUTI HARRISON (b. 1934), a feminist writer and critical observer of the American scene, was born in Brooklyn, New York. Roman Catholic for her first nine years, Harrison, together with her mother, converted to the Jehovah's Witnesses. At the age of twenty-two, she rejected the faith. She wrote an account of her religious upbringing in *Visions of Glory: A History and a Memory of Jehovah's Witness* (1978). Always sensitive to women's issues, Harrison examined the effects of public education in *Unlearning the Lie: Sexism in School* (1973). Her essays on literature, politics, and popular culture have appeared in magazines such as *Ms.*, *Esquire*, and *The New Republic*, and they have been collected in *Off Center* (1980). She recounts her travels through the land of her ancestry in *Italian Days* (1989). Two years after the following autobiographical essay first appeared in *Ms.* in 1975, Harrison converted back to Catholicism — a "return," she notes, that surprised her.

"The trouble with you," Anna said, in a voice in which compassion, 1 disgust, and reproach fought for equal time, "is that you can't remember what it was like to be young. And even if you could remember — well, when you were my age, you were in that crazy Jehovah's Witness religion, and you probably didn't even play spin the bottle."

Anna, my prepubescent eleven-year-old, feels sorry for me because I did 2 not have "a normal childhood." It has never occurred to her to question whether her childhood is "normal" . . . which is to say, she is happy. She cannot conceive of a life in which one is not free to move around, explore, argue, flirt with ideas and dismiss them, form passionate alliances and friendships according to no imperative but one's own nature and volition; she regards love as unconditional, she expects nurturance as her birthright. It fills her with terror and pity that anyone — especially her mother — could have grown up any differently — could have grown up in a religion where love was conditional upon rigid adherence to dogma and established practice . . . where approval had to be bought from authoritarian sources . . . where people did not fight openly and love fiercely and forgive generously and make decisions of their own and mistakes of their own and have adventures of their own.

"Poor Mommy," she says. To have spent one's childhood in love 3 with/tyrannized by a vengeful Jehovah is not Anna's idea of a good time — nor is it her idea of goodness. As, in her considered opinion, my having been a proselytizing Jehovah's Witness for thirteen years was about as good a preparation for real life as spending a commensurate amount of time in a Skinner box on the North Pole, she makes allowances for me. And so, when Anna came home recently from a boy-girl party to tell me that she had kissed a boy ("interesting," she pronounced the experiment), and I heard my mouth ask that atavistic mother-question, "And what else did you do?" Anna was inclined to be charitable with me: "Oh, for goodness' sake, what do you think we did, screw? The trouble with you is . . ." And then she explained to me about spin the bottle.

I do worry about Anna. She is, as I once explained drunkenly to someone 4 who thought that she might be the better for a little vigorous repression, a teleological child. She is concerned with final causes, with ends and purposes and means; she would like to see evidence of design and order in the world; and all her adventures are means to that end. That, combined with her love for the music, color, poetry, ritual, and drama of religion, might, I think, if she were at all inclined to bow her back to authority — and if she didn't have my childhood as an example of the perils thereof — have made her ripe for conversion to an apocalyptic, messianic sect.

That fear may be evidence of my special paranoia, but it is not an entirely 5 frivolous conjecture. Ardent preadolescent girls whose temperament tends toward the ecstatic are peculiarly prone to conversion to fancy religions.

I know. My mother and I became Jehovah's Witnesses in 1944, when I 6 was nine years old. I grew up drenched in the dark blood-poetry of a fierce messianic sect. Shortly after my conversion, I got my first period. We used to sing this hymn: "Here is He who comes from Eden / all His raiment stained with blood." My raiments were stained with blood, too. But the blood of the Son of Man was purifying, redemptive, cleansing, sacrificial. Mine was filthy — proof of my having inherited the curse placed upon the seductress Eve. I used to "read" my used Kotexes compulsively, as if the secret of life — or a harbinger of death — were to be found in that dull, mysterious effluence.

My brother, at the time of our conversion, was four. After a few years of 7 listlessly following my mother and me around in our door-to-door and street-corner proselytizing, he allied himself with my father, who had been driven to noisy, militant atheism by the presence of two female religious fanatics in his hitherto patriarchal household. When your wife and daughter are in love with God, it's hard to compete — particularly since God is good enough not to require messy sex as proof or expression of love. As a child, I observed that it was not extraordinary for women who became Jehovah's Witnesses to remove themselves from their husband's bed as a first step to getting closer to God. For women whose experience had taught them that all human relationships were treacherous and capricious and frighteningly volatile, an escape from the confusions of the world into the certainties of a fundamentalist religion provided the illusion of safety and of rest. It is not too simple to say that the reason many unhappily married and sexually embittered women fell in love with Jehovah was that they didn't have to go to bed with Him.

Apocalyptic religions are, by their nature, antierotic. Jehovah's Witnesses believe that the world — or, as they would have it, "this evil system under Satan the Devil" — will end in our lifetime. After the slaughter Jehovah has arranged for his enemies at Armageddon, say the Witnesses, this quintessentially masculine God — vengeful in battle, benevolent to survivors — will turn the earth into an Edenic paradise for true believers. I grew up under the umbrella of the slogan, "Millions Now Living Will Never Die," convinced that 1914 marked "the beginning of the times of the end." So firmly did Jehovah's Witnesses believe this to be true that there were those who, in 1944, refused to get their teeth filled, postponing all care of their bodies until God saw to their regeneration in His New World, which was just around the corner. 8

Some corner. 9

Despite the fact that their hopes were not immediately rewarded, Jehovah's Witnesses have persevered with increasing fervor and conviction, and their attitude toward the world remains the same: Because all their longing is for the future, they are bound to hate the present — the material, the sexual, the flesh. It's impossible, of course, truly to savor and enjoy the present, or to bend one's energies to shape and mold the world into the form of goodness, if you are only waiting for it to be smashed by God. There is a kind of ruthless glee in the way in which Jehovah's Witnesses point to earthquakes, race riots, heroin addiction, the failure of the United Nations, divorce, famine, and liberalized abortion laws as proof of the nearest Armageddon. 10

The world will end, according to the Witnesses, in a great shaking and rending and tearing of unbelieving flesh, with unsanctified babies swimming in blood — torrents of blood. They await God's Big Bang — the final orgasmic burst of violence, after which all things will come together in a cosmic orgasm of joy. In the meantime, they have disgust and contempt for the world; and freedom and spontaneity, even playfulness, in sex are explicitly frowned upon. 11

When I was ten, it would have been more than my life was worth to acknowledge, as Anna does so casually, that I knew what *screwing* was. (Ignorance, however, delivered me from that grave error.) Once, having read somewhere that Hitler had a mistress, I asked my mother what a mistress was. (I had an inkling that it was some kind of sinister superhousekeeper, like Judith Anderson in *Rebecca*.) I knew from my mother's silence, and from her cold, hard, and frightened face, that the question was somehow a grievous offense. I knew that I had done something terribly wrong, but as usual, I didn't know what. The fact was that I never knew how to buy God's — or my mother's — approval. There were sins I consciously and knowingly commit- 12 ted. That was bad, but it was bearable. I could always pray to God to forgive me, say, for reading the Bible for its "dirty parts" (to prefer the Song of Solomon to all the begats of Genesis was proof absolute of the sinfulness of my nature.) But the offenses that made me most cringingly guilty were those I had committed unconsciously; as an imperfect human being descended from the wretched Eve, I was bound — so I had been taught — to offend Jehovah seventy-seven times a day without my even knowing what I was doing wrong.

I knew that good Christians didn't commit "unnatural acts"; but I didn't   13
know what "unnatural" acts were. I knew that an increase in the number of rapes was one of the signs heralding the end of the world, but I didn't know what rape was. Consequently, I spent a lot of time praying that I was not committing unnatural acts or rape.

My ignorance of all things sexual was so profound that it frequently led to   14
comedies of error. Nothing I've ever read has inclined me to believe that Jehovah has a sense of humor, and I must say that I consider it a strike against Him that He wouldn't find this story funny: One night shortly after my conversion, a visiting elder of the congregation, as he was avuncularly tucking me in bed, asked me if I were guilty of performing evil practices with my hands under the covers at night. I was puzzled. He was persistent. Finally, I thought I understood. And I burst into wild tears of self-recrimination: What I did under the covers at night was bite my cuticles — a practice which, in fact, did afford me a kind of sensual pleasure. I didn't learn about masturbation — which the Witnesses call "idolatry" because "the masturbator's affection is diverted away from the Creator and is bestowed upon a coveted object . . . his genitals" — until much later. So, having confessed to a sin that I didn't even know existed, I was advised of the necessity of keeping one's body pure from sin; cold baths were recommended. I couldn't see the connection between cold baths and my cuticles, but no one ever questioned the imperatives of an elder. So I subjected my impure body, in midwinter, to so many icy baths that I began to look like a bleached prune. My mother thought I was demented. But I couldn't tell her that I'd been biting my cuticles, because to have incurred God's wrath — and to see the beady eye of the elder steadfastly upon me at every religious meeting I went to — was torment enough. There was no way to win.

One never questioned the imperatives of an elder. I learned as a very small   15
child that it was my primary duty in life to "make nice." When I was little, I was required to respond to inquiries about my health in this manner: "Fine and dandy, just like sugar candy, thank you." And to curtsy. If that sounds like something from a Shirley Temple movie, it's because it is. Having been brought up to be the Italian working-class Shirley Temple from Bensonhurst, it was not terribly difficult for me to learn to "make nice" for God and the elders. Behaving well was relatively easy. The passionate desire to win approval guaranteed my conforming. But behaving well never made me feel good. I always felt as if I were a bad person.

I ask myself why it was that my brother was not hounded by the obsessive 16
guilt and the desperate desire for approval that informed all my actions.
Partly, I suppose, luck, and an accident of temperament, but also because of
the peculiarly guilt-inspiring double message girls received. Girls were taught
that it was their nature to be spiritual, but paradoxically that they were more
prone to absolute depravity than were boys.

In my religion, everything beautiful and noble and spiritual and good was 17
represented by a woman; and everything evil and depraved and monstrous
was represented by a woman. I learned that "God's organization," the "bride
of Christ," or His 144,000 heavenly co-rulers were represented by a "chaste
virgin." I also learned that "Babylon the Great," or "false religion," was "the
mother of the abominations or the 'disgusting things of the earth' . . . She
likes to get drunk on human blood. . . . Babylon the Great is . . . pictured
as a woman, an international harlot."

Young girls were thought not to have the "urges" boys had. They were not 18
only caretakers of their own sleepy sexuality but protectors of boys' vital male
animal impulses as well. They were thus doubly responsible, and, if they fell,
doubly damned. Girls were taught that, simply by existing, they were pro-
voking male sexuality . . . which it was their job then to subdue.

To be female, I learned, was to be Temptation; nothing short of 19
death — the transformation of your atoms into a lilac bush — could
change that. (I used to dream deliciously of dying, of being as inert — and
as unaccountable — as the dust I came from.) Inasmuch as males naturally "wanted it" more, when a female "wanted it" she was doubly depraved, unnatural as well as sinful. She was the receptacle for male lust,
"the weaker vessel." If the vessel, created by God for the use of males,
presumed to have desires of its own, it was perforce consigned to the
consuming fires of God's wrath. If then, a woman were to fall from grace,
her fall would be mighty indeed — and her willful nature would lead her
into that awful abyss where she would be deprived of the redemptive love
of God and the validating love of man. Whereas, were a man to fall, he
would be merely stumbling over his own feet of clay.

(Can this be accident? My brother, when he was young, was always falling 20
over his own feet. I, on the other hand, to this day sweat with terror at the
prospect of going down escalators or long flights of stairs. I cannot fly; I am
afraid of the fall.)

I spent my childhood walking a religious tightrope, maintaining a difficult 21
dizzying balance. I was, for example, expected to perform well at school, so
that glory would accrue to Jehovah and "His organization." But I was also
made continually aware of the perils of falling prey to "the wisdom of this world
which is foolishness to God." I had constantly to defend myself against the
danger of trusting my own judgment. To question or to criticize God's "earthly
representatives" was a sure sign of "demonic influence"; to express doubt
openly was to risk being treated like a spiritual leper. I was always an honor
student at school; but this was hardly an occasion for unqualified joy. I felt,

rather, as if I were courting spiritual disaster: While I was congratulated for having "given a witness" by virtue of my academic excellence, I was, in the next breath, warned against the danger of supposing that my intelligence could function independently of God's. The effect of all this was to convince me that my intelligence was like some kind of tricky, predatory animal, which, if it were not kept firmly reined, would surely spring on and destroy me.

"Vanity, thy name is woman." I learned very early what happened to women with "independent spirits" who opposed the will and imperatives of male elders. They were disfellowshipped (excommunicated) and thrown into "outer darkness." Held up as an example of such perfidious conduct was Maria Frances Russell, the wife of Charles Taze Russell, charismatic founder of the sect.   22

Russell charged his wife with "the same malady which has smitted oth-   23
ers — *ambition*." Complaining of a "female conspiracy" against the Lord's organization, he wrote: "The result was a considerable stirring up of slander and misrepresentation, for of course it would not suit (her) purposes to tell the plain unvarnished truth, that Sister Russell was ambitious. . . . When she desired to come back, I totally refused, except upon a promise that she should make reasonable acknowledgment of the wrong course she had been pursuing." Ambition in a woman was, by implication, so reprehensible as to exact from Jehovah the punishment of death.

(What the Witnesses appeared less eager to publicize about the Russells'   24
spiritual-cum-marital problems is that in April, 1906, Mrs. Russell, having filed suit for legal separation, told a jury that her husband had once remarked to a young orphan woman the Russells had reared: "I am like a jellyfish. I float around here and there. I touch this one and that one, and if she responds I take her to me, and if not I float on to others." Mrs. Russell was unable to prove her charge.)

I remember a line in *A Nun's Story:* "Dear God," the disaffected Belgian   25
nun anguished, "forgive me. I will never be able to love a Nazi." I, conversely, prayed tormentedly for many years, "Dear God, forgive me, I am not able to hate what you hate. I love the world." As a Witness I was taught that "friendship with the world" was "spiritual adultery." The world was crawling with Satan's agents. But Satan's agents — evolutionists, "false religionists," and all those who opposed, or were indifferent to, "Jehovah's message" — often seemed like perfectly nice, decent, indeed lovable people to me. (They were certainly interesting.) As I went from door to door, ostensibly to help the Lord divide the "goats" from the "sheep," I found that I was more and more listening to *their* lives; and I became increasingly more tentative about telling them that I had *The* Truth. As I grew older, I found it more and more difficult to eschew their company. I entertained fantasies, at one time or another, about a handsome, ascetic Jesuit priest I had met in my preaching work and about Albert Schweitzer, J. D. Salinger, E. B. White, and Frank Sinatra; in fact, I was committing "spiritual adultery" all over the place. And then, when I was fifteen, I fell in love with an "unbeliever."

If I felt — before having met and loved Arnold Horowitz, English 31,   26
New Utrecht High School — that life was a tightrope, I felt afterward that my
life was perpetually being lived on a high wire, with no safety net to catch
me. I was obliged, by every tenet of my faith, to despise him: to be "yoked
with an unbeliever," an atheist and an intellectual . . . the pain was exquisite.

He was the essential person, the person who taught me how to love, and   27
how to doubt. Arnold became interested in me because I was smart; he loved
me because he thought I was good. He nourished me. He nurtured me. He
paid me the irresistible compliment of totally comprehending me. He hated
my religion. He railed against the sect that would rather see babies die than
permit them to have blood transfusions, which were regarded as unscriptural;
he had boundless contempt for my overseers, who would not permit me to
go to college — the "Devil's playground," which would fill my head with
wicked, ungodly nonsense; he protested mightily, with the rage that springs
from genuine compassion, against a religion that could tolerate segregation
and apartheid, sneer at martyred revolutionaries, dismiss social reform and
material charity as "irrelevant," a religion that — waiting for God to cure all
human ills — would act by default to maintain the status quo, while regarding human pain and struggle without pity and without generosity. He loathed
the world view that had been imposed on me, a black-and-white view that
allowed no complexities, no moral dilemmas, that disdained metaphysical or
philosophical or psychological inquiry; he loathed the bloated simplicities
that held me in thrall. But he loved *me*. I had never before felt loved
unconditionally.

This was a measure of his love: Jehovah's Witnesses are not permitted to   28
salute the flag. Arnold came, unbidden, to sit with me at every school
assembly, to hold my hand, while everyone else stood at rigid salute. We
were very visible; and I was very comforted. And this was during the
McCarthy era. Arnold had a great deal to lose, and he risked it all for me.
Nobody had ever risked anything for me before. How could I believe that he
was wicked?

We drank malteds on his porch and read T. S. Eliot and listened to   29
Mozart. We walked for hours, talking of God and goodness and happiness
and death. We met surreptitiously. (My mother so feared and hated the man
who was leading me into apostasy that she once threw a loaf of Arnold bread
out the window; his very name was loathsome to her.) Arnold treated me
with infinite tenderness; he was the least alarming man I had ever known.
His fierce concentration on me, his solicitous care uncoupled with sexual
aggression, was the gentlest — and most thrilling — love I had ever known.
He made me feel what I had never felt before — valuable, and good.

It was very hard. All my dreams centered around Arnold, who was   30
becoming more important, certainly more real to me, than God. All my
dreams were blood-colored. I would fantasize about Arnold's being converted and surviving Armageddon and living forever with me in the New

World. Or I would fantasize about my dying with Arnold, in fire and flames, at Armageddon. I would try to make bargains with God — my life for his. When I confessed my terrors to the men in charge of my spiritual welfare — when I said that I knew I could not rejoice in the destruction of the "wicked" at Armageddon — I was told that I was presuming to be "more compassionate than Jehovah," the deadliest sin against the holy spirit. I was reminded that, being a woman and therefore weak and sentimental, I would have to go against my sinful nature and listen to their superior wisdom, which consisted of my never seeing Arnold again. I was also reminded of the perils of being over-smart: If I hadn't been such a good student, none of this would have happened to me.

I felt as if I were leading a double life, as indeed I was. I viewed the world 31 as beautifully various, as a blemished but mysteriously wonderful place, as savable by humans, who were neither good nor bad but imperfectly wise; but I *acted* as if the world were fit for nothing but destruction, as if all human efforts to purchase happiness and goodness were doomed to failure and deserving of contempt, as if all people could be categorized as "sheep" or "goats" and herded into their appropriate destinies by a judgmental Jehovah, the all-seeing Father who knew better than His children what was good for them.

As I had when I was a little girl, I "made nice" as best I could. I 32 maintained the appearance of "goodness," that is, of religiosity, although it violated my truest feelings. When I left high school, I went into the full-time preaching work. I spent a minimum of five hours a day ringing doorbells and conducting home Bible studies. I went to three religious meetings a week. I prayed that my outward conformity would lead to inner peace. I met Arnold very occasionally, when my need to see him overcame my elders' imperatives and my own devastating fears. He was always accessible to me. Our meetings partook equally of misery and joy. I tried, by my busyness, to lock all my doubts into an attic of my mind.

And for a while, and in a way, it "took." I derived sustenance from 33 communal surges of revivalist fervor at religious conventions and from the conviction that I was united, in a common cause, with a tiny minority of persecuted and comradely brothers and sisters whose approval became both my safety net and the Iron Curtain that shut me off from the world. I felt that I had chosen Jehovah, and that my salvation, while not assured, was at least a possibility; perhaps He would choose me. I vowed finally never to see Arnold again, hoping, by this sacrifice, to gain God's approval for him as well as for me.

I began to understand that for anyone so obviously weak and irresponsible 34 as I, only a life of self-sacrifice and abnegation could work. I wanted to be consumed by Jehovah, to be locked so closely into the straitjacket of His embrace that I would be impervious to the devilish temptations my irritable, independent intelligence threw up in my path.

I wished to be eaten up alive; and my wish was granted. When I was 35 nineteen, I was accepted into Bethel, the headquarters organization of Jehovah's Witnesses, where I worked and lived, one of twelve young women among two hundred and fifty men, for three years. "Making nice" had paid off. Every minute of my waking life was accounted for, there was no leisure in which to cultivate vice or reflection. I called myself happy. I worked as a housekeeper for my brothers, making thirty beds a day, sweeping and vacuuming and waxing and washing fifteen rooms a day (in addition to proselytizing in my "free time"); I daily washed the bathtub thirty men had bathed in. In fact, the one demurral I made during those years was to ask — I found it so onerous — if perhaps the brothers, many of whom worked in the Witnesses' factory, could not clean out their own bathtub (thirty layers of grease is a lot of grease). I was told by the male overseer who supervised housekeepers that Jehovah had assigned me this "privilege." And I told myself I was lucky.

I felt myself to be even luckier — indeed, blessed — when, after two years   36 of this servant's work, one of Jehovah's middlemen, the president of the Watch Tower Bible and Tract Society, told me that he was assigning me to proofread Watch Tower publications. He accompanied this benediction with a warning: This new honor, I was told, was to be a test of my integrity — "Remember in all things to defer to the brothers; you will have to guard your spirit against pride and vanity. Satan will try now to tempt you as never before."

And defer I did. There were days when I felt literally as if my eternal   37 destiny hung upon a comma: If the brother with whom I worked decided a comma should go out where I wanted to put one in, I prayed to Jehovah to forgive me for that presumptuous comma. I was perfectly willing to deny the existence of a split infinitive if that would placate my brother. I denied and denied — commas, split infinitives, my sexuality, my intelligence, my femaleness, my yearning to be part of the world — until suddenly with a great silent shifting and shuddering, and with more pain than I had ever experienced or expect to experience again, I broke. I woke up one morning, packed my bags, and walked out of that place. I was twenty-two; and I had to learn how to begin to live. It required a great deal of courage; I do not think I will ever be capable of that much courage again.

The full story of life in that institution and the ramifications of my   38 decision to leave it is too long to tell here; and it will take me the rest of my life to understand fully the ways in which everything I have ever done since has been colored and informed by the guilt that was my daily bread for so many dry years, by the desperate need for approval that allowed me to be swallowed up whole by a devouring religion, by the carefully fostered desire to "make nice" and to be "a good girl," by the conviction that I was nothing and nobody unless I served a cause superior to that of my own necessities.

Arnold, of course, foresaw the difficulty; when I left religion, he said,   39 "Now you will be just like the rest of us." With no guiding passion, he meant; uncertain, he meant, and often muddled and confused, and always struggling. And he wept.

Analyzing This Selection

1. What are the author's tone and attitudes toward Anna? What is the author's purpose in presenting her relationship with her daughter?

2. In Harrison's view, what are the attractions of religious cults and sects? How do they differ from or resemble the attractions of other religions?

3. How did her relationship with Arnold challenge Harrison's religious beliefs? How did she attempt to resolve this spiritual crisis?

4. Clarify Arnold's attitude in the final paragraph. Is he congratulating or criticizing Harrison? What are the overtones of the final sentence?

Analyzing Connections

5. Harrison and Susan Allen Toth (see "Boyfriends," p. 132) reminisce about their first teenage boyfriends. What changes in themselves are the authors recalling? How do they respond to the changes?

Analyzing by Writing

6. In the religion you know best, what signs of sexism do you find expressed in specific customs, doctrines, stories, or images? If the assumptions about women contradict its other religious values, explain the inconsistency of beliefs. If you find the signs of woman's separateness equalized by other advantages, explain the balance.

Patricia Hampl

PARISH STREETS

◇

PATRICIA HAMPL (b. 1946) was raised in St. Paul, Minnesota. She graduated
from the University of Minnesota and earned a master's degree in the writers'
program at the University of Iowa. Her poetry and prose have appeared in
magazines such as *The New Yorker, Granta, Antaeus,* and the *Paris Review.*
Her first memoir, A *Romantic Education* (1981), explores connections between her European heritage and her American experience. "Parish Streets" is
excerpted from her second memoir, *Virgin Time* (1992), which focuses on her
religious upbringing. She is a professor at the University of Minnesota and lives
in her native St. Paul. She has won a Guggenheim Fellowship (1988) and a
MacArthur Foundation Fellowship (1990).

Lexington, Oxford, Chatsworth, continuing down Grand Avenue to Mil- 1
ton and Avon, as far as St. Albans — the streets of our neighborhood had an
English, even an Anglican, ring to them. But we were Catholic, and the
parishes of the diocese, unmarked and ghostly as they were, posted borders
more decisive than the street signs we passed on our way to St. Luke's grade
school, or, later, walking in the other direction to Visitation Convent for
high school.

We were like people with dual citizenship. I *lived* on Linwood Avenue, 2
but I *belonged* to St. Luke's. That was the lingo. Mothers spoke of daughters
who were going to the junior-senior prom with boys "from Nativity" or "from
St. Mark's," as if from feifdoms across the sea.

"Where you from?" a boy livid with acne asked when we startled each 3
other lurking behind a pillar in the St. Thomas Academy gym at a Friday
night freshman mixer.

"Ladies' choice!" one the mothers cried from a dim corner where a 4
portable high-fi was set up. She rasped the needle over the vinyl, and Fats
Domino came on, insinuating a heavier pleasure than I yet knew: *I found my
thrill . . . on Blueberry Hill.*

"I'm from Holy Spirit," the boy said, as if he'd been beamed in to stand 5
by the tepid Cokes and tuna sandwiches and the bowls of sweating potato
chips on the refreshments table.

Parish members did not blush to describe themselves as being "from 6
Immaculate Conception." Somewhere north, near the city line, there was

even a parish frankly named Maternity of Mary. But then, in those years, the 1950s and early 1960s, breeding was a low-grade fever pulsing amongst us unmentioned, like a buzz or hum you get used to and cease to hear. The white noise of matrimonial sex.

On Sundays the gray stone nave of St. Luke's church, big as a warehouse, 7 was packed with families of eight or ten sitting in the honey-colored pews. The fathers wore brown suits. In memory they appear spectrally thin, wraith-like and spent, like trees hollowed of their pulp. The wives were petite and cheerful with helmet-like haircuts. Perkiness was their main trait. But what did they say, these small women, how did they talk? Mrs. Healy, mother of fourteen ("They can afford them," my mother said, as if to excuse her paltry two. "He's a doctor."), never uttered a word, as far as I remember. Even pregnant, she was somehow wiry, as if poised for a tennis match. Maybe these women only wore a *look* of perkiness, and like their lean husbands, they were sapped of personal strength. Maybe they were simply tense.

Not everyone around us was Catholic. Mr. Kirby, a widower who was our 8 next door neighbor, was Methodist — whatever that was. The Nugents across the street behind their cement retaining wall and double row of giant saliva, were Lutheran, more or less. The Williams family, who subscribed to *The New Yorker* and had a living room outfitted with spare Danish furniture, were Episcopalian. They referred to their minister as a priest — a plagiarism that embarrassed me for them because I liked them and their light, airy ways.

As for the Bertrams, our nearest neighbors to the west, it could only be 9 said that Mrs. Bertram, dressed in a narrow suit with a peplum jacket and a hat made of the same heathery wool, went *somewhere* via taxi on Sunday mornings. Mr. Bertram went nowhere — on Sunday or on any other day. He was understood, during my entire girlhood, to be indoors, resting.

Weekdays, Mrs. Bertram took the bus to her job downtown. Mr. Bertram 10 stayed home behind their birchwood Venetian blinds in an aquarium half-light, not an invalid (we never thought of him that way), but a man whose occupation it was to rest. Sometimes in the summer he ventured forth with a large wrench-like gadget to root out the masses of dandelions that gave the Bertram lawn a temporary brilliance in June.

I associated him with the Wizard of Oz. He was small and mild-looking, 11 going bald. He gave the impression of extreme pallor except for small, very dark eyes.

It was a firm neighborhood rumor that Mr. Bertram had been a screen- 12 writer in Hollywood. Yes, that pallor was a writer's pallor; those small dark eyes were a writer's eyes. They saw, they noted.

He allowed me to assist him in the rooting-out of his dandelions. I wanted 13 to ask him about Hollywood — had he met Audrey Hepburn? I couldn't bring myself to maneuver for information on such an important subject. But I did feel something serious was called for here. I introduced religion while he plunged the dandelion gadget deep into the lawn.

No, he said, he did not go to church. "But you do believe in God?" I 14
asked, hardly daring to hope he did not. I longed for novelty.

He paused for a moment and looked up at the sky where big, spreading 15
clouds streamed by. "God isn't the problem," he said.

Some ancient fissure split open, a fine crack in reality: so there *was* a 16
problem. Just as I'd always felt. Beneath the family solidity, the claustro-
phobia of mother-and-father-brother-me, past the emphatic certainties of St.
Luke's catechism class, there was a problem that would never go away. Mr.
Bertram stood amid his dandelions, resigned as a Buddha, looking up at the
sky which gave back nothing but drifting white shapes on the blue.

What alarmed me was my feeling of recognition. Of course there was 17
a problem. It wasn't God. Life itself was a problem. Something was not
right, would never be right. I'd sensed it all along, some kind of fishy
vestigial quiver in the spine. It was bred in the bone, way past thought.
Life, deep down, lacked the substantiality that it *seemed* to display. The
physical world, full of detail and interest, was a parched topsoil that could
be blown away.

This lack, this blankness akin to chronic disappointment, was everywhere, 18
under the perkiness, lurking even within my own happiness. "What are you
going to do today?" my father said when he saw me digging in the backyard
on his way to work at the greenhouse.

"I'm digging to China," I said. 19

"Well, I'll see you at lunch," he said, "if you're still here." 20

I wouldn't bite. I frowned and went back to work with the bent tablespoon 21
my mother had given me. It wasn't a game. I wanted out. I was on a
desperate journey that only looked like play. I couldn't explain.

The blank disappointment, masked as weariness, played on the faces of 22
people on the St. Clair bus. They looked out the windows, coming home
from downtown, unseeing: clearly nothing interested them. What were they
thinking of? The passing scene was not beautiful enough — was that it? — to
catch their eye. Like the empty clouds Mr. Bertram turned to, their blank
looks gave back nothing. There was an unshivered shiver in each of us, a
shudder we managed to hold back.

We got off the bus at Oxford where, one spring, in the lime green house 23
behind the catalpa tree on the corner, Mr. Lenart (whom we didn't know
well) had slung a pair of tire chains over a rafter in the basement and hanged
himself. Such things happened. Only the tight clutch of family life ("The
family that prays together stays together") could keep things rolling along.
Step out of the tight, bright circle, and you might find yourself dragging your
chains down to the basement.

The perverse insubstantiality of the material world was the problem: 24
Reality refused to be real enough. Nothing could keep you steadfastly happy.
That was clear. Some people blamed God. But I sensed that Mr. Bertram
was right not to take that tack. *God is not the problem.* The clouds passing in

the big sky kept dissipating, changing form. That was the problem — but so what? Such worries resolved nothing, and were best left unworried — the unshivered shiver.

There was no one to blame. You could only retire, like Mr. Bertram, stay 25 indoors behind your birchwood blinds, and contemplate the impossibility of things, allowing the Holywood glitter of reality to fade away and become a vague local rumor.

There were other ways of coping. Mrs. Krueger, several houses down with 26 a big garden rolling with hydrangea bushes, held as her faith a passionate belief in knowledge. She sold *World Book* encyclopedias. After trying Christian Science and a stint with the Unitarians, she had settled down as an agnostic. There seemed to be a lot of reading involved with being an agnostic, pamphlets and books, long citations on cultural anthropology in the *World Book*. It was an abstruse religion, and Mrs. Krueger seemed to belong to some ladies' auxiliary of disbelief.

But it didn't really matter what Mrs. Krueger decided about "the deity- 27 idea," as she called God. No matter what they believed, our neighbors lived not just on Linwood Avenue; they were in St. Luke's parish too, whether they knew it or not. We claimed the territory. And we claimed them — even as we dismissed them. They were all non-Catholics, the term that disposed nicely of all spiritual otherness.

Let the Protestants go their schismatic ways; the Lutherans could splice 28 themselves into synods any which way. Believers, nonbelievers, even Jews (the Kroners on the corner) or a breed as rare as the Greek Orthodox whose church was across the street from St. Luke's — they were all non-Catholics, just so much extraneous spiritual matter orbiting the nethersphere.

Or maybe it was more intimate than that, and we dismissed the rest of the 29 world as we would our own serfs. We saw the Lutherans and Presbyterians, even those snobbish Episcopalians, as rude colonials, non-Catholics all, doing the best they could out there in the bush to imitate the ways of the homeland. *We* were the homeland. . . .

The hierarchy we lived in, a great linked chain of religious being, seemed 30 set to control every entrance and exit to and from the mind and heart. The buff-colored *Baltimore Catechism*, small and square, read like an owner's manual for a very complicated vehicle. There was something pleasant, lulling and rhythmic, like heavily rhymed poetry, about the sing-song Q-and-A format. Who would not give over heart, if not mind, to the brisk nannyish assurance of the Baltimore prose:

Who made you?
God made me.

Why did God make you?
God made me to know, love, and serve Him in this world, in order to
be happy with him forever in the next.

What pleasant lines to commit to memory. And how harmless our Jesu- 31
itical discussions about what, exactly, constituted a meatless spaghetti sauce
on Friday. Strict constructionists said no meat of any kind should ever, at any
time, have made its way into the tomato sauce; easy liberals held with the
notion that meatballs could be lurking around in the sauce, as long as you
didn't eat them. My brother lobbied valiantly for the meatball *intactus* but
present. My mother said nothing doing. They raged for years.

Father Flannery, who owned his own airplane and drove a sports car, had 32
given Peter some ammunition when he'd been asked to rule on the meatball
question in the confessional. My mother would hear none of it. "I don't want
to know what goes on between you and your confessor," she said, taking the
high road.

"A priest, Ma, a *priest*," my brother cried. "This is an ordained priest 33
saying right there in the sanctity of the confessional that meatballs were OK."

But we were going to heaven my mother's way. 34

Life was like that — crazy. Full of hair-splitting, and odd rituals. We got 35
our throats blessed on St. Blaise day in February, with the priest holding
oversized bees-wax candles in an X around our necks, to ward off death by
choking on fishbones. There were smudged foreheads on Ash Wednesday,
and home May altars with plaster statuettes of the Virgin festooned with
lilacs. Advent wreaths and nightly family rosary vigils during October (Rosary
Month), the entire family on their knees in the living room.

There were snatches of stories about nuns who beat kids with rulers in the 36
coat room; the priest who had a twenty-year affair with a member of the Altar
and Rosary Society; the other priest in love with an altar boy — they'd had
to send him away. Not St. Luke's stories — oh no, certainly not — but
stories, floating, as stories do, from inner ear to inner ear, respecting no
parish boundaries. Part of the ether.

And with it all, a relentless xenophobia about other religions. "It's 37
going to be a mixed marriage, I understand," one of my aunts murmured
about a friend's daughter who was marrying an Episcopalian. So what if
he called himself High Church? What did that change? He was a non-
Catholic.

And now, educated out of it all, well climbed into the professions, the 38
Catholics find each other at cocktail parties and get going. The nun stories,
the first confession traumas — and a tone of rage and dismay that seems to
bewilder even the tellers of these tales.

Nobody says, when asked, "I'm Catholic." It's always, "Yes, I was brought 39
up Catholic." Anything to put it at a distance, to diminish the presence of
that grabby heritage that is not racial but acts as if it were. "You never get
over it, you know," a fortyish lawyer told me a while ago at a party where we
found ourselves huddled by the chips and dip, as if we were at a St. Thomas
mixer once again.

He seemed to feel he was speaking to someone with the same hopeless 40 congenital condition. "It's different now, of course," he said. "But when we were growing up back there. . . ." Ah yes, the past isn't a time. It's a place. And it's always there. . . .

"I'm divorced," he said. We both smiled: there's no going to hell any- 41 more. "Do they still have mortal sin?" he asked wistfully.

The love-hate lurch of a Catholic upbringing, like having an extra set of 42 parents to contend with. Or an added national allegiance — not to the Vatican, as we were warned that the Baptists thought during John Kennedy's campaign for president. The allegiance was to a different realm. It was the implacable loyalty of faith, that flawless relation between self and existence which we were born into. A strange country where people prayed and believed impossible things.

The nuns who taught us, rigged up in their bold black habits with the big 43 round wimples stiff as frisbees, walked our parish streets; they moved from convent to church in twos or threes, dipping in the side door of the huge church "for a little adoration," as they would say. The roly-poly Irish-born monsignor told us to stand straight and proud when he met us slouching along Summit toward class. And fashionable Father Flannery who, every night, took a gentle, companionable walk with the old Irish pastor, the two of them taking out white handkerchiefs, waving them for safety, as they crossed the busy avenue on the way home in the dark, swallowed in their black suits and cassocks, invisible in the gloom.

But the one I would like to summon up most and to have pass me on 44 Oxford as I head off to St. Luke's in the early morning mist, one of those mid-May weekdays, the lilacs just starting to spill, that one I want most to materialize from "back there" — I don't know her name, where, exactly, she lived, or who she was. We never spoke, in fact. We just passed each other, she coming home from six o'clock daily Mass, I going early to school to practice the piano for an hour before class began.

She was a "parish lady," part of the anonymous population that thickened 45 our world, people who were always there, who were solidly part of us, part of what we were, but who never emerged beyond the bounds of being parishioners to become persons.

We met every morning, just past the Healy's low brick wall. She wore a 46 librarian's cardigan sweater. She must have been about forty-five, and I sensed she was not married. Unlike Dr. and Mrs. Harrigan who walked smartly along Summit holding hands, their bright Irish setter accompanying them as far as the church door where he waited till Mass was over, the lady in the cardigan was always alone.

I saw her coming all the way from Grand where she had to pause for the 47 traffic. She never rushed across the street, zipping past a truck, but waited until the coast was completely clear, and passed across keeping her slow, almost floating pace. A lovely, peaceful gait, no rush to it.

When finally we were close enough to make eye contact, she looked up, 48 straight into my face, and smiled. It was such a *complete* smile, so entire, that it startled me every time, as if I'd heard my name called out on the street of a foreign city.

She was a homely woman, plain and pale, unnoticeable. But I felt — how 49 to put it — that she shed light. The mornings were often frail with mist, the light uncertain and tender. The smile was a brief flood of light. She loved me, I felt.

I knew what it was about. She was praying. Her hand, stuck in her 50 cardigan pocket, held one of the crystal beads of her rosary. I knew this. I'd once seen her take it out of the left pocket and quickly replace it after she had found the handkerchief she needed.

If I had seen a nun mumbling the rosary along Summit (and that did 51 happen), it would not have meant much to me. But here on Oxford, the side street we used as a sleepy corridor to St. Luke's, it was a different thing. The parish lady was not a nun. She was a person who prayed, who prayed alone, for no reason that I understood. But there was no question that she prayed without ceasing, as the strange scriptural line instructed.

She didn't look up to the blank clouds for a response, as Mr. Bertram did 52 in his stoic way. Her head was bowed, quite unconsciously. And when she raised it, keeping her hand in her pocket where the clear beads were, she looked straight into the eyes of the person passing by. It was not an invasive look, but one brimming with a secret which, if only she had words, it was clear she would like to tell.

Analyzing This Selection

1. What were the differences between the author's neighborhood and parish? How does Hampl make one region more interesting than the other?

2. What dissatisfactions prompted her childhood religious doubts? What gave her reassurances as a child?

3. Do you think Hampl's young life was troubled or serene?

4. Explain what the anonymous parish lady meant to Hampl as a child and, in retrospect, what she means to her now.

Analyzing Connections

5. For Hampl and Barbara Grizzuti Harrison (in the preceding selection), society was defined by their religions. Explain how their religious groups viewed and connected with the rest of society.

Analyzing by Writing

6. Hampl refers to her religious upbringing as a "dual citizenship." The sense of inhabiting double spheres, or parallel worlds, can arise for young people in religious, ethnic, and racial groups — or in any strongly defined cultural

grouping such as the children of military families or of Americans employed abroad. Analyze your own experience of dual citizenship. Explain the differing dimensions, expectations, styles, and manners of the two realms. How did you bridge them? Were you a full citizen in both realms? or partly an alien in one or both? What were the temporary or long-lasting effects of dual citizenship?

Henry Louis Gates, Jr.

IN THE KITCHEN

◊

HENRY LOUIS GATES, JR. (b. 1950) was born and raised in West Virginia. He graduated from Yale University. After serving as a London correspondent for *Time* magazine, Gates earned a Ph.D. in English from Cambridge University. He has taught at Duke University and Harvard University, where he is now the chairman of Afro-American Studies. His *The Signifying Monkey: A Theory of African-American Literary Criticism* won a National Book Award in 1989. Gates writes on issues of popular culture and race relations, contributing to magazines such as *Harper's*, the *Village Voice*, and *The New Yorker*. The following essay is part of his memoir *Colored People* (1994).

We always had a gas stove in the kitchen, in our house in Piedmont, West 1 Virginia, where I grew up. Never electric, though using electric became fashionable in Piedmont in the sixties, like using Crest toothpaste rather than Colgate, or watching Huntley and Brinkley rather than Walter Cronkite. But not us: gas, Colgate, and good ole Walter Cronkite, come what may. We used gas partly out of loyalty to Big Mom, Mama's Mama, because she was mostly blind and still loved to cook, and could feel her way more easily with gas than with electric. But the most important thing about our gas-equipped kitchen was that Mama used to do hair there. The "hot comb" was a fine-toothed iron instrument with a long wooden handle and a pair of iron curlers that opened and closed like scissors. Mama would put it in the gas fire until it glowed. You could smell those prongs heating up.

I liked that smell. Not the smell so much, I guess, as what the smell meant 2 for the shape of my day. There was an intimate warmth in the women's tones as they talked with my Mama, doing their hair. I knew what the women had been through to get their hair ready to be "done," because I would watch Mama do it to herself. How that kink could be transformed through grease and fire into that magnificent head of wavy hair was a miracle to me, and still is.

Mama would wash her hair over the sink, a towel wrapped around her 3 shoulders, wearing just her slip and her white bra. (We had no shower — just a galvanized tub that we stored in the kitchen — until we moved down Rat Tail Road into Doc Wolverton's house, in 1954.) After she dried it, she would grease her scalp thoroughly with blue Bergamot hair grease, which came in a short, fat jar with a picture of a beautiful colored lady on it. It's important to grease your scalp real good, my Mama would explain, to keep from burning yourself. Of course, her hair would return to its natural kink almost as soon as the hot water and shampoo hit it. To me, it was another miracle how hair so "straight" would so quickly become kinky again the second it even approached some water.

My Mama had only a few "clients" whose heads she "did" — did, I think, because she enjoyed it, rather than for the few pennies it brought in. They would sit on one of our red plastic kitchen chairs, the kind with the shiny metal legs, and brace themselves for the process. Mama would stroke that red-hot iron — which by this time had been in the gas fire for half an hour or more — slowly but firmly through their hair, from scalp to strand's end. It made a scorching, crinkly sound, the hot iron did, as it burned its way through kink, leaving in its wake straight strands of hair, standing long and tall but drooping over at the ends, their shape like the top of a heavy willow tree. Slowly, steadily, Mama's hands would transform a round mound of Odetta kink into a darkened swamp of everglades. The Bergamot made the hair shiny; the heat of the hot iron gave it a brownish-red cast. Once all the hair was as straight as God allows kink to get, Mama would take the well-heated curling iron and twirl the straightened strands into more or less loosely wrapped curls. She claimed that she owed her skill as a hairdresser to the strength in her wrists, and as she worked her little finger would poke out, the way it did when she sipped tea. Mama was a southpaw, and wrote upside down and backward to produce the cleanest, roundest letters you've ever seen.

The "kitchen" she would all but remove from sight with a handheld pair of shears, bought just for this purpose. Now, the kitchen was the room in which we were sitting — the room where Mama did her hair and washed clothes, and where we all took a bath in that galvanized tub. But the word has another meaning, and the kitchen that I'm speaking of is the very kinky bit of hair at the back of your head, where your neck meets your shirt collar. If there was ever a part of our African past that resisted assimilation, it was the kitchen. No matter how hot the iron, no matter how powerful the chemical, no matter how stringent the mashed-potatoes-and-lye formula of a man's "process," neither God nor woman nor Sammy Davis, Jr., could straighten the kitchen. The kitchen was permanent, irredeemable, irresistible kink. Unassimilably African. No matter what you did, no matter how hard you tried, you couldn't de-kink a person's kitchen. So you trimmed it off as best you could.

When hair had begun to "turn," as they'd say — to return to its natural kinky glory — it was the kitchen that turned first (the kitchen around the back, and nappy edges at the temples). When the kitchen started creeping up the back of the neck, it was time to get your hair done again.

Sometimes, after dark, a man would come to have his hair done. It was Mr. Charlie Carroll. He was very light-complected and had a ruddy nose — it made me think of Edmund Gwenn, who played Kris Kringle in "Miracle on 34th Street." At first, Mama did him after my brother, Rocky, and I had gone to sleep. It was only later that we found out that he had come to our house so Mama could iron his hair — not with a hot comb or a curling iron but with our very own Proctor-Silex steam iron. For some reason I never understood, Mr. Charlie could conceal his Frederick Douglass-like mane under a big white Stetson hat. I never saw him take it off except when he came to our house, at night, to have his hair pressed. (Later, Daddy would tell us about Mr. Charlie's most prized piece of knowledge, something that the man would only confide after his hair had been pressed, as a token of intimacy. "Not many people know this," he'd say, in a tone of circumspection, "but George Washington was Abraham Lincoln's daddy." Nodding solemnly, he'd add the clincher: "A white man told me." Though he was in dead earnest, this became a humorous refrain around our house — "a white man told me" — which we used to punctuate especially preposterous assertions.)

My mother examined my daughters' kitchens whenever we went home to 8
visit, in the early eighties. It became a game between us. I had told her not to do it, because I didn't like the politics it suggested — the notion of "good" and "bad" hair. "Good" hair was "straight," "bad" hair kinky. Even in the late sixties, at the height of Black Power, almost nobody could bring themselves to say "bad" for good and "good" for bad. People still said that hair like white people's hair was "good," even if they encapsulated it in a disclaimer, like "what we used to call 'good.' "

Maggie would be seated in her high chair, throwing food this way and 9
that, and Mama would be coming about how cute it all was, how I used to do just like Maggie was doing, and wondering whether her flinging her food with her left hand meant that she was going to be left-handed like Mama. When my daughter was just about covered with Chef Boyardee Spaghetti-O's, Mama would seize the opportunity: wiping her clean, she would tilt Maggie's head to one side and reach down the back of her neck. Sometimes Mama would even rub a curl between her fingers, just to make sure that her bifocals had not deceived her. Then she'd sigh with satisfaction and relief: No kink . . . yet. Mama! I'd shout, pretending to be angry. Every once in a while, if no one was looking, I'd peek, too.

I say "yet" because most black babies are born with soft, silken hair. But 10
after a few months it begins to turn, as inevitably as do the seasons or the leaves on a tree. People once thought baby oil would stop it. They were wrong.

Everybody I knew as a child wanted to have good hair. You could be as 11
ugly as homemade sin dipped in misery and still be thought attractive if you had good hair. "Jesus moss," the girls at Camp Lee, Virginia, had called Daddy's naturally "good" hair during the war. I know that he played that thick head of hair for all it was worth, too. My own hair was "not a bad grade," as barbers would tell me when they cut it for the first time. It was like

a doctor reporting the results of the first full physical he has given you. Like "You're in good shape" or "Blood pressure's kind of high — better cut down on salt."

I spent most of my childhood and adolescence messing with my hair. I   12 definitely wanted straight hair. Like Pop's. When I was about three, I tried to stick a wad of Bazooka bubble gum to that straight hair of his. I suppose what fixed that memory for me is the spanking I got for doing so: he turned me upside down, holding me by my feet, the better to paddle my behind. Little *nigger*, he had shouted, walloping away. I started to laugh about it two days later, when my behind stopped hurting.

When black people say "straight," of course, they don't usually mean   13 literally straight — they're not describing hair like, say, Peggy Lipton's (she was the white girl on "The Mod Squad"), or like Mary's of Peter, Paul & Mary fame; black people call that "stringy" hair. No, "straight" just means not kinky, no matter what contours the curl may take. I would have done *anything* to have straight hair — and I used to try everything, short of getting a process.

Of the wide variety of techniques and methods I came to master in the   14 challenging prestidigitation of the follicle, almost all had two things in common: a heavy grease and the application of pressure. It's not an accident that some of the biggest black-owned companies in the fifties and sixties made hair products. And I tried them all, in search of that certain silken touch, the one that would leave neither the hand nor the pillow sullied by grease.

I always wondered what Frederick Douglass put on *his* hair, or what   15 Phillis Wheatley put on hers. Or why Wheatley has that rag on her head in the little engraving in the frontispiece of her book. One thing is for sure: you can bet that when Phillis Wheatley went to England and saw the Countess of Huntingdon she did not stop by the Queen's coiffeur on her way there. So many black people still get their hair straightened that it's a wonder we don't have a national holiday for Madame C. J. Walker, the woman who invented the process of straightening kinky hair. Call it Jheri-Kurled or call it "relaxed," it's still fried hair.

I used all the greases, from sea-blue Bergamot and creamy vanilla Duke   16 (in its clear jar with the orange-white-and-green label) to the godfather of grease, the formidable Murray's. Now, Murray's was some *serious* grease. Whereas Bergamot was like oily jello, and Duke was viscous and sickly sweet, Murray's was light brown and *hard*. Hard as lard and twice as greasy, Daddy used to say. Murray's came in an orange can with a press-on top. It was so hard that some people would put a match to the can, just to soften the stuff and make it more manageable. Then, in the late sixties, when Afros came into style, I used Afro Sheen. From Murray's to Duke to Afro Sheen: that was my progression in black consciousness.

We used to put hot towels or wash rags over our Murray-coated heads, in   17 order to melt the wax into the scalp and the follicles. Unfortunately, the wax also had the habit of running down your neck, ears, and forehead. Not to mention your pillowcase. Another problem was that if you put two palmfuls of Murray's on your head your hair turned white. (Duke did the same thing.) The challenge was to get rid of that white color. Because if you got rid of the white stuff you had a magnificent head of wavy hair. That was the beauty of it: Murray's was so hard that it froze your hair into the wavy style you brushed it into. It looked really good if you wore a part. A lot of guys had parts *cut* into their hair by a barber, either with the clippers or with a straightedge razor. Especially if you had kinky hair — then you'd generally wear a short razor cut, or what we called a Quo Vadis.

We tried to be as innovative as possible. Everyone knew about using a   18 stocking cap, because your father or your uncle wore one whenever something really big was about to happen, whether sacred or secular: a funeral or a dance, a wedding or a trip in which you confronted official white people. Any time you were trying to look really sharp, you wore a stocking cap in preparation. And if the event was really a big one, you made a new cap. You asked your mother for a pair of her hose, and cut it with scissors about six inches or so from the open end — the end with the elastic that goes up to the top of the thigh. Then you knotted the cut end, and it became a beehive-shaped hat, with an elastic band that you pulled down low on your forehead and down around your neck in the back. To work well, the cap had to fit tightly and snugly, like a press. And it had to fit that tightly because it *was* a press: it pressed your hair with the force of the hose's elastic. If you greased your hair down real good, and left the stocking cap on long enough, voilà: you got a head of pressed-against-the-scalp waves. (You also got a ring around your forehead when you woke up, but it went away.) And then you could enjoy your concrete do. Swore we were bad, too, with all that grease and those flat heads. My brother and I would brush it out a bit in the mornings, so that it looked — well, "natural." Grown men still wear stocking caps — especially older men, who generally keep their stocking caps in their top drawers, along with their cufflinks and their see-through silk socks, their "Maverick" ties, their silk handkerchiefs, and whatever else they prize the most.

A Murrayed-down stocking cap was the respectable version of the process,   19 which, by contrast, was most definitely not a cool thing to have unless you were an entertainer by trade. Zeke and Keith and Poochie and a few other stars of the high-school basketball team all used to get a process once or twice a year. It was expensive, and you had to go somewhere like Pittsburgh or D.C. or Uniontown — somewhere where there were enough colored people to support a trade. The guys would disappear, then reappear a day or two later, strutting like peacocks, their hair burned slightly red from the lye base. They'd also wear "rags" — cloths or handkerchiefs — around their heads when they slept or played basketball. Do-rags, they were called. But the result was straight hair, with just a hint of wave. No curl. Do-it-yourselfers took their chances at home with a concoction of mashed potatoes and lye.

The most famous process of all, however, outside of the process Malcolm 20
X describes in his "Autobiography," and maybe the process of Sammy Davis,
Jr., was Nat King Cole's process. Nat King Cole had patent-leather hair.
That man's got the finest process money can buy, or so Daddy said the night
we saw Cole's TV show on NBC. It was November 5, 1956. I remember the
date because everyone came to our house to watch it and to celebrate one of
Daddy's buddies' birthdays. Yeah, Uncle Joe chimed in, they can do shit to
his hair that the average Negro can't even *think* about — secret shit.

Nat King Cole was *clean*. I've had an ongoing argument with a Nigerian 21
friend about Nat King Cole for twenty years now. Not about whether he
could sing — any fool knows that he could — but about whether or not he
was a handkerchief head for wearing that patent-leather process.

Sammy Davis, Jr.'s, process was the one I detested. It didn't look good on 22
him. Worse still, he liked to have a fried strand dangling down the middle
of his forehead, so he could shake it out from the crown when he sang. But
Nat King Cole's hair was a thing unto itself, a beautifully sculpted work of art
that he and he alone had the right to wear. The only difference between a
process and a stocking cap, really, was taste; but Nat King Cole, unlike, say,
Michael Jackson, looked *good* in his. His head looked like Valentino's head
in the twenties, and some say it was Valentino the process was imitating. But
Nat King Cole wore a process because it suited his face, his demeanor, his
name, his style. He was as clean as he wanted to be.

I had forgotten all about that patent-leather look until one day in 1971, 23
when I was sitting in an Arab restaurant on the island of Zanzibar surrounded
by men in fezzes and white caftans, trying to learn how to eat curried goat
and rice with the fingers of my right hand and feeling two million miles from
home. All of a sudden, an old transistor radio sitting on top of a china
cupboard stopped blaring out its Swahili music and started playing "Fly Me
to the Moon," by Nat King Cole. The restaurant's din was not affected at all,
but in my mind's eye I saw it: the King's magnificent sleek black tiara. I
managed, barely, to blink back the tears.

Analyzing This Selection

1. What were Gates's boyhood attitudes toward his mother's hairstyling business?
   Find words and phrases that suggest the sort of child he was.

2. How does the other meaning of "kitchen" affect the essay's title?

3. Why couldn't black people easily switch their definitions of "good" and "bad"
   hair? What were the complications in using these terms?

4. When and why did Gates first accept the natural style of his hair? Why doesn't the author give more emphasis to his change in attitude?

5. What seemed so great about Nat King Cole's hair? Why does the author nearly weep when reminded of it?

Analyzing Connections

6. What views and explanations can Marcia Aldrich add (see "Hair," p. 36) to help Gates understand some nonracial meanings of a hairdo? Does Gates's perspective on blacks add another dimension to Aldrich's view of women's hairdressing?

Analyzing by Writing

7. Do young people (adolescents through twenty-somethings) need to identify with or be liberated from their ancestral cultures? What individual strengths and vulnerabilities increase or decrease from drawing close — or from pulling farther away? Discuss one connection to your ethnic, racial, or religious heritage that you have either willingly adopted or resisted for personal reasons. Fully explain why you made the choices you did.

Andrew Hacker

RACISM AS A
CONSOLATION PRIZE[1]

◇

ANDREW HACKER (b. 1929) is a professor of political science at Queens College, New York City. He graduated from Amherst College and completed his doctoral degree at Princeton University. His books include *The End of the American Era* (1970). Hacker's essays on economic and political issues appear in magazines such as *Newsweek, The Atlantic Monthly, Harper's,* and *The Nation.* The following selection is excerpted from his recent analysis of racial divisions in the United States, *Two Nations: Black and White, Separate, Hostile, Unequal* (1992).

America has always been the most competitive of societies. It poises its 1 citizens against one another, with the warning that they must make it on their own. Hence the stress on moving past others, driven by a fear of falling behind. No other nation so rates its residents as winners or losers.

If white America orchestrates this arena, it cannot guarantee full security 2 to every member of its own race. Still, while some of its members may fail, there is a limit to how far they can fall. For white America has agreed to provide a consolation prize: No matter to what depths one descends, no white person can ever become black. As James Baldwin has pointed out, white people need the presence of black people as a reminder of what providence has spared them from becoming.

If white people are compelled to compete against one another, they are 3 also urged to believe that any advances blacks may make will be at their expense. Here government and politics reflect a harsh economy. Indeed, this country is less a society, certainly less a community, than any of the countries with which it compares itself. A reason commonly given is that the United States is a large and diverse country. What is less commonly acknowledged is that its culture makes a point of exaggerating differences and exacerbating frictions. This appears most vividly in the stress placed on race.

Competition and whites' fears of failure help to explain the resistance to 4 ensuring opportunities for black Americans, let alone more equitable outcomes. Even allowing for interludes like the New Deal and the Great

[1]Editor's title.

Society, government is expected to take on obligations only as a late and last resort. Hence the presence in the United States of more violent crime, more of its people in prison, more homeless families and individuals, more children created virtually by accident, more fatal addiction and disease, more dirt and disorder — why prolong the list? — than any other nation deemed industrially advanced and socially civilized.

A society that places so great a premium on "getting ahead" cannot afford   5
to spare much compassion for those who fall behind. If the contest were racially fair, it would at least be true to its own principle of assessing all individuals solely on talent and effort. But keeping black Americans so far behind the starting line means most of the outcomes will be racially foreordained. . . .

Most white Americans will say that, all things considered, things aren't so   6
bad for black people in the United States. Of course, they will grant that many problems remain. Still, whites feel there has been steady improvement, bringing blacks closer to parity, especially when compared with conditions in the past. Some have even been heard to muse that it's better to be black, since affirmative action policies make it a disadvantage to be white.

What white people seldom stop to ask is how they may benefit from   7
belonging to their race. Nor is this surprising. People who can see do not regard their vision as a gift for which they should offer thanks. It may also be replied that having a white skin does not immunize a person from misfortune or failure. Yet even for those who fall to the bottom, being white has a worth. What could that value be?

Let us try to find out by means of a parable: Suspend disbelief for a   8
moment, and assume that what follows might actually happen:

The Visit

You will be visited tonight by an official you have never met. He begins by telling you that he is extremely embarrassed. The organization he represents has made a mistake, something that hardly ever happens.

According to their records, he goes on, you were to have been born black: to another set of parents, far from where you were raised.

However, the rules being what they are, this error must be rectified, and as soon as possible. So at midnight tonight, you will become black. And this will mean not simply a darker skin, but the bodily and facial features associated with African ancestry. However, inside you will be the person you always were. Your knowledge and ideas will remain intact. But outwardly you will not be recognizable to anyone you now know.

Your visitor emphasizes that being born to the wrong parents was in no way your fault. Consequently, his organization is prepared to offer you some reasonable recompense. Would you, he asks, care to name a sum of money you might consider appropriate? He adds that his group is by no means poor. It can be quite generous when the circumstances warrant, as they seem to in your case. He finishes by saying that their records show you are scheduled to live another fifty years — as a black man or woman in America.

How much financial recompense would you request?

When this parable has been put to white students, most seemed to feel 9 that it would not be out of place to ask for $50 million, or $1 million for each coming black year. And this calculation conveys, as well as anything, the value that white people place on their own skins. Indeed, to be white is to possess a gift whose value can be appreciated only after it has been taken away. And why ask so large a sum? Surely this needs no detailing. The money would be used, as best it could, to buy protection from the discriminations and dangers white people know they would face once they were perceived to be black. . . .

Hence, the weight Americans have chosen to give to race, in particular to 10 the artifact of "whiteness," sets a floor on how far people of that complexion can fall. No matter how degraded their lives, white people are still allowed to believe that they possess the blood, the genes, the patrimony of superiority. No matter what happens, they can never become "black." White Americans of all classes have found it comforting to preserve blacks as a subordinate caste: a presence, which despite all its pain and problems, still provides whites with some solace in a stressful world.

Analyzing This Selection

1. What is Hacker's charge against America's competitiveness? What historical and political evidence from less competitive countries could corroborate or challenge his assumption?

2. The parable suggests that a person changed from white to black would face additional costs of living. On what things might this person spend money in order "to buy protection from the discriminations and dangers" of being black?

Analyzing Connections

3. Hacker and Maya Angelou (see "Graduation," p. 193) perceive rivalries at the center of racism. Do the authors hold similar or contrasting views about competitiveness?

4. Would Alexis de Tocqueville (see Insights, p. 244) agree or disagree with Hacker's view of American society? In your opinion, has Hacker updated or refuted Tocqueville's view?

Analyzing by Writing

5. Hacker points out that whiteness is a privileged caste in America. In your view, what are some white privileges (that is, assumed preferential treatment) that pervade the whole society? What are the white privileges on campus? Does competition tend to solidify or reduce this caste system?

Shelby Steele

THE NEW SOVEREIGNTY

◇

SHELBY STEELE (b. 1946), grew up in a black community in Chicago. He earned his Ph.D. in history from the University of Utah, and he teaches English at San Jose State University in California. His essays on race relations have appeared in magazines such as *Harper's*, the *New York Times Magazine*, *Commentary*, and *Black World*. His criticisms of both white and black social policies on affirmative action and other issues are collected in *The Content of Our Character: A New Vision of Race in America* (1990), which won a National Book Critics Circle Award. The following essay was selected for *The Best American Essays of 1993*.

Toward the end of a talk I gave recently at a large Midwestern university 1 I noticed a distinct tension in the audience. All respectful audiences are quiet, but I've come to understand that when there is disagreement with what's being said at the podium the silence can become pure enough to constitute a statement. Fidgeting and whispering cease, pencils stay still in notetakers' hands — you sense the quiet filling your pauses as a sign of disquiet, even resistance. A speaker can feel ganged-up on by such a silence.

I had gotten myself into this spot by challenging the orthodoxy of diversity 2 that is now so common on university campuses — not the *notion* of diversity, which I wholly subscribe to, but the rigid means by which it is pursued. I had told the students and faculty members on hand that in the late 1960s, without much public debate but with many good intentions, America had embarked upon one of the most dramatic social experiments in its history. The federal government, radically and officially, began to alter and expand the concept of entitlement in America. Rights to justice and to government benefits were henceforth to be extended not simply to individuals but to racial, ethnic, and other groups. Moreover, the essential basis of all entitlement in America — the guarantees of the Constitution — had apparently been found wanting; there was to be redress and reparation of past grievances, and the Constitution had nothing to say about that.

I went on to explain that Martin Luther King and the early civil rights 3 leaders had demanded only constitutional rights; they had been found wanting, too. By the late Sixties, among a new set of black leaders, there had developed a presumption of collective entitlement (based on the redress of

275

past grievances) that made blacks eligible for rights beyond those provided for in the Constitution, and thus beyond those afforded the nation's non-black citizens. Thanks to the civil rights movement, a young black citizen as well as a young white citizen could not be turned away from a college because of the color of his or her skin; by the early Seventies a young black citizen, poor or wealthy, now qualified for certain grants and scholarships — might even be accepted for admission — simply *because* of the color of his or her skin. I made the point that this new and rather unexamined principle of collective entitlement had led America to pursue a democracy of groups as well as of individuals — that collective entitlement enfranchised groups just as the Constitution enfranchised individuals.

It was when I introduced a concept I call the New Sovereignty that my   4
audience's silence became most audible. In America today, I said, sovereignty — that is, power to act autonomously — is bestowed upon any group that is able to construct itself around a perceived grievance. With the concept of collective entitlement now accepted not only at the federal level but casually at all levels of society, any aggrieved group — and, for that matter, any assemblage of citizens that might or might not have previously been thought of as such a group — could make its case, attract attention and funding, and build a constituency that, in turn, would increase attention and funding. Soon this organized group of aggrieved citizens would achieve sovereignty, functioning without our long-sovereign nation and negotiating with that nation for a separate, exclusive set of entitlements. And here I pointed to America's university campuses, where, in the name of grievances, blacks, women, Hispanics, Asians, Native Americans, gays, and lesbians had hardened into sovereign constituencies that vied for the entitlements of sovereignty — separate "studies" departments for each group, "ethnic" theme dorms, preferential admissions and financial-aid policies, a proportionate number of faculty of their own group, separate student lounges and campus centers, and so on. This push for equality among groups, I said, necessarily made for an inequality among individuals that prepared the ground for precisely the racial, gender, and ethnic divisiveness that, back in the Sixties, we all said we wanted to move beyond.

At the reception that followed the talk I was approached by a tall, elegant   5
woman who introduced herself as the chairperson of the women's-studies department. Anger and the will to be polite were at war in her face so that her courteous smile at times became a leer. She wanted to "inform" me that she was proud of the fact that women's studies was a separate department unto itself at her university. I asked her what could be studied in this department that could not studied in other departments. Take the case of, say, Virginia Woolf: In what way would a female academic teaching in a women's-studies department have a different approach to Woolf's writing than a woman professor in the English department? Above her determined smile her eyes became fierce. "You must know as a black that they won't accept us" — meaning women, blacks, presumably others — "in the En-

glish department. It's an oppressive environment for women scholars. We're not taken seriously there." I asked her if that wasn't all the more reason to be there, to fight the good fight, and to work to have the contributions of women broaden the entire discipline of literary studies. She said I was naive. I said her strategy left the oppressiveness she talked about unchallenged. She said it was a waste of valuable energy to spend time fighting "old white males." I said that if women were oppressed, there was nothing to do *but* fight.

We each held tiny paper plates with celery sticks and little bricks of 6 cheese, and I'm sure much body language was subdued by the tea-party postures these plates imposed on us. But her last word was not actually a word. It was a look. She parodied an epiphany of disappointment in herself, as if she'd caught herself in a bizarre foolishness. *Of course, this guy is the enemy. He is the very oppressiveness I'm talking about. How could I have missed it?* And so, suddenly comfortable in the understanding that I was hopeless, she let her smile become gracious. Grace was something she could afford now. An excuse was made, a hand extended, and then she was gone. Holding my little plate, I watched her disappear into the crowd.

Today there are more than five hundred separate women's-studies depart- 7 ments or programs in American colleges and universities. There are nearly four hundred independent black-studies departments or programs, and hundreds of Hispanic, Asian, and Native American programs. Given this degree of entrenchment, it is no wonder this woman found our little debate a waste of her time. She would have had urgent administrative tasks awaiting her attention — grant proposals to write, budget requests to work up, personnel matters to attend to. And suppose I had won the debate? Would she have rushed back to her office and begun to dismantle the women's-studies department by doling out its courses and faculty to long-standing departments like English and history? Would she have given her secretary notice and relinquished her office equipment? I don't think so.

I do think I know how it all came to this — how what began as an attempt 8 to address the very real grievances of women wound up creating newly sovereign fiefdoms like this women's-studies department. First there was collective entitlement. Then, since sovereignty requires autonomy, there had to be a demand for separate and independent stature within the university (or some other institution of society). There would have to be a separate territory, with the trappings that certify sovereignty and are concrete recognition of the grievance identity — a building or suite of offices, a budget, faculty, staff, office supplies, letterhead, et cetera.

And so the justification for separate women's- and ethnic-studies programs 9 has virtually nothing to do with strictly academic matters and everything to do with the kind of group-identity politics in which the principle of collective entitlement has resulted. My feeling is that there can be no full redress of the woeful neglect of women's intellectual contributions until those contributions are entirely integrated into the very departments that neglected them in the first place. The same is true for America's minorities. Only inclusion answers history's exclusion. But now the sovereignty of grievance-group identities has confused all this.

It was the sovereignty issue that squelched my talk with the women's-studies chairperson. She came to see me as an enemy not because I denied that women writers had been neglected historically; I was the enemy because my questions challenged the territorial sovereignty of her department and of the larger grievance identity of women. It was not a matter of fairness — of justice — but of power. She would not put it that way, of course. For in order to rule over her sovereign fiefdom it remains important that she seem to represent the powerless, the aggrieved. It remains important, too, that my objection to the New Sovereignty can be interpreted by her as sexist. When I failed to concede sovereignty, I became an enemy of women.

In our age of the New Sovereignty the original grievances — those having to do with fundamental questions such as basic rights — have in large measure been addressed, if not entirely redressed. But that is of little matter now. The sovereign fiefdoms are ends in themselves — providing career tracks and bases of power. This power tends to be used now mostly to defend and extend the fiefdom, often by exaggerating and exploiting secondary, amorphous, or largely symbolic complaints. In this way, America has increasingly become an uneasy federation of newly sovereign nations. . . .

In a liberal democracy, collective entitlements based upon race, gender, ethnicity, or some other group grievance are always undemocratic expedients. Integration, on the other hand, is the most difficult and inexpedient expansion of the democratic ideal; for in opting for integration, a citizen denies his or her impulse to use our most arbitrary characteristics — race, ethnicity, gender, sexual preference — as the basis for identity, as a key to status, or for claims to entitlement. Integration is twentieth-century America's elaboration of democracy. It eliminates such things as race and gender as oppressive barriers to freedom, as democrats of an earlier epoch eliminated religion and property. Our mistake has been to think of integration only as a utopian vision of perfect racial harmony. I think it is better to see integration as the inclusion of all citizens into the same sphere of rights, the same range of opportunities and possibilities that our Founding Fathers themselves enjoyed. Integration is not social engineering or group entitlements; it is a fundamental *absence* of arbitrary barriers to freedom.

If we can understand integration as an absence of barriers that has the effect of integrating all citizens into the same sphere of rights, then it can serve as a principle of democratic conduct. Anything that pushes anybody out of this sphere is undemocratic and must be checked, no matter the good intentions that seem to justify it. Understood in this light, collective entitlements are as undemocratic as racial and gender discrimination, and a group grievance is no more a justification for entitlement than the notion of white supremacy was at an earlier time. We are wrong to think of democracy as a gift of freedom; it is really a kind of discipline that avails freedom. Sometimes its enemy is racism and sexism; other times the enemy is our expedient attempts to correct these ills.

I think it is time for those who seek identity and power through grievance 14 groups to fashion identities apart from grievance, to grant themselves the widest range of freedom, and to assume responsibility for that freedom. Victimhood lasts only as long as it is accepted, and to exploit it for an empty sovereignty is to accept it. The New Sovereignty is ultimately about vanity. It is the narcissism of victims, and it brings only a negligible power at the exorbitant price of continued victimhood. And all the while integration remains the real work.

Analyzing This Selection

1. Steele opposes "collective entitlement," yet he subscribes to "diversity." Does he appear to be for or against affirmative action laws and programs as the means to achieve diversity?

2. According to Steele, how is the New Sovereignty divisive? Explain why he thinks that separate turfs create barriers to equality. Do you agree with Steele?

3. In his account of his conversation with the women's studies chairperson, does the author give the participants a level playing field?

4. What does Steele favor as America's form of democracy? What is your view of his goal for society?

Analyzing Connections

5. The women's studies chairperson called Steele "naive." Would Andrew Hacker (in the preceding selection) also call him naive? or wise? or perhaps something else? Bring Hacker's viewpoint into Steele's consideration of remedies for minority grievances.

Analyzing by Writing

6. Explain both the benefits and the disadvantages of making full participation an entitlement. Use your contact with ethnic or minority groups on campus, or use your experience in other collective enfranchisements. For instance, when you participated in sports and/or music education programs as a young person, did everyone in your group — your team, family, or class — get to play? What are the good and bad effects of affirming full participation by all members? What conflicts arise between two equally good purposes? How have you seen them resolved?

7. Do you think that separate "studies" departments, ethnic theme dorms, and other separate organizations for ethnic, racial, and gender groups have a place in the university, or do you agree with Steele that such organizations are counterproductive? Explain and support your assertion, perhaps drawing on observations of your own campus.

Lucy Honig

ENGLISH AS A
SECOND LANGUAGE

◇

Lucy Honig grew up in Maine. After moving to Brooklyn, she began teaching
English to adult immigrants. The following story grew out of that experience.
According to the author, her students "were not yet saturated with American
media hype, and . . . they could usually tell the difference between real feeling
and baloney." Honig's stories have appeared in the *Georgia Review*, the
Gettysburg Review, and *The Best American Short Stories of 1988*. Honig now
lives in a small town in upstate New York, where she directs a local human
rights agency.

Inside Room 824, Maria parked the vacuum cleaner, fastened all the locks   1
and the safety chain and kicked off her shoes. Carefully she lay a stack of
fluffy towels on the bathroom vanity. She turned the air conditioning up
high and the lights down low. Then she hoisted up the skirt of her uniform
and settled all the way back on the king-sized bed with her legs straight out
in front of her. Her feet and ankles were swollen. She wriggled her toes. She
threw her arms out in each direction and still her hands did not come near
the edges of the bed. From here she could see, out the picture window, the
puffs of green treetops in Central Park, the tiny people circling along the
paths below. She tore open a small foil bag of cocktail peanuts and ate them
very slowly, turning each one over separately with her tongue until the salt
dissolved. She snapped on the TV with the remote control and flipped
channels.

The big mouth game show host was kissing and hugging a woman playing   2
on the left-hand team. Her husband and children were right there with her,
and *still* he encircled her with his arms. Then he sidled up to the daughter,
a girl younger than her own Giuliette, and *hugged* her and kept *holding* her,
asking questions. None of his business, if this girl had a boyfriend back in
Saginaw!

"Mama, you just don't understand!" That's what Jorge always said when   3
she watched TV at home. He and his teenaged friends would sit around in
their torn bluejeans dropping potato chips between the cushions of her couch
and laughing, writhing with laughter while she sat like a stone.

Now the team on the right were hugging each other, squealing, jumping 4
up and down. They'd just won a whole new kitchen — refrigerator, dish-
washer, microwave, *everything!* Maria could win a whole new kitchen too,
someday. You just spun a wheel, picked some words. She could do that.

She saw herself on TV with Carmen and Giuliette and Jorge. Her hand- 5
some children were so quick to press the buzzers the other team never had
a chance to answer first. And they got every single answer right. Her children
shrieked and clapped and jumped up and down each time the board lit up.
They kissed and hugged that man whenever they won a prize. That man put
his hands on her beautiful young daughters. That man pinched and kissed
her, an old woman, in front of the whole world! Imagine seeing *this* back
home! Maria frowned, chewing on the foil wrapper. There was nobody left
at home in Guatemala, nobody to care if a strange man squeezed her
wrinkled flesh on the TV.

"Forget it, Mama. They don't let poor people on these programs," Jorge 6
said one day.

"But poor people need the money, they can win it here!" 7

Jorge sighed impatiently. "They don't give it away because you *need* it!" 8

It was true, she had never seen a woman with her kids say on a show: My 9
husband's dead. Jorge knew. They made sure before they invited you that
you were the right kind of people and you said the right things. Where would
she put a new kitchen in her cramped apartment anyway! No hookups for a
washer, no space for a two-door refrigerator . . .

She slid sideways off the bed, carefully smoothed out the quilted spread, 10
and squeezed her feet into her shoes. Back out in the hall she counted the
bath towels in her cart to see if there were enough for the next wing. Then
she wheeled the cart down the long corridor, silent on the deep blue rug.

Maria pulled the new pink dress on over her head, eased her arms into the 11
sleeves, then let the skirt slide into place. In the mirror she saw a small dark
protrusion from a large pink flower. She struggled to zip up in back, then she
fixed the neck, attaching the white collar she had crocheted. She pinned the
rhinestone brooch on next. Shaking the pantyhose out of the package, she
remembered the phrase: the cow before the horse, wasn't that it? She should
have put these on first. Well, so what. She rolled down the left leg of the
nylons, stuck her big toe in, and drew the sheer fabric around her foot,
unrolling it up past her knee. Then she did the right foot, careful not to catch
the hose on the small flap of scar.

The right foot bled badly when she ran over the broken glass, over what 12
had been the only window of the house. It had shattered from gunshots
across the dirt yard. The chickens dashed around frantically, squawking,
trying to fly, spraying brown feathers into the air. When she had seen Pedro's
head turn to blood and the two oldest boys dragged away, she swallowed
every word, every cry, and ran with the two girls. The fragments of glass

stayed in her foot for all the days of hiding. They ran and ran and ran and somehow Jorge caught up and they were found by their own side and smuggled out. And still she was silent, until the nurse at the border went after the glass and drained the mess inside her foot. Then she had sobbed and screamed, "Aaiiiee!"

"Mama, stop thinking and get ready," said Carmen.   13
"It is too short, your skirt," Maria said in Spanish. "What will they say?"   14
Carmen laughed. "It's what they all wear, except for you old ladies."   15
"Not to work! Not to school!"   16
"Yes, to work, to school! And Mama, you are going for an award for your   17
English, for all you've learned, so please speak English!"
Maria squeezed into the pink high heels and held each foot out, one by   18
one, so she could admire the beautiful slim arch of her own instep, like the feet of the American ladies on Fifth Avenue. Carmen laughed when she saw her mother take the first faltering steps, and Maria laughed too. How much she had already practiced in secret, and still it was so hard! She teetered on them back and forth from the kitchen to the bedroom, trying to feel steady, until Carmen finally sighed and said, "Mama, quick now or you'll be late!"

She didn't know if it was a good omen or a bad one, the two Indian   19
women on the subway. They could have been sitting on the dusty ground at the market in San _____, selling corn or clay pots, with the bright-colored striped shawls and full skirts, the black hair pulled into two braids down each back, the deeply furrowed square faces set in those impassive expressions, seeing everything, seeing nothing. They were exactly as they must have been back home, but she was seeing them *here*, on the downtown IRT from the Bronx, surrounded by businessmen in suits, kids with big radio boxes, girls in skin-tight jeans and dark purple lipstick. Above them, advertisements for family planning and TWA. They were like stone-age men sitting on the train in loincloths made from animal skins, so out of place, out of time. Yet timeless. Maria thought, they are timeless guardian spirits, here to accompany me to my honors. Did anyone else see them? As strange as they were, nobody looked. Maria's heart pounded faster. The boys with the radios were standing right over them and never saw them. They were invisible to everyone but her: Maria was utterly convinced of it. The spirit world had come back to life, here on the number 4 train! It was a miracle!

"Mama, look, you see the grandmothers?" said Carmen.   20
"Of course I see them," Maria replied, trying to hide the disappointment   21
in her voice. So Carmen saw them too. They were not invisible. Carmen rolled her eyes and smirked derisively as she nodded in their direction, but before she could put her derision into words, Maria became stern. "Have respect," she said. "They are the same as your father's people." Carmen's face sobered at once.

She panicked when they got to the big school by the river. "Like the 22
United Nations," she said, seeing so much glass and brick, an endless
esplanade of concrete.

"It's only a college, Mama. People learn English here, too. And more, 23
like nursing, electronics. This is where Anna's brother came for computers."

"Las Naciones Unidas," Maria repeated, and when the guard stopped 24
them to ask where they were going, she answered in Spanish: to the literacy
award ceremony.

"*English*, Mama!" whispered Carmen. 25

But the guard also spoke in Spanish: Take the escalator to the third floor. 26

"See, he knows," Maria retorted. 27

"That's not the point," murmured Carmen, taking her mother by the 28
hand.

Every inch of the enormous room was packed with people. She clung to 29
Carmen and stood by the door paralyzed until Cheryl, her teacher, pushed
her way to them and greeted Maria with a kiss. Then she led Maria back
through the press of people to the small group of award winners from other
programs. Maria smiled shakily and nodded hello.

"They're all here now!" Cheryl called out. A photographer rushed over 30
and began to move the students closer together for a picture.

"Hey Bernie, wait for the Mayor!" someone shouted to him. He spun 31
around, called out some words Maria did not understand, and without even
turning back to them, he disappeared. But they stayed there, huddled close,
not knowing if they could move. The Chinese man kept smiling, the tall
black man stayed slightly crouched, the Vietnamese woman squinted, confused, her glasses still hidden in her fist. Maria saw all the cameras along the
sides of the crowd, and the lights, and the people from television with video
machines, and more lights. Her stomach began to jump up and down.
Would she be on television, in the newspapers? Still smiling, holding his
pose, the Chinese man next to her asked, "Are you nervous?"

"Oh yes," she said. She tried to remember the expression Cheryl had 32
taught them. "I have worms in my stomach," she said.

He was a much bigger man than she had imagined from seeing him on 33
TV. His face was bright red as they ushered him into the room and quickly
through the crowd, just as it was his turn to take the podium. He said hello
to the other speakers and called them by their first names. The crowd drew
closer to the little stage, the people standing farthest in the back pushed in.
Maria tried hard to listen to the Mayor's words. "Great occasion . . . pride
of our city . . . ever since I created the program . . . people who have worked
so hard . . . overcoming hardship . . . come so far." Was that them? Was he
talking about them already? Why were the people out there all starting to
laugh? She strained to understand, but still caught only fragments of his
words. "My mother used to say . . . and I said, Look, Mama . . ." He was

talking about *his* mother now; he called her Mama, just like Maria's kids called *her*. But everyone laughed so hard. At his mother? She forced herself to smile; up front, near the podium, everyone could see her. She should seem to pay attention and understand. Looking out into the crowd she felt dizzy. She tried to find Carmen among all the pretty young women with big eyes and dark hair. There she was! Carmen's eyes met Maria's; Carmen waved. Maria beamed out at her. For a moment she felt like she belonged there, in this crowd. Everyone was smiling, everyone was so happy while the Mayor of New York stood at the podium telling jokes. How happy Maria felt too!

"Maria Perez grew up in the countryside of Guatemala, the oldest daugh- 34 ter in a family of 19 children," read the Mayor as Maria stood quaking by his side. She noticed he made a slight wheezing noise when he breathed between words. She saw the hairs in his nostrils, black and white and wiry. He paused. "Nineteen children!" he exclaimed, looking at the audience. A small gasp was passed along through the crowd. Then the Mayor looked back at the sheet of paper before him. "Maria never had a chance to learn to read and write, and she was already the mother of five children of her own when she fled Guatemala in 1980 and made her way to New York for a new start."

It was her own story, but Maria had a hard time following. She had to 35 stand next to him while he read it, and her feet had started to hurt, crammed into the new shoes. She shifted her weight from one foot to the other.

"At the age of 45, while working as a chambermaid and sending her 36 children through school, Maria herself started school for the first time. In night courses she learned to read and write in her native Spanish. Later, as she was pursuing her G.E.D. in Spanish, she began studying English as a Second Language. This meant Maria was going to school five nights a week! Still she worked as many as 60 hours cleaning rooms at the Plaza Hotel.

"Maria's ESL teacher, Cheryl Sands, says — and I quote — 'Maria works 37 harder than any student I have ever had. She is an inspiration to her classmates. Not only has she learned to read and write in her new language, but she initiated an oral history project in which she taped and transcribed interviews with other students, who have told their stories from around the world.' Maria was also one of the first in New York to apply for amnesty under the 1986 Immigration Act. Meanwhile, she has passed her enthusiasm for education to her children: Her son is now a junior in high school, her youngest daughter attends the State University, and her oldest daughter, who we are proud to have with us today, is in her second year of law school on a scholarship."

Two older sons were dragged through the dirt, chickens squawking in mad 38 confusion, feathers flying. She heard more gunshots in the distance, screams, chickens squawking. She heard, she ran. Maria looked down at her bleeding feet. Wedged tightly into the pink high heels, they throbbed.

The Mayor turned toward her. "Maria, I think it's wonderful that you 39
have taken the trouble to preserve the folklore of students from so many
countries." He paused. Was she supposed to say something? Her heart
stopped beating. What was folklore? What was preserved? She smiled up at
him, hoping that was all she needed to do.

"Maria, tell us now, if you can, what was one of the stories you collected 40
in your project?"

This was definitely a question, meant to be answered. Maria tried to smile 41
again. She strained on tiptoes to reach the microphone, pinching her toes
even more tightly in her shoes. "Okay," she said, setting off a high-pitched
ringing from the microphone.

The Mayor said, "Stand back," and tugged at her collar. She quickly 42
stepped away from the microphone.

"Okay," she said again, and this time there was no shrill sound. "One of 43
my stories, from Guatemala. You want to hear?"

The Mayor put his arm around her shoulder and squeezed hard. Her first 44
impulse was to wriggle away, but he held tight. "Isn't she wonderful?" he
asked the audience. There was a low ripple of applause. "Yes, we want to
hear!"

She turned and looked up at his face. Perspiration was shining on his 45
forehead and she could see by the bright red bulge of his neck that his collar
was too tight. "In my village in Guatemala," she began, "the mayor did not
go along — get along — with the government so good."

"Hey, Maria," said the Mayor, "I know exactly how he felt!" The people 46
in the audience laughed. Maria waited until they were quiet again.

"One day our mayor met with the people in the village. Like you meet 47
people here. A big crowd in the square."

"The people liked him, your mayor?" 48

"Oh, yes," said Maria. "Very much. He was very good. He tried for more 49
roads, more doctors, new farms. He cared very much about his people."

The Mayor shook his head up and down. "Of course," he said, and again 50
the audience laughed.

Maria said, "The next day after the meeting, the meeting in the square 51
with all the people, soldiers come and shoot him dead."

For a second there was total silence. Maria realized she had not used the 52
past tense and felt a deep, horrible stab of shame for herself, shame for her
teacher. She was a disgrace! But she did not have more than a second of this
horror before the whole audience began to laugh. What was happening?
They couldn't be laughing at her bad verbs? They couldn't be laughing at her
dead mayor! They laughed louder and louder and suddenly flashbulbs were
going off around her, the TV cameras swung in close, too close, and the
Mayor was grabbing her by the shoulders again, holding her tight, posing for
one camera after another as the audience burst into wild applause. But she
hadn't even finished! Why were they laughing?

"What timing, huh?" said the Mayor over the uproar. "What d'ya think, 53
the Republicans put her here, or maybe the Board of Estimate?" Everyone
laughed even louder and he still clung to her and cameras still moved in
close, lights kept going off in her face and she could see nothing but the sharp
white poof! of light over and over again. She looked for Carmen and Cheryl,
but the white poof! poof! poof! blinded her. She closed her eyes and listened
to the uproar, now beginning to subside, and in her mind's eye saw chickens
trying to fly, chickens fluttering around the yard littered with broken glass.

He squeezed her shoulders again and leaned into the microphone. "There 54
are ways to get rid of mayors, and ways to get rid of mayors, huh Maria?"

The surge of laughter rose once more, reached a crescendo, and then 55
began to subside again. "But wait," said the Mayor. The cameramen stepped
back a bit, poising themselves for something new.

"I want to know just one more thing, Maria," said the Mayor, turning to 56
face her directly again. The crowd quieted. He waited a few seconds more,
then asked his question. "It says here 19 children. What was it like growing
up in a house with 19 children? How many *bathrooms* did you have?"

Her stomach dropped and twisted as the mayor put his hand firmly on the 57
back of her neck and pushed her toward the microphone again. It was
absolutely quiet now in the huge room. Everyone was waiting for her to
speak. She cleared her throat and made the microphone do the shrill hum.
Startled, she jumped back. Then there was silence. She took a big, trembling
breath.

"We had no bathrooms there, Mister Mayor," she said. "Only the out- 58
doors."

The clapping started immediately, then the flashbulbs burning up in her 59
face. The Mayor turned to her, put a hand on each of her shoulders, bent
lower and kissed her! Kissed her on the cheek!

"Isn't she terrific!" he asked the audience, his hand on the back of her 60
neck again, drawing her closer to him. The audience clapped louder, faster.
"Isn't she just the greatest?"

She tried to smile and open her eyes, but the lights were still going 61
off — poof! poof! — and the noise was deafening.

"Mama, look, your eyes were closed *there*, too," chided Jorge, sitting on 62
the floor in front of the television set.

Maria had watched the camera move from the announcer at the studio 63
desk to her own stout form in bright pink, standing by the Mayor.

"In my village in Guatemala," she heard herself say, and the camera 64
showed her wrinkled face close up, eyes open now and looking nowhere.
Then the mayor's face filled the screen, his forehead glistening, and then
suddenly all the people in the audience, looking ahead, enrapt, took his
place. Then there was her wrinkled face again, talking without a smile. ". . .
soldiers come and shoot him dead." Maria winced, hearing the wrong tense

of her verbs. The camera shifted from her face to the Mayor. In the brief moment of shamed silence after she'd uttered those words, the Mayor drew his finger like a knife across his throat. And the audience began to laugh.

"Turn it off!" she yelled to Jorge. "Off! This minute!"   65

Late that night she sat alone in the unlighted room, soaking her feet in   66 Epsom salts. The glow of the television threw shadows across the wall, but the sound was off. The man called Johnny was on the screen, talking. The people in the audience and the men in the band and the movie stars sitting on the couch all had their mouths wide open in what she knew were screams of laughter while Johnny wagged his tongue. Maria heard nothing except brakes squealing below on the street and the lonely clanging of garbage cans in the alley.

She thought about her English class and remembered the pretty   67 woman, Ling, who often fell asleep in the middle of a lesson. The other Chinese students all teased her. Everyone knew that she sewed coats in a sweatshop all day. After the night class she took the subway to the Staten Island Ferry, and after the ferry crossing she had to take a bus home. Her parents were old and sick and she did all their cooking and cleaning late at night. She struggled to keep awake in class; it seemed to take all her energy simply to smile and listen. She said very little and the teacher never forced her, but she fell further and further behind. They called her the Quiet One.

One day just before the course came to an end the Quiet One asked to   68 speak. There was no reason, no provocation — they'd been talking informally about their summer plans — but Ling spoke with a sudden urgency. Her English was very slow. Seeing what a terrible effort it was for her, the classmates all tried to help when she searched for words.

"In my China village there was a teacher," Ling began. "Man teacher."   69 She paused. "All children love him. He teached mathematic. He very — " She stopped and looked up toward the ceiling. Then she gestured with her fingers around her face.

"Handsome!" said Charlene, the oldest of the three Haitian sisters in the   70 class.

Ling smiled broadly. "Handsome! Yes, he very handsome. Family very   71 rich before. He have sister go to Hong Kong who have many, many money."

"*Much* money," said Maria.   72

"Much, much money," repeated Ling thoughtfully. "Teacher live in big   73 house."

"In China? Near you?"   74

"Yes. Big house with much old picture." She stopped and furrowed her   75 forehead, as if to gather words inside of it.

"Art? Paint? Pictures like that?" asked Xavier.   76

Ling nodded eagerly. "Yes. In big house. Most big house in village."   77

"But big house, money, rich like that, bad in China," said Fu Wu. 78
"Those year, Government bad to you. How they let him do?"

"In *my* country," said Carlos, "government bad to you if you got *small* 79
house, *no* money."

"Me too," said Maria. 80

"Me too," said Charlene. 81

The Chinese students laughed. 82

Ling shrugged and shook her head. "Don't know. He have big house. 83
Money gone, but keep big house. Then I am little girl." She held her hand
low to the floor.

"I *was* a little girl," Charlene said gently. 84

"I *was*," said Ling. "Was, was." She giggled for a moment, then seemed 85
to spend some time in thought. "We love him. All children love — all
children did love him. He giving tea in house. He was — was — so handsome!" She giggled. All the women in the class giggled. "He very nice. He
learn music, he go . . . he went to school far away."

"America?" 86

Ling shook her head. "Oh no, no. You know, another . . . west." 87

"Europa!" exclaimed Maria proudly. "Espain!" 88

"No, no, another." 89

"France!" said Patricia, Charlene's sister. "He went to school in France?" 90

"Yes, France," said Ling. Then she stopped again, this time for a whole 91
minute. The others waited patiently. No one said a word. Finally she continued. "But big boys in more old school not like him. He too handsome."

"Oooh!" sang out a chorus of women. "Too handsome!" 92

"The boys were jealous," said Carlos. 93

Ling seized the word. "Jealous! Jealous! They very jealous. He handsome, 94
he study France, he very nice to children, he give tea and cake in big house,
he show picture on the wall." Her torrent of words came to an end and she
began to think again, visibly, her brow furrowing. "Big school boys, they
. . ." She stopped.

"Jealous!" sang out the others. 95

"Yes," she said, shaking her head "no." "But more. More bad. Hate. 96
They hate him."

"That's bad," said Patricia. 97

"Yes, very bad." Ling paused, looking at the floor. "And they heat." 98

"Hate." 99

"No, they heat." 100

All the class looked puzzled. Heat? Heat? They turned to Cheryl. 101

The teacher spoke for the first time. "Hit! Ling, do you mean hit? They 102
hit him?" Cheryl slapped the air with her hand.

Ling nodded, her face somehow serious and smiling at the same time. 103
"Hit many time. And also so." She scooted her feet back and forth along the
floor.

"Oooh," exclaimed Charlene, frowning. "They kicked him with the 104 feet."

"Yes," said Ling. "They kicked him with the feet and hit him with the 105 hands, many many time they hit, they kick."

"Where this happened?" asked Xavier. 106

"In the school. In classroom like . . ." She gestured to mean their room. 107

"In the school?" asked Xavier. "But other people were they there? They 108 say stop, no?"

"No. Little children in room. They cry, they . . ." She covered her eyes 109 with her hand, then uncovered them. "Big boys kick and hit. No one stop. No one help."

Everyone in class fell silent. Maria remembered: they could not look at 110 one another then. They could not look at their teacher.

Ling continued. "They break him, very hurt much place." She stopped. 111 They all fixed their stares on Ling, they could bear looking only at her. "Many place," she said. Her face had not changed, it was still half smiling. But now there were drops coming from her eyes, a single tear down each side of her nose. Maria would never forget it. Ling's face did not move or wrinkle or frown. Her body was absolutely still. Her shoulders did not quake. Nothing in the shape or motion of her eyes or mouth changed. None of the things that Maria had always known happened when you cry happened when Ling shed tears. Just two drops rolled slowly down her two pale cheeks as she smiled.

"He very hurt. He *was* very hurt. He blood many place. Boys go away. 112 Children cry. Teacher break and hurt. Later he in hospital. I go there visit him." She stopped, looking thoughtful. "I went there." One continuous line of wetness glistened down each cheek. "My mother, my father say don't go, but I see him. I say, 'You be better?' But he hurt. Doctors no did helped. He alone. No doctor. No nurse. No medicine. No family." She stopped. They all stared in silence for several moments.

Finally Carlos said, "Did he went home?" 113

Ling shook her head. "He go home but no walk." She stopped. Maria 114 could not help watching those single lines of tears moving down the pale round face. "A year, more, no walk. Then go."

"Go where?" 115

"End." 116

Again there was a deep silence. Ling looked down, away from them, her 117 head bent low.

"Oh, no," murmured Charlene. "He died." 118

Maria felt the catch in her throat, the sudden wetness of tears on her own 119 two cheeks, and when she looked up she saw that all the other students, men and women both, were crying too.

Maria wiped her eyes. Suddenly all her limbs ached, her bones felt stiff 120 and old. She took her feet from the basin and dried them with a towel. Then she turned off the television and went to bed.

Analyzing This Selection

1. Maria perceives that television quiz shows select "the right kind of people." Who are they? What are "the right things" for contestants to say?

2. The prize citation relates part of Maria's history. How does this biographical sketch differ from Maria's own story of herself? What is her own attitude toward her life?

3. At the climax of Ling's story, the other immigrants cannot look at one another or at their teacher. Explain their reactions.

4. Reconsider the story's title. Why is English a *second* language?

Analyzing Connections

5. What would Amy Tan and Tan's mother (see "Mother Tongue," p. 226) say about the style of this story? Do you think the style serves Honig's purpose in writing?

Analyzing by Writing

6. Write a set of *Four Guidelines for Coping with the United States*. Explain four things that a newcomer has to know and understand in order to recognize American realities. Address yourself to young adults who are as well educated as yourself. Discuss what may be unfamiliar to an outsider. Your guidelines may explain positive or negative features of society.

7. Four selections in this book depict the difficulties immigrants have acquiring English and assimilating American culture. Looking back on Honig's story and the essays by Kingston (p. 203), Rodriguez (p. 208), and Tan (p. 226), examine the difficulties of entering our society. How does assimilation affect such matters as family ties, group identity, and self-awareness? What is gained and what is lost in the process of assimilating? Use evidence and illustrations from the selections to make your point. If you have personal knowledge of the assimilation process, add your information.

PART 6

POSSESSIONS

INSIGHTS

It is easier for a camel to go through the eye of a needle, than for a rich man to enter into the kingdom of God.

— MATTHEW 19:24

◇

A man is rich in proportion to the number of things which he can afford to let alone.

— HENRY DAVID THOREAU

◇

There is something about holding on to things that I find therapeutic.

— EDNA O'BRIEN

◇

I call people rich when they're able to meet the requirements of their imagination.

— HENRY JAMES

◇

I instinctively like to acquire and store up what promises to outlast me.

— COLETTE

◇

It is ironic that the very kind of thinking which produces all our riches also renders them unable to satisfy us. Our restless desire for more and more has been a major dynamic for economic growth, but it has made the achievement of that growth largely a hollow victory. Our sense of contentment and satisfaction is not a simple result of any absolute level of what we acquire or achieve. It depends upon our frame of reference, on how what we attain compares to what we expected. If we get farther than we expected we tend to feel good. If we expected to go farther than we have then even a rather high level of success can be experienced as disappointing. In America, we keep upping the ante. Our expectations keep accommodating to what we have attained. "Enough" is always just over the horizon, and like the horizon it recedes as we approach it.

We do not tend to think in terms of a particular set of conditions and amenities that we regard as sufficient and appropriate for a good life. Our calculations tend to be relative. It is not what we have that determines whether we think we are doing well; it is whether we have *more* — more than our parents, more than we had ten years ago, perhaps more than our neighbors. This latter source of relativity, keeping up with (or ahead of) the Joneses, is the most frequently commented upon. But it is probably less important, and less destructive, than our comparisons with our own previous levels and with the new expectations they generate. Wanting more remains a constant, regardless of what we have.

— PAUL WACHTEL

◇

Increasing familiarity with the curative powers of human tissues is likely, in the opinion of many, to foster a public attitude under which citizens will be considered to have a duty to make their dead bodies available for the aid of the sick, and the community will have valid claims upon its dead for the same purpose. It is well within contemplation that, as medicine continues to find greater and greater uses for human tissues, we will come to see these claims upon the dead assuming the aspect of a public entitlement. If this happened, the human body would acquire some of the attitudes of property. The possibility of such a climate of opinion makes it necessary to re-examine the strength of our beliefs in personal autonomy and individual freedom.

— RUSSELL SCOTT

◇

People who have lived for centuries in poverty in the relative isolation of the rural village have come to terms with this existence. It would be astonishing were it otherwise. People do not strive, generation after generation, century after century, against circumstances that are so constituted as to defeat them. They accept. Nor is such acceptance a sign of weakness of character. Rather, it is a profoundly rational response. Given the formidable hold of the . . . poverty within which they live, accommodation is the optimal solution. Poverty is cruel. A continuing struggle to escape that is continuously frustrated is more cruel. It is more civilized, more intelligent, as well as more plausible, that people, out of the experience of centuries, should reconcile themselves to what has for so long been the inevitable.

The deeply rational character of accommodation lies back, at least in part, of the central instruction of the principal world religions. All, without exception, urge acquiescence, some in remarkably specific form. The blessedness that Christianity accords to the meek is categorical. The pain of poverty is not denied, but its compensatory spiritual reward is very high. The poor pass through the eye of the needle into Paradise; the rich remain outside with the camels. Acquiescence is equally urged, or as in the case of Hinduism compelled, by the other ancient faiths. There has long been a suspicion, notably enhanced by Marx, that the contentment urged by religion is a design for diverting attention from the realities of class and exploitation — it is the opiate of the people. It is, more specifically, a formula for making the best of a usually hopeless situation.

— JOHN KENNETH GALBRAITH

◇

A Summer Morning

Her young employers, having got in late
From seeing friends in town
And scraped the right front fender on the gate,
Will not, the cook expects, be coming down.

She makes a quiet breakfast for herself.
The coffee-pot is bright,
The jelly where it should be on the shelf.
She breaks an egg into the morning light,

Then, with the bread-knife lifted stands and hears
The sweet efficient sounds
Of thrush and catbird, and the snip of shears
Where, in the terraced backward of the grounds,

A gardener works before the heat of day.
He straightens for a view
Of the big house ascending stony-gray
Out of his beds mosaic with the dew.

His young employers having got in late,
He and the cook alone
Receive the morning on their old estate,
Possessing what the owners can but own.

— RICHARD WILBUR

FOCUSING BY WRITING

1. Our possessions can possess us — and they frequently do, sometimes delightfully, sometimes harmfully. Nearly everyone has felt that the essence of life was summed up for the moment by having a dog, a record collection, a pair of skis, or earrings, or special jeans. In a brief essay, define your past or present obsession with a special personal belonging that affects your life.

2. Examine the effects of telephone technology on your life. Consider the beneficial and negative ways that an answering machine, a cordless phone, a car phone, voice mail, or some other telecommunication device plays a part in your friendships or family relations. Consider your gains and losses in matters affecting your freedom, vulnerability to others, and social status.

3. In many households there is some treasured object that is associated with earlier generations or with an important period in the recent family past. Perhaps it is a vase or lamp, a Bible or jewelry, a piece of furniture or a rug. The object comes to be treated as something precious and irre-placeable — even though it may be fairly common — because it embodies certain ideals or meanings. Select any single object that holds special status in your household; explain its meanings and how they are kept alive by customs and habits.

4. Going to look at other people's great wealth — for instance, the elegant houses of the very rich, royalty's crown jewels, or boats in a yacht basin — can sometimes be enjoyable and sometimes disturbing. Whatever the reaction, images of other people's wealth affect how we feel about ourselves. Describe an example of great wealth that stimulated you favorably or made you feel uncomfortable. Clarify the meaning of its effect on you.

Harry Crews

THE CAR

◇

HARRY CREWS (b. 1935), who was raised in Georgia, joined the Marine Corps after high school and became a sergeant before he left the corps to go to college. He was educated at the University of Florida, where he now teaches writing. His novels include CAR (1972), A *Feast of Snakes* (1976), and *The Knockout Artist* (1988). He often writes for magazines such as *Playboy* and *Esquire*, in the latter of which this essay first appeared.

The other day, there arrived in the mail a clipping sent by a friend of 1 mine. It had been cut from a Long Beach, California, newspaper and dealt with a young man who had eluded police for fifty-five minutes while he raced over freeways and through city streets at speeds up to 130 miles per hour. During the entire time, he ripped his clothes off and threw them out the window bit by bit. It finally took twenty-five patrol cars and a helicopter to catch him. When they did, he said that God had given him the car, and that he had "found God."

I don't want to hit too hard on a young man who obviously has his own 2 troubles, maybe even is a little sick with it all, but when I read that he had found God in the car, my response was: So *say we all*. We have found God in cars, or if not the true God, one so satisfying, so powerful, and awe-inspiring that the distinction is too fine to matter. Except perhaps ultimately, but pray we must not think too much on that.

The operative word in all this is *we*. It will not do for me to maintain that 3 I have been above it all, that somehow I've managed to remain aloof from the national love affair with cars. It is true that I got a late start. I did not learn to drive until I was twenty-one; my brother was twenty-five before he learned. The reason is simple enough. In Bacon County, Georgia, where I grew up, many families had nothing with a motor in it. Ours was one such family. But starting as late as I did, I still had my share, and I've remembered them all, the cars I've owned. I remember them in just the concrete specific way you remember anything that changed your life. Especially I remember the early ones.

The first car I ever owned was a 1938 Ford coupe. It had no low gear and 4 the door on the passenger side wouldn't open. I eventually put a low gear in it, but I never did get the door to work. One hot summer night on a clay road a young lady whom I'll never forget had herself braced and ready with one foot on the rearview mirror and the other foot on the wind vent. In the first few lovely frantic moments, she pushed out the wing vent, broke off the rearview mirror, and left her little footprints all over the ceiling. The memory of it was so affecting that I could never bring myself to repair the vent or replace the headliner she had walked all over upside down.

Eight months later I lost the car on a rain-slick road between Folkston, Georgia, and Waycross. I'd just stopped to buy a stalk of bananas (to a boy raised in the hookworm and rickets belt of the South, bananas will always remain an incredibly exotic fruit, causing him to buy whole stalks at a time), and back on the road again I was only going about fifty in a misting rain when I looked over to say something to my buddy, whose nickname was Bonehead and who was half drunk in the seat beside me. For some reason I'll never understand, I felt the back end of the car get loose and start to come up on us in the other lane. Not having driven very long, I overcorrected and stepped on the brake. We turned over four times. Bonehead flew out of the car and shot down a muddy ditch about forty yards before he stopped, sober and unhurt. I ended up under the front seat, thinking I was covered with gouts of blood. As it turned out, I didn't have much wrong with me and what I was covered with was gouts of mashed banana.

The second car I had was a 1940 Buick, square, impossibly heavy, built like a Sherman tank, but it had a '52 engine in it. Even though it took about ten miles to get her open full bore, she'd do over a hundred miles an hour on flat ground. It was so big inside that in an emergency it could sleep six. I tended to live in that Buick for almost a year and no telling how long I would have kept it if a boy who was not a friend of mine and who owned an International Harvester pickup truck hadn't said in mixed company that he could make the run from New Lacy in Coffee County, Georgia, to Jacksonville, Florida, quicker than I could. He lost the bet, but I wrung the speedometer off the Buick, and also — since the run was made on a blistering day in July — melted four inner tubes, causing them to fuse with the tires, which were already slick when the run started. Four new tires and tubes cost more than I had or expected to have anytime soon, so I sadly put that old honey up on blocks until I could sell it to a boy who lived up toward Macon.

After the Buick, I owned a 1953 Mercury with three-inch lowering blocks, fender skirts, twin aerials, and custom upholstering made of rolled Naugahyde. Staring into the bathroom mirror for long periods of time I practiced expressions to drive it with. It was that kind of car. It looked mean, and it was mean. Consequently, it had to be handled with a certain style. One-handing it through a ninety-degree turn on city streets in a power slide where you were in danger of losing your ass as well as the car, you were obligated to have your left arm hanging half out the window and a very *bored* expression on your face. That kind of thing.

Those were the sweetest cars I was ever to know because they were my   8
first. I remember them like people — like long-ago lovers — their idiosyn-
crasies, what they liked and what they didn't. With my hands deep in
crankcases, I was initiated into their warm greasy mysteries. Nothing in
the world was more satisfying than winching the front end up under the
shade of a chinaberry tree and sliding down the chassis on a burlap sack
with a few tools to see if the car would not yield to me and my expert
ways.

The only thing that approached working on a car was talking about one.   9
We'd stand about for hours, hustling our balls and spitting, telling stories
about how it had been somewhere, sometime, with the car we were driving.
It gave our lies a little focus and our talk a little credibility, if only because
we could point to the evidence.

"But, hell, don't it rain in with that wing vent broke out like that?"   10

"Don't mean nothing to me. Soon's Shirley kicked it out, I known I was   11
in love. I ain't about to put it back."

Usually we met to talk at night behind the A&W Root Beer stand, with   12
the air heavy with the smell of grease and just a hint of burned French fries
and burned hamburgers and burned hot dogs. It remains one of the most
sensuous, erotic smells in my memory because through it, their tight little
asses ticking like clocks, walked the sweetest softest short-skirted carhops in
the world. I knew what it was to stand for hours with my buddies, leaning
nonchalant as hell on a fender, pretending not to look at the carhops, and
saying things like: "This little baby don't look like much, but she'll git rubber
in three gears." And when I said it, it was somehow my own body I was
talking about. It was *my* speed and *my* strength that got rubber in three gears.
In the mystery of that love affair, the car and I merged.

But, like many another love affair, it has soured considerably. Maybe it   13
would have been different if I had known cars sooner. I was already out of the
Marine Corps and twenty-two years old before I could stand behind the
A&W Root Beer and lean on the fender of a 1938 coupe. That seems pretty
old to me to be talking about getting rubber in three gears, and I'm certain
it is *very* old to feel your own muscle tingle and flush with blood when you
say it. As is obvious, I was what used to be charitably called a late bloomer.
But at some point I did become just perceptive enough to recognize bullshit
when I was neck deep in it.

The 1953 Mercury was responsible for my ultimate disenchantment with   14
cars. I had already bored and stroked the engine and contrived to place a
six-speaker sound system in it when I finally started to paint it. I spent the
better half of a year painting that car. A friend of mine owned a body shop
and he let me use the shop on weekends. I sanded the Mercury down to raw
metal, primed it, and painted it. Then I painted it again. And again. And
then again. I went a little nuts, as I am prone to do, because I'm the kind of
guy who if he can't have too much of a thing doesn't want any at all. So one

day I came out of the house (I was in college then) and saw it, the '53 Mercury, the car upon which I had heaped more attention and time and love than I had ever given a human being. It sat at the curb, its black surface a shimmering of the air, like hundreds of mirrors turned to catch the sun. It had twenty-seven coats of paint, each coat laboriously hand-rubbed. It seemed to glow, not with reflected light, but with some internal light of its own.

I stood staring, and it turned into one of those great scary rare moments   15
when you are privileged to see into your own predicament. Clearly, there were two ways I could go. I could sell the car, or I could keep on painting it for the rest of my life. If twenty-seven coats of paint, why not a hundred and twenty-seven? The moment was brief and I understand it better now than I did then, but I did realize, if imperfectly, that something was dreadfully wrong, that the car owned me much more than I would ever own the car, no matter how long I kept it. The next day I drove to Jacksonville and left the Mercury on a used-car lot. It was an easy thing to do.

Since that day, I've never confused myself with a car, a confusion com-   16
mon everywhere about us — or so it seems to me. I have a car now, but I use it like a beast, the way I've used all cars since the Mercury, like a beast unlovely and unlikable but necessary. True as all that is, though, God knows I'm in the car's debt for that blistering winning July run to Jacksonville, and the pushed-out wing vent, and finally for that greasy air heavy with the odor of burned meat and potatoes there behind the A&W Root Beer. I'll never smell anything that good again.

Analyzing This Selection

1. What does Crews mean in saying, "We have found God in cars"? Why does the thought lead him to say, in almost the same breath, "pray we must not think too much on that"?

2. Crews seems to be exaggerating some details in his descriptions of his cars and in his accounts of his experiences. What kinds of exaggerations does he lard into his essay, and what effects do they have on our response to him as a writer? What qualities of his might be objectionable? What qualities might be thought of as attractive?

3. At what point did Crews begin to realize that he was identifying himself too closely with his cars? What other realization is this one linked with?

4. In the final paragraph, Crews says that people around him seem to be confusing themselves with their cars — in what ways? What features of common American life is he alluding to in that observation?

5. The tone of the essay includes some nostalgia — over what, precisely? What broader theme is included in his treatment of the main topic?

Analyzing Connections

6. Compare the ways that Crews and Thomas Simmons (see "Motorcycle Talk," p. 67) were changed by their vehicles. What aspects of themselves did they come to possess through their possessions?

Analyzing by Writing

7. Do young Americans currently idolize cars? What are contemporary teenage attitudes and expectations about cars? Discuss the role of the car in male or female rites of passage, new freedoms, and social relations, and consider its other symbolic and practical roles. If you think the thrill of cars has diminished for American youth (since Crews's generation), try to explain reasons for the decline.

Fred Davis

BLUE JEANS AND IDENTITY[1]

◇

FRED DAVIS (1925–1993) was a professor of sociology at the University of California at San Diego. He was raised in Brooklyn and graduated from Brooklyn College. He earned his doctoral degree at the University of Chicago. His main research areas were in nursing and physical disabilities. Recently, Davis turned to research on public moods and fashions, culminating in his final book *Fashion, Culture, and Identity* (1992), from which this selection is excerpted.

The new clothes [jeans] express profoundly democratic values. There are no distinctions of wealth or status, no elitism; people confront one another shorn of these distinctions.

— CHARLES A. REICH
The Greening of America

Throughout the world, the young and their allies are drawn hypnotically to denim's code of hope and solidarity — to an undefined vision of the energetic and fraternal Americanness inherent in them all.

— KENNEDY FRASER
"That Missing Button"

Karl Lagerfeld for Chanel shapes a classic suit from blue and white denim, $960, with denim bustier, $360, . . . and denim hat, $400. All at Chanel Boutique, Beverly Hills.

— Photograph caption in *Los Angeles Times Magazine*
for article "Dressed-Up Denims," April 19, 1987

Since the dawn of fashion in the West some seven hundred years ago, 1 probably no other article of clothing has in the course of its evolution more fully served as a vehicle for the expression of status ambivalences and ambiguities than blue jeans. Some of the social history supporting this statement is by now generally well known. First fashioned in the mid-nineteenth-century American West by Morris Levi Strauss, a Bavarian Jewish peddler

[1]Editor's title.

newly arrived in San Francisco, the trousers then as now were made from a sturdy, indigo-dyed cotton cloth said to have originated in Nimes, France. (Hence the anglicized contraction to *denim* from the French *de Nimes*. A garment similar to that manufactured by Levi Strauss for goldminers and outdoor laborers is said to have been worn earlier in France by sailors and dockworkers from Genoa, Italy, who were referred to as "genes"; hence the term *jeans*. The distinctive copper riveting at the pants pockets and other stress points were the invention of Jacob Davis, a tailor from Carson City, Nevada, who joined the Levi Strauss firm in 1873, some twenty years after the garment's introduction.

More than a century went by, however, before this working-man's gar- 2 ment attained the prominence and near-universal recognition it possesses today. For it was not until the late 1960s that blue jeans, after several failed moves in previous decades into a broader mass market, strikingly crossed over nearly all class, gender, age, regional, national, and ideological lines to become the universally worn and widely accepted item of apparel they are today. And since the crossover, enthusiasm for them has by no means been confined to North America and Western Europe. In former Soviet bloc countries and much of the Third World, too, where they have generally been in short supply, they remain highly sought after and hotly bargained over.

A critical feature of this cultural breakthrough is, of course, blue jeans's 3 identity change from a garment associated exclusively with work (and hard work, at that) to one invested with many of the symbolic attributes of leisure: ease, comfort, casualness, sociability, and the outdoors. . . . In bridging the work/leisure divide when it did, it tapped into the new, consumer-goods-oriented, postindustrial affluence of the West on a massive scale. Soon thereafter it penetrated those many other parts of the world that emulate the West.

But this still fails to answer the questions of why so rough-hewn, drably 4 hued, and crudely tailored a piece of clothing should come to exercise the fascination it has for so many diverse societies and peoples, or why within a relatively short time of breaking out of its narrow occupational locus it spread so quickly throughout the world. . . . Considering its origins and longtime association with workingmen, hard physical labor, the outdoors, and the American West, much of the blue jeans's fundamental mystique seems to emanate from populist sentiments of democracy, independence, equality, freedom, and fraternity. This makes for a sartorial symbolic complex at war . . . with class distinctions, elitism, and snobbism, dispositions extant nearly as much in jeans-originating America as in the Old World. It is not surprising, therefore, that the first non–"working stiffs" to become attached to blue jeans and associated denim wear were painters and other artists, mainly in the southwest United States, in the late 1930s and 1940s. These were soon followed by "hoodlum" motorcycle gangs ("bikers") in the 1950s and by New Left activists and hippies in the 1960s. All these groups (each in its own way, of course) stood strongly in opposition to the dominant conservative, middle-class, consumer-oriented culture of American society. Blue jeans, given their origins and historic associations, offered a visible means for announcing such antiestablishment sentiments. Besides, jeans were cheap, and, at least at first, good fit hardly mattered. . . .

Notwithstanding the symbolic elaborations and revisions (some would say   5 perversions) to which fashion and the mass market have in the intervening years subjected the garment, there can be little doubt that . . . its underlying symbolic appeal derived from its antifashion significations: its visually persuasive historic allusions to rural democracy, the common man, simplicity, unpretentiousness, and, for many, especially Europeans long captivated by it, the romance of the American West with its figure of the free-spirited, self-reliant cowboy.

But as the history of fashion has demonstrated time and again, no vest-   6 mental symbol is inviolable. All can, and usually will be, subjected to the whims of those who wish to convey more or different things about their person than the "pure" symbol in its initial state of signification communicates. Democratic, egalitarian sentiments notwithstanding, social status still counts for too much in Western society to permanently suffer the proletarianization that an unmodified blue-jean declaration of equality and fraternity projected. No sooner, then, had jeans made their way into the mass marketplace than myriad devices were employed for muting and mixing messages, readmitting evicted symbolic allusions, and, in general, promoting invidious distinctions among classes and coteries of jean wearers. Indeed, to the extent that their very acceptance was propelled by fashion as such, it can be said an element of invidiousness was already at play. For, other things being equal and regardless of the "message" a new fashion sends, merely to be "in fashion" is to be one up on those who are not as yet. . . .

A host of stratagems and devices . . . sought . . . to de-democratize jeans   7 while capitalizing on the ecumenical appeal they had attained: designer jeans, which prominently displayed the label of the designer; jeans bearing factory sewn-in embroidering, nailheads, rhinestones, and other decorative additions; specially cut and sized jeans for women, children, and older persons; in general, jeans combined (with fashion's sanction) with items of clothing standing in sharp symbolic contradiction of them, e.g., sports jackets, furs, dress shoes, spiked heels, ruffled shirts, or silk blouses.

Paralleling the de-democratization of the jean, by the 1970s strong   8 currents toward its eroticization were also evident. These, of course, contravened the unisex, de-gendered associations the garment initially held for many: the relative unconcern for fit and emphasis on comfort;

the fly front for both male and female; the coarse denim material, which, though it chafed some, particularly women, was still suffered willingly. Numerous means were found to invest the jean and its associated wear with gender-specific, eroticized meaning. In the instance of women — and this is more salient sociologically since it was they who had been defemininized by donning the blatantly masculine blue jeans in the first place — these included the fashioning of denim material into skirts, the "jeans for gals" sales pitches of manufacturers, the use of softer materials, cutting jeans so short as to expose the buttocks, and, in general, the transmogrification of jeans from loose-fitting, baggy trousers into pants so snugly pulled over the posterior as to require some women to lie down to get into them. So much for comfort, so much for unisexuality! . . .

Of all of the modifications wrought upon it, the phenomenon of designer 9 jeans speaks most directly to the garment's encoding of status ambivalences. The very act of affixing a well-known designer's label — and some of the world's leading hautes couturiers in time did so — to the back side of a pair of jeans has to be interpreted . . . as an instance of conspicuous consumption; in effect, a muting of the underlying rough-hewn proletarian connotation of the garment through the introduction of a prominent status marker. True, sewing an exterior designer label onto jeans — a practice designers never resort to with other garments — was facilitated psychologically by the prominent Levi Strauss & Co. label, which had from the beginning been sewn above the right hip pocket of that firm's denim jeans and had over the years become an inseparable part of the garment's image. It could then be argued, as it sometimes was, that the outside sewing of a designer label was consistent with the traditional image of blue jeans. Still, Yves Saint Laurent, Oscar de la Renta, or Gloria Vanderbilt, for that matter, are not names to assimilate easily with Levi Strauss, Lee, or Wrangler, a distinction hardly lost on most consumers.

But as is so characteristic of fashion, every action elicits its reaction. No 10 sooner had the snoblike, status-conscious symbolism of designer jeans made its impact on the market than dress coteries emerged whose sartorial stock-in-trade was a display of disdain for the invidious distinctions registered by so obvious a status ploy. This was accomplished mainly through a demonstration of hyperloyalty to the original, underlying egalitarian message of denim blue jeans. . . . "Positively baggy denims" . . . were . . . assimilated into the fashion cycle. Then those "into" denim styles could by "dressing down" stay ahead of — as had their older, first-time-around denim-clad siblings of the sixties — their more conformist, "properly dressed" alters. . . . The dialectics of status and antistatus, democracy and distinction, inclusiveness and exclusiveness pervade fashion's twists and turns; as much, or even more, with the workingman's humble blue jeans as with formal dinner wear and the evening gown.

Analyzing This Selection

1. The first sentence makes a very large claim about blue jeans. What part of that assertion does the essay support?

2. What different groups adopted blue jeans in the 1930s, 1940s, 1950s, and 1960s? What attitudes did these groups have in common?

3. What messages about social status are conveyed by fashion jeans? by designer jeans? and by "positively baggy" jeans?

Analyzing Connections

4. Do jeans facilitate the forming of male friendships? What would Marc Feigen Fasteau observe (see "Friendships Among Men," p. 168) about the status symbolism of jeans? Would Fasteau and Barbara Ehrenreich (see "In Praise of 'Best Friends,'" p. 163) interpret their status symbolism differently for women?

Analyzing by Writing

5. In your view, is wearing jeans a rebellious or a conformist action? Analyze and explain the mixed messages about inclusiveness and exclusiveness, and other symbolic meanings, that jeans currently express. Consider their messages not only about the individuals wearing them but also about society.

6. Analyze the fashion statement by the motorbiker in the photograph on page 292. What "status ambivalences and ambiguities" are expressed by her clothes and her other possessions?

Jamaica Kincaid

BIOGRAPHY OF A DRESS

◇

See the earlier headnote about Jamaica Kincaid on page 90. The following
essay appeared first in *Grand Street* (1992).

The dress I am wearing in this black-and-white photograph (p. 309), taken 1
when I was two years old, was a yellow dress made of cotton poplin (a fabric
with a slightly unsmooth texture first manufactured in the French town of
Avignon and brought to England by the Huguenots, but I could not have
known that at the time), and it was made for me by my mother. This shade
of yellow, the color of my dress that I am wearing when I was two years old,
was the same shade of yellow as boiled cornmeal, a food that my mother was
always eager for me to eat in one form (as a porridge) or another (as fongie,
the starchy part of my midday meal) because it was cheap and therefore easily
available (but I did not know that at the time), and because she thought that
foods bearing the colors yellow, green, or orange were particularly rich in
vitamins and so boiled cornmeal would be particularly good for me. But I
was then (not so now) extremely particular about what I would eat, not
knowing then (but I do now) of shortages and abundance, having no consciousness of the idea of rich and poor (but I know now that we were poor
then), and would eat only boiled beef (which I required my mother to chew
for me first and, after she had made it soft, remove it from her mouth and
place it in mine), certain kinds of boiled fish (doctor or angel), hard-boiled
eggs (from hens, not ducks), poached calf's liver and the milk from cows, and
so would not even look at the boiled cornmeal (porridge or fongie). There
was not one single thing that I could isolate and say I did not like about the
boiled cornmeal (porridge or fongie) because I could not isolate parts of
things then (though I can and do now), but whenever I saw this bowl of
trembling yellow substance before me I would grow still and silent, I did not
cry, that did not make me cry. My mother told me this then (she does not
tell me this now, she does not remember this now, she does not remember
telling me this now): She knew of a man who had eaten boiled cornmeal at
least once a day from the time he was my age then, two years old, and he
lived for a very long time, finally dying when he was almost one hundred
years old, and when he died he had looked rosy and new, with the springy

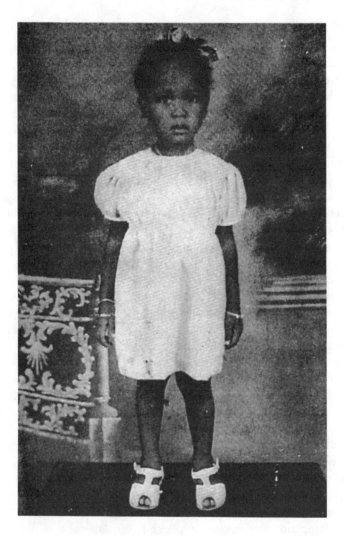

wrinkles of the newborn, not the slack pleats of skin of the aged; as he lay dead his stomach was cut open, and all his insides were a beautiful shade of yellow, the same shade of yellow as boiled cornmeal. I was powerless then (though not so now) to like or dislike this story; it was beyond me then (though not so now) to understand the span of my lifetime then, two years old, and it was beyond me then (though not so now), the span of time called almost one hundred years old; I did not know then (though I do now) that there was such a thing as an inside to anybody, and that this inside would have a color, and that if the insides were the same shade of yellow as the yellow of boiled cornmeal my mother would want me to know about it.

On a day when it was not raining (that would have been unusual, that would have been out of the ordinary, ruining the fixed form of the day), my mother walked to one of the Harneys' stores (there were many Harneys who owned stores, and they sold the same things, but I did not know then and I do not know now if they were all of the same people) and bought one-and-a-half yards of this yellow cotton poplin to make a dress for me, a dress I would wear to have my picture taken on the day I turned two years old. Inside, the store was cool and dark, and this was a good thing because outside was hot and overly bright. Someone named Harney did not wait on my mother, but someone named Miss Verna did and she was very nice still, so nice that she tickled my cheek as she spoke to my mother, and I reached forward as if to kiss her, but when her cheek met my lips I opened my mouth and bit her hard with my small child's teeth. Her cry of surprise did not pierce the air, but she looked at me hard, as if she knew me very, very well; and later, much later, when I was about twelve years old or so and she was always in and out of the crazy house, I would pass her on the street and throw stones at her, and she would turn and look at me hard, but she did not know who I was, she did not know who anyone was at all, not at all. Miss Verna showed my mother five flat thick bolts of cloth, white, blue (sea), blue (sky), yellow, and pink, and my mother chose the yellow after holding it up against the rich copper color that my hair was then (it is not so now); she paid for it with a one-pound note that had an engraving of the king George Fifth on it (an ugly man with a cruel, sharp, bony nose, not the kind, soft, fleshy noses I was then used to), and she received change that included crowns, shillings, florins, and farthings.

My mother, carrying me and the just-bought piece of yellow poplin wrapped in coarse brown paper in her arms, walked out of Mr. Harney's store, up the street a few doors away, and into a store called Murdoch's (because the family who owned it were the Murdochs), and there my mother bought two skeins of yellow thread, the kind used for embroidering and a shade of yellow almost identical to the yellow poplin. My mother not only took me with her everywhere she went, she carried me, sometimes in her arms, sometimes on her back; for this errand she carried me in her arms; she did not complain, she never complained (but later she refused to do it anymore and never gave an explanation, at least not one that I can remember now); as usual, she spoke to me and sang to me in French patois (but I did not understand French patois then and I do not now and so I can never know what exactly she said to me then). She walked back to our house on Dickenson Bay Street, stopping often to hold conversations with people (men and women) she knew, speaking to them sometimes in English, sometimes in French; and if after they said how beautiful I was (for people would often say that about me then but they do not say that about me now), she would laugh and say that I did not like to be kissed (and I don't know if that was really true then but it is not so now). And that night after we had eaten our supper (boiled fish in a butter-and-lemon-juice sauce) and her husband (who was not my father but I did not know that at the time, I know that now) had gone for a walk (to the jetty), she removed the yellow poplin from its brown wrapper and folded and made creases in it and with scissors made holes (for the arms and neck) and slashes (for an opening in the back and the shoulders); she then placed it along with some ordinary thread (yellow), the thread for embroidering, the scissors and a needle in a basket that she had brought with her from her home in Dominica when she first left it at sixteen years of age.

For days afterward, my mother, after she had finished her usual chores 4 (clothes washing, dish washing, floor scrubbing, bathing me, her only child, feeding me a teaspoon of cod-liver oil), sat on the sill of the doorway, half in the sun, half out of the sun, and sewed together the various parts that would make up altogether my dress of yellow poplin; she gathered and hemmed and made tucks; she was just in the early stages of teaching herself how to make smocking and so was confined to making straight stitches (up-cable, down-cable, outline, stem, chain); the bodice of the dress appeared simple, plain, and the detail and pattern can only be seen close up and in real life, not from far away and not in a photograph; and much later, when she grew in confidence with this craft, the bodice of my dresses became overburdened with the stitches chevron, trellis, diamonds, Vandyke, and species of birds she had never seen (swan) and species of flowers she had never seen (tulip) and species of animals she had never seen (bear) in real life, only in a picture in a book.

My skin was not the color of cream in the process of spoiling, my hair was 5 not the texture of silk and the color of flax, my eyes did not gleam like blue jewels in a crown, the afternoons in which I sat watching my mother make me this dress were not cool, and verdant lawns and pastures and hills and dales did not stretch out before me; but it was the picture of such a girl at two years old — a girl whose skin was the color of cream in the process of spoiling, whose hair was the texture of silk and the color of flax, a girl whose eyes gleamed like blue jewels in a crown, a girl whose afternoons (and mornings and nights) were cool, and before whom stretched verdant lawns and pastures and hills and dales — that my mother saw, a picture on an almanac advertising a particularly fine and scented soap (a soap she could not afford to buy then but I can now), and this picture of this girl wearing a yellow dress with smocking on the front bodice perhaps created in my mother that desire to have a daughter who looked like that or perhaps created the desire in my mother to try and make the daughter she already had look like that. I do not know now and I did not know then. And who was that girl really? (I did not ask then because I could not ask then but I ask now.) And who made her dress? And this girl would have had a mother; did the mother then have some friends, other women, and did they sit together under a tree (or sit somewhere else) and compare strengths of positions used to throw away a child, or weigh the satisfactions to be had from the chaos of revenge or the smooth order of forgiveness; and this girl with skin of cream on its way to spoiling and hair the color of flax, what did her insides look like, what did she eat? (I did not ask then because I could not ask then and I ask now but no one can answer me, really answer me.)

My second birthday was not a major event in anyone's life, certainly not 6 my own (it was not my first and it was not my last, I am now forty-three years old), but my mother, perhaps because of circumstances (I would not have known then and to know now is not a help), perhaps only because of an established custom (but only in her family, other people didn't do this), to mark the occasion of my turning two years old had my ears pierced. One day, at dusk (I would not have called it that then), I was taken to someone's house (a woman from Dominica, a woman who was as dark as my mother was fair, and yet they were so similar that I am sure now as I was then that they shared the same tongue), and two thorns that had been heated in a fire were pierced through my earlobes. I do not now know (and could not have known then) if the pain I experienced resembled in any way the pain my mother experienced while giving birth to me or even if my mother, in having my ears bored in that way, at that time, meant to express hostility or aggression toward me (but without meaning to and without knowing that it was possible to mean to). For days afterward my earlobes were swollen and covered with a golden crust (which might have glistened in the harsh sunlight, but I can only imagine that now), and the pain of my earlobes must have filled up all that made up my entire being then and the pain of my earlobes must have been unbearable, because it was then that was the first time that I separated myself from myself, and I became two people (two small children then, I was two years old), one having the experience, the other observing the one having the experience. And the observer, perhaps because it was an act of my own will (strong then, but stronger now), my first and only real act of self-invention, is the one of the two I most rely on, the one of the two whose voice I believe is to be the true voice; and of course it is the observer who cannot be relied on as the final truth to be believed, for the observer has woven between myself and the person who is having an experience a protective membrane, which allows me to see but only feel as much as I can handle at any given moment. And so . . .

. . . On the day I turned two years old, the twenty-fifth of May 1951, a pair   7
of earrings, small hoops made of gold from British Guiana (it was called that then, it is not called that now), were placed in the bored holes in my earlobes (which by then had healed); a pair of bracelets made of silver from someplace other than British Guiana (and that place too was called one thing then, something else now) was placed one on each wrist; a pair of new shoes bought from Bata's was placed on my feet. That afternoon, I was bathed and powdered, and the dress of yellow poplin, completed, its seams all stitched together with a certainty found only in the natural world (I now realize), was placed over my head, and it is quite possible that this entire act had about it the feeling of being draped in a shroud. My mother, carrying me in her arms (as usual), took me to the studio of a photographer, a man named Mr. Walker, to have my picture taken. As she walked along with me in her arms (not complaining), with the heat of the sun still so overwhelming that it, not gravity, seemed to be the force that kept us pinned to the earth's surface, I placed my lips against one side of her head (the temple) and could feel the rhythm of the blood pulsing through her body; I placed my lips against her throat and could hear her swallow saliva that had collected in her mouth; I

placed my face against her neck and inhaled deeply a scent that I could not identify then (how could I, there was nothing to compare it to) and cannot now, because it is not of animal or place or thing, it was (and is) a scent unique to her, and it left a mark of such depth that it eventually became a part of my other senses, and even now (yes, now) that scent is also taste, touch, sight, and sound.

And Mr. Walker lived on Church Street in a house that was mysterious 8 to me (then, not now) because it had a veranda (unlike my own house) and it had many rooms (unlike my own house, but really Mr. Walker's house had only four rooms, my own house had one) and the windows were closed (the windows in my house were always open). He spoke to my mother, I did not understand what they said, they did not share the same tongue. I knew Mr. Walker was a man, but how I knew that I cannot say (now, then, sometime to come). It is possible that because he touched his hair often, smoothing down, caressing, the forcibly straightened strands, and because he admired and said that he admired my dress of yellow poplin with its simple smocking (giving to me a false air of delicacy), and because he admired and said that he admired the plaid taffeta ribbon in my hair, I thought that he perhaps wasn't a man at all, I had never seen a man do or say any of those things, I had then only seen a woman do or say those things. He (Mr. Walker) stood next to a black box which had a curtain at its back (this was his camera but I did not know that at the time, I only know it now) and he asked my mother to stand me on a table, a small table, a table that made me taller, because the scene in the background, against which I was to be photographed, was so vast, it overwhelmed my two-year-old frame, making me seem a mere figurine, not a child at all; and when my mother picked me up, holding me by the armpits with her hands, her thumb accidentally (it could have been deliberate, how could someone who loved me inflict so much pain just in passing?) pressed deeply into my shoulder, and I cried out and then (and still now) looked up at her face and couldn't find any reason in it, and could find no malice in it, only that her eyes were full of something, a feeling that I thought then (and am convinced now) had nothing to do with me; and of course it is possible that just at that moment she had realized that she was exhausted, not physically, but just exhausted by this whole process, celebrating my second birthday, commemorating an event, my birth, that she may not have wished to occur in the first place and may have tried repeatedly to prevent, and then, finally, in trying to find some beauty in it, ended up with a yard and a half of yellow poplin being shaped into a dress, teaching herself smocking and purchasing gold hoops from places whose names never remained the same and silver bracelets from places whose names never remained the same. And Mr. Walker, who was not at all interested in my mother's ups and downs and would never have dreamed of taking in the haphazard mess of her life (but there was nothing so unusual about that, every life, I now know, is a haphazard mess), looked on for a moment as my mother, belying the look in her eyes, said kind and loving words to me in a kind and loving voice, and then he walked over to a looking glass that hung on a wall and squeezed with two of his fingers a lump the size of a pinch of sand that was on his cheek; the lump had a shiny white surface and it broke, emitting a tiny plap sound, and from it came a long ribbon of thick, yellow pus that curled on Mr. Walker's cheek imitating, almost, the decoration on the birthday cake that awaited me at home, and my birthday cake was decorated with a series of species of flora and fauna my mother had never seen (and still has not seen to this day, she is seventy-three years old).

After that day I never again wore my yellow poplin dress with the smocking 9 my mother had just taught herself to make. It was carefully put aside, saved for me to wear to another special occasion; but by the time another special occasion came (I could say quite clearly then what the special occasion was and can say quite clearly now what the special occasion was but I do not want to), the dress could no longer fit me, I had grown too big for it.

Analyzing This Selection

1. Kincaid uses a great many parentheses, more than are usually considered good style. What does she put into parentheses? What is the cumulative effect of multiplying these parentheses?

2. What is the child's sense of her connection to her mother? What details support Kincaid's memory?

3. How did her mother respond to the picture of the girl in the almanac? What does Kincaid now perceive in that almanac picture?

4. What seems to have happened at the photographer's house? Is Kincaid's memory dim, or what?

5. In the essay as a whole, is Kincaid's attitude toward her past nostalgic? critical? or some other tone?

Analyzing Connections

6. In "A Walk to the Jetty" (see p. 90), Kincaid writes about her departure from home at the age of fifteen. How does Annie John's personality clarify some of Kincaid's recollections in this biography of her dress? How does Kincaid's view of Antigua in "Biography of a Dress" differ from the view in "A Walk to the Jetty"? How has her viewpoint expanded?

Analyzing by Writing

7. Based on a photograph of yourself at a very early age (before six, if possible), write a biographical sketch of an article of clothing or a toy that is prominent in your memory. Keep distinct, but also combine, the concrete experiences of the child and your present, broader understanding of the elements of the picture.

(You need not write long, complex, highly digressive sentences. They are difficult to control. But you might like to try constructing one or two sentences like Kincaid's.)

E. M. Forster

MY WOOD

◇

E. M. FORSTER (1879–1970) was a British novelist and essayist who was educated at Cambridge University. Except for periods of travel to India and the Mediterranean, where he was deeply affected by his contacts with ancient cultures, he continued to live at his college through most of his adulthood. His fiction is often about conventionally educated young English people discovering something unconventional in themselves in response to symbolic places, such as other countries or old houses. Even the titles of his novels suggest traveling to take up a fresh perspective on things: *Where Angels Fear to Tread* (1905), *The Longest Journey* (1907), *A Room with a View* (1908), *Howards End* (1910), and *A Passage to India* (1924), which is the book Forster mentions in the first sentence of this selection from his collection of essays *Abinger Harvest* (1936).

A few years ago I wrote a book which dealt in part with the difficulties of 1
the English in India. Feeling that they would have had no difficulties in India themselves, the Americans read the book freely. The more they read it the better it made them feel, and a check to the author was the result. I bought a wood with the check. It is not a large wood — it contains scarcely any trees, and it is intersected, blast it, by a public footpath. Still, it is the first property that I have owned, so it is right that other people should participate in my shame, and should ask themselves, in accents that will vary in horror, this very important question: What is the effect of property upon the character? Don't let's touch economics; the effect of private ownership upon the community as a whole is another question — a more important question, perhaps, but another one. Let's keep to psychology. If you own things, what's their effect on you? What's the effect on me of my wood?

In the first place, it makes me feel heavy. Property does have this effect. 2
Property produces men of weight, and it was a man of weight who failed to get into the Kingdom of Heaven. He was not wicked, that unfortunate millionaire in the parable, he was only stout; he stuck out in front, not to mention behind, and as he wedged himself this way and that in the crystalline entrance and bruised his well-fed flanks, he saw beneath him a comparatively slim camel passing through the eye of a needle and being woven into the robe of God. The Gospels all through couple stoutness and slowness.

They point out what is perfectly obvious, yet seldom realized: that if you have a lot of things you cannot move about a lot, that furniture requires dusting, dusters require servants, servants require insurance stamps, and the whole tangle of them makes you think twice before you accept an invitation to dinner or go for a bathe in the Jordan. Sometimes the Gospels proceed further and say with Tolstoy that property is sinful; they approach the difficult ground of asceticism here, where I cannot follow them. But as to the immediate effects of property on people, they just show straightforward logic. It produces men of weight. Men of weight cannot, by definition, move like the lightning from the East unto the West, and the ascent of a fourteen-stone bishop into a pulpit is thus the exact antithesis of the coming of the Son of Man. My wood makes me feel heavy.

In the second place, it makes me feel it ought to be larger.   3

The other day I heard a twig snap in it. I was annoyed at first, for I thought   4
that someone was blackberrying, and depreciating the value of the under-growth. On coming nearer, I saw it was not a man who had trodden on the twig and snapped it, but a bird, and I felt pleased. My bird. The bird was not equally pleased. Ignoring the relation between us, it took fright as soon as it saw the shape of my face, and flew straight over the boundary hedge into a field, the property of Mrs. Henessy, where it sat down with a loud squawk. It had become Mrs. Henessy's bird. Something seemed grossly amiss here, something that would not have occurred had the wood been larger. I could not afford to buy Mrs. Henessy out, I dared not murder her, and limitations of this sort beset me on every side. . . .

In the third place, property makes its owner feel that he ought to do   5
something to it. Yet he isn't sure what. A restlessness comes over him, a vague sense that he has a personality to express — the same sense which, without any vagueness, leads the artist to an act of creation. Sometimes I think I will cut down such trees as remain in the wood, at other times I want to fill up the gaps between them with new trees. Both impulses are pretentious and empty. They are not honest movements toward money-making or beauty. They sprang from a foolish desire to express myself and from an inability to enjoy what I have got. Creation, property, enjoyment form a sinister trinity in the human mind. Creation and enjoyment are both very, very good, yet they are often unattainable without a material basis, and at such moments property pushes itself in as a substitute, saying, "Accept me instead — I'm good enough for all three." It is not enough. It is, as Shakespeare said of lust, "The expense of spirit in a waste of shame": it is "Before, a joy proposed; behind, a dream." Yet we don't know how to shun it. It is forced on us by our economic system as the alternative to starvation. It is also forced on us by an internal defect in the soul, by the feeling that in property may lie the germs of self-development and of exquisite or heroic deeds. Our life on earth is, and ought to be, material and carnal. But we have not yet learned to manage our materialism and carnality properly; they are still entangled with the desire for ownership, where (in the words of Dante) "Possession is one with loss."

And this brings us to our fourth and final point: the blackberries.   6

Blackberries are not plentiful in this meagre grove, but they are easily seen   7
from the public footpath which traverses it, and all too easily gathered.
Foxgloves, too — people will pull up the foxgloves, and ladies of an educational tendency even grub for toadstools to show them on the Monday in
class. Other ladies, less educated, roll down the bracken in the arms of their
gentlemen friends. There is paper, there are tins. Pray, does my wood belong
to me or doesn't it? And, if it does, should I not own it best by allowing no
one else to walk there? There is a wood near Lyme Regis, also cursed by a
public footpath, where the owner has not hesitated on this point. He had
built high stone walls each side of the path, and has spanned it by bridges,
so that the public circulate like termites while he gorges on the blackberries
unseen. He really does own his wood, this able chap. And perhaps I shall
come to this in time. I shall wall in and fence out until I really taste the
sweets of property. Enormously stout, endlessly avaricious, pseudo-creative,
intensely selfish, I shall weave upon my forehead the quadruple crown of
possession until those nasty Bolshies come and take it off again and thrust me
aside into the outer darkness.

Analyzing This Selection

1. In the second paragraph, the terms "heavy" and "weight" include nonliteral
   meanings. Give a literal explanation of this first effect of property on Forster's
   character. What is added by Forster's figurative presentation?

2. In paragraph 4, explain the effect of the short sentence "My bird."

3. Explain Forster's somewhat difficult point about property becoming a substitute
   for creativity and enjoyment. From his viewpoint, how is that to be avoided?

4. The essay includes an abundance of references to history, literature, and religion,
   and they occur without much introduction or clarification. What is their purpose? And what is the effect of their suddenness?

Analyzing Connections

5. In the Insights (p. 294), Paul Wachtel offers an explanation of why riches fail to
   satisfy. Does Wachtel's theory about possessions explain Forster's reactions to his
   property? How much or how little does Forster's experience illustrate Wachtel's
   point?

Analyzing by Writing

6. If you were designing a better society, what would you allow individuals to own
   privately? Conversely, what should be owned publicly? Would you change the
   status of utilities, transportation systems, communication networks, hospitals,
   schools, shorelines, family housing, or any other major components of present
   society? Explain why your plan for ownership would be good for people.

Toni Cade Bambara

THE LESSON

◇

Toni Cade Bambara (b. 1939) grew up in the black districts of New York City, where she experienced racism and poverty set in sharp contrast to the opulence of white Manhattan, as the following story reflects. After graduating from Queens College, she studied dance and acting in Italy and France before returning to New York, where she took an M.A. degree at City College. Bambara worked as a welfare investigator and youth counselor while writing short stories. She has taught English at Duke University and Spelman College and is the editor of an anthology of essays, *The Black Woman* (1970). Her fiction has been collected in *The Sea Birds Are Still Alive: Collected Stories* (1977).

Back in the days when everyone was old and stupid or young and foolish and me and Sugar were the only ones just right, this lady moved on our block with nappy hair and proper speech and no makeup. And quite naturally we laughed at her, laughed the way we did at the junk man who went about his business like he was some big-time president and his sorry-ass horse his secretary. And we kinda hated her too, hated the way we did the winos who cluttered up our parks and pissed on our handball walls and stank up our hallways and stairs so you couldn't halfway play hide-and-seek without a goddamn gas mask. Miss Moore was her name. The only woman on the block with no first name. And she was black as hell, cept for her feet, which were fish-white and spooky. And she was always planning these boring-ass things for us to do, us being my cousin, mostly, who lived on the block cause we all moved North the same time and to the same apartment then spread out gradual to breathe. And our parents would yank our heads into some kinda shape and crisp up our clothes so we'd be presentable for travel with Miss Moore, who always looked like she was going to church, though she never did. Which is just one of the things the grownups talked about when they talked behind her back like a dog. But when she came calling with some sachet she'd sewed up or some gingerbread she'd made or some book, why then they'd all be too embarrassed to turn her down and we'd get handed over all spruced up. She'd been to college and said it was only right that she should take responsibility for the young ones' education, and she not even related by marriage or blood. So they'd go for it. Specially Aunt Gretchen.

She was the main gofer in the family. You got some ole dumb shit foolishness you want somebody to go for, you send for Aunt Gretchen. She been screwed into the go-along for so long, it's a blood-deep natural thing with her. Which is how she got saddled with me and Sugar and Junior in the first place while our mothers were in a la-de-da apartment up the block having a good ole time.

So this one day Miss Moore rounds us all up at the mailbox and it's 2 puredee hot and she's knockin herself out about arithmetic. And school suppose to let up in the summer I heard, but she don't never let up. And the starch in my pinafore scratching the shit outta me and I'm really hating this nappy-head bitch and her goddamn college degree. I'd much rather go to the pool or to the show where it's cool. So me and Sugar leaning on the mailbox being surly, which is a Miss Moore word. And Flyboy checking out what everybody brought for lunch. And Fat Butt already wasting his peanut-butter-and-jelly sandwich like the pig he is. And Junebug punchin on Q.T.'s arm for potato chips. And Rosie Giraffe shifting from one hip to the other waiting for somebody to step on her foot or ask if she from Georgia so she can kick ass, preferably Mercedes'. And Miss Moore asking us do we know what money is, like we a bunch of retards. I mean real money, she say, like it's only poker chips or monopoly papers we lay on the grocer. So right away I'm tired of this and say so. And would much rather snatch Sugar and go to the Sunset and terrorize the West Indian kids and take their hair ribbons and their money too. And Miss Moore files that remark away for next week's lesson on brotherhood, I can tell. And finally I say we oughta get to the subway cause it's cooler and besides we might meet some cute boys. Sugar done swiped her mama's lipstick, so we ready.

So we heading down the street and she's boring us silly about what things 3 cost and what our parents make and how much goes for rent and how money ain't divided up right in this country. And then she gets to the part about we all poor and live in the slums, which I don't feature. And I'm ready to speak on that, but she steps out in the street and hails two cabs just like that. Then she hustles half the crew in with her and hands me a five-dollar bill and tells me to calculate 10 percent tip for the driver. And we're off. Me and Sugar and Junebug and Flyboy hanging out the window and hollering to everybody, putting lipstick on each other cause Flyboy a faggot anyway, and making farts with our sweaty armpits. But I'm mostly trying to figure how to spend this money. But they all fascinated with the meter ticking and Junebug starts laying bets as to how much it'll read when Flyboy can't hold his breath no more. Then Sugar lay bets as to how much it'll be when we get there. So I'm stuck. Don't nobody want to go for my plan, which is to jump out at the next light and run off to the first bar-b-que we can find. Then the driver tells us to get the hell out cause we there already. And the meter reads eight-five cents. And I'm stalling to figure out the tip and Sugar say give him a dime. And I decide he don't need it bad as I do, so later for him. But then he tries to take off with Junebug foot still in the door so we talk about his mama something ferocious. Then we check out that we on Fifth Avenue and everybody dressed up in stockings. One lady in a fur coat, hot as it is. White folks crazy.

"This is the place," Miss Moore say, presenting it to us in the voice she 4
uses at the museum. "Let's look in the windows before we go in."

"Can we steal?" Sugar asks very serious like she's getting the ground rules 5
squared away before she plays. "I beg your pardon," say Miss Moore, and we fall out. So she leads us around the windows of the toy store and me and Sugar screamin, "This is mine, that's mine, I gotta have that, that was made for me, I was born for that," till Big Butt drowns us out.

"Hey, I'm goin to buy that there."   6

"That there? You don't even know what it is, stupid."   7

"I do so," he say punchin on Rosie Giraffe. "It's a microscope."   8

"Whatcha gonna do with a microscope, fool?"   9

"Look at things."   10

"Like what, Ronald?" ask Miss Moore. And Big Butt ain't got the first   11
notion. So here go Miss Moore gabbing about the thousands of bacteria in a drop of water and the somethinorother in a speck of blood and the million and one living things in the air around us is invisible to the naked eye. And what she say that for? Junebug go to town on that "naked" and we rolling. Then Miss Moore ask what it cost. So we all jam into the window smudgin it up and the price tag say $300. So then she ask how long'd take for Big Butt and Junebug to save up their allowances. "Too long," I say. "Yeh," adds Sugar, "outgrown it by that time." And Miss Moore say no, you never outgrow learning instruments. "Why, even medical students and interns and," blah, blah, blah. And we ready to choke Big Butt for bringing it up in the first damn place.

"This here costs four hundred eighty dollars," say Rosie Giraffe. So we   12
pile up all over her to see what she pointin out. My eyes tell me it's a chunk of glass cracked with something heavy, and different-color inks dripped into the splits, then the whole thing put into a oven or something. But for $480 it don't make sense.

"That's a paperweight made of semi-precious stones fused together under   13
tremendous pressure," she explains slowly, with her hands doing the mining and all the factory work.

"So what's a paperweight?" asks Rosie Giraffe.   14

"To weigh paper with, dumbbell," say Flyboy, the wise man from the   15
East.

"Not exactly," say Miss Moore, which is what she say when you warm or   16
way off too. "It's to weigh paper down so it won't scatter and make your desk untidy." So right away me and Sugar curtsy to each other and then to Mercedes who is more the tidy type.

"We don't keep paper on top of the desk in my class," say Junebug,   17
figuring Miss Moore crazy or lyin one.

"At home, then," she say. "Don't you have a calendar and a pencil case   18 and a blotter and a letter-opener on your desk at home where you do your homework?" And she know damn well what our homes look like cause she nosys around in them every chance she gets.

"I don't even have a desk," say Junebug. "Do we?" 19

"No. And I don't get no homework neither," says Big Butt. 20

"And I don't even have a home," say Flyboy like he do at school to keep 21 the white folks off his back and sorry for him. Send this poor kid to camp posters, is his specialty.

"I do," says Mercedes. "I have a box of stationery on my desk and a picture 22 of my cat. My godmother bought the stationery and the desk. There's a big rose on each sheet and the envelopes smell like roses."

"Who wants to know about your smelly-ass stationery," say Rosie Giraffe 23 fore I can get my two cents in.

"It's important to have a work area all your own so that . . ." 24

"Will you look at this sailboat, please," say Flyboy, cuttin her off and 25 pointin to the thing like it was his. So once again we tumble all over each other to gaze at this magnificent thing in the toy store which is just big enough to maybe sail two kittens across the pond if you strap them to the posts tight. We all start reciting the price tag like we in assembly. "Handcrafted sailboat of fiberglass at one thousand one hundred ninety-five dollars."

"Unbelievable," I hear myself say and am really stunned. I read it again 26 for myself just in case the group recitation put me in a trance. Same thing. For some reason this pisses me off. We look at Miss Moore and she lookin at us, waiting for I dunno what.

"Who'd pay all that when you can buy a sailboat set for a quarter at Pop's, 27 a tube of glue for a dime, and a ball of string for eight cents? It must have a motor and a whole lot besides," I say. "My sailboat cost me about fifty cents."

"But will it take water?" say Mercedes with her smart ass. 28

"Took mine to Alley Pond Park once," say Flyboy. "String broke. Lost it. 29 Pity."

"Sailed mine in Central Park and it keeled over and sank. Had to ask my 30 father for another dollar."

"And you got the strap," laugh Big Butt. "The jerk didn't even have a 31 string on it. My old man wailed on his behind."

Little Q.T. was staring hard at the sailboat and you could see he wanted 32 it bad. But he too little and somebody'd just take it from him. So what the hell. "This boat for kids, Miss Moore?"

"Parents silly to buy something like that just to get all broke up," say Rosie 33 Giraffe.

"That much money it should last forever," I figure. 34

"My father'd buy it for me if I wanted it." 35

"Your father, my ass," say Rosie Giraffe getting a chance to finally push 36 Mercedes.

"Must be rich people shop here," say Q.T. 37

"You are a very bright boy," say Flyboy. "What was your first clue?" And 38 he rap him on the head with the back of his knuckles, since Q.T. the only one he could get away with. Though Q.T. liable to come up behind you years later and get his licks in when you half expect it.

"What I want to know is," I says to Miss Moore though I never talk to her, **39** I wouldn't give the bitch that satisfaction, "is how much a real boat costs? I figure a thousand'd get you a yacht any day?"

"Why don't you check that out," she says, "and report back to the group?" **40** Which really pains my ass. If you gonna mess up a perfectly good swim day least you could do is have some answers. "Let's go in," she say like she got something up her sleeve. Only she don't lead the way. So me and Sugar turn the corner to where the entrance is, but when we get there I kinda hang back. Not that I'm scared, what's there to be afraid of, just a toy store. But I feel funny, shame. But what I got to be shamed about? Got as much right to go in as anybody. But somehow I can't seem to get hold of the door, so I step away for Sugar to lead. But she hangs back too. And I look at her and she looks at me and this is ridiculous. I mean, damn, I have never ever been shy about doing nothing or going nowhere. But then Mercedes steps up and then Rosie Giraffe and Big Butt crowd in behind and shove, and next thing we all stuffed into the doorway with only Mercedes squeezing past us, smoothing out her jumper and walking right down the aisle. Then the rest of us tumble in like a glued-together jigsaw done all wrong. And people lookin at us. And it's like the time me and Sugar crashed into the Catholic church on a dare. But once we got in there and everything so hushed and holy and the candles and the bowin and the handkerchiefs on all the drooping heads, I just couldn't go through with the plan. Which was for me to run up to the altar and do a tap dance while Sugar played the nose flute and messed around in the holy waters. And Sugar kept givin me the elbow. Then later teased me so bad I tied her up in the shower and turned it on and locked her in. And she'd be there till this day if Aunt Gretchen hadn't finally figured I was lyin about the boarder takin a shower.

Same thing in the store. We all walkin on tiptoe and hardly touchin the **41** games and puzzles and things. And I watched Miss Moore who is steady watchin us like she waiting for a sign. Like Mama Drewery watches the sky and sniffs the air and takes note of just how much slant is in the bird formation. Then me and Sugar bump smack into each other, so busy gazing at the toys, 'specially the sailboat. But we don't laugh and go into our fat-lady bump-stomach routine. We just stare at that price tag. Then Sugar run a finger over the whole boat. And I'm jealous and want to hit her. Maybe not her, but I sure want to punch somebody in the mouth.

"Watcha bring us here for, Miss Moore?" **42**

"You sound angry, Sylvia. Are you mad about something?" Givin me one **43** of them grins like she tellin a grown-up joke that never turns out to be funny. And she's lookin very closely at me like maybe she plannin to do my portrait from memory. I'm mad, but I won't give her that satisfaction. So I slouch around the store bein very bored and say, "Let's go."

Me and Sugar at the back of the train watchin the tracks whizzin by large   44
then small then gettin gobbled up in the dark. I'm thinkin about this tricky
toy I saw in the store. A clown that somersaults on a bar then does chin-ups
just cause you yank lightly at his leg. Cost $35. I could see me askin my
mother for a $35 birthday clown. "You wanna who that costs what?" she'd
say, cocking her head to the side to get a better view of the hole in my head.
Thirty-five dollars and the whole household could go visit Grandaddy Nelson
in the country. Thirty-five dollars would pay for the rent and the piano bill
too. Who are these people that spend that much for performing clowns and
$1000 for toy sailboats? What kinda work they do and how they live and how
come we ain't in on it? Where we are is who we are, Miss Moore always
pointin out. But it don't necessarily have to be that way, she always adds then
waits for somebody to say that poor people have to wake up and demand their
share of the pie and don't none of us know what kind of pie she talkin about
in the first damn place. But she ain't so smart cause I still got her four dollars
from the taxi and she sure ain't gettin it. Messin up my day with this shit.
Sugar nudges me in my pocket and winks.

Miss Moore lines us up in front of the mailbox where we started from,   45
seem like years ago, and I got a headache for thinkin so hard. And we lean
all over each other so we can hold up under the draggy-ass lecture she always
finishes us off with at the end before we thank her for borin us to tears. But
she just looks at us like she readin tea leaves. Finally she say, "Well, what did
you think of F.A.O. Schwartz?"

Rosie Giraffe mumbles, "White folks crazy."   46

"I'd like to go there again when I get my birthday money," says Mercedes,   47
and we shove her out the pack so she has to lean on the mailbox by herself.

"I'd like a shower. Tiring day," say Flyboy.   48

Then Sugar surprises me by saying, "You know, Miss Moore, I don't   49
think all of us here put together eat in a year what that sailboat costs." And
Miss Moore lights up like something goosed her. "And?" she say, urging
Sugar on. Only I'm standin on her foot so she don't continue.

"Imagine for a minute what kind of society it is in which some people can   50
spend on a toy what it would cost to feed a family of six or seven. What do
you think?"

"I think," say Sugar pushing me off her feet like she never done before,   51
cause I whip her ass in a minute, "that this is not much of a democracy if you
ask me. Equal chance to pursue happiness means an equal crack at the
dough, don't it?" Miss Moore is besides herself and I am disgusted with
Sugar's treachery. So I stand on her foot one more time to see if she'll shove
me. She shuts up, and Miss Moore looks at me, sorrowfully I'm thinkin. And
somethin weird is goin on. I can feel it in my chest.

"Anybody else learn anything today?" lookin dead at me. I walk away and   52
Sugar has to run to catch up and don't even seem to notice when I shrug her
arm off my shoulder.

"Well, we got four dollars anyway," she says.   53

"Uh hunh."   54

"We could go to Hascombs and get half a chocolate layer and then to the   55
Sunset and still have plenty of money for potato chips and ice cream sodas."

"Uh hunh."   56

"Race you to Hascombs," she say.   57

We start down the block and she gets ahead which is O.K. by me cause   58
I'm goin to the West End and then over to the Drive to think this day
through. She can run if she want to and even run faster. But ain't nobody
gonna beat me at nuthin.

Analyzing This Selection

1. Based on details in the first paragraph, about how old is the narrator? What
   particular characteristics lead you to this informed guess?

2. At what point in the story does Miss Moore's lesson begin to take hold of Sylvia?
   What are Sylvia's specific reactions at that moment?

3. Why does Sylvia continue to resist Miss Moore's efforts to teach the children?

4. Who learns the author's intended lesson, Sugar or Sylvia?

5. What tone do the slang and obscenities add to the story? What attitudes do you
   think the author has toward the kids?

Analyzing Connections

6. Sylvia and the chambermaid Maria in "English as a Second Langauge" (p. 280)
   contemplate the extreme inequities of wealth in America. How are the injustices
   in each story remediable? What different things need to be changed?

Analyzing by Writing

7. In the concluding paragraph Sylvia says that she is going to "the Drive" to think
   the day through. Continue her story. Let Sylvia seriously reconsider the particular
   facts of her life that are suggested by details in the story's first paragraph. How
   might her experience with Miss Moore and the other kids change her attitude
   toward her life?

William Ian Miller

GIFTS AND HONOR:
AN EXCHANGE[1]

◊

WILLIAM IAN MILLER (b. 1946) is a professor of law at the University of Michigan. He earned a Ph.D. in English at Yale University before turning to scholarship on ancient and modern law. His books include *Bloodtaking and Peacemaking: Feud, Law, and Society in Saga Iceland* (1990). The following selection is excerpted from his most recent book, *Humiliation: And other essays on Honor, Social Discomfort, and Violence* (1993).

One Valentine's Day the doorbell rang around six in the evening. At the 1 door were the four-year-old boy who lived around the corner and his mother. My wife answered the door, and seeing that they had a valentine for Bess, my three-year-old daughter, got the valentine she had had Bess make for the boy that afternoon. I marveled at my wife's skill in handling this. How in the world did she know to be ready for this exchange? The boy, a year older than our daughter, was not a very frequent playmate of Bess's and we were only on cordial but standoffishly neighborly terms with his parents. What luck, I thought, that she had thought to have something ready for the boy. Then the glitch occurred. What Bobby handed over to Bess was an expensive doll, some twenty dollars' worth, clearly bought for this occasion. What Bess handed Bobby was some scribbling, representing an attempt to draw a heart, and a cookie that my wife, with Bess's indispensable assistance, had baked that afternoon. The visit broke up quickly after the exchange. We had been fixing dinner when they appeared, and Bobby and his mother only got far enough beyond the threshold so that we could close the storm door on the cold air outside. There was an undeniable look of disappointment on the boy's face when he left, and Bess, though hardly disappointed, was mildly bewildered at having gotten such a nice gift out of the blue. As soon as the door closed my wife expressed her embarrassment and acute discomfort. What could we do? How could we repay them? How could we rectify the situation? I too felt embarrassed although not quite to the same extent as Kathy; for it was not me who was going to have to have future dealings with

[1]Editor's title.

Bobby and his mother. It is also true that Kathy and I felt some amusement with our embarrassment. Discomfitures of this sort are funny even at the cost of your own pain. And of course, academic that I am, I started immediately wondering why we felt acutely embarrassed and maybe even shamed and Bobby's mother did not, because she did not manifest any sense that something had not been quite right in the exchange.

The structure of the valentine exchange can be described as a simple 2
game. The players each have one move and each must make that move (in this instance the move is giving a gift to the other) without knowledge of what the other has given. The object of the game is to match the value of the other's move. Both players lose if there is great discrepancy between their moves. Both win if there is a small increment between their moves. Normal social interaction presents various versions of this game fairly frequently. Christmas-gift exchanges and choosing how to dress for a party or other social function in which it is not totally clear that there is one correct way of attiring oneself follow this pattern. (Birthday-gift exchanges, however, follow a different structure unless the players celebrate their birthdays on the same day.) This game requires certain broad skills no matter what its particular setting may be. Adept players must understand the norms that govern the situation; they must also have the ability to judge the other party's understanding of those norms and his or her willingness to adhere to them even if understood, and they must make reasonably accurate assessments of the other party's assessments of themselves in these same matters.

Winning in the gift exchange does not mean getting the best present. That 3
is what Kathy and I understood to be a loss. Winning is guessing what the other will give and giving a gift adequate to requite it. Social norms do the work of coordinating people's behavior so that most of the time these interactions pass without glitch. We know what to give and how much to spend and we reasonably expect that others know what we know and that they will act accordingly. Small variations can be tolerated; they are even desired to some extent. If, for instance, you want to dress at a level of formality that will accord with that of everyone else, you might still want to wear something more tasteful or nicer than what others have on. If I give you a gift costing twelve dollars and you give me one costing ten dollars, no one is embarrassed, and I might even exact a very small amount of greater gratitude than the gratitude I have to give you to make up the difference. But when my gift to you cost a dime and your gift to me cost twenty dollars we should, if we are properly socialized, feel awkward and embarrassed. The embarrassment, however, will not be equally distributed. The person who spent the most will feel the least embarrassed, generally speaking. Why? We can even make the question a little harder by referring back to Bess's valentine. Why was it that my wife and I felt greater unpleasant feelings, when we followed the norms governing the situation, than I am supposing Bobby's mother did, who clearly broke the rules by vastly exceeding the appropriate amount of expenditure for little kids on Valentine's Day?

Just what are the sources of embarrassment, shame, humiliation, and 4
even guilt (perhaps) that were provoked by this situation? The lowrollers
cannot feel embarrassed that they broke the rules of the Valentine game,
because they did not. By one account the highrollers, if embarrassed, are
embarrassed more because they caused the lowroller's embarrassment than
because they exceeded the norms of propriety governing the game. No doubt
there is a causal connection between the highrollers' embarrassment and
their failure to adhere to the norms of the Valentine game inasmuch as that
was what caused the lowrollers' embarrassment, but that would be getting the
psychology of it wrong. Their experience is one of second-order embarrassment, the embarrassment of witnessing another's embarrassment, not the
primary embarrassment of having done something embarrassing. It seems
that what is going on here is that there is more than one game being played
and that there are more than one set of norms governing the transaction. The
true source of the lowrollers' embarrassment is that they have also been
shamed by being bested in the much more primitive game of gift exchange. . . . The simple fact remains that a gift demands an adequate return
even if that gift, by its size, breaks the rules governing the particular exchange. The norms of adequate reciprocity trumped the norms of Valentine's Day. Yet there is a cost here borne by the highrollers. Because the
highrollers defied the normal expectation they do not acquire honor to the
extent that they caused shame. Their action, in effect, has made the whole
transaction less than zero-sum.

A somewhat difficult account also suggests itself. I have been supposing 5
the giver's lack of primary embarrassment. But it might be that Bobby's
mother was more than embarrassed by embarrassing us, she might have felt
humiliated, not by breaking the rules of the Valentine's Day game but by
having to realize how much more greatly she valued us than we valued her.
Her pain then, if pain she felt, was not really a function of misplaying the
Valentine game in the same way ours was. To be sure, the game provided the
setting for her humiliation but it needn't have. Her pain, in other words, was
not caused because she violated the norms of Valentine's Day, but because
she overvalued us. In contrast, our pain was solely a function of the Valentine's Day glitch. Yet I suspect that she felt no humiliation whatsoever, for
the situation provided her with an adequate nondemeaning explanation for
the smallness of our gift. Our gift, she would know, was exactly what the
situation called for. The normal expectations of the situation thus shielded
her from more painful knowledge.

The peculiar facts of Bess's gift show us also that who ends up bearing the 6
costs of norm transgression will depend on the makeup of the opposing sides.
The discussion above assumed highroller and lower to be individual actors in
a one-on-one game, but in our Valentine situation there were mother and
son on one side and mother and daughter on the other. If we look now only
at the emotions engendered by the exchange, Bobby's mother felt no shame
and only a little embarrassment. Bess's mother felt much embarrassment.

Bess felt quite pleased. But Bobby, alas poor Bobby. Here was the true bearer of the cost of his mother's indiscretion. Bobby, one can reasonably suppose, was deeply envious of the gift Bess was to receive and had been sick with desire for a similar gift. Recall, when you were little, the painful experience of being the guest watching the birthday child open the presents. But Bobby can console himself that this Valentine gift will lead to an immediate return and not be miserably deferred as with birthday gifts. And what has Bobby's mother led him to believe he will be receiving? I would guess it was a little more exciting than Bess's scribblings and one chocolate chip cookie (made according to a health-food recipe no less).

Our discomfort was utterly unassuaged by the knowledge that our gifts 7 involved our own efforts (or at least Bess's and Kathy's). Our personalized efforts did not match the larger money expenditure of the other party. The issue wasn't just the money, because if Bobby had handed Bess a twenty-dollar bill we would have refused the gift without much anxiety. Here a breach of norms governing the form of the gift (e.g., no money unless under very certain conditions) is not as capable of embarrassing the receiver, if at all, as are breaches of norms governing the value of the gift. But we need to be more specific. The failure to abide by the norms governing the value of a gift only embarrasses the receiver if it exceeds the value of a normal gift; embarrassment is the lot of the giver if the gift's value is less than the norm. It seems in the end that our judgments are also quite particularized, taking into account not only the money spent but time and energy expended, the uniqueness of the gift, the seriousness of it, how individualized it is, how much such things mean to the giver, how much they mean to the receiver, the state of relations between the parties, and so on. Our cookie and Bess's scribbling were not going to balance the money and the time Bobby's mother took in picking out a gift for Bess. Our cookies were promiscuous, meant to be eaten by us and by anyone who stumbled by when we were eating them. When it is not clear that the personalized effort of one party was significant, when the labors engaged in could also be interpreted as an attempt to avoid spending money or were not engaged in specifically for the recipient, then monetary value will probably trump mere expenditures of effort. Obviously these rankings can undergo readjustment. If Bess were a recognized art prodigy, if Kathy were a professional cook, then our gifts would carry other meanings, as they would, too, if Bobby were the Cookie Monster.

One of the immediate moves that the embarrassed recipient makes is 8 desperately to try to reconstruct a plausible account for the breach, to attempt to interpret it away by supposing legitimizing or justifying states of mind for the giver. Perhaps she was playing a different game. Could the value of the gift be partially excused because Bobby was a year older than Bess, or because Bobby was a boy, or because his mother had a warm spot for Kathy or a warm spot for Bess? Was this really a gift initiating a youthful courtship in which gifts do not demand returns in the same specie? Was it simply that Bobby's mother never stinted in buying Bobby anything and that the toy she bought Bess had a much lower value to her than it did to us? Was she known to be inept in these kinds of things and hence each subsequent ineptitude bore a diminishing power to humiliate and embarrass? Or was the embarrassment that we thought she might be making a pitiable attempt to buy our friendship, in which case our very palpable embarrassment at our own failings would be compounded with our embarrassment for her as well. Whatever, no amount of such explanation for her action made us feel any less embarrassed. And we had played by the rules! But, as it turns out, only by the rules of the Valentine game. This game, as we discovered, was nested within a larger game of honor that demanded that each gift be requited with an adequate return, and that game we had lost.

The cost of our losing was our minor humiliation and shame and our 9 great embarrassment. In our culture in that particular setting it was a cost we could bear. In other settings we may have had to suffer the sanction of being reputed cheap and even ostracized on account of it. In other cultures humiliation and shame exact a greater toll. Reuters recently published the following story picked up by papers as column filler:

> *Monday June 10, 1991:* **Scorn over gift leads to double suicide.** Beijing: A couple from northern China committed suicide on their nephew's wedding day after relatives scoffed at the value of their gift to him, a Shanghai newspaper said.
> Following custom, the couple from the province of Shanxi wrote in a gift book that they were giving a total of $3.70 as a wedding gift, less than half the $8.50 other relatives gave, said the Xinmin Evening News.
> Unable to bear their relatives' scorn and worried about future wedding gifts for their other nephews and nieces, husband Yang Baosheng hanged himself after his wife, Qu Junmei, drowned herself in a vat, the newspaper said.

For Reuters and the newspapers that printed it, the story was clearly intended to be comical in a black way, an example of the strange behavior of people with strange names (note that giving the names of the suicides is part of the process of ridicule). The story is told as one of silly people who kill themselves for trifles. Any possibility of tragedy is skillfully prevented by several devices. There are the strange names already mentioned. There is the detail of drowning in a vat, which carries with it all the indignities of pure farce. Above all, there are the money amounts involved: these people committed suicide because of $4.80. And therein lies the real comedy of the presentation. Such levels of poverty and economic underdevelopment are so unthinkable for us to be a source of amusement and wonder. But anyone . . . should be able to discern the unfathomable shame and the desperate reassertion of dignity which these people tried to accomplish with their suicides. Suicide proved them anything but shameless and hence showed them to be people of honor. Reuters got their genre wrong. This is not comedy, but the stuff of epic and tragedy.

Analyzing This Selection

1. Explain the rules of gift exchange. Why did both parties lose in the Valentine episode? What constitutes "winning"?

2. What is the author's use or purpose for the exhaustive abstract analysis of the episode? How does he win our patience for it?

3. Does the author approve of the suicide of the Chinese couple? What does their story illustrate to him? How does it affect you?

Analyzing Connections

4. Construct the "game theory" that structures our wearing jeans *fashionably* (see "Blue Jeans and Identity," p. 303). Set the rules of the game and explain the social norms that regulate this behavior.

Analyzing by Writing

5. Writing as an observer of the customs of high school seniors, explain the system of gift exchange that operated among your friends during your final year in high school. At Christmas, at graduation, or on birthdays, did you pay more than usual attention to expecting and giving gifts? How did you deal with problems involving esteem, embarrassment, and shame? Did some people receive gifts only because they were part of a group including other, more valued friends? How did you negotiate exchanges of adequate reciprocity among all your friends?

Thomas H. Murray

THE GIFT OF LIFE
MUST ALWAYS REMAIN A GIFT

◇

THOMAS H. MURRAY (b. 1946) was educated at Temple University and Princeton, where he did his graduate work in psychology. His major interests focus upon the ethical issues that scientists must confront in their relationship with patients as they develop new technologies. Until 1986 Murray taught ethics at the University of Texas Medical School in Galveston, where he founded and edited *Medical Humanities Review*. He is now director of the Center for Biomedical Ethics at Case Western Reserve University.

The call came early in the morning. It was a staffer from a congressional 1
subcommittee. The chairman had become interested in the issues raised by the Mo Cell case. Would I come to Washington and testify?

My first reaction was to laugh. I knew the case. John Moore had been a 2
cancer patient with hairy-cell leukemia. There was no treatment for it except to remove his dangerously enlarged spleen. So they had plucked it out, and some scientists at UCLA had managed to grow Moore's cells — labeled Mo for short — in the laboratory; an immortal cell line, they called it, because, unlike most cells from mammals, Moore's cancerous spleen cells didn't stop replicating after a few dozen divisions. None of that was so new; immortal cell lines have contributed vastly to medical research. What made the case noteworthy was that UCLA and the scientists patented the Mo line — and then John Moore sued them.

The Mo Cell case seemed to belong in the Mondo Ethico category — a 3
name coined by a friend and me for bizarre cases in bioethics. That was why I laughed. But when Congress calls, the least you owe them is to think it over. So I said I would brood about it, and talk to them later in the day.

Once I began to think about the case, though, it obsessed me. The 4
questions were so provocative: What is our relationship with diseased parts of our bodies once they have been removed? Do scientists have any right to get rich from our misfortune? Are there any good analogies for thinking about these issues?

Such questions wouldn't have been raised ten or twenty years ago, before 5
biotechnology captured the imagination of the American public — and Wall

Street. No one worried about winning any biotechnology lottery, because there was nothing to win. Like most basic researchers, biologists labored in relative anonymity and poverty. Yet with the sudden blossoming of genetic engineering, monoclonal antibodies, and other technologies, biologists have found that the distance from the lab to the condo in St. Moritz isn't so far.

However, the birth of biotechnology only explains why the question of who should profit from human cell lines hasn't arisen before now. While modern biology's age of innocence may have passed, we must still decide how it should behave as a responsible adult. The Mo Cell case may be one of its severest tests.   6

The first thing I realized about this case was that we needed models for thinking about our relationship with our body parts once they were no longer joined with the living whole. There seemed to be three possibilities: the body as property, as surplus, and as a gift.   7

If the body is property, then it can be bought and sold like other commodities. The only question in the Mo Cell case then would be who owns it *now*? Did Moore abandon or transfer title to his spleen cells when he let UCLA remove them?   8

There are reasons for thinking of the body as property. We allow the sale of such things as hair, sperm, and blood. But these are all replenishable (usually), and that may be the vital difference. Also, those of us who work at hazardous occupations risk our bodies, or at least our health, for money every workday. But risking our health isn't really the same thing as selling our bodies. Imagine someone making a living by betting his pancreas against someone else's cash. Even if the odds were awfully good, I suspect we would see that as wrong. It's one thing to risk our health at work, quite another to wager our bodies.   9

In fact, there are better reasons for thinking that we don't regard the body as commercial property. Even in the culture that spawned *Let's Make a Deal*, not everything is for sale. We aren't permitted to sell our freedom, our children, or, most recently, our transplantable organs — though the shortage of human organs has led to a couple of lamentable efforts. In one case, ads appeared in the classified sections of newspapers offering kidneys for sale. (We have two kidneys but can live with just one.) In another, a man tried to peddle his liver, until it was pointed out to him that we're not born with spares. A Virginia physician, who had set himself up as a broker in human organs, went so far as to procure a license to import organs from overseas.   10

This was too much for Congress, which in 1984 passed a bill banning the buying or selling of organs for transplant. (People just don't take kindly to the thought of an organ mogul sipping champagne next to his kidney- or heart-shaped swimming pool.)   11

Why the moral repugnance toward trading in human organs? One reason may be fear of the development of a market in which the poor do the selling and the rich the buying. Our consciences can tolerate considerable injustice,   12 but such naked, undisguised profiteering in life would be too much for most of us.

And even if everyone had an equal chance to buy and sell, I doubt that 13 we'd countenance a market in human organs. The notion that people are special, that they have a dignity and moral worth that sets them apart, is deeply woven into our religious, legal, and political traditions. We may be more than mere protoplasm, but we're nothing without our bodies (at least in this world). Putting a price on the priceless, even a high price, actually cheapens it. So we don't approve of selling our body parts; and the body isn't quite property.

Of course, when a piece of us had been taken out, we're none too eager 14 to have it back. The psychologist Gordon Allport once proposed a thought experiment: Imagine filling a tumbler with your own saliva. Now consider drinking it. Not a pleasant thought. The same saliva was in our mouth just a moment before, and not at all foreign to us. Yet we'd much rather see it disappear down the sink than be forced to reclaim it. Should we think of separated body parts as surplus, then?

Surplus is something we have no use for and would like to be rid of. That 15 may be true for our saliva, or for our tonsils, once they've been removed. But does that mean we've abandoned all interest in what was once a part of us? Perhaps so for some replenishable body products. We don't really get bent out of shape when the barber sweeps our hair off the floor and into a wastebasket — unless we're bemoaning the loss of our hair generally. But we don't relinquish our interest so readily if the part was more intimate, less dispensable.

Do you know what happens to your appendix or other tissue after the 16 surgeon has removed it? First, it's examined by pathologists to make sure it was diseased, as your physician thought: a form of quality control on med-icine. You probably signed a consent for surgery that contained a vague statement permitting your tissue to be used for research or education, and then disposed of respectfully (usually by incineration). Indeed, that's just what ordinarily happens. It's a system marked by respect for the human origin of the specimens handled. And most of us seem quite content with the way it works. Scientists and medical educators get the materials they need to do their work. And we're assured that our tissues are being handled properly, and perhaps pleased that some good may come from our misfortune.

Imagine, however, that your appendix wound up as a decoration on the 17 pathology department's Christmas tree? You'd have a right to be indignant (which means, after all, that you felt your dignity had been wounded). You surely wouldn't feel this way if our body parts were truly surplus. Plainly, we retain an interest in having our tissues treated respectfully. But if our parts are neither property nor surplus, then what are they? I think the model that best depicts how we actually act and feel toward our organs and tissues is that they are a very special sort of gift.

A physician friend once told me of a young boy with a rare blood 18
deficiency. His blood lacked one of the factors that enables it to clot, though
not the one (Factor VIII) whose absence commonly causes hemophilia. The
blood's unusual properties made it exceedingly valuable to medical researchers, and for about a year the boy came regularly to the medical center to
donate blood for research. Then a pharmaceutical company learned of the
youngster, and hit upon a way to use his blood profitably. They asked him
for it and he agreed to give it — for a stiff price. The same blood that had
been donated to the scientists suddenly became a commodity. The boy and
his family apparently felt that it was right, even noble, to give the blood
without remuneration to the scientists. With equal conviction, they also
apparently believed that it would be foolish to make a gift of it to a company
that planned to sell it to make money.

This story tells us that people regard their relationships with scientific 19
researchers as drastically different from their relationships with profit-
seeking corporations. Scientists are engaged in a socially valued enterprise
in which they aren't expected to grow wealthy; corporations exist to max-
imize their wealth. We can have a relationship with scientists based on
gifts; nobody has a gift relationship with General Dynamics (except perhaps the Pentagon).

Nothing more clearly illuminates the gift nature of transactions involving 20
our organs than the "gift of life" itself — donating organs for transplantation.
Most organs come from cadavers, although roughly a third of the kidneys
come from live donors, almost always close kin of the recipients. The model
law authorizing organ donation is called the Uniform Anatomical *Gift* Act.
The organ banks responsible for procuring organs go to great lengths to make
certain that while the donors or their heirs aren't financially penalized for
their generosity, neither are they given monetary inducements. The itemized
hospital bill is carefully examined; only those charges relating to the organ
donation are paid by the organ bank. Our culture works awfully hard to avoid
the taint of money in organ donations. The gift of life must always remain
a gift.

Similar norms, unspoken and even unacknowledged at times, govern 21
tissue donations to medical researchers and educators. When we consent to
the use of our removed appendix or ulcerous stomach tissue to further the
goals of medicine, we do so with the implicit understanding that we're
making a gift of it to people who'll employ it in socially valuable ways.

The question posed by the Mo Cell case boils down to this: What are the 22
ethics when one person makes a gift to another, who then attempts to use it
for personal enrichment?

Again, we need an analogy to clarify the issue. Imagine that you've made 23
a gift of a set of treasured family recipes to a neighbor. A couple of years later
you discover that the neighbor has written a cookbook in which your recipes
are the feature attraction. Chances are you'd do a slow burn; your neighbor

hadn't asked permission to use your recipes in this way or offered to share the profits from the book with you.

But before anyone could draw any conclusions from this example, they'd want to know a number of things. For one, what were the implied understandings accompanying the gift? Probably no mention was made of the possibility that the recipes would show up in a cookbook. The donor hadn't forbidden it; he probably never even considered the possibility. But it would surely make a difference if he had known beforehand that the neighbor wrote cookbooks; it would have made even more of a difference if he had known that the recipe collector had made similar use of other friends' family recipes. In any case, implied understanding would be important in judging whether an injustice had been done. 24

Another factor that would influence our reaction is if the recipes had been altered. Our indignation would be heightened if the published versions were word-for-word copies of the originals. If, on the other hand, they showed evidence of months of experimentation in the author's kitchen and were substantially modified, we would have less reason for indignation. The author's contribution, then, is another significant consideration. 25

It might also make a difference if the recipes were more or less generic for your ethnic group — in my family, tomato sauce or pizzelles — and could have been gotten from almost anybody from your culture. But if the recipes were unique, treasured secrets — and the author simply couldn't have produced his book without them — we would have much more reason to complain. 26

The test of an analogy is its fruitfulness — whether it leads us to ask significant questions about the primary issue. The cookbook analogy does this for biotechnology. Look at the first factor, implied understanding. If we regard the donation of our organs and tissues to science as a gift to a socially valuable endeavor and not as a contribution to someone's personal fortune, then we're likely to be offended when that gift is claimed as property by someone else, especially property that might have great commercial value. On the other hand, if we knew that patenting and profit were always possibilities and still made the gift, our complaint would ring hollow. 27

How much or how little our contribution had been modified would matter too. If our tissue had merely been the starting point for a complex series of manipulations that transformed the original gift into something wholly unrecognizable, we'd have little claim on it. But if all the researcher had done was to plop some cells into a culture medium and watch them grow, unaltered, the identity of the original gift would have been little changed. 28

Finally, if almost any starting point could have been used, and it was only by chance that ours was chosen, then our contribution isn't unique. By contrast, if our gift was uniquely suited to the research, our claim is stronger. This last factor speaks to the use of cloned genes to produce human growth 29 hormone, which the bioengineering firm Genentech has recently received approval from the Food and Drug Administration to market. All healthy nucleated human cells contain the gene that produces growth hormone. The gene used for cloning might have come from anyone's body. So, my contribution wouldn't have been unique. (The recipe idea may come to be known as the biotechnology-as-tuna-hot-dish analogy.)

At the congressional hearings, David Blake of the Johns Hopkins University School of Medicine offered a different analogy. He suggested that the donor was merely the supplier of the raw material: "This is no different from the owner of a farm who sells the property to a developer who in turn builds houses and retains the profits without returning a share to the original owner." While Blake acknowledges that tissues are donated and not sold, he doesn't think this fact is relevant. More important for him is that no deception was involved.

There are two problems with his analogy. First, contrary to his belief, a great deal hinges on whether the object is sold or presented as a gift. Imagine that we had donated the property to the pastor of a church, only to find out that he had set himself up as a real estate developer, and was turning a neat profit on our gift. We had assumed the gift was going to be used exclusively to benefit the work of the church, though we never explicitly noted that when we made the gift. After we complain, the minister assures us that he will share the profits with the church. This analogy is much closer to the facts in the Moore case than in Blake's analogy. And I suspect most of us would feel offended by the minister's conduct.

The second problem also emerges from the modified analogy. As in John Moore's situation, no deception was involved (at least initially — there's dispute over who knew what and when). But the lack of active deception isn't an adequate excuse if important information was withheld from the donor, or if the donor's reasonable expectations about what would be done with the gift were mistaken and the recipient never corrected them.

The real danger from the Mo Cell case and others that may follow is that they threaten to transform the nature of the relationship between scientists and the public. People have been generous with science, especially in making gifts of themselves in the form of tissues and organs. If they begin to see scientists as greedy players in a biotechnology lottery with tickets provided by public generosity, this relationship stands to change, and not for the better.

Whether or not John Moore wins his suit isn't the fundamental issue. His case will probably be decided more by the vagaries of the patent laws than by any ethical analysis. At the heart of the matter is whether the gift relationship between science and the public can continue, or whether *caveat donor* becomes the new rule. Scientists are going to have to face this issue squarely. If public trust, esteem, and generosity are important to them, then a little generosity in turn is a small price to pay for sustaining a mutually satisfying relationship. Otherwise, this could be the beginning of the end of a beautiful friendship.

Analyzing This Selection

1. Describe the tone of Murray's essay, and consider whether or not it is appropriate for the subject matter.

2. Summarize the three "models" Murray uses to discuss the bioethical issues raised by the disposition of human body parts once they are removed from the body. Can you think of additional models for considering these issues?

3. Do you agree with Murray that most people think it would be *wrong* to wager or sell our bodies? Why or why not?

4. What analogies does Murray use to present his arguments? How do they serve to clarify the issues he raises?

5. Do you think you have any obligation to donate a kidney (Murray points out you can live with just one) to a patient who would die without a new kidney?

Analyzing Connections

6. If the body is property, what are the possible effects on an individual's character? Evaluate the problem in the personal way that E. M. Forster considers the effects of private ownership of land in "My Wood" (p. 315). If the body is not our property at all, how can we claim the right to control abortions, euthanasia, and other exercises of personal autonomy?

Analyzing by Writing

7. In view of the curative power of tissues and organs from the dead and from unborn fetuses, what guidelines should govern society's needs and uses for these materials? There are questions other than *ownership* at issue here. Argue in favor of a principle or standard that acknowledges conflicting values.

PART 7

MEDIA IMAGES

INSIGHTS

Memory, as the ultimate in private property, is a vestige of a vanished century. In the new civilization, half the faces in the memory bank are of public personalities, actors playing fictional characters. The farmer plowing his field in the Housatonic Valley in 1803 had how many names in his head? Family, neighbors, people he passed on the road going to and from market, the prosperous and powerful of nearby counties, a certain number of state and national political figures, the characters in the Bible, Washington and Jefferson and other outstanding patriots. He had heard some stories, some ballads, some episodes of history. He may have heard of some actors, some travelers, some outlaws.

But if you went into the street right now and stopped anyone at random you could tap into a knowledge of hundreds, thousands, of familiar strangers: people who do Nike ads, people who present clips from forthcoming summer releases, the aspiring sons and daughters of well-known and game-show hosts, people who sold the rights to their murder trial to a famous tabloid. Every single person in the subway station is a walking encyclopedia, a directory of show-biz personalities and celebrity criminals.

They live the consequences of an inner-population explosion, a proliferation of internalized three-dimensional holograms. How can they think straight with all those people running around in their heads? And the people in their heads, they too have people in their heads. They talk about nothing else in their all-night talk shows. "I saw him on your show last night talking about seeing her on his show last week." It breeds a nostalgia for the present moment; if only you could really be in the room where you are, laughing along with the laughers in the televised auditorium. They are with you, they are inside you, but you can't make contact with them.

Instead of memory there is the culture of permanent playback. The past hardly needs to be recaptured: It never goes away. The loops go incessantly around until the last possible ounce of sympathy or curiosity has been exhausted. As in the behavior-modification therapy to which the hero of *A Clockwork Orange* was subjected, the rotating images teach the art of numbness.

— GEOFFREY O'BRIEN

◇

It should not be surprising that all sorts of Americans — not only the bed- and house-ridden — find solace in the mythically stable communities of soap operas. Some soap communities, after all, have lasted over thirty years. All potential viewers are members of a society that has been in constant transformation through geographic mobility and the loss of extended families. Loneliness, we are repeatedly told, has become pandemic in America, and the longing for community is a palpable need. Whether through religion, clubs, associations, or support groups — or through daily immersion in a favorite soap — many Americans search for some kind of communal life to counter varying degrees of social isolation and alienation.

— RUTH ROSEN

◇

The Miss America pageant is the worst sort of "Americanism," the soft smile of sex and the hard sell of toothpaste and hair dye ads wrapped in the dreamy ideological gauze of "making it through one's own effort." In a perverse way, I like the show; it is the only live television left other than sports, news broadcasts, performing arts awards programs, and speeches by the president. I miss live TV. It was the closest thing to theater for the masses. And the Miss America contest is, as it has been for some time, the most perfectly rendered theater in our culture, for it so perfectly captures what we yearn for: a low-class ritual, a polished restatement of vulgarity, that wants to open the door to high-class respectability by way of plain middle-class anxiety and ambition. "Am I doing all right?" the contestants seem to ask in a kind of reassuring, if numbed, way. The contest brings together all the American classes in a show-biz spectacle of classlessness and tastelessness.

— GERALD EARLY

◇

The movies are an encyclopedia of gestures. They fix indelibly the look of things — a woman throwing her drink in a man's face, someone being shot through the head, a swimmer wrestling a crocodile, a police car flying off the side of the road and executing a slow half twist before landing on its roof — that, if you are halfway lucky, you can pass a lifetime without seeing anywhere except in the movies. But the movies make these things familiar. They can even, through endless repetition, make them boring. If you have seen a swimmer wrestling a crocodile twice, you may choose the third occasion to go out for popcorn.

Some movie-made gestures never become boring, of course. They're returned to again and again, and are even incorporated into your own repertoire. One of the important social services the movies have performed over the years, for example, is the instruction of generations of interested pre-adolescents in the mechanics of kissing — from the early-movie manner, in which the man rather suddenly and violently mashes his face onto the woman's and grinds slowly against it (are both mouths wide open, or only his?), to more recent representations, in which sheer face-swallowing is less emphasized and a good deal of nibbling and tongue work are indicated. It's not that you would never have figured out how to kiss (or to perform related activities, since kissing in the movies is usually a synecdoche for intimacies that cannot be shown: as above, so below) if you hadn't had Gary Cooper or Ellen Barkin to help you out. It's that it is impossible to say what in your knowledge of kissing comes from kissing and what comes from movies of people kissing.

— LOUIS MENAND

◇

Dear John Wayne

August and the drive-in picture is packed.
We lounge on the hood of the Pontiac
surrounded by the slow-burning spirals they sell
at the window, to vanquish the hordes of mosquitoes.
Nothing works. They break through the smoke-screen for blood.

Always the look-out spots the Indians first,
spread north to south, barring progress.
The Sioux, or Cheyenne, or some bunch
in spectacular columns, arranged like SAC missiles,
their feathers bristling in the meaningful sunset.

The drum breaks. There will be no parlance.
Only the arrows whining, a death-cloud of nerves
swarming down on the settlers
who die beautifully, tumbling like dust weeds
into the history that brought us all here
together: this wide screen beneath the sign of the bear.

The sky fills, acres of blue squint and eye
that the crowd cheers. His face moves over us,
a thick cloud of vengeance, pitted
like the land that was once flesh. Each rut,
each scar makes a promise: *It is
not over, this fight, not as long as you resist.*

Everything we see belongs to us.
A few laughing Indians fall over the hood
slipping in the hot spilled butter.
The eye sees a lot, John, but the heart is so blind.
How will you know what you own?

He smiles, a horizon of teeth
the credits reel over, and then the white fields
again blowing in the true-to-life dark.
The dark films over everything.
We get into the car
scratching our mosquito bites, speechless and small
as people are when the movie is done.
We are back in ourselves.

How can we help but keep hearing his voice,
the flip side of the sound-track, still playing:
Come on, boys, we've got them
where we want them, drunk, running.
They will give us what we want, what we need:
The heart is a strange wood inside of everything
we see, burning, doubling, splitting out of its skin.

                                 — LOUISE ERDRICH

FOCUSING BY WRITING

1. Talk shows on television and radio offer a public forum for discussing controversial personal and national issues. They air diverse opinions from hosts, studio guests, and call-in listeners, and sometimes heated discussions get out of control. Are talk shows valuable as democratic forums of debate, or do they trivialize opinions into statements that shock but have no social or moral consequences? Consider a recent talk show that you have seen or heard. How did the program affect you? Did you become more or less concerned to form an opinion on the issues that were discussed?

2. What was the dominant impression you received during your visit to a Disney park or other entertainment park? Consider what details of the place created the atmosphere. (It is possible that the atmosphere you felt was not the one intended by the park.) Is your present memory of the park significantly different from your response to it at the time?

3. Some people prefer to watch or hear an event on television or radio rather than actually to be present at a ball game, concert, or political rally. Do you prefer the broadcast version or the actual event? What are the important advantages or disadvantages that lead to your preference?

4. Explain the status-appeal of two dissimilar television celebrities. Mix your selection among entertainers, advertising figures, and news reporters, and possibly include a cartoon or puppet personality. What personal qualities appear in their aura? What, if any, similarities underlie their status-appeal?

Louise Erdrich

Z: THE MOVIE
THAT CHANGED MY LIFE

◇

LOUISE ERDRICH (b. 1954) grew up in Wahpeton, North Dakota, the eldest child
of a Chippewa Indian mother and a German-American teacher at the Bureau
of Indian Affairs school. Erdrich entered Dartmouth College in 1972, the year
women were first admitted and the year the Native American Studies department was established. She earned a master's degree in the writing program at
the Johns Hopkins University. Her first novel, *Love Medicine* (1984), won a
National Book Critics Circle award and other prizes. Erdrich received a
Guggenheim Fellowship in 1985. Her fiction often deals with contemporary
Indian life in tribal communities and in urban settings. Her most recent novel
is *The Bingo Palace* (1994). The following essay was commissioned for the
collection *The Movie That Changed My Life* (1991), in which writers reflect
on the unexpected personal impact of a film they saw.

Next to writing full-time, the best job I ever had combined two pas- 1
sions — popcorn and narrative. At fourteen, I was hired as a concessioner at
the Gilles Theater in Wahpeton, North Dakota. Behind a counter of black
marbleized glass, I sold Dots, Red Hot Tamales, Jujubes, Orange Crush,
and, of course, hot buttered popcorn. My little stand was surrounded by art
deco mirrors, and my post, next to the machine itself, was bathed in an aura
of salt and butter. All of my sophomore year, I exuded a light nutty fragrance
that turned, on my coats and dresses, to the stale odor of mouse nests. The
best thing about the job was that, once I had wiped the counters, dismantled
the machines, washed the stainless steel parts, totaled up the take and refilled
the syrup canisters and wiped off the soft drink machine, I could watch the
show, free.

I saw everything that came to Wahpeton in 1969 — watched every movie 2
seven times, in fact, since each one played a full week. I saw Zeffirelli's
Romeo and Juliet, and did not weep. I sighed over Charlton Heston in *Planet
of the Apes*, and ground my teeth at the irony of the ending shot. But the one
that really got to me was Costa-Gavras's Z.

Nobody in Wahpeton walked into the Gilles knowing that the film was 3
about the assassination in Greece of a leftist peace leader by a secret right-

wing organization and the subsequent investigation that ended in a bloody coup. The ad in the paper said only "Love Thriller" and listed Yves Montand and Irene Papas as the stars.

"Dear Diary," I wrote the morning after I'd seen Z for the first time. "The hypocrites are exposed. He is alive! Just saw the best movie of my life. Must remember to dye my bra and underwear to match my cheerleading outfit."

I forgot to rinse out the extra color, so during the week that Z was playing, I had purple breasts. The school color of my schizophrenic adolescence. My parents strictly opposed my career as a wrestling cheerleader, on the grounds that it would change me into someone they wouldn't recognize. Now, they were right, though of course I had never let anyone know my secret.

I had changed in other ways, too. Until I was fourteen, my dad and I would go hunting on weekends or skating in the winter. Now I practiced screaming S-U-C-C-E-S-S and K-I-L-L for hours, and then, of course, had to run to work during the matinee. Not that I was utterly socialized. Over my cheerleading outfit I wore Dad's army jacket, and on my ankle, a bracelet made of twisted blasting-wire given to me by a guitar-playing Teen Corps volunteer, Kurt, who hailed from The Valley of the Jolly Green Giant, a real town in eastern Minnesota.

No, I was not yet completely subsumed into small-town femalehood. I knew there was more to life than the stag leap, or the flying T, but it wasn't until I saw Z that I learned language for what that "more" was.

After the third viewing, phrases began to whirl in my head. "The forces of greed and hatred cannot tolerate us"; "There are not enough hospitals, not enough doctors, yet one half of the budget goes to the military"; "Peace at all costs"; and, of course, the final words, "He is alive!" But there was more to it than the language. It was the first *real* movie I had ever seen — one with a cynical, unromantic, deflating ending.

At the fourth viewing of the movie, I had a terrible argument with Vincent, the Gilles's pale, sad ticket taker, who was also responsible for changing the wooden letters on the marquee. At the beginning of the week, he had been pleased. It was he who thought of the ad copy, "Love Thriller." By the middle of the run, he was unhappy, for he sided with the generals, just as he sided with our boss.

Vincent always wore a suit and stood erect. He was officious, a tiger with gatecrashers and tough with those who had misplaced their stubs while going to the bathroom. I, on the other hand, waved people in free when I was left in charge, and regarded our boss with absolute and burning hatred, for he was a piddling authority, a man who enjoyed setting meaningless tasks. I hated being made to rewash the butter dispenser. Vincent liked being scolded for not tearing the tickets exactly in half. Ours was an argument of more than foreign ideologies.

Vincent insisted that the boss was a fair man who made lots of money. I maintained that we were exploited. Vincent said the film was lies, while I insisted it was based on fact. Neither of us checked for the truth in the library.

Neither of us knew the first thing about modern Greece, yet I began comparing the generals to our boss. Their pompous egotism, the way they bumbled and puffed when they were accused of duplicity, their self-righteous hatred of "long-haired hippies and dope addicts of indefinite sex."

When I talked behind the boss's back, Vincent was worse than horrified; 12 he was incensed.

"Put what's-his-name in a uniform and he'd be the head of the security 13 police," I told Vincent, who looked like he wanted to pound my head.

But I knew what he knew. I had my reasons. Afraid that I might eat him 14 out of Junior Mints, the boss kept a running tab of how many boxes of each type of candy reposed in the bright glass case. Every day, I had to count the boxes and officially request more to fill the spaces. I couldn't be off by so much as a nickel at closing.

One night, made bold by Z, I opened each candy box and ate one Jujube, 15 one Jordan Almond, one Black Crow, and so on, out of each box, just to accomplish something subversive. When I bragged, Vincent cruelly pointed out that I had just cheated all my proletarian customers. I allowed that he was right, and stuck to popcorn after that, eating handfuls directly out of the machine. I had to count the boxes, and the buckets, too, and empty out the ones unsold and fold them flat again and mark them. There was an awful lot of paperwork involved in being a concessioner.

As I watched Z again and again, the generals took on aspects of other 16 authorities. I memorized the beginning, where the military officers, in a secret meeting, speak of the left as "political mildew" and deplored "the dry rot of subversive ideologies." It sounded just like the morning farm report on our local radio, with all the dire warnings of cow brucellosis and exhortations to mobilize against the invasion of wild oats. I knew nothing about metaphor, nothing, in fact, of communism or what a dictatorship was, but the language grabbed me and would not let go. Without consciously intending it, I had taken sides.

Then, halfway into Christmas vacation, Vincent told on me. The boss 17 took me down into his neat little office in the basement and confronted me with the denouncement that I had eaten one piece of candy from every box in the glass case. I denied it.

"Vincent does it all the time," I lied with a clear conscience. 18

So there we were, a nest of informers and counterinformers, each waiting 19 to betray the other over a Red Hot Tamale. It was sad. I accused Vincent of snitching; he accused me of the same. We no longer had any pretense of solidarity. He didn't help me when I had a line of customers, and I didn't give him free pop.

Before watching Z again the other night, I took a straw poll of people I knew 20 to have been conscientious in 1969, asking them what they remembered about the movie. It was almost unanimous. People running, darkness, a little blue truck, and Irene Papas. Michael and I sat down and put the rented tape of Z into the video recorder. Between us we shared a bowl of air-popped corn. No salt. No butter anymore. Back in 1969, Michael had purchased the soundtrack to the movie and reviewed it for his school newspaper. It had obviously had an effect on both of us, and yet we recalled no more about it than the viewers in our poll. My memories were more intense because of the argument that almost got me fired from my first indoor job, but all was very blurred except for Irene Papas. As the credits rolled I looked forward to seeing the star. Moment after moment went by, and she did not appear. The leftist organizer went to the airport to pick up the peace leader, and somehow I expected Irene to get off the plane and stun everyone with her tragic, moral gaze.

Of course, Yves was the big star, the peace leader. We watched. I waited   21 for Irene, and then, when it became clear she was only a prop for Yves, I began to watch for *any* woman with a speaking role.

The first one who appeared spoke into a phone. The second woman was   22 a maid, the third a secretary, then a stewardess, then finally, briefly, Irene, looking grim, and then a woman in a pink suit handing out leaflets. Finally, a woman appeared in a demonstration, only to get kicked in the rear end.

Not only that, the man who kicked her was gay, and much was made of   23 his seduction of a pinball-playing boy, his evil fey grin, his monstrosity. To the Costa-Gavras of 1969, at least, the lone gay man was a vicious goon, immoral and perverted.

Once Yves was killed, Irene was called in to mourn, on cue. Her main   24 contribution to the rest of the movie was to stare inscrutably, to weep uncomfortably, and to smell her deceased husband's after-shave. How had I gotten the movie so wrong?

By the end, I knew I hadn't gotten it so wrong after all. In spite of all that   25 is lacking from the perspective of twenty years, Z is still a good political film. It still holds evil to the light and makes hypocrisy transparent. The witnesses who come forward to expose the assassination are bravely credible, and their loss at the end is terrible and stunning. Z remains a moral tale, a story of justice done and vengeance sought. It deals with stupidity and avarice, with hidden motives and the impact that one human being can have on others' lives. I still got a thrill when the last line was spoken, telling us that Z, in the language of the ancient Greeks, means "He is alive." I remember feeling that the first time I saw the movie, and now I recalled one other thing. The second evening the movie showed, I watched Vincent, who hadn't even waited for the end, unhook the red velvet rope from its silver post.

Our argument was just starting in earnest. Normally, after everyone was   26 gone and the outside lights were doused, he spent an hour, maybe two if a Disney had played, cleaning up after the crowd. He took his time. After eleven o'clock, the place was his. He had the keys and the boss was gone. Those nights, Vincent walked down each aisle with a bag, a mop, and a bucket filled with the same pink soapy solution I used on the butter machine. He went after the spilled Coke, the mashed chocolate, the Jujubes pressed flat. He scraped the gum off the chairs before it hardened. And there were things people left, things so inconsequential that the movie goers rarely bothered to claim them — handkerchiefs, lipsticks, buttons, pens, and small change. One of the things I knew Vincent liked best about his job was that he always got to keep what he found.

There was nothing to find that night, however, not a chewed pencil or a 27 hairpin. No one had come. We'd have only a few stragglers the next few nights, then the boss canceled the film. Vincent and I locked the theater and stood for a moment beneath the dark marquee, arguing. Dumb as it was, it was the first time I'd disagreed with anyone over anything but hurt feelings and boyfriends. It was intoxicating. It seemed like we were the only people in the town.

There have been many revolutions, but never one that so thoroughly 28 changed the way women are perceived and depicted as the movement of the last twenty years. In Costa-Gavra's *Missing*, *Betrayed*, and *Music Box*, strong women are the protagonists, the jugglers of complicated moral dilemmas. These are not women who dye their underwear to lead cheers, and neither am I anymore, metaphorically I mean, but it is hard to escape from expectations. The impulse never stops. Watching Z in an empty North Dakota theater was one of those small, incremental experiences that fed into personal doubt, the necessary seed of any change or growth. The country in Z seemed terribly foreign, exotic, a large and threatened place — deceptive, dangerous, passionate. As it turned out, it was my first view of the world.

Analyzing This Selection

1. How did Z stimulate Erdrich at age fourteen? Why did she immediately think that it was the best movie she had seen?

2. Twenty years later, did Erdrich's view of the movie change or remain the same? How has Erdrich personally changed or remained the same?

3. Readers don't learn until paragraph 27 that almost nobody else in Wahpeton saw the movie. What are the effects of delaying this unexpected information?

Analyzing Connections

4. How does Erdrich's response to a John Wayne movie (see Insights, p. 342) indicate a larger personal and social context for her excitement about Z? What do her contrasting responses imply about the messages conveyed by movies?

Analyzing by Writing

5. Consider a movie that illuminated or jolted you into a larger, truer "view of the world." Examine the way it entered your life during a period of specific changes. Explain how it encouraged new attitudes, challenged old expectations, or supplied fresh perceptions.

Following Erdrich's example, do not summarize the movie. Include, as she does, enough synopsis to help your reader grasp the story line. But analyze your experience, not the movie.

Andrea Freud Loewenstein

SISTER FROM ANOTHER PLANET PROBES THE SOAPS

◇

ANDREA FREUD LOEWENSTEIN (b. 1949) grew up in a Boston suburb, a community she wrote about in her collection of autobiographical stories, *The Worry
Girl* (1992). She attended Clark University and received a doctorate in English
at the University of Sussex, England. Her book *Loathsome Jews and Engulfing
Women* (1993) is a criticism of misogyny and anti-Semitism in modern British
literature. Loewenstein has taught writing to people in prisons, recovery centers, and housing projects as well as to college students at Goddard College and
Brooklyn College. The following essay appeared first in *Ms.* magazine (1993).

Dear Professor:

Enclosed is my research paper. As you may remember, I attended every one
of your lectures (I float at a right angle in the front row; last Thursday I was an
iridescent green with ocher spots) on that most fascinating subject, the human
species North Americanus Soapus. For my research project, I viewed several
weeks' worth of documentary videotapes from four different "Soaps," chosen
because they were among the most widely watched programs in the Earthling
year 1993, with some 50 million viewers combined. I will hereafter refer to the
humanoids whose acquaintance I made in *The Young and the Restless, The
Bold and the Beautiful, All My Children,* and *General Hospital* as "Soapoids."

The name "Soaps," by the way, appears to derive from the obsessional
recurrence of the cleanliness theme in the "commercials," which occur at
rhythmic intervals throughout the tapes. These are short, ritualized hymns of
thanksgiving and praise to select objects of worship, such as toilet bowl cleaners
and vaginal deodorants.

I must admit that during the first week of viewing, in which I used all 17 1
of my sensors, I was unable to distinguish one Soapoid from another. The
only distinction I was immediately able to make was between male and
female — the Soapoids' preoccupation with ritual ownership of the opposite
sex causes them to go to amazing lengths to signal gender distinction. These
signals include the compulsory arrangement and selective removal of facial
and head hair, distinctive body coverings, and (for the adult female) symbolic facial markings and mutilations.

This species, in contrast to our own, is subdivided into a mere two fixed 2
gender groupings: male and female. Contrary to the lecture in which you

informed us that occasionally both male and female choose to couple with their own kind and that those humanoids tend to be ostracized by the majority, I observed no variation in gender identity or object choice. On the contrary, all of my sample were hostile toward their own gender, whom they perceived as rivals in their never-ending fight to possess the opposite sex. Although this goal appears to be the Soapoids' overwhelming motivational force, the humans in my sample spent almost no time actually copulating. Instead, their main behavior consisted of endless discussions of, preparations for, and references to the act.

Nevertheless, copulation, when it does occur, often leads to trouble and 3 confusion, even for the viewer. I spent a great deal of time attempting to determine the name of the young woman from *All My Children* who works in a police station, is the daughter of one of the two possible fathers of Mimi's unborn child, and nosily looked up information to determine the date of conception. Since the records revealed that she had copulated with both men during the same week, Mimi was forced to confess and call off her wedding the day it was scheduled. I never did get the young woman's name.

Copulation does allow the females to exert ownership over the males. You 4 had informed us that males are the dominant gender, and that their inability to express their feelings verbally leads to frequent acts of violence. I regret to inform you that this conclusion is no longer valid. Soapoid males are quite gentle and verbally expressive. Their preferred behavior consists of lengthy expositions on their feelings toward the females. The male is especially prone to elaborate courtship rituals in preparation for copulation. These include the repetition of such submissive phrases as: "I love you so much," "You're my whole life," and "You were amazing last night, darling!" In one typical behavior, a male in *The Bold and the Beautiful* prepared for intercourse by placing at least 20 floating water lilies containing small lit candles in a pool of water upon which floated an inflatable rubber raft, the intended scene of sexual activity.

The far more complex females are the actual aggressors. In a lecture, you 5 had mentioned that some women, referred to as "feminists," join with one another toward a common goal. No such movement was evident in this sample. In fact, the females' most favored posture was the standoff, a highly aggressive position in which two women position themselves from one to two feet apart and emit such statements as "I hated you the first time I saw you." This is accompanied by a full range of physical expressions, including crossing of the arms, curling of the lip, and advancing in a menacing manner.

Unlike the male, the female can be classified into several subtypes, all 6 arranged around the notions of "good" and "evil." These inborn tendencies emerge at puberty, apparently along with the mammary glands. The Good Female mitigates her natural dominance by an exaggerated concern for the welfare and nourishment of "her" male. She is especially solicitous of his title — Writer, Actor, Businessman, Doctor, Lawyer, or Policeman — and is always ready to abandon her own title to have more time to support his efforts. In *The Young and the Restless*, for example, Nikki, a Businesswoman, repeatedly interrupts her own work to service Cole, a Writer who is also a Groomer of Horses. Attired in a series of low-cut red evening gowns, she waits on him at his workplace in the horse stable, serving him champagne and caviar, assuring him that publishers from the mythical city of New York will turn his novel into a "best-seller."

It is important to note, however, that these work titles are symbolic. 7 Soapoids, who possess a limited will to action and often require several hours of "processing" conversation to accomplish a simple task, must limit themselves to the all-important Preparation for Copulation. They have neither the time nor the energy to engage in actual "work." (The now meaningless title *General Hospital* indicates that Soapoids did work at one time.)

Good Females can be recognized by their wide-open, forward-gazing 8 eyes, modest demeanor, and light pink lip-paint. In old age they become wrinkled. Evil Females, on the other hand, remain slim, highly polished, and brightly painted throughout life, a certain tautness of the facial skin being the only visible sign of aging. The Evil Females' characteristics include unfaithfulness, sexual rapacity, and the need to manipulate others. Most Evil Females confine their ambition to collecting a large number of men, but a few exhibit a further will to power through the ownership of Titles, Land, Factories, Businesses, or Patents. These women, whom I call Controllers, have destroyed the lives of generations of Soapoids.

In your lecture on racial and ethnic diversity, you brought us almost to 9 jellification with your tale of the oppression of darker-hued or "African American" humanoids at the hands of the lighter ones whom you labeled the subspecies "European American." I am happy to inform you that no such oppression exists among modern-day Soapoids. In fact, there seems to be no difference between the darker and lighter types. All hues mix and converse on terms of perfect equality and good-will and hold titles of equal symbolic significance. Dark-skinned females (who exhibit a wide range of coloration, unlike the more muted light-skinned humanoids) wear their head hair in the same fashion as all other females — raised two or three inches from the head, then flowing to the shoulders. Darker and lighter humanoids do not mate, and appear to have no desire to do so. Whether this is because of the force of taboo or physical incompatibility cannot be determined at this juncture. It should be noted, however, that none of the African American females had attained the status of Controller, perhaps because they lack the necessary icy blue eyes.

Saul, an elderly male from *The Bold and the Beautiful*, speaks with an 10 accent, wears a pink shirt, highly ornamented necktie, and thick spectacles; he appears to be a eunuch. My ethnosensor identified him as a member of the subspecies "Jew." Whether these characteristics are an honest reflection of this identity is hard for me to determine — he was the only member of the group in this sample. Maria from *All My Children* was identified as a member of the subspecies "Latina"; as far as I can tell from my viewing, this group is notable for wavy head hair and the ability to ride a Horse without a saddle. Unlike African Americans, these Latinas appear able to mate with the "European Americans."

The photographs you showed us of the unsavory dwelling places 11 (known as "Ghettos") of some humanoids also appear to be out of date. As of now, all Soapoids inhabit spacious, carefully color-coordinated cubes filled with plastic flowers and bright modular furniture, in which they engage in their activities of arguing, preparing for copulation, and discussing their feelings for one another. Since eating, cleaning, and evacuation are not part of these sequences (being reserved for the "commercials"), no rooms are provided for these activities. It is unclear whether this is by choice or necessity (perhaps the atmosphere outside these cubes is not pure enough to breathe).

No analysis of Soapoid society would be complete without a mention of 12 the interlacing "commercials." These mini-documentaries demonstrate the Soapoids' unique ability to encapsulate and split off areas of behavior and their need to control their errant bodies. The mini-docs also provide a neat solution for any scholars who may, thus far in my narrative, have been puzzled by the absence of ingestion and excretion in the lives of these living organisms. All such functions are reserved for the mini-docs, during which Soapoids frantically ingest pre-packaged, slimness-controlling nourishments and rid their cubes, their eating utensils, their garments, and their bodies of all superfluous liquids and imperfections. "Dirty on the outside!" exclaims a voice-over as a female handles her mate's garment in horror. "Uh, oh, what about the inside!" A typical hour in the lives of Soapoids contains countless mini-docs that utilize not only a cleaning fluid that will purify garments on the inside, but also: a garment the can absorb the excretions of even the most wiggly of infant young; a tablet that cleans the excreting instrument by providing 2,000 flushes; another tablet to be ingested by the enemy species Cockroach; and yet another to be taken by the female Soapoid in order to soften her stools and ease excretion.

The lower body of the female seems to be especially in need of such 13 devices. A sequence that begins with the frightening words "Out of control!" introduces tablets that will "take control" of diarrhea in one day. The vaginal area is serviced by a pellet that cures yeast infections, a deodorant designed to "intercede" between the female's odor and her undergarments, and — for those who would seem to have the opposite problem — an ointment for vaginal dryness. Is it because the female Soapoid's vagina is the seat of her dominance over the male, and thus the location of her power, that it requires such constant servicing? Or is the female's verbal aggression yet another mark of her need to "stay in control" of her wayward body?

I end this paper with a conscience: I entered my research project with a 14 certain amount of bias against humanoids, whom I had been taught to regard as primitive, quarrelsome creatures, frozen in their limited natures and bodily forms, unable to regulate their own lives and affairs. But slowly, I grew increasingly susceptible to the charm of these beings. Before long, I found myself growing impatient with the time spent in my ordinary occupations. As I went about my daily tasks, I couldn't wait to join those beings who, never challenging, always predictable, asked nothing more from me than to watch them. Now that the viewing is over, I feel empathy.

As I beam this paper to your neurotransmitters and project it into the   15 ozone, it is with both fondness and regret that, amid the busy whirl of my life, I pause to remember the Soapoids, a matriarchal people whose lives drag out in long luxurious segments lived within color-coordinated cubes, and who relegate the more messy business of life to quick one-minute segments, thus freeing themselves for a stress-free, germ-free, moisture-controlled existence.

Analyzing This Selection

1. What tone does the author adopt through her fantasy role? Find several words and phrases that establish this tone. How does the author want us to respond to that tone?

2. How do the student's specific findings differ from her professor's lectures? How does she explain those differences? How do we explain them?

3. How is the student changed by her long-term viewing? What is the author's point about the effect of television in our society?

Analyzing Connections

4. Loewenstein and Marcia Aldrich in "Hair" (see p. 36) use comic irony and fantasy to comment on our lives. Which selection is more amusing? Which makes its intended point more effectively?

Analyzing by Writing

5. Review one episode of a soap-opera or situation comedy. Watch the program closely and take ample notes. Then, in an essay, identify the main interests and issues that were treated directly or indirectly. Explain how the program illuminates or trivializes the moral and social significance of its content. Take into account some effects of technical features such as canned audience responses, studio settings, and interruptions for commercials.

Hanif Kureishi

EIGHT ARMS TO HOLD YOU

◇

HANIF KUREISHI (b. 1954) is a British novelist, playwright, and screenwriter. He
is best known in the United States for his screenplay for *My Beautiful Laun-
drette* (1986). He has been the resident writer at the Royal Court Theatre,
London. His first novel, *The Buddha of Suburbia* (1990), was recently made
into a film. The following essay appeared first in *Granta* magazine (1993).

One day at school — an all-boys comprehensive on the border between 1
London and Kent — our music teacher told us that John Lennon and Paul
McCartney didn't actually write those famous Beatles songs we love so much.

It was 1968 and I was thirteen. For the first time in music appreciation class 2
we were to listen to the Beatles — "She's Leaving Home," with the bass turned
off. The previous week, after some Brahms, we'd been allowed to hear a Frank
Zappa record, again baseless. For Mr. Hogg, our music and religious instruction teacher, the bass guitar 'obscured' the music. But hearing anything by the
Beatles at school was uplifting, an act so unusually liberal it was confusing.

Mr. Hogg prised open the lid of the school "stereophonic equipment," 3
which was kept in a big, dark wooden box and wheeled around the premises
by the much-abused war-wounded caretaker. Hogg put on "She's Leaving
Home" without introduction, but as soon as it began he started his Beatles
analysis.

What he said was devastating, though it was put simply, as if he were 4
stating the obvious. These were the facts: Lennon and McCartney could not
possibly have written the songs ascribed to them; it was a con — we should
not be taken in by the "Beatles," they were only the front-men.

Those of us who weren't irritated by his prattling through the tune were 5
giggling. Certainly, for a change, most of us were listening to teacher. I was
perplexed. Why would anyone want to think anything so ludicrous? What
was really behind this idea?

"Who did write the Beatles' songs, then, sir?" someone asked bravely. And 6
Paul McCartney sang:

> We struggled hard all our lives to get by,
> She's leaving home after living alone,
> For so many years.

Mr. Hogg told us that Brian Epstein and George Martin wrote the Lennon /McCartney songs. The Fabs only played on the records — if they did anything at all. (Hogg doubted whether their hands had actually touched the instruments.) "Real musicians were playing on those records," he said. Then he put the record back in its famous sleeve and changed the subject.

But I worried about Hogg's theory for days; on several occasions I was 7 tempted to buttonhole him in the corridor and discuss it further. The more I dwelt on it alone, the more it revealed. The Mopheads couldn't even read music — how could they be geniuses?

It was unbearable to Mr. Hogg that four young men without significant 8 education could be the bearers of such talent and critical acclaim. But then Hogg had a somewhat holy attitude to culture. "He's cultured," he'd say of someone, the antonym of, "He's common." Culture, even popular culture — folk-singing, for instance — was something you put on a special face for, after years of wearisome study. Culture involved a particular twitching of the nose, a faraway look (into the sublime) and a fruity pursing of the lips. Hogg knew. There was, too, a sartorial vocabulary of knowingness, with leather patches sewn on to the elbows of shiny, rancid jackets.

Obviously this was not something the Beatles had been born into. Nor had 9 they acquired it in any recognized academy or university. No, in their early twenties, the Fabs made culture again and again, seemingly without effort, even as they mugged and winked at the cameras like schoolboys.

Sitting in my bedroom listening to the Beatles on a Grundig reel-to-reel 10 tape-recorder, I began to see that to admit to the Beatles' genius would devastate Hogg. It would take too much else away with it. The songs that were so perfect and about recognizable common feelings — "She Loves You," "Please, Please Me," "I Wanna Hold Your Hand" — were all written by Brian Epstein and George Martin because the Beatles were only boys like us: ignorant, bad-mannered, and rude; boys who'd never, in a just world, do anything interesting with their lives. This implicit belief, or form of contempt, was not abstract. We felt and sometimes recognized — and Hogg's attitude toward the Beatles exemplified this — that our teachers had no respect for us as people capable of learning, of finding the world compelling and wanting to know it.

The Beatles would also be difficult for Hogg to swallow because for him 11 there was a hierarchy among the arts. At the top were stationed classical music and poetry, beside the literary novel and great painting. In the middle would be not-so-good examples of these forms. At the bottom of the list, and scarcely considered art forms at all, were films ("the pictures"), television and, finally, the most derided — pop music.

But in that post-modern dawn — the late 1960s — I like to think that 12 Hogg was starting to experience cultural vertigo — which was why he worried about the Beatles in the first place. He thought he knew what culture was, what counted in history, what had weight and what you needed to know to be educated. These things were not relative, not a question of taste or decision. Notions of objectivity did exist; there were criteria and Hogg knew what the criteria were. Or at least he thought he did. But the particular form of certainty, of intellectual authority, along with many other forms of authority, was shifting. People didn't know where they were anymore.

Not that you could ignore the Beatles even if you wanted to. Those rockers 13 in suits were unique in English popular music, bigger than anyone had seen before. What a pleasure it was to swing past Buckingham Palace in the bus knowing the Queen was indoors, in her slippers, watching her favorite film, *Yellow Submarine,* and humming along to "Eleanor Rigby." ("*All the lonely people . . .*")

The Beatles couldn't be as easily dismissed as the Rolling Stones, who 14 often seemed like an ersatz American group, especially when Mick Jagger started to sing with an American accent. The Beatles' music was supernaturally beautiful and it was English music. In it you could hear cheeky music-hall songs and send-ups, pub ballads and, more importantly, hymns. The Fabs had the voices and looks of choirboys, and their talent was so broad they could do anything — love songs, comic songs, kids' songs, and sing-alongs for football crowds (at White Hart Lane, Tottenham Hotspur's ground, we sang: "Here, there, and every-fucking-where, Jimmy Greaves, Jimmy Greaves"). They could do rock 'n' roll too, though they tended to parody it, having mastered it early on.

One lunch-time in the school library, not long after the incident with 15 Hogg, I came across a copy of *Life* magazine which included hefty extracts from Hunter Davies's biography of the Beatles, the first major book about them and their childhoods. It was soon stolen from the library and passed around the school, a contemporary *Lives of the Saints.* (On the curriculum we were required to read Gerald Durrell and C. S. Forester, but we had our own books, which we discussed, just as we exchanged and discussed records. We liked *Candy, Lord of the Flies,* James Bond, Mervyn Peake, and *Sex Manners for Men,* among other things.)

Finally my parents brought the biography for my birthday. It was the first 16 hardback I possessed and, pretending to be sick, I took the day off to read it, with long breaks between chapters to prolong the pleasure. But *The Beatles* didn't satisfy me as I'd imagined it would. It wasn't like listening to *Revolver,* for instance, after which you felt satisfied and uplifted. The book disturbed and intoxicated me; it made me feel restless and dissatisfied with my life. After reading about the Beatles' achievements I began to think I didn't expect enough of myself, that none of us at school did really. In two years we'd start work; soon after all that we'd get married and buy a small house nearby. The form of life was decided before it was properly begun.

To my surprise it turned out that the Fabs were lower-middle-class pro- 17 vincial boys; neither rich nor poor, their music didn't come out of hardship and nor were they culturally privileged. Lennon was rough, but it wasn't poverty that made him hard-edged. The Liverpool Institute, attended by Paul and George, was a good grammar school. McCartney's father had been well enough off for Paul and his brother Michael to have piano lessons. Later, his father bought him a guitar.

We had no life guides or role models among politicians, military types, or   18
religious figures, or even film stars for that matter, as our parents did. Footballers and pop stars were the revered figures of my generation, and the Beatles, more than anyone, were exemplary for countless young people. If coming from the wrong class restricts your sense of what you can be, then none of us thought we'd become doctors, lawyers, scientists, politicians. We were scheduled to be clerks, civil servants, insurance managers, and travel agents.

Not that leading some kind of creative life was entirely impossible. In the   19
mid-1960s the media was starting to grow. There was a demand for designers, graphic artists, and the like. In our art lessons we designed toothpaste boxes and record sleeves to prepare for the possibility of going to art school. Now, these were very highly regarded among the kids; they were known to be anarchic places, the sources of British pop art, numerous pop groups, and the generators of such luminaries as Pete Townshend, Keith Richards, Ray Davies, and John Lennon. Along with the Royal Court and the drama corridor of the BBC, the art schools were the most important post-war British cultural institution, and some lucky kids escaped into them. Once, I ran away from school to spend the day at the local art college. In the corridors where they sat cross-legged on the floor, the kids had disheveled hair and paint-splattered clothes. A band was rehearsing in the dining-hall. They liked being there so much they stayed till midnight. Round the back entrance there were condoms in the grass.

But these kids were destined to be commercial artists, which was, at least,   20
"proper work." Commercial art was OK but anything that veered too closely toward pure art caused embarrassment; it was pretentious. Even education fell into this trap. When, later, I went to college, our neighbors would turn in their furry slippers and housecoats to stare and tut-tut to each other as I walked down the street in my army-surplus greatcoat, carrying a pile of library books. I like to think it was the books rather than the coat they were objecting to — the idea that they were financing my uselessness through their taxes. Surely nurturing my brain could be of no possible benefit to the world; it would only render me more argumentative — create an intelligentsia and you're only producing criticism for the future. . . .

I could, then, at least have been training to be an apprentice. But,   21
unfortunately for the neighbors, we had seen *A Hard Day's Night* at Bromley Odeon. Along with our mothers, we screamed all through it, fingers stuck in our ears. And afterwards we didn't know what to do with ourselves, where to go, how to exorcize this passion the Beatles had stoked up. The ordinary wasn't enough; we couldn't accept only the everyday now! We desired ecstasy, the extraordinary, magnificence — today!

For most, this pleasure lasted only a few hours and then faded. But for 22 others it opened a door to the sort of life that might, one day, be lived. And so the Beatles came to represent opportunity and possibility. They were carefree offers, a myth for us to live by, a light for us to follow.

How could this be? How was it that of all the groups to emerge from that 23 great pop period the Beatles were the most dangerous, the most threatening, the most subversive? Until they met Dylan and, later, dropped acid, the Beatles wore matching suits and wrote harmless love songs offering little ambiguity and no call to rebellion. They lacked Elvis's sexuality, Dylan's introspection, and Jagger's surly danger. And yet . . . and yet — this is the thing — everything about the Beatles represented pleasure, and for the provincial and suburban young pleasure was only the outcome and justification of work. Pleasure was work's reward and it occurred only at weekends and after work.

But when you looked at *A Hard Day's Night* or *Help!*, it was clear that 24 those four boys were having the time of their life: The films radiated freedom and good times. In them there was no sign of the long, slow accumulation of security and status, the year-after-year movement toward satisfaction, that we were expected to ask of life. Without conscience, duty, or concern for the future, everything about the Beatles spoke of enjoyment, abandon, and attention to the needs of the self. The Beatles became heroes to the young because they were not deferential: No authority had broken their spirit; they were confident and funny; they answered back; no one put them down. It was this independence, creativity, and earning-power that worried Hogg about the Beatles. Their naive hedonism and dazzling accomplishments were too paradoxical. For Hogg to approve of them wholeheartedly was like saying crime paid. But to dismiss the new world of the 1960s was to admit to being old and out of touch. . . .

The Beatles could seduce the world partly because of their innocence. 25 They were, basically, good boys who became bad boys. And when they became bad boys, they took a lot of people with them.

Lennon claimed to have "tripped" hundreds of times, and he was just the 26 sort to become interested in unusual states of mind. LSD creates euphoria and suspends inhibition; it may make us aware of life's intense flavor. In the tripper's escalation of awareness, the memory is stimulated too. Lennon knew the source of his art was the past, and his acid songs were full of melancholy, self-examination, and regret. It's no surprise that *Sergeant Pepper*, which at one time was to include "Strawberry Fields" and "Penny Lane," was originally intended to be an album of songs about Lennon and McCartney's Liverpool childhood.

Soon the Beatles started to wear clothes designed to be read by people who 27 were stoned. . . . John Lennon in 1967, . . . was reportedly wearing a green flower-patterned shirt, red cord trousers, yellow socks, and a sporran in which he carried his loose change and keys. These weren't the cheap but hip adaptations of work clothes that young males had worn since the late 1940s — Levi jackets and jeans, sneakers, work boots or DMs, baseball caps, leather jackets — democratic styles practical for work. The Beatles had rejected this conception of work. Like Baudelairean dandies they could afford to dress ironically and effeminately, for each other, for fun, beyond the constraints of the ordinary. Stepping out into that struggling post-war world steeped in memories of recent devastation and fear — the war was closer to them than *Sergeant Pepper* is to me today — wearing shimmering bandsman's outfits, crushed velvet, peach-colored silk and long hair, their clothes were gloriously nonfunctional, identifying their creativity and the pleasures of drug-taking.

By 1966 the Beatles behaved as if they spoke directly to the whole world. 28 This was not a mistake: They were at the center of life for millions of young people in the West. And certainly they're the only mere pop group you could remove from history and suggest that culturally, without them, things would have been significantly different. All this meant that what they did was influential and important. At this time, before people were aware of the power of the media, the social changes the Beatles sanctioned had happened practically before anyone noticed. Musicians have always been involved with drugs, but the Beatles were the first to parade their particular drug-use — marijuana and LSD — publicly and without shame. They never claimed, as musicians do now — when found out — that drugs were a "problem" for them. And unlike the Rolling Stones, they were never humiliated for drug-taking or turned into outlaws. . . . The Beatles made taking drugs seem an enjoyable, fashionable, and liberating experience: Like them you would see and feel in ways you hadn't imagined possible. Their endorsement, far more than that of any other group or individual, removed drugs from their subcultural, avant-garde, and generally squalid associations, making them part of mainstream youth activity. Since then, illegal drugs have accompanied music, fashion, and dance as part of what it is to be young in the West. . . .

Whatever they did and however it went wrong, the Beatles were always on 29 top of things musically, and perhaps it is this, paradoxically, that made their end inevitable. The loss of control that psychedelic drugs can involve, the political anger of the 1960s and its antiauthoritarian violence, the foolishness and inauthenticity of being pop stars at all, rarely violates the highly finished surface of their music. Songs like "Revolution" and "Helter Skelter" attempt to express unstructured or deeply felt passions, but the Beatles are too controlled to let their music fray. It never felt as though the bad was going to disintegrate through sheer force of feeling, as with Hendrix, the Who, or the Velvet Underground. Their ability was so extensive that all madness could be contained within a song. Even "Strawberry Fields" and "I Am the Walrus" are finely engineered and controlled. The exception is "Revolution No. 9," which Lennon had to fight to keep on the *White Album*; he wanted to smash through the organization and accomplished form of his pop music. But Lennon had to leave the Beatles to continue in that direction and it wasn't until his first solo album that he was able to strip away the Beatle frippery for the raw feeling he was after.

At least, Lennon wanted to do this. In the 1970s, the liberation tendencies 30 of the 1960s bifurcated into two streams — hedonism, self-aggrandizement, and decay, represented by the Stones; and serious politics and self-exploration, represented by Lennon. He continued to be actively involved in the obsessions of the time, both as initiate and leader, which is what makes him the central cultural figure of the age. . . .

But to continue to develop, Lennon had to leave the containment of the 31 Beatles and move to America. He had to break up the Beatles to lead an interesting life. . . .

Since Hogg played "She's Leaving Home," the media has expanded 32 unimaginably, but pop music remains one area accessible to all, both to spectators and, especially, to participants. The cinema is too expensive, the novel too refined and exclusive, the theater too poor and middle class, and television too complicated and rigid. Music is simpler to get into. And pop musicians never have to ask themselves — in the way that writers, for instance, constantly have to — who is my audience, who am I writing for, and what am I trying to say? It is art for their own sakes, and art which connects with a substantial audience hungry for a new product, an audience which is, by now, soaked in the history of pop music and is sophisticated, responsive, and knowledgeable.

And so there has been in Britain since the mid-1960s a stream of fantas- 33 tically accomplished music, encompassing punk and new wave, northern soul, reggae, hip-hop, rap, acid jazz, and house. The Left, in its puritanical way, has frequently dismissed pop as capitalist pap, preferring folk and other "traditional" music. But it is pop that has spoken of ordinary experience with far more precision, real knowledge, and wit than, say, British fiction of the equivalent period. And you can't dance to fiction.

Analyzing This Selection

1. What were the reasons for Mr. Hogg's attitude toward the Beatles? Which of these reasons does the author view sympathetically? What is the author's attitude toward the other reasons?

2. In the author's youth, what were the ordinary expectations and limits of his social class? How did young people usually pursue their ambitions?

3. Why were the Beatles more influential than other pop singers? Do you agree with the author's analysis of their importance?

4. Kureishi says that the breakup of the group was inevitable. In his view, what alternatives would have been worse than their breakup?

Analyzing Connections

5. Kureishi and Louise Erdrich in "Z: The Movie That Changed My Life" (see p. 345) affirm that the media revolutionized their lives. As adolescents, what were their similar and different responses to the media? As adults, how do they evaluate their adolescent experiences? Who sees the changes as more liberating?

Analyzing by Writing

6. Can today's popular entertainers achieve the influence that the Beatles, Bob Dylan, the Rolling Stones, and Elvis Presley had twenty to thirty years ago? Kureishi implies that the culture of the young has completely changed. Using his analysis of the appeal of earlier singers, explain why you think pop music or other popular entertainment can or cannot presently define "what it is to be young in the West."

Stephan Talty

FAMILY RECORD

◇

STEPHAN TALTY (b. 1964) was raised in Buffalo, New York. He graduated from Amherst College. He began his career as a free-lance writer by writing on crime and music for the *Miami Herald*. He has worked as a free-lancer in Dublin, Ireland, and New York City. Talty has contributed to the *Boston Globe*, the Irish *Times*, *Musician*, *American Film*, and *Film Comment*, in which the following essay first appeared (1991).

They've stopped their conversation, quickly smoothed their hair, and turned toward us in the quiet room. Or they've come spilling out of the farmhouse onto the sun and lined up, all twelve of them, against the rough wall and squinted at us. Their faces grow somber, shy, or excessively proud. The flash pops in the silence. They blow out their breaths in a strange cheer and turn back.

When, later, they died and became our ancestors, the people in the photographs had forgotten the few flashes of light that gave us an idea of them. And yet, for the last hundred years or so, it's been the photograph alone that has shown us our forefathers and lightly etched our individual pasts against the collective history. And that produced in us the purest physical sensation of the past that we know. Now that is beginning to change, as we videotape one another for generation 2100, and the power of the American family album gives way to the new home movies.

Home video is in its rambling adolescent days, a great tragicomic tool disguised as a novelty toy. Theoretically, a well-used family videocamera could provide the kid of 2150 with an idea of his or her past that would seem incomprehensibly rich to us today. As a hint of the possibilities, imagine a video of your family including footage from 1900 to the present. The first scenes show, say, your farmer ancestors in rural Wales. Your grandfather as a boy is the first to appear, eagerly leading the operator on a tour of the house: describing the brothers and sisters who are working or have gone to America, showing the camera his rough wooden toys. He leads us outside to the back pasture, where sheep are grazing under a lead sky. The operator asks him about school. He says that he likes math but has missed two years to work at plowing and harvesting. He stares down at his hands for a moment, then turns and looks for his father in the fields.

The tape then cuts to a different house (the quality of light in the picture   4
changes subtly). The technical ace in the family has intercut another video:
These scenes are from the other side of the family and show your grandmother as a young girl. The scene is a middle-class Boston home, circa 1900;
your grandmother, holding the videocam, walks into the livingroom, where
her mother and three friends sit talking. The mother arches her eyebrows in
feigned annoyance as the girl sits herself in an armchair and begins to
question the women about their lives with great seriousness. They look at
each other, and smile. . . .

Those are the beginnings of what a family film might be like: full portraits   5
of the generations by an unsentimental eye. There could be something
revolutionary in that, clear knowledge instead of nostalgia.

Then again, and far more likely, the kid of 2150 could be handed a tape   6
in which it appears he or she dropped from a long straight line of jackasses
with frozen smiles, endlessly repeating a few lousy jokes, the family hand-
gestures of terror, and the same four or five expressions. For that's what so
many of our home movies are: a terrible dumb show. If he can stand the
guilt, the kid of the future can always erase the family tapes; but the evidence
would certainly poison the memory with its images of worthless lives. Along
with that old sawhorse, "a reverence for the past," something large and
necessary would pass out of his life: a valued connection with his or her dead.

The point is not to get serious about family films. In fact, the best would   7
not be the earnest interviews of high-school AV projects. Nor does video's
arrival mean family photos are doomed; the two will probably coexist in the
American home. But video will likely win any contest of memory between
the technologies: the great-grandmother watched on video will hold the
imagination longer than the great-grandmother in the photo album. The gap
between the persons portrayed — and between the portrayals and the individual — is enormous. Photos froze life into small, mysterious squares; the
other promises to free it up once again and record it faithfully. The individual waits to see if she will survive either with any honesty at all.

The photographs in the family album stopped precisely at the brink of   8
giving us real knowledge of our forebears. They gave us physical details only
to deny us the emotional life, the group portrait without telling us anything
about family character and chemistry. So around the mystery of lives interrupted — the people turned to us in the quiet room — our imaginations
ceaselessly returned to try to animate the past, with guilt, love, romantic
pain, and, above all, ignorance.

This power has been magnified to perhaps its highest intensity in Amer-   9
ica's emigrant culture. We look hard for our past in the clothes our great-
grandparents wore, in the curl of smoke over rooftops, in the jut of bones in
faces, in landscape after landscape. If anything has come to embody and store
up the past of the individual American, it is these few black-and-whites.

The early pictures have immense power that springs up at us every time   10 we page through them. Unfamiliar with the technology, our forefathers stared off into the skies, letting the photographer take a picture of their bodies as their personalities withdrew. They come to us in their tragic, vaguely militaristic stances, from a time before actorly posing. The last wisps of an antitechnological holiness cling to them, along with the signs of exposure and long wars. There is the sense, almost inevitably, of lost nobility or lost honesty, or a lost sense of living, in the pictures: Whatever is missing in 1991 can mysteriously appear in a photograph in 1907.

The new technology may change this; but first it must be considered that   11 technology may not be the point and a change threatens nothing. There was a chance for generation-to-generation memory when pen and paper came into existence, and before that with oral storytelling. Even Thomas Edison, on inventing sound recording, thought of family history as one use for his new machines: "The Family Record: a registry of sayings, reminiscences, etc., by members of a family in their own voices, and the last words of dying persons."

That last part is strange — as if Edison thought that whatever tenderness   12 a family had for the dying person would be overruled by their desire for a few last words. It's a brutally foreshortened view from the lab. But Edison's impulse remains intact: to find a trail back in the darkness of family life and history. The danger also remains, and has increased dramatically: invasiveness.

The reputation video has earned in its first decade centers on carnality and   13 betrayal. Our first real introductions to video images were shots of FBI stings, bank holdups, the spectrum of American ripoffs that reached a new highwater mark with the tapes of Marion Barry. Time after time we have seen, in the murky black and white of early video, doors kicked down on private moments, private faces. The crime being investigated often lost importance, even with Barry, as we watched something worse — the broadcasting of an intimate violation. Something in us flinched at these invasions, but something else in us was fascinated. It is the second impulse that grew stronger.

When the video came into the home, a few things changed, most stayed   14 the same. Many videocam operators (almost always men, whereas it was the family women who were caretakers of the photos) treated the videos as *home movies* — which they are not. The zooming and the swooping and corkscrewing of the picture — similar to Hollywood shots of a baby being carried off by a mountain eagle — is the sign of a brother or uncle "making movies." It's a technical fault that is mirrored in the shots themselves: The people in the videos think of them not as recording the event itself, but as a kind of accompanying film. They act or they freeze in their inability to act. Behavior is bludgeoned into two camps — the shrill and the mortified.

The result is that most home videos are sad and wrong. If photos were   15 unlike life in ways that enhanced and mystified life, videos ridicule and reduce it. There is an astonishing lack of variety in them: the same types of bright, dry-throated response, vacant looks, and forced humor. The only absolute law seems to be that sincerity is out of the question. What we see ourselves doing isn't acting, exactly — it's closer to the patter of a badly frightened salesman.

It takes only ten good seconds of home video to make one feel in one's gut   16 how much we are deprived of. I have seen videos in which fully all of the medium's promise is fulfilled. One of a relative, the night after having her first baby, waiting in a darkened hospital room for the nurse to bring her daughter to bring home. It was silent and the woman, with a nervous, bowed head, stood by the door, obviously thinking about this package that was to be handed to her (hers, all alone) to keep. Her back to the camera, she kept looking agitatedly at the closed door as footsteps approached and then passed. Watching the video, we could feel her deep seriousness, the rising-up of responsibilities, and the realization that a way of life was ending and a new one beginning. It was a memory, absolutely true.

Personal memories like these are the final raise in the stakes between video   17 and photographs. In a lucid moment, John Berger writes about what we are moving away from:

> The private photograph — the portrait of a mother, a picture of a daughter, a group photo of one's team — is appreciated and read in a context which is continuous with that from which the camera removed it. Such a photograph remains surrounded by the meaning from which it was severed. A mechanical device, the camera, has been used as an instrument to contribute to a living memory. The photograph is a memento from a life being lived.

Eloquent and right. But now, with video, we have a tool that theoretically   18 removes nothing from life.

Photos do not eventually become our memories. Often, they give us a   19 dissenting opinion on what the past was really like. We are stunned that we look unhappy in a picture of a summer that we remembered as a streak of laughter, or that we are laughing at the prom an hour before the disaster.

Video, on the other hand, may come close to actually being a kind of   20 physical memory. It is, after all, "real life" being sucked into the ports of a new technology: sound, sight, color, dimension, real time. But will this add up to a vivid memory for the person sitting down thirty years later to watch his life again? I think it takes only a quick memory of the things we rarely see in family video — men razzing each other at a barbecue, spontaneous fun, spontaneous anger, quiet conversation in a livingroom between uncle and aunt — to get our answer.

What, then, can we do? There is a danger about offering practical advice   21 for making better videos, as all the advice offered so far in the media has been practical. There has been no talk about what spirit to take videos in, how to make ones that will catch life and not force people into simulating it. But we have to want a new kind of home video; above all, to make the videocam more than a toy, we need the strength to ignore it.

The videocam is the technological eye of the family, and that causes acute   22
shortness of breath in most people. In fact, family tapes a hundred years on will probably begin with scenes of this generation's nervousness, and we shall be seen the same way as those grandparents who were so stiff before the camera. But this time the effect will be more devastating than moving. Naturalness is the only way to get true videos (true meaning not "artistic" or "educational" but watchable and honest); and the first step is to change the understanding that passes between the uncle approaching with the videocam and the person being filmed. In those seconds before the lens is adjusted and you are brought into focus, the silent contract should be made: that this will not crash through the thing it is to preserve.

The operators also need a change of heart. I have seen people with   23
videocams acquire a new humility, standing back and filming a scene that is allowed to happen without being re-created. They've stopped charging through the party like a Beirut film crew, so that the videos are freed from the curse of the amateur and gather a great deal of the humor, the rhythm, the true unexpectedness of a piece of unravelling life. Some of that, I am sure, grows out of watching those awful early videos. There is a drunkenness with the power of the *moviemaker* that is instantly seen, and embarrassment teaches. One look at them and people realize: Good home videos are not made, they are received into the camera.

Video could be a tool to humanize the monumental past. Written history,   24
art, advertising, film, and literature will redraw our age, but these videos will reproduce the neighborhood, the slang, the clan in that time. When we begin to get videos that entertain and satisfy us individually as self-historians, we shall be on our way to breathing some life into the format. Video could be immense and lyric. It could be anything more than what it is now, which is a deadly bore.

Analyzing This Selection

1. What is Talty's main criticism of family videos? What makes them unsatisfactory?

2. According to Talty, how do photographs engage us in a sense of the past? Does he think videos — if they are perfected — will affect us in the same way, or in a different way?

Analyzing Connections

3. In the Insights, Geoffrey O'Brien says that films and videos numb our responses to others (see p. 340). Talty believes that videos can increase our empathy for others. Which writer's view seems more plausible to you?

Analyzing by Writing

4. Write the scenario for a short videotape of yourself at present, which you would bequeath to the future. Beware: This video will be the only remaining photographic record of your life.

5. Consider the personal and cultural effects of audiotape recordings of voices — another type of technology that our ancestors did not have. What are some misuses of tape recordings in preserving family histories? How do the effects of audiotape differ, if at all, from effects of videotape? How do voice recordings affect our sense of a family and a national past?

Oscar Hijuelos

THE MAMBO KINGS
PLAY SONGS OF LOVE

◇

OSCAR HIJUELOS (b. 1951) was born of Cuban parents in New York City. He graduated from City College, where he also earned a master's degree. He has won several fiction awards, including a National Endowment for the Arts fellowship and a Pulitzer Prize for his second novel, *The Mambo Kings Play Songs of Love* (1989), from which this story was excerpted. His most recent novel is *Fourteen Sisters of Emilio Montez O'Brien* (1993).

It was a Saturday afternoon on La Salle Street, years and years ago when 1
I was a little kid, and around three o'clock Mrs. Shannon, the heavy Irish
woman in her perpetually soup-stained dress, opened her back window and
shouted out into the courtyard, "Hey, Cesar, yoo-hoo, I think you're on
television, I swear it's you!" When I heard the opening strains of the *I Love
Lucy* show I got excited because I knew she was referring to an item of
eternity, that episode in which my dead father and my Uncle Cesar had
appeared, playing Ricky Ricardo's singing cousins fresh off the farm in
Oriente Province, Cuba, and north in New York for an engagement at
Ricky's nightclub, the Tropicana.

This was close enough to the truth about their real lives — they were 2
musicians and songwriters who had left Havana for New York in 1949, the
year they formed the Mambo Kings, an orchestra that packed clubs, dance
halls, and theaters around the East Coast — and, excitement of excitements,
they even made a fabled journey in a flamingo-pink bus out to Sweet's
Ballroom in San Francisco, playing on an all-star mambo night, a beautiful
night of glory, beyond death, beyond pain, beyond all stillness.

Desi Arnaz had caught their act one night in a supper club on the West 3
Side, and because they had perhaps already known each from Havana or
Oriente Province, where Arnaz, like the brothers, was born, it was natural
that he ask them to sing on his show. He liked one of their songs in
particular, a romantic bolero written by them, "Beautiful Maria of My
Soul."

Some months later (I don't know how many, I wasn't five years old yet) 4
they began to rehearse for the immortal appearance of my father on this

show. For me, my father's gentle rapping on Ricky Ricardo's door has always been a call from the beyond, as in Dracula films, or films of the walking dead, in which spirits ooze out from behind tombstones and through the cracked windows and rotted floors of gloomy antique halls: Lucille Ball, the lovely red-headed actress and comedienne who played Ricky's wife, was housecleaning when she heard the rapping of my father's knuckles against that door.

"I'm commmmmming," in her singsong voice.   5

Standing in her entrance, two men in white silk suits and butterfly-looking 6
lace bow ties, black instrument cases by their side and black-brimmed white hats in their hands — my father, Nestor Castillo, thin and broad-shouldered, and Uncle Cesar, thickset and immense.

My uncle: "Mrs. Ricardo? My name is Alfonso and this is my brother 7
Manny . . ."

And her face lights up and she says, "Oh, yes, the fellows from Cuba. 8
Ricky told me all about you."

Then, just like that, they're sitting on the couch when Ricky Ricardo 9
walks in and says something like, "Manny, Alfonso! Gee, it's really swell that you fellas could make it up here from Havana for the show."

That's when my father smiled. The first time I saw a rerun of this, I could 10
remember other things about him — his lifting me up, his smell of cologne, his patting my head, his handing me a dime, his touching my face, his whistling, his taking me and my little sister, Leticia, for a walk in the park, and so many other moments happening in my thoughts simultaneously that it was like watching something momentous, say the Resurrection, as if Christ had stepped out of his sepulcher, flooding the world with light — what we were taught in the local church with the big red doors — because my father was now newly alive and could take off his hat and sit down on the couch in Ricky's living room, resting his black instrument case on his lap. He could play the trumpet, move his head, blink his eyes, nod, walk across the room, and say "Thank you" when offered a cup of coffee. For me, the room was suddenly bursting with a silvery radiance. And now I knew that we could see it again. Mrs. Shannon had called out into the courtyard alerting my uncle: I was already in his apartment.

With my heart racing, I turned on the big black-and-white television set 11
in his living room and tried to wake him. My uncle had fallen asleep in the kitchen — having worked really late the night before, some job in a Bronx social club, singing and playing the horn with a pickup group of musicians. He was snoring, his shirt was open, a few buttons had popped out on his belly. Between the delicate-looking index and forefingers of his right hand, a Chesterfield cigarette burning down to the filter, that hand still holding a half glass of rye whiskey, which he used to drink like crazy because in recent years he had been suffering from bad dreams, saw apparitions, felt cursed, and, despite all the women he took to bed, found his life of bachelorhood solitary and wearisome. But I didn't know this at the time, I thought he was

sleeping because he had worked so hard the night before, singing and playing the trumpet for seven or eight hours. I'm talking about a wedding party in a crowded, smoke-filled room (with bolted-shut fire doors), lasting from nine at night to four, five o'clock in the morning, the band playing one-, two-hour sets. I thought he just needed the rest. How could I have known that he would come home and, in the name of unwinding, throw back a glass of rye, then a second, and then a third, and so on, until he'd plant his elbow on the table and use it to steady his chin, as he couldn't hold his head up otherwise. But that day I ran into the kitchen to wake him up so that he could see the episode, too, shaking him gently and tugging at his elbow, which was a mistake, because it was as if I had pulled loose the support columns of a five-hundred-year-old church: He simply fell over and crashed to the floor.

A commercial was running on the television, and so, as I knew I wouldn't 12 have much time, I began to slap his face, pull on his burning red-hot ears, tugging on them until he finally opened one eye. In the act of focusing he apparently did not recognize me, because he asked, "Nestor, what are you doing here?"

"It's me, Uncle, it's Eugenio." 13

I said this in a really earnest tone of voice, just like the kid who hangs out 14 with Spencer Tracy in the movie of *The Old Man and the Sea*, really believing in my uncle and clinging on to his every word in life, his every touch like nourishment from a realm of great beauty, far beyond me, his heart. I tugged at him again, and he opened his eyes. This time he recognized me.

He said, "You?" 15

"Yes, Uncle, get up! Please get up! You're on television again. Come on." 16

One thing I have to say about my Uncle Cesar, there was very little he 17 wouldn't do for me in those days, and so he nodded, tried to push himself off the floor, got to his knees, had trouble balancing, and then fell backwards. His head must have hurt: His face was a wince of pain. Then he seemed to be sleeping again. From the living room came the voice of Ricky's wife, plotting as usual with her neighbor Ethel Mertz about how to get a part on Ricky's show at the Tropicana, and I knew that the brothers had already been to the apartment — that's when Mrs. Shannon had called out into the courtyard — that in about five more minutes my father and uncle would be standing on the stage of the Tropicana, ready to perform that song again. Ricky would take hold of the microphone and say, "Well, folks, now I have a real treat for you. Ladies and gentlemen, Alfonso and Manny Reyes, let's hear it!" And soon my father and uncle would be standing side by side, living, breathing beings, for all the world to see, harmonizing in a duet of that *canción*.

As I shook my uncle, he opened his eyes and gave me his hand, hard and 18 callused from his other job in those days, as superintendent, and he said, "Eugenio, help me. Help me."

I tugged with all my strength, but it was hopeless. Still he tried: With great 19 effort he made it to one knee, and then, with his hand braced on the floor, he started to push himself up again. As I gave him another tug, he began miraculously to rise. Then he pushed my hand away and said, "I'll be okay, kid."

With one hand on the table and the other on the steam pipe, he pulled 20 himself to his feet. For a moment he towered over me, wobbling as if powerful winds were rushing through the apartment. Happily I led him down the hallway and into the living room, but he fell over again by the door — not fell over, but rushed forward as if the floor had abruptly tilted, as if he had been shot out of a cannon, and, wham, he hit the bookcase in the hall. He kept piles of records there, among them a number of the black and brittle 78s he had recorded with my father and their group, the Mambo Kings. These came crashing down, the bookcase's glass doors jerking open, the records shooting out and spinning like flying saucers in the movies and splintering into pieces. Then the bookcase followed, slamming into the floor beside him: The songs "Bésame Mucho," "Acérate Más," "Juventud," "Twilight in Havana," "Mambo Nine," "Mambo Number Eight," "Mambo for a Hot Night," and their fine version of "Beautiful María of My Soul" — all these were smashed up. This crash had a sobering effect on my uncle. Suddenly he got to one knee by himself, and then the other, stood, leaned against the wall, and shook his head.

"Bueno," he said. 21

He followed me into the living room and plopped down on the couch 22 behind me. I sat on a big stuffed chair that we'd hauled up out of the basement. He squinted at the screen, watching himself and his younger brother, whom, despite their troubles, he loved very much. He seemed to be dreaming.

"Well, folks," Ricky Ricardo said, "and now I have a real treat for 23 you . . ."

The two musicians in white silk suits and big butterfly-looking lace bow 24 ties, marching toward the microphone, my uncle holding a guitar, my father a trumpet.

"Thank you, thank you. And now a little number that we composed . . ." 25 And Cesar started to strum the guitar and my father lifted his trumpet to his lips, playing the opening of "Beautiful María of My Soul," a lovely, soaring melody line filling the room.

They were singing the song as it had been written — in Spanish. With the 26 Ricky Ricardo Orchestra behind them, they came into a turnaround and began harmonizing a line that translates roughly into English as: "What delicious pain love has brought to me in the form of a woman."

My father . . . He looked so alive! 27

"Uncle!" 28

Uncle Cesar had lit a cigarette and fallen asleep. His cigarette had slid out 29 of his fingers and now was burning into the starched cuff of his white shirt. I put the cigarette out, and then my uncle, opening his eyes again, smiled. "Eugenio, do me a favor. Get me a drink."

"But, Uncle, don't you want to watch the show?"   30

He tried really hard to pay attention, to focus on it.   31

"Look, it's you and Poppy."   32

"Coño, si . . ."   33

My father's face with his horsey grin, arching eyebrows, big fleshy ears — a   34
family trait — that slight look of pain, his quivering vocal cords, how beautiful it all seemed to me then . . .

And so I rushed into the kitchen and came back with a glass of rye   35
whiskey, charging as fast as I could without spilling it. Ricky had joined the brothers onstage. He was definitely pleased with their performance and showed it, because as the last note sounded he whipped up his hand and shouted "Olé!" a big lock of his thick black hair falling over his brows. Then they bowed and the audience applauded.

The show continued on its course. A few gags followed: A costumed bull   36
with flowers wrapped around its horns came out dancing an Irish jig, its horns poking into Ricky's bottom and so exasperating him that his eyes bugged out, he slapped his forehead and started speaking a-thousand-words-a-second Spanish. But at that point it made no difference to me, the miracle had passed, the resurrection of a man, Our Lord's promise which I then believed, with its release from pain, release from the troubles of this world.

Analyzing This Selection

1. Based on your impression of the story as a whole, what sort of boy is Eugenio? Find details in the first four paragraphs that support your view of his personality. What did these details first lead you to expect from the character and the story?

2. What is the significance of the falling bookcase? Explain the uncle's reaction. What tone of voice would you give his remark?

3. For the boy, what is the connection between television and his religion? What attitude does the story express about this connection? Find details that support your interpretation.

Analyzing Connections

4. In the preceding selection, "Family Record," Stephan Talty says that videos may begin to displace memory in shaping our self-history. What frictions between memory and video occur in Eugenio? Does video have the effect Talty predicts?

Analyzing by Writing

5. Much of our sense of history comes from movie and television dramas. For instance, the Civil War, World War II, and the Holocaust are imprinted in public memory by films and mini-series. Consequently, our beliefs about their substance comes from the entertainment industry. By contrast, in school, our

knowledge of history comes for the most part from reading and lectures, not screening. What is contributed by each medium of presentation? Choose one historical topic (you are not limited to the examples given) and consider its presentation in both books and film. How have film versions enhanced or distorted the views of the past that you formed through reading? How did your reading knowledge affect your response to the screened version?

David Gelman

THE VIOLENCE IN OUR HEADS

◇

DAVID GELMAN was raised in Brooklyn and graduated from Brooklyn College. As a journalist, Gelman won awards for his Vietnam reporting and for his analysis of topics such as mental health. He joined the staff of *Newsweek* in 1975 and was a senior writer until his recent retirement. The following article appeared first in *Newsweek* (1993).

Teenagers don't invent violence, they learn it. To a considerable extent, they act out the attitudes and ethics of the adults closest to them. Thus any study of the causes of teen crime might look first at the violence that grown-ups have been carrying in their heads. In the last 30 years, Americans have developed a culture of violence surpassing in its pervasiveness anything we experienced before. It shows up in our speech, in our play, more than ever in the entertainments we fashion and fancy, in business style. "There's an extraordinary degree of violence in the language, and it's the window to the actual feelings and mores of the culture," says Dr. Robert Phillips, director of forensic services for the Connecticut Department of Public Health. "You get a sense of how the social fabric is beginning to wear thin — a lot of it is directed at minorities."

Everyone seems aggressively on the defensive these days. A rampant "make my day" ethic expressed at various levels of the culture may be largely to blame for both the rise in teen crime and its increasing callousness, says Deborah Prothrow-Stith, an assistant dean at the Harvard School of Public Health. Our national icons tend to be men who excel at violence, from John Wayne to Clint Eastwood. When President Clinton ordered a retaliatory airstrike on Baghdad because of an alleged plot against George Bush, his popularity rating took a leap, just as Bush's had when, as president, he ordered up the gulf war, in which an estimated 100,000 Iraqi civilians were killed by bombs and missiles.

Ironically, a quarter century of feminist consciousness-raising has managed, among worthier achievements, to bring us back to a macho mystique. Meanwhile the Schwarzenegger generation is pumping iron and signaling "Don't mess with me." T-shirts are broadcasting more direct messages — and so are rap lyrics: "Beat that bitch with a bat," one of them urges. "Violence is hip right now," says Jack Levin, a professor of sociology and criminology at Northeastern University. Better than hip: It's commercial.

In her 1991 book, "Deadly Consequences," Prothrow-Stith says that, for 4 adolescents, an attraction to violence is developmentally normal. But what accounts for adults' voyeuristic fascination with it? Are Rambo and RoboCop our surrogate avengers, as one psychologist suggests? It's not only teenagers who flock to the latest kung fu epic. It's certainly not teenagers alone who are guzzling beer and starting brawls at sports contests that are themselves turning ever more violent.

With new, improved technology, films grow more and more like demo- 5 lition derbies. Trailers for these movies are edited to breathing montages of blazing guns, exploding cars and heads, and bodies hurtling out of windows. The destruction is cartoonish, but the shattered glass and bodies look real enough to leave disturbing afterimages. On the tube, growly-voiced promos whip up viewers lust for bone-crunching, bloodletting sports contests to come. Videos capture football's hardest hits, complete with spliced-in grunts and groans. On the field, despite a belated ban, players still dance the obscene little touchdown shimmy that is intended to add manly insult to injury. If that doesn't sate your appetite, you can always attend the fights, at the hockey game — and, lately, at basketball and baseball games as well. Fans seem to love them. The danger, psychiatrists say, is that the constant repetition of violence and violent imagery desensitizes us in much the way a therapist desensitizes a phobia patient: by deliberate exposure to what's scary.

Images are not reality, but they feed into the perception many people have 6 of an inescapable, "out of control" violence in the country. And it would be a mistake to think this sensory inundation doesn't have an impact on the young. By now, the media-violence relationship is one of the best-researched connections in social science, says Myriam Miedzian, author of "Boys Will Be Boys: Breaking the Link Between Masculinity and Violence." But it is also, she adds, one of the best-kept secrets. "There's been an enormous reluctance to deal with this. Mothers will still say, 'Oh, I took the kids to see the Slasher, and they came home and had milkshakes and cookies.' "

In fact, milkshakes and cookies may not be such a bad idea. The impact 7 of violent movies and TV — almost impossible to put off-limits since the advent of VCRs — can be mitigated by a caring parent who sits down with the children and helps put things in perspective. That, of course, assumes a caring parent is available. "It's virtually impossible when the parent is working 50 or 60 hours a week," says Stephen Klineberg, a professor of sociology at Rice University, in Texas. In 1974, for the first time, 50 percent of American children had nobody at home when school let out at 3 o'clock. Now, it's closer to 80 percent, but schools still kick kids out at 3. "While the family has undergone a revolution, there's been a failure of these other structures to change accordingly," says Klineberg. "It's what sociologists call a cultural lag."

The failure of schools to adapt is only one example of what social analysts 8 believe is a general failure of will, a kind of paralysis in the face of the growing dimensions of the problem. The token gesture of the TV networks in volunteering parental-guidance labels for certain shows scarcely changes the picture. There are obvious dangers in imposing more aggressive restraints and flinging the doors open wider to censorship. But meanwhile, the levels of tolerated violence in the media, in sports, and in the real world keep ratcheting upward. When do we stop feeling helpless and start doing something? "The surgeon general's reports for years have said that violence on television is related to violence in children," says Carol Nagy Jacklin, dean of the division of social science and communication at the University of Southern California. "It's so upsetting that, on the one hand, we seem to deplore this violence but, on the other, we are not stopping it in the ways that we know it needs to be stopped."

Taken down to cases, there are more proximate causes of adolescent crime   9 in this country — guns and drugs, to name just two. But in the longer view, they may be no more responsible than the cultural violence of which we are the principal makers and consumers, and which we still hesitate to bring under effective control.

Analyzing This Selection

1. According to the author, is teenage violence caused mainly by social disorders, by the appeal of violent entertainment, or by the influence of adults? What order of importance does Gelman give these causes? What order do you give them?

2. In paragraph 8, Gelman refers to "the failure of the schools to adapt." To what? What adaptive changes is Gelman suggesting for schools?

3. How would you improve the list of authorities Gelman quotes? Suggest changes that strengthen, not weaken, the author's argument.

Analyzing Connections

4. Gelman and Hanif Kureishi in "Eight Arms to Hold You" (see p. 355) consider the rebellious youth cultures of generations thirty years apart. What social conditions appear to have changed? What insights about adolescents could Kureishi add to Gelman's view of teenagers?

Analyzing by Writing

5. Consider a nationally popular spectator sport such as baseball, football, basketball, or hockey that embodies values people want confirmed by their entertainment. Perhaps the sport expresses an ideal of physical perfection, team cooperation, control of power, or a similar quality that people may not find in their work or home life. Perhaps the sport expresses impulses that are malignant or destructive. Examine the sport from the viewpoint of a social scientist who is trying to find the values and stresses of a society reflected in popular sports events.

Andrea Dworkin

LETTER FROM A WAR ZONE

◇

ANDREA DWORKIN (b. 1946) was raised in Camden, New Jersey, and attended Bennington College. She lived in Crete and Amsterdam. Returning to New York, Dworkin worked as a free-lance writer and began her career of activism against pornography. Her first feminist book, *Woman Hating* (1974), won her a nationwide audience. In 1978 Dworkin participated in the first Take Back the Night March to protest urban districts that harbor prostitution and pornography. In *Intercourse* (1987), Dworkin attacks possessive and contemptuous attitudes in the way ordinary men write and speak about sexual intercourse. She has also published two novels, *Ice and Fire* (1987) and *Mercy* (1991). Dworkin's essays and speeches have been collected in *Letters from a War Zone* (1989).

It is late 1986 now, and we are losing. The war is men against women; the country is the United States. Here, a woman is beaten every eighteen seconds: by her husband or the man she lives with, not by a psychotic stranger in an alley. Understand: Women are also beaten by strangers in alleys but that is counted in a different category — gender-neutral assault, crime in the streets, big-city violence. Woman-beating, the intimate kind, is the most commonly committed violent crime in the country, according to the FBI, not feminists. A woman is raped every three minutes, nearly half the rapes committed by someone the woman knows. Forty-four percent of the adult women in the United States have been raped at least once. Forty-one percent (in some studies seventy-one percent) of all rapes are committed by two or more men; so the question is not how many rapes there are, but how many rapists. There are an estimated 16,000 new cases of father-daughter incest each year; and in the current generation of children, thirty-eight percent of girls are sexually molested. Here, now, less than eight percent of women have not had some form of unwanted sex (from assault to obscene harassment) forced on them. 1

We keep calling this war normal life. Everyone's ignorant; no one knows; the men don't mean it. In this war, the pimps who make pornography are the SS, an élite, sadistic, military, organized vanguard. They run an efficient and expanding system of exploitation and abuse in which women and children, as lower life forms, are brutalized. This year they will gross $10 billion. 2

We have been slow to understand. For fun they gag us and tie us up as if 3 we were dead meat and hang us from trees and ceilings and door frames and meat hooks; but many say the lynched women probably like it and we don't have any right to interfere with them (the women) having a good time. For fun they rape us or have other men, or sometimes animals, rape us and film the rapes and show the rapes in movie theaters or publish them in magazines, and the normal men who are not pimps (who don't know, don't mean it) pay money to watch; and we are told that the pimps and the normal men are free citizens in a free society exercising rights and that we are prudes because this is sex and real women don't mind a little force and the women get paid anyway so what's the big deal? The pimps and the normal men have a constitution that says the filmed rapes are "protected speech" or "free speech." Well, it doesn't actually *say* that — cameras, after all, hadn't been invented yet; but they interpret their constitution to protect their fun. They have laws and judges that call the women hanging from the trees "free speech." There are films in which women are urinated on, defecated on, cut, maimed, and scholars and politicians call them "free speech." The politicians, of course, deplore them. There are photographs in which women's breasts are slammed in rat traps — in which things (including knives, guns, glass) are stuffed in our vaginas — in which we are gang-banged, beaten, tortured — and journalists and intellectuals say: Well, there is a lot of violence against women *but* . . . But what, prick? But we run this country, cunt.

If you are going to hurt a woman in the United States, be sure to take a 4 photograph. This will confirm that the injury you did to her expressed a point-of-view, sacrosanct in a free society. Hey, you have a right not to like women in a democracy, man. In the very unlikely event that the victim can nail you for committing a crime of violence against her, your photograph is still constitutionally protected, since it communicates so eloquently. The woman, her brutalization, the pain, the humiliation, her smile — because you did force her to smile, didn't you? — can be sold forever to millions of normal men (them again) who — so the happy theory goes — are having a "cathartic" experience all over her. It's the same with snuff films, by the way. You can torture and disembowel a woman, ejaculate on her dismembered uterus, and even if they do put you away someday for murder (a rather simple-minded euphemism), the film is legally *speech. Speech.*

In the early days, feminism was primitive. If something hurt women, 5 feminists were against it, not for it. In 1970, radical feminists forcibly occupied the offices of the ostensibly radical Grove Press because Grove published pornography marketed as sexual liberation and exploited its female employees. Grove's publisher, an eminent boy-revolutionary, considered the hostile demonstration CIA-inspired. His pristine radicalism did not stop him from calling the very brutal New York City police and having the women physically dragged out and locked up for trespassing on his private property. Also in 1970, radical feminists seized *Rat*, an underground rag that devoted itself, in the name of revolution, to pornography and male chauvinism equally, the only attention gender got on the radical left. The pornographers, who think strategically, and actually do know what they are doing, were quick to react. "These chicks are our natural enemy," wrote Hugh Hefner in a secret memo leaked to feminists by secretaries at *Playboy*. "It is time we do battle with them. . . . What I want is a devastating piece that takes the militant feminists apart." What he got were huge, raucous demonstrations at Playboy Clubs in big cities.

Activism against pornography continued, organized locally, ignored by   6 the media but an intrinsic part of the feminist resistance to rape. Groups called Women Against Violence Against Women formed independently in many cities. Pornography was understood by feminists (without any known exception) as woman-hating, violent, rapist. Robin Morgan pinpointed pornography as the theory, rape as the practice. Susan Brownmiller, later a founder of the immensely influential Women Against Pornography, saw pornography as woman-hating propaganda that promoted rape. These insights were not banal to feminists who were beginning to comprehend the gynocidal and terrorist implications of rape for all women. These were *emerging* political insights, not learned-by-rote slogans.

Sometime in 1975, newspapers in Chicago and New York City revealed   7 the existence of snuff films. Police detectives, trying to track down distribution networks, said that prostitutes, probably in Central America, were being tortured, slowly dismembered, then killed, for the camera. Prints of the films were being sold by organized crime to private pornography collectors in the United States.

In February 1976, a day or two before Susan B. Anthony's birthday, a   8 snazzy, first-run movie house in Times Square showed what purported to be a real snuff film. The marquee towered above the vast Times Square area, the word *Snuff* several feet high in neon, next to the title the words "made in South America where life is cheap." In the ads that blanketed the subways, a woman's body was cut in half.

We felt despair, rage, pain, grief. We picketed every night. It rained every   9 night. We marched round and round in small circles. We watched men take women in on dates. We watched the women come out, physically sick, and still go home with the men. We leafleted. We screamed out of control on street corners. There was some vandalism: not enough to close it down. We tried to get the police to close it down. We tried to get the District Attorney to close it down. You have no idea what respect those guys have for free speech.

The pimp who distributed the film would come to watch the picket line   10 and laugh at us. Men who went in laughed at us. Men who walked by laughed at us. Columnists in newspapers laughed at us. The American Civil Liberties Union ridiculed us through various spokesmen (in those days, they used men). The police did more than laugh at us. They formed a barricade with their bodies, guns, and nightsticks — to protect the film from women. One threw me in front of an oncoming car. Three protestors were arrested and *locked up* for using obscene language to the theater manager. Under the United States Constitution, obscene language is not speech. Understand: It is not that obscene language is unprotected speech; it is not considered speech at all. The protestors, talking, used obscene language that was not speech; the maiming in the snuff film, the knife eviscerating the woman, was speech. All this we had to learn.

We learned a lot, of course. Life may be cheap, but knowledge never is. 11 We learned that the police protect property and that pornography is property. We learned that the civil liberties people didn't give a damn, my dear: A woman's murder, filmed to bring on orgasm, was speech, and they didn't even *mind* (these were the days before they learned that they had to say it was bad to hurt women). The ACLU did not have a crisis of conscience. The District Attorney went so far as to find a woman he claimed was "the actress" in the film to show she was alive. He held a press conference. He said that the only law the film broke was the law against fraud. He virtually challenged us to try to get the pimps on fraud, while making clear that if the film had been real, no United States law would have been broken because the murder would have occurred elsewhere. So we learned that. During the time *Snuff* showed in New York City, the bodies of several women, hacked to pieces, were found in the East River and several prostitutes were decapitated. We also learned that.

When we started protesting *Snuff*, so-called feminist lawyers, many still 12 leftists at heart, were on our side: No woman could sit this one out. We watched the radical boy lawyers pressure, threaten, ridicule, insult, and intimidate them; and they did abandon us. They went home. They never came back. We saw them learn to love free speech above women. Having hardened their radical little hearts to *Snuff*, what could ever make them put women first again?

There were great events. In November 1978, the first feminist conference 13 on pornography was held in San Francisco. It culminated in the country's first Take Back the Night March: Well over 3,000 women shut down San Francisco's pornography district for one night. In October 1978, over 5,000 women and men marched on Time Square. One documentary of the march shows a man who had come to Times Square to buy sex looking at the sea of women extending twenty city blocks and saying, bewildered and dismayed: "I can't find one fucking woman." In 1980, Linda Marchiano published *Ordeal*. World-famous as Linda Lovelace, the porn-queen extraordinaire of *Deep Throat*, Marchiano revealed that she had been forced into prostitution and pornography by brute terrorism. Gang-raped, beaten, kept in sexual slavery by her pimp/husband (who had legal rights over her as her husband), forced to have intercourse with a dog for a film, subjected to sustained sadism rarely found by Amnesty International with regard to political prisoners, she dared to survive, escape, and expose the men who had sexually used her (including *Playboy*'s Hugh Hefner and *Screw*'s Al Goldstein). The world of normal men (the consumers) did not believe her; they believed *Deep Throat*.

Feminists did believe her. Today Marchiano is a strong feminist fighting pornography.

In 1980, when I read *Ordeal*, I understood from it that every civil right 14 protected by law in this country had been broken on Linda's prostituted body. I began to see gang rape, marital rape and battery, prostitution, and other forms of sexual abuse as civil rights violations which, in pornography, were systemic and intrinsic (the pornography could not exist without them). The pornographers, it was clear, violated the civil rights of women much as the Ku Klux Klan in this country had violated the civil rights of blacks. The pornographers were domestic terrorists determined to enforce, through violence, an inferior status on people born female. The second-class status of women itself was constructed through sexual abuse; and the name of the whole system of female subordination was *pornography* — men's orgasm and sexual pleasure synonymous with women's sexually explicit inequality. Either we were human, equal, citizens, in which case the pornographers could do to us what they did with impunity and, frankly, constitutional protection; or we were inferior, not protected as equal persons by law, and so the pimps could brutalize us, the normal men could have a good time, the pimps and their lawyers and the normal men could call it free speech, and we could live in hell. Either the pornographers and the pornography did violate the civil rights of women, or women had no rights of equality.

I asked Catharine A. MacKinnon, who had pioneered sexual harassment 15 litigation, if we could mount a civil rights suit in Linda's behalf. Kitty worked with me, Gloria Steinem (an early and brave champion of Linda), and several lawyers for well over a year to construct a civil rights suit. It could not, finally, be brought, because the statute of limitations on every atrocity committed against Linda had expired; and there was no law against showing or profiting from the films she was coerced into making. Kitty and I were despondent; Gloria said our day would come. It did — in Minneapolis on December 30, 1983, when the City Council passed the first human rights legislation ever to recognize pornography as a violation of the civil rights of all women. In Minneapolis, a politically progressive city, pornography had been attacked as a *class* issue for many years. Politicians cynically zoned adult bookstores into poor and black areas of the city. Violence against the already disenfranchised women and children increased massively; and the neighborhoods experienced economic devastation as legitimate businesses moved elsewhere. The civil rights legislation was passed in Minneapolis because poor people, people of color (especially Native Americans and blacks), and feminists demanded justice.

But first, understand this. Since 1970, but especially after *Snuff*, feminist 16 confrontations with pornographers had been head-on: militant, aggressive, dangerous, defiant. We had thousands of demonstrations. Some were inside theaters where, for instance, feminists in the audience would scream like hell when a woman was being hurt on the screen. Feminists were physically dragged from the theaters by police who found the celluloid screams to be *speech* and the feminist screams to be *disturbing the peace*. Banners were unfurled in front of ongoing films. Blood was poured on magazines and sex paraphernalia designed to hurt women. Civil disobedience, sit-ins, destruction of magazines and property, photographing consumers, as well as picketing, leafleting, letter-writing, and debating in public forums, have all been engaged in over all these years without respite. Women have been arrested repeatedly: the police protecting, always, the pornographers. In one jury trial, three women, charged with two felonies and one misdemeanor for pouring blood over pornography, said that they were acting to prevent a greater harm — rape; they also said that the blood was already there, they were just making it visible. They were acquitted when the jury heard testimony about the actual use of pornography in rape and incest *from the victims:* a raped woman; an incestuously abused teenager.

So understand this too: *Feminism works*; at least primitive feminism 17 works. We used militant activism to defy and to try to destroy the men who exist to hurt women, that is, the pimps who make pornography. We wanted to destroy — not just put some polite limits on but *destroy* — their power to hurt us; and millions of women, each alone at first, one at a time, began to remember, or understand, or find words for how she herself had been hurt by pornography, what had happened to her because of it. Before feminists took on the pornographers, each woman, as always, had thought that only she had been abused in, with, or because of pornography. Each woman lived in isolation, fear, shame. Terror creates silence. Each woman had lived in unbreachable silence. Each woman had been deeply hurt by rape, the incest, the battery; but something more had happened too, and there was no name for it and no description of it. Once the role of pornography in *creating* sexual abuse was exposed — rape by rape, beating by beating, victim by victim — our understanding of the nature of sexual abuse itself changed. To talk about rape alone, or battery alone, or incest alone, was not to talk about the totality of how the women had been violated. Rape or wife-beating or prostitution or incest were not discrete or free-standing phenomena. We had thought: Some men rape; some men batter; some men fuck little girls. We had accepted an inert model of male sexuality: Men have fetishes; the women must always be blond, for instance; the act that brings on orgasm must always be the same. But abuse created by pornography was different: The abuse was multifaceted, complex, the violations of each individual woman were many and interconnected; the sadism was exceptionally dynamic. We found that when pornography created sexual abuse, men learned any new tricks the pornographers had to teach. We learned that anything that hurt or humiliated women could be sex for men who used pornography; and male sexual practice would change dramatically to accommodate violations and degradations promoted by pornography. We found that sexual abuses in a woman's life were intricately and complexly connected when pornography was a factor: Pornography was used to accomplish incest and then the child would be used to make pornography; the pornography-consuming husband would not just beat his wife but would tie her, hang her, torture her, force her into prostitution, and film her for pornography; pornography used in gang rape meant that the gang rape was enacted according to an already existing script, the sadism of the gang rape enhanced by the contributions of the pornographers. The forced filming of forced sex became a new sexual violation of women. In sexual terms, pornography created for women and children concentration camp conditions. This is not hyperbole.

One psychologist told the Minneapolis City Council about three cases 18 involving pornography used as "recipe books": "Presently or recently I have worked with clients who have been sodomized by broom handles, forced to have sex with over twenty dogs in the back seat of their car, tied up and then electrocuted on their genitals. These are children [all] in the ages of fourteen to eighteen . . . where the perpetrator has read the manuals and manuscripts at night and used these as recipe books by day or had the pornography present at the time of the sexual violence."

A social worker who works exclusively with adolescent female prostitutes 19 testified: "I can say almost categorically never have I had a client who has not been exposed to prostitution through pornography. . . . For some young women that means that they are shown pornography, either films, videotapes, or pictures as this is how you do it, almost as a training manual in how to perform acts of prostitution. . . . In addition, out on the street when a young woman is [working], many of her tricks or customers will come up to her with little pieces of paper, pictures that were torn from a magazine and say, I want this . . . it is like a mail order catalogue of sex acts, and that is what she is expected to perform. . . . Another aspect that plays a bit part in my work . . . is that on many occasions my clients are multi, many rape victims. These rapes are often either taped or have photographs taken of the event. The young woman when she tries to escape [is blackmailed]."

A former prostitute, testifying on behalf of a group of former prostitutes 20 afraid of exposure, confirmed: "[W]e were all introduced to prostitution through pornography, there were no exceptions in our group, and we were all under eighteen." Everything done to women in pornography was done to these young prostitutes by the normal men. To them the prostitutes were synonymous with the pornography but so were all women, including wives and daughters. The abuses of prostitutes were not qualitatively different from the abuses of other women. Out of a compendium of pain, this is one incident: "[A] woman met a man in a hotel room in the 5th Ward. When he got there she was tied up while sitting on a chair nude. She was gagged and left alone in the dark for what she believed to be an hour. The man returned with two other men. They burned her with cigarettes and attached nipple clips to her breasts. They had many S and M magazines with them and showed her many pictures of women appearing to consent, enjoy, and encourage this abuse. She was held for twelve hours, continuously raped and beaten. She was paid $50 or about $2.33 per hour."

Racist violation is actively promoted in pornography; and the abuse has 21
pornography's distinctive dynamic — an annihilating sadism, the brutality
and concept taken wholesale from the pornography itself. The pornographic video game "Custer's Revenge" generated many gang rapes of
Native American women. In the game, men try to capture a "squaw," tie
her to a tree, and rape her. In the sexually explicit game, the penis goes in
and out, in and out. One victim of the "game" said: "When I was first
asked to testify I resisted some because the memories are so painful and so
recent. I am here because of my four-year-old daughter and other Indian
children. . . . I was attacked by two white men and from the beginning
they let me know they hated my people. . . . And they let me know that
the rape of a 'squaw' by white men was practically honored by white
society. In fact, it had been made into a video game called 'Custer's Last
Stand' [*sic*]. They held me down and as one was running the tip of his
knife across my face and throat he said, 'Do you want to play Custer's Last
Stand? It's great, you lose but you don't care, do you? You like a little
pain, don't you, squaw?' They both laughed and then he said, 'There is a
lot of cock in Custer's Last Stand. You should be grateful, squaw, that
all-American boys like us want you. Maybe we will tie you to a tree and
start a fire around you.'"

The same sadistic intensity and arrogance is evident in this pornography- 22
generated gang rape of a thirteen-year-old girl. Three deer hunters, in the
woods, looking at pornography magazines, looked up and saw the blond
child. "There's a live one," one said. The three hunters chased the child,
gang-raped her, pistol-whipped her breasts, all the while calling her names
from the pornography magazines scattered at their campsite — Golden Girl,
Little Godiva, and so on. "All three of them had hunting rifles. They, two
men held their guns at my head and the first man hit my breast with his rifle
and they continued to laugh. And then the first man raped me and when he
was finished they started making jokes about how I was a virgin. . . . The
second man then raped me. . . . The third man forced his penis into my
mouth and told me to do it and I didn't know how to do it. I did not know
what I was supposed to be doing . . . one of the men pulled the trigger on
his gun so I tried harder. Then when he had an erection, he raped me. They
continued to make jokes about how lucky they were to have found me when
they did and they made jokes about being a virgin. They started . . . kicking
me and told me that if I wanted more, I could come back the next day. . . .
I didn't tell anyone that I was raped until I was twenty years old." These men,
like the men who gang-raped the Native American woman, had fun; they
were playing a game.

I am quoting from some representative but still relatively *simple* cases. 23
Once the role of pornography in the abuse is exposed, we no longer have just
rape or gang rape or child abuse or prostitution. We have, instead, sustained
an intricate sadism with no inherent or predictable limits on the kinds of

degrees of brutality that will be used on women or girls. We have torture; we have killer-hostility.

Pornography-saturated abuse is specific and recognizable because it is   24
Nazism on women's bodies: The hostility and sadism it generates are car-
nivorous. Interviewing 200 working prostitutes in San Francisco, Mimi H.
Silbert and Ayala M. Pines discovered astonishing patterns of hostility related
to pornography. No questions were asked about pornography. But so much
information was given casually by the women about the role of pornography
in assaults on them that Silbert and Pines published the data they had
stumbled on. Of the 200 women, 193 had been raped as adults and 178 had
been sexually assaulted as children. That is 371 cases of sexual assault on a
population of 200 women. Twenty-four percent of those who had been raped
mentioned that the rapist made specific references to pornography during the
rape: "The assailant referred to pornographic materials he had seen or read
and then insisted that the victims not only enjoyed the rape but also the
extreme violence." When a victim, in some cases, told the rapist that she was
a prostitute and would perform whatever sex act he wanted (to dissuade him
from using violence), *in all cases* the rapists responded in these ways: "(1)
their language became more abusive, (2) they became significantly more
violent, beating and punching the women excessively, often using weapons
they had shown the women, (3) they mentioned having seen prostitutes in
pornographic films, the majority of them mentioning specific pornographic
literature, and (4) after completing the forced vaginal penetration, they
continued to assault the women sexually in ways they claimed they had seen
prostitutes enjoy in the pornographic literature they cited." Examples include forced and anal penetration with a gun, beatings all over the body with
a gun, breaking bones, holding a loaded pistol at the woman's vagina "in-
sisting this was the way she had died in the film he had seen."

Studies show that between sixty-five and seventy-five percent of women in   25
pornography were sexually abused as children, often incestuously, many put
into pornography as children. One woman, for instance, endured this: "I'm
an incest survivor, ex-pornography model, and ex-prostitute. My incest story
begins before pre-school and ends many years later — this was with my
father. I was also molested by an uncle and a minister . . . my father forced
me to perform sexual acts with men at a stag party when I was a teenager. I
am from a 'nice' middle-class family. . . . My father is an $80,000 a year
corporate executive, lay minister, and alcoholic. . . . My father was my
pimp in pornography. There were three occasions from ages nine to sixteen
when he forced me to be a pornography model . . . in Nebraska, so, yes, it
does happen here." This woman is now a feminist fighting pornography. She
listens to men mostly debate whether or not there is any social harm connected to pornography. People want experts. We have experts. Society says
we have to prove harm. We have proved harm. What we have to prove is that
women are human enough for harm to matter. As one liberal so-called
feminist said recently: "What's the harm of pornography? A paper cut?" This

woman was a Commissioner on the so-called Meese commission.[1] She had spent a year of her life looking at the brutalization of women in pornography and hearing the life-stories of pornography-abused women. Women were not very human to her.

In pain and in privacy, women began to face, then to tell, the truth, first 26 to themselves, then to others. Now, women have testified before governmental bodies, in public meetings, on radio, on television, in workshops at conventions of liberal feminists who find all this so messy, so declassé, *so unfortunate.* Especially, the liberal feminists hate it that this mess of pornography — having to do something about these abuses of women — might interfere with their quite comfortable political alliances with all those normal men, the consumers — who also happen to be, well, friends. They don't want the stink of this kind of sexual abuse — the down-and-dirty kind for fun and profit — to rub off on them. Feminism to them means getting success, not fighting oppression.

Here we are: Weep for us. Society, with the acquiescence of too many 27 liberal-left feminists, says that pornographers must *not* be stopped because the freedom of everyone depends on the freedom of the pornographers to exercise speech. The woman gagged and hanging remains the speech they exercise. In liberal-left lingo, stopping them is called *censorship.*

The civil rights law — a modest approach, since it is not the barrel of a 28 gun — was passed twice in Minneapolis, vetoed twice there by the mayor. In Indianapolis, a more conservative city (where even liberal feminists are registered Republicans), a narrower version was adopted: *Narrower* means that only very violent pornography was covered by the law. In Indianapolis, pornography was defined as the graphic, sexually explicit subordination of women in pictures and/or words that also included rape, humiliation, penetration by objects or animals, or dismemberment. Men, children, and transsexuals used in these ways could also use this law. The law made pornographers legally and economically responsible for the harm they did to women. Makers of pornography, exhibitors, sellers, and distributors could be sued for trafficking in pornography. Anyone coerced into pornography could hold the makers, sellers, distributors, or exhibitors liable for profiting from the coercion and could have the coerced product removed from the marketplace. Anyone forced to watch pornography in their home, place of work or education, or in public, could sue whoever forces them and any institution that sanctions the force (for instance, a university or an employer). Anyone physically assaulted or injured because of a specific piece of pornography could sue the pornographer for money damages and get the pornography off the shelves. Under this law, pornography is correctly understood and recognized as a practice of sex discrimination. Pornography's impact on the status

---

[1]Named by the pornographers and their friends after their very right-wing Edwin Meese, the Commission was actually set up by the moderate former Attorney General William French Smith. [Au.]

of women is to keep all women second-class: targets of aggression and civilly inferior.

The United States courts have declared the Indianapolis civil rights law 29 unconstitutional. A Federal Appeals Court said that pornography did all the harm to women we said it did — causing us both physical injury and civil inferiority — but its success in hurting us only proved its power as speech. Therefore, it is protected speech. Compared with the pimps, women have no rights.

The good news is that the pornographers are in real trouble and that we 30 made the trouble. *Playboy* and *Penthouse* are both in deep financial trouble. *Playboy* has been losing subscribers, and thus its advertising base, for years; both *Playboy* and *Penthouse* have lost thousands of retail outlets for their wares in the last few years. We have cost them their legitimacy.

The bad news is that we are in trouble. There is much violence against us, 31 pornography-inspired. They make us, our bodies, pornography in their magazines and tell the normal men to get us good. We are followed, attacked, threatened. Bullets were shot into one feminist antipornography center. Feminists have been harassed out of their homes, forced to move. And the pornographers have found a bunch of girls (as the women call themselves) to work for them: not the chickenshit liberals, but real collaborators who have organized specifically to oppose the civil rights legislation and to protect the pornographers from our political activism — pornography should not be a feminist issue, these so-called feminists say. They say: Pornography is misogynist *but* . . . The *but* in this case is that it derepresses us. The victims of pornography can testify, and have, that when men get derepressed, women get hurt. These women say they are feminists. Some have worked for the defeated Equal Rights Amendment or for abortion rights or for equal pay or for lesbian and gay rights. But these days, they organize to stop us from stopping the pornographers.

Most of the women who say they are feminists but work to protect 32 pornography are lawyers or academics: lawyers like the ones who walked away from *Snuff*; academics who think prostitution is romantic, an unrepressed female sexuality. But whoever they are, whatever they think they are doing, the outstanding fact about them is that they are ignoring the women who have been hurt in order to help the pimps who do the hurting. They are collaborators, not feminists.

The pornographers may well destroy us. The violence against us — in the 33 pornography, in the general media, among men — is escalating rapidly and dangerously. Sometimes our despair is horrible. We haven't given in yet. There is a resistance here, a real one. I can't tell you how brave and brilliant the resisters are. Or how powerless and hurt. Surely it is clear: The most powerless women, the most exploited women, are the women fighting the pornographers. Our more privileged sisters prefer not to take sides. It's a nasty fight, all right. Feminism is dying here because so many women who say they are feminists are collaborators or cowards. Feminism is magnificent and militant here because the most powerless women are putting their lives on the line to confront the most powerful men for the sake of all women. Be proud of us for fighting. Be proud of us for getting so far. Help us if you can. The pornographers will have to stop us. We will not give in. They know that and now so do you.

Love,
Andrea Dworkin

Analyzing This Selection

1. Describe the tone and explain the effect on you of Dworkin's letter. What did you find disturbing?

2. What is the effect of the statistics cited in the first paragraph? According to the author, why aren't these facts better known?

3. In the essay as a whole, how does Dworkin show that reading and viewing pornography affect men's actual behavior? Which kinds of evidence are more convincing, and why?

4. What does Dworkin imply by the terms "radical" and "liberal"? What do these terms mean to you? Does either term apply to you?

5. What is the author's recommendation for dealing legally with pornography? What has frustrated such attempts?

Analyzing Connections

6. Dworkin and David Gelman, in the preceding selection, point out that violence is commercially profitable. According to each author, in addition to the profit motive, what are the aims and purposes of violence in our entertainment?

Analyzing by Writing

7. Examine mixed attitudes about sex in a recent issue of *Playboy* or *Cosmopolitan* magazine (or another glossy magazine that has an erotic but socially acceptable appeal). Take into consideration not only the articles and the photographs but also the advertising. Analyze the tone and other connotations as well as what is explicitly said and pictured. You will probably find a wide range of attitudes, from pleasing to offensive and from exalting to degrading, that will require careful differentiation. Try to identify and define different kinds and levels of erotic appeal to the audience.

8. What are the problems of defining pornography? (Consider the definition given by Dworkin in paragraph 28.) Assuming that a ban on pornography could lead to censorship of any controversial, offensive, sexual material, what great harm would be done? Is freedom of speech as important as protecting people's lives? In an essay, present your viewpoint on the conflict between restricting pornography and guaranteeing free speech.

PART 8

DILEMMAS

INSIGHTS

If I had to choose between betraying my country and betraying my friend, I hope I should have the guts to betray my country.

— E. M. FORSTER

◇

It grieves me to say that, to the best of our knowledge, hate is as much a part of man as hunger. You can no more stop a child from hating than you can stop him from dreaming. So we must each learn how to manage hate, how to channel it, how to use it where hate is justified — and how to teach our children to do these things, too.

To raise children by drumming into their minds that they do not "really" hate is to tell them a fearful lie. To moon benignly to the child who cries, "I *hate* you!" that (at that moment) he does not — not *really* — is to confuse a child about an emotion he really feels, knows he possesses, and cannot avoid harboring.

The opposite of hate, in this context, is not love; it is hypocrisy. And children loathe the mealymouthed.

— LEO ROSTEN

◇

In our age there is no such thing as "keeping out of politics." All issues are political issues, and politics itself is a mass of lies, evasions, folly, hatred, and schizophrenia. When the general atmosphere is bad, language must suffer. . . . Political language — and with variations this is true of all political parties, from Conservatives to Anarchists — is designed to make lies sound truthful and murder respectable, and to give an appearance of solidity to pure wind.

— GEORGE ORWELL

◇

In sheer quantity, household labor, including child care, constitutes a huge amount of socially necessary production. Nevertheless, in a society based on commodity production, it is not usually considered as "real work" since it is outside of trade and the marketplace. . . . In a society in which money determines value, women are a group who work outside the money economy.

— MARGARET LOWE BENSTON

◇

The Road Not Taken

Two roads diverged in a yellow wood,
And sorry I could not travel both
And be one traveller, long I stood
And looked down one as far as I could
To where it bent in the undergrowth;

Then took the other, as just as fair,
And having perhaps the better claim,
Because it was grassy and wanted wear;
Though as for that the passing there
Had worn them really about the same,

And both that morning equally lay
In leaves no step had trodden black.
Oh, I kept the first for another day!
Yet knowing how way leads on to way,
I doubted if I should ever come back.

I shall be telling this with a sigh
Somewhere ages and ages hence:
Two roads diverged in a wood, and I —
I took the one less travelled by,
And that has made all the difference.

— ROBERT FROST

◇

No trumpets sound when the important decisions of our life are made. Destiny is made known silently.

— AGNES DE MILLE

FOCUSING BY WRITING

1. Everyone has felt the lure of winning big money in a lottery, a prize contest, or a bet on a long shot. Gambling casinos are highly popular entertainment in every part of the country; many states conduct public lotteries and offer daily gambling on the numbers game; food companies sponsor contests with labels or matching tickets; horse races and many other sports events include the possibility of big payoffs. Does mass gambling mean that, for Americans, getting lucky is the remedy for life's problems and dissatisfactions? Or does mass gambling stimulate positive things as well? Is it good entertainment or irresponsibility? Consider the good and bad effects on character and social policy of the national craze over sudden big winnings.

2. Where did you go right or wrong in life? Develop your second thoughts about a choice, a direction, or an action you once took that you now see from a different perspective. What was the strongest factor in your decision at the time? What other factor would gain importance now? As you look back on the decision or action, do you now feel mainly regret, pride, embarrassment, relief, resentment, nostalgia, resignation, or some other attitude?

3. We are asked to support, endorse, or contribute to many more good causes than we actually join in. How do you usually decide? Does your response depend mainly on the issue involved, the people involved, or the possible misinterpretations of your support or refusal? Examine all the elements that entered your recent decision to participate or not to participate in a cause.

4. Are restrictions on advertising a form of censorship of speech? In what circumstances, if any, are advertising restrictions justified? Consider the problem with regard to beer advertisements, which are targeted at young people. Are there reasons why restrictions on television and magazine advertising for liquor should not apply also to beer? Should restrictions on alcohol advertisements be completely removed? Or should restrictions be broadened to include beer? Consider that among college students, drinking is often connected to accidental deaths, serious injuries, and sexual assaults. What, if anything, should be done to modify or to deregulate the advertising of alcohol?

Peter Marin

HELPING AND HATING
THE HOMELESS

◇

PETER MARIN (b. 1936) is a free-lance writer living in Santa Barbara, California. He took his undergraduate degree from Swarthmore College in 1955 and his master's degree from Columbia University in 1958, both in literature. During the sixties and seventies, he taught at several colleges and universities and was awarded fellowships by the Guggenheim Foundation, the National Endowment for the Arts, and the Center for the Study of Democratic Institutions. He has published several books, including *In a Man's Time*, an autobiographical novel (1972); *Divided Conscience*, a book of poems (1972); *The Limits of Schooling* (1975), and *The World of the Homeless* (1986). His articles have appeared in a wide range of national periodicals, and since 1982 he has been a contributing editor to *Harper's*, where the following essay appeared in 1987.

When I was a child, I had a recurring vision of how I would end as an old   1
man: alone, in a sparsely furnished second-story room I could picture quite
precisely, in a walk-up on Fourth Avenue in New York, where the secondhand bookstores then were. It was not a picture which frightened me. I liked
it. The idea of anonymity and solitude and marginality must have seemed to
me, back then, for reasons I do not care to remember, both inviting and
inevitable. Later, out of college, I took to the road, hitchhiking and traveling
on freights, doing odd jobs here and there, crisscrossing the country. I liked
that too: the anonymity and the absence of constraint and the rough community I sometimes found. I felt at home on the road, perhaps because I felt
at home nowhere else, and periodically, for years, I would return to that
world, always with a sense of relief and release.

I have been thinking a lot about that these days, now that transience and   2
homelessness have made their way into the national consciousness, and
especially since the town I live in, Santa Barbara, has become well known
because of the recent successful campaign to do away with the meanest
aspects of its "sleeping ordinances" — a set of foolish laws making it illegal
for the homeless to sleep at night in public places. During that campaign I
got to know many of the homeless men and women in Santa Barbara, who
tend to gather, night and day, in a small park at the lower end of town, not

far from the tracks and the harbor, under the rooflike, overarching branches of a gigantic fig tree, said to be the oldest on the continent. There one enters much the same world I thought, as a child, I would die in, and the one in which I traveled as a young man: a "marginal" world inhabited by all those unable to find a place in "our" world. Sometimes, standing on the tracks close to the park, you can sense in the wind, or in the smell of tar and ties, the presence and age of that marginal world: the way it stretches backward and inevitably forward in time, parallel to our own world, always present, always close, and yet separated from us — at least in the mind — by a gulf few of us are interested in crossing.

Late last summer, at a city council meeting here in Santa Barbara, I saw, 3 close up, the consequences of that strange combination of proximity and distance. The council was meeting to vote on the repeal of the sleeping ordinances, though not out of any sudden sense of compassion or justice. Council members had been pressured into it by the threat of massive demonstrations — "The Selma of the Eighties" was the slogan one heard among the homeless. But this threat that frightened the council enraged the town's citizens. Hundreds of them turned out for the meeting. One by one they filed to the microphone to curse the council and castigate the homeless. Drinking, doping, loitering, panhandling, defecating, urinating, molesting, stealing — the litany went on and on, was repeated over and over, accompanied by fantasies of disaster: the barbarian hordes at the gates, civilization ended.

What astonished me about the meeting was not what was said; one could 4 have predicted that. It was the power and depth of the emotion revealed: the mindlessness of the fear, the vengefulness of the fury. Also, almost none of what was said had anything to do with the homeless people I know — not the ones I once traveled with, not the ones in town. They, the actual homeless men and women, might not have existed at all.

If I write about Santa Barbara, it is not because I think the attitudes at work 5 here are unique. They are not. You find them everywhere in America. In the last few months I have visited several cities around the country, and in each of them I have found the same thing: more and more people in the streets, more and more suffering. (There are at least 350,000 homeless people in the country, perhaps as many as 3 million.) And, in talking to the good citizens of these cities, I found, almost always, the same thing: confusion and ignorance, or simple indifference, but anger too, and fear.

What follows here is an attempt to explain at least some of that anger and 6 fear, to clear up some of the confusion, to chip away at the indifference. It is not meant to be definitive; how could it be? The point is to try to illuminate some of the darker corners of homelessness, those we ordinarily ignore, and those in which the keys to much that is now going on may be hidden.

The trouble begins with the word "homeless." It has become such an 7 abstraction, and is applied to so many different kinds of people, with so many different histories and problems, that it is almost meaningless.

Homelessness, in itself, is nothing more than a condition visited upon 8 men and women (and, increasingly, children) as the final stage of a variety of problems about which the word "homelessness" tells us almost nothing. Or, to put it another way, it is a catch basin into which pour all of the people, disenfranchised or marginalized or scared off by processes beyond their control, those which lie close to the heart of American life. Here are the groups packed into the single category of "the homeless":

- Veterans, mainly from the war in Vietnam. In many American cities, vets make up close to 50 percent of all homeless males.
- The mentally ill. In some parts of the country, roughly a quarter of the homeless would, a couple of decades ago, have been institutionalized.
- The physically disabled or chronically ill, who do not receive any benefits or whose benefits do not enable them to afford permanent shelter.
- The elderly on fixed incomes whose funds are no longer sufficient for their needs.
- Men, women, and whole families pauperized by the loss of a job.
- Single parents, usually women, without the resources or skills to establish new lives.
- Runaway children, many of whom have been abused.
- Alcoholics and those in trouble with drugs (whose troubles often begin with one of the other conditions listed here).
- Immigrants, both legal and illegal, who often are not counted among the homeless because they constitute a "problem" in their own right.
- Traditional tramps, hobos, and transients, who have taken to the road or the streets for a variety of reasons and who prefer to be there.

You can quickly learn two things about the homeless from this list. First, 9 you can learn that many of the homeless, before they were homeless, were people more or less like ourselves: members of the working or middle class. And you can learn that the world of the homeless has its roots in various policies, events, and ways of life for which some of us are responsible and from which some of us actually prosper.

We decide, as a people, to go to war, we ask our children to kill and to die, 10 and the result, years later, is grown men homeless on the street.

We change, with the best intentions, the laws pertaining to the mentally 11 ill, and then, without intention, neglect to provide them with services; and the result, in our streets, drives some of us crazy with rage.

We cut taxes and prune budgets, we modernize industry and shift the 12 balance of trade, and the result of all these actions and errors can be read, sleeping form by sleeping form, on our city streets.

The liberals cannot blame the conservatives. The conservatives cannot 13 blame the liberals. Homelessness is the *sum total* of our dreams, policies, intentions, errors, omissions, cruelties, kindnesses, all of it recorded, in flesh, in the life of the streets.

You can also learn from this list one of the most important things there is 14 to know about the homeless — that they can be roughly divided into two groups: those who have had homelessness forced upon them and want nothing more than to escape it; and those who have at least in part *chosen* it for themselves, and now accept, or in some cases, embrace it.

I understand how dangerous it is to introduce the idea of choice into a   15 discussion of homelessness. It can all too easily be used to justify indifference or brutality toward the homeless, or to argue that they are only getting what they "deserve." And yet it seems to me that it is only by taking choice into account, in all of the intricacies of its various forms and expressions, that one can really understand certain kinds of homelessess.

The fact is, many of the homeless are not only hapless victims but   16 voluntary exiles, "domestic refugees," people who have turned not against life but against *us*, our life, American life. Look for a moment at the vets. The price of returning to America was to forget what they had seen or learned in Vietnam, to "put it behind them." But some could not do that, and the stress of trying showed up as alcoholism, broken marriages, drug addiction, crime. And it showed up too as life on the street, which was for some vets a desperate choice made in the name of life — the best they could manage. It was a way of avoiding what might have occurred had they stayed where they were: suicide, or violence done to others.

We must learn to accept that there may indeed be people, and not only   17 vets, who have seen so much of our world, or seen it so clearly, that to live in it becomes impossible. Here, for example, is the story of Alice, a homeless middle-aged woman in Los Angeles, where there are, perhaps, 50,000 homeless people. It was set down a few months ago by one of my students at the University of California, Santa Barbara, where I taught for a semester. I had encouraged them to go find the homeless and listen to their stories. And so, one day, when this student saw Alice foraging in a dumpster outside a McDonald's, he stopped and talked to her:

> She told me she had led a pretty normal life as she grew up and eventually went to college. From there she went on to Chicago to teach school. She was single and lived in a small apartment.
>
> One night, after she got off the train after school, a man began to follow her to her apartment building. When she got to her door she saw a knife and the man hovering behind her. She had no choice but to let him in. The man raped her.
>
> After that, things got steadily worse. She had a nervous breakdown. She went to a mental institution for three months, and when she went back to her apartment she found her belongings gone. The landlord had sold them to cover the rent she hadn't paid.
>
> She had no place to go and no job because the school had terminated her employment. She slipped into depression. She lived with friends until she could muster enough money for a ticket to Los Angeles. She said she no longer wanted to burden her friends, and that if she had to live outside, at least Los Angeles was warmer than Chicago.

It is as if she began back then to take on the mentality of a street person. She resolved herself to homelessness. She's been out West since 1980, without a home or job. She seems happy, with her best friend being her cat. But the scars of memories still haunt her, and she is running from them, or should I say *him*.

This is, in essence, the same story one hears over and over again on the 18 street. You begin with an ordinary life; then an event occurs — traumatic, catastrophic; smaller events follow, each one deepening the original wound; finally, homelessness becomes inevitable, or begins to *seem* inevitable to the person involved — the only way out of an intolerable situation. You are struck continually, hearing these stories, by something seemingly unique in American life, the absolute isolation involved. In what other culture would there be such an absence or failure of support from familial, social, or institutional sources? Even more disturbing is the fact that it is often our supposed sources of support — family, friends, government organizations — that have caused the problem in the first place.

Everything that happened to Alice — the rape, the loss of job and apart- 19 ment, the breakdown — was part and parcel of a world gone radically wrong, a world, for Alice, no longer to be counted on, no longer worth living in. Her homelessness can be seen as flight, as failure of will or nerve, even, perhaps, as *disease*. But it can also be seen as a mute, furious refusal, a self-imposed exile far less appealing to the rest of us than ordinary life, but *better*, in Alice's terms.

We like to think, in America, that everything is redeemable, that every- 20 thing broken can be magically made whole again, and that what has been "dirtied" can be cleansed. Recently I saw on television that one of the soaps had introduced the character of a homeless old woman. A woman in her thirties discovers that her long-lost mother has appeared in town, on the streets. After much searching the mother is located and identified and embraced; and then she is scrubbed and dressed in style, restored in a matter of days to her former upper-class habits and role.

A triumph — but one more likely to occur on television than in real life. 21 Yes, many of those on the streets could be transformed, rehabilitated. But there are others whose lives have been irrevocably changed, damaged beyond repair, and who no longer want help, who no longer recognize the *need* for help, and whose experience in our world has made them want only to be left alone. How, for instance, would one restore Alice's life, or reshape it in a way that would satisfy *our* notion of what a life should be? What would it take to return her to the fold? How to erase the four years of homelessness, which have become as familiar to her, and as much a home, as her "normal" life once was? Whatever we think of the way in which she has resolved her difficulties, it constitutes a sad peace made with the world. Intruding ourselves upon it in the name of redemption is by no means as simple a task — or as justifiable a task — as one might think.

It is important to understand too that however disorderly and dirty and   22
unmanageable the world of homeless men and women like Alice appears to
us, it is not without its significance, and its rules and rituals. The homeless
in our cities mark out for themselves particular neighborhoods, blocks,
buildings, doorways. They impose on themselves often obsessively strict
routines. They reduce their world to a small area, and thereby protect
themselves from a world that might otherwise be too much to bear.

Daily the city eddies around the homeless. The crowds flowing past leave   23
a few feet, a gap. We do not touch the homeless world. Perhaps we cannot
touch it. It remains separate even as the city surrounds it.

The homeless, simply because they are homeless, are strangers, alien —   24
and therefore a threat. Their presence, in itself, comes to constitute a kind of
violence; it deprives us of our sense of safety. Let me use myself as an example.
I know, and respect, many of those now homeless on the streets of Santa
Barbara. Twenty years ago, some of them would have been my companions
and friends. And yet, these days, if I walk through the park near my home and
see strangers bedding down for the night, my first reaction, if not fear, is a sense
of annoyance and intrusion, of worry and alarm. I think of my teenage
daughter, who often walks through the park, and then of my house, a hundred yards away, and I am tempted — only tempted, but tempted, still — to
call the "proper" authorities to have the strangers moved on. Out of sight, out
of mind.

Notice: I do not bring them food. I do not offer them shelter or a shower   25
in the morning. I do not even stop to talk. Instead, I think: my daughter, my
house, my privacy. What moves me is not the threat of *danger* — nothing as
animal as that. Instead there pops up inside of me, neatly in a row, a set of
anxieties, ones you might arrange in a dollhouse living room and label:
Family of bourgeois fears. The point is this: Our response to the homeless is
fed by a complex set of cultural attitudes, habits of thought, and fantasies and
fears so familiar to us, so common, that they have become a *second* nature
and might as well be instinctive, for all the control we have over them. And
it is by no means easy to untangle this snarl of responses. What does seem
clear is that the homeless embody all that bourgeois culture has for centuries
tried to eradicate and destroy.

If you look to the history of Europe you find that homelessness first appeared   26
(or is first acknowledged) at the very same moment that bourgeois culture
begins to appear. The same processes produced them both: the breakup of
feudalism, the rise of commerce and cities, the combined triumphs of capitalism, industrialism, and individualism. The historian Fernand Braudel, in
The Wheels of Commerce, describes, for instance, the armies of impoverished
men and women who began to haunt Europe as far back as the eleventh
century. And the makeup of these masses? Essentially the same then as it is
now: the unfortunates, the throwaways, the misfits, the deviants.

In the eighteenth century, all sorts and conditions were to be found in this human dross . . . widows, orphans, cripples, . . . journeymen who had broken their contracts, out-of-work labourers, homeless priests with no living, old men, fire victims, . . . war victims, deserters, discharged soldiers, would-be vendors of useless articles, vagrant preachers with or without licenses, "pregnant servant-girls and unmarried mothers driven from home," children sent out to "find bread or to maraud."

Then, as now, distinctions were made between the "homeless" and the   27 supposedly "deserving" poor, those who knew their place and willingly sustained, with their labors, the emergent bourgeois world.

The good paupers were accepted, lined up and registered on the official list; they had a right to public charity and were sometimes allowed to solicit it outside churches in prosperous districts, when the congregation came out, or in market places. . . .

When it comes to beggars and vagrants, it is a very different story, and different pictures meet the eye: crowds, mobs, processions, sometimes mass emigrations, "along the country highways or the streets of the Towns and Villages," by beggars "whom hunger and nakedness has driven from home." . . . The towns dreaded these alarming visitors and drove them out as soon as they appeared on the horizon.

And just as the distinction made about these masses were the same then   28 as they are now, so too was the way society saw them. They seemed to bourgeois eyes (as they still do) the one segment of society that remained resistant to progress, unassimilable and incorrigible, inimical to all order.

It is in the nineteenth century, in the Victorian era, that you can find the   29 beginnings of our modern strategies for dealing with the homeless: the notion that they should be controlled and perhaps eliminated through "help." With the Victorians we begin to see the entangling of self-protection with social obligation, the strategy of masking self-interest and the urge to control as *moral duty.* Michel Foucault has spelled this out in his books on madness and punishment: the zeal with which the overseers of early bourgeois culture tried to purge, improve, and purify all of urban civilization — whether through schools and prisons, or, quite literally, with public baths and massive new water and sewage systems. Order, ordure — this is, in essence, the tension at the heart of bourgeois culture, and it was the singular genius of the Victorians to make it the main component of their medical, aesthetic, *and* moral systems. It was not a sense of justice or even empathy which called for charity or new attitudes toward the poor; it was *hygiene.* The very same attitudes toward the poor; it was *hygiene.* The very same attitudes appear in nineteenth-century America. Charles Loring Brace, in an essay on homeless and vagrant children written in 1876, described the treatment of delinquents in this way: "Many of their vices drop from them like the old and verminous clothing they left behind. . . . The entire change of circumstances seems to cleanse them of bad habits." Here you have it all: *vices, verminous clothing,*

cleansing them of bad habits — the triple association of poverty with vice
with dirt, an equation in which each term comes to stand for all of them.

These attitudes are with us still; that is the point. In our own century the   30
person who has written most revealingly about such things is George Orwell,
who tried to analyze his own middle-class attitudes toward the poor. In 1933,
in *Down and Out in Paris and London,* he wrote about tramps:

> In childhood we are taught that tramps are blackguards, . . . a repulsive,
> rather dangerous creature, who would rather die than work or wash, and wants
> nothing but to beg, drink, or rob hen-houses. The tramp monster is no truer
> to life than the sinister Chinaman of the magazines, but he is very hard to get
> rid of. The very word "tramp" evokes his image.

All of this is still true in America, though now it is not the word "tramp"   31
but the word "homeless" that evokes the images we fear. It is the homeless
who smell. Here, for instance, is part of a paper a student of mine wrote
about her first visit to a Rescue Mission on skid row.

> The sermon began. The room was stuffy and smelly. The mixture of body
> odors and cooking was nauseating. I remember thinking: How can these people
> share this facility? They must be repulsed by each other. They had strange
> habits and dispositions. They were a group of dirty, dishonored, weird people
> to me.
>
> When it was over I ran to my car, went home, and took a shower. I felt
> extremely dirty. Through the day I would get flashes of that disgusting smell.

To put it as bluntly as I can, for many of us the homeless are *shit*. And our   32
policies toward them, our spontaneous sense of disgust and horror, our wish
to be rid of them — all of this has hidden in it, close to its heart, our feelings
about excrement. Even Marx, that most bourgeois of revolutionaries, described the deviant *lumpen* in *The Eighteenth Brumaire of Louis Bonaparte*
as "scum, offal, refuse of all classes." These days, in puritanical Marxist
nations, they are called "parasites" — a word, perhaps not incidentally, one
also associates with human waste.

What I am getting at here is the *nature* of the desire to help the home-   33
less — what is hidden behind it and why it so often does harm. Every
government program, almost every private project, is geared as much to the
needs of those giving help as it is to the needs of the homeless. Go to any
government agency, or, for that matter, to most private charities, and you
will find yourself enmeshed, at once, in a bureaucracy so tangled and
oppressive, or confronted with so much moral arrogance and contempt, that
you will be driven back out into the streets for relief.

Santa Barbara, where I live, is as good an example as any. There are three   34
main shelters in the city — all of them private. Between them they provide
fewer than a hundred beds a night for the homeless. Two of the three shelters
are religious in nature: the Rescue Mission and the Salvation Army. In the
mission, as in most places in the country, there are elaborate and stringent
rules. Beds go first to those who have not been there for two months, and you

can stay for only two nights in any two-month period. No shelter is given to those who are not sober. Even if you go to the mission only for a meal, you are required to listen to sermons and participate in prayer, and you are regularly proselytized — sometimes overtly, sometimes subtly. There are obligatory, regimented showers. You go to bed precisely at ten: lights out, no reading, no talking. After the lights go out you will find fifteen men in a room with double-decker bunks. As the night progresses the room grows stuffier and hotter. Men toss, turn, cough, and moan. In the morning you are awakened precisely at five forty-five. Then breakfast. At seven-thirty you are back on the street.

The town's newest shelter was opened almost a year ago by a consortium 35 of local churches. Families and those who are employed have first call on the beds — a policy which excludes the congenitally homeless. Alcohol is not simply forbidden *in* the shelter; those with a history of alcoholism must sign a "contract" pledging to remain sober and chemical-free. Finally, in a paroxysm of therapeutic bullying, the shelter has added a new wrinkle: If you stay more than two days you are required to fill out and then discuss with a social worker a complex form listing what you perceive as your personal failings, goals, and strategies — all of this for men and women who simply want a place to lie down out of the rain!

It is these attitudes, in various forms and permutations, that you find 36 repeated endlessly in America. We are moved either to "redeem" the homeless or to punish them. Perhaps there is nothing consciously hostile about it. Perhaps it is simply that as the machinery of bureaucracy cranks itself up to deal with these problems, attitudes assert themselves automatically. But whatever the case, the fact remains that almost every one of our strategies for helping the homeless is simply an attempt to rearrange the world *cosmetically*, in terms of how it looks and smells to *us*. Compassion is little more than the passion for control.

The central question emerging from all this is, What does a society owe 37 to its members in trouble, and *how* is that debt to be paid? It is a question which must be answered in two parts: first, in relation to the men and women who have been marginalized against their will, and then, in a slightly different way, in relation to those who have chosen (or accept or even prize) their marginality.

As for those who have been marginalized against their wills, I think the 38 general answer is obvious: A society owes its members whatever it takes for them to regain their places in the social order. And when it comes to specific remedies, one need only read backward the various processes which have created homelessness and then figure out where help is likely to do the most good. But the real point here is not the specific remedies required — affordable housing, say — but the basis upon which they must be offered, the necessary underlying ethical notion we seem in this nation unable to grasp: that those who are the inevitable casualties of modern industrial capitalism and the free-market system are entitled, *by right*, and by the simple virtue of their participation in that system, to whatever help they need. They are entitled to help to find and hold their places in the society whose social contract they have, in effect, signed and observed.

Look at that for just a moment: the notion of a contract. The majority of 39 homeless Americans have kept, insofar as they could, to the terms of that contract. In any shelter these days you can find men and women who have worked ten, twenty, forty years, and whose lives have nonetheless come to nothing. These are people who cannot afford a place in the world they helped create. And in return? Is it life on the street they have earned? Or the cruel charity we so grudgingly grant them?

But those marginalized against their will are only half the problem. There 40 remains, still, the question of whether we owe anything to those who are voluntarily marginal. What about them: the street people, the rebels, and the recalcitrants, those who have torn up their social contracts or returned them unsigned?

I was in Las Vegas last fall, and I went out to the Rescue Mission at the 41 lower end of town, on the edge of the black ghetto, where I first stayed years ago on my way west. It was twilight, still hot; in the vacant lot next-door to the mission 200 men were lining up for supper. A warm wind blew along the street lined with small houses and salvage yards, and in the distance I could see the desert's edge and the smudge of low hills in the fading light. There were elderly alcoholics in line, and derelicts, but mainly the men were the same sort I had seen here years ago: youngish, out of work, restless and talkative, the drifters and wanderers for whom the word "wanderlust" was invented.

At supper — long communal tables, thin gruel, stale sweet rolls, ice 42 water — a huge black man in his twenties, fierce and muscular, sat across from me. "I'm from the Coast, man," he said. "Never been away from home before. Ain't sure I like it. Sure don't like *this* place. But I lost my job back home a couple of weeks ago and figured, why wait around for another. I thought I'd come out here, see me something of the world."

After supper, a squat Portuguese man in his mid-thirties, hunkered down 43 against the mission wall, offered me a smoke and told me: "Been sleeping in my car, up the street, for a week. Had my own business back in Omaha. But I got bored, man. Sold everything, got a little dough, came out here. Thought I'd work construction. Let me tell you, this is one tough town."

In a world better than ours, I suppose, men (or women) like this might not 44 exist. Conservatives seem to have no trouble imagining a society so well disciplined and moral that deviance of this kind would disappear. And leftists envision a world so just, so generous, that deviance would vanish along with inequity. But I suspect that there will always be something at work in some men and women to make them restless with the systems others devise for them, and to move them outward toward the edges of the world, where life is always riskier, less organized, and easier going.

Do we owe anything to these men and women, who reject our company 45
and what we offer and yet nonetheless seem to demand *something* from us?

We owe them, I think, at least a place to exist, a way to exist. That may 46
not be a *moral* obligation, in the sense that our obligation to the involuntarily
marginal is clearly a moral one, but it is an obligation nevertheless, one you
might call an existential obligation.

Of course, it may be that I think we owe these men something because I 47
have liked men like them, and because I want their world to be there always,
as a place to hide or rest. But there is more to it than that. I think we as a
society need men like these. A society needs its margins as much as it needs
art and literature. It needs holes and gaps, *breathing spaces*, let us say, into
which men and women can escape and live, when necessary, in ways
otherwise denied them. Margins guarantee to society a flexibility, an elas-
ticity, and allow it to accommodate itself to the natures and needs of its
members. When margins vanish, society becomes too rigid, too oppressive
by far, and therefore inimical to life.

It is for such reasons that, in cultures like our own, marginal men and 48
women take on a special significance. They are all we have left to remind us
of the narrowness of the received truths we take for granted. "Beyond the
pale," they somehow redefine the pale, or remind us, at least, that *something*
is still out there, beyond the pale. They preserve, perhaps unconsciously, a
dream that would otherwise cease to exist, the dream of having a place in the
world, and of being *left alone*.

Quixotic? Infantile? Perhaps. But remember. . . . [w]hat we are talking 49
about here is *freedom*, and with it, perhaps, an echo of the dream men
brought, long ago, to wilderness America. I use the word "freedom" gingerly,
in relation to lives like these: skewed, crippled, emptied of everything we
associate with a full, or realized, freedom. But perhaps this is the condition
into which freedom has fallen among us. Art has been "appreciated" out of
existence; literature has become an extension of the university, replete with
tenure and pensions; and as for politics, the ideologies which ring us round
seem too silly or shrill by far to speak for life. What is left, then, is this mute
and intransigent independence, this "waste" of life which refuses even interpretation, and which cannot be assimilated to any ideology, and which
therefore can be put to no one's use. In its crippled innocence and the
perfection of its superfluity it amounts, almost, to a rebellion against history,
and that is no small thing.

Let me put it as simply as I can: What we see on the streets of our cities 50
are two dramas, both of which cut to the troubled heart of the culture and
demand from us a response we may not be able to make. There is the drama
of those struggling to survive by regaining their place in the social order. And
there is the drama of those struggling to survive outside of it.

The resolution of both struggles depends on a third drama occurring at the 51
heart of the culture: the tension and contention between the magnanimity we
owe to life and the darker tendings of the human psyche: our fear of

strangeness, our hatred of deviance, our love of order and control. How we mediate by default or design between those contrary forces will determine not only the destinies of the homeless, but also something crucial about the nation, and perhaps — let me say it — about our own souls.

Analyzing This Selection

1. From the first two paragraphs, what were the attractions of the "marginal world" for Marin as a young person? What attracts him as an adult?

2. According to the author, how are the homeless unfairly characterized? How does Marin characterize them? What makes his viewpoint convincing?

3. Marin's sympathetic retelling of Alice's story (paragraphs 17–22) explains why she lives a homeless life. Do you think Alice had alternatives to living on the street? Explain why or why not.

4. According to Marin, what are the causes of homelessness? What personal causes does he view in a social context?

5. What is Marin's major objection to the nature of the government and private charity programs supposedly designed to help the homeless?

6. Why does Marin believe it important for society to make room for "marginal men and women"? Can you think of other means to achieve that same end?

Analyzing Connections

7. Examine the photograph of the homeless woman on page 390. What details characterize her? How does she resemble or differ from Marin's characterization of the homeless? How does the photograph's "viewpoint" resemble or differ from Marin's viewpoint?

8. How do our "bourgeois fears" of the homeless resemble or differ from American attitudes toward racial minorities? What explanations of "bourgeois fears" are offered by Andrew Hacker (see p. 272) and by Brent Staples (see p. 46)?

9. Alexis de Tocqueville (see Insights, p. 244) comments on general strengths and weaknesses of democratic societies. What perspectives does he add to the social problem of homelessness? Does Marin's modern outlook on American society differ from Tocqueville's?

Analyzing by Writing

10. What portions, if any, of your campus and college services would you make available to the homeless? Should they be permitted to sleep in sheltered areas? Congregate around the quad or plaza? Expect food, money, and other assistance from students? What are some likely reactions to their sharing your turf? Discuss the problems that might arise in the college, and consider the limits of any proposed solution.

Jonathan Swift

A MODEST PROPOSAL

◊

JONATHAN SWIFT (1667–1745) has been called "the greatest satirist in the English language." Born in Ireland to English parents, he was educated at Kilkenny School and Trinity College, Dublin, and later spent much of his time in England. An active participant in the political and literary life of London, Swift became a brilliant political pamphleteer. In 1713, he obtained the deanery of St. Patrick's Cathedral in Dublin and later published several books, including his masterpiece, *Gulliver's Travels* (1726). "A Modest Proposal," published in 1729, was Swift's response to extreme poverty in Ireland, brought on by drought and exploitation by the English, who controlled a large proportion of Irish farm land.

It is a melancholy object to those who walk through this great town or travel in the country, when they see the streets, the roads, and cabin doors, crowded with beggars of the female sex, followed by three, four, or six children, all in rags and importuning every passenger for an alms. These mothers, instead of being able to work for their honest livelihood, are forced to employ all their time in strolling to beg sustenance for their helpless infants, who, as they grow up, either turn thieves for want of work, or leave their dear native country to fight for the Pretender[1] in Spain, or sell themselves to the Barbados.[2]

I think it is agreed by all parties that this prodigious number of children in the arms, or on the backs, or at the heels of their mothers, and frequently of their fathers, is in the present deplorable state of the kingdom a very great additional grievance; and therefore whoever could find out a fair, cheap, or easy method of making these children sound, useful members of the commonwealth would deserve so well of the public as to have his statue set up for a preserver of the nation.

But my intention is very far from being confined to provide only for the children of professed beggars; it is of a much greater extent, and shall take in

---

[1]James Edward Stuart (1688–1766), "the Old Pretender," a Catholic who claimed the British throne from exile in France. [Ed.]

[2]In Swift's time, many Irish sailed to Barbados, exchanging labor there for their passage. [Ed.]

the whole number of infants at a certain age who are born of parents in effect as little able to support them as those who demand our charity in the streets.

As to my own part, having turned my thoughts for many years upon this 4 important subject, and maturely weighed the several schemes of other projectors, I have always found them grossly mistaken in their computation. It is true, a child just dropped from its dam may be supported by her milk for a solar year, with little other nourishment; at most not above the value of two shillings, which the mother may certainly get, or the value in scraps, by her lawful occupation of begging; and it is exactly at one year that I propose to provide for them in such a manner as instead of being a charge upon their parents or the parish, or wanting food and raiment for the rest of their lives, they shall on the contrary contribute to the feeding, and partly to the clothing, of many thousands.

There is likewise another great advantage in my scheme, that it will 5 prevent those voluntary abortions, and that horrid practice of women murdering their bastard children, alas, too frequent among us, sacrificing the poor innocent babes, I doubt, more to avoid the expense than the shame, which would move tears and pity in the most savage and inhuman breast.

The number of souls in this kingdom being usually reckoned one million 6 and a half, of these I calculate there may be about two hundred thousand couples whose wives are breeders; from which number I subtract thirty thousand couples who are able to maintain their own children, although I apprehend there cannot be so many under the present distress of the kingdom; but this being granted, there will remain an hundred and seventy thousand breeders. I again subtract fifty thousand of those women who miscarry, or whose children die by accident or disease within the year. There only remain an hundred and twenty thousand children of poor parents annually born. The question therefore is, how this number shall be reared and provided for, which, as I have already said, under the present situation of affairs, is utterly impossible by all the methods hitherto proposed. For we can neither employ them in handicraft or agriculture; we neither build houses (I mean in the country) nor cultivate land. They can very seldom pick up a livelihood by stealing till they arrive at six years old, except where they are of towardly parts; although I confess they learn the rudiments much earlier, during which time they can however be looked upon only as probationers, as I have been informed by a principal gentleman in the country of Cavan, who protested to me that he never knew above one or two instances under the age of six, even in a part of the kingdom so renowned for the quickest proficiency in that art.

I am assured by our merchants that a boy or a girl before twelve years old 7 is no salable commodity; and even when they come to this age they will not yield above three pounds; or three pounds and half a crown at most on the Exchange; which cannot turn to account either to the parents or the kingdom, the charge of nutriment and rags having been at least four times that value.

I shall now therefore humbly propose my own thoughts, which I hope will 8 not be liable to the least objection.

I have been assured by a very knowing American of my acquaintance in 9 London, that a young healthy child well nursed is at a year old a most delicious, nourishing, and wholesome food, whether stewed, roasted, baked, or boiled; and I make no doubt that it will equally serve in a fricasee or a ragout.

I do therefore humbly offer it to public consideration that of the hundred 10 and twenty thousand children, already computed, twenty thousand may be reserved for breed, whereof only one fourth part to be males, which is more than we allow to sheep, black cattle, or swine; and my reason is that these children are seldom the fruits of marriage, a circumstance not much regarded by our savages, therefore one male will be sufficient to serve four females. That the remaining hundred thousand may at a year old be offered in sale to the persons of quality and fortune through the kingdom, always advising the mother to let them suck plentifully in the last month, so as to render them plump and fat for a good table. The child will make two dishes at an entertainment for friends; and when the family dines alone, the fore or hind quarter will make a reasonable dish, and seasoned with a little pepper or salt will be very good boiled on the fourth day, especially in winter.

I have reckoned upon a medium that a child just born will weigh twelve 11 pounds, and in a solar year if tolerably nursed increaseth to twenty-eight pounds.

I grant this food will be somewhat dear, and therefore very proper for 12 landlords, who, as they have already devoured most of the parents, seem to have the best title to the children.

Infant's flesh will be in season throughout the year, but more plentiful in 13 March, and a little before and after. For we are told by a grave author, an eminent French physician, that fish being a prolific diet, there are more children born in Roman Catholic countries about nine months after Lent than at any other season; therefore, reckoning a year after Lent, the market will be more glutted than usual, because the number of popish infants is at least three to one in this kingdom; and therefore it will have one other collateral advantage, by lessening the number of Papists among us.

I have already computed the charge of nursing a beggar's child (in which 14 list I reckon all cottagers, laborers, and four-fifths of the farmers) to be about two shillings per annum, rags included; and I believe no gentleman would repine to give ten shillings for the carcass of a good fat child, which, as I have said, will make four dishes of excellent nutritive meat, when he hath only some particular friend or his own family to dine with him. Thus the squire will learn to be a good landlord, and grow popular among the tenants; the mother will have eight shillings net profit, and be fit for work till she produces another child.

Those who are more thrifty (as I must confess the times require) may flay 15 the carcass; the skin of which artificially dressed will make admirable gloves for ladies, and summer boots for fine gentlemen.

As to our city of Dublin, shambles[3] may be appointed for this purpose in 16 the most convenient parts of it, and butchers we may be assured will not be wanting; although I rather recommend buying the children live, and dressing them hot from the knife as we do roasting pigs.

A very worthy person, a true lover of his country, and whose virtues I highly 17 esteem, was lately pleased in discoursing on this matter to offer a refinement upon my scheme. He said that many gentlemen of his kingdom, having of late destroyed their deer, he conceived that the want of venison might well be supplied by the bodies of young lads and maidens, not exceeding fourteen years of age nor under twelve, so great a number of both sexes in every county being now ready to starve for want of work and service; and these to be disposed of by their parents, if alive, or otherwise by their nearest relations. But with due deference to so excellent a friend and so deserving a patriot, I cannot be altogether in his sentiments; for as to the males, my American acquaintance assured me from frequent experience that their flesh was generally tough and lean, like that of our schoolboys, by continual exercise, and their taste disagreeable; and to fatten them would not answer the charge. Then as to the females, it would, I think with humble submission, be a loss to the public, because they soon would become breeders themselves; and besides, it is not improbable that some scrupulous people might be apt to censure such a practice (although indeed very unjustly) as a little bordering upon cruelty; which, I confess, hath always been with me the strongest objection against any project, how well soever intended.

But in order to justify my friend, he confessed that this expedient was put 18 into his head by the famous Psalmanazar, a native of the island of Formosa, who came from thence to London above twenty years ago, and in conversation told my friend that in his country when any young person happened to be put to death, the executioner sold the carcass to persons of quality as a prime dainty; and that in his time the body of a plump girl of fifteen, who was crucified for an attempt to poison the emperor, was sold to his Imperial Majesty's prime minister of state, and other great mandarins of the court, in joints from the gibbet, at four hundred crowns. Neither indeed can I deny that if the same use were made of several plump young girls in this town, who without one single groat to their fortunes cannot stir abroad without a chair,[4] and appear at the playhouse and assemblies in foreign fineries which they never will pay for, the kingdom would not be the worse.

Some persons of a desponding spirit are in great concern about the vast 19 number of poor people who are aged, diseased, or maimed, and I have been desired to employ my thoughts what course may be taken to ease the nation of so grievous an encumbrance. But I am not in the least pain upon the matter, because it is very well known that they are every day dying and rotting

---

[3]Slaughterhouses. [Ed.]

[4]A portable chair in which the passenger is carried by two people on foot. [Ed.]

by cold and famine, and filth and vermin, as fast as can be reasonably expected. And as to the younger laborers, they are now in almost as hopeful a condition. They cannot get work, and consequently pine away for want of nourishment to a degree that if any time they are accidentally hired to common labor, they have not strength to perform it; and thus the country and themselves are happily delivered from the evils to come.

I have too long digressed, and therefore shall return to my subject. I think 20 the advantages by the proposal which I have made are obvious and many, as well as of the highest importance.

For first, as I have already observed, it would greatly lessen the number of 21 Papists, with whom we are yearly overrun, being the principal breeders of the nation as well as our most dangerous enemies; and who stay at home on purpose to deliver the kingdom to the Pretender, hoping to take their advantage by the absence of so many good Protestants, who have chosen rather to leave their country than to stay at home and pay tithes against their conscience to an Episcopal curate.

Secondly, the poorer tenants will have something valuable of their own, 22 which by law may be made liable to distress, and help to pay their landlord's rent, their corn and cattle being already seized and money a thing unknown.

Thirdly, whereas the maintenance of an hundred thousand children, 23 from two years old and upwards, cannot be computed at less than ten shillings per annum, the nation's stock will be thereby increased fifty thousand pounds per annum, besides the profit of a new dish introduced to the tables of all gentlemen of fortune in the kingdom who have any refinement in taste. And the money will circulate among ourselves, the goods being entirely of our own growth and manufacture.

Fourthly, the constant breeders, besides the gain of eight shillings sterling 24 per annum by the sale of their children, will be rid of the charge of maintaining them after the first year.

Fifthly, this food would likewise bring great custom to taverns, where the 25 vintners will certainly be so prudent as to procure the best receipts for dressing it to perfection, and consequently have their houses frequented by all the fine gentlemen, who justly value themselves upon their knowledge in good eating; and a skillful cook, who understands how to oblige his guests, will contrive to make it as expensive as they please.

Sixthly, this would be a great inducement to marriage, which all wise 26 nations have either encouraged by rewards or enforced by laws and penalties. It would increase the care and tenderness of mothers toward their children, when they were sure of a settlement for life to the poor babes, provided in some sort by the public, to their annual profit instead of expense. We should see an honest emulation among the married women, which of them could bring the fattest child to the market. Men would become as fond of their wives during the time of their pregnancy as they are now of their mares in foal, their cows in calf, or sows when they are ready to farrow; nor offer to beat or kick them (as is too frequent a practice) for fear of a miscarriage.

Many other advantages might be enumerated. For instance, the addition   27
of some thousand carcasses in our exportation of barreled beef, the propa-
gation of swine's flesh, and improvements in the art of making good bacon,
so much wanted among us by the great destruction of pigs, too frequent at
our tables, which are no way comparable in taste or magnificence to a
well-grown, fat, yearling child, which roasted whole will make a considerable figure at a lord mayor's feast or any other public entertainment. But this
and many others I omit, being studious of brevity.

Supposing that one thousand families in this city would be constant   28
customers for infants' flesh, besides others who might have it at merry
meetings, particularly weddings and christenings, I compute that Dublin
would take off annually about twenty thousand carcasses, and the rest of the
kingdom (where probably they will be sold somewhat cheaper) the remaining
eighty thousand.

I can think of no one objection that will possibly be raised against this   29
proposal, unless it should be urged that the number of people will be thereby
much lessened in the kingdom. This I freely own, and it was indeed one
principal design in offering it to the world. I desire the reader will observe,
that I calculate my remedy for this one individual kingdom of Ireland and for
no other that ever was, is, or I think ever can be upon earth. Therefore let
no man talk to me of other expedients: of taxing our absentees at five shillings
a pound: of using neither clothes nor household furniture except what is of
our own growth and manufacture: of utterly rejecting the materials and
instruments that promote foreign luxury: of curing the expensiveness of
pride, vanity, idleness, and gaming in our women: of introducing a vein of
parsimony, prudence, and temperance: of learning to love our country, in
the want of which we differ even from Laplanders and the inhabitants of
Topinamboo: of quitting our animosities and factions, nor acting any longer
like Jews, who were murdering one another at the very moment their city was
taken: of being a little cautious not to sell our country and conscience for
nothing: of teaching landlords to have at least one degree of mercy toward
their tenants: lastly, of putting a spirit of honesty, industry, and skill into our
shopkeepers; who, if a resolution could not be taken to buy only our native
goods, would immediately unite to cheat and exact upon us in the price, the
measure, and the goodness, nor could ever yet be brought to make one fair
proposal of just dealing, though often and earnestly invited to it.

Therefore I repeat, let no man talk to me of these and the like expedients,   30
till he hath at least some glimpse of hope that there will be some hearty and
sincere attempt to put them in practice.

But as to myself, having been wearied out for many years with offering   31
vain, idle, visionary thoughts, and at length utterly despairing of success, I
fortunately fell upon this proposal, which, as it is wholly new, so it hath
something solid and real, and of expense and little trouble, full in our own
power, and whereby we can incur no danger in disobliging England. For this

kind of commodity will not bear exportation, the flesh being of too tender a consistence to admit a long continuance in salt, although perhaps I could name a country which would be glad to eat up our whole nation without it.

After all, I am not so violently bent upon my own opinion as to reject any   32 offer proposed by wise men, which shall be found equally innocent, cheap, easy, and effectual. But before something of that kind shall be advanced in contradiction to my scheme, and offering a better, I desire the author or authors will be pleased maturely to consider two points. First, as things now stand, how they will be able to find food and raiment for an hundred thousand useless mouths and backs. And secondly, there being a round million of creatures in human figure throughout this kingdom, whose sole subsistence put into a common stock would leave them in debt two millions of pounds sterling, adding those who are beggars by profession to the bulk of farmers, cottagers, and laborers, with their wives and children who are beggars in effect; I desire those politicians who dislike my overture, and may perhaps be so bold to attempt an answer, that they will first ask the parents of these mortals whether they would not at this day think it a great happiness to have been sold for food at a year old in this manner I prescribe, and thereby have avoided such a perpetual scene of misfortunes as they have since gone through by the oppression of landlords, the impossibility of paying rent without money or trade, the want of common sustenance, with neither house nor clothes to cover them from the inclemencies of the weather, and the most inevitable prospect of entailing the like or greater miseries upon their breed forever.

I profess, in the sincerity of my heart, that I have not the least personal   33 interest in endeavoring to promote this necessary work, having no other motive than the public good of my country, by advancing our trade, providing for infants, relieving the poor, and giving some pleasure to the rich. I have no children by which I can propose to get a single penny; the youngest being nine years old, and my wife past childbearing.

Analyzing This Selection

1. The first three paragraphs straightforwardly express concern for the poor. What details in paragraph 4 begin to raise our suspicions about the speaker's concern for poor people?

2. What abilities and traits comprise the speaker's view of himself? What is our view of him? At what point in the essay are we fully shocked by his discussion of the problem?

3. Why is the idea of cannibalism first suggested to him by an American? Why would his references to Americans be amusing to Swift's contemporaries?

4. What are the causes of poverty in Swift's Ireland?

Analyzing Connections

5. In opposite ways, Swift and Peter Marin (in the preceding selection) rouse concern over the large numbers of destitute people in their countries. What reaction to the problem does each writer stimulate? Without his ironic mask, would Swift agree with Marin's attitude toward the homeless?

Analyzing by Writing

6. In addition to attacking the problem of poverty, Swift satirizes the kind of reasoning that is rational without being moral, and logical without being ethical. Point out some absurdities of the so-called objective "reasonableness" that you find in current controversy over a public issue such as pornography (see "Letter from a War Zone," p. 378), gun control, welfare reform, capital punishment, drug legalization, doctor-assisted suicide, or perhaps a campus issue. (You may wish to take an ironic stance as an advocate of a "reasonable" position that you find absurd.)

Martin Green

DYING — AND KILLING? — FOR ONE'S COUNTRY[1]

◇

MARTIN GREEN (b. 1927) is an English professor and a critic of modern literature and culture. He was born in London and graduated from Cambridge
University. After serving in the Royal Air Force, Green came to the United
States to earn his Ph.D. at the University of Michigan. He has taught at
Wellesley College, the University of Birmingham, and Tufts University, receiving numerous academic awards and two Guggenheim Fellowships. Green
retained his British citizenship until recently, and the occasion of his becoming an American gave rise to the following observations about obedience to the
law and allegiance to a nation. These moral and political issues are also
addressed in several of his books, such as *The Problem of Boston* (1966),
Children of the Sun: A Narrative of "Decadence" in England after 1918
(1976), *The Challenge of the Mahatmas* (1978), *Dreams of Adventure, Deeds
of Empire* (1979), *The Great American Adventure* (1984), *The Origins of
Nonviolence: Tolstoy and Gandhi in Their Historical Setting* (1986), and *The
Robinson Crusoe Story* (1991). In a slightly different form, this essay appeared
in the *Boston Review* in 1990.

A recent stay in England showed me how many of my loyalties had 1
unconsciously shifted away from my native land and become American, and
on December 15 I took an oath of allegiance to the U.S.A.

The ceremony took place in Faneuil Hall in Boston, full of memories of 2
the Revolution. We sat in front of a large dim painting of a debate in the Hall
featuring a fiery orator, and the legend beneath ran "Liberty and Union,
Now and Forever." Busts of John Adams and other revolutionary heroes
stood there for us to contemplate. At the first Continental Congress, I
remembered, John Adams grew impatient with "those who shuddered at the
prospect of blood." He regretted New England's pietism, and "longed more
ardently to be a soldier."

There were over four hundred and sixty of us being naturalized, including 3
a hundred and fifty who were also changing their names, so it was a long
ceremony. We were there from 9:30 to 12:30, although all that *I* did was

[1]Editor's title.

hand in a form and an Alien Registration Card at one table, getting a certificate in return, which at another table was stamped six times. The rest was waiting, in line and on chairs.

We were all sorts and conditions of men and women. I shuffled up the 4 gangway behind a young man with a razor haircut, scarred cheeks, and a topcoat as broad in the shoulders as it was long in the skirt. He was jigging as well as shuffling, his ears plugged, a thin ghost of rock music washing around him. Behind him I was the professor, the Brahmin, with a thin ghost of book language around me.

We came from all the corners of the earth. The judge welcoming us 5 alluded to Vietnamese boat people, Cambodian camp refugees, and Soviet Jews. Without quoting "your huddled masses, yearning to be free," he found equivalent phrases. He spoke of our struggles at home against tyranny, our struggles over here against prejudice, and the long effort to learn English.

From all this I, naturally, was excluded by my privileges. The rhetoric of 6 America names only the disadvantaged. But for all of us equally the ceremony itself was an ordeal of birth. A very mild one, of course, but as we sat waiting for the judge — there was a full hour to wait, after the certificates were stamped — people kept twisting their heads to watch the door. The chairs all faced the painting, the busts, the platform from which the judge would address us, and the doors were behind us. We felt exposed as well as impatient. At any moment, of the hundred or so heads in front of me, maybe fifteen were twisted round to look. We were anxious.

Jammed so close together, our frames of reference were jolted askew, and 7 without those frames (our friends, our car, our workshop) we couldn't establish our characters, make our gestures of patience, impatience, determination, irony. Without my frame, that lift of my eyebrow, that swell of my bicep, might not convey my meaning.

Of course, in any major ordeal characters vanish, at least temporarily. If 8 a bomb exploded in the hall, or terrorists mounted the platform with machine guns, the differences between me and my right-hand neighbor, so brawny and scowling, might fade to nothing. This event just put our characters briefly in suspense, put us on hold.

But I thought of it as a kind of birth. Friends of mine had adopted a 9 Colombian baby a few weeks before. They had to spend a week in Medellín, filling out applications, getting vital documents, dealing with government offices. They described the night drive into the city along unlighted roads, the nine armed soldiers standing outside their hotel, and the week's mounting tension till they finally flew out again, with their baby, to their homeland. For them, it was an experience more like birth than birth itself. Our experience in Faneuil Hall was a bit like that; dimly, shadowily, briefly, we passed into unreality, and then back into reality, with a new identity.

In Faneuil Hall there were no men with guns, but the question of arms 10 was in the air. When I filled in my first application, nearly eighteen months before, I refused to promise to defend the U.S.A. with arms, and this involved me in various detours and delays — an essay defining my position, an interview defending it. The oath itself is largely about bearing arms. Of course what could be more central to the constitution of a state? There would be no U.S.A. if the American colonists had not taken up arms. And thereafter, as John Adams said, the independent America had to adopt "the great, manly, and martial virtues."

There was, as it turned out, no *real* difficulty for me. I am far too old to 11
be called on to fight, and the oath is nowadays (though this is recent) understood to postpone the crucial decision about fighting till the moment of conscription.

My eighteen-month naturalization process was not a trial to recall that of 12
Socrates or Joan of Arc. It did have its mild agonies, but they were of uncertainty (you can't find out when to expect the next step) and of bad manners (the clerks who deal with immigrants can be very nasty to them). There is some black humor to the daily conflicts between the bewildered (but not always innocent) applicants and the bored and harassed (but often malevolent) officials. When confronted by a Brahmin, of course, the clerks' sourness takes another turn. They are reminded that *they* don't get a large slice of the American pie, after all.

For me the ordeal was, however theoretically, a matter of principle. My 13
examiner hinted, more than once, that I and he could save each other a lot of trouble if I would just take the oath. Nuns, he told me, took it without hesitation, and no one expected them, or me, actually to spray an enemy battalion with bullets, or to napalm a leaf-thatched village. But for me it was time to give my ideas about nonviolence a little edge of definition. If the U.S.A. would not take me without this oath, then I would do without citizenship. To put it more positively, I wanted my new country to acknowledge, in principle, the contribution a nonviolent person could make to citizenship.

The examination was easy for me partly because what the examinee has 14
mostly to do is show that his or her convictions are well-considered and long-held, not conjured up on the spur of the moment for ignoble motives. For most people it must be very hard to date or demonstrate a growing conviction, but luckily I had made declarations in print, in writing about Tolstoy and Gandhi. I sat there in the examiner's room, pulling copies of my books out of my briefcase, and he took them away and photocopied passages. At the Faneuil Hall ceremony he recognized me — "Ah, the man with several volumes."

What Tolstoy and Gandhi teach us is that the question of nonviolence, 15
and therefore the question of violence, is the absolutely crucial one. Most philosophies teach us to avoid violence wherever we can and point to our enemies as violent, but imply that we must be ready, sooner or later, to kill them. This means not thinking too much about violence. For Tolstoy and Gandhi, violence is that about which one cannot think too much. It has the place for them which economic injustice has for Marx.

Gandhi and Tolstoy recognized that our deep attraction to violence is not 16
merely to be wished down or prayed away — unlike most "moderates," who

simply avert their eyes and hope such things will disappear. Gandhi and Tolstoy honored soldiers and armies, among other human types. Gandhi even wanted to make his followers capable of violence, saying that otherwise they would not be capable of nonviolence. He recruited for the British army in India in 1918, because he, like John Adams, wanted his countrymen to show themselves worthy of freedom. So these are hard and puzzling moral questions, even for someone who thinks he has made up his mind about them.

So in Faneuil Hall I took what is called a partial or qualified oath. As we   17 repeated the words, clause by clause, after an officer of the court, I lowered my hand and closed my mouth during the clause about bearing arms. Nobody noticed.

As it happens, December 15 is Bill of Rights Day, and the day of my   18 naturalization the *Boston Globe* ran a full-page advertisement about that, paid for by Philip Morris. There was a photograph of Franklin Roosevelt instituting that day in 1941, and saying, "Those who have long enjoyed such privileges as we enjoy forget in time that men have died to win them."

The word "died" of course is a flip-flop, the other side of which is "killed."   19 Heroes, not martyrs, found political institutions. We are all aware of such verbal flip-flops, as necessary to our comfort. We have a Department of Defense, not of War, much less of Attack. So it must be; nobody wants to be reminded while eating that a steak comes from a killed cow, and roast lamb is dead lamb. But by that token, we need to listen to those who *do* remind us (on occasion with angry passion) that we *mean* to kill and to make war; that being a law-abiding citizen does not make one nonviolent; that, in fact, the reverse is true.

Analyzing This Selection

1. Identify three or four ways in which the author appears unlike others at the naturalization ceremony. What reflections about these differences arise in Green's thoughts?

2. Why does Green insist on his principle? Explain what he hopes to signify by his action. What is its significance to you?

3. According to Green, how do the ideas of Tolstoy and Gandhi differ from most other condemnations of violence?

4. What relevance does Green give to the ceremony's date and location?

Analyzing Connections

5. Green and Peter Marin in "Helping and Hating the Homeless" (see p. 395) argue that nonconformists and dissenters improve the society that tries to condemn them. What contributions to citizenship, according to Green, come from the

nonviolent? According to Marin, what contributions come from the homeless? Which writer's view is more convincing to you? Explain why you agree with one, both, or neither.

Analyzing by Writing

6. Even if you have never participated in a political protest, you have probably openly or privately opposed something on grounds that were *political* to you because the situation involved issues of justice, power, equality, or rights. Perhaps it involved your parents or your school. Analyze your role as a participant in and/or observer of a politicized confrontation. Be specific about the stages of your commitment to the issues, and be clear about your response to the outcome or current state of affairs.

7. Should young people be drafted into military service? Is universal military service moral and legal in a society dedicated to individual conscience and personal liberty? What are the moral and social effects of an entirely volunteer military? Argue for or against the principle of a military draft.

George Orwell

SHOOTING AN ELEPHANT

◇

GEORGE ORWELL (1903–1950) was the pen name of Eric Blair, who was born in India and sent by his English parents to England for his education at Eton. He returned to India as an officer in the Imperial Police, but be became bitterly disenchanted with service to the Empire and he soon abandoned his career in the government. His first book, *Down and Out in Paris and London* (1933), recounts his struggles to support himself while he learned to write. His lifelong subject, however, is not bohemian life as a writer but his personal encounters with totalitarianism, which he addressed in his novel *Burmese Days* (1935) and his book *Homage to Catalonia* (1938), a chronicle of his developing despair over all political parties after he participated in the Spanish Civil War. His feelings toward politics and government are also expressed in his fiction, *Animal Farm* (1945) and *1984* (1949). The following essay is a memoir of his early period of conflicting loyalties as a British magistrate in Burma.

In Moulmein, in lower Burma, I was hated by large numbers of people 1 — the only time in my life that I have been important enough for this to happen to me. I was subdivisional police officer of the town, and in an aimless, petty kind of way anti-European feeling was very bitter. No one had the guts to raise a riot, but if a European woman went through the bazaars alone somebody would probably spit betel juice over her dress. As a police officer I was an obvious target and was baited whenever it seemed safe to do so. When a nimble Burman tripped me up on the football field and the referee (another Burman) looked the other way, the crowd yelled with hideous laughter. This happened more than once. In the end the sneering yellow faces of young men that met me everywhere, the insults hooted after me when I was at a safe distance, got badly on my nerves. The young Buddhist priests were the worst of all. There were several thousands of them in the town and none of them seemed to have anything to do except stand on street corners and jeer at Europeans.

All this was perplexing and upsetting. For at that time I had already made 2 up my mind that imperialism was an evil thing and the sooner I chucked up my job and got out of it the better. Theoretically — and secretly, of course — I was all for the Burmese and all against their oppressors, the British. As for the job I was doing, I hated it more bitterly than I can perhaps make clear. In a job like that you see the dirty work of Empire at close quarters. The wretched prisoners huddling in the stinking cages of the lock-ups, the grey, cowed faces of the long-term convicts, the scarred buttocks of the men who had been flogged with bamboos — all these oppressed me with an intolerable sense of guilt. But I could get nothing into perspective. I was young and ill-educated and I had had to think out my problems in the utter silence that is imposed on every Englishman in the East. I did not even know that the British Empire is dying, still less did I know that it is a great deal better than the younger empires that are going to supplant it. All I knew was that I was stuck between my hatred of the empire I served and my rage against the evil-spirited little beasts who tried to make my job impossible. With one part of my mind I thought of the British Raj as an unbreakable tyranny, as something clamped down, in *saecula saeculorum*, upon the will of prostrate peoples; with another part I thought that the greatest joy in the world would be to drive a bayonet into a Buddhist priest's guts. Feelings like these are the normal byproducts of imperialism; ask any Anglo-Indian official, if you can catch him off duty.

One day something happened which in a roundabout way was enlight- 3 ening. It was a tiny incident in itself, but it gave me a better glimpse than I had had before of the real nature of imperialism — the real motives for which despotic governments act. Early one morning the subinspector at a police station the other end of the town rang me up on the phone and said that an elephant was ravaging the bazaar. Would I please come and do something about it? I did not know what I could do, but I wanted to see what was happening and I got on to a pony and started out. I took my rifle, an old .44 Winchester and much too small to kill an elephant, but I thought the noise might be useful *in terrorem*. Various Burmans stopped me on the way and told me about the elephant's doings. It was not, of course, a wild elephant, but a tame one which had gone "must." It had been chained up, as tame elephants always are when their attack of "must" is due, but on the previous night it had broken its chain and escaped. Its mahout, the only person who could manage it when it was in that state, had set out in pursuit, but had taken the wrong direction and was now twelve hours' journey away, and in the morning the elephant had suddenly reappeared in the town. The Burmese population had no weapons and were quite helpless against it. It had already destroyed somebody's bamboo hut, killed a cow, and raided some fruit-stalls and devoured the stock; also it had met the municipal rubbish van and, when the driver jumped out and took to his heels, had turned the van over and inflicted violences upon it.

The Burmese subinspector and some Indian constables were waiting for 4 me in the quarter where the elephant had been seen. It was a very poor quarter, a labyrinth of squalid bamboo huts, thatched with palm-leaf, winding all over a steep hillside. I remember that it was a cloudy, stuffy morning at the beginning of the rains. We began questioning the people as to where the elephant had gone and, as usual, failed to get any definite information.

That is invariably the case in the East; a story always sounds clear enough at a distance, but the nearer you get to the scene of events the vaguer it becomes. Some of the people said that the elephant had gone in one direction, some said that he had gone in another, some professed not even to have heard of any elephant. I had almost made up my mind that the whole story was a pack of lies, when we heard yells a little distance away. There was a loud, scandalized cry of "Go away, child! Go away this instant!" and an old woman with a switch in her hand came round the corner of a hut, violently shooing away a crowd of naked children. Some more women followed, clicking their tongues and exclaiming; evidently there was something that the children ought not to have seen. I rounded the hut and saw a man's dead body sprawling in the mud. He was an Indian, a black Dravidian coolie, almost naked, and he could not have been dead many minutes. The people said that the elephant had come suddenly upon him round the corner of the hut, caught him with its trunk, put its foot on his back, and ground him into the earth. This was the rainy season and the ground was soft, and his face had scored a trench a foot deep and a couple of yards long. He was lying on his belly with arms crucified and head sharply twisted to one side. His face was coated with mud, the eyes wide open, the teeth bared and grinning with an expression of unendurable agony. (Never tell me, by the way, that the dead look peaceful. Most of the corpses I have seen looked devilish.) The friction of the great beast's foot had stripped the skin from his back as neatly as one skins a rabbit. As soon as I saw the dead man I sent an orderly to a friend's house nearby to borrow an elephant rifle. I had already sent back the pony, not wanting it to go mad with fright and throw me if it smelt the elephant.

The orderly came back in a few minutes with a rifle and five cartridges,   5 and meanwhile some Burmans had arrived and told us that the elephant was in the paddy fields below, only a few hundred yards away. As I started forward practically the whole population of the quarter flocked out of the houses and followed me. They had seen the rifle and were all shouting excitedly that I was going to shoot the elephant. They had not shown much interest in the elephant when he was merely ravaging their homes, but it was different now that he was going to be shot. It was a bit of fun to them, as it would be to an English crowd; besides they wanted the meat. It made me vaguely uneasy. I had no intention of shooting the elephant — I had merely sent for the rifle to defend myself if necessary — and it is always unnerving to have a crowd following you. I marched down the hill, looking and feeling a fool, with the rifle over my shoulder and an ever-growing army of people jostling at my heels. At the bottom, when you got away from the huts, there was a metalled road and beyond that a miry waste of paddy fields a thousand yards across, not yet ploughed but soggy from the first rains and dotted with coarse grass. The elephant was standing eight yards from the road, his left side towards us. He took not the slightest notice of the crowd's approach. He was tearing up bunches of grass, beating them against his knees to clean them and stuffing them into his mouth.

I had halted on the road. As soon as I saw the elephant I knew with perfect   6 certainty that I ought not to shoot him. It is a serious matter to shoot a working elephant — it is comparable to destroying a huge and costly piece of machinery — and obviously one ought not to do it if it can possibly be avoided. And at that distance, peacefully eating, the elephant looked no more dangerous than a cow. I thought then and I think now that his attack of "must" was already passing off; in which case he would merely wander harmlessly about until the mahout came back and caught him. Moreover, I did not in the least want to shoot him. I decided that I would watch him for a little while to make sure that he did not turn savage again, and then go home.

But at that moment I glanced round at the crowd that had followed me. It was an immense crowd, two thousand at the least and growing every minute. It blocked the road for a long distance on either side. I looked at the sea of yellow faces above the garish clothes — faces all happy and excited over this bit of fun, all certain that the elephant was going to be shot. They were watching me as they would watch a conjurer about to perform a trick. They did not like me, but with the magical rifle in my hands I was momentarily worth watching. And suddenly I realized that I should have to shoot the elephant after all. The people expected it of me and I had got to do it; I could feel their two thousand wills pressing me forward, irresistibly. And it was at this moment, as I stood there with the rifle in my hands, that I first grasped the hollowness, the futility of the white man's dominion in the East. Here was I, the white man with his gun, standing in front of the unarmed native crowd — seemingly the leading actor of the piece; but in reality I was only an absurd puppet pushed to and fro by the will of those yellow faces behind. I perceived in this moment that when the white man turns tyrant it is his own freedom that he destroys. He becomes a sort of hollow, posing dummy, the conventionalized figure of a sahib. For it is the condition of his rule that he shall spend his life in trying to impress the "natives," and so in every crisis he has got to do what the "natives" expect of him. He wears a mask, and his face grows to fit in. I had got to shoot the elephant. I had committed myself to doing it when I sent for the rifle. A sahib has got to act like a sahib; he has got to appear resolute, to know his own mind and do definite things. To come all that way, rifle in hand, with two thousand people marching at my heels, and then to trail feebly away, having done nothing — no, that was impossible. The crowd would laugh at me. And my whole life, every white man's life in the East, was one long struggle not to be laughed at.

But I did not want to shoot the elephant. I watching him beating his bunch of grass against his knees, with that preoccupied grandmotherly air that elephants have. It seemed to me that it would be murder to shoot him. At that age I was not squeamish about killing animals, but I had never shot an elephant and never wanted to. (Somehow it always seems worse to kill a *large* animal.) Besides, there was the beast's owner to be considered. Alive, the elephant was worth at least a hundred pounds; dead, he would only be worth the value of his tusks, five pounds, possibly. But I had got to act quickly. I turned to some experienced-looking Burmans who had been there when we arrived, and asked them how the elephant had been behaving.

They all said the same thing: He took no notice of you if you left him alone, but he might charge if you went too close to him.

It was perfectly clear to me what I ought to do. I ought to walk up to 9 within, say, twenty-five yards of the elephant and test his behavior. If he charged, I could shoot; if he took no notice of me, it would be safe to leave him until the mahout came back. But also I knew that I was going to do no such thing. I was a poor shot with a rifle and the ground was soft mud into which one would sink at every step. If the elephant charged and I missed him, I should have about as much chance as a toad under a steam-roller. But even then I was not thinking particularly of my own skin, only of the watchful yellow faces behind. For at that moment, with the crowd watching me, I was not afraid in the ordinary sense, as I would have been if I had been alone. A white man mustn't be frightened in front of "natives"; and so, in general, he isn't frightened. The sole thought in my mind was that if anything went wrong those two thousand Burmans would see me pursued, caught, trampled on, and reduced to a grinning corpse like that Indian up the hill. And if that happened it was quite probable that some of them would laugh. That would never do. There was only one alternative. I shoved the cartridges into the magazine and lay down on the road to get a better aim.

The crowd grew very still, and a deep, low, happy sigh, as of people who 10 see the theater curtain go up at last, breathed from innumerable throats. They were going to have their bit of fun after all. The rifle was a beautiful German thing with cross-hair sights. I did not then know that in shooting an elephant one would shoot to cut an imaginary bar running from ear-hole to ear-hole. I ought, therefore, as the elephant was sideways on, to have aimed straight at his ear-hole; actually I aimed several inches in front of this, thinking the brain would be further forward.

When I pulled the trigger I did not hear the bang or feel the kick — one 11 never does when a shot goes home — but I heard the devilish roar of glee that went up from the crowd. In that instant, in too short a time, one would have thought, even for the bullet to get there, a mysterious, terrible change had come over the elephant. He neither stirred nor fell, but every line of his body had altered. He looked suddenly stricken, shrunken, immensely old, as though the frightful impact of the bullet had paralysed him without knocking him down. At last, after what seemed a long time — it might have been five seconds, I dare say — he sagged flabbily to his knees. His mouth slobbered. An enormous senility seemed to have settled upon him. One could have imagined him thousands of years old. I fired again into the same spot. At the second shot he did not collapse but climbed with desperate slowness to his feet and stood weakly upright, with legs sagging and head drooping. I fired a third time. That was the shot that did for him. You could see the agony of it jolt his whole body and knock the last remnant of strength from his legs. But in falling he seemed for a moment to rise, for as his hind legs collapsed beneath him he seemed to tower upward like a huge rock toppling, his trunk reaching skywards like a tree. He trumpeted, for the first and only time. And then down he came, his belly towards me, with a crash that seemed to shake the ground even where I lay.

I got up. The Burmans were already racing past me across the mud. It was obvious that the elephant would never rise again, but he was not dead. He was breathing very rhythmically with long rattling gasps, his great mound of a side painfully rising and falling. His mouth was wide open — I could see far down into caverns of pale pink throat. I waited a long time for him to die, but his breathing did not weaken. Finally I fired my two remaining shots into the spot where I thought his heart must be. The thick blood welled out of him like red velvet, but still he did not die. His body did not even jerk when the shots hit him, the tortured breathing continued without a pause. He was dying, very slowly and in great agony, but in some world remote from me where not even a bullet could damage him further. I felt that I had got to put an end to that dreadful noise. It seemed dreadful to see the great beast lying there, powerless to move and yet powerless to die, and not even to be able to finish him. I sent back for my small rifle and poured shot after shot into his heart and down his throat. They seemed to make no impression. The tortured gasps continued as steadily as the ticking of a clock.

In the end I could not stand it any longer and went away. I heard later that it took him half an hour to die. Burmans were bringing dahs[1] and baskets even before I left, and I was told they had stripped his body almost to the bones by the afternoon.

Afterwards, of course, there were endless discussions about the shooting of the elephant. The owner was furious, but he was only an Indian and could do nothing. Besides, legally I had done the right thing, for a mad elephant has to be killed, like a mad dog, if its owner fails to control it. Among the Europeans opinion was divided. The older men said I was right, the younger men said it was a damn shame to shoot an elephant for killing a coolie, because an elephant was worth more than any damn Coringhee coolie. And afterwards I was very glad that the coolie had been killed; it put me legally in the right and it gave me a sufficient pretext for shooting the elephant. I often wondered whether any of the others grasped that I had done it solely to avoid looking a fool.

Analyzing This Selection

1. Why did Orwell hate his job even before this incident occurred? What effect was the job having on his feelings and attitudes? How would you describe his state of mind at the time?

2. Why does the Burman subinspector have to call Orwell? Why can't the Burmans themselves take care of the problem?

[1]Large knives. [Ed.]

3. What details in the descriptions of the elephant connect it with human life? What details in the descriptions of the Burmans connect them with animals? What evokes Orwell's humane, sympathetic responses?

4. Orwell says that he acted "solely to avoid looking a fool." If he had believed in the goals and values of British imperialism, would his actions have had more integrity?

Analyzing Connections

5. In Insights, Orwell says that "all issues are political" (see p. 392). In this essay are there issues that are nonpolitical? Any that go beyond the political? For what reasons, political or otherwise, are issues in this essay important to *you*?

Analyzing by Writing

6. In paragraph 7, Orwell observes that "when the white man turns tyrant it is his own freedom that he destroys." In what ways might Andrew Hacker ("Racism as a Consolation Prize," p. 272) oppose, support, or modify this statement?

7. Orwell was not able to "just say no." Internal and external complications led him to knowingly do a "dumb" thing. Describe your dilemma at a time when you were being coerced to do what others wanted. What possible advantages, embarrassments, dangers, and resentments did you think about? At the time, what part of your problem felt entirely personal and internal? What part of the problem came from external circumstances? Analyze the issues as you understand them now.

Bel Kaufman

SUNDAY IN THE PARK

◇

BEL KAUFMAN, granddaughter of the Yiddish humorist Sholem Aleichem, was born in Berlin, and she spent her childhood in Russia before coming to the United States at the age of twelve. She graduated magna cum laude from Hunter College and earned a master's degree from Columbia University. From 1949 Kaufman taught English in New York City high schools, an experience that led to her best-selling novel, *Up the Down Staircase* (1964), which was later made into a popular film. Kaufman has written another novel, *Love, etc.* (1979), and many essays and short stories. She has taught writing at the City University of New York.

It was still warm in the late-afternoon sun, and the city noises came 1 muffled through the trees in the park. She put her book down on the bench, removed her sunglasses, and sighed contentedly. Morton was reading the *Times Magazine* section, one arm flung around her shoulder; their three-year-old son, Larry, was playing in the sandbox: A faint breeze fanned her hair softly against her cheek. It was five-thirty on a Sunday afternoon, and the small playground, tucked away in a corner of the park, was all but deserted. The swings and seesaws stood motionless and abandoned, the slides were empty, and only in the sandbox two little boys squatted diligently side by side. *How good this is,* she thought, and almost smiled at her sense of well-being. They must go out in the sun more often; Morton was so city-pale, cooped up all week inside the gray factorylike university. She squeezed his arm affectionately and glanced at Larry, delighting in the pointed little face frowning in concentration over the tunnel he was digging. The other boy suddenly stood up and with a quick, deliberate swing of his chubby arm threw a spadeful of sand at Larry. It just missed his head. Larry continued digging; the boy remained standing, shovel raised, stolid and impassive.

"No, no, little boy." She shook her finger at him, her eyes searching for 2 the child's mother or nurse. "We mustn't throw sand. It may get in some-one's eyes and hurt. We must play nicely in the nice sandbox." The boy looked at her in unblinking expectancy. He was about Larry's age but perhaps ten pounds heavier, a husky little boy with none of Larry's quickness and sensitivity in his face. Where was his mother? The only other people left in the playground were two women and a little girl on roller skates leaving now through the gate, and a man on a bench a few feet away. He was a big man, and he seemed to be taking up the whole bench as he held the Sunday comics close to his face. She supposed he was the child's father. He did not look up from his comics, but spat once deftly out of the corner of his mouth. She turned her eyes away.

At that moment, as swiftly as before, the fat little boy threw another 3 spadeful of sand at Larry. This time some of it landed on his hair and forehead. Larry looked up at his mother, his mouth tentative; her expression would tell him whether to cry or not.

Her first instinct was to rush to her son, brush the sand out of his hair, and 4 punish the other child, but she controlled it. She always said that she wanted Larry to learn to fight his own battles.

"Don't *do* that, little boy," she said sharply, leaning forward on the bench. 5 "You mustn't throw sand!"

The man on the bench moved his mouth as if to spit again, but instead 6 he spoke. He did not look at her, but at the boy only.

"You go right ahead, Joe," he said loudly. "Throw all you want. This here 7 is a *public* sandbox."

She felt a sudden weakness in her knees as she glanced at Morton. He had 8 become aware of what was happening. He put his *Times* down carefully on his lap and turned his fine, lean face toward the man, smiling the shy, apologetic smile he might have offered a student in pointing out an error in his thinking. When he spoke to the man, it was with his usual reasonableness.

"You're quite right," he said pleasantly, "but just because this is a public 9 place. . . ."

The man lowered his funnies and looked at Morton. He looked at him 10 from head to foot, slowly and deliberately. "Yeah?" His insolent voice was edged with menace. "My kid's got just as good right here as yours, and if he feels like throwing sand, he'll throw it, and if you don't like it, you can take your kid the hell out of here."

The children were listening, their eyes and mouths wide open, their 11 spades forgotten in small fists. She noticed the muscle in Morton's jaw tighten. He was rarely angry; he seldom lost his temper. She was suffused with a tenderness for her husband and an impotent rage against the man for involving him in a situation so alien and so distasteful to him.

"Now, just a minute," Morton said courteously, "you must realize . . ." 12

"Aw, shut up," said the man. 13

Her heart began to pound. Morton half rose; the *Times* slid to the ground. 14 Slowly the other man stood up. He took a couple of steps toward Morton, then stopped. He flexed his great arms, waiting. She pressed her trembling knees together. Would there be violence, fighting? How dreadful, how incredible. . . . She must do something, stop them, call for help. She wanted to put her hand on her husband's sleeve, to pull him down, but for some reason she didn't.

Morton adjusted his glasses. He was very pale. "This is ridiculous," he 15 said unevenly. "I must ask you . . ."

"Oh, yeah?" said the man. He stood with his legs spread apart, rocking a 16 little, looking at Morton with utter scorn. "You and who else?"

For a moment the two men looked at each other nakedly. Then Morton 17 turned his back on the man and said quietly, "Come on, let's get out of here." He walked awkwardly, almost limping with self-consciousness, to the sandbox. He stooped and lifted Larry and his shovel out.

At once Larry came to life, his face lost its rapt expression and he began 18 to kick and cry. "I don't *want* to go home, I want to play better, I don't *want* any supper, I don't *like* supper. . . ." It became a chant as they walked, pulling their child between them, his feet dragging on the ground. In order to get to the exit gate they had to pass the bench where the man sat sprawling again. She was careful not to look at him. With all the dignity she could summon, she pulled Larry's sandy, perspiring little hand, while Morton pulled the other. Slowly and with head high she walked with her husband and child out of the playground.

Her first feeling was one of relief that a fight had been avoided, that no one 19 was hurt. Yet beneath it there was a layer of something else, something heavy and inescapable. She sensed that it was more than just an unpleasant incident, more than defeat of reason by force. She felt dimly it had something to do with her and Morton, something acutely personal, familiar, and important.

Suddenly Morton spoke. "It wouldn't have proved anything." 20

"What?" she asked. 21

"A fight. It wouldn't have proved anything beyond the fact that he's bigger 22 than I am."

"Of course," she said. 23

"The only possible outcome," he continued reasonably, "would have 24 been — what? My glasses broken, perhaps a tooth or two replaced, a couple of days' work missed — and for what? For justice? For truth?"

"Of course," she repeated. She quickened her step. She wanted only to get 25 home and to busy herself with her familiar tasks; perhaps then the feeling, glued like heavy plaster on her heart, would be gone. *Of all the stupid, despicable bullies*, she thought, pulling harder on Larry's hand. The child was still crying. Always before she had felt a tender pity for his defenseless little body, the frail arms, the narrow shoulders with sharp, winglike shoulder blades, the thin and unsure legs, but now her mouth tightened in resentment.

"Stop crying," she said sharply. "I'm ashamed of you!" She felt as if all 26 three of them were tracking mud along the street. The child cried louder.

If there had been an issue involved, she thought, *if there had been some- 27 thing to fight for. . . . But what else could he possibly have done? Allow himself to be beaten? Attempt to educate the man? Call a policeman? "Officer, there's a man in the park who won't stop his child from throwing sand on mine. . . ."* The whole thing was as silly as that, and not worth thinking about.

"Can't you keep him quiet, for Pete's sake?" Morton asked irritably. 28

"What do you suppose I've been trying to do?" she said. 29

Larry pulled back, dragging his feet.   30

"If you can't discipline this child, I will," Morton snapped, making a   31
move toward the boy.

But her voice stopped him. She was shocked to hear it, thin and cold and   32
penetrating with contempt. "Indeed?" she heard herself say. "You and who
else?"

Analyzing This Selection

1. Before the bully speaks, what are the positive and negative aspects of the woman's frame of mind?

2. Toward the end the woman wonders what there was to fight over. In your opinion, was anything really at stake?

3. At the end, what is your attitude toward Morton? toward the woman? How do you account for these attitudes?

Analyzing Connections

4. Martin Green maintains in "Dying — and Killing? — for One's Country" (p. 415) that the problem of violence is "the absolutely crucial one" for humankind. How would Green's nonviolent doctrine affect the situation and/or the outcome of this story? What moral elements are present or missing in the situation that make nonviolence an effective response?

5. In Kaufman's story and in Stephen Dixon's "Interstate 7" (p. 50), the main characters must cope with situations in which expectations about acceptable behavior are challenged, where "rules" are broken. What similarities do you see in the main characters' reactions? What can we conclude about human reactions to such startling, unpleasant incidents?

Analyzing by Writing

6. Violent force is widely accepted if the violence is used to preserve "the nation's honor" or a person's "manly honor." Also, violence confers honor in film and video entertainment. Less acceptable but equally pervasive uses of violence are linked with honor among members of neighborhood gangs and organized crime families. What, if any, positive human attributes are contained in the link between violence and honor? What honorable goals and ideals might be separable from the violence? Try to define a concept of honor that does not depend on violence for confirmation.

   For details to illustrate your points, use "Sunday in the Park," news stories, videos, or just your imagination.

7. How should one act toward unreasonable, hostile behavior? One precept is to "turn the other cheek." Do you think that is good or bad advice? Explain the moral effects of choosing either nonviolence or force in response to a situation similar to that in "Sunday in the Park."

Sallie Tisdale

WE DO ABORTIONS HERE

◇

Sallie Tisdale (b. 1957), a writer and part-time nurse, has written two studies of the nursing profession, *The Sorcerer's Apprentice* (1986) and *Harvest Moon* (1987). She has written about health also in *Lot's Wife: Salt and the Human Condition* (1988). Her most recent book is *Stepping Westward: The Long Search for Home in the Pacific Northwest* (1991). Tisdale frequently writes for *Harper's*, and *The New Yorker*, contributing essays on health care and social services for the mentally retarded. She lives in Portland, Oregon. Tisdale was a registered nurse in an abortion clinic when she wrote the following reflections about the tasks, the suffering, and the moral issues involved in that work.

We do abortions here; that is all we do. There are weary, grim moments 1
when I think I cannot bear another basin of bloody remains, utter another
kind phrase of reassurance. So I leave the procedure room in the back and
reach for a new chart. Soon I am talking to an eighteen-year-old woman
pregnant for the fourth time. I push up her sleeve to check her blood pressure
and find row upon row of needle marks, neat and parallel and discolored.
She has been so hungry for her drug for so long that she has taken to using
the loose skin of her upper arms; her elbows are already a permanent ruin of
bruises. She is surprised to find herself nearly four months pregnant. I
suspect she is often surprised, in a mild way, by the blows she is dealt. I
prepare myself for another basin, another brief and chafing loss.

"How can you stand it?" Even the clients ask. They see the machine, the 2
strange instruments, the blood, the final stroke that wipes away the promise
of pregnancy. Sometimes I see that too: I watch a woman's swollen abdomen
sink to softness in a few stuttering moments and my own belly flip-flops with
sorrow. But all it takes for me to catch my breath is another interview, one
more story that sounds so much like the last one. There is a numbing
sameness lurking in this job: the same questions, the same answers, even the
same trembling tone in the voices. The worst is the sameness of human
failure, of inadequacy in the face of each day's dull demands.

In describing this work, I find it difficult to explain how much I enjoy it 3
most of the time. We laugh a lot here, as friends and as professional peers.
It's nice to be with women all day. I like the sudden, transient bonds I forge
with some clients: moments when I am in my strength, remembering weak-

ness, and a woman in weakness reaches out for my strength. What I offer is not power, but solidness, offered almost eagerly. Certain clients waken in me every tender urge I have — others make me wince and bite my tongue. Both challenge me to find a balance. It is a sweet brutality we practice here, a stark and loving dispassion.

I look at abortion as if I am standing on a cliff with a telescope, gazing at   4
some great vista. I can sweep the horizon with both eyes, survey the scene in all its distance and size. Or I can put my eye to the lens and focus on the small details, suddenly so close. In abortion the absolute must always be tempered by the contextual, because both are real, both valid, both hard. How can we do this? How can we refuse? Each abortion is a measure of our failure to protect, to nourish our own. Each basin I empty is a promise — but a promise broken a long time ago.

I grew up on the great promise of birth control. Like many women my   5
age, I took the pill as soon as I was sexually active. To risk pregnancy when it was so easy to avoid seemed stupid, and my contraceptive success, as it were, was part of the promise of social enlightenment. But birth control fails, far more frequently than laboratory trials predict. Many of our clients take the pill; its failure to protect them is a shocking realization. We have clients who have been sterilized, whose husbands have had vasectomies; each one is a statistical misfit, fine print come to life. The anger and shame of these women I hold in one hand, and the basin in the other. The distance between the two, the length I pace and try to measure, is the size of an abortion.

The procedure is disarmingly simple. Women are surprised, as though the   6
mystery of conception, a dark and hidden genesis, requires an elaborate finale. In the first trimester of pregnancy, it's a mere few minutes of vacuuming, a neat tidying up. I give a woman a small yellow Valium, and when it has begun to relax her, I lead her into the back, into bareness, the stirrups. The doctor reaches in her, opening the narrow tunnel to the uterus with a succession of slim, smooth bars of steel. He inserts a plastic tube and hooks it to a hose on the machine. The woman is framed against white paper that crackles as she moves, the light bright in her eyes. Then the machine rumbles low and loud in the small windowless room; the doctor moves the tube back and forth with an efficient rhythm, and the long tail of it fills with blood that spurts and stumbles along into a jar. He is usually finished in a few minutes. They are long minutes for the woman; her uterus frequently reacts to its abrupt emptying with a powerful, unceasing cramp, which cuts off the blood vessels and enfolds the irritated, bleeding tissue.

I am learning to recognize the shadows that cross the faces of the women   7
I hold. While the doctor works between her spread legs, the paper drape hiding his intent expression, I stand beside the table. I hold the woman's hands in mine, resting them just below her ribs. I watch her eyes, finger her necklace, stroke her hair. I ask about her job, her family; in a haze she answers me; we chatter, faces close, eyes meeting and sliding apart.

I watch the shadows that creep up unnoticed and suddenly darken her face   8
as she screws up her features and pushes a tear out each side to slide down
her cheeks. I have learned to anticipate the quiver of chin, the rapid intake
of breath, and the surprising sobs that rise soon after the machine starts to
drum. I know this is when the cramp deepens, and the tears are partly the
tears that follow pain — the sharp, childish crying when one bumps one's
head on a cabinet door. But a well of woe seems to open beneath many
women when they hear that thumping sound. The anticipation of the
moment has finally come to fruit; the moment has arrived when the loss is
no longer an imagined one. It has come true.

I am struck by the sameness and I am struck every day by the variety   9
here — how this commonplace dilemma can so display the differences of
women. A twenty-one-year-old woman, unemployed, uneducated, without
family, in the fifth month of her pregnancy. A forty-two-year-old mother of
teenagers, shocked by her condition, refusing to tell her husband. A twenty-
three-year-old mother of two having her seventh abortion, and many women
in their thirties having their first. Some are stoic, some hysterical, a few
giggle uncontrollably, many cry.

I talk to a sixteen-year-old uneducated girl who was raped. She has   10
gonorrhea. She describes blinding headaches, attacks of breathlessness, nausea. "Sometimes I feel like two different people," she tells me with a calm
smile, "and I talk to myself."

I pull out my plastic models. She listens patiently for a time, and then   11
holds out her hands wide in front of her stomach.

"When's the baby going to go up into my stomach?" she asks.   12

I blink. "What do you mean?"   13

"Well," she says, still smiling, "when women get so big, isn't the baby in   14
your stomach? Doesn't it hatch out of an egg there?"

My first question in an interview is always the same. As I walk down the   15
hall with the woman, as we get settled in chairs and I glance through her
files, I am trying to gauge her, to get a sense of the words, and the tone, I
should use. With some I joke, and others I chat, sometimes I fall into a brisk,
business-like patter. But I ask every woman, "Are you sure you want to have
an abortion?" Most nod with grim knowing smiles. "Oh, yes," they sigh.
Some seek forgiveness, offer excuses. Occasionally a woman will flinch and
say, "Please don't use that word."

Later I describe the procedure to come, using care with my language. I   16
don't say "pain" any more than I would say "baby." So many are afraid to ask
how much it will hurt. "My sister told me — " I hear. "A friend of mine
said — " and the dire expectations unravel. I prick the index finger of a
woman for a drop of blood to test, and as the tiny lancet approaches the skin
she averts her eyes, holding her trembling hand out to me and jumping at my
touch.

It is when I am holding a plastic uterus in one hand, a suction tube in the   17
other, moving them together in imitation of the scrubbing to come, that

women ask the most secret question. I am speaking in a matter-of-fact voice about "the tissue" and "the contents" when the woman suddenly catches my eye and asks, "How big is the baby now?" These words suggest a quiet need for a definition of the boundaries being drawn. It isn't so odd, after all, that she feels relief when I describe the growing bud's bulbous shape, its miniature nature. Again I gauge, and sometimes lie a little, weaseling around its infantile features until its clinging power slackens.

But when I look in the basin, among the curdlike blood clots, I see an 18 elfin thorax, attenuated, its pencilline ribs all in parallel rows with tiny knobs of spine rounding upwards. A translucent arm and hand swim beside.

A sleepy-eyed girl, just fourteen, watched me with a slight and goofy smile 19 all through her abortion. "Does it have little feet and little fingers and all?" she'd asked earlier. When the suction was over she sat up woozily at the end of the table and murmured, "Can I see it?" I shook my head firmly.

"It's not allowed," I told her sternly, because I knew she didn't really want 20 to see what was left. She accepted this statement of authority, and a shadow of confused relief crossed her plain, pale face.

Privately, even grudgingly, my colleagues might admit the power of 21 abortion to provoke emotion. But they seem to prefer the broad view and disdain the telescope. Abortion is a matter of choice, privacy, control. Its uncertainty lies in specific cases: retarded women and girls too young to give consent for surgery, women who are ill or hostile or psychotic. Such common dilemmas are met with both compassion and impatience; they slow things down. We are too busy to chew over ethics. One person might discuss certain concerns, behind closed doors, or describe a particularly disturbing dream. But generally there is to be no ambivalence.

Every day I take calls from women who are annoyed that we cannot see 22 them, cannot do their abortion today, this morning, now. They argue the price, demand that we stay after hours to accommodate their job or class schedule. Abortion is so routine that one expects it to be like a manicure; quick, cheap, and painless.

Still, I've cultivated a certain disregard. It isn't negligence, but I don't 23 always pay attention. I couldn't be here if I tried to judge each case on its merits; after all, we do over a hundred abortions a week. At some point each individual in this line of work draws a boundary and adheres to it. For one physician the boundary is a particular week of gestation; for another, it is a certain number of repeated abortions. But these boundaries can be fluid too: One physician overruled his own limit to abort a mature but severely malformed fetus. For me, the limit is allowing my clients to carry their own burden, shoulder the responsibility themselves. I shoulder the burden of trying not to judge them.

This city has several "crisis pregnancy centers" advertised in the Yellow 24 Pages. They are small offices staffed by volunteers, and they offer free pregnancy testing, glossy photos of dead fetuses, and movies. I had a client recently whose mother is active in the antiabortion movement. The young woman went to the local crisis center and was told that the doctor would make her touch her dismembered baby, that the pain would be the most horrible she could imagine, and that she might, after an abortion, never be able to have children. All lies. They called her at home and at work, over and over and over, but she had been wise enough to give a false name. She came to us a fugitive. We who do abortions are marked, by some, as impure. It's dirty work.

When a deliveryman comes to the sliding glass window by the reception 25 desk and tilts a box toward me, I hesitate. I read the packing slips, assess the shape and weight of the box in the light of its supposed contents. We request familiar faces. The doors are carefully locked; I have learned to half glance around at bags and boxes, looking for a telltale sign. I register with security when I arrive, and I am careful not to bang a door. We are a little on edge here.

Concern about size and shape seem to be natural, and so is the relief that 26 follows. We make the powerful assumption that the fetus is different from us, and even when we admit the similarities, it is too simplistic to be seduced by form alone. But the form is enormously potent — humanoid, powerless, palm-sized, and pure, it evokes an almost fierce tenderness when viewed simply as what it appears to be. But appearance, and even potential, aren't enough. The fetus, in becoming itself, can ruin others; its utter dependence has a sinister side. When I am struck in the moment by the contents in the basin, I am careful to remember the context, to note the tearful teenager and the woman sighing with something more than relief. One kind of question, though, I find considerably trickier.

"Can you tell what it is?" I am asked, and this means gender. This 27 question is asked by couples, not women alone. Always couples would abort a girl and keep a boy. I have been asked about twins, and even if I could tell what race the father was.

An eighteen-year-old woman with three daughters brought her husband to 28 the interview. He glared first at me, then at his wife, as he sank lower and lower in the chair, picking his teeth with a toothpick. He interrupted a conversation with his wife to ask if I could tell whether the baby would be a boy or a girl. I told him I could not.

"Good," he replied in a slow and strangely malevolent voice, " 'cause if 29 it was a boy I'd wring her neck."

In a literal sense, abortion exists because we are able to ask such questions, 30 able to assign a value to the fetus which can shift with changing circumstances. If the human bond to a child were as primitive and unflinchingly narrow as that of other animals, there would be no abortion. There would be no abortion because there would be nothing more important than caring for the young and perpetuating the species, no reason for sex but to make babies. I sense this sometimes, this wordless organic duty, when I do ultrasounds.

We do ultrasound, a sound-wave test that paints a faint, gray picture of the   31
fetus, whenever we're uncertain of gestation. Age is measured by the width
of the skull and confirmed by the length of the femur or thighbone; we speak
of a pregnancy as being a certain "femur length" in weeks. The usual
concern is whether a pregnancy is within the legal limit for an abortion.
Women this far along have bellies which swell out round and tight like trim
muscles. When they lie flat, the mound rises softly above the hips, pressing
the umbilicus upward.

It takes practice to read an ultrasound picture, which is grainy and etched   32
as though in strokes of charcoal. But suddenly a rapid rhythmic motion
appears — the beating heart. Nearby is a soft oval, scratched with lines — the
skull. The leg is harder to find, and then suddenly the fetus moves, bobbing
in the surf. The skull turns away, an arm slides across the screen, the torso rolls.
I know the weight of a baby's head on my shoulder, the whisper of lips on ears,
the delicate curve of a fragile spine in my hand. I know how heavy and correct
a newborn cradled feels. The creature I watch in secret requires nothing from
me but to be left alone, and that is precisely what won't be done.

These inadvertently made beings are caught in a twisting web of motive   33
and desire. They are at least inconvenient, sometimes quite literally dangerous in the womb, but most often they fall somewhere in between — consequences never quite believed in come to roost. Their virtue rises and falls
outside their own nature: They become only what we make them. A fetus
created by accident is the most absolute kind of surprise. Whether the blame
lies in a failed IUD, a slipped condom, or a false impression of safety, that
fetus is a thing whose creation has been actively worked against. Its existence
is an error. I think this is why so few women, even late in a pregnancy, will
consider giving a baby up for adoption. To do so means making the fetus
real — imagining it as something whole and outside oneself. The decision to
terminate a pregnancy is sometimes so difficult and confounding that it
creates an enormous demand for immediate action. The decision is a rejec-
tion; the pregnancy has become something to be rid of, a condition to be
ended. It is a burden, a weight, a thing separate.

Women have abortions because they are too old, and too young, too poor,   34
and too rich, too stupid, and too smart. I see women who berate themselves
with violent emotions for their first and only abortion, and others who return
three times, five times, hauling two or three children, who cannot remember
to take a pill or where they put the diaphragm. We talk glibly about choice.
But the choice for what? I see all the broken promises in lives lived like a
series of impromptu obstacles. There are the sweet, light promises of love and
intimacy, the glittering promise of education and progress, the warm promise
of safe families, long years of innocence and community. And there is the
promise of freedom: freedom from failure, from faithlessness. Freedom from
biology. The early feminist defense of abortion asked many questions, but
the one I remember is this: Is biology destiny? And the answer is yes,

sometimes it is. Women who have the fewest choices of all exercise their right to abortion the most.

Oh, the ignorance. I take a woman to the back room and ask her to undress;   35
a few minutes later I return and find her positioned discreetly behind a drape, still wearing underpants. "Do I have to take these off too?" she asks, a little shocked. Some swear they have not had sex, many do not know what a uterus is, how sperm and egg meet, how sex makes babies. Some late seekers do not believe themselves pregnant; they believe themselves *impregnable*. I was chastised when I began this job for referring to some clients as girls: It is a feminist heresy. They come so young, snapping gum, sockless and sneakered, and their shakily applied eyeliner smears when they cry. I call them girls with maternal benignity. I cannot imagine them as mothers.

The doctor seats himself between the woman's thighs and reaches into the   36
dilated opening of a five-month pregnant uterus. Quickly he grabs and crushes the fetus in several places, and the room is filled with a low clatter and snap of forceps, the click of the tanaculum, and a pulling, sucking sound. The paper crinkles as the drugged and sleepy woman shifts, the nurse's low, honey-brown voice explains each step in delicate words.

I have fetus dreams, we all do here: dreams of abortions one after the   37
other; of buckets of blood splashed on the walls; trees full of crawling fetuses. I dreamed that two men grabbed me and began to drag me away: "Let's do an abortion," they said with a sickening leer, and I began to scream, plunged into a vision of sucking, scraping pain, of being spread and torn by impartial instruments that do only what they are bidden. I woke from this dream barely able to breathe and thought of kitchen tables and coat hangers, knitting needles striped with blood, and women all alone clutching a pillow in their teeth to keep the screams from piercing the apartment-house walls. Abortion is the narrowest edge between kindness and cruelty. Done as well as it can be, it is still violence — merciful violence, like putting a suffering animal to death.

Maggie, one of the nurses, received a call at midnight not long ago. It was   38
a woman in her twentieth week of pregnancy; the necessarily gradual process of cervical dilation begun the day before had stimulated labor, as it sometimes does. Maggie and one of the doctors met the woman at the office in the night. Maggie helped her onto the table, and as she lay down the fetus was delivered into Maggie's hands. When Maggie told me about it the next day, she cupped her hands into a small bowl — "It was just like a small kitten," she said softly, wonderingly. "Everything was still attached."

At the end of the day I clean out the suction jars, pouring blood into the   39
sink, splashing the sides with flecks of tissue. From the sink rises a rich and humid smell, hot, earthy, and moldering; it is the smell of something recently alive beginning to decay. I take care of the plastic tub on the floor, filled with pieces too big to be trusted to the trash. The law defines the

contents of the bucket I hold protectively against my chest as "tissue." Some would say my complicity in filling that bucket gives me no right to call it anything else. I slip the tissue gently into a bag and place it in the freezer, to be burned at another time. Abortion requires of me an entirely new set of assumptions. It requires a willingness to live with conflict, fearlessness, and grief. As I close the freezer door, I imagine a world where this won't be necessary, and then return to the world where it is.

Analyzing This Selection

1. In the detailed description of an abortion, what does the author want the reader to recognize? How does her description affect you?

2. What attitude toward her clients does Tisdale reject? What attitude does she uphold? What problems does she have in controlling her attitudes? How do your responses to her clients differ from hers?

3. Explain Tisdale's stance on the public controversy over abortion. What is her attitude toward antiabortionists?

4. What is the author's outlook on humanity? What generalizations does Tisdale assert or imply about the human race?

Analyzing Connections

5. In "The Gift of Life Must Always Remain a Gift" (see p. 331), Thomas H. Murray says that we can think of our body and its parts as *property*, as *surplus*, or as a *gift*. Which category is farthest from Tisdale's view of abortion? Which is closest?

Analyzing by Writing

6. Construct a *balanced* view of a controversial issue such as abortion, banning pornography, or capital punishment. Explain one good reason on each side of the issue. Do not make the arguments mere opposites, but give each side a prime justification, the rationale that is most valid in your judgment.

Stephen L. Carter

SCHOOLS OF DISBELIEF[1]

◇

STEPHEN L. CARTER (b. 1954) was educated in the public schools of Washington, D.C., New York City, and Ithaca, New York. He graduated from Stanford University and received his law degree from Yale University. After serving as law clerk to Supreme Court Justice Thurgood Marshall, Carter joined the Yale faculty, where he teaches constitutional law. His articles and legal research have been published widely. His first book was *Reflections of an Affirmative Action Baby* (1991). The following essay is excerpted from *The Culture of Disbelief: How American Law and Politics Trivialize Religious Devotion* (1993).

Contemporary American politics faces few greater dilemmas than deciding how to deal with the resurgence of religious belief. On the one hand, American ideology cherishes religion, as it does all matters of private conscience, which is why we justly celebrate a strong tradition against state interference with private religious choice. At the same time, many political leaders, commentators, scholars, and voters are coming to view any religious element in public moral discourse as a tool of the radical right for reshaping American society. But the effort to banish religion for politics' sake has led us astray: In our sensible zeal to keep religion from dominating our politics, we have created a political and legal culture that presses the religiously faithful to be other than themselves, to act publicly, and sometimes privately as well, as though their faith does not matter to them. . . .

Religion is the first subject of the First Amendment. The amendment begins with the Establishment Clause ("Congress shall make no law respecting an establishment of religion . . .") which is immediately followed by the Free Exercise Clause ("or prohibiting the free exercise thereof"). Although one might scarcely know it from the zeal with which the primacy of the other First Amendment freedoms (free press, free speech) is often asserted, those protections come *after* the clauses that were designed to secure religious liberty, which Thomas Jefferson called "the most inalienable and sacred of all human rights." What this means in practice, however, is often quite complicated.

[1]Editor's title.

Consider an example: At a dinner party in New York City a few years ago, 3
I met a Christian minister who told me about a drug-rehabilitation program
that he runs in the inner city. His claim — I cannot document it — was that
his program had a success rate much higher than other programs. The secret,
he insisted, was prayer. It was not just that he and his staff prayed for the drug
abusers they were trying to help, he told me, although they naturally did
that. But the reason for the program's success, he proclaimed, was that he
and his staff taught those who came to them for assistance to pray as well; in
other words, they converted their charges, if not to Christianity, then at least
to religiosity. But this program, he went on with something close to bitterness, could receive no state funding, because of its religious nature.

Well, all right. To decide that the program should not receive any funds, 4
despite the success of its approach, might seem to be a straightforward
application of the doctrine holding that the Constitution sets up a wall of
separation between church and state. After all, the program is frankly religious: It uses prayer, and even teaches prayer to its clients. What could be
more threatening to the separation of church and state than to provide a
government subsidy for it? The Supreme Court has said many times that the
government may neither "advance" religion nor engage in an "excessive
entanglement" with it. On its face, a program of drug-rehabilitation therapy
that relies on teaching people to pray would seem to do both.

It is doubtless frustrating to believe deeply that one has a call from God to 5
do what one does, and then to discover that the secular society often will not
support that work, no matter how important it is to the individual. Yet that
frustration is itself a sign of the robustness of religious pluralism in America.
For the most significant aspect of the separation of church and state is not,
as some seem to think, the shielding of the secular world from too strong a
religious influence; the principal task of the separation of church and state is
to secure religious liberty.

The separation of church and state is one of the great gifts that American 6
political philosophy has presented to the world, and if it has few emulators,
that is the world's loss. Culled from the writings of Roger Williams and
Thomas Jefferson, the concept of a "wall of separation" finds its constitutional moorings in the First Amendment's firm statement that the "Congress
shall make no law respecting any establishment of religion." Although it
begins with the word "Congress," the Establishment Clause for decades has
been quite sensibly interpreted by the Supreme Court as applying to states as
well as to the federal government.

For most of American history, the principal purpose of the Establishment 7
Clause has been understood as the protection of the religious world against
the secular government. A century ago, Philip Schaff of Union Seminary in
New York celebrated the clause as "the Magna Carta of religious freedom,"
representing as it did "the first example in history of a government deliberately depriving itself of all legislative control over religion." Note the word-
ing: not religious control over government — government control over
religion. . . .

Over the years, the Supreme Court has handed down any number of controversial decisions under the Establishment Clause, many of them landmarks of our democratic culture. The best known are the cases in which the Justices struck down the recital of organized prayer in the public school classrooms, decisions that for three decades have ranked (in surveys) as among the most unpopular in our history. But the decisions were plainly right, for if the state is either able to prescribe a prayer to begin the school day or to select a holy book from which a prayer must be taken, it is casting exercising control over the religious aspects of the life of its people — precisely what the Establishment Clause was written to forbid. But although the separation of church and state is essential to the success of a vibrant, pluralistic democracy, the doctrine does not entail all that is done in its name. . . . [A] school district in Colorado . . . thought it the better part of valor to forbid a teacher to add books on Christianity to a classroom library that already included works on other religions. The town of Hamden, Connecticut, where I live, briefly ruled that a church group could not rent an empty schoolhouse for Sunday services. (Cooler heads in the end prevailed.) These rulings were both defended as required by the separation of church and state; so is the intermittent litigation to strike the legend IN GOD WE TRUST from America's coins or the phrase "under God" from the Pledge of Allegiance, an effort, if successful, that would wipe away even the civil religion. In short, it is not hard to understand the frequent complaints that the secular world acts as though the constitutional command is that the nation and its people must keep religion under wraps. . . . 8

Justice Hugo Black, in *Everson* v. *Board of Education* (1947), . . . wrote these words: "The First Amendment has erected a wall between church and state. That wall must be kept high and impregnable. We could not approve the slightest breach." A year later, Justice Stanley Reed warned that "a rule of law should not be drawn from a figure of speech." One critic wrote years later that Black had simply penned a few "lines of fiction." The critics are not quite right, but they are not quite wrong, either. There is nothing wrong with the metaphor of a wall of separation. The trouble is that in order to make the Founders' vision compatible with the structure and needs of modern society, the wall has to have a few doors in it. . . . 9

What *should* the public schools say about religion generally? One problem with the public school curriculum — a problem, happily, that has lately had much attention — is that the concern to avoid even a hint of forbidden *endorsement* of religion has led to a climate in which teachers are loath to *mention* religion. A number of studies have concluded that the public school curriculum is actually biased against religion. But one need not to go that far in order to appreciate the importance of teaching children about the role of religion at crucial junctures in the nation's history, from the openly religious rhetoric of the Founding Generation, through the religious justifications for the abolition of slavery, the "social gospel" movement to reform American society and industry, or even the civil rights movement of the 1950s and 10

1960s. (Of course, children should study the negative side as well: from the religion-based prohibition movement that culminated in the Eighteenth Amendment and the Volstead Act to the destruction of many Native American religious traditions to what the historian Jon Butler has called the "African spiritual holocaust" — that is, the willed destruction during the nineteenth century of the African religious traditions that the slaves brought with them and tried to preserve.)

The movement to teach about religions in the public schools is not, as some 11 might imagine, a smokescreen for infiltration of the education system by the religious right. On the contrary, John Buchanan of People for the American Way — a liberal organization that normally exists in a relationship of mutual antipathy with the right — agrees that there is a problem. Says Buchanan: "You can't have an accurate portrayal of history and leave out religion."

Both supporters and opponents of teaching about religion in the classroom 12 have worried about the constitutional status of such instruction. But there is nothing to worry about, and, indeed, it would be bizarre if the command of the Establishment Clause turned out to be that religion may never be mentioned in the classroom, even when it is historically relevant. Nothing in the Supreme Court's decisions on school prayer or school curriculum is inconsistent with the idea that public schools can teach about religion, or even that the schools can use religious materials and texts in doing so. . . .

It ought to be embarrassing, in this age of celebration of America's 13 diversity, that the schools have been so slow to move toward teaching about our nation's diverse religious traditions. But matters are beginning to change. In 1988, a gathering of business, political, and religious leaders produced the Williamsburg Charter, which calls for greater attention to the role of religion in American life, including the establishment of a public school curriculum on the history of religions. That same year, a diverse group of religious and education organizations joined to issue a set of guidelines for teaching "about" religion without indoctrination. And all across the country, public schools are working to incorporate into their curricula a more sensitive understanding of the role of religion in American history and culture. In 1991, schools across the country began using new primary school textbooks developed by Houghton Mifflin Company (in response to pressure from California, the largest market for school texts). The new books emphasize the contributions of Christianity, Judaism, and many of the nation's other religious traditions.

Still, the new goal of teaching about religion is not without its problems 14 — especially if the goal remains, as advocates insist it does, to teach about religion "objectively." Richard Baer of Cornell University has warned that although teaching respect for all religions "has a nice democratic ring to it," it could, if taken literally, lead to "intolerable consequences for those persons who take seriously the truth claims of the Christian gospel." Baer worries that a requirement of "objectivity" would make it illegitimate for teachers to criticize any religions, including Satanism, fanatical apocalypticism, or snake handling.

There is, moreover, the tricky problem of what to do when children begin 15 to ask the hard questions. After all, if the material is well taught, many children will surely be intrigued by what will be for many their first exposure to religious traditions different than their own — or, in some instances, to any religious traditions at all. Sooner or later, teachers using the new books and other programs will be asked questions like, "But is it true?" or "What happens when we die?" or "Who made God?" The only safe answers will be those that so frustrate school children searching for certainty: "Well, many people believe that . . . and on the other hand, many others think. . . ." Few teachers are likely to enjoy picking their way through this particular minefield, but keeping the nation's religious heritage out of the classroom is not the answer. As one observer has put it, "The challenge will be finding consensus on an educational approach that describes religious doctrine without indoctrinating. But the option, denying children a piece of their culture and past, is more dangerous."

Analyzing This Selection

1. What is the intended audience for this essay? Find details that give you an impression of Carter's targeted audience.

2. Which clause in the First Amendment does Carter think is currently undermined?

3. What is Carter's main argument in favor of presenting religion in schools? What problems does he foresee?

Analyzing Connections

4. Barbara Grizzuti Harrison (see "Growing Up Apocalyptic," p. 247) and Patricia Hampl (see "Parish Streets," p. 257) grew up in intensely religious communities. How would their communities possibly accept or reject Carter's proposed educational goals? Would Carter's proposal favor one or balance both sects? Is it an even-handed proposal?

Analyzing by Writing

5. Analyze a few differences between *knowing about* and *believing in* a concept of God or a specific religious text (such as the Book of Exodus, the Gospels, or the Koran). In your experience, do knowledge and belief develop simultaneously, or sequentially? mutually, or antithetically? Consider *knowing* and *believing* as comparable but distinct activities of mind, and try to characterize them.

6. Propose your solution to what Carter regards as a great American dilemma. Where and how, if at all, should religion be taught? Explain why the legal and moral principles that guide your solution are more valid than other guidelines that would lead to other educational results.

Martin Green, "Dying — and Killing? — for One's Country." First appeared in *Boston Review* under the title "Arts and Arms." Reprinted by permission of the author.

Andrew Hacker, "Racism as a Consolation Prize." Excerpted from *Two Nations: Black and White, Separate, Hostile, Unequal* by Andrew Hacker. Copyright © 1992 by Andrew Hacker. Reprinted with the permission of Charles Scribner's Sons, an imprint of Macmillan Publishing.

Patricia Hampl, "Parish Streets." Excerpted from *The Graywolf Annual Three: Essays, Memoirs, and Reflections.* Copyright 1986 by Patricia Hampl. Reprinted with the permission of Graywolf Press, Saint Paul, Minnesota.

Joy Harjo, "Three Generations of Native American Women's Birth Experience." First appeared in *Ms.* July/August 1991). Reprinted by permission of *Ms.* Magazine, © 1991.

Barbara Grizzuti Harrison, "Growing Up Apocalyptic." From *Off Center* by Barbara Grizzuti Harrison. Copyright © 1980 by Barbara Grizzuti Harrison. Used by permission of Doubleday, a division of Bantam Doubleday Dell Publishing Group, Inc.

Steven Harvey, "The Nuclear Family." From *A Geometry of Lilies: Life and Death in an American Family* by Stephen Harvey. Copyright © 1993 by the University of South Carolina Press. Reprinted by permission.

Robert Hayden, "Those Winter Sundays." Reprinted from *Angle of Ascent: New and Selected Poems* by Robert Hayden, with the permission of Liveright Publishing Corporation. Copyright © 1966 by Robert Hayden.

Oscar Hijuelos, "The Mambo Kings Play Songs of Love." Excerpted from *The Mambo Kings Play Songs of Love* by Oscar Hijuelos. Copyright © 1989 by Oscar Hijuelos. Reprinted by permission of Farrar, Straus & Giroux, Inc.

Linda Hogan, "Walking." First appeared in *Parabola* Magazine, Vol. XV, No. 2 (Summer 1990). Reprinted by permission of the author.

Andrew Holleran, "The Fear." Copyright © 1988 by Andrew Holleran. Reprinted by permission of the author.

Lucy Honig, "English as a Second Language." First published in *Witness*, Vol. IV, No. 1 (1990). Copyright © Lucy Honig. Reprinted by permission of the author and *Witness*, Oakland Community College, 27055 Orchard Lake Road, Farmington Hills, MI 48334.

Kazuo Ishiguro, "A Family Supper." Copyright © 1982 by Kazuo Ishiguro. Reprinted by permission of the author c/o International Creative Management, Inc., in association with Rogers, Coleridge & White.

James Weldon Johnson, "Lift Ev'ry Voice and Sing." Copyright © Edward B. Marks Music Company. Used by permission.

Bel Kaufman, "Sunday in the Park." Reprinted by permission of the author.

Jamaica Kincaid, "Biography of a Dress." Copyright © 1992 by Jamaica Kincaid. First printed in *Grand Street*. Reprinted with the permission of Wylie, Aitken & Stone, Inc. Photograph on p. 309 reprinted by permission of the author. "A Walk to the Jetty." From *Annie John* by Jamaica Kincaid. Copyright © 1984, 1985 by Jamaica Kincaid. Reprinted by permission of Farrar, Straus & Giroux, Inc.

Maxine Hong Kingston, "The Misery of Silence." From *The Woman Warrior* by Maxine Hong Kingston. Copyright © 1975, 1976 by Maxine Hong Kingston. Reprinted by permission of Alfred A. Knopf, Inc.

Hanif Kureishi, "Eight Arms to Hold You." From *London Kills Me* by Hanif Kureishi. Copyright © 1991 by Hanif Kureishi. Used by permission of Viking Penguin, a division of Penguin Books USA, Inc.

D. H. Lawrence, "A Letter to Ernest Collings." From *The Letters of D. H. Lawrence, Vol. 1*, edited by James T. Boulton. Copyright 1932 by the estate of D. H. Lawrence; copyright 1934 by Frieda Lawrence; copyright 1933, 1948, 1953, 1954, © 1956, 1957, 1958, 1959, 1960, 1961, 1962, 1967, 1969 by Angelo Ravagli and C. Montague Weekley, executors of the estate of Frieda Lawrence Ravagli; © the estate of Frieda Lawrence Ravagli 1979. Reprinted with the permission of Cambridge University Press.

Andrea Freud Loewenstein, "Sister from Another Planet Probes the Soaps." First appeared in *Ms.* (November/December 1993). Reprinted by permission of *Ms.* Magazine, © 1993.

Peter Marin, "Helping and Hating the Homeless." Copyright © 1986 by *Harper's* Magazine. All rights reserved. Reprinted from the January 1987 issue by special permission.

Edward C. Martin, "Being Junior High." Reprinted by permission of *Daedalus: Journal of the American Academy of Arts and Sciences*, Vol. 100, No. 4 (Fall 1971), Boston, MA. The article is a condensation of an article that appeared under the original title of "Reflections on the Early Adolescent in School."

Louis Menand, "That's Entertainment." Originally in *The New Yorker* (22 Nov. 1993). Reprinted by permission; © 1993 Louis Menand. All rights reserved.

William Ian Miller, "Gifts and Honor: An Exchange." Reprinted from *Humiliation: And Other Essays on Honor, Social Discomfort, and Violence* by William Ian Miller. Copyright © 1993 by Cornell University. Used by permission of the publisher, Cornell University Press.

Michael Moffatt, "Coming of Age in a College Dorm." From *Coming of Age in New Jersey: College and American Culture* by Michael Moffatt. Copyright © 1989 by Rutgers, The State University. Reprinted by permission of Rutgers University Press.

N. Scott Momaday, "The Eagle Feather Fan." Reprinted by permission of the author.

Thomas H. Murray, "The Gift of Life Must Always Remain a Gift." Copyright © 1986 by *Discover* Magazine. Reprinted by permission.

Geoffrey O'Brien, excerpt reprinted from *The Phantom Empire* by Geoffrey O'Brien, with the permission of W. W. Norton & Company, Inc. Copyright © 1993 by Geoffrey O'Brien.

Sharon Olds, "Sex Without Love." From *The Dead and the Living* by Sharon Olds. Copyright © 1983 by Sharon Olds. Reprinted by permission of Alfred A. Knopf, Inc.

Tillie Olsen, "I Stand Here Ironing." From *Tell Me a Riddle* by Tillie Olsen. Copyright © 1956, 1957, 1960, 1961 by Tillie Olsen. Used by permission of Delacorte Press/Seymour Lawrence, a division of Bantam Doubleday Dell Publishing Group, Inc.

George Orwell, "Shooting an Elephant." From *Shooting an Elephant and Other Essays* by George Orwell. Copyright © 1950 by Sonia Brownell Orwell and renewed 1978 by Sonia Pitt-Rivers. Reprinted by permission of Harcourt Brace & Company, the estate of the late Sonia Brownell Orwell, and Martin Secker and Warburg.

J. H. Plumb, excerpt from "The Dying Family." Copyright © J. H. Plumb. Reprinted by permission of the author.

Richard Rodriguez, "Reading for Success." From *Hunger of Memory* by Richard Rodriguez. Copyright © 1981 by Richard Rodriguez. Reprinted by permission of David R. Godine, Publisher, Inc.

Ruth Rosen, excerpt from "Search for Yesterday" by Ruth Rosen in *Watching Television*, edited by Todd Gitlin. "Search for Yesterday" copyright © 1986 by Ruth Rosen. Compilation copyright © 1986 by Todd Gitlin. Reprinted by permission of Pantheon Books, a division of Random House, Inc.

Thomas Simmons, "Motorcycle Talk," from *The Unseen Shore: Memories of a Christian Science Childhood* by Thomas Simmons. Copyright © 1991 by Thomas Simmons. Reprinted by permission of Beacon Press.

Brent Staples, "Black Men and Public Space." Reprinted by permission of the author.

Shelby Steele, "The New Sovereignty." Copyright © 1992 by *Harper's* Magazine. Reprinted from the July 1992 issue by special permission.

Stephan Talty, "Family Record." Originally appeared in *Film Comment* (May/June 1991). Reprinted by permission of the author.

Amy Tan, "Mother Tongue." First appeared in *The Threepenny Review*. Copyright © 1989 by Amy Tan. Reprinted by permission of the author and the Sandra Dijkstra Literary Agency.

Sallie Tisdale, "We Do Abortions Here." First published in *Harper's* magazine, October 1987. Reprinted by permission of the author.

Alexis de Tocqueville, excerpt from *Democracy in America* by Alexis de Tocqueville. Edited by J. P. Mayer and Max Lerner. Translated by George Lawrence. English translation copyright © 1965 by Harper & Row, Publishers, Inc. Copyright renewed. Reprinted by permission of HarperCollins Publishers, Inc.

Susan Allen Toth, "Boyfriends." From *Blooming: A Small-Town Girlhood* by Susan Allen Toth. Copyright © 1978, 1981 by Susan Allen Toth. Reprinted by permission of Little, Brown and Company.

Calvin Trillin, "It's Just Too Late." Appears in his book entitled *Killings*, published by Ticknor & Fields. Copyright © 1984 by Calvin Trillin. Reprinted by permission.

Lindsy Van Gelder, "Marriage as a Restricted Club." Originally appeared in *Ms.* Reprinted by permission of the author.

Alice Walker, "Brothers and Sisters." From *In Search of Our Mothers' Gardens: Womanist Prose,* copyright © 1975 by Alice Walker. Reprinted by permission of Harcourt Brace & Company.

Richard Wilbur, "A Summer Morning." From *Advice to a Prophet and Other Poems* by Richard Wilbur. Copyright © 1960 and renewed 1988 by Richard Wilbur. Reprinted by permission of Harcourt Brace & Company.

Virginia Woolf, "Professions for Women." From *The Death of the Moth and Other Essays* by Virginia Woolf. Copyright 1942 by Harcourt Brace & Company and renewed 1970 by Marjorie T. Parsons, Executrix. Reprinted by permission of the publisher.

RHETORICAL INDEX

◊

449

Comparison and Contrast

Definition

Description

Division and Classification

Example

* Story

INDEX OF
AUTHORS AND TITLES

◇